And others, John Tremaine

# Pleas of the Crown in Matters Criminal and Civil - Containing a Large Collection of Modern Precedents

Part the Second

And others, John Tremaine

**Pleas of the Crown in Matters Criminal and Civil - Containing a Large Collection of Modern Precedents**
*Part the Second*

ISBN/EAN: 9783337268022

Printed in Europe, USA, Canada, Australia, Japan

Cover: Foto ©Suzi / pixelio.de

More available books at **www.hansebooks.com**

# PLEAS OF THE CROWN,

## IN MATTERS CRIMINAL AND CIVIL:

CONTAINING

## A LARGE COLLECTION OF MODERN PRECEDENTS,

TO WIT.

Appeals,
Certiorari's,
Convictions,
Demurrers,
Indictments,
Informations,
Pleas in abatement,
——— Bar,
Replications,
Rejoynders, &c.
Traverses,
Writs of habeas corpus,
——— mandamus,
——— quo warranto,
——— restitution, &c.
and pleadings thereupon.

With a great Variety of Precedents under many other Heads, relating to the CROWN LAW.

The Whole collected

By the Late Sir JOHN TREMAINE, Kt. Serjeant at Law.

Digested and Revised

By the Late Mr. JOHN RICE, of Furnival's Inn.

And translated into English

By THOMAS VICKERS, Esq. Barrister at Law.

PART THE SECOND.

With a New INDEX.

—DUBLIN:—

BY H. WATTS, LAW BOOKSELLER, NO. 3, CHRIST CHURCH-LANE;

1794.

To this Part are added the Pleadings in the KING against THOMAS AMERY and JOHN MONK.

# E R R A T A.

Page.
364, l. 47, for *fuifter* read *finifter*
370, l. 12, for *ard* read *and*
371, l. 3, fide note read *bill* inftead of *writ*
376, l. 6, for *in* read *into*
389, l. 24, for *ana* read *and*
l. 41, in fame page for *ana* read *and*
396, l. 13, after admittance read *or*
400, l. 20, for *paliate* read *palliate*
404, l. 35, for *forfeiturs* read *forfeitures*
406, l. 24, for *Henry* read *Henley*
420, l. 20, for *ophans* read *orphans*
425, l. 29, after *of the* read *city*
428, l. 43, for *words* read *word*
430, l. 34, for *whereby* read *whereupon*
437, l. 16, in fide note for *twenty* read *thirty*
443, l. 40, for *the* read *his*
446, l. 35, *wanting in all* read *wanting all*
455, the laft line but one, inftead of *to* read *to the great*
460, the laft line but three, inftead of *he reign* read *the reign*
461, l. 18, for *beeaufe* read *becaufe*
the laft line of fame page inftead of *vinters* read *vintners*
464, l. 24, for *eftablifh* read *eftablifhed*
472, l. 32, for *our writ* read *our command*
475, l. 10, *to the fellows* read *to be fellows*
476, l. 19, for *profident* read *prefident.*

Page.
496, l. 20, for *pyhfick* read *phyfick*
502, l. 34, *herefore* read *therefore*
505, the laft line but one, *in the fame* read *this fame*
508, l. 29, for *hts* read *his*
512, l. 25, after queen infert *in*
516, l. 22, read *into* inftead of *unto*
520, l. 4, after perfon infert *or*
551, l. 27, for *fummaned* read *fummoned*
557, l. 5, England *not for* read *for*
fide note in fame page, l. 6, *do concern* read *do not concern*
559, l. 16, in fide note for *deereed* read *decrees*
578, l. 26, for *takne* read *taken*
585, l. 24, for *ord* read *lord*
595, l. 19, for *method* read *methods*
596, l. 32, for *complain* read *complains*
601, l. 8, *we willing* read *we being willing*
604, l. 31, *fupply the* read *fupply of the*
619, l. 21, for *inquifitions the* read *inquifitions aforefaid the*
626, l. 41, *or in part* read *or or in any part*
639, l. 2, *on the writ* read *in the writ*
641, l. 38, for *received* read *viewed*
659, l. 22, for *manifefted* read *manifeft*
684, l. 8, *office of the* read *office of one of the*
688, the laft line but three read *before you.*

In Part I. p. 295, l. 31, after *ment* read "*and whereas the power*".

# PLEAS of the CROWN, * P. 351

## IN

## Matters Criminal and Civil.

### Habeas Corpus and Returns thereto.

### The King *against* Keyser.

### *Michaelmas* 5th Edward 4th. Roll 143.

THE lord the king hath sent to the keeper of his gaol of Maidstone in the county of Kent or to his deputy, his writ close in these words: Edward by the grace of God, king of England and France, and lord of Ireland, to the keeper of our gaol of Maidstone in the county of Kent, or to his deputy greeting:—We command you that the body of John Keyser executor of the testament of John Keyser late of East Peckham his father, in our prison under your custody detain'd as it is said, under a safe and sure conduct, together with the cause of his detention, by whatsoever name the said John may be called in the same; you have before us at Westminster on the Tuesday next after the morrow of St. Martin, to prosecute our certain writ, in our court before us against Thomas Stephens of Aylesford in the county of Kent shipman, and Isabella his wife of a plea, wherefore when pleas of the reasonable part of the goods and chattels coming to the children after the decease of their parents according to the custom of our kingdom of England, especially belong to us our crown and dignity, the said Isabella hath prosecuted her suit in the court Christian before Thomas archbishop of Canterbury, and his auditor of causes and businesses auditory against the said executor, for this that the said executor should render to the said Isabella the reasonable part of all the goods and chattels which were the said John Keyser's deceased her father coming to her according to the custom in the county of Kent hitherto used and approved of; to the injury of our crown and dignity, to the great damage of the said executor, and against our prohibition, and have there this writ wit-

Habeas corpus to the gaoler of Maidstone to bring up the body of a prisoner to prosecute his writ of prohibition.

Return—Commitment by the commissioners of the archbishop of Canterbury, by virtue of his commission to them directed.

ness J. Markham at Westminster, the 14th day of November, in the 5th year of our reign; and the indorsement on the said writ follows in these words, to wit, John Keyser within written, was taken at East Peckham by John Bromston, by virtue of a certain commission from Thomas by divine permission archbishop of Canterbury, primate of all England, and legate of the apostolick see, to the said John Bromston and others in the said commission specified directed, the transcript of which is annexed to this writ, and is detained by the said cause and no other, in the prison of the lord the king under my custody, whose body before the lord the king at the day and place within contained, I have ready as the said writ in itself commands and requires; and the tenor of the transcript in the said indosement specified follows in these words, to wit, Thomas by divine permission archbishop of Canterbury, primate of all England, and legate of the apostolick see, to all and singular * bailiffs and constables, stewards, and other officers and ministers, and to Richard Culpepper and John Bromston esquires, health, grace and good will; we have received the grievous complaint of our beloved in Christ Isabella Stephens of Alyesford in our diocese, stating that John Keyser of East Peckham, within our immediate jurisdiction for his manifest contumacy, rebellion and offence in not obeying our certain lawful monitions to him at the instance of the said Isabella rightly and lawfully made, is by our ordinary authority involved in the greater excommunication, and in such greater excommunication rightly, duly and lawfully denounced for eight months and more, hath hardily persevered, and as yet doth persevere with incorigiblo disposition, wickedly despising the authority of the holy mother church, and the said John Keyser as publick fame reports, and as we understand by the notoriety of facts, and by the evidence of witnesses worthy of belief, advisedly asserts, declares and affirms that such mandates are not to be feared, and that he doth not fear the same, and although we or our commissaries have excommunicated him, that he doth not care for the same, because as to God he is not excommunicated, and that this was true as he asserted it, plainly appeared from this, that in last autumn so standing excommunicated he had as great a plenty of corn and of other grain for the quantity of his land as any of his neighbours, and he shows his field of corn to his neighbours, saying to them in derision, that an excommunicated person ought not to have such corn, from which premisses and others we have justly suspected the said John of heresy, to you, therefore by the authority of the letters of our lord the king of England to us in this behalf granted, we commit and command that you arrest or cause to be arrested the said John Keyser suspected of heresy as aforesaid, and cause him faithfully to be kept in the goal of Maidstone, personally to answer certain articles concerning such crime of heresy

*-P. 352.

* This precedent is in the original in some places mis-printed, *ex. gr. minime* is put for *animo*.

heresy to him by our official, at the promotion of the said party, the said Isabella to be objected, and further to do and receive that which justice in this behalf demands. And what you shall do in the premisses you shall duly certify by letters to us or our commissaries, when you shall be rightly required by the party the said Isabella, or you shall in like manner certify how our present command hath been executed by your letters containing the tenor of these letters patent authenticated with your seal, at the same time returning these presents given at our manor of Lambeth the 24th day of October, in the year of our lord 1465, and in the 12th year of our translation; and thereupon the said John Keyser present here in court brought to the bar by the said keeper of the said goal is delivered on bail to John Sampson of East Peckham in the county of Kent gent. and to Henry Reynolds of London, dyer, who mainprized to have the body of the said John Keyser before the lord the king from the day of *St. Hilary* in fifteen days, wheresoever, &c. to wit. each of the mainpernors aforesaid under the pain of 10l. and the said John Keyser undertook for himself under the pain of 40l. to be before the lord the king at the said term wheresoever, &c. which sums of 10l. each of the mainpernors aforesaid for himself, and the said John Keyser the said sum of 40l. granted of their lands and chattels should be made and levied to the use of the lord the king, if it should happen that the said John Keyser at the same term should make default; at which day before the lord the king at Westminster comes the said John Keyser in his proper person, and thereupon the said John Keyser is * further delivered on bail to the said John Sampson, and to one John Benge of Wadherst in the county of Sussex, gent. who mainprized to have the body of the said John Keyser before the lord the king from the day of *Easter*, in one month, wheresoever, &c. to wit, each of the mainpernors aforesaid under the pain of 10l. and the said John Keyser undertook for himself under the pain of 40l. to be before the lord the king at the said one month, &c. wheresoever, &c. which sums of 10l. each of the mainpernors aforesaid for himself, and the said John Keyser the said sum of 40l. granted of their goods and chattels should be made and levied to the use of the lord the king, if it should happen that the said John Keyser at the said one month, &c. should make default. At which day before the lord the king at Westminster, comes the said John Keyser in his proper person, and thereupon the said John Keyser produced here in court, the letters of the said venerable father Thomas archbishop of Canterbury, sealed with his seal, testifying that the said John Keyser from the court of the said archbishop in respect of the premisses was dismissed; whereupon it is considered by the court here,

Defendant admitted to bail.

* P. 353.

Defendant discharged on bringing into court the letters of the archbishop testifying that he was discharged from the archbishop's court in respect of the premisses.

here, that the ſaid John Keyſer from the court of the lord the king here in reſpect of the premiſſes be diſmiſſed, quit, and diſcharged, and that he go thence without day, &c.

---

## The King *againſt* Maddox.

### *Eaſter*, 22d. James I.

Return to an habeas corpus; commitment for a fine at the goal delivery for Middleſex upon a conviction for a cheat.

*Middleſex.* To wit. } WILLIAM MADDOX, by Randolph Freeman and Thomas Moulſon, ſheriff of the ſaid county, by virtue of the writ of the lord the king, of habeas corpus ad ſubjiciendum, &c. to him thereupon directed, and brought before the lord the king at Weſtminſter, with the cauſe to wit, that before the coming of the ſaid writ, to wit, at the ſeſſion of the peace held at Hicks-Hall, in St. John-ſtreet, in the ſaid county, on Monday the 16th day of February, in the 21ſt year of the reign of the lord James, now king of England, &c. before T.F. knight, J. H. knight, and others their fellows, juſtices of the ſaid lord the king, to preſerve the peace in the ſaid county, &c. the ſaid William Maddox is indicted for this, that he had obtained into his hands by ſubtile and deceitful practice with falſe dice at the game of paſſage 30l. of one Nicholas Ferrowe, and afterwards at the delivery of the goal of the lord the king of Newgate for the county aforeſaid, before the mayor of the city of London, and others his fellows, juſtices, &c. is convicted and attainted, and for the ſame cauſe is committed to the priſon of the lord the king of Newgate under the cuſtody of the ſame ſheriff, there to remain until that he ſhould pay to the lord the king the ſum of 50l. and ſhould ſatisfy the ſaid Nicholas Ferrowe, which William Maddox is committed to the marſhal, &c. and afterwards is delivered on bail.

The

## * The King *against* Gardiner.

* P. 354.

## *Easter*, 43d Elizabeth. Roll 49.

*Cambridge,* To wit. } THE lady the queen hath sent to the sheriff of the said county her writ close in these words, Elizabeth, by the grace of God of England, &c. to the sheriff of Cambridge greeting. We command you that the body of John Gardiner in our prison under your custody detained, as it is said, together with the cause of his detention, by whatsoever name the said John may be called in the same, you have before Francis Gawdy, one of our justices assigned to hold pleas before us, at his house in Chancery-lane London, immediately after the receipt of this writ, to submit to and receive those things which our said justice concerning him then and there shall consider in this behalf, and this in no manner omit at your peril, and have there this writ. Witness, &c.

Writ of habeas corpus to the sheriff of Cambridge returnable immediately before a judge of the queen's bench.

Giles Allington Esquire, Sheriff.

By virtue of the warrant to this writ annexed, the body of the within named John Gardiner is detained in the prison of the lady the queen of her castle of Cambridge, as appears by the said warrant, and by virtue of the said writ to me directed, I certify to the lady the queen, that the body of the said John Gardiner is detained for the same occasion, and for no other, whose body together with the cause of his detention I have ready at the day and place within contained, as I am within commanded, Cambridge.——*Forasmuch as Edward Taylor of Hatley St. George in the county of Cambridge, yeoman, did bring before me at Hatley aforesaid, one John Gardiner of London, sadler, whom he hath seen and found the same at Hatley aforesaid, carrying and having about him in his journey one hand-gun, being stock and all, under the length of three quarters of a yard, charged with powder, contrary to the laws of the realm; and therefore hath prayed me that justice might be done: I John St. George being the next justice of the peace in the said county to the place aforesaid, did then, upon the said request, at Hatley aforesaid, take the examination of the said John Gardiner, and did also then and there hear the proofs of the said Edward Taylor, concerning the said offence, and for that it did manifestly appear unto me that the said John Gardiner had not then lands or tenements, fees, annuities or offices to the yearly value of* 100l. *and by his own confession, and by the proofs of the said Edward Taylor, that he did then carry about*

Return. Commitment by a warant of a justice of peace on a conviction before the said justice for carrying a hand gun.

*about him the said gun, charged in manner aforesaid, I do send you herewith the body of the said John Gardiner, as convicted of the said offence requiring you in her Majesty's name to receive him into your said gaol, and him there safely to keep as her Majesty's prisoner, until* * *that he shall have truly paid the pain and forfeit of* 10l. *of lawful money of England, laid upon him for the said offence by the statute thereof made in the 33d year of the reign of the late King Henry the Eighth, that is to say, the one half to our said sovereign lady, and the other moiety, to the said Edward Taylor, the first bringer of him before me, and this shall be your sufficient warrant on that behalf. Hereof fail not, as you will answer at your peril. Given at Hatley, the twenty-eighth day of November, in the 43d year of our soverign lady Elizabeth, by the grace of God of England, France, and Ireland, Queen, Defender, of the Faith, &c.*

* P. 355.

JOHN St. GEORGE.

Defendant appears in court upon a recognizance, and prays oyer of the writ and return and justifies the carrying the hand gun in defence of himself and another sheriff's bailiff in the execution of a warrant upon a fieri facias.

And now to wit, on the Wednesday next after 15 days of Easter, in this same term, before the lady the Queen at Westminster, comes the said John Gardiner, according to his recognizance, before the said lady the queen, in this behalf before acknowledged, in his proper person, and prays oyer of the said writ and of the return of the same, which being read and heard, he saith that he doth not apprehend that the said lady the queen, or the said Edward Taylor, in the return of the said writ mentioned, ought to have the said 10l. in the return of the said writ in like manner specified, or one penny thereof, because he saith, that heretofore, to wit, in the term of St. Michael, in the 42d and 43d years of the reign of the lady Elizabeth, the now queen of England, &c. before the lady the queen at Westminster, one Thomas Gardiner, sued out a certain writ of the said lady the queen of fieri facias directed to the sheriff of Cambridge against the said John St. George, returnable before the justices of the said lady the queen at Westminster, from the day of St. Hilary, in 15 days thence next following, which writ, afterwards to wit, on the 26th day of November in the 43d year of the reign of the said lady the queen aforesaid, was delivered to Giles Allington, esquire, then sheriff of the county of Cambridge, to be executed in the form of law, by virtue of which writ of fieri facias the said Giles Allington, afterwards to wit, on the said 26th day of November in the 43d year of the reign of the said lady the now queen aforesaid, made his certain warrant to the said John Gardiner, and to one Henry Carter, his bailiffs for that time only, on behalf of the said lady the queen, commanding them, that of the lands and chattles of the said John St. George, they should cause to be made as well a certain debt of 13l. which the said Thomas Gardiner, in in the court of the ſaid lady the queen, before the juſtices of the ſaid lady the queen, at Weſtminſter aforeſaid, had recovered againſt him, as the ſum of 100 ſhillings, which were adjudged to the ſaid Thomas, in the ſaid court, for his damages which he had by reaſon of the detention of the ſaid debt, ſo that he ſhould have that money before the ſaid juſtices at Weſtminſter from the day of St. Hilary in 15 days aforeſaid, to be paid to the ſaid Thomas Gardiner, according to the command of the ſaid writ, by virtue of which warrant, they the ſaid bailiffs afterwards, to wit, on the 28th day of the ſaid month of November, in the 43d year aforeſaid, at Ampthill, in the county of Bedford, proceeded on their journey towards the manſion houſe of the ſaid John St. George, ſituate and being at Hatly St. George, in the ſaid county of Cambridge, for the execution of the ſaid warrant. And the ſaid John Gardiner, then as well in the defence of the ſaid John Gardiner, and of the ſaid other bailiff, as for the more ſure and better execution of the * ſaid warrant, carried with him on his ſaid journey the ſaid dagge, called a hand gun, or piſtol, in the return of the ſaid writ ſpecified as it was well lawful for him ſo to do, and this he is ready to verify, wherefore he prays judgment, and that he of the premiſes may be diſmiſſed by the court here. And David Waterhouſe, eſquire, coroner aud attorney of the ſaid lady the queen, before the queen herſelf, who for the ſaid lady the queen in this behalf proſecutes, the plea of the ſaid John Gardiner being ſeen, and by him well underſtood, becauſe that it ſufficiently appears to him, by the relation and teſtimony of divers faithful ſubjects of the ſaid lady the queen, that the ſaid John Gardiner carried with him on his journey the ſaid dagge, called a hand gun, charged with powder, in the return of the ſaid writ mentioned, as well in defence of the ſaid John Gardiner and the other bailiff aforeſaid, as for the more ſure and better execution of the ſaid warrant in the manner and form as the ſaid John Gardiner above by pleading hath alledged, this the ſaid attorney of the ſaid lady the queen doth not deny, but the ſaid plea by him the ſaid John as aforeſaid above pleaded, on behalf of the ſaid lady the queen, altogether confeſſes, and acknowledges to be true. Whereupon as well the ſaid plea of the ſaid John Gardiner, above by him in the manner aforeſaid pleaded, as the confeſſion of the ſaid plea of the ſaid attorney of the ſaid lady the queen, and all and ſingular the premiſſes being ſeen, and by the court here underſtood, it is conſidered that the ſaid John Gardiner of the premiſſes may go thence without day, &c. &c.

* P. 356.

The queen's coroner and attorney confeſſes the plea and thereupon defendant is diſcharged.

Judgment.

Reported in 5th Coke's Reports 71.—See 2d Blackſtone's Reports 1209.

The

## The King *against* Fox, and others.

Return by the sheriff of Worcester to an habeas corpus; commitment of the defendant, by a warrant of a justice of peace for holding a conventicle.

*Worcester.* } I THOMAS FOLEY, the younger, esquire,
To wit. } sheriff of the said county, most humbly certify to the most serene lord the king at Westminster, that before the coming of the said writ of the said lord the king to me directed, and to this schedule annexed, to wit, on the 17th day of September, in the 25th year of the reign of the said lord the king, George Fox, in the said writ named, was committed to the gaol of the said lord the king, at the city of Worcester, in the said county, under my custody, and there is detained by virtue of a certain warrant of Henry Parker, esquire, one of the justices of the said lord the king, assigned to preserve the peace in the said county, and also to hear and determine divers felonies, trespasses, and other misdeeds, in the said county perpetrated, for the cause in the said warrant contained. The tenor of which warrant follows in these words, to wit.—Worcestershire to wit. *To the constable of Treddington, in the said county of Worcester, and to all the constables and tithing men of the several townships and vills, within the said parish of Treddington, and to the keeper of the gaol for the said county of Worcester; complaint being made to me being one of his majesty's justices of the peace for the said county of Worcester, that within the said parish of Treddington there hath of late been several meetings of divers persons, to the number of* 400 *persons and upwards at a time, upon pretence of exercising religion otherwise than what is established by the laws of England; and many of the said persons, some of which were teachers, and came from the north, and others * from remote parts of the kingdom, which tends to the prejudice of the reformed and established religion, and may prove prejudicial to the public peace. And it appearing to me that there was this present day such a meeting as aforesaid, to the number of the* 200 *or thereabouts, at Arscott, in the said parish of Treddington, and that George Fox, of London, and Thomas Lower, of the parish of Creid, in the county of Cornwall, were present at the said meeting, and the said George Fox, was teacher or speaker at the said meeting, and no satisfactory account of their settlement or place of habitation appearing to me. And forasmuch as the said George Fox and Thomas Lower, refused to give securities to appear at the next sessions of the peace to be holden for the said county, to answer the breach of the common laws of England, and what other matters should be objected against him. These are therefore in his majesty's name, to will and require you or either of you, forthwith to convey the bodies of the said George Fox and*

* P. 357.

*Thomas*

*Thomas Lower to the county-goal of Worcester aforesaid, and there safely to be kept until they shall be from thence delivered in due course of law, for which this shall be your sufficient warrant in this behalf, dated the 17th day of December, in the 25th year of the reign of his majesty over England, &c. 1673.* And afterwards, to wit, at the general quarter session of the peace of the said lord the king, held for the county of Worcester aforesaid, at W. in the said county, on Tuesday next after the feast of the Epiphany, to wit, on the 13th day of January, in the 25th year of the reign of the said lord the now king, &c. before L. Simpson esquire, J. Winford knight, and others their fellows, justices of the said lord the king, assigned to preserve the peace in the said county of Worcester, and also to hear and determine divers felonies, trespasses, and other misdeeds in the said county perpetrated, because that the said George Fox, the oath of obedience contained in a certain act made and provided in the parliament of the lord James the late king of England, held at Westminster, in the county of Middlesex, on the 5th day of November, in the 3d year of his reign, to the said George by the said justices in the open court aforesaid, then and there being duly tendered, and required by him to be taken upon the holy gospel of God, then and there did refuse to take, against the form of the said statute; the said George by the order of the said court there, for the want of mainpernors was remanded to the said goal, there to remain until that he should be delivered by the due form of law, and these are the causes of the caption and detention of the said George Fox, but his body before the lord the king at the day and place in the writ to this schedule annexed named, I have ready, as I am commanded by the said writ.

Afterwards charged in custody with an order at the quarter sessions for not taking the oath required by the stat. 3d. James 1st.

THOMAS FOLEY the younger, esquire sheriff.

---

## * The King *against* the Lady Dowager Rochester.

* P. 358.

### *Trinity*, 1st James 2d.

Writ of habeas corpus to the lady Rochester to have the body of the lady Mallet Wilmot in the court of king's bench on a certain day.

JAMES the 2d. &c. To Anna, lady dowager of Rochester, greeting: We command you that the body of the lady Mallet Wilmot being confined and detained under your custody, as it is said, together with the day and cause of her caption and detention, by whatsoever name the said lady Mallet

Mallet Wilmot may be called in the ſame, you have before us at Weſtminſter, on the Wedneſday next after 3 weeks of the Holy Trinity, to ſubmit to, and receive what our court then and there concerning her ſhall conſider in this behalf, and have there this writ, &c. The execution of this writ appears in a certain ſchedule to this writ annexed; the anſwer of Anna Rocheſter. England, to wit. I Anna, lady dowager of Rocheſter, moſt humbly certify and return to the moſt ſerene lord the king named in the writ to this ſchedule annexed, that Mallet Wilmot in the ſaid writ named, is one of the three daughters and coheireſſes of the moſt noble John, earl of Rocheſter, deceaſed, and is ſeized of a third part of the manor of Eumore, in the county of Somerſet, by hereditary deſcent from the ſaid John, and is within the age of 14 years, to wit, of the age of 10 years and not more, and at the time of the iſſuing of the ſaid writ was, and yet is in the cuſtody of the ſaid Anna, lady dowager of Rocheſter, the grandmother of the ſaid Mallet, of her father's ſide, to wit, the mother of the ſaid John, the father of the ſaid Mallet, as guardian of the ſaid Mallet, in ſocage, and this is the cauſe of the detention of the ſaid Mallet Wilmot, whoſe body at the day and place named in the ſaid writ, I have ready, as by the ſaid writ I am within commanded.

Return. That ſhe keeps the lady Mallet as guardian to her in ſocage.

ANNA ROCHESTER.

---

* P. 359.

## * The King *againſt* Hill and others.

Return to an habeas corpus; that war was proclaimed and is continued between England and France, and that the priſoners were ſubjects of the king of France, and were arreſted and kept in cuſtody by a warrant from the king's privy council.

The execution of this writ appears in a certain ſchedule to the ſaid writ annexed. The anſwer of Nicholas Hill, James Hetſon, and John Thompſon.

*England,* To wit } WE N.H. J.H. and J.T. named in the writ to this ſchedule annexed, moſt humbly certify and return to the lord the king, and to the lady the queen, that Bartholomew Medy, Nicholas Medy, Anthony Didier, and John, otherwiſe Peter Deprement, at the time of their caption and detention, and alſo at the time of the obtaining and ſuing out of the ſaid writ, were and as yet are foreigners, and born out of the allegiance of the lord the king and the lady the queen of England, and within the allegiance of Lewis king of France, to wit, at Pontoys, within the kingdom of France, under the obedience of Lewis king of of France, which Lewis king of France and the men of the ſaid country, at the time of the caption and detention aforeſaid and long before, and always afterwards hitherto, were and as yet are enemies and adverſaries to the lord the king and to the lady the queen, and to their kingdom of England, and to all the people of the ſaid lord the king and the ſaid lady the queen of their ſaid kingdom of England, and that long before the ſaid B. M. N. M. A. D. J. otherwiſe P. D. were taken, detained, or impriſoned, or any or either of them was, or were taken, detained, or impriſoned, war between the ſaid lord the king and the lady the queen of England, and the ſaid Lewis king of France was begun and proclaimed, and always afterwards hitherto was and is continued; and that before the taking and detention aforeſaid, and before the iſſuing of the ſaid writ, and during the war between them the ſaid lord the king and the lady the queen of England, and the ſaid Lewis king of France, they the ſaid B. M. N. M. A. D. J. otherwiſe P. D. did preſume to remain within this kingdom of England, and thereupon before the iſſuing of the ſaid writ, to wit, on the 25th day of January, in the firſt year of the reign of the ſaid lord the king and the lady the queen, they the ſaid B. M. N. M. A. D. and J. otherwiſe P. D. being of the country at war with the ſaid lord the king and the lady the queen, as enemies of the ſaid lord the now king and the lady the now queen of England, &c. were taken and committed into our cuſtody, and there now remain and are detained, by virtue of a certain warrant dated the 23d day of January, in the firſt year of the reign of the ſaid lord the now king, and the lady the now queen of England, made by the moſt noble Thomas marquis of Carmarthen, preſident of the council of the ſaid lord the king of England, [and others of the privy council,] lords of the privy council of the ſaid lord the king, in their council at Whitehall, then and there being aſſembled, and to us in that behalf directed, the tenor of which warrant follows in theſe words: "*Whereas his majeſty has been informed, that twelve Engliſh merchants are made priſoners of war at Morlaix, in France, theſe are therefore by his majeſty's command in council, to will and require you forthwith to apprehend and take into your cuſtody, the bodies of Bartholomew Medy, Nicholas Medy, Anthony Didier, and Peter Deprement, and them ſafely keep in your cuſtody until his majeſty's ſaid ſubjects* * *ſhall be releaſed in France, or until you ſhall receive further orders from this board, for which this ſhall be your warrant. From the court at Whitehall, the 23d January 1689. To Nicholas Hill, James Hetſon, and John Thompſon, meſſengers of his majeſty's chamber;*" and this is the cauſe of the caption and detention of the ſaid Bartholomew Medy,

* P. 362.

 Nicholas

Medy, Anthony Didier, and John otherwise Peter Dupre-ment, in prison under our custody, whose bodies before the lord the king and the lady the queen, at the day and place in the said writ mentioned, we have ready, as by the said writ we are commanded.

---

## The King *against* Pell and Orton.

Writ of habeas corpora to the chancellor of the county palatine of Durham, returnable into the king's bench.

CHARLES the 2d. &c. To our chancellor of our county Palatine of Durham, or his deputy there, greeting: We command you that by our writ of mandare facias, to be made in the due manner, under the seal of the county Palatine aforesaid, to the sheriff of the county Palatine aforesaid directed, the bodies of William Pell, clerk, and John Orton, gentleman, in our prison, under his custody committed and detained, as it is said, together with the day and cause of their caption and detention, by whatsoever names the said John and William may be called in the same, you have before us at Westminster, on the Tuesday next after the octave of the blessed Virgin Mary, to submit to and receive those things which our said court concerning them then and there shall ordain in this behalf, and this in no wise omit at your peril, and have there this writ. Witness M. Hale, knight, at Westminster, the 23d day of January, in the 35th year of our reign, by the court, Fanshawe. The execution of this writ appears in a certain schedule annexed.

Return.

That by the custom of the county palatine, if any person be excommunicated by the bishop of Durham, or by the dean and chapter (sede vacante) and that it is signified into the court of chancery of Durham, a writ de excommunicato capiendo is issued out of the said court directed to the sheriff of Durham.

The answer of John Otway, knight, chancellor of the county Palatine of Durham, to the writ of habeas corpora cum causâ, to this schedule annexed. By virtue of this writ of habeas corpora, to me directed, and to this schedule annexed, I certify to the lord the king in the said writ named, at the day and place in the said writ mentioned, that the county of Durham is, and from the whole time whereof the memory of man is not to the contrary, hath been an antient county Palatine, and that within the said county Palatine, there is held, and also for the whole time aforesaid, was held a certain antient court of chancery, commonly called the court of chancery of Durham, held before the Chancellor of the county Palatine aforesaid, for the time being, and that also within the said county Palatine, there is held, and also for the whole time aforesaid was held, a certain antient cuſtom uſed and approved in the ſaid county, that if the biſhop of Durham for the time being, or the dean and chapter of Durham of the cathedral church of Chriſt and the bleſſed Virgin Mary, for the time being, the epiſcopal ſee of Durham being vacant (to which dean and chapter of Durham, all and every juriſdiction, ſpiritual and eccleſiaſtical, which hath belonged to the biſhop of Durham, the ſee being full; the epiſcopal ſee of Durham being vacant doth belong, and for the whole time aforeſaid did belong) by their reſpective letters * under their reſpective * P. 361. epiſcopal and chapter ſeals; into the court of chancery aforeſaid, have ſignified to the lord the king, that any perſon or perſons inhabiting within the county Palatine aforeſaid, by the authority of the ſaid biſhop for the time being, or by the authority of the ſaid dean and chapter of Durham aforeſaid, for the time being, (the epiſcopal ſee of Durham aforeſaid being vacant) hath or have been excommunicated, and that ſuch perſon or perſons under the ſentence of excommunication aforeſaid for 40 days after the publiſhing of the ſame, hath or have ſtood excommunicated, that then from time to time, for the whole time aforeſaid, according to the ſaid cuſtom upon ſuch letters of ſignificavit, a writ or writs of the ſaid lord the king de excommunicato capiendo have been awarded out of the ſaid court of chancery, and for the whole time aforeſaid, have been accuſtomed to be awarded to the ſheriff of the county Palatine aforeſaid directed, for the taking and arreſting of ſuch perſon or perſons, ſo as aforeſaid ſignified to be excommunicated, by the body or bodies, until that the holy church ſhould be ſatisfied of the contempt and injury done to her by ſuch excommunicated perſon or perſons; and further, to the ſaid lord the now king I certify, that before the coming of the ſaid writ of habeas corpus to this ſchedule annexed, to wit, on the 4th day of December, in the 25th year of the reign of the ſaid lord the now king, (the epiſcopal ſee of Durham then and as yet being vacant) John Sudbury, doctor in divinity, then and as yet dean, and the chapter of the cathedral church of Durham aforeſaid, by their letters patent, ſealed with the chapter ſeal of the ſaid dean and chapter aforeſaid, to the ſaid lord the now king, into the court of chancery of the ſaid county Palatine, according to the ſaid cuſtom did ſignify, that William Pell, clerk, of the pariſh of St. Oſwald, Durham, in the county of Durham, and John Orton, gent. of the pariſh of St. Oſwald aforeſaid, Durham aforeſaid, in the ſaid county of Durham, for their manifold contumacies and offences, in not appearing before Thomas Cartwright, official of the ſaid dean and chapter, or his deputy, on a certain day and hour then paſt, to anſwer certain

That the dean and chapter ſignified into chancery, that the defendants were by them excommunicated.

tain articles, heads or interrogatories, concerning their souls health, and the reformation of their manners and excesses, and also because of certain ecclesiastical crimes and offences by them respectively perpetrated, at his visitation after the feast of Easter last past, exercised and celebrated, to him presented and disclosed, and especially in entirely absenting themselves from their parochial church of St. Oswald aforesaid, and in not being present at the prayers in the book of common prayer and of the liturgy of the church of England, injoined by act of parliament, and in not receiving the sacrament of the holy eucharist, or the supper of our Lord at the feast of Easter then last past, according to the command of law in that behalf, and having been publickly called, and long waited for, and in no wise appearing, in the sentence of the greater excommunication by the authority of the said dean and chapter were and are involved, and each of them was and is involved, in which sentence of the greater excommunication for 40 days and more, after the denouncing of the same, they have stood, and as yet stand and persist, and each of them hath stood, stands, and persists, with obstinate and incorrigible dispositions, wickedly despising the authority of the mother church, to the pernicious example of

* P. 362. other good christians, and to the great danger of their * own souls, which letters patent afterwards, to wit, on the said 4th day of December, in the 25th year of the reign of the now king, &c. aforesaid, into the court of chancery aforesaid, held at the city of Durham, in the county Palatine aforesaid were delivered, and in the said court of chancery remain of record, and thereupon afterwards, to wit, on the said 4th day of December, according to the said custom, certain writs of the said lord the now king of excommunicato capiendo issued out of the said court of chancery, held at the city of Durham aforesaid, in the county of Durham, aforesaid, against the said W. Pell, clerk, and John Orton, gent. respectively, in the said letters patent named, to the then sheriff of the said county directed, the tenor of which several writs of excommunicato capiendo, follows in these words, to wit, Charles the 2d. &c. To the sheriff of Durham, greeting: John Sudbury, doctor in divinity, dean, and the chapter of the cathedral church of Christ and the blessed Virgin Mary of Durham, to whom all and every the jurisdiction spiritual and ecclesiastical, which hath belonged to the bishop of Durham [the see being full] that see then, and as yet being vacant, is manifestly known to belong, have signified to us by their letters patent, under the chapter seal of the said dean and chapter of Durham, that one William Pell, of the parish of St. Oswald, Durham, in the county of Durham, clerk, for his manifest contumacy,

*That writs of excommunicato capiendo issued out of chancery directed to the sheriff of Durham.*

*The tenor of the writs.*

*1st writ.*

tumacy, by the ordinary authority of the ſaid dean and chapter is excommunicated, nor will by eccleſiaſtical cenſure be brought to juſtice, and becauſe that the holy church ought not to be without the royal power in their complaints: We command you, that you attach the ſaid William Pell by his body, according to the cuſtom of England, until that he ſhall ſatisfy the holy church, as well of the contempt as of the injury by him done to her; witneſs, J. Otway, knight, chancellor of the county Palatine of Durham, at Durham, on the 4th day of December, in the 25th year of the reign of Charles the 2d. Croſby. Charles the 2d, &c. To the ſheriff of Durham, greeting:—John Sudbury, doctor in divinity, dean, and the chapter of the cathedral church of Chriſt and the bleſſed Virgin Mary, of Durham, to whom all and every the juriſdiction ſpiritual and eccleſiaſtical which hath belonged to the biſhop of Durham, (the ſee being full) that ſee then and as yet being vacant, is manifeſtly known to belong, have ſignified to us by their letters patent, under the chapter ſeal of the dean and chapter of Durham, that one John Orton, gentleman, of the pariſh of St. Oſwald, Durham, in the county of Durham, for his manifeſt contumacy, by the ordinary authority of the ſaid dean and chapter is excommunicated, nor will by eccleſiaſtical cenſure be brought to juſtice; and becauſe the holy church ought not to be without the royal power in their complaints, we command you, that you attach the ſaid John Orton by his body, according to the cuſtom of England, until that he ſhall ſatisfy the holy church, as well of the contempt as of the injury by him done to her. Witneſs, J. Otway, knight, &c. as aforeſaid. And to the ſaid lord the now king I further certify, that by virtue of the ſaid writ of habeas corpora, aforeſaid, to this ſchedule as aforeſaid annexed, by the writ of the lord the king, under the ſeal of the county Palatine, aforeſaid, in the due manner made, I have commanded James Clavering, baronet, ſheriff of the county Palatine of Durham, aforeſaid, * that he ſhould duly execute the ſaid writ of habeas corpora in all things, who anſwers to me, that William Pell, clerk, and John Orton, gentleman, in the ſaid writ of habeas corpora named, ſeverally and reſpectively were taken, on the 5th day of December laſt paſt, and were detained in the priſon of the lord the king, at Durham, by virtue of the ſaid ſeveral writs of the ſaid lord the king of excommunicato capiendo, and that the bodies of the ſaid William Pell and John Orton, at the day and place in the ſaid writ of habeas corpora contained, he hath ready, as in the ſaid writ of habeas corpora is commanded, and this is the cauſe of the caption and detention of the ſaid William Pell and John Orton.

2d. Writ.

The chancellor upon the ſaid writ of habeas corpora, made his mandate to the ſheriff of Durham, who returned that the priſoners were taken and detained by virtue of the ſaid writ of ex. cap.

* P. 363

*The principal exception to this return was, that the chancellor only returned the sheriff's answer to him, quod corpora parata habet, and does not say, corpora, &c. parato habeo; and therefore the prisoners were remanded, as is reported, 3 Keble 279.*

---

## The King *against* Barrington.

Writ of habeas corpus to the keeper of a goal near Canterbury, returnable into the king's bench.

CHARLES the 2d, &c. To the keeper of the gaol in St. Dunstan, nigh to the city of Canterbury, in the county of Kent, greeting: We command you, that the body of J. Barrington, in our prison, under your custody detained, as it is said, together with the day and cause of his caption and detention, by whatsoever name the said John may be called in the same, you have before us at Westminster, on the Thursday next after one month of Easter, to submit to and receive whatever our court concerning him then and there shall consider in this behalf, and this in no wise omit at your peril, and have there this writ, &c. The execution of this writ appears in a certain schedule to this writ annexed. The answer of Henry Lenman, keeper of the within written goal.

Return. Imprisonment by virtue of a warrant from two justices of peace, founded on a certificate of the official of the archdeacon of Canterbury, stating a contempt to the authority of the ecclesiastical laws, in a suit for sequestration of tithes; against the statute 27 H. 8. c. 20.

Kent, to wit, I Henry Lenman, keeper of the goal in St. Dunstan, nigh the city of Canterbury, in the county of Kent, most humbly certify to the most serene lord the king, Charles the 2d. in the writ to this schedule annexed mentioned, that before the coming of the said writ to me directed, the body of the said John Barrington, in the said writ named, was taken and detained under my custody, by virtue of a certain warrant under the hands and seals of Norton Knatchbull, bart. and Richard Hulse, esquire, two of the justices of the said lord the king, assigned to preserve the peace in the said county of Kent, and also to hear and determine divers felonies, trespasses, and other misdeeds in the said county perpetrated, the tenor of which warrant follows in these words, to wit,—"*To the constables and borsholders whom these may concern, within the said county, whereas we have received a certificate from Thomas Bouchieva, doctor of laws, and official of the archdeaconry of Canterbury, under his seal of office, bearing date the 19th day of November, last past, of the wilful contumacy and* * *contempt of John Barrington, in the parish of Kennington, in the archdeaconry of Canterbury, yeoman, against the power, authority and jurisdiction of the laws ecclesiastical, in a suit there depending, between William Wilkins, clerk, sequestrator of the tithes*

* P. 364

*tithes belonging to the vicarage of Kennington aforeſaid, plaintiff, and the ſaid John Barrington, defendant, contrary to the ſtatute of the 27th of Henry the eighth, chap. 20th. made in the caſe of ſubſtraction of tithes. Theſe are therefore to will and require you, by virtue of the ſaid act, and in his majeſty's name ſtrictly to command you, and every of you, immediately upon the ſight hereof, to attach the body of the ſaid John Barrington, and him ſafely to convey unto his majeſty's goal in St. Dunſtan's, near Canterbury, and deliver him to the keeper of the ſame, who is hereby commanded him to receive and keep a priſoner without bail or mainprize, until he ſhall give ſufficient caution before us, by recognizance or otherwiſe to his majeſty's uſe, for his future obedience to the laws eccleſiaſtical in the cauſe aforeſaid, according to the true intent and meaning of the aforeſaid ſtatute: and hereof fail you not, as you and every of you will anſwer the ſame at your utmoſt perils. Given under our hands and ſeals at Aſhford, the 10th day of December, in the 20th year of his majeſty's reign, and in the year of our Lord, 1673. NORTON KNATCHBULL, RICHARD HULSE."* And this the cauſe of the caption and detention of the ſaid John Barrington, the body of which John Barrington, before the lord the king, at the day and place mentioned in the writ to this ſchedule annexed, I have ready, as by the ſaid writ I am commanded.

HENRY LENMAN, keeper of the ſaid goal.

---

## The King *againſt* Lloyd.

THE king, &c. To the conſtable of our priſon of the caſtle of Cheſter, or to his deputy there, greeting:— We command you, that the body of John Lloyd, in our priſon under your cuſtody detained, as it is ſaid, together with the cauſe of his caption and detention, by whatſoever name the ſaid John may be called in the ſame, you have before us at Weſtminſter, on the Wedneſday next after fifteen days of Eaſter, to ſubmit to and receive whatever our court concerning him then and there ſhall conſider in this behalf, and this in no wiſe omit under the pain of 40l. and have there this writ, &c. The anſwer of Randolph Metcalfe, conſtable of the caſtle of Cheſter, within written, and keeper of the priſon of the lord the king of the ſaid caſtle,

Writ of habeas corpus to the conſtable of Cheſter caſtle, returnable into the king's bench.

castle, appears in a certain schedule to this writ annexed. The execution of this writ, appears in a certain schedule to this writ annexed, R. Metcalfe, J. Randolph Metcalfe, constable of the castle of the lord the king of Chester, and keeper of the prison of the lord the king of the said castle of the lord the king, on the day in the writ to this schedule annexed, certify, that the county of Chester is, and from the time whereof the * memory of man is not to the contrary, hath been an antient county Palatine, whereof the said lord the king now is, and his progenitors, kings and queens of this kingdom of England, were seized as of fee and right, and that the said lord the now king, and all his progenitors, kings and queens of England, from the whole time aforesaid, have had, and have been accustomed to have the said county Palatine, and many antient customs, liberties, rights, and privileges, and all other rights, royalties and liberties, and royal jurisdictions, exercised and used within and throughout the said county Palatine, and all places which to the said county Palatine appertain; and that within the said county Palatine there is held, and for the whole time aforesaid hath been held, a certain court of record, called the exchequer of Chester, held at the castle of Chester aforesaid, before the chamberlain of the said county Palatine of Chester, for the time being, or his deputy, which chamberlain for the time being, has, and for the whole time aforesaid hath had, all the jurisdiction of a chancellor, within the said county Palatine, and that there is held, and for the whole time aforesaid hath been held, within the said county Palatine, a certain other court of record, called the court of the great session of Chester, as well for pleas of the crown, as for all other pleas, as well real as personal, and mixt, arising within the said county Palatine, held before the justice of the said lord the king of Chester, for the time being, or his deputy, so that every subject of the said lord the king, might and could fully obtain in the said court compleat justice in their certain causes, according to their cases, and according to the laws and customs of the said county Palatine, from antient time used and approved; and that as well all pleas of the crown, as all other pleas concerning lands and tenements, and all contracts, causes and matters, arising within the said county Palatine, are pleadable and ought to be pleaded, heard, and judicially determined, in certain courts within the said county Palatine, and not elsewhere out of the said county Palatine; and that if any such are pleaded, heard, or determined, out of the said county Palatine, the same are void, and coram non judice, (writs of error, and cases of foreign plea, and foreign suit, only excepted) so that any writ of the said lord the king ought not, and hath not been accustomed to run into the said county

Special return That all pleas of the crown, and all actions, real, personal, and mixt, (except, &c.) arising within the county Palatine of Chester, ought to be tried and determined in the court of the county Palatine, and not elsewhere. That the prisoner was committed to his custody on an attachment out of the court of exchequer of the county Palatine, for a cause arising within the county Palatine.

* P. 365

county Palatine, out of any other court, nor ought any other justices of the said lord the king, or of his progenitors, kings and queens of England, in any other manner intermeddle with the said pleas, held in the county aforesaid; (The writs running within the said county Palatine, only under the seal of the said county Palatine, writs of proclamation by the statute enacted in the 1st year of the reign of Edward the 6th only excepted.) And I the said constable, and keeper of the said prison to the said lord the king, further certify, that John Lloyd, in the writ aforesaid to this schedule annexed named, before the issuing of the said writ, to wit, on the 18th day of November, in the 16th year of the reign of the said lord the now king, then being an inhabitant within the said county Palatine, and servant of one William Edwards, of the city of Chester, within the county Palatine aforesaid, merchant, by virtue of a certain writ of the lord the king of attachment, out of the said court of exchequer of the said county Palatine issuing, (being process issuing according to the custom of the said county Palatine, upon a petition of the said William Edwards, against the said John Lloyd, for an account upon certain causes within the said county Palatine, and not without arising, then in the said court depending) was taken, and by the court of exchequer aforesaid, was committed to the custody of me, the said constable and keeper of the said prison, safely to be kept until that the said court further thereupon in like manner should ordain: wherefore I, the said constable and keeper of the said prison, the body of the said John Lloyd, together with the day and cause of the caption and detention of the said John, cannot have before the lord the king at the day in the said writ contained, without violating, injuring, and enervating the said antient customs, liberties and privileges, of the said county Palatine, as within I am commanded.

And that he cannot have the body without injuring the customs, liberties and privileges of the said co. Palatine.

---

## Habeas Corpus *for* King.

THE keepers of the liberties of England, by the authority of parliament, to the mayor, aldermen, and sheriffs of London, greeting: We command you, that the body of John King, otherwise L'Roy, in our prison under your custody detained, as it is said, under a safe and sure conduct,

Writ of habeas corpus to the mayor, aldermen, and sheriffs of London, returnable before the chief justice of the upper bench.



together

together with the day and cause of his caption and detention, by whatever name the said John may be called in the same, you have before Henry Rolle, chief justice, assigned to hold pleas in the court of upper bench, before us, at his chamber in Serjeant's-inn, in Fleet-street, London, immediately after the receipt of this writ, to do and receive, then and there, all and singular the things which the said chief justice concerning him, then and there shall consider in this behalf; and have there then this writ. Witness, &c.

The execution of this writ appears in a certain schedule to this writ annexed. The answer of Thomas Foot, mayor, and of the aldermen of the city of London, and of Christopher Pack, and Rowland Wilson, sheriffs of the said city.

Return. Imprisonment by virtue of an original bill in debt for 10l. levied in the court of the lord mayor and aldermen of London, at the suit of the chamberlain of London, upon an act of common council, made pursuant to the custom of London, against exercising a trade within the city, not being a freeman.

Custom to make bye-laws.

We, Thomas Foot, mayor, and the aldermen of the city of London, and Christopher Pack and Rowland Wilson, of the said city, sheriffs, to Henry Rolle, chief justice of the keepers of the liberties of England, by authority of parliament, assigned to hold pleas before them in the court of the upper bench, immediately certify at his chamber in Serjeant's-inn, in Fleet-street, London: That the city of London is, and from the whole time whereof the memory of man is not to the contrary, hath been an antient city, and that within the said city, and the liberties and franchises of the same, there is had, and also from the time whereof the memory of man is not to the contrary, was had a * custom, and the citizens of the said city, from the whole time aforesaid, hitherto have used and enjoyed the franchises and liberties: that no person who was not a freeman of the said city, within the said city, or the liberties or franchises of the same, by himself or by any other, by any colour, ways and means, directly or indirectly, hath kept, or may keep, or hath been accustomed to keep, any shop or other place, inwards or outwards, for the shewing, selling, or exposing to sale, any wares or merchandize whatsoever, by retail, or hath used and exercised any trade, mystery, or handicraft whatsoever, within the said city, or the liberties or franchises of the same: and that within the said city there is had, and from the whole time aforesaid was had such custom, used and approved, to wit, that if any custom, obtained and approved in the said city, is or was hard or defective in any part, or any things in the said city newly arising, where remedy is not, or was not before ordained, should want amendment, then that the mayor and aldermen of the said city, for the time being, with the consent of the commonalty of the said city, fit remedy, consonant to good faith and reason, for the common profit of the citizens of the said city, and of other faithful people repairing to the same, may appoint, and have appointed, and for

* P. 367

for the whole time aforesaid have been used to appoint by ordinance, under a reasonable penalty, to be forfeited by the transgressors of such ordinance, and to be recovered by action of debt by the chamberlain of the said city for the time being, in the court of the lord the king for the time being, before the mayor and aldermen of the said city for the time being, to be held, and for the whole time aforesaid accustomed to be held, and this as often as, and whensoever it shall seem to them necessary, provided, that such ordinance be profitable and consonant to good faith and reason. And we further signify, that the said customs, and all other customs of the said city, from the time aforesaid, &c. used, by the authority of the parliament of the lord Richard, late king of England, the 2d after the conquest, held at Westminster, in the 7th year of his reign, were ratified and confirmed to the then mayor, and commonalty of the said city, and to their successors: And we the said mayor, aldermen and sheriffs, of the city of London, aforesaid, further signify, that in the common council held according to the custom of the city of London, in the chamber of the Guildhall of the said city, on the 15th day of April, in the 4th year of the reign of the lord James, late king of England, &c. by Leonard Holliday, knight, then mayor of the said city, and the aldermen of the said city, with the assent of the commonalty of the said city, in the said common council being assembled, according to the said custom of the said city it was ordained, enacted and established, in the manner and form as here follows, to wit:—"*Whereas, by the antient charters, customs, franchises and liberties of the city of London, confirmed by sundry acts of parliament, no person not being free of the city of London, may or ought to sell, or put to sale, any wares or merchandizes, within the said city or liberties of the same, by retail, or keeping an open or inward shop, or other inward place or room for shew, sale, or putting to sale of any wares or merchandizes, or for use of any art, trade, or occupation, mystery* * *or handicraft within the same. And whereas also Edward, sometimes king of England, of famous memory, the third of that name, by his charter made and granted to the said city, in the fifteenth year of his reign, confirmed also by parliament, amongst other things granted, that if any customs in the said city, before that time obtained and used, were in any part hard or defective, or any things in the same city newly arising, where remedy before that time was not ordained, should need amendment, the mayor and aldermen of the same city, and their successors, with the assent of the commonalty of the said city, might put and ordain thereto fit remedy as often as it should seem expedient to them, so that such ordinances should be profitable to the king, for the profit of his citizens, and other his people repairing to the said city, and agreeable to reason. And whereas by force of*

Customs confirmed by act of parliament.

Bye-law made the 15th April, 4th James 1st.

* P. 368

*of the said customs, franchises and liberties and of the charter last afore-mentioned, confirmed as is before specified by parliament. The lord mayor, aldermen, and commons of the said city, did the 12th day of October, in the third year of the reign of Edward, sometime king of England the 4th, as a thing thought fit and convenient for that time, amongst other things agree and ordain, that the basket-makers and gold-wire drawers, and other foreigners, contrary to the liberties of the said city, holding open shops in divers places of the said city, and using mysteries within the said city, should not from thenceforth hold shops within the liberties of the said city aforesaid, but if they would hold any shop or dwell in the liberty of the same city, they should dwell at Blanch Appleton, and there hold shops, so as they might have sufficient dwellings there. And whereas also, the lord mayor, aldermen, and commons of the said city, did afterwards, the 16th day of May, in the 17th year of the reign of our late sovereign lord, of famous memory, king Henry the eighth, as a course thought fit and agreeable for that time, ordain, establish, and enact, that no manner of person or persons, being estrange from the liberties of the city, from thenceforth should hold or keep an open shop or shops, within the said city or liberties of the same, neither with lattices before, nor yet without lattices (certain number of poor men occupying the seat of botchers, taylors and coblers only excepted) upon pain of imprisonment, and also to forfeit and pay 40s. to the use of the commonalty of this city, as oftentimes as he or they should do to the contrary. And also whereas, the lord mayor, aldermen, and commons of the said city, did afterwards, the 20th day of January, in the said 17th year of king Henry the eighth, reciting, That whereas at a common council, holden the 16th day of May, in the 17th year of the reign of king Henry the eighth, it was ordained and enacted, that no manner of person or persons, being estrange from the liberties of this city, from thenceforth should hold or keep open any shop or shops within this city, or the liberties of the same, neither with any lattices before, nor yet without any lattices, upon pain of imprisonment, further ordain and establish, that if any person or persons being foreign, should hold and keep open any shop or shops, as is aforesaid, he shall forfeit for every time so doing 40s. to be levied by distress, to the use of the commonalty of the said city; to the chamberlain for the time being, or other officer of this city; as also have imprisonment by the discretion of the mayor and aldermen for the time being. Now forasmuch as divers and sundry strangers and foreigners from the liberties of the said city, not regarding the said antient charters, franchises, customs or liberties of the said city, and acts and ordinances heretofore made according to the same, but wholly intending their private profit, have of late years devised and practised by all sinister and subtle means, how to defeat and defraud the said charters, liberties and customs, good orders*

*orders and ordinances; and to that end do now inwardly, in private and secret places, usually and ordinarily shew, sell, and put to sale their wares and merchandizes, and use trades, arts, occupations, mysteries and handicrafts, within the said city and liberties of the same, to the great detriment and hurt of the freemen of the said city, who pay lot and scot, bear offices and undergo other charges, which strangers and others not free, are not chargeable withal nor will perform. For reformation of which disorders, and for avoiding such prejudice and damage, as thereby groweth to the freemen of the said city, and is now more of late used than was in any time heretofore suffered; and to provide for the common profit and good of the freemen and citizens of this city, it is therefore by the lord mayor and aldermen, and commons of this common council assembled, ordained and established, that no person whatsoever, not being free of the city of London, shall at any time after the feast of St. Michael, now next ensuing, by any colour, way, or means whatsoever, either directly or indirectly, by himself, or by any other, shall sell or put to sale, any wares or merchandizes whatsoever, by retail, within the city of London, or liberties or suburbs of the same, upon pain to forfeit to the chamberlain of the city of London, for the time being, to the use of the mayor and commonalty, and citizens of the said city, the sum of 5l. of lawful money of England, for every time wherein such person shall shew, sell, or put to sale, any wares or merchandizes, by retail, within the said city, liberties or suburbs thereof, contrary to the true intent and meaning hereof. And it is further ordained and established, that no person whatsoever, not being free of the city of London, shall at any time after the feast of St. Michael, now next ensuing, by any colour, way, or means, whatsoever, directly or indirectly, by himself or by any other person, keep any shop or other place whatsoever, inward or outward, for shew, sale, or putting to sale, any wares or merchandizes whatsoever, by way of retail, or use any art, trade, occupation, mystery or handicraft whatsoever, within the said city, or the liberties and suburbs of the same, upon pain to forfeit the sum of 5l. of lawful money of England, for every time wherein such person shall keep any shop or other place whatsoever, inward or outward, for shew, sale, or putting to sale, * of any wares or merchandizes whatsoever, by way of retail, or use any art, trade, occupation, mystery, or handicraft, whatsoever, within the said city, liberties, or suburbs of the same, contrary to the true intent and meaning hereof. All which pains, penalties, forfeitures, and sums of money, to be forfeited by virtue of this act or ordinance, shall be recovered by action of debt, bill or plaint, to be commenced and prosecuted in the name of the chamberlain of the city of London, for the time being, in the king's majesty's court, to be holden in the chamber of the Guildhall of the city of London, before the lord mayor and aldermen of the same city, wherein no essoin or wager*

* P. 370

*wager of the law ſhall be admitted or allowed for the defendant, and that the ſaid chamberlain of the ſaid city, for the time being, ſhall in all ſuits to be proſecuted by virtue of this act or ordinance, againſt any offender, recover the ordinary coſts of ſuit, to be expended in and about the proſecution thereof: and further, that one equal third part of all forfeitures, to be recovered by virtue hereof (the coſts of ſuit for the recovery of the ſame being deducted and allowed) ſhall after the recovery and receipt thereof, be paid and delivered to the governors of Chriſt's hoſpital, to be employed towards the relief of the poor children, to be brought up and maintained in the ſaid hoſpital; and one other equal third part to him or them who ſhall firſt give information of the offences for which ſuch forfeitures ſhall grow, and proſecute ſuit in the name of the chamberlain of the ſaid city, for recovery of the ſame, any thing in this act to the contrary notwithſtanding. Provided always, that this act, or any thing herein contained, ſhall not extend to any perſon or perſons for bringing, or cauſing to be brought, any victuals to be ſold within the ſaid city, and the liberties thereof, but that they and every of them, may ſell victuals within the ſaid city and the liberties thereof, as they might have lawfully done before the making hereof; any thing to the contrary thereof in any wiſe notwithſtanding:"* And further, we the ſaid mayor, aldermen, and ſheriffs, of the ſaid city, now certify, that the ſaid ordinance was, and is profitable and conſonant to good faith and reaſon, and that before the coming of the ſaid writ of the keepers of the liberties of England, by the authority of parliament to us directed, and to this ſchedule annexed, James King, otherwiſe L'Roy, in the ſaid writ named, was taken in the ſaid city, and in the priſon of the ſaid keepers of the liberties of England, by the authority of parliament, under the cuſtody of us the ſaid ſheriffs now is detained, by virtue of a certain original bill in a plea of debt, upon a demand of 10l. of the lawful money of England, brought againſt him on the 27th day of the month of September, in the year of our Lord 1649, at the court of the ſaid keepers of the liberties of England, by the authority of parliament, held before Thomas Andrews, then mayor, and the aldermen of the city of London, in the ſaid chamber of the Guildhall of the ſaid city, according to the cuſtom of the ſaid city, at the ſuit of Gilbert Harriſon, chamberlain of the city of London, upon the act of the common council aforeſaid, made as aforeſaid, on the 15th day of April, in the 4th year of the reign of the lord James the 1ſt, aforeſaid, the tenor of which original bill follows in theſe words, to wit, Gilbert Harriſon, chamberlain of the city of London, who on the 20th day of * April, in the year of our Lord, 1648, and always afterwards hitherto was, and as yet is chamberlain of the ſaid city, by George May, his attorney, demands againſt

[Margin: Impriſonment on a writ of debt on the ſaid bye-law.]

[Margin: Tenor, in hæc verba.]

[Margin: * P. 371]

against John King, otherwise L'Roy, 10l. of the lawful money of England, which he owes to him, and unjustly detains, because that whereas, in the common council held according to the custom of the city of London, in the chamber of the Guildhall of the said city, situate in the parish of St. Michael, Bassishaw, in the ward of Bassishaw, London, aforesaid, on the 15th day of April, in the 4th year of the reign of the lord James, the late king of England, &c. by the power and authority of the said common council it was ordained and enacted, that no person whatsoever, not being free of the city of London, at any time after the feast of St. Michael the arch angel, then next ensuing, by any colour, way, or means, whatsoever, either directly or indirectly, by himself or by any other, should shew, sell, or put to sale, any wares or merchandize whatsoever, by retail, within the said city of London, the liberties or suburbs of the same, upon pain to forfeit to the chamberlain of London, for the time being, to the use of the mayor, commonalty, and citizens of the said city, the sum of 5l. of the lawful money of England, for every time wherein such person should shew, sell, or expose to sale, any wares or merchandizes whatsoever, by way of retail, within the said city, the liberties or suburbs of the same, against the true intent of the act of common council aforesaid, and then and there by the said authority it is further ordained and established, that no person whatever, not being free of the city of London, at any time after the said feast of St. Michael, then next ensuing, by any colour, way or means whatsoever, either directly or indirectly, by himself or by any other, should keep any shop, or other place whatsoever, inward or outward, for the shew, sale, or putting to sale, of any wares or merchandizes whatsoever, by way of retail, or should use any art, trade, occupation, mystery, or handicraft whatsoever, within the said city, the liberties and suburbs of the same, upon pain to forfeit the sum of 5l. of the lawful money of England, for every time wherein such person should keep any shop or other place whatsoever, inward or outward, for the shew, sale, or putting to sale, of any wares or merchandizes whatsoever, by way of retail, or should use any art, trade, occupation, mystery, or handicraft, whatsoever, within the said city, the liberties or suburbs of the same, against the true intent of the said act; and whereas, then and there by the said authority it was further enacted, that all the pains, penalties, forfeitures, and sums of money to be forfeited, by virtue of the said act or ordinance, should be recovered by action of debt, bill or plaint, to be commenced and prosecuted in the name of the chamberlain of the city of London, for the time being, in the court to be holden in the chamber of the Guildhall, of the city of London, before the lord mayor and the aldermen of the ſaid city, for the time being, in which no eſſoin or wager of law ſhould be admitted or allowed, for the defendant, and that the chamberlain of the ſaid city, for the * time being, in all ſuits to be proſecuted by virtue of the ſaid act or ordinance, againſt any offender, ſhould recover the ordinary coſts of ſuit, to be expended in and about the proſecution of the ſame; and further, that one equal third part of all forfeitures to be recovered by virtue of the ſaid act or ordinance, (the coſts of ſuit for the recovery of the ſame being deducted and allowed) after the recovery and receipt thereof, ſhould be paid and delivered to the treaſurer of Chriſt's hoſpital, to be employed towards the relief of the poor children to be brought up and maintained in the ſaid hoſpital; and another equal third part thereof, to him or them, who firſt ſhould give information of the offences for which ſuch forfeitures ſhould grow, and ſhould proſecute ſuit in the name of the chamberlain of the ſaid city, for the recovery of the ſame, any thing in the ſaid act to the contrary thereof notwithſtanding, as by the ſaid act of common council aforeſaid, fully appeareth: Nevertheleſs, the ſaid defendant, not regarding the ſaid act of common council, nor in any manner fearing the penalty in the ſame contained, after the ſaid feaſt of St. Michael the arch-angel, in the ſaid act mentioned, and before the bringing of this original bill, to wit, on the 20th day of September, in the year of our Lord, 1649, and at divers other days and times, between the ſaid 20th day of April, in the year of our Lord, 1648, aforeſaid, and the ſaid 20th day of September, in the year of our Lord, 1649, aforeſaid, within the ſaid city of London, to wit, in the pariſh of St. Chriſtopher, London, not being at the ſaid feaſt of St. Michael the arch-angel, in the ſaid act mentioned, nor at any time afterwards. a perſon free of the ſaid city, uſed the myſtery, art, or handicraft of a working goldſmith, for his own lucre and profit to be made thereby: and alſo, on the 21ſt day of September, in the year of our Lord, 1649, aforeſaid, in the pariſh laſt mentioned, the ſaid defendant uſed the myſtery, art, or handicraft, of a working jeweller, for his own lucre and profit to be made thereby, againſt the true intent of the act of common council, aforeſaid, whereby an action hath accrued to the ſaid plaintiff, to ſue for, demand, and have of the ſaid defendant, the ſaid 10l. now demanded, which the ſaid defendant to the ſaid plaintiff hath not paid, although often, &c. to the ſaid plaintiff's damage of twenty ſhillings, and thereupon he produces his ſuit, &c." Upon which original bill, the ſaid parties pleaded to the country, and ſo that matter before the ſaid mayor and aldermen in the ſaid court depends undetermined; alſo,

also, the said John King, otherwise L'Roy, is detained in prison under custody aforesaid, by virtue of a certain original bill in a plea of debt, upon the demand of 10l. of the lawful money of England, brought in the said court before us the said mayor and aldermen, held in the chamber of the Guildhall of the said city, on the 6th day of November, in the year of our lord, 1649, aforesaid, at the suit of the said Gilbert Harrison, chamberlain of the city of London, and which in like manner depends undetermined: and these are the causes of the caption and detention of the said John King otherwise L'Roy in prison, under the custody aforesaid, which together with the body of the said John King otherwise L'Roy, at the day and place in the said writ contained we have ready, as by the said writ we are commanded.

Another bill of debt at the suit of the chamberlain.

---

## * The Chamberlain of London *against* Drinkwater. * P. 373.

JAMES the 2d. to the mayor, aldermen, and sheriffs of London, greeting: We command you, that the body of John Drinkwater, in our prison, under your custody detained, as it is said, under a safe and sure conduct, together with the day and cause of his caption and detention, by whatsoever name the said John may be called in the same, you have before our beloved and faithful Edward Herbert, knight, our chief justice, assigned to hold pleas in our court before us, at his chamber situate in Serjeant's Inn, in Fleet-street, London, immediately after the receipt of this writ, to do and receive all and singular the things which our said chief justice concerning him then and there shall consider in this behalf, and have there then this writ, witness, &c. The execution of this writ appears in a certain schedule to this writ annexed. The answer of John Peake, knight, mayor, and of the aldermen of the city of London, and also of Thomas Rawlinson, knight, and Thomas Fowle, knight, sheriffs of the said city. London, to wit. We John Peake, knight, mayor, and the aldermen of the city of London, and also T. Rawlinson, knight, and T. Fowle, knight, sheriffs of the said city, to Edward Herbert, knight, chief justice of our lord James the 2d. the now king of England, &c. assigned to hold pleas in the court of the said lord the king, before the king himself, at his chamber situate in Serjant's Inn, in Fleet-street, London, immediately certify,

Writ of habeas corpus to the lord mayor, aldermen and sheriffs of London, returnable immediately before the lord chief justice of B. R. at his chamber.

Return. Imprisonment on an original bill of debt in the court of the lord mayor and aldermen, at the suit of the chamberlain of London, for a penalty in an act of common council for exercising the business of a porter by landing merchandizes in the city not being free of the porters company.

certify, that the city of London is, and from the time whereof the memory of man is not to the contrary, hath been an antient city, and that the citizens and freemen of the city of London aforesaid, from the whole time aforesaid whereof the memory of man is not to the contrary until, to and unto the term of the Holy Trinity, in the 35th year of the reign of the lord Charles the 2d. the late king of England, &c. were incorporated as well by the name of the mayor and commonalty and citizens of the city of London, as by the name of the mayor and commonalty of the city of London; and that in the said city there is had, and from the whole time whereof the memory of man is not to the contrary was had, until to and unto the said term of the Holy Trinity, in the 35th year of the reign of the said lord Charles the 2d. the late king of England aforesaid, a custom used and approved, to wit, that the measuring, portage, and carriage of all coals, corn and grain of whatsoever kind, and of all salt of what sort soever, and of all kinds of apples, peas, plums, onions, and of roots to be eaten, and of all other merchandizes measurable, or to be measured, arriving or brought into the city of London, upon or by water, or by the river Thames, and going out of the ports from the bridge of the town of Stains in the county of Middlesex, unto London bridge, and from thence into a certain place called Yendall, otherwise Yendland, otherwise Yendeele, towards the sea in the county of Kent, in any ship, boat, barge or vessel whatsoever, floating, loading, remaining or being of what side soever of the said river Thames, and upon any bank, wharf or shore of the said * river, which shall happen there to remain, and to be delivered or landed, or to be carried outward, or from the said city, from the said bridge of the town of Stains aforesaid, unto London bridge, and from thence to said place called Yendall, otherwise Yendland, otherwise Yendeele, from the time whereof the memory of man is not to the contrary until, to, and unto the said term of the Holy Trinity, have belonged to the mayor and commonalty and citizens of London, and always until, to, and unto the said term of the Holy Trinity, were used and exercised by their officers and ministers, and by certain porters freemen of the said city, called and known by the name of the corn and salt porters. And we further signify, that in the said city there is had, and from the whole time aforesaid whereof the memory of man is not to the contrary until, to and unto the said term of the Holy Trinity was had a certain other custom used and approved, to wit, that if any customs in the said city obtained and approved in any part were difficult and defective, or any things in the said city newly arising where remedy

The Citizens and freemen of London a corporation by prescription until Trinity term 35 Ch. 2.

Custom of the city until that time as to the measuring and portage of goods, &c. brought to London by water.

P. 374.

Custom to make bye laws.

medy was not before ordained should want amendment, the mayor and aldermen of the said city for the time being, with the assent of the commons of the common council of the said city, may and can appoint and ordain apt remedy consonant to good faith and reason, for the common profit of the citizens of the said city, and others coming to the same, as often as and whenever it shall seem to them expedient; provided nevertheless, that such ordinance be profitable to the laws of this kingdom of England, and to the progenitors of the said lord the king, and to his people, and be consonant to good faith and reason, which several customs, and all the other customs of the said city from the whole time aforesaid used and approved, by the authority of the parliament of the lord Richard, late king of England, &c. the 2d. after the conquest, held at Westminster, in the 7th year of his reign, to the then mayor and commonalty of the said city, and to their successors were ratified and confirmed. And we the said mayor and aldermen and sheriffs of the said city further certify, that in the common council held according to the custom of the city of London, in the chamber of the Guildhall of the said city, on the 5th day of October, in the 18th year of the reign of the lord James the late king of England, &c. by William Cockham, knight, then mayor, and the aldermen of the said city, with the assent of the commons in the common council of the said city then and there assembled, it was enacted by the said mayor and aldermen, with the assent of the said commons, by the authority of the said common council, in the manner and form as follows, to wit: "*Whereas the measuring, portage and carriage of all coals, corn and grain of what kind soever, and of all salt of what sort soever, and of all kinds of apples, pears, plums, onions, and of roots to be eaten, and of all other merchandizes, measurable or to be measured, arriving or brought into the port of the city of London, upon or by water, or by the river Thames, and going out of the said ports within the limits hereafter mentioned, in any ship, boat, barge or vessel whatsoever, floating, loading, remaining or being, of what side soever of the river of Thames, or upon any bank, wharf, or shore of the* * *said river, which shall happen there to remain and to be delivered or landed, or be carried outward, or from the said city from the bridge of the town of Staines, in the county of Middlesex unto London-bridge, and from thence into a certain place called Yendall, otherwise Yendland, otherwise Yendeele, towards the sea in the county of Kent, have time out of mind belonged, and yet do belong unto the mayor and commonality and citizens of London, and always have been and now are exercised and used by their officers and ministers, and by certain porters freemen of this city, called and known by the name of corn and salt porters, taking*

The customs of the city confirmed by parliament.

Act of common council 5th Oct. 18th James 1st.

* P. 375.

taking their denomination from the chief of the merchandizes aforesaid, antiently established and appointed to and for their labour and work of portage, by orders of the court of lord mayor and aldermen of this city, until of late, certain foreign porters not lawfully allowed and authorised by the said lord mayor and court of aldermen, have intruded in the labour of the said free porters in divers parts within the said city's limits and jurisdictions upon the river of Thames, to the manifest wrong and prejudice of the city's antient liberties and privileges, to the great hindrance of the poor freemen of this city, who being by great casualties decayed in their estates, have for relief by the allowance aforesaid, undertaken the said hard labour, by reason whereof much disturbance hath often arisen, and the said free porters have been much hindered in the due discharge and performance of the labour aforesaid; for prevention whereof, and for the better directing, settling and establishing of the said company of corn and salt porters, commonly called the porters of Billingsgate. It is now ordained and enacted by the right honourable Sir William Cockham, knight, lord mayor of the city of London, and his right worshipful brethren the aldermen of the said city, and by the commons of this present common council assembled, and by the authority of the same, that the company and fellowship of the porters of Billingsgate, commonly called by the name of corn and salt porters, or by any other name whatsoever, shall remain, continue, and be from henceforth one company or brotherhood, and be called by the name of the porters of Billingsgate, as antiently they have been. And whereas the said company of porters was heretofore appointed to consist of the number of 120 persons; now forasmuch as it is thought fit and necessary, for the better and speedy dispatch of the merchants and victuallers, and merchants of sea coal, repairing and bringing the several commodities aforesaid into and within the ports of this city by water, within the limits aforesaid, that the said number of 120 persons shall from henceforth be encreased and aug-
* P. 376. mented to the number of 400 able and sufficient men that * shall work in the said labour within the limits aforesaid and no more. And the said company of porters shall from henceforth consist of 400 persons, freemen of this city, and not to exceed the same without the allowance of the alderman of the ward of Billingsgate for the time being, of which number of 400 persons, 24 of the saddest, discreetest and meetest persons, shall from time to time, be and continue assistants, and bear the name of four and twenty assistants of the said fellowship, and they shall be elected of such of the said fellowship as shall be free of the said city, and none other, and that as often as it shall happen any of the said 24 persons to decease, or depart this city, or otherwise be removed from being of the said assistants, that then the whole company or the greater part of them, shall be called together and shall nominate

*nominate one or more other sad and discreet person or persons in his or their places, and present him or them to the alderman of the said ward of Billingsgate for the time being, and in his absence to his deputy, there to be allowed by the said alderman or deputy, if he or they shall seem to him to be meet and able thereunto: and that the whole company may from henceforth on midsummer-day every year, or at any other time as they or the greatest part of them shall think fit to appoint, in quiet sort, assemble themselves together in such convenient place as shall seem to them meet. And there the said four and twenty assistants, together with such as have been, or hereafter shall have been rulers of the said company, and of the said brotherhood or fraternity by their mutual assent, to elect and nominate six of the saddest and discreetest persons of and amongst the said company, all freemen of the said city of London, to be rulers and governors of the said company for one whole year then next ensuing, of which said number of six governors to be chosen as aforesaid, three of them shall be of the number of six that remained governors the year before; which governors so to be nominated and chosen, shall be presented to the alderman of the said ward, or in his absence to his deputy, to be allowed and confirmed to be meet men to serve in the said rooms. And if the said alderman, or in his absence his deputy, shall mislike of any of the said six rulers to be nominated as aforesaid, or any of the said twenty four persons to be named and appointed for assistants, then the company and the assistants aforesaid, shall eftsoons assemble themselves, and nominate such other discreet person or persons, either for rulers or for assistants, as the said alderman, or in his absence his deputy shall think meet to be allowed. And that upon every such allowance of the rulers and assistants, or any of them as aforesaid, they shall present themselves before the lord mayor and aldermen of the said city for the time * being in the Utter-court, and* * P. 377.
*there the said rulers and assistants, and every of them, shall receive their several oaths for the due execution of the said offices and rooms accordingly, as antiently hath been used, and every of them to pay for their oath two pence. And that the said company, and all the members thereof, shall be subject to all such ordinances and rules, as shall be from time to time made and set down by the court of lord mayor and aldermen of this city, in the council-chamber of this city, for the good government of the men of the said fellowship, under such reasonable pains, penalties and forfeitures as the said court shall limit and appoint. Also be it further ordained, enacted established by the authority aforesaid, That the porters of Billingsgate, shall have and receive for their travel in bearing burdens of corn, salt, and sea coals, or any other things, such wages and sums of money as hereafter particularly ensue; that is to say, for the carriage of wheat, rye, peas, beans and barley out of any vessel at the water side within*

*in*

*in the limits and places of the river Thames, as aforesaid, on both sides the river of Thames into any granary, loft or sacks upon any wharf or key, or out of any loft or granary, or sacks into any vessel, boat or lighter, being next to any such wharf or key, for every quarter of grain so carried two pence, and for the lifting or carrying of any of the said grains out of one small vessel, boat or lighter into another, if it be bought and sold, or to be passed away from London two pence. Item. For malt, oats and beer-corn carried into or from any the places aforesaid, for the quarter three half-pence; and for such as shall be lifted or carried overboard out of any ship, hoy, barge, lighter or boat into another if it be bought and sold, or to be passed away from London for the quarter one penny. Item. For carriage of four bushels of oats from Galley-key and Porters-key, or any other key, to any citizen's house, being distant as far from the water side as the Cross in Cheap-side is from any of the said keys, four pence. Item, it is further ordered, that touching the carriage of wheat, rye, peas, beans and malt, or any other the grains before mentioned, to any place or places further distant from the water-side than aforesaid, it is then thought meet, and enacted by the authority aforesaid, that the same be left to the agreement of the parties as they can compound; or if they cannot agree therein, then the same to be referred to the alderman of the ward for the time being, or his deputy in his absence, to decide the same. Item, For all light burthens, called catching-burthens, that are carried so far as is distant from Billingsgate to Leaden-hall in London, or the like distance from the water-side within the city of London, for every burthen two pence. Item,*
* P. 378. *The * said burthens being salt, for one bushel one penny, for two bushels two pence, for three bushels three pence, and if it be carried any further, then to agree with the porters for carrying thereof. Item, for carrying of salt within the limits or places aforesaid, on both sides the river of Thames, out of any vessel into any shop or cellar upon the wharf or key next adjoining to the same from the water-side, two pence, and also the like sum for recarrying of the same into any vessel from the places aforesaid, for every weight of salt so carried or passed away from London, and out of one vessel into another lying side by side, eight pence, or within the length of a plank of one another. Item, of every poor man, woman or child of the said city, as also of the country, for a bushel of corn, or a bushel of salt out of any vessel into any car or sack, or a horseback upon the key, for every bushel one halfpenny. Item, for oysters, muscles, onions and carrots, or any other burthen carried or put out of any vessel into another, or to be laid upon horse or cart, being at the same wharf or key, the one with the other, the burthen one penny. Also, it is enacted, ordained and established by the authority aforesaid, that the said porters shall have for the carriage of*

*sea*

*sea coal out of any vessel within the limits and places aforesaid, on both sides the river Thames, upon any wharf, yard or court adjoining to the river Thames, fifteen foot of planks and eighteen foot of shore or less, (the buyer and seller finding fillers, as they always have done) for every chaldron carrying to the places aforesaid four pence, and for the recarrying of the said coals of the like distance, the sum of four pence. Item, Whereas, heretofore they have been ordered to take but six pence for the carrying of a chaldron of sea coals in the Bridge-house and at Broken-wharf, and they do usually receive eight pence the chaldron, it is thought meet that they continue the said eight pence, and that they shall in respect of that increase of two pence upon the chaldron, either fill the sacks themselves, or else provide fillers at their own charge for filling thereof; and likewise, the porters to have and receive for the carriage of every chaldron of coals, from the water-side out of the vessel or lighter there, into the cellar or house under the granaries at Bridewell, and filling and trimming them up to the floor, as high as they can in the cellar or house, nine pence as they have used to have, and to other men's houses, as the said porters have for carrying of salt, and besides if up stairs, for every pair of stairs two pence; and for the carriage of every quarter of corn from the water-side, at Bridewell, out of the vessel, barge, or lighter there, into the granaries there, one with another, two pence halfpenny; and so after that rate into the other granaries within the limits aforesaid, and on both sides the river Thames, according to that order as it is * used for the granaries at Bridewell; and for the carriage of every quarter of corn from the water side into the granaries at the Bridge-house, being nearer to the water-side than the Bell-garner, two pence; and for carrying the like quantity of corn into any other granaries that are as far from the water-side as the Bell-garner, or further on the Bridge-house wharf one with another two pence halfpenny: and it is further ordained, enacted and established by the authority aforesaid, that the owner or merchant, or loader of any French, Dutch, Scotch, Hull or Lynn, or double decked ship, or any bark, except Kentish or Essex hoys, shall pay to the said porters, for every quarter of corn, beans, peas, oats and malt (the said porters fetching them out of the hold) a halfpenny a quarter, as always heretofore hath been paid, or else the ship's company to heave it up out of the said hold; also it is ordained, enacted and established, by the authority aforesaid, that the meters as well of corn as of salt and coals, or their deputies, or any fillers, shall at any time hereafter, when either salt or corn shall come to be discharged at any of the places above specified, call the rulers of the said porters at Billingsgate, where one of the rulers is always to give his attendance, and one other of them at Porter's-key, unto them, or otherwise give them knowledge of the quantity of corn or salt, or sea coals so come, that they the same rulers may appoint such* 

* P. 379



*number*

*number of the porters to the ſaid work, as ſhall be ſufficient to ſerve for the diſcharge of the ſame; and that the ſaid meters, or their deputies or fillers, ſhall not of themſelves, ſet any other perſon to work at any time, but call the rulers of the ſaid company of porters, and they to appoint them porters for the ſame work as hath been uſed, upon pain to forfeit and loſe the ſum of* 20 *ſhillings for every ſuch offence, one half of ſuch forfeiture to be for the uſe of the poor children now harboured or hereafter to be harboured in Chriſt's hoſpital, aud the other half for the uſe of the ſaid company or fellowſhip; alſo it is enacted, ordained and eſtabliſhed, by the authority aforeſaid, that the meters of ſea coals, or their deputies, ſhall call one of the rulers of the ſaid fellowſhip to appoint them porters for the carriage of ſea coals, as the meters of corn and ſalt, and to ſet them on work ſo as their turns may be ſerved; alſo it is ordained and enacted, by the authority aforeſaid, that touching the carriage of all kinds of grain to be carried from off the water into any loft or garner, or from any wharf into any cart, or out of any garner or loft into another, or into any ſhip, lighter or other veſſel, or out of any ſhip or veſſel into another, the ſaid porters ſhall have the carriage thereof ſo often as it is to be carried or removed, and after every ſale or*
* P. 380 ** change of the property of the ſame, as heretofore they have uſed to have, if it be to be carried (except any bakers, being freemen of this city, that carry it by their millers or domeſtical ſervants out of their granaries to be carried to the mill) And that if any perſon or perſons ſhall refuſe to yield to any of the ſaid fellowſhip, the benefit of this order, then ſuch as ſhall ſo refuſe ſhall upon complaint thereof be puniſhed by the diſcretion of the court of the lord mayor and aldermen of the ſaid city, for the time being; provided nevertheleſs, that notwithſtanding any thing contained in this act, it ſhall be lawful for any carrier of the country to ſend by his ordinary porter, being a freeman of this city, or allowed to be a porter according to the laws and ordinances of this act, from his inn to Billingſgate or Queenhith, for ſuch proviſions as he ſhall think meet, and ſuch porter ſhall not be reſtrained, hindered or letted by reaſon of this act, or any thing herein contained, but that he may quietly carry his burthen to ſuch carrier to his inn, or any other place which he ſhall appoint, as he lawfully might have done before the making of theſe ordinances; Alſo it is further enacted, ordained and eſtabliſhed, by the authority of this common council, that all brewers, bakers, merchants and others, who are or ſhall be owners, ſellers or buyers, of wheat, rye, malt, or other grain, or of ſalt or ſea coals, ſhall not retain or ſet on work, nor ſuffer to be retained or ſet on work, to carry it as porters, any ſtranger, foreigner, or other, to carry their wheat, rye, malt, or other grain, or ſalt or ſea coal, or other things as aforeſaid, other than ſuch as be or ſhall be of the ſaid fellowſhip, (except ſuch porters as have for the ſpace of ten years at*

*the*

*the least, now past, at Billingsgate, used to carry butter, cheese, iron, hemp, roots, sprats, sand, or burthens called catching burthens, and are now grown old and cannot take any other course to live) and except it be upon an extraordinary, or needful, or urgent necessity, occasion or casualty; And that no measurer of corn, salt or sea coals, or other the things aforesaid, or their deputies, measure any corn, salt or sea coal, or other the things aforesaid, but only the porters of the said fellowship to have the landing and carrying thereof, upon pain to forfeit and lose the sum of 20 shillings for every the offences aforesaid, the one half of which penalty to the use of the poor harboured in Christ's hospital, and the other half to the use of the said fellowship; And be it further enacted by the authority aforesaid, that no foreigner, bargeman, hoyman or waterman, or any person or persons whatsoever, not being of the said fellowship, shall intermeddle with the landing, carrying or recarrying up or down, in or out of any ship, barge, boat or lighter, or any other vessel into * another upon the said* P. 381 river Thames, within the limits aforesaid, or out of any garner, loft or warehouse, to the said river near adjoining, within the limits and places aforesaid, any corn, grain, salt or sea coals, unless he be a fellow or brother of the said company, upon pain to forfeit and lose every time he shall offend therein 20 shillings, unless it be in time of danger of the loss or hurt of the commodities, by foul weather or leaking, or other urgent necessity; and it is likewise enacted by the authority aforesaid, that if any bargeman, hoyman, maltman, or other person or persons, shall convey away any corn, malt, salt, or any fruit whatsoever, by land or by water, either by day or by night, without a bill from the lord mayor of this city for the time being, and paying the due fees for metage, fillage and porterage, that then they shall forfeit and lose for every time he or they shall offend therein 20 shillings, one half of which forfeiture to be to the use of the poor children harboured or hereafter to be harboured in Christ's hospital, and the other half to the use of the said company. And whereas there hath always been a difference in that brotherhood, concerning their kind of labour, which the rulers and assistants always upheld and continued for the good of the old and antient, viz. that the men of the antientest standing are called corn porters, and men of the younger sort are called salt porters or quarter men, and every Midsummer there is to be taken in to carry corn six of the antientest of salt porters; it is now enacted by the authority aforesaid, that the said orders be from henceforth duly observed and kept by the rulers, assistants and others of the said company; Also it is ordained and enacted by the authority aforesaid, that no deputy coal meters, or salt meters, or corn fillers, shall be hereafter received, admitted or allowed, by any master corn meter, coal meter, or salt meter, or corn filler, or salt filler, but only such as are or shall be of the said fellowship or brotherhood, and known to be of honest life and*

*conversation, upon pain to forfeit and lose the sum of five pounds the one half of which to be to the use of the poor harboured or hereafter to be harboured in Christ's hospital, and the other half to the use of the said fellowship; All which pains and penalties and sums of money so to be forfeited by virtue of this act, shall be recovered by and in the name of the chamberlain of this city, for the time being, in the king's majesty's court, holden before the lord mayor and aldermen of the city of London, in the chamber of the Guildhall of the same city, by action, bill or information, wherein no protection, essoin, or wager of law, shall be admitted or allowed for the defendant, and if the suit shall pass for the plaintiff, he shall recover against the defendant his ordinary costs of suit; and after the recovery had the forfeiture so recovered to be employed according to the true intent and meaning of this act; and if the suit shall pass against the plaintiff, the defendant shall recover*
* P. 382. *his ordinary costs against * the plaintiff."* And we further certify, that in the term of St. Michael, in the 33d year of the reign of the said lord Charles the 2d, king, &c. Robert Sawyer, knight, attorney-general of the said lord the late king, who for the said late king in that behalf, did prosecute in his proper person, came into the court of the said late king, before the said late lord the king himself, then held at Westminster, in the county of Middlesex, on the Monday next after 15 days of St. Martin, in that same term, and for the said late king then exhibited in the court there, a certain information against the then mayor, and commonalty, and citizens, of the city of London, aforesaid, and in the said information then gave the court there to understand and to be informed, that the then mayor, and commonalty, and citizens of the said city of London, for the space of one month then last past, and more, had used, and then did use, and had claimed to have and use, without any warrant or royal grant, within the city of London, aforesaid, and the liberties and precincts of the said city, divers liberties, privileges and franchises, in that information specified, without any commission or other authority from the said lord the late king, in that behalf granted or obtained, all and singular which liberties, privileges, and franchises, they the said mayor, and commonalty, and citizens, of the city of London, aforesaid, for the whole time aforesaid, against the said lord the late king, had usurped, and until then did usurp; and thereupon afterwards, to wit, on the Monday next after the octave of St. Hillary, in the 33d year of the reign of the said late lord the king, aforesaid, in the court of the said late lord the king, before the said late lord the king himself, at Westminster, (the said court then being held at Westminster, in the county of Middlesex) came the said mayor, and commonalty, and citizens, of the city of London, by Benedict Brown,

In Michaelmas term 33d Ch. 2d the attorney general exhibited a quo warranto against the lord mayor, commonalty and citizens of London, for usurping divers liberties, privileges, &c.

Who appeared.

Brown, then their attorney, and having had oyer of the ſaid information, they the ſaid then mayor, and commonalty, and citizens, of the city of London, prayed day to imparl thereto, until, &c. from the day of Eaſter in 15 days then next coming, and it was granted to them, before the ſaid lord the king, whereſoever, &c. And thereupon it was in ſuch ſort proceeded in the ſaid court, before the ſaid late king, at Weſtminſter, aforeſaid; that afterwards, to wit, in the ſaid term of the Holy Trinity, in the 35th year of the reign of the ſaid lord Charles the 2d, the late king of England, &c. aforeſaid, in the ſaid court of the ſaid late lord the king, before the ſaid late lord the king, then being held at Weſtminſter, in the county of Middleſex, becauſe that it ſeemed to the ſaid court then there, that the ſaid then mayor, and commonalty, and citizens, of the city of London, aforeſaid, had forfeited to the ſaid late lord the king, their liberties, privileges, and franchiſes, aforeſaid; it was conſidered by the ſaid court there, that the liberties, privileges, and franchiſes, of being in themſelves one body corporate and politick, in deed, fact and name, by the name of the mayor, and commonalty, and citizens of London, and by the ſaid name to plead, and to be impleaded, to anſwer, and to be anſwered, by the ſaid mayor, commonalty, and citizens, of the ſaid city, claimed ſhould be taken and ſeized into the hands of the ſaid late lord the king, whereof they are convicted, as by the record and proceedings thereupon in the court of the lord the now king, before the king himſelf, to wit, at Weſtminſter, aforeſaid, fully appears of record, which judgment as yet remains in its full * force and effect, not reverſed or annulled; by virtue whereof the ſaid late lord the king Charles the 2d, was ſeized of the liberties, privileges and franchiſes aforeſaid; and we further certify, that the moſt illuſtrious lord James the 2d, the now king of England, &c. according to, and by his royal good pleaſure, willing that the government and adminiſtration of the ſaid city, and of the citizens of the ſaid city, in all things ſhould be continued, exerciſed and uſed, for the honour of the ſaid city, and for the advantage of the citizens of the ſaid city, and the other ſubjects of the ſaid lord the now king, in the ſame manner in which at and before the time of the giving of the ſaid judgment it was uſed; and that the good and laudable cuſtoms and laws, uſed and conſtituted within the ſaid city, before the giving of the ſaid judgment, and being in force at the time of the giving of the ſaid judgment, as yet ſhould be held, exerciſed and obſerved, afterwards, to wit, by his letters patent, made under his great ſeal of England, bearing date at Weſtminſter, aforeſaid, in the county of Middleſex, the 17th day of January, in the 2d year of his reign, aſſigned, conſtituted and made, his beloved John Peake,

*Margin notes:* and obtain'd imparlance until Eaſter term following. — In Trinity term 35 of Ch. 2d. judgment for the king. — That their privileges, liberties and franchiſes ſhould be ſeized into the king's hands. — * P. 383. — Whereby the king was ſeized of the franchiſes, &c. — That James the 2d by his letters patent, granted that the city ſhould be governed in the ſame manner as before the judgment, and ſhould enjoy all their antient cuſtoms, courts, liberties, &c.

Peake, knight, then mayor, and William Turner, knight, and 24 others, then aldermen of the ſaid city, to continue and to be aldermen of the ſaid city of London, aforeſaid, and to have, enjoy, and execute, all and the like authorities, powers and privileges, as the reſpective aldermen aforeſaid, at the time of the giving of the ſaid judgment of right had executed or could execute; to have, enjoy, perform and execute the ſame offices, authorities, powers and privileges, with all and ſingular the things appertaining and belonging to the ſame, as well within their wards, reſpectively, as in any courts held, or to be held before the mayor and aldermen of the ſaid city, or elſewhere within the ſaid city and the liberties of the ſame, and in all other places, and to all intentions and purpoſes, in as ample manner and form in all things as they or any of them, or any other aldermen, or alderman of the ſaid city, before that time had enjoyed, performed and executed, or of right ought to have, enjoy, perform and execute; and further, the ſaid lord James the 2d, &c. by his ſaid letters patent willed, conſtituted, eſtabliſhed and declared, that the mayor, aldermen, recorder, ſheriffs, chamberlain, and all the other officers of the ſaid city, who then were, and afterwards ſhould be, and every of them, ſhould have, hold, enjoy and exerciſe, all courts as well of record as not of record, juriſdictions, powers and authorities, in their ſtations reſpectively, as well within the city of London, as without, which the mayor, aldermen, recorder, ſheriffs, chamberlain, and other officers of the ſaid city, or any of them, at the time of the giving of the ſaid judgment, or before or afterwards reſpectively had and exerciſed, or lawfully could have and exerciſe; and alſo, that the mayor and aldermen of the ſaid city, for the time being, or any thirteen of them (of whom he willed that the mayor of the ſaid city, or one of the two ſenior aldermen for the time being ſhould be one) might and could ordain, decree and provide, for the good government of the ſaid city, and of the citizens and other his ſubjects in the ſaid city, or the liberties
* P. 384 of the ſame; and the ſaid lord James the 2d, * by his ſaid letters patent further ordained, conſtituted and eſtabliſhed, that all the good cuſtoms, preſcriptions, acts, laws of common council, and conſtitutions exerciſed, conſtituted and eſtabliſhed in the ſaid city, before the giving of the ſaid judgment, and at the time of the ſaid judgment being in force, of and concerning the widows and orphans of the citizens of the ſaid city, and of the guardianſhip of the ſaid orphans, and of their goods and effects, and of or concerning admiſſion into the freedom of the ſaid city, and the prohibition and puniſhment of thoſe who not before admitted, or afterwards to be admitted, did keep or afterwards might keep

ſhop,

ſhop, or did ſell, or afterwards might ſell, goods or merchandize by retail, or did exerciſe or uſe, or afterwards might exerciſe or uſe, any art or occupation within the ſaid city or the liberties of the ſame, againſt the laws, or cuſtoms, or privileges, of the ſaid city; and for the regulation of the hire of cars and carts, and coaches, or carriages, and for the reſtraining and puniſhing nuiſances and other obſtructions, of whatſoever kind, in the ſtreets and public ways, within the ſaid city and the liberties of the ſame, and for the regulation and government of all and ſingular courts, fairs and markets, of what kind ſoever, public ſcales and weights, watches, priſoners, brokers, porters, officers, and miniſters, whatſoever, within the ſaid city, or the liberties of the ſame, or of or concerning any other thing, cauſe or matter, whatſoever, (the cuſtoms and conſtitutions of or concerning the election of the mayor, aldermen, recorder and ſheriffs, of the ſaid city, and for holding the common council excepted) firmly, for ever afterwards, ſhould be held, obſerved, exerciſed and uſed, in all things, as fully and entirely, and by ſuch perſon or perſons, and in as ample manner and form, as they by any of them reſpectively, before the giving of the ſaid judgment were held, obſerved, exerciſed or uſed, or ought, or of right might be held, obſerved, exerciſed or uſed; and we further certify, that before the coming of the ſaid writ, of the ſaid lord the king, to us directed, and to this ſchedule annexed, John Drinkwater, in the ſaid writ named, was taken by the name of John Drinkwater, within the ſaid city, and is detained in the priſon of the ſaid lord the king, under the cuſtody of us the ſaid ſheriffs, by virtue of a certain original bill, in a plea of debt, upon a demand of 40 ſhillings, of the lawful money of England, againſt him the ſaid John Drinkwater, on the 18th day of March, in the 3d year of the reign of our ſaid lord James the 2d, &c. before us the ſaid mayor and aldermen of the ſaid city, in the ſaid chamber of the Guildhall of the ſaid city then held, according to the cuſtom of the ſaid city, at the ſuit of Henry Loads, eſquire, chamberlain of the ſaid city, brought upon the act of common council aforeſaid, made as aforeſaid, on the 5th day of October, in the 18th year of the reign of the ſaid lord James, late king of England, &c. aforeſaid; the tenor of which original bill, follows in theſe words, to wit,—" Henry Loads, eſquire, chamberlain of the city of London, by James Gibſon, his attorney, demands againſt John Drinkwater, 40 ſhillings, of the lawful money of England, which he owes to him and unjuſtly detains, &c. for this, becauſe, that in the common council held according to the cuſtom of the city of London, aforeſaid, uſed and approved from the whole time whereof the memory of * man is not to the contrary, in

Defendant impriſoned upon a bill of debt, founded on the ſaid act of common council, made in the 18th year of the reign of James 1ſt.

Tenor of the bill.

* P. 385

in the chamber of the Guildhall of the ſaid city, ſituate in the pariſh of St. Michael, Baſſiſhaw, in the ward of Baſſiſhaw, London, aforeſaid, on the 5th day of October, in the 18th year of the reign of the lord James, the late king of England, &c. by a certain act of the common council then and there made, reciting, that whereas the meaſuring, portage, and carriage of all coals, corn and grain, of whatſoever kind, and of all ſalt of what ſort ſoever, and of all kinds of apples, pears, plumbs, onions, and of roots to be eaten, and of all other merchandizes meaſurable, or to be meaſured, arriving or brought into the port of London, upon or by water, or by the river Thames, and going out of the ports, within the limits afterwards in the ſaid act mentioned, in any ſhip, boat, barge or veſſel, whatſoever, floating, loading, remaining or being, on what ſide ſoever of the ſaid river Thames, and upon any bank, wharf, or ſhore, of the ſaid river, which ſhall there happen to remain, and to be delivered or landed, or to be carried outward, or from the ſaid city, from the bridge of the town of Stains, in the county of Middleſex, unto London Bridge, and from thence into a certain place called Yendall, otherwiſe Yendland, otherwiſe Yendeele, towards the ſea in the county of Kent, from the time whereof the memory of man is not to the contrary, have belonged and as yet belong, to the mayor, commonalty and citizens of London, and always were, and then were exerciſed and uſed by their officers and miniſters, and by certain porters, freemen of the ſaid city, called and known by the name of the corn and ſalt porters; among other things it is enacted and ordained, by the authority of the ſaid common council, that the company and fellowſhip of the porters of Billingſgate, called by the name of the corn and ſalt porters, or by any other name whatſoever, ſhall remain and continue, and from thence ſhould be one ſociety or brotherhood, and ſhould be called by the name of the porters of Billingſgate, as they antiently were; and whereas the ſaid company of porters before that time, conſiſted of the number of 120 perſons, by the ſaid act it is ordained and appointed, that for the better diſpatch of the merchants, and others bringing the ſaid ſeveral commodities to the port of the city of London, within the ſaid limits, that the ſaid number ſhould be increaſed and augmented to the number of 400 able and ſufficient men; and alſo the reaſonable prices, which the ſaid ſociety of porters ſhould have, for the carrying the ſaid ſeveral commodities, are expreſſly mentioned and appointed in the ſaid act; and then and there, by the ſaid act of the common council, aforeſaid, it is further enacted by the ſaid authority, that no foreign bargeman, hoyman, or waterman, or any other perſon or perſons whatſoever, not being of the

ſaid

ſaid fellowſhip, ſhould intermeddle with the landing, carrying, or recarrying up or down, in or out of any ſhip, boat, barge, hoy or other veſſel, into another, upon the ſaid river Thames, within the limits * aforeſaid, or out of any garner, loft or warehouſe, to the ſaid river near adjoining, within the limits and places aforeſaid, any corn, grain, ſalt or ſea coals, unleſs he be a fellow or brother of the ſaid company, upon pain to forfeit and loſe for every time that he ſhall offend therein 20 ſhillings, unleſs it be in time of danger of the loſs or hurt of the commodities aforeſaid, by foul weather or leaking, or other urgent neceſſity, one moiety of which penalty ſhall be to the uſe of the poor harboured in Chriſt's hoſpital, and the other moiety to the uſe of the ſaid ſociety, all which pains, penalties, and ſums of money, to be forfeited by virtue of the ſaid act, ſhould be recovered by and in the name of the chamberlain of the ſaid city, for the time being, in the court of the king's majeſty, held before the lord mayor and aldermen of the city of London, in the chamber of the Guildhall of the ſaid city, by action, bill or information, in which no protection, eſſoin, or wager of law, ſhould be admitted and allowed for the defendant; and if the ſuit ſhall paſs for the plaintiff, he ſhall recover againſt the defendant his ordinary coſts of ſuit, and after the recovery had, the forfeiture ſo recovered to be employed according to the true intent and meaning of the ſaid act; and if the ſuit ſhall paſs againſt the plaintiff, the defendant ſhall recover his ordinary coſt againſt the plaintiff, as by the ſaid act of common council among other things more fully appears; and the ſaid plaintiff ſaith, that the ſaid John Drinkwater, not being a freeman, nor brother of the ſaid ſociety, not regarding the act of common council aforeſaid, nor in any manner fearing the penalty in the ſame contained, after the making and enacting of the ſaid act of common council, and before the bringing of this original bill, to wit, on the 4th day of November, in the 1ſt year of the reign of our lord James the 2d, &c. in the pariſh of St. Bridget, otherwiſe Bride's, London, and within the juriſdiction of this court, no danger of the loſs or hurt of the malt after mentioned, or of any part thereof then being by foul weather, or leaking, or other urgent neceſſity; 150 quarters of malt, out of a certain boat then and there being in and upon the ſaid river, within the limits in the ſaid act mentioned, and within the juriſdiction of this court, did land againſt the true intent of the ſaid act, whereby an action hath accrued to the ſaid plaintiff, to demand and have of the ſaid defendant 20 ſhillings, parcel of the ſaid 40 ſhillings; and the ſaid John Drinkwater, not being a freeman or brother of the ſaid ſociety, not regarding the ſaid act of common council, nor in

* P. 386

Aſſignment of the facts againſt the act.

any manner fearing the penalty in the fame contained, after the making and enacting of the faid act of common council, aforefaid, and before the bringing of this original bill, to wit, on the 10th day of Auguft, in the 2d year of the reign of our lord James the 2d, &c. in the parifh of St. Bridget, otherwife Bride's, London, and within the jurifdiction of this court, no danger of the lofs or hurt of the malt after mentioned, or of any part thereof then being, by foul wea-
*P. 387 ther, or leaking, or other urgent neceffity, 100 other * quarters of malt, out of a certain barge, then and there upon the faid river, within the faid limits remaining, did land againft the true intent of the faid act, whereby an action hath accrued to the faid plaintiff, to demand and have of the faid defendant 20 fhillings, the refidue of the faid 40 fhillings, with this, that he the faid Henry will verify, that the faid number of 400 porters is fufficient to carry, load and unload, all quantities of the faid commodities in the faid act mentioned, to be brought to the faid ports, within the faid limits, or to be exported from the faid ports; neverthelefs, the faid defendant hath not paid the faid plaintiff the faid fum of 40 fhillings, or one penny thereof, although often requefted, to the faid plaintiff's damage of 20 fhillings; and thereupon he produces his fuit, &c. and fo the faid caufe depends as yet undetermined, &c. And this is the only caufe of the caption and detention of the faid John Drinkwater, in the faid writ named, which together with his body, we have ready as we are commanded by the faid writ.

Et hæc eft caufa, &c.

---

## Habeas Corpus *for* Bradnox.

Writ of habeas corpus to the mayor, aldermen and fheriffs of London, returnable before a judge of the king's bench immediately.

CHARLES the 2d, &c. To the mayor, aldermen and fheriffs of London, greeting:—We command you, that the body of Henry Bradnox, in our prifon under your cuftody detained, as it is faid, under a fafe and fure conduct, together with the day and caufe of his caption and detention, by whatfoever name the faid Henry may be called in the fame, you have before our beloved and faithful Thomas Twyfden, knight and baronet, one of our juftices affigned to hold pleas in our court before us, at his houfe in the Inner Temple, London, immediately after the receipt of this writ, to do and receive all and fingular the things which our faid juftice concerning him then and there fhall confider in this behalf, and have there then this writ, &c.

The

The execution of this writ appears in a certain ſchedule to this writ annexed. The anſwer of Richard Ford, knight, mayor, and of the aldermen of the city of London, and alſo of Danett Forth and Patience Ward, of the ſaid city, ſheriffs.

Return of the lord mayor, aldermen and ſheriffs.

We, Richard Ford, knight, mayor, and the aldermen of the city of London, and alſo Danett Forth, eſquire, and Patience Ward, eſquire, of the ſaid city, ſheriffs, to Thomas Twyſden, knight and baronet, one of the juſtices of our lord Charles the 2d, &c. aſſigned to hold pleas in the court of the lord the king, before the king himſelf, at his houſe in the Inner Temple, immediately ſignify; that the city of London is, and from the whole time whereof the memory of man is not to the contrary, hath been an antient * city, and that the mayor and commonalty, and citizens of the city of London, are, and from the whole time aforeſaid, have been, a body politick and corporate, and for the whole time aforeſaid, known by the name of the citizens of London; of the citizens of the city of London; of the barons of the king, of the city of the lord the king, of London, of the mayor and citizens of London, of the mayor and commonalty of the city of London, of the mayor and commonalty and citizens, of the city of London; and that within the ſaid city there is had, and from the whole time aforeſaid, was had, a cuſtom uſed and approved, to wit, that the mayor and commonalty and citizens of the city of London, by themſelves, or by ſuch other perſon or perſons, as by the mayor and aldermen of the city of London, aforeſaid, with the aſſent of the commons of the ſaid city, they ſhould appoint, ſhould have the right of regulating, ordering and diſpoſing of cars, carts, carrooms, carters and carmen, and of all other perſon or perſons whatſoever, working any car or cart, within the city of London and the liberties of the ſame city; and we further ſignify, that in the ſaid city there is had, and from the whole time aforeſaid was had ſuch cuſtom, uſed and approved, to wit, that if any cuſtoms obtained and approved in the ſaid city, are or were in any part difficult and defective, or any thing in the ſaid commonalty newly ariſing, where remedy was not before ordained, want or ſhould want amendment, that the mayor and aldermen of the ſaid city, for the time being, with the aſſent of the commons of the ſaid city, may and ought to appoint and ordain apt remedy, conſonant to good faith and reaſon, for the common profit of the citizens of the ſaid city, and the other faithful ſubjects of the ſaid lord the king and his progenitors, repairing to the ſaid city, as often as and whenſoever it ſhall ſeem expedient to them, and to make and ordain orders and ordinances, for the good government of the ſaid city; provided nevertheleſs,

Return. That the defendant was arreſted and impriſoned upon an original bill of debt, exhibited in the court of the lord mayor of London, at the ſuit of the chamberlain, for a penalty in an act of common council, againſt working of carts within the city, by any perſons but thoſe appointed by the lord mayor, aldermen and commons.

* P. 388.

Corporation by ſeveral names.

By cuſtom the mayor and commonalty and citizens have the ordinance and diſpoſal of carts, cars, &c. within the city.

Cuſtom to make bye-laws.

nevertheless, that such ordinances be profitable to the lord the now king, and to his progenitors, and to his people, and be consonant to good faith and reason, which customs and all the other customs of the said city, from the whole time aforesaid, used and approved by the authority of the parliament of the lord Richard, late king of England, &c. the 2d after the conquest, held at Westminster, in the 7th year of his reign, to the then mayor and commonalty of the said city, and to their successors, were ratified and confirmed; and we the said mayor and aldermen, and sheriffs of London, aforesaid, further signify, that in the common council held according to the custom of the city of London, in the chamber of the Guildhall of the said city, on the 21st day of June, in the year of our lord 1665, by John Lawrence, knight, then mayor of the said city, and the aldermen of the said city, with the assent of the commons in the common council of the said city, then and there assembled, a certain ordinance was made by the said mayor and aldermen, with the assent of the said commons, by the authority of the said common council, in the form following, and containing the matter following, to wit:—" *Whereas the right of ordering and disposing of cars, carts,* * *carrooms, carters and carmen, and of all other person or persons whatsoever, working any cars or carts within the city of London or the liberties thereof, is (and from the time whereof the memory of man is not to the contrary) hath been in the mayor and commonalty, and the citizens of this city, and in pursuance thereof the government of the said cars, carts, carrooms, carters and carmen, hath from time to time, by several acts of common council, been disposed and committed sometimes to the president and governors of Christ's hospital, and at other times to the master, wardens and fellowship of woodmongers, London, and in the year* 1658, *to the late president and governors for the poor of the said city, and last of all was again committed to the master, wardens and assistants of the said fellowship of woodmongers, by act of common council, made the* 10*th of May,* 1661, *in the mayoralty of sir Richard Brown, knight and baronet, and divers rules, directions and provisions and penalties thereby given, made and set down, touching the licensing and regulation of carmen, and several other matters; and the master, wardens and assistants of the said company of woodmongers, by the act impowered for licensing and allowing of the said carmen, and to several other purposes, as in and by the said act more fully may appear. And forasmuch as complaint hath been made by divers citizens and others, of sundry abuses committed in the government of the carmen, and of many inconveniences and grievances brought upon the citizens and inhabitants of this city and liberties and parts adjacent, in raising the price, and using deceits in the weight and measure of coals, by means and pretence of the privilege*

Customs confirmed by act of parliament.

Act of common council, 21st June, 1665.

* P. 389

*privilege and power granted in and by the said act of common council, as in and by a report of certain committees, appointed to examine the said grievances and abuses, read and allowed in this court, more particularly and fully may appear; Be it therefore enacted, granted and agreed, by the right honourable the lord mayor, the right worshipful the aldermen his brethren, and the commons in this common council assembled, and by the authority of the same, that the before-mentioned act, made in the mayoralty of sir Richard Brown, and every clause, article and thing therein contained, shall from henceforth be utterly repealed, and made void to all intents and purposes. And that the president and governors of Christ's hospital, London, shall from time to time hereafter, have the rule, oversight and government of the said cars, carts, carters and carmen, and of all other person or persons whatsoever, working any cars or carts within the city of London, and the liberties thereof, during the pleasure of this court and no longer, and according to the rules, directions and provisions in this present act mentioned and comprised, and such other orders, rules, directions and limitations, as by this court, or the lord mayor and court of aldermen, shall hereafter upon further considerations be made and provided in this behalf. And it is enacted, that no more than 420 cars shall by the mayor, * commonalty and citizens* * P. 390.
*of this city, or any other person or persons, claiming by, from and under them, be allowed and permitted to work within this city and the liberties thereof, and that 17s. 4d. per annum, and no more, shall be paid or received for a carroom, and 20s. and no more or greater fine, upon an admittance or alienation of a carroom. And that if any person or persons shall presume to work any car or cars, by himself or servants, not being duly allowed as aforesaid, such person or persons for every time so offending, shall forfeit and pay the sum of 40s. to be recovered, received and obtained, as hereafter mentioned. Also it is enacted, that there shall not hereafter be any car, cart or carts, permitted or allowed to any wharf, wharfingers or woodmongers, or kept or worked by any wharfinger or woodmonger, after the first day of August next, but by licence of the said president and governors of Christ's hospital, and the same to be part of the said number of 420 carts, and that all the street-cars, or residue of the said 420 cars to be licensed as aforesaid, shall or may be used or allowed to work within this city or the liberties thereof, for the carriage of all wood, coals and other fuel, within the same city and liberties at such rates, and in all other respects, as all goods and commodities have used and ought to be carried, and not otherwise. Provided nevertheless, that it shall be lawful for every person or persons, to send his and their own, or other cart or cars, out of the country to bring coals from wharfs, and also to bring his and their own coals home, to his and their house or houses in London, with his and their own cart or carts, not being traders in fuel by retailing*

*retailing the same. And if any wharfinger, woodmonger or other shall presume to work and keep any car, cart or carts, contrary to the true meaning hereof, such person or persons for every time so offending, shall forfeit and pay for the first offence the sum of* 40 *shillings, to be recovered and obtained as is hereafter mentioned; and for the second and every other offence afterwards, the said car or cars to be seized and carried to the new storeyard on the Postern, and there kept and detained according to the custom of the city of London. And be it hereby further enacted, that such as have any carroom or carrooms, duly allowed, shall not directly or indirectly set them out for hire at any time hereafter, without the approbation and allowance of the said president and governors of Christ's hospital for the time being, first had and obtained, and attested in writing under the said president's hand, to the end that none may be admitted to work any car, but such as shall be found of civil carriage, and able and meet for that employment, upon pain that every person offending therein, shall forfeit the sum of* 10*s. a day, for every day he shall let to hire the said car, to be recovered as is hereafter mentioned: And that the prices of carriages may be moderate, as well for the people as for the carmen, it is enacted, that forthwith this present year, and hereafter always from year to year, in the month of September, the rates and*
* P. 391. *prices of carriages, within this city and liberties, shall be * set and appointed by the court of aldermen, and such of the commons and others as they shall think fit to call before them for their information; and the said prices to be printed and set upon posts in public places: And if any carman shall demand or take more than according to such rates and prices so to be set down, such person or persons so offending, shall forfeit and pay for such offence the sum of* 10*s. to be had and recovered as hereafter is mentioned. And it is hereby further enacted, that it shall and may be lawful for any of the marshalls of this city, and their men respectively, who are hereby authorized and appointed, to assist the said president and governors of Christ's hospital, and whom they the said president and governors shall appoint, from time to time, to take and seize all the supernumerary cars not allowed, which shall be found working in the said city and the liberties thereof; and according to the antient custom of this city in that behalf used, to impound them in the new storeyard at the Postern belonging to this city, there to remain till the respective owners of them shall conform themselves to the government of the said president and governors. It is also hereby further enacted, that if any person or persons, authorized to work any car or cars, by himself or his servants, shall neglect or refuse duly to pay the said yearly rent of* 17*s.* 4*d. a piece to the said president and governors, for all and every the said car and carts, as is before mentioned, the carroom,* [*that is*] *the licence of such person or persons to work any such car or carts shall forthwith be suspended, and such person or persons be disabled*

*abled to work any longer by virtue of the same licence, until he or they shall conform to the payment of the said duty of 17s. 4d. respectively. And if any person or persons, for the cause before mentioned being so disabled before conformity, shall presume after such disallowance to use or work any car or cars, either in their own person or persons, or by his or their servant or servants, agent or agents, then such person and persons shall respectively forfeit and lose the sum of 40s. for every time they shall so work, as in working without licence or allowance. And for the prevention of such deceit hereafter, as divers woodmongers have practised in the sale and measure of their coals, it is enacted, that all sea coals hereafter to be sold or uttered by retail, by any person or persons whatsoever, shall be filled or brought home to the buyers in the sea coal meters sacks, and are or shall be marked by the keeper of the Guildhall for the time being, according to an order of the court of aldermen, made the 21st day of October, in the time of the mayoralty of sir Thomas Campbell, knight, deceased, and carried by some street-car or cars of persons duly licenced and allowed as aforesaid, and bearing upon the same cars the mark of the red cross for a note of their allowance, as hath antiently been accustomed: And that all person and persons vending or uttering sea coals by retail, and their carmen, servants and agents, shall hereafter from * time to time, and at all times, when they carry or send abroad any coals within the city of London or the liberties thereof, carry along in their car or cars, together with their sea coals, a good and lawful bushel, sealed according to the bushel in Guildhall allowed for the measuring of sea coals, which agreeth with the fat antiently used for the measuring of sea coals; which shall be and contain in breadth from out to out, the ring not exceeding half an inch, nineteen inches and a half, and in depth within the bushel, seven inches and a half, and if any person or persons shall bring home in his or their cart or car to any buyer, any coals in any other sack or sacks, and without such bushel as are before mentioned and appointed, such persons so offending shall forfeit and pay 10s. for the first and second offence respectively, for the third and every other offence, the car or cars of the offender to be seized and carried to the new storeyard on the Postern, as is aforesaid. And be it enacted by the authority aforesaid, that the said president and governors of Christ's hospital, shall from time to time observe, perform and execute, such acts, orders and rules, as have been, or shall hereafter from time to time be further made, published or enjoined by the common council, or by the lord mayor and court of aldermen of this city for the time being, for touching and concerning the government and regulation of cars, carts, carters and carmen, touching or concerning the price, measure or assise of coal sacks, or other fuel, or any matter or thing to the same, or any of them in any wise belonging or appertaining. And for a constant store and provision of sea coals to be had, and*

* P. 392.

*made*

*made hereafter for the supply of this city, and especially for the benefit and relief of the poor in times of dearth and scarcity, which hath happened in this and many other years heretofore, by reason of wars and troubles at sea, or by the subtle combinations and practice of the retailers at home, for their private gain and profit, to the common abuse and detriment of the citizens and other his majesty's subjects; be it enacted by the authority aforesaid, that besides the general stock employed by this city for the provision of coals, for the benefit of the poor within the said city and liberties, there shall be provided yearly hereafter, at the best hand, betwixt Lady-day and Michaelmas, by the several companies of this city, the several chaldrons of sea coals hereafter mentioned, that is to say, mercers* 488 *chaldrons, grocers* 675, *drapers* 562, *fishmongers* 465, *goldsmiths* 525, *skinners* 315, *merchant-taylors* 750, *haberdashere* 578, *salters* 360, *ironmongers* 255, *vintners* 375, *cloth-workers* 412, *dyers* 105, *brewers* 104, *leather-sellers* 210, *pewterers* 52, *cutlers* 75, *white-bakers* 45, *wax-chandlers* 19, *tallow-chandlers* 97, *armourers* 19, *girdlers*
* P. 393. 105, *butchers* 22, *sadlers* 90, *carpenters* 38, *cordwainers* * 60, *barber-surgeons* 60, *painter-stainers* 12, *curriers* 11, *masons* 22, *plumbers* 19, *innholders* 45, *founders* 7, *poulterers* 12, *cooks* 30, *coopers* 52, *tylers and bricklayers* 19, *bowyers* 3, *fletchers* 3, *blacksmiths* 15, *apothecaries* 45, *joiners* 22, *weavers* 27, *woolmen* 3, *woodmongers* 60, *scriveners* 60, *fruiterers* 7, *plaisterers* 8, *brown-bakers* 12, *stationers* 75, *embroiderers* 30, *upholsterers* 9, *musicians* 6, *turners* 13, *basket-makers* 6, *glaziers* 6. *And that the said quantity of sea coals shall be stored or laid up in convenient places by every the said companies respectively, and brought out, sold and uttered at other hard and dear seasons of the year, in such manner and at such prices as the lord mayor aud court of aldermen of this city for the time being, shall judge most requisite and convenient, and by their precepts in writing shall direct and require, for the end and purposes before mentioned, so as such companies as aforesaid, be not by such prices ordered to sell the same coals at loss. And whereas divers woodmongers and others, using to sell and utter coals by retail within this city and liberties, in design to raise and enhance the prices thereof for their own private gain and commodity, have commonly heretofore gone or sent down the river of Thames, or otherwise travelled and employed their agents to meet the ships and vessels coming from Newcastle and other parts, towards this city of London with coals, and at distant places from the said city, or by pre-contract within the same city and liberties, have bought up, forestalled and engrossed, great quantities of coals, which should have been brought to the said city by the owners and sellers thereof, to be there sold and uttered at reasonable prices, and the same have conveyed and brought to the said city to sell again at high and excessive prices, against the custom and privileges of this city, and to the publick detriment*

*detriment and oppression of the poor, and great charge of all others, inhabiting and dwelling within the said city and liberties thereof. For reformation whereof, be it enacted, ordained and established by the authority aforesaid, that no person or persons whatsoever, inhabiting or dwelling, or that hereafter shall inhabit or dwell within the said city or the liberties thereof, shall from and after the feast of the nativity of St. John the Baptist, now next ensuing, either by themselves, or any for them, or to their use, provide, buy, bargain or contract for any sea-coals, scotch-coals, pit-coals, or other coals coming towards this city to be sold, other than such as shall be provided and brought to be spent within their own private houses, nor shall sell or utter the same by retail or in gross, within this city or liberties, to any person or persons, but that the owners and sellers thereof at their own costs and charges shall and may * bring the same coals to the city themselves, here by themselves to be sold upon pain, that all and every person and persons whatsoever that shall offend contrary to the true intent and meaning thereof, shall forfeit and lose 5l. for every chaldron of sea-coals, and the like sum for every ton of Scotch or pit-coals that shall be bought, bargained or contracted for, contrary to the intent and true meaning of this act, to be recovered as is hereafter mentioned. And it is enacted, that the yeomen of the wood-wharfs of this city for the time being, shall from time to time, diligently oversee that all persons, coming and repairing to this city with any manner of coals before mentioned to be sold, do and shall observe and keep the orders, rules and directions beforegoing, and shall use like diligence for the discovery and punishment of all offenders in and about any particular thereof according to the intent and meaning of this act. And lastly, it is enacted, that all pain, penalties and forfeitures in and by this act before limited and appointed, shall and may be recovered by action of debt, bill or information in the name of the chamberlain of the city for the time being, in his majesty's court holden by the mayor and aldermen of the said city, in the chamber of the Guildhal of the city of London, wherein no essoin or wager of law shall be admitted or allowed for the defendant; and after the recovery thereof one moiety [after all charges deducted] shall be to the informer, and the other moiety to the poor of Christ's Hospital in London, to be employed for and towards their relief. In all which suits to be brought by this act, the chamberlain shall recover his ordinary costs and charges to be expended in and for the recovery of all such forfeitures against the offender or offenders. Weld.* And further, we the said mayor and aldermen and sheriffs of the said city certify, that the act of common council aforesaid, was in the due manner proclaimed and published in the said city, according to the custom of the said city, and from the whole time aforesaid used and approved; and that the said limitation of the number of

* P. 394.

That the act was published.

That the limitation of cars was necessary, and that 420 was a sufficient number for the business of the city, that defendant wrought a car against the intent of the act of common coucil.

cars was expedient for the good government of the cars in the said city, and that 420 cars was a sufficient and competent number of cars, to perform all business to be performed by cars in the said city, and that before the coming of the said writ of the lord the king to us directed, and to this schedule annexed, to wit, on the 14th day of April, in the 23d year of the reign of the lord Charles the 2d, the now king of England, &c. Henry Bradnox, in the said writ named, being an inhabitant in the said city, and not being allowed to work any car within the said city or the liberties of the same, after the making of the said act, wrought a car within the said city and the limits of the same, for his own proper gain, to wit, from a certain wharf situate in the said city, to wit, in the parish of St. Mary, Somerset, in the ward of London, to the parish of St. Mildred, * Bread-

* P. 395. street, in the said city against the true intent of the act of common council aforesaid, and thereupon afterwards the said Henry Bradnox then being a citizen and freeman, and inhabitant of the said city, was taken in the said city, and in the prison of the said lord the king, under the custody of us the said sheriffs is detained by virtue of a certain original bill in a plea of debt, upon a demand of 40 shillings, of the lawful money of England, against him the said Henry Bradnox, in the court of the lord the king, before us the said mayor and aldermen, held in the chamber of the Guildhall of the said city, according to the custom of the said city, being a court of record, and having sufficient jurisdiction in that behalf, at the suit of Thomas Player, knight, chamberlain of the said city, in a plea of debt, brought upon the act of common council aforesaid, the tenor of which original bill follows in these words, to wit, Thomas Player, knight, chamberlain of the said city, by William Lightfoot, his attorney, demands against Henry Bradnox 40 shillings, which he owes him, and unjustly detains, for this, to wit, that whereas in the common council held according to the custom of the said city, from the time whereof the memory of man is not to the contrary, in the Guildhall of the said city, situate in the parish of St. Michael Bassishaw, in the ward of Bassishaw, London, on 21st day of June, in the year of our lord 1665, before John Lawrence, knight, then mayor of the said city, T. Adams, and others then aldermen of the said city, and also the sheriffs of the said city, and the major part of the commons of the common council of the said city then and there assembled, among other things it was enacted, by the said mayor, aldermen and commons in the said common council assembled, and by the authority of the same, that the president and governors of Christ's Hospital, London, from time to time, from that

Defendant arrested on original bill in debt.

The tenor in hæc verba.

that time afterwards ſhould have the rule, overſight and government of cars, carts, carters and carmen, and of all other perſon or perſons whatſoever, working any cars or carts within the ſaid city or the liberties of the ſame, during the pleaſure of the ſaid court of common council, and no longer; and it was further enacted by the ſaid authority, that no more than 420 cars by the mayor, commonalty and citizens of the ſaid city, or by any other perſon or perſons claiming by, from or under them, ſhould be allowed or permitted to work within the ſaid city or the liberties of the ſame, and that 17s. 4d. per annum, and no more, ſhould be received or paid for the licence of a car, called a carroom, and 20 ſhillings and no more, or greater fine upon any admittance alienation of a carroom. And it was further enacted by the ſaid authority, by the ſaid act, that if any perſon or perſon ſhould preſume to work any car or cars by himſelf or his ſervants, not being duly allowed as is aforeſaid, that ſuch perſon or perſons for the time being ſo offending, ſhould forfeit and pay the ſum of 40 ſhillings to be recovered, received and obtained as in the ſaid act is after mentioned; and it was further enacted by the ſaid authority by the ſaid act, that all pains, penalties and forfeitures, in and by the * ſaid act limited and appointed, ſhould be recovered by action of debt, bill, or information in the name of the chamberlain of the ſaid city for the time being, in the court of the lord the now king, to be held before the mayor and aldermen of the ſaid city, in the chamber of the Guildhall of the ſaid city, in which no eſſoin or wager of law ſhould be admitted or allowed for the defendant, and that after the recovery thereof, one moiety after all expences deducted ſhould be to the informer, and the other moiety to the poor of Chriſt's Hoſpital, to be employed for and towards their relief, in all which ſuits to be proſecuted by virtue of the ſaid act, the ſaid chamberlain ſhould recover his ordinary coſts and charges to be expended in and for the recovery of all ſuch forfeitures againſt the offender and offenders, as by the ſaid act of common council in the due manner made and enacted, and alſo in the due manner publiſhed and proclaimed within the ſaid city, among other things by the ſaid act enacted more fully appears; and the ſaid Thomas ſaith that in fact the ſaid preſident and governors of Chriſt's Hoſpital London, aforeſaid, from the time of the making and enacting of the ſaid act of common council, have had, and as yet have the rule, overſight and government of the cars, carts, carters and carmen aforeſaid, and of all other perſon and perſons whatſoever, working any cart or car within the ſaid city and the liberties of the ſame, by the aſſent and conſent of the ſaid court of common council

* P. 396.

 aforeſaid,

aforesaid, and that the said Henry Bradnox, neither at the time of the making and enacting of the said act, nor at any time afterwards, was allowed by the mayor, commonalty and citizens of the said city, or by the said president and governors of Christ's Hospital London, aforesaid, or by any other person or persons claiming by or under them, nor by any other person having sufficient authority in that behalf, to work any car within the said city, or the liberties of the same: but the said Henry as aforesaid, not being allowed to work any car within the said city, or the liberties of the same, after the making and enacting of the said act, and before the exhibition of this original bill; to wit, on the 14th day of April, in the 23d year of the reign of the said lord the now king, at the parish of St. Mary Somerset, in the ward of                within the city aforesaid, having sufficient notice of the act of common council aforesaid, against the true intent of the act of common council aforesaid, did work one car, and upon the said car, then and there within the city of London aforesaid, to wit, at the parish of St. Mary Somerset, aforesaid, did take up a carload of sea coals, and then and there did carry for his own proper gain, upon the said car, the said carload of sea coals to a certain place within the said city, to wit, within the parish of St. Mildred, Bread-street, and then and there did lay down the said load of sea coal, whereby and by force of the said act, an action hath accrued to the said T. Player, to demand and have of the said H. B. the said 40 shillings as aforesaid forfeited, and now demanded, which the said H. although often requested, hath not paid to the said T. P, but the same to him hitherto to pay altogther hath refused, and as yet doth refuse to the said T. P. damage of 20 shillings, and thereupon he produces his suit,
* P. 397. &c. with this that the said * T. P. will verify that 420 cars are a sufficient number of cars for the city of London, and the suburbs and liberties thereof, to do all business in the city of London, and the suburbs and liberties of the same to be done with cars; and so depends undetermined; and this is the only cause of the caption and detention of the said H. B. in prison under our custody, which together with the body of the said H. we have ready at the day and place in the said writ as by the said writ we are commanded.

## Habeas Corpus and Returns thereto.

# Habeas Corpus for Seaman, a Debtor of the Lord the King.

Writ of habeas corpus to the mayor, aldermen and sheriffs of London, returnable into the court of exchequer.

CHARLES the 2d. &c. To the mayor, aldermen and sheriffs of London, and to every of them, greeting: We command you, that the body of Edward Seaman, our debtor, or by what other name or addition of name the said Edward may be called, taken and in our prison, under your custody, or under the custody of one of you detained, as it is said, together with the cause of the caption and detention of the said Edward in the same, you have before the barons of our exchequer at Westminster, on Saturday the 5th day of February next coming, to do and receive what our said court concerning him then and there shall think fit to ordain, and have there then this writ, witness Mathew Hale, knight, at Westminster, the 28th day of January, in the 21st year of our reign.

*ARDEN,*
*BERESFORD.*

The execution of this writ appears in a certain schedule to this writ annexed. The answer of Samuel Sterling, knight, mayor, and of the aldermen of the city of London, and also of James Edwards, and John Smith, of the said city, sheriffs.

Return. Imprisonment of a foreigner on an action of debt at the suit of the chamberlain of London for the penalty imposed in an act of common council against selling goods and merchandize in London till they are first weighed at the king's beames.

*London*, to wit, We, Samuel Sterling, knight, mayor of the city of London, the aldermen of the same, and James Edwards, and John Smith, of the said city of London, sheriffs, to the barons of the exchequer of the lord the king at Westminster certify, that the city of London is, and for the whole time whereof the memory of man is not to the contrary, hath been an antient city, and that the freemen of the said city are, and for the whole time aforesaid, have been incorporated as well by the name of the mayor and commonalty and citizens of the city of London, as by the name of the mayor and commonalty of the said city, as also by the name of the citizens of the said city; and we further certify, that for * the more indifferent and just weighing of goods and merchandizes used to be bought and sold by by weight, within the said city and the liberties of the same, there is had, and for the whole time aforesaid was had, a certain custom used and approved within the said city, and the liberties of the same, That all merchandizes of any foreigner, not being a freeman of the said city, sold within the said city and the liberties of the same by weight, ought, and have been accustomed, at, or before the delivery

* P. 398.

Custom of London that the goods, &c. of a foreigner ſold within the city ſhould before delivery be weighed at the King's beams.

of the ſame to the buyer thereof, there to be weighed at certain common beams of the ſaid city, commonly called the King's Beams, or at ſome one of them within the ſaid city, or the liberties of the ſame; and we further certify, that there are had, and for the whole time aforeſaid, was had within the ſaid city and the liberties thereof, certain common beams commonly called the King's Beams, uſed and occupied for the true and juſt weighing of all goods, wares and merchandizes bought by the freemen of the ſaid city, or others of foreigners, aliens and ſtrangers, within the liberties of the ſaid city, which uſually have been accuſtomed to be bought and ſold by the weight, and officers ſworn and appointed by the mayor, commonalty, and citizens of the ſaid city, attending the ſaid beams for the weighing of the ſaid goods, wares, and merchandizes indifferently between buyer and ſeller: And we further certify, that Edward the 4th, heretofore king of England, by his certain charter bearing date the 22d day of July, in the 18th year of his reign, among other things, granted and confirmed to the mayor, and commonalty of the ſaid city, and to their ſucceſſors, the weighing of the ſaid merchandizes, which charter in the parliament of the lord Henry the 8th, late king of England, in the 3d year of his reign is confirmed: And further, we certify, that the ſaid late king Henry the 8th, by his charter bearing date the 13th day of April in the 22d year of his reign, reciting, that it manifeſtly and without difficulty appeared to the ſaid late king, that the office of keeper of the great beam, and of the common ſcales ordained for weighing between merchant and merchant, and the iſſues and profits thereof ariſing appertained, and of antient right belonged to the ſaid mayor and commonalty, and citizens, and to their ſucceſſors; granted and confirmed to the ſaid mayor and commonalty, and to the citizens of the ſaid city, and to their ſucceſſors, that the ſaid weights and beams for the weighing of merchandizes between merchant and merchant, the iſſues ariſing from them and the perception of the ſame, which belonged to the commonalty of the ſaid city, ſhould remain in the cuſtody of good and ſufficient men of the ſaid city, expert in that office, and for this purpoſe elected by the ſaid commonalty, to be kept at the will of the ſaid commonalty, and that in no wiſe they ſhould be committed to others than to thoſe ſo elected, and that they ſhould have toll, to wit, for the weighing of lead, hides, pepper, allum, madder, and of all other ſuch wares, within the ſaid city for ever: And he further granted to the ſaid mayor and commonalty, and citizens, and to their ſucceſſors, the office of keeper of the great beams and of the common ſcales ordained for weighing

The cuſtom confirmed by the charter of Edward the 4th, which charter was confirm'd by parliament in the 3d of Hen 8th. and the ſaid privilege enlarged by charter of the ſaid H. 8th in the 22d year of his reign.

ing

ing between merchant and merchant, and alfo the office of keeper of the public fcales or weights * within the faid city for weighing of all mercandizes by averdupois, and alfo of all kinds of fpices, wares, and things in the faid city there to be weighed; and alfo the faid late king Henry the 8th, by the faid letters patent, gave and granted to the faid mayor, commonalty and citizens of his city of London, the authority and power of making, nominating and affigning from time to time, all and all manner of clerks, porters, fervants and minifters, of the great beam and fcales, and of the iron beam, and of the hanging beam, called the ftill-yard beam, and of the faid weights, and alfo all other clerks, fervants, porters and minifters to the faid office appertaining. And we further certify, that within the faid city there is had, and from the time whereof the memory of man is not to the contrary, was had a certain cuftom ufed and approved, to wit, that if any cuftom in the faid city obtained and approved in any part fhould be defective, or any thing in the faid city newly arifing, where remedy before that time was not ordained fhould want amendment, that then the mayor and aldermen of the faid city for the time being, with the affent of the faid commons of the faid city in the common council affembled, were ufed to ordain, and could ordain apt remedy confonant to good faith and reafon, for the common profit of the faid commonalty of the faid city, and of the other faithful fubjects repairing to the faid city, as often as it fhould feem fit to them, provided neverthelefs, that the faid ordinances fhould be profitable to the people, and confonant to good faith and reafon; and we further certify, that the faid cuftoms, and all the other cuftoms of the faid city, from the whole time aforefaid, ufed and approved by the authority of the parliament held at Weftminfter, in the 7th year of the reign of Richard, late king of England, the 2d after the conqueft, to the then mayor and commonalty of the faid city, and to their fucceffors were confirmed; we alfo certify, that in the common council held according to the cuftom of the city of London, in the chamber of the Guildhall of the faid city, on the 2d day of February, in the year of our Lord 1658, before John Ireton, then mayor of the faid city, and the aldermen of the faid city, with the affent of the commons of the faid city, in the faid common council affembled, according to the cuftom of the faid city, by the power and authority of the faid court of common council, it was then and there ordained in thefe words following, to wit. *Whereas for the more indifferent and juft weighing of goods and merchandizes, which ufed to be bought and fold by weight, within the city of London and liberties thereof, there are, and from*

* P. 399.

Cuftoms to make bye laws or acts of common council.

Cuftoms of London confirmed by the parliament of the 7th R. 2d.

An act of common council 2d February 1658.

*from the time whereof the memory of man is not to the contrary, have been certain common beams, within the same city and liberties, commonly called the king's beams, at which there are and have been during all the time aforesaid, certain sworn officers attending, and who by the duty of their places, have used and ought to attend for the weighing of such goods and merchandizes:*
* P. 400. *And whereas all such goods * and merchandizes of all foreigners, not being free of the city aforesaid, which have been sold or bartered within the said city or liberties, to any person or persons whatsoever, as well freemen as others, ought and during all the time aforesaid, have been accustomed to be weighed at one of the said beams, at or before the sale and delivery thereof; and whereas divers foreigners of late times, not minding or regarding the good and wholsome customs of the said city, but out of a covetous desire by sinister ways and means to promote their own interest, have oftentimes sold and delivered their goods and merchandizes within the said city, as well to freemen of the said city as others, by other false and unjust weights and beams, without weighing the same at any of the said common beams; and the better to paliate their offences and avoid suspicion, do sometimes by confederacy and practice with some freemen of the said city, cause fraudulent sale to be made of such their goods and merchandizes to freemen of the said city, before the said goods and merchandizes do come to the said city or liberties, contrary to the oath of such freemen; and sometimes do mix their goods with the goods of other persons that are free of the said city, that so the distinct property of the foreigners may not be known from that of the freemen; and at other times do procure freemen to be partners with them in such goods and merchandizes, who many times have but a small and inconsiderable share therein with such foreigners; and upon such and other groundless pretences, hold themselves discharged from the duty of weighing any such goods at any of the said beams; whereas in truth, they are not, nor ought by any such pretences, be at all discharged from the said duty. For remedy whereof it is hereby enacted, ordained and declared by the lord mayor, aldermen and commons of the said city of London, in common council assembled, and by the authority of the same as followeth: First, that all goods, wares, or merchandizes of all person or persons being a foreigner or foreigners, and not free of this city, of what kind soever, which used to be bought and sold by weight, which at any time after the tenth day of February now next ensuing, being within the said city or liberties thereof, shall be sold or bartered to any freeman or freemen of the said city, or to any other person or persons whatsoever within the said city or liberties thereof, shall at or before the delivery thereof to such freeman or freemen, or other person or persons, be weighed at the said common beams, called the king's beams, or one of them, upon pain of forfeiture*

*feiture*

*feiture of thirteen ſhillings and four pence, for every five hundred weight of ſuch wares and merchandizes by the ſeller or barterer thereof, and ſo after that rate for a greater or leſſer quantity. Item, That if any covinous or fraudulent ſale ſhall be made by any ſuch foreigner or foreigners, to any freeman or freemen of this city, of any ſuch goods or merchandizes before the ſame goods or merchandizes come to this city or the liberties thereof, to the intent to avoid the duty of weighing ſuch goods or merchandizes * at one of the ſaid beams, and ſuch goods and merchandizes as ſhall afterwards come to this city, or the liberties thereof, and ſhall after the tenth day of February, be ſold or bartered, and delivered by ſuch foreigner or foreigners, freeman or freemen or any other perſon or perſons whatſoever, within the ſaid city or the liberties thereof, then ſuch goods and merchandizes ſhall, at or before the delivery thereof to ſuch perſon or perſons, be weighed at the ſaid common beams, called the king's beams, or one of them, upon pain of the forfeiture of thirteen ſhillings and four pence, for every five hundred weight of ſuch wares and merchandizes by the ſeller or barterer thereof, and ſo after that rate for a greater or leſſer quantity as aforeſaid, notwithſtanding any ſuch covinous or fraudulent ſale as aforeſaid. Item, That if any freeman or freemen of this city to whom ſuch fraudulent ſale of ſuch goods and merchandizes ſhall be made as aforeſaid, knowing the ſame, ſhall wittingly or willingly after the ſaid tenth day of February, put in uſe, juſtify or maintain ſuch fraudulent ſale as true, and made bona fide, to the intent to avoid the ſaid duty of weighing ſuch goods and merchandizes, then all and every ſuch freeman or freemen ſhall forfeit for every ſuch offence the ſum of five pounds a piece. Item, If any ſuch goods or merchandizes of any freeman or freemen of this city, ſhall be mixed with the goods and merchandizes of any foreigner or foreigners from the liberties of the ſame city, being of the ſame kind, ſo that the diſtinct properties and proportion of ſuch freeman or freemen in ſuch goods or merchandizes, from the property and proportion of ſuch foreigner or foreigners in ſuch goods and merchandizes cannot be known; and ſuch goods and merchandizes being within the ſaid city or liberties, ſhall at any time after the ſaid tenth day of February, be ſold or bartered by ſuch freeman or freemen and ſuch foreigner or foreigners, to any other perſon or perſons, before any partition, diviſion or ſeparation be made of ſuch goods or merchandizes of ſuch freeman or freemen, from ſuch goods or merchandizes of ſuch foreigner or foreigners, then all ſuch goods and merchandizes, as well of ſuch freeman or freemen, as of ſuch foreigner or foreigners, ſhall at or before the delivery thereof to any other perſon or perſons be weighed at the common beams called the king's beams, or one of them, upon pain of forfeiture of thirteen ſhillings and four pence, for every five hundred weight of*

* P. 401.

of such wares and merchandizes, by the seller or barterer thereof, and so after that rate for a greater or lesser quantity as aforesaid. Item, If any such goods or merchandizes of any such freeman or freemen, shall be mixed as aforesaid, with such goods or merchandizes of such foreigner or foreigners, and such goods and merchandizes of such foreigner or foreigners shall at any time after the said tenth day of February, be sold or bartered within the said city or liberties, to any person or persons before any partition, division, or separation thereof shall be made as aforesaid, then such goods and merchandizes of such foreigner or
* P. 402. foreigners so sold as * aforesaid, shall after partition, division, or separation thereof to be made as aforesaid, from such goods of such freeman or freemen, in case such separation or division shall be thereof made, before any sale or barter shall be made by such foreigner or foreigners, of such goods or merchandizes of such foreigner or foreigners, be weighed at the said common beams, or one of them, upon pain of forfeiture of thirteen shillings and four pence, for every five hundred weight of such merchandizes by the seller or barterer thereof, and so after that rate for a greater or lesser quantity thereof; but in case such wares and merchandizes of such freeman or freemen so mixed as aforesaid, shall be likewise sold within the said city or liberties thereof, to any person or persons, before any separation and division thereof shall be made as aforesaid, then all such merchandizes so mixed and sold as aforesaid, as well of such freeman or freemen, as of such foreigner or foreigners, shall at or before the said delivery thereof to any person or persons be weighed at the common beams, or one of them, upon pain of forfeiture of thirteen shillings and four pence, for every five hundred weight of such wares and merchandizes by the last sellers or barterers thereof; and so after that rate, for a greater or lesser quantity as aforesaid. Item, That all such goods and merchandizes usually sold by weight, whereof any freeman or freemen, or any foreigner or foreigners shall be possessed in copartnership, or in common, by equal moieties, or by any other share or shares, which at any time after the said tenth day of February, shall be sold or bartered to any person or persons whatsoever, within the said city or the liberties thereof, shall at or before the delivery thereof, be weighed at the said common beams, or one of them, upon pain of forfeiture of thirteen shillings and four pence, for every five hundred weight of such wares or merchandizes by the sellers or barterers thereof, and so after that rate for a greater or lesser quantity as aforesaid. Item, It is hereby further enacted, that the buyer or buyers whether he or they be foreigners or freemen, of the wares and merchandizes aforesaid, which shall be sold and not weighed according to the respective provisions aforesaid, shall forfeit and incur the penalties and forfeitures as by the seller or sellers hereof are before ordained to be forfeited. Item, It is further hereby

*hereby enacted, that all and singular the penalties and forfeitures aforesaid, shall and may be recovered by action of debt, to be commenced in the name of the chamberlain of the city of London for the time being. Item, It is hereby further enacted, that such action of debt shall and may be commenced in * any of the courts of record within the city of London, and that no essoin or wager of the law shall be admitted or allowed; and that the plaintiff, if he recover in such action, shall recover his ordinary costs of suit. Item, It is hereby further enacted, that the several forfeitures so to be recovered, charges of suit being deducted, shall be paid to the treasurer of St. Bartholomew's Hospital, near West-Smithfield, London, for the time being, for the use of the poor, sick, sore, and diseased people there harboured. Item, To the intent that the officer or officers who shall weigh such goods and merchandizes at the said common beams, may be paid or satisfied the duties due and accustomed for weighing thereof, without being put to the charges of suit for the same: It is hereby enacted and declared, that it shall and may be lawful to and for such officer or officers, his or their deputy or deputies, servant or servants, to detain such goods and merchandizes so to be weighed by them or any of them, in his or their hands or custody, until the respective duties for weighing thereof of right due and accustomed shall be paid or satisfied; provided, that nothing contained in this act shall extend to charge any person or persons whatsoever, unless the action thereupon to be brought shall be commenced within the space of one year, next after the offence abovesaid committed.* And we, the said mayor and aldermen, and sheriffs of the said city, further signify, that before the coming of the said writ of the lord the king to us directed, and here to this schedule annexed, Edward Seaman in the said writ named, was taken in the said city, and in the prison of the said lord the king, under the custody of us the said sheriffs is detained, by virtue of a certain original bill in a plea of debt, upon a demand of four pounds, thirteen shillings, and four pence, of the lawful money of England, against him the said Edward Seaman, on the 24th day of December, in the 21st year of the reign of our lord Charles the 2d. the now king of England, &c. before us the said mayor and aldermen, in the chamber of the Guildhall of the said city, held according to the custom of the said city, at the suit of Thomas Player, knight, chamberlain of the said city, brought upon the said act of common council aforesaid, the tenor of which original bill follows in these words, to wit, "Before the mayor and aldermen in the chamber of the Guildhall of the city of London, Thomas Player, knight, chamberlain of the said city, who on the 1st day of December, in the 21st year of the reign of our lord Charles the 2d the now king of England, &c. and al-

* P. 403

The defendant arrested on an original bill in debt founded on the said act of common council.

Tenor of the bill.

 ways

ways afterwards hitherto was, and as yet is chamberlain of the ſaid city of London, by Robert Rawlins, his attorney, demands againſt Edward Seaman four pounds, thirteen ſhillings, and four pence, of the lawful money of England, which he owes him, and unjuſtly detains, &c. For this becauſe that in the common council held according to the cuſtom of the ſaid city, uſed and approved in the ſame from the time whereof the memory of man is not to the
* P. 404. contrary, in the chamber of the * Guildhall of the ſaid city, ſituate in the pariſh of St. Michael Baſſiſhaw, in the ward of Baſſiſhaw, London, aforeſaid, on the 2d day of February, in the year of our Lord 1658, by a certain act of the ſaid council then and there made, it is enacted, ordained, and declared by the mayor, aldermen, and commons of the city of London aforeſaid, in the ſaid common council then and there aſſembled, and by the power and authority of the ſame, that all goods, wares and merchandizes, of any perſon or perſons, being foreigner or foreigners, and not free of the ſaid city, of whatſoever kind which were accuſtomed to be bought and ſold by weight, which at any time after the 10th day of February then next following, after the making of the ſaid act of common council, being within the ſaid city or the liberties of the ſame, ſhould be ſold or bartered to any freeman or freemen of the ſaid city, or to any other perſon or perſons whatſoever, within the ſaid city, or the liberties of the ſame, at or before the delivery thereof to ſuch freeman or freemen, or to ſuch perſon or perſons ſhould be weighed at the public beams, called the king's beams, or at one of them, upon pain of forfeiture of thirteen ſhillings and four pence, for every five hundred weight of ſuch wares or merchandizes by the ſeller or barterer of the ſame, and ſo after that rate for a greater or leſſer quantity; and by the ſaid common council and by the authority of the ſame, it is further enacted, that all and ſingular the penalties and forfeiturs aforeſaid, ſhould and might be recovered by action of debt, to be commenced in the name of the chamberlain of the city of London for the time being; and by the ſaid common council, and by the authority of the ſame, it is further enacted, that ſuch action of debt ſhould and might be commenced in any of the courts of record within the city of London, and that no eſſoin or wager of law ſhould be admitted or allowed, and that the plaintiff, if in ſuch action he ſhould recover, ſhould recover his ordinary coſts of ſuit; and it was provided in and by the ſaid act of common council, that nothing in the ſaid act contained ſhould extend to charge any perſon or perſons whatſoever, unleſs the action thereupon to be brought, ſhould be commenced within the

ſpace of one year next after the offence committed, as by the ſaid act of common council, among other things, more fully appeareth: And the ſaid Thomas Player in fact ſayeth, that the ſaid Edward Seaman, not conſidering the ſaid act of common council, nor in any manner fearing the penalty in the ſame contained, after the ſaid 10th day of February next following the making of the ſaid act of common council, and within the ſpace of one year before the bringing of this original bill, to wit, on the 21ſt day of December, in the 21ſt year of the reign of our lord Charles the 2d the now king of England, &c. aforeſaid, three thouſand five hundred pounds weight of figs, within the city of London aforeſaid, and the liberties of the ſame, to wit, in the pariſh of St. Hellen, London, the ſaid figs then and there being the goods of the ſaid Edward Seaman, and he the ſaid * Edward Seaman, then and as yet being a foreigner from the liberty of the city of London, and not free of the ſaid city, then and there ſold to divers perſons to the ſaid Thomas unknown, being freemen of the ſaid city, which three thouſand five hundred pounds weight of figs on the 23d day of the ſaid month of December, in the year laſt aforeſaid, and in the pariſh laſt aforeſaid, were delivered to the ſaid divers perſons to the ſaid Thomas unknown, and at or before the ſaid delivery thereof, to the ſaid divers perſons to the ſaid Thomas unknown, were not weighed, nor was any parcel thereof weighed at the common beams, in the ſaid act of common council aforeſaid mentioned, nor at any of the ſaid beams, according to the tenor of the ſaid act; and the ſaid plaintiff, alſo in fact ſaith, that the ſaid figs from the whole time aforeſaid, were accuſtomed to be bought and ſold by weight within the ſaid city of London, to wit, in the pariſh of St. Hellen aforeſaid, and that from the whole time aforeſaid, always hitherto, there were, and as yet are certain common beams, called the king's beams, uſed within the ſaid city, to wit, in the pariſh laſt aforeſaid, for the weighing of the figs aforeſaid, and of other merchandize, and during the whole time aforeſaid there were, and yet are in the ſaid pariſh, certain ſworn officers attending the ſaid king's beams, ready to weigh figs and other merchandize, whereby an action hath accrued to the ſaid plaintiff to aſk, demand, and have of the ſaid Edward Seaman, the pain and forfeiture of thirteen ſhillings and four pence, for every five hundred pound weight of the ſaid three thouſand five hundred pounds weight of the ſaid figs, whereupon the whole ſum amounts to the ſaid four pounds, thirteen ſhillings, and four pence, now demanded, which the ſaid defendant to the ſaid plaintiff hath not yet paid, although often, &c. to the damage of the ſaid plaintiff of twenty

* P. 405.

twenty shillings, and thereupon he produces suit, &c. and so the said cause depends between the said parties undetermined, &c. and this is the only cause of the caption and detention of the said Edward Seaman, in prison, and under custody as aforesaid, which together with his body, we have ready, as by the said writ we are commanded.

Et hæc est causa.

---

## Player, Knight, *against* Bringhman.

Writ of habeas corpus to the lord mayor, aldermen and sheriffs of London, returnable before the lord chief justice of B. R.

CHARLES the second, &c. To our mayor, aldermen and sheriffs of London, greeting: We command you, that the body of James Bringhman, in our prison, under your custody detained, as it is said, under a safe and sure conduct, together with the day and cause of his caption and detention, by whatever name the said James may be called in the same, you have before our beloved and faithful Mathew Hale, knight, our chief justice, assigned to hold pleas before us at his chamber in Serjeants-Inn, in Cancery-lane, London, immediately after the receipt of this writ, to do and * receive all and singular the things which our said chief justice concerning him, then and there shall consider in this behalf, and have there then this writ. Witness Mathew Hale, knight, at Westminster, the 12th day of February, in the 23d year of our reign.

* P. 406.

*BRINGHURST*, Attorney,
*HENBY*.

The execution of this writ appears in a certain schedule this writ annexed; the answer of George Waterman, knight, mayor, and of the aldermen of the city of London, and also of John Dawes, knight, and Robert Clayton, knight, of the said city sheriffs.

*WAGSTAFFE*,
*TRAVERS*.

*London*,

*London*, to wit. We George Waterman, knight, mayor, and the aldermen of the city of London, and alſo John Dawes, knight, and Robert Clayton, knight, of the ſaid city, ſheriffs, to Mathew Hale, knight, chief juſtice of our lord Charles II. the now king of England, &c. aſſigned to hold pleas before the lord the king himſelf, at his chamber, ſituate in Serjeant's Inn, in Chancery Lane, London, immediately certify that the city of London is, and from the whole time whereof, the memory of man is not to the contrary, hath been an antient city, and that the mayor, and commonalty, and citizens of the ſaid city are, and from the whole time aforeſaid have been one body politic, and corporate, and from the whole time aforeſaid, known by the name of the citizens of London, of the citizens of the city of London, of the barons of the king, of the city of the lord the king of London, of the mayor, and citizens of London, of the mayor, and commonalty, of the city of London, of the mayor, and commonalty, and citizens of the city of London; and that within the ſaid city there is had, and from the whole time aforeſaid was had, a cuſtom uſed and approved, to wit, that if any cuſtoms in the ſaid city obtained or approved, in any part, are, or ſhould be difficult or defective, or any thing in the ſaid city newly ariſing, where remedy was not before ordained, ſhould want amendment, that the mayor, and aldermen of the ſaid city, for the time being, with the aſſent of the commons of the ſaid city, might, and could appoint and ordain, apt remedy conſonant to good faith and reaſon, for the common profit of the citizens of the ſaid city, and the other faithful ſubjects of the ſaid lord the king, and his progenitors arriving at the ſame, as often as and whenſoever it ſhall ſeem to them expedient, provided nevertheleſs, that ſuch ordinance be profitable to the ſaid lord, the now king, and to his progenitors, and to his people, and conſonant to good faith and reaſon, which cuſtoms, and all the other cuſtoms of the ſaid city, from the whole time aforeſaid, uſed and approved by the authority of the parliament, of the lord Richard, late king of England, &c. the * ſecond after the conqueſt, held at Weſtminſter, in the ſeventh year of his reign, to the then mayor, and commonalty of the ſaid city, and to their ſucceſſors, were ratified and confirmed; and we the ſaid mayor, and aldermen, and ſheriffs of the ſaid city of London, further ſignify, that in the common-council held, according to the cuſtom of the ſaid city of London, in the chamber of the Guildhall of the ſaid city, on the twenty ſeventh day of October, in the twenty-third year of the reign of our lord Charles II. the now king of England, &c. by the then mayor, and aldermen of the ſaid city, with the aſſent of the commons, of the common-council of the ſaid city, then and there aſſembled, it was enacted by the ſaid mayor and aldermen, with the aſſent of the

Return. Impriſonment of the defendant, upon an action of debt in the mayor's court, at the ſuit of the chamberlain of London, founded on an act of common-council, againſt exerciſing the office of a broker, without being firſt admitted by the lord mayor and aldermen.

Cuſtom to make bye-laws, or acts of common-council.

Cuſtoms confirmed by parliament, ſeventh Rich. II.

* P. 407

27 October, 23 Char. II. act of common-council againſt any foreigners or others, exerciſing the office of broker within London, unleſs admitted and ſworn before the lord mayor and aldermen.

the ſaid commons, by the authority of the ſaid common-council as follows, to wit, *Whereas by antient cuſtom of this city of London, and by charter of ſeveral kings of England, confirmed by parliament, no perſon ought to exerciſe brocage within the ſaid city, unleſs the ſame perſon be thereunto admitted, and ſworn before the lord mayor and aldermen of the ſame city, yet notwithſtanding of late times very many perſons, contrary to the ſaid cuſtom and charters, have taken upon them and do daily take upon them, the uſe and exerciſe of the ſame office and employment of their own authority, not being firſt admitted and ſworn as aforeſaid, whereby manifold evils and inconveniencies have enſued, and do daily happen both to the brokers duly admitted, allowed and ſworn, as alſo to the merchants, traders and owners of ſhipping and mariners, between whom ſuch brokers not admitted, have negotiated and do deal, whilſt they remain free and looſe from that oath and obligation, for their faithful and honeſt demeanour in the ſaid employment, which is taken and entered into by the lawful brokers, at their admittance into the ſaid office, for remedy whereof, and for the better eſchewing and preventing for the future, contracts and bargains of uſury, falſe clearance, and other corrupt devices and crafty deceits which have been invented, deviſed and practiſed by the great number and multitude of ſuch common brokers, both Engliſh and aliens, not admitted, ſworn or bound as aforeſaid. Be it enacted, ordained and eſtabliſhed by the right honourable the lord mayor, the aldermen, and commons, in this common council aſſembled, and by the authority of the ſame; and it is hereby enacted, that no perſon or perſons Engliſh or alien, free of the city of London, or foreign from the liberties thereof, after the firſt day of the month of December now next coming, ſhall take upon him or them, the uſe and exerciſe of the office of a broker, or brocage, between any manner of perſons within the ſaid city of London, or the liberties thereof, nor ſhall preſume as a broker or ſolicitor, to make any manner of bargain or bargains, contract or contracts in or relating to the art or trade of merchandizing by exchange, or for letting of ſhips to freight or hire, or other-*

* P. 408. *wiſe, between any manner of perſons, within the * ſaid city and liberties thereof, unleſs he, or they, be or ſhall be, firſt admitted and ſworn before the lord mayor, and aldermen of this city of London, for the time being, or before the ſaid mayor, and the more part of the ſaid aldermen, for the time being, a common broker to exerciſe brocage within the ſaid city and liberties thereof, and be bound with good ſecurities for him or them, for the due execution of the ſame office, upon pain of forfeiting the ſum of twenty pounds, of lawful money of England, for every time that ſuch perſon or perſons, ſhall offend, commit, or do contrary to the purport, true intent and effect of this preſent act. And it is further enacted by the authority aforeſaid, that no perſon, or perſons whatſoever, after the firſt day of December, now next coming, employ, or ſet on work,*

*work, any person or persons, as a broker, to make any other bargain with any other person or persons, within this city of London, or the liberties thereof, unless such person or persons, so employed, or to be employed as a broker, be or shall be first admitted, and sworn before the mayor and aldermen of the said city, for the time being, a common broker, and be bound as aforesaid, upon pain of forfeiting the sum of five pounds of lawful money of England, for every time that such person or persons, shall offend therein, and further to prevent all pretence, that the persons are not known who are duly admitted and sworn brokers; and that it may appear to the merchants and others, who shall use and employ any brokers, that the same brokers are duly admitted to exercise the same office, it is enacted by the authority aforesaid, that a fair table of the names of all such persons, in writing or in print, who are and shall be duly admitted and sworn brokers as aforesaid, be made and published by being hung up at the entrance of the Royal Exchange, and from time to time there to be continued, and that the said brokers who are or shall be duly admitted and sworn, do bear about with them a medal of silver, with the city arms, to hang before their breasts, and also to carry along with them authentic copies, under the seal of the mayoralty of this city, of their said admittances for their authority, and for the satisfaction of all persons concerned to know the same. And be it further enacted by the authority aforesaid, that all and every the pains, penalties and forfeitures in and by this act of common-council as aforesaid, limited and appointed, the charges of the suit for the recovery thereof being first deducted, shall be divided into two equal moieties, or half parts, whereof one equal moiety, or half part shall be to the use of the hospitals and prisons belonging to this city, to be distributed as the said mayor and court of aldermen for the time * being shall direct and appoint; and the other equal moiety or half part thereof, shall be to the use of the first presenter of the same offence. And that all and every such pains, penalties and forfeitures, shall be recovered by action of debt, bill, plaint or information, to be commenced and prosecuted in the name of the chamberlain of this city for the time being, in the king's majesty court, holden before the lord mayor and aldermen of this city of London, in the chamber of the Guildhall of the same city for the time being, in all which actions and suits to be commenced and prosecuted by virtue of this present act, against the offender or offenders, the said chamberlain shall recover his reasonable costs of suit, to be expended in and about the prosecution of such actions and suits, wherein no essoign or wager of the law, shall be admitted or allowed for the defendant: and it is further enacted by the authority aforesaid, that the number of the said brokers so to be admitted, shall not exceed the number of one hundred persons, born within this kingdom, and the number of twelve alien-born, being members of the French and Dutch congregations, and six others*

* P. 409.

*being aliens born, as the court of aldermen from time to time shall think fit; and that every broker as well native as foreign born, shall enter into one obligation, with two sufficient sureties unto the chamberlain of London for the time being, in the sum or penalty of two hundred pounds, with condition there under written, that so long as he shall occupy and enjoy the office of brocage within the said city and liberties thereof, he do neither buy nor sell, nor any other for him, by fraud or collusion, any manner of merchandize for his own proper use, nor for his own store or proper expences, within the franchises of the said city, without the special licence of the lord mayor and court of aldermen of the same city for the time being, first had and obtained, nor do at any time hereafter, within the franchise of the same city or the liberties thereof, make or cause to be made any manner of bargain between foreigner and foreigner, or foreigner and stranger within the said city and liberties thereof, (the delivery of money by exchange, and the sale of lands only excepted) and if he know of any merchandize foreign bought, or foreign sold, he shall give notice thereof to the lord mayor for the time being; and also that during the time of his said office, he shall not at any time buy any manner of merchandizes of any manner of person or persons, within the franchise and liberties of the said city, or without, to the use of any person or persons, but that he bring the buyer and seller thereof, or their sufficient deputy or deputies together, or having sufficient warrant from any*
* P. 410 *such buyer or seller, (being * absent) in writing or otherwise, make a rightful bargain between them; and that he shall from time to time, give knowledge to the lord mayor and aldermen of the said city for the time being, of all and every such person and persons, as he at any time during the time of his office, shall know to use or occupy brocage within the said city of London or liberties thereof, not being lawfully admitted so to do. And that he be not livery with any person or persons, nor be host to lodge any manner of stranger or alien-born, within the said city or liberties thereof; at any time during the said office, nor colour nor conceal the goods of any alien or foreigner, whereby the king's majesty, or the city may lose any of their customs or duties, and also that he shall cause all such bargains as he, at any time during his said office, shall make between party and party to be truly and wholly written into a fair book, ready to be shewed to the lord mayor and aldermen, whensoever it shall be called for by them, for the testimony and declaration of the said bargains; and that he shall not dwell, or be harboured, or lodged, with any manner of merchant stranger, nor with any other stranger, within the said city of London, and the liberties thereof, and in case he shall know of any persons concealing or colouring of aliens, or foreigners goods, he shall give the lord mayor notice thereof; and that he shall not go or send out of the said city and liberties thereof, to buy or forestall any merchandize or victuals, at any time hereafter, during*

*during the time of his said office of brocage.* And we the said mayor, and aldermen of the said city, and the sheriffs of the said city, further certify, that before the coming of the writ of the lord the king to us directed, and to this schedule annexed, James Bringhman in the said writ named, was taken in the said city, and in the prison of the said lord the king, under the custody of us the said sheriff is detained, by virtue of a certain original bill in a plea of debt, upon a demand of twenty pounds, of the lawful money of England, against him the said James B. on the fourteenth day of February, in the twenty-fourth year of the reign of the said lord the now king, &c. at the court of the said lord the king, before us, the said George Waterman, knight, mayor, and the aldermen of the city aforesaid, in the said chamber of the Guildhall, of the said city then held, according to the custom of the said city at the suit of Thomas Player, knight, chamberlain of the city of London, brought upon the act of common-council aforesaid, made as aforesaid, upon the said twenty-seventh day of October, in the twenty-third year of the reign of the said lord the now king aforesaid; the tenor of which original bill follows in these words, to wit, Thomas Player, knight, chamberlain of the city of London, by William Lightfoot his attorney, demands against James Bringhman, twenty pounds of the lawful money of England, which he owes him, and unjustly detains &c. for this, * that whereas in the common-council held according to the custom of the city of London aforesaid, used and approved from the time whereof the memory of man is not to the contrary, in the chamber of the Guildall of the said city, situate in the parish of St. Michael, in Bassishaw, in the ward of Bassishaw London, aforesaid, on the twenty-seventh day of October, in the twenty-third year of the reign of our lord Charles II. the now king of England, &c. by a certain act of the said common-council, then and there made among other things, it was ordained, enacted and established, by the mayor, aldermen and commons of the said city, in the said common-council then and there assembled, and by the authority of the same, that no person or persons English or alien, free of the city of London, or foreign from the liberties thereof, after the first day of the month of December, then next coming should take upon him or them, the use and exercise of the office of a broker, or brocage, between any manner of persons within the said city of London, or the liberties thereof, nor should presume as a broker or solicitor, to make any manner of bargain or bargains, contract or contracts, in or relating to the art or trade of merchandizing by exchange, or for letting of ships to freight, or hire, or otherwise between any manner

Defendant arrested upon an original bill of debt, founded on the said act of common-council.

Tenor of the bill.

* P. 411.

of perſons within the ſaid city or the liberties thereof, unleſs he or they be, or ſhould be firſt admitted and ſworn before the mayor and aldermen of the ſaid city of London for the time being, or before the ſaid mayor and the more part of the ſaid aldermen for the time being, a common broker to exerciſe brocage within the ſaid city and the liberties thereof, and be bound with good ſureties for him or them, for the due execution of the ſame office, upon pain of forfeiting the ſum of twenty pounds of lawful money of England, for every time that ſuch perſon or perſons ſhould offend, commit or do contrary to the purport, true intent and effect of the ſaid act; And it was further enacted by the ſaid authority, that all and every the pains, penalties and forfeitures, in and by the ſaid act of common council aforeſaid limited and appointed, the charges of the ſuit for the recovery thereof being firſt deducted, ſhould be divided into two equal moieties or half parts, whereof one equal moiety, or half, ſhould be to the uſe of the hoſpitals and priſons belonging to the ſaid city, to be diſtributed as the lord mayor and the court of aldermen for the time being, ſhould direct and appoint, and the other equal moiety or half part thereof, ſhould be to the uſe of the preſenter of the ſaid offence; and that all and every ſuch pains, penalties, and forfeitures ſhould be recovered by action of debt, bill, plaint or information, to be commenced and proſecuted in the name of the chamberlain of the ſaid city for the time being, in the king's majeſty's court, holden before the mayor and aldermen of the city of London aforeſaid, in the chamber of the Guildhall of the ſaid city, for the time being, in all which actions and ſuits to be commenced and proſecuted by virtue of the ſaid
* P. 412. act againſt the offender * or offenders, the ſaid chamberlain ſhould recover his reaſonable coſts of ſuit to be expended in and about the proſecution of ſuch action, and in which no eſſoign or wager of law ſhould be allowed or admitted, for the defendant, as by the ſaid act of common council, made and enacted in the due manner, and alſo in the due manner proclaimed and publiſhed within the ſaid city, among other things, by the ſaid act enacted more fully appears. Nevertheleſs, the ſaid James Bringhman being an alien, and foreign from the liberties of the ſaid city, not regarding the ſaid act of common council, nor in any manner fearing the pain in the ſame contained, after the making and enacting of the ſaid act of common council, and after the ſaid firſt day of the month of December next coming, after the 27th day of October, in the 23d year aforeſaid, and before the exhibition of this original bill, to wit, on the 15th day of December, in the 23d year of the reign of our ſaid lord Charles

Breach of the act of common council.

Charles the 2d, the now king of England, &c. did take upon him the ufe and exercife of the office of a broker and brocage, between James Davidfon, and certain other perfons to the faid Thomas Player unknown, within the faid city of London, to wit, in the parifh aforefaid, and then and there did prefume as a broker and folicitor, to make a certain bargain and contract, in and relating to the art or trade of merchandizing, for letting a certain fhip, called the King David of Rotterdam, to freight and hire, between the faid James Davifon, and the faid other perfons, to the faid Thomas Player unknown, within the faid city, to wit, in the parifh aforefaid, he the faid James Bringhman, not then, nor as yet, being firft admitted and fworn before the mayor and aldermen of the faid city of London for the time being, nor before the faid mayor, and the more part of the faid aldermen for the time being, a common broker to exercife brocage within the faid city and the liberties of the fame, againft the purport, true intent and effect of the act aforefaid, whereby an action hath accrued to the faid Thomas Player, knight, chamberlain, &c. to afk, demand, and have of the faid James Bringhman, the faid twenty pounds now demanded, which the faid James, to the faid Thomas Player knight, chamberlain, &c. hath not paid, although often, &c. to the damage of the faid Thomas Player, knight, chamberlain, &c. of forty fhillings, and therefore he produces his fuit, &c. and the faid bill original aforefaid, depends undetermined, &c. and this is the only caufe of the caption and detention of the faid James Bringhman, in prifon, and under cuftody as aforefaid, which together with the body of the faid James, at the day and place in the faid writ contained, we have ready, as we are within commanded by the faid writ.

* P. 413.

# * HABEAS CORPUS.

## The King *against* Wood and Chambers.

Return to an habeas corpus; That the defendants were committed to Newgate by the lord mayor and aldermen at their court upon the complaint of the bailiffs and wardens of the company of weavers, for a disturbance at an election of bailiffs and wardens of the said company.

Michaelmas the 21ſt Charles, &c. *London*, to wit. } WE Thomas Adams, mayor, and the aldermen of the city of London, and Thomas Foot, and John Kenrick, ſheriffs of the ſaid city, and alſo Henry Woolaſton, keeper of the goal of the lord the king of Newgate, certify, to the lord the king at Weſtminſter, that the city of London is an antient city, and that the freemen of the ſaid city, from the time whereof the memory of man is not to the contrary, have been, and as yet are incorporated as well by the name of the mayor and commonalty and citizens of the city of London, as by the name of the mayor and commonalty of the city of London, and that there are, and from the whole time aforeſaid, have been certain aldermen within the ſaid city, and that the ſaid aldermen from the whole time aforeſaid, have been, and are part and member of the ſaid mayor and commonalty and citizens of the ſaid city, and that the ſaid mayor and commonalty and citizens, ſo incorporated from the whole time aforeſaid, have been, and have conſiſted of, and as yet are, and conſiſt of ſeveral companies, guilds, myſteries and fraternities, of freemen of the ſaid city; and that every ſuch freeman at the time of his admiſſion into the freedom of the ſaid city, according to the cuſtom from the whole time aforeſaid, in the ſaid city uſed and approved, takes and ought, and hath been accuſtomed to take his corporal oath, before the chamberlain of the ſaid city for the time being, in the chamber of the Guildhall of the ſaid city, ſituate in the pariſh of St. Michael, in Baſſiſhaw, in the ward of Baſſiſhaw, London, that he would maintain the franchiſes and cuſtoms of the ſaid city, and would ſave the ſaid city harmleſs as much as in him lay, and that there is, and from the whole time aforeſaid hath been, a certain antient court of the lord the king, of record held, and to be held before the mayor and aldermen of the ſaid city for the time being, in the chamber of the Guildhall of the ſaid city, ſituate in the ſaid pariſh of St. Michael in Baſſiſhaw, in the ward of Baſſiſhaw, London, aforeſaid, to wit, upon every Tueſday, and every Thurſday in every week, at the leaſt, and that the ſaid ſeveral guilds, fraternities, myſteries and companies of the ſaid city are, and from the

the whole time aforeſaid, have been accuſtomed to be under the rule, government, and ordinance of the ſaid court of the ſaid mayor and aldermen of the ſaid city, in the elections of the governors of the ſeveral guilds, fraternities, myſteries and companies aforeſaid, and that the ſaid mayor and aldermen accuſtomed to the peaceable government of the ſaid guilds, according to the cuſtom of the ſaid city, in the ſaid court are uſed, and for the whole time aforeſaid, have been uſed and accuſtomed to inſpect and hear, examine and determine complaints between the guilds or fraternities aforeſaid, and the freemen of the ſaid ſeveral guilds or fraternities, or any of them, concerning the elections of the governors of the ſaid ſeveral guilds, or fraternities, * and con- * P. 414.
tempts committed againſt the governors of the ſaid ſeſeveral guilds, or fraternities, and diſturbances made in ſuch elections; and to puniſh and correct ſuch freemen, whom upon complaint, they ſhould find to have diſturbed ſuch elections, or in ſuch elections exciting ſedition againſt the accuſtomed government of the ſaid guilds, by impriſonment of their bodies, until they ſhould declare that they will not afterwards unduly diſturb ſuch elections, or until the ſaid court ſhould otherwiſe ordain, which cuſtoms, and all the other cuſtoms, privileges, and liberties of the ſaid city of London aforeſaid, by the authority of the parliament of the lord Richard, late king of England, the 2d after the conqueſt, held at Weſtminſter, in the 7th year of his reign, to the then mayor and commonalty and citizens of the ſaid city, were ratified and confirmed; and we further certify, that within the ſaid city from the whole time whereof the memory of man is not to the contrary, there hath been a certain antient guild, or fraternity of the art or miſtery of weavers, freemen of the ſaid city, conſiſting of two bailiffs, two wardens, certain aſſiſtants and liverymen, and of the community of the guild or fraternity aforeſaid; and from the whole time aforeſaid, being member and part of the ſaid body corporate aforeſaid, of the mayor, and commonalty and citizens of the ſaid city aforeſaid, and that every freeman of the ſaid guild or fraternity aforeſaid, at the time of his admiſſion into the ſaid guild or fraternity, from the whole time aforeſaid, hath taken, and hath been accuſtomed to take, his corporal oath upon the holy Goſpel of God, before the bailiffs and wardens of the ſaid guild or fraternity for the time being, to be obedient from time to time, to the bailiffs and wardens of the ſaid guild for the time being, and to obſerve the good orders of the ſaid guild or fraternity, as much as in him lay; in which guild or fraternity, for the better rule, government, direction and order of the ſame, and of the men, things, and buſineſs touching and con-

cerning

cerning the mistery of the said guild or fraternity, for the whole time aforesaid, four governors, to wit, two bailiffs, and two wardens, annually chosen, are elected, and have been accustomed to be elected by the said assistants, and livery of the said guild or fraternity, or by the major part of the same, assembled in their common hall, situate in the said parish of St. Michael, in Bassishaw, in the ward of Bassishaw London, aforesaid, upon the 25th day of July in every year annually, and so being elected and duly sworn, according to the custom of the said guild, in their said offices, ought and have been accustomed to continue until other bailiffs and wardens respectively elected to the several offices aforesaid, according to the custom of the said guild, and into the same according to the said custom, should be duly sworn; and we further certify, to the lord the king, that on the 25th day of July, in the 21st year of the reign of our lord Charles, the now king of England, &c. last past, one Richard Worsam and Gratian Allen, freemen of the city and guild aforesaid, were bailiffs of the said guild before that time duly elected, appointed and sworn, according to the custom of the said guild, and that on the
* P. 415. said 25th day of * July in the 21st year aforesaid, George Davis and William Bolnest, freemen of the city and guild aforesaid, were wardens of the said guild before that time duly elected, appointed and sworn, and that on the said 25th day of July, in the 21st year aforesaid, and from that time hitherto, there were, and as yet are, assistants to the said bailiffs and wardens, and divers others of the livery of the said guild, or fraternity duly elected and sworn; and that John Wood, in the writ named, on the 26th day of July, in the 6th year of the reign of our lord Charles, &c. at the common hall of the said guild or fraternity aforesaid, situate in the parish and ward aforesaid, according to the custom of the said guild, was admitted and sworn a freeman of the guild or fraternity aforesaid; and John Chambers, in the said writ also named, on the 2d day of October, in the 8th year of the reign of our lord Charles, &c. at the common hall of the said guild was admitted and sworn a freeman of the guild or fraternity aforesaid, according to the custom aforesaid, and then and there the said John Wood, and John Chambers respectively, did take their corporal oaths upon the holy Gospel of God, to be obedient to the bailiffs and wardens of the said guild or fraternity, for the time being, and to observe the orders of the said fraternity as much as in them lay, and have been, and as yet are freemen of the said city, duly elected and sworn according to the custom aforesaid; and we further certify, that the said Richard Worsam, and Gratian Allen, so as aforesaid, being bailiffs

bailiffs of the ſaid guild, and the ſaid George Davis, and William Bolneſt, ſo as aforeſaid, being wardens of the ſaid guild, afterwards, to wit, on the ſaid 25th day of July, in the 21ſt year of the reign of the lord Charles, king of England, &c. aforeſaid, the ſaid bailiffs, wardens, aſſiſtants and livery, being aſſembled at the common hall of the guild or fraternity aforeſaid, according to the cuſtom aforeſaid, for the election of bailiffs and wardens for the enſuing year, then and there proceeded to the election of the ſaid bailiffs and wardens; and they the ſaid John Wood and John Chambers, being freemen of the city and fraternity aforeſaid, as aforeſaid, and not being bailiffs or wardens, nor of the aſſiſtants, nor of the livery of the guild or fraternity aforeſaid, then and there came into the common hall aforeſaid, and then and unduly and tumultuouſly diſturbed and confounded the election aforeſaid, and then and there made a great hue and cry, contradicting and oppoſing themſelves againſt the quiet election of the baliffs and wardens of the fraternity aforeſaid, to the great diſturbance of the ſaid company, and of the ſaid election then to be made, and then and there exciting ſedition againſt the accuſtomed government of the ſaid guild; and the ſaid John Wood and John Chambers then and there being requeſted that they would retire, and deſiſt from making further ſuch diſturbance, nevertheleſs, they then and there entirely refuſed to deſiſt or retire, then and there calling and ſhouting that the ſaid bailiffs, wardens, aſſiſtants and others of the ſaid livery, ought not to proceed, and ſhould not proceed to make the ſaid election without them, and the others of the * community of the ſaid guild, not being bailiffs, wardens, aſſiſtants, nor of the livery aforeſaid, and that they and others of the community of the guild aforeſaid, who were not bailiffs, wardens, aſſiſtants, nor of the ſaid livery, would make the election of the ſaid bailiffs, and wardens, and would, and ought to be preſent at the ſaid election for the preſent, and in future, and that the election of bailiffs, and wardens whatſoever, without them, would and ought to be void; whereby not only the election of bailiffs and wardens aforeſaid, to be made for the preſent, was then and there obſtructed and diſturbed, but alſo in future times great diſturbance and ſedition was about to ariſe between the members of the ſaid guild, and of other guilds of the aforeſaid city, to the evil example of all others in the like caſe, offending againſt the laudable cuſtoms of the ſaid city, and to the weakening of the government of the guild and city aforeſaid, unleſs apt remedy ſhould be applied in this behalf, according to the cuſtoms of the city aforeſaid, whereupon the ſaid bailiffs and wardens of the ſaid guild or fraternity aforeſaid, exhibited complaint con-

* P. 416.

cerning the premisses, to the mayor and aldermen of the city aforesaid, for apt remedy upon the premisses, to be applied according to the custom of the city aforesaid; and we further certify, that at the court of the said lord the king, holden before the mayor and aldermen of the said city, in the said chamber of the Guildhall of the said city, situate in the parish and ward aforesaid, on the 4th day of September, in the 21st year of the reign of our lord Charles, the now king of England, &c. and then and there the said complaint so made by the said bailiffs and wardens, against the said John Wood and John Chambers, to the said mayor and aldermen in the said court held before them was heard, and upon the hearing of the said John Wood and John Chambers, and examination of the complaint and matter aforesaid, the mayor and aldermen in the said court found the said complaint to be true, and the said John Wood and John Chambers not only did not deny, nor did either of them deny the matter of the said complaint, but hardily and contemptuously then and there in the said court did affirm, and each of them did affirm, that they and others of the community of the said guild, who were not bailiffs, wardens, assistants or of the livery aforesaid, would be voters in such election to be made in future, whereupon by the said court then and there, according to the custom of the said city, they were and each of them was commanded, that they should desist, and should promise to desist from such undue disturbance in such election to be made in future, which to do they the said John Wood and John Chambers, then and there in contempt of the court aforesaid, and to the evil example of others, refused, and each of them for himself refused; whereupon consideration of the premisses by the said court then and there being had, and because the said John Wood and John Chambers, had disturbed the said election as aforesaid, and declared that they would persist in their purpose of disturbing as well the rule and govern-
* P. 417. ment of the said guild, as * other such elections, it was
considered then and there by the said court, that the said John Wood should be committed to the goal of the said lord the king, until that in the said court, afterwards he should declare that he would not unduly disturb any more the election of the bailiffs and wardens of the said guild, against the customs of the city and guild aforesaid, or the said court should otherwise ordain, and that the said John Chambers should be committed to the said goal, until that in the said court afterwards he should declare that he would not unduly disturb any more the election of the bailiffs and wardens, of the said guild against the customs of the city and guild aforesaid, or the said court should otherwise ordain; and then

then and there the said John Wood and John Chambers, were committed to the said prison under the custody of me Henry Woolaston, by the said court for the causes aforesaid; and we further certify, that the said John Wood and John Chambers have not as yet declared that they will not, nor hath either of them declared that he will not unduly disturb the election of the bailiffs and wardens of the guild aforesaid, against the customs of the said city, nor hath the said court concerning them the said John Wood and John Chambers, nor either of them, otherwise as yet ordained; and this is the cause of the caption and detention of the bodies of the said John Wood and John Chambers, in prison and under custody as aforesaid, nevertheless, the bodies of the said John Wood and John Chambers before the lord the king at the day and place in the said writ contained we have ready, as by the said writ we are commanded.

---

## The Mayor and Sheriffs of London *against* Coles.

Return to an Habeas Corpus; a commitment of a fishmonger, by the court of the lord mayor and aldermen of London, for forestalling fish.

*London, To wit.* WE Richard Ford, knight, mayor, and the aldermen of the city of London, and Dannett Forth, and Patience Ward, of the said city sheriffs, to the most serene lord the king, certify that the city of London is an antient city, and that the freemen of the said city, from the whole time whereof the memory of man is not to the contrary, have been and as yet are incorporated, by the name of the mayor and commonalty of the city of London, and that the said freemen so incorporated from the whole time aforesaid, have been and have consisted, and as yet do consist of several companies, guilds and fraternities, using several arts, mysteries, and handicrafts within the said city, the liberties and suburbs of the same, and that the mystery of a fish-monger, within the said city is, and from the whole time aforesaid, hath been one of the mysteries of the said city, and that within the said city there are, and from the whole time aforesaid there hath been, divers common public and open markets for the selling of fish and other food *, and that from the whole time aforesaid within the said city, there was had and as yet is had, a certain court of the said lord the king, and of his ancestors of record holden weekly, on every Tuesday and every Thursday, before the mayor and aldermen of the city aforesaid, for the time being, in the chamber of the Guildhall of the said city, situate in the parish of St. Michael,

* P. 418.

 Bassishaw,

Baſſiſhaw, in the ward of Baſſiſhaw London, in which court the mayor and aldermen of the ſaid city for the time being, from the whole time aforeſaid have been uſed, and accuſtomed, and as yet are uſed to order and ordain, as well thoſe things which belong to, and concern the regulation and preſervation of the ſeveral markets within the ſaid city, as well as thoſe things which have belonged, or do belong to the good rule and government of the ſaid city, and of the freemen of the ſaid city, uſing their ſeveral arts, myſteries and handicrafts within the ſaid city, in any thing touching or concerning the ſaid freemen, in their ſeveral arts, myſteries and handicrafts, for the public good and the quiet government of the ſaid city, and of the ſaid freemen of the ſaid city; and that the freemen of the ſeveral arts, myſteries and handicrafts within the ſaid city, from the whole time aforeſaid, have been and as yet are, under the rule, government, correction and puniſhment of the ſaid mayor and aldermen of the ſaid city, in the ſaid court, for their miſdeeds and offences, committed in their ſeveral arts, myſteries and handicrafts, within the ſaid city; and that within the ſaid city there is had, and from the whole time aforeſaid was had, a certain antient and laudable cuſtom, uſed and approved, to wit, that if any freeman of the ſaid city, within the ſaid city and the liberties of the ſame, hath foreſtalled fiſh or food, coming to any of the markets of the ſaid city, and if complaint hath been made in the ſaid court of ſuch foreſtalling, the ſaid court upon ſuch complaint, and upon the confeſſion of ſuch freemen in the ſaid court, of ſuch foreſtalling by him, ſo as aforeſaid committed, hath ordained that ſuch freeman in future, ſhould abſtain and deſiſt from ſuch foreſtalling, and if ſuch freeman being preſent in the ſaid court, and upon notice given to him by the ſaid court of ſuch their order, hath been required by the ſaid court, to conform himſelf and to yield obedience to ſuch order, and ſuch freeman then and there, not only obſtinately and wilfully hath refuſed to conform himſelf, and to yield obedience to ſuch order, but alſo obſtinately and contemptuouſly then hath declared to the ſaid court, that he in future would do the contrary of the ſaid order, that then the ſaid court for the whole time aforeſaid, hath been uſed and accuſtomed to commit ſuch freemen to ſome priſon within the ſaid city, there to remain until that ſuch freeman voluntarily ſhould declare or ſignify to the ſaid court, that he for the future time would conform himſelf, and render obedience to ſuch order, which cuſtom and all the other cuſtoms of the ſaid city, from the whole time whereof the memory of man is not to the contrary uſed in the ſame, by the authority of the parliament of the lord
* P. 419. Richard, late king of England, * the ſecond after the conqueſt,

queſt, held at Weſtminſter, in the county of Middleſex, in the ſeventh year of his reign, to then mayor and commonalty of the ſaid city, were ratified and confirmed; and we further certify that before the coming of the writ, of the ſaid lord the king, to us the ſaid mayor, and aldermen, and ſheriffs of London, directed, and to this ſchedule annexed, to wit, on the twentieth day of March, in the twenty-third year of the reign, of our lord Charles II. &c. William Coles in the ſaid writ named, then and as yet being a freeman of the ſaid city, and then and as yet exerciſing the art of a fiſhmonger within the ſaid city, foreſtalled divers great quantities of fiſh, coming to the public market within the ſaid city, to be expoſed to ſale, and that afterwards and before the coming of the ſaid writ to us, to wit, at the ſaid court of the ſaid lord the now king, before us the ſaid mayor, and aldermen of the ſaid city, held according to the cuſtoms of the ſaid city, in the ſaid chamber of the Guildhall, of the ſaid city, on Thurſday the twenty third day of March, in the year laſt aforeſaid, a certain complaint was made to us, the ſaid mayor and aldermen, in the ſaid court, againſt the ſaid William Coles, in the ſaid writ named for the foreſtalling aforeſaid, which foreſtalling the ſaid William Coles, then in the ſaid court before us the ſaid mayor and aldermen, confeſſed and affirmed, upon which complaint, and upon the confeſſion and affirmation aforeſaid, the ſaid court then and there ordained, that the ſaid William Coles ſhould in future, abſtain and deſiſt from ſuch foreſtalling of fiſh, and to the ſaid William Coles then and there being preſent in the ſaid court, gave notice of their order aforeſaid, and then and there required the ſaid William Coles to conform himſelf, and to yield obedience to their order aforeſaid, and becauſe the ſaid William Coles being a freeman of the ſaid city, then and there in the ſaid court, not only obſtinately and wilfully refuſed to conform himſelf, and to yield obedience to the ſaid order, but alſo obſtinately and contemptuouſly then declared to the ſaid court, that he ſaid William Coles in future, would do contrary to the ſaid order, and would not abſtain from ſuch foreſtalling of fiſh, he the ſaid William Coles according to the ſaid cuſtom of the ſaid city, from the whole time aforeſaid, in the ſame uſed and approved, and by the authority of parliament in the manner and form aforeſaid, ratified and confirmed then and there by the ſaid court, was committed to the priſon of the ſaid lord the king, of Newgate, within the city of London aforeſaid, under the cuſtody of us the ſaid ſheriffs, there to remain until that he ſhould declare or ſignify to the ſaid court, that he for the future time would yield obedience to the ſaid order, or otherwiſe ſhould be diſcharged from thence by the due courſe of law, and finally, we certi

fy

ſy that the ſaid W. C. hitherto hath not declared nor ſignified to the ſaid court, that he for the future time would yield obedience to the ſaid order, and this is the cauſe of th ecaption and detention, &c.

---

* P. 420.

## * Habeas Corpus *for* Harwood.

Return to an Habeas Corpus; commitment of the defendant by the court of the lord mayor and aldermen of London, for non-payment of a fine impoſed by them on the defendant, for marrying the orphan of a freeman of the ſaid city, without the leave of the ſaid mayor and aldermen.

*London*, To wit. } WE Jonathan Dawes, knight, and Robert Clayton, knight, ſheriffs of the city of London, to the lord the king, moſt humbly certify that the city of London is, and from the whole time whereof the memory of man is not to the contrary, hath been an antient city, and that the mayor, and commonalty, and citizens of the city of London are, and from the whole time aforeſaid have been, a body politic, and corporate, and that in the ſaid city there are, and from the whole time aforeſaid have been, twenty-four aldermen of the ſaid city, and that in the ſaid city there is had, and from the whole time whereof the memory of man is not to the contrary, was had ſuch cuſtom uſed and approved within the ſaid city, to wit, that if any citizen and freeman of the ſaid city ſhould die, having at the time of his death an orphan, or ophans, being within the age of twenty-one years and unmarried, immediately after the death of ſuch freeman, the mayor, and aldermen of the ſaid city for the time being, have had, and from the whole time aforeſaid, have been accuſtomed to have the wardſhip, as well of the body or bodies of ſuch orphan or orphans, as of the goods and chattles, lands and tenements in any wiſe belonging or appertaining to ſuch orphan or orphans, to the uſe and behoof of ſuch orphan or orphans, until ſuch orphan or orphans, if male or males, ſhall have arrived at the age of twenty-one years, and if female or females, until ſhe or they ſhall be married, or ſhall have arrived at the age of twenty-one years, whichſoever ſhall firſt happen, and that in the ſaid city there is, and from the whole time aforeſaid, hath been, a certain antient court of the lord the king, and of his progenitors late kings and queens of England of record, called and named the court of the orphans of the ſaid city, held before the mayor and aldermen of the ſaid city, for the time being, in the chamber of the Guildhall, of the ſaid city, ſituate in the pariſh of St. Michael, Baſſiſhaw, in the ward of Baſſiſhaw, London, aforeſaid, for the determination of all and ſingular the cauſes and matters whatſoever, touching or concerning ſuch orphans, their goods and chattles, lands and tenements whatſoever; and that the mayor, and aldermen of the ſaid city, for the time

time being, in the ſaid court from the whole time aforeſaid, have been uſed and accuſtomed to give, or for reaſonable cauſe to deny leave to ſuch female orphan, or female orphans, being within the age of twenty-one years, to eſpouſe and to take to huſband any perſon, and alſo to give or for reaſonable cauſe to deny leave to any perſon or perſons, to take to wife ſuch female orphan or female orphans, being within the age of twenty-one years as aforeſaid, and that within the ſaid city there is, and from the whole time aforeſaid hath been, a certain other cuſtom uſed and approved in the ſaid city, that if any perſon hath taken to wife any ſuch female orphan, being within the age of twenty-one years *, without the leave of the mayor, and aldermen of the ſaid city, for the time being, in the ſaid court of the orphans firſt had and obtained, that the mayor and aldermen of the ſaid city for the time being, in the ſaid court from the whole time aforeſaid, have been uſed and accuſtomed to impoſe and aſſeſs a reaſonable fine, upon ſuch perſon who hath ſo taken to wife ſuch female orphan being within the age of twenty-one years, without the leave of the mayor, and aldermen of the ſaid city, for the time being, in the ſaid court firſt had and obtained for his contempt in that behalf; and if ſuch perſon upon whom ſuch fine hath been impoſed and aſſeſſed, being perſonally preſent in the ſaid court, and having notice of ſuch fine upon him ſo as aforeſaid impoſed and aſſeſſed, hath refuſed to pay ſuch fine, or give ſecurity by his writing obligatory for the payment thereof, to the mayor, and aldermen of the ſaid city, for the time being, within a reaſonable time then next enſuing, that then the ſaid mayor, and aldermen of the ſaid city, for the time being, could and from the whole time aforeſaid have been uſed and accuſtomed, to commit ſuch perſon ſo refuſing to pay ſuch fine, or to give ſecurity as aforeſaid for the payment thereof, to the priſon of the lord the king, of Newgate, ſituate in the pariſh of St. Sepulchre, in the ward of Farringdore, without London, there to remain until that ſuch perſon ſhould pay ſuch fine, or until ſuch perſon ſhould be diſcharged from the ſaid priſon by the due courſe of law; which cuſtoms and all the other cuſtoms of the ſaid city, by the authority of the parliament of lord Richard, late king of England, the ſecond after the conqueſt, held at Weſtminſter, in the county of Middleſex, in the ſeventh year of his reign, to the then mayor, and commonalty, and citizens of the ſaid city, and to their ſucceſſors were ratified; and confirmed, and further we moſt humbly certify to the lord the king, that before the coming of the ſaid writ, to wit, on the thirteenth day of November, in the twenty-third year of the reign, of our lord Charles II. the now king of England, &c. One Ralph Harwood, of London

* P. 421.

London, merchant, took to his wife one Martha Offley, daughter and orphan of one Robert Offley, lately deceased, who whilst he lived and at the time of his death, was a citizen and freeman of the said city, to wit, of the company of cloathworkers within the said city, she the said Martha, at the time of her said marriage being within the age of twenty-one years, without the leave of the mayor, and aldermen of the said city, for the time being, in the said court had and obtained, and that the marriage portion of the said Martha, then amounted to eight hundred pounds, of the lawful money of England, and thereupon at the said court of the orphans, held in the chamber of the Guildhall, of the said city, on Tuesday the fourteenth day of November, in the twenty-third year of the reign, of the lord the now king, &c. before George Waterman, knight, then and as yet mayor, and the aldermen of the said city, upon the examination of the said matter in the said court, it sufficiently appeared to the said court, that the said Ralph Harwood, had taken to his wife the said Martha, the said orphan, without any leave
* P. 422. of the mayor, and aldermen of the said * city, for the time being, in the said court had and obtained, and that the marriage portion of the said Martha, amounted to eight hundred pounds; whereupon then and there by the said court, the fine of forty pounds (being a reasonable fine for the contempt aforesaid) was imposed and assessed upon the said Ralph Harwood, for his contempt aforesaid, and that the said Ralph then and there, was personally present in the said court, and had notice of the said fine upon him as aforesaid, imposed and assessed, and then and there was requested by the said court, to pay the said fine upon him as aforesaid imposed, or to give security in the form aforesaid for the payment thereof, to the mayor, and aldermen of the said city, within a reasonable time, then next ensuing, which to do the said Ralph, then and there entirely denied and refused, wherefore the said Ralph Harwood, then and there by the said mayor, and aldermen of the said city, in the said court was committed to the said prison, of the lord the king, of Newgate, there to remain until that the said Ralph, should pay the said fine upon him as aforesaid imposed, or until the said Ralph, from the said prison, should be discharged by the due course of law, and this is the cause of the caption and detention of the said Ralph, in the said prison, under the custody of us the said sheriffs, whose body nevertheless we have ready before the lord the king, as by the said writ we are commanded, &c.

*This case is reported 2 Levinz. 32. and for aught that appears to the contrary, the return was adjudged good.*

Habeas

# Habeas Corpus and Returns thereto.

## Habeas Corpus *for* Clarke.

*London,* } WE Thomas Davies knight, mayor, and the
To wit. } aldermen of the city of London, by virtue of the writ of the lord the king to us now directed, and to this ſchedule annexed, to the lord the king humbly certify, that the city of London is an antient city, and that in the ſaid city there is, and from the whole time whereof the memory of man is not to the contrary, there hath been a certain antient court of record, held before the mayor and aldermen of the ſaid city for the time being, in the chamber of the Guildhall of the ſaid city, according to the cuſtom of the ſaid city; and that within the ſaid city there is had, and from the whole time aforeſaid was had, a cuſtom uſed and approved, to wit, that if any citizen or freeman of the ſaid city hath miſdemeaned himſelf towards any of the aldermen of the ſaid city, to the ſcandal and reproach of his eſtate, of an alderman, or to the ignominy, diſgrace, or diſhonour of ſuch alderman, or if ſuch citizen and freeman of the ſaid city, hath maliciouſly ſaid, or ſpoken contemptuous, reproachful, ſcandalous and defamatory words to the diſhonour and contempt of ſuch alderman, or if ſuch citizen and freeman of the ſaid * city hath maliciouſly charged to ſuch alderman, any ſcandal or reproach to the diſhonour and contempt of ſuch alderman, the common ſerjeant at law of the ſaid city for the time being, for the whole time aforeſaid, hath been uſed and accuſtomed, for the mayor and commonalty and citizens of the city of London, aforeſaid, in the ſaid court of the ſaid lord the king, and of his progenitors, kings and queens of this kingdom of England, before the mayor and aldermen of the ſaid city for the time being, held in the chamber of the Guildhall of the ſaid city, according to the cuſtom of the ſaid city, to exhibit and proſecute an information or informations againſt ſuch delinquent or delinquents, for ſuch crime and crimes by him or them ſo as aforeſaid committed or perpetrated; and if ſuch citizen and freeman of ſuch offence or crime, by his own proper confeſſion or by the verdict of twelve good and lawful men of the ſaid city, in the ſaid court be convicted, then ſuch citizen and freeman ſo as aforeſaid convicted for his crime aforeſaid, in that behalf from the whole time aforeſaid, by the judgment of the ſaid court, might and hath been accuſtomed to be puniſhed by reaſonable fine, according to the demerit of ſuch delinquent; which cuſtom, and all the other cuſtoms of the ſaid city, by the authority of the parliament of the lord Richard the late king of England, the ſecond after the conqueſt, held at Weſtminſter, in the ſeventh year of his reign,

Return to an Habeas Corpus; That the defendant was committed by the court of the lord mayor and aldermen of London, on an information before them exhibited against the defendant by the common ſerjeant, for ſpeaking re- * P. 423. flecting words of one of the aldermen of London.

to the then mayor and commonalty and citizens of the said city, and to their successors, were ratified and confirmed; and we further signify, that on the twenty-third day of January, in the twenty-eighth year of the reign of our lord Charles II. by the grace of God of England, &c. king, &c. George Jeffreys, esquire, then and as yet common serjeant of the said city of London, who, according to the custom of the said city, for the mayor and commonalty and citizens of the said city of London prosecuted, in his proper person came into the court of the said lord the king, in the chamber of the Guildhall of the said city of London before us, the said Thomas Davies knight, mayor, of the city of London, and the aldermen of the said city, held according to the custom of the said city, and exhibited a certain information against John Clarke in the said writ named, which John Clarke on the twentieth day of November, in the twenty-eighth year of the reign of our lord Charles II. was, and as yet is a citizen and freeman of the city of London aforesaid, which information follows in these words, to wit, " Be it remembered, that on the twenty-third day of January in the twenty-eighth year of the reign of our lord Charles II. the now king of England, &c. George Jeffreys, esquire, common serjeant at law of the city of London, who for the mayor and commonalty and citizens of the city of London prosecutes, in his proper person comes here into the court of the said lord the now king, held in the chamber of the Guildhall of the said city, situate in the parish of St. Michael, Bassishaw, in the ward of Bassishaw London, before Thomas Davies, knight, mayor of the said city, and the aldermen of the said city, according to the custom of the said city, and gives the court here to understand, and to be informed that one John Lawrence, knight citizen and alderman of the city of London, from the time of his nativity, always hitherto hath been of good name fame and credit *, and the duty and office of sheriff of the city of London, and of the county of Middlesex, and also of mayor of the city of London, faithfully and praise-worthily lately hath borne and exercised, and whereas also the said John Lawrence, knight, for the space of divers years now last past, to wit, for seven years and more, was and now is an alderman of the said city, and unto the said office according to the custom of the said city lawfully was admitted and sworn, and by reason of his office of alderman, for the whole time aforesaid, was and as yet is one of the justices of the said lord the now king, assigned to preserve the peace in the said city, and also to hear and determine divers felonies, trespasses, and other misdeeds in the said city perpetrated, and in the offices aforesaid well and honourably hath demeaned himself without any mark or suspicion of guilt, deceit or falsity whatsoever, but for his good demeanour in the offices aforesaid, with all the faithful

* P. 424.

subjects

ſubjects of the ſaid lord the king within the ſaid city hath deſerved well, and by reaſon thereof not only with the ſaid lord the king, and the lords of the privy council of the ſaid lord the now king, and the other peers and nobles of this kingdom, but alſo with the citizens of the ſaid city, and the other faithful ſubjects of the ſaid lord the now king deſervedly hath obtained great praiſe, eſteem and commendation; and whereas alſo the ſaid John Lawrence, on the twentieth day of November in the twenty-eighth year of the reign of the ſaid lord the now king, at the pariſh of St. Michael Baſſiſhaw in the ward of Baſſiſhaw London, was one of the committee to try and examine the meaſures within the ſaid city uſed for buying and ſelling coals, for this purpoſe lawfully appointed, and whereas on that occaſion the ſaid John Lawrence knight, then came to the ſitting of the ſaid committee, then held at the Guildhall of the ſaid city, to wit, in the pariſh aforeſaid, and then and long before and afterwards, there was with the other commiſſioners executing the ſaid buſineſs, nevertheleſs one John Clarke, citizen and freeman of the city of London, then and as yet uſing the art or myſtery of a woodmonger in ſelling wood, and alſo in ſelling coals by the meaſure there, on the ſaid twentieth day of November, in the twenty-eighth year of the reign of the ſaid lord the now king aforeſaid, not being ignorant of the premiſſes, but knowing that the ſaid John Lawrence knight, then was an alderman of the ſaid city, and one of the juſtices of the ſaid lord the now king, aſſigned as aforeſaid to preſerve the peace in the ſaid city, and one of the ſaid committee nevertheleſs contriving and intending the authority, magiſtracy, governance, and rule of the ſaid John Lawrence knight, as one of the aldermen of the ſaid city, and as one of the juſtices aſſigned to preſerve the peace in the ſaid city, and as one of the committee aforeſaid, to draw into hatred, diſgrace and contempt, and him as much as it was in the power of the ſaid John Clarke, with the laſting mark of infamy, deceit, and falſity to ſtain, and the ſtate and dignity of an alderman and magiſtrate of the ſaid city, to ſcandalize, depreſs and diminiſh, of his malice aforethought, in the ſaid pariſh of St. Michael Baſſiſhaw, in the ward of Baſſiſhaw London aforeſaid, having then and there * a diſcourſe with the ſaid John Lawrence knight, concerning the ſaid buſineſs of trying the ſaid meaſures, and the things to be inquired into and done by the ſaid John Lawrence knight, and one of the ſaid committee for the public good of the ſaid city, theſe falſe feigned, ſcandalous and opprobrious Engliſh words following, of the ſaid John Lawrence knight, in the preſence and in the hearing of divers liege ſubjects of the ſaid lord the now king, then and there being and hearing falſly, and maliciouſly did ſay, aſſert, * P. 425.

 publiſh

publish and with a loud voice pronounce, to wit "*he*" (meaning the said J. L. knight) "*comes to ruin the wood-mongers and the city*" (meaning the said city of London) "*he*" (meaning the said John Lawrence knight) "*studies to destroy the city*" (meaning the city of London aforesaid) and "*he*" (meaning the said John Lawrence knight) "*durst not stay to do justice,*" "*he*" (meaning the said John Lawrence knight) "*was a knave,*" "*he,*" (again meaning the said John Lawrence knight) "*is a knave;*" and further the said John Clarke, then and there of his further malice aforethought, these wicked, false, feigned, scandalous, and opprobrious English words following, to the said John Lawrence knight, and concerning the said John Lawrence knight, in the presence and hearing of divers faithful subjects of the said lord the now king, then and there present, and hearing falsly and maliciously, did say, assert, and with a loud voice pronounce, to wit, "*you*" (meaning the said John Lawrence knight) "*are a knave*" against the peace of the said lord the now king his crown and dignity, in contempt, dishonour, and disgrace of the said John Lawrence knight, and of the estate of an alderman and magistrate of the said city, and to the reproach and scandal of the government of the said city, and to the pernicious example of all others in the like case offending, and also against the customs of the said city, with this that the said George Jeffreys will verify, that the said John Clarke on the said twentieth day of November in the twenty-eighth year aforesaid, to wit, at the said time of the speaking and publishing of the said words and long before, and continually afterwards, hitherto was and as yet is a freeman and citizen of the aforesaid, wherefore the said George Jeffreys, for the mayor and commonalty and citizens of the said city prays the consideration of the court here in the premisses, and that the said John Clarke may come here into court to answer concerning the premisses, &c. To which information so as aforesaid exhibited against the said John Clarke, in the court of the said lord the king before us, the said mayor and aldermen of the said city, as well the said George Jeffreys, who &c by William Lightfoot and Thomas Monk his attorneys, as the said John Clarke by Peter King his attorney, severally have appeared, &c. And this is the information which depends before us the said mayor and aldermen of the said city, against the said John Clarke, whereof in the said writ mention is made, which we send to the said lord the king, under our seals, from the day of Easter in fifteen days wheresoever, &c. &c. &c.

* *This case is reported 3 Keble, 764, 799, 811, who says a procedendo was denied by the court, who judged it unreasonable for a man to be disfranchised for words, and that the aldermen should be judges in their own case; and that they could not commit for any contempt out of court, according to Cro. El. 78, Simmons against Sweet; and 689 Dean's case, and Moor 247. Pl. 389. The Serjeant in his notes says, that after several motions for a procedendo, the case was referred and agreed, and then a procedendo was granted, no defence being made; this was Trinity, 30th Charles 2d.* * P. 426.

*This case is also reported 2 Levinz, 200.*

---

## Habeas Corpus for Smartfoote.

Writ of pluries habeas corpus subpœna to to the mayor, aldermen and sheriffs of London, returnable into B. R.

CHARLES the 2d &c. to the mayor, aldermen and sheriffs of London, greeting: We command you, as we have often times commanded you, that the body of Francis Smartfoote in our prison under your custody detained, as it is said, together with the day and cause of his caption and detention, by whatsoever name the said Francis may be called in the same, you have before us at Westminster on the Saturday next after the octave of the blessed Virgin Mary, next ensuing, to submit to and receive all and singular those things which our court concerning him then and there shall ordain in this behalf, and this in no wise omit under the pain of 20l. and have there then this writ. Witness R. Rainsford, at Westminster, the 9th day of February, in the 30th year of our reign.

The execution of this writ appears in a certain schedule to this writ annexed.

The Answer of the Mayor, Aldermen and Sheriffs of London.

To

Return—That the defendant was committed by the court of the lord mayor and aldermen of London upon a complaint before them ore tenus, by the master and wardens of the company of merchant taylors against the defendant, one of their company for refusing to take upon him the office of a liveryman of that company tho' thereto duly elected.

* P. 427.

TO our most serene lord Charles the second——By the grace of God, of England, Scotland, France and Ireland, king, defender of the faith, &c. WE Thomas Davis, knight, mayor of the city of London, and the aldermen of the said city, and John Peake, knight, and Thomas Stampe, knight, sheriffs of the said city, most humbly certify, that the city of London is, and from the time whereof the memory of man is not to the contrary, hath been an antient city, and that the citizens and freemen of the said city from the whole time whereof the memory of man is not to the contrary, have been, and as yet * are incorporated as well by the name of the mayor, commonalty and citizens of the city of London, as by the name of the mayor, and commonalty of the city of London, and that of the said citizens and freeman so incorporated from the whole time aforesaid, there have been several guilds, companies, and fraternities within the said city, whereof the company of merchant taylors, the fraternity of St. John the Baptist, in the city of London, who for the whole time aforesaid, have been incorporated by the name of the master and wardens of the merchant taylors the fraternity of St. John the Baptist, in the city of London, now is, and from the whole time aforesaid hath been one; and that as well of and in the said company of merchant taylors, as in all the other companies, guilds and fraternities, in the said city there are, and from the whole time aforesaid, have been certain men, being citizens and freemen of the city aforesaid, and freemen of the said companies, guilds and fraternities respectively, called liverymen, who, from time to time, from the whole time aforesaid, have been elected, and have been accustomed to be elected by the company, guild or fraternity whereof such men are free, and whereof each and every of them is free respectively, into the livery of the said guild, company or fraternity, whereof they respectively so as aforesaid are freemen, which men, and every of them respectively so elected, and not having any reasonable cause or excuse to the contrary thereof, the office or place of a liveryman of that guild, company or fraternity respectively, in which every such man hath been elected to be of the livery thereof from the whole time aforesaid, ought and have been accustomed to take upon themselves, and that office, and the burden of that office or place to undergo and sustain, which men so elected and undertaking the said office, by reason of the said

ſaid office or place, greater burdens and expences and ſums of money towards the ſupport, and in and for the public good, and better government of the ſaid company reſpectively, whereof every ſuch man is of the livery thereof, than the other freemen of the ſaid company reſpectively not being of the livery thereof, from the whole time aforeſaid have been uſed, and ought to pay and contribute: And we further moſt humbly certify, to the ſaid lord the now king, that within the ſaid city there is had, and from the whole time aforeſaid, whereof the memory of man is not to the contrary was had, a certain court of the lord the now king, and of his anceſtors heretofore kings and queens of England, of record, held weekly on every Tueſday and every Thurſday, before the mayor and aldermen of the ſaid city for the time being, in the chamber of the Guildhall of the ſaid city, ſituate in the pariſh of St. Michael Baſſiſhaw, in the ward of Baſſiſhaw, in which court the mayor and aldermen of the ſaid city for the time being, from the whole time aforeſaid, have managed, regulated, and ordained, and have been uſed and accuſtomed to manage, regulate, and ordain all things for the time being, touching, appertaining to, or in any manner concerning the ſaid ſeveral companies, guilds and fraternities of the ſaid city, which have been brought before them for the better rule and government thereof to the * ſupport of the honour and * P. 428 dignity of the ſaid city; and that the freemen being citizens and freemen of the city of London aforeſaid, of whatſoever company, guild, or fraternity of the city of London aforeſaid, each and every of them are, and from the whole time aforeſaid have been, and have been accuſtomed to be under the rule, government, correction and puniſhment of the ſaid mayor and aldermen of the ſaid city for the time being, in the court aforeſaid, in the form aforeſaid held, for all and ſingular the matters by any ſuch freeman thereupon done, or omitted to be done againſt or to the prejudice of the good government, and rule of the ſaid company, guild, or fraternity of the city aforeſaid: And we further moſt humbly certiſy to the ſaid lord the now king, that within the ſaid city there is had, and alſo from the whole time aforeſaid there was had a certain other cuſtom within the ſaid city, from the whole time aforeſaid, hitherto uſed and approved, that if any complaint be made in writing, or by words of mouth, to the ſaid mayor and aldermen of the ſaid city for the time being, in the court aforeſaid, ſo as aforeſaid, held before them according to the cuſtom aforeſaid, by the maſter and wardens of any company of the ſaid city, within the ſaid city, or by the principle members of any company of the ſaid city within the ſaid city, in which there are not maſters and wardens, or by any of them, ſhowing that any perſon being a citizen and freeman of the ſaid city, and a member of the ſaid company, hath been elected by that company to the livery of the ſaid company, whereof he is a member, and hath been requeſted to undertake the office or place of a liveryman of the ſaid company, and to undergo and ſuſtain the burden of that office or place, and that ſuch citizen and freeman of the ſaid city and member of ſuch company, without any reaſonable cauſe and excuſe to the contrary thereof, hath refuſed to be of the livery of the ſaid company, to undertake that office or place, and to undergo and ſuſtain the burden of that office or place, and thereupon praying remedy, relief, aid and juſtice from the ſaid court, before the ſaid mayor and aldermen of the ſaid city for the time being, held as aforeſaid, according to the ſaid cuſtom, in the premiſſes againſt ſuch perſon ſo refuſing, and thereupon ſuch perſon againſt whom ſuch complaint hath been made, being a citizen and freeman of the ſaid city, and member of ſuch company, being before the mayor and aldermen of the ſaid city for the time being, in the ſaid court aſſembled, before the ſaid mayor and aldermen in the ſaid court hath confeſſed or hath not denyed the premiſſes, but being admoniſhed by the ſaid court to conform himſelf in that behalf, and to take upon himſelf the ſaid office or place, and to undergo and ſuſtain the burden of that office or place, openly, wilfully, obſtinately and contemptuouſly without any cauſe or excuſe whatſoever to the contrary thereof, hath refuſed in the ſaid court to be of the livery of the ſaid company whereof he as aforeſaid is a member, and to take upon himſelf that office or place, then the ſaid mayor and aldermen of the city of London aforeſaid, for the time being, in the ſaid court held as aforeſaid, have charged and committed ſuch perſon ſo refuſing * to priſon under the cuſtody of the ſheriffs of the city of London for the time being, there to remain under their cuſtody, and to be detained until the ſaid perſon ſo committed to priſon, would conſent and declare that he would take upon himſelf the ſaid office or place, and would undergo and ſuſtain the burden of that office of place, or otherwiſe ſuch perſon ſhould be delivered and diſcharged out of the priſon and cuſtody of the ſaid ſheriffs of the ſaid city by the due courſe of law; which ſeveral cuſtoms above mentioned, and all the other cuſtoms and frank uſages of the ſaid city within the ſaid city uſed, by the authority of the parliament of the lord Richard late king of England, the ſecond after the conqueſt, held at Weſtminſter in the county of Middleſex, in the ſeventh year of his reign to the then mayor and commonalty of the ſaid city, were ratified.

* P. 429.

tified and confirmed; and further to the ſaid lord the now king we moſt humbly certify, that before the coming of the ſaid writ of Habeas Corpus, and alſo before the coming of the firſt writ of Habeas Corpus to us in this behalf directed, to wit, on the ſixteenth day of January, in the twenty-eighth year of the reign of the ſaid lord the now king, Francis Smartfoot, in the writ to this ſchedule annexed named, who then and long before and continually afterwards hitherto was and as yet is a citizen and freeman of the city aforeſaid and a freeman and member of the ſaid company of merchant taylors the fraternity of St. John the baptiſt, in the city of London aforeſaid, by that company in the due manner was elected into the livery of the ſaid fraternity, and whereof the ſaid Francis Smartfoote then had notice, and thereupon was requeſted to take upon himſelf the office or place of a livery man of the ſaid fraternity, and to undergo and ſuſtain the burden of that office or place, according to the cuſtoms of the ſaid city, from the whole time aforeſaid hitherto uſed and approved in the ſame, but ſo to do he entirely hath refuſed; whereupon afterwards and before the coming of the ſaid firſt writ of Habeas Corpus, to us in this behalf directed, to wit, on Thurſday the firſt day of February, in the twenty-ninth year of the reign of the ſaid lord the now king, a certain complaint was made by word of mouth to us the ſaid Thomas Davies, then and as yet mayor and to the then aldermen of the ſaid city, in the ſaid court then held before us, the ſaid mayor and aldermen of the ſaid city, by one John White then maſter, and by Edward Harvey, George Archer, John Wallis and John Clift then wardens of the company of merchant taylors the fraternity of St. John the baptiſt, in the city of London aforeſaid, being one of the companies of the city of London aforeſaid, ſhewing that the ſaid Francis Smartfoote, being a citizen and freeman of the ſaid city, and a member of the company of merchant taylors the fraternity of St. John the Baptiſt in the city of London aforeſaid, was elected by that company into the livery of the ſaid company, and was requeſted to take upon him the office or place of one of the livery of the ſaid company, and to undergo and ſuſtain the burden of that office or place; nevertheleſs the ſaid Francis Smartfoote being a citizen and freeman of the ſaid city, and a member of the ſaid company without any reaſonable cauſe or excuſe to the contrary thereof, had entirely refuſed to be of the livery of the ſaid company, and to take upon himſelf that * office or place, and to undergo and ſuſ- * P. 430.
tain the burden of that office or place, and thereupon the ſaid maſter and wardens by that complaint, prayed remedy, aid, and juſtice of the ſaid court, before the mayor and aldermen aforeſaid, then held according to the cuſtom aforeſaid,

upon the ſaid premiſſes, againſt the ſaid Francis Smar t ſoote and thereupon the ſaid Francis Smartfoote being before us the ſaid mayor and aldermen of the ſaid city aſſembled in the ſaid court, then and there held before us according to the cuſtom aforeſaid, and perſonally appearing before us the ſaid mayor and aldermen of the ſaid city in the ſaid court, the premiſſes aforeſaid to wit, that he being a citizen and freeman of the ſaid city, and being a member and freeman of the ſaid company laſt named, was elected by that company into the livery of the ſaid company, and was required to take upon himſelf the office or place of one of the livery of the ſaid company, and to undergo and ſuſtain the burden of that office or place, nevertheleſs that he the ſaid Francis Smartfoote being a citizen and freeman of the ſaid city, and a member of the ſaid company, had refuſed to take upon himſelf that office or place and to undergo and ſuſtain the burden of that office or place, before us the ſaid mayor and aldermen of the ſaid city, in the open court aforeſaid, held before us on the day and place laſt aforeſaid named, expreſsly acknowledged and confeſſed, whereupon the ſaid Francis Smartfoote then and there in the ſaid court by us the ſaid mayor and aldermen of the ſaid city, often times in the ſaid court, was admoniſhed to conform himſelf in that behalf, and to take upon himſelf that office or place, and to undergo and ſuſtain the burden of that office or place, nevertheleſs the ſaid F. S. not having or alledging any cauſe or excuſe whatſoever to the contrary thereof, after ſuch admonition to him in the form aforeſaid made, not having nor alledging any cauſe or excuſe to the contrary thereof, to be of the livery of the company laſt aforeſaid, or to take upon himſelf that office or place, and to undergo and ſuſtain the burden of that office or place, in the ſaid court there openly, wilfully obſtinately and contemptuouſly without any cauſe or excuſe whatſoever to the contrary thereof, denied and expreſsly refuſed; whereby we the ſaid mayor and aldermen of the city of London aforeſaid, then and there in the ſaid court before the coming of the ſaid writ of Habeas Corpus, and alſo before the coming of the ſaid firſt writ of Habeas Corpus in that behalf, him the ſaid Francis Smartfoote ſo refuſing according to the cuſtom aforeſaid, to priſon under the cuſtody of us the ſaid ſheriffs have charged and committed, there to remain and to be detained, until that the ſaid F. S. hath conſented and declared, that he would take upon himſelf the office or place aforeſaid, and that he would ſuſtain and undergo the burden of that office or place, or until the ſaid F. S. otherwiſe out of the ſaid priſon, and out of the cuſtody of the ſaid ſheriffs of the ſaid city for the time being, by the due courſe of law, ſhould be delivered and diſcharged; and we further moſt humbly certify to the ſaid lord the king, that the ſaid F. S. at any time hitherto hath not conſented

Defendant before the lord mayor and aldermen confeſſes the election, &c. but refuſes to take the office upon him.

ſented and declared that he was willing to take upon himſelf the ſaid office or place, or to undergo and ſuſtain the burden of that office or place, nor hath he taken * upon himſelf that office and place; and this is the cauſe of the caption and detention of the ſaid F. S. &c. * P. 431.

The Anſwer of the Mayor, Aldermen and Sheriffs of the ſaid City.

*After debate of this caſe, a procedendo was granted, caſes cited for the defendant againſt the procedendo, 1 Leon. 103. Jerome againſt Neale and others. 2 Leon. 34, 35. Collet againſt the bailiffs of Shrewſbury.*

---

## Habeas Corpus for Taverner returnable into the Common Pleas.

Return—The like return for refuſing the office of a liveryman of the vintners company.

WE Simon Lewis, and Jonathan Raymond, knights, ſheriffs of the city of London, to the juſtices of the lord the king, at the day and place in the writ to this ſchedule annexed named, moſt humbly certify; that the city of London is, and from the whole time whereof the memory of man is not to the contrary; hath been an antient city, and that the citizens and freemen of the ſaid city from the whole time whereof the memory of man is not to the contrary, have been, and as yet are incorporated as well by the name of the mayor and commonalty, and citizens of the city of London, as by the name of the mayor and commonalty of the city of London, and that of the ſaid citizens and freemen ſo incorporated from the whole time aforeſaid, there have been ſeveral companies, guilds and fraternities within the ſaid city, whereof the company of the miſtery of vintners, in the city of London, who from the whole time aforeſaid, have been incorporated by the name of the maſter, wardens, and freemen and community of the miſtery of vintners of the city of London, is and from the whole time aforeſaid hath been one; and that of and in the ſaid company of vintners, as well as in all the other companies, guilds or fraternities within the ſaid city, there are, and from the whole time aforeſaid, have been certain men being citizens and freemen of the ſaid city, and freemen of the ſaid companies, guilds or fraternities reſpectively, called liverymen, who from time to time, for the whole time aforeſaid have been elected, and have been accuſtomed to be elected by the company, guild or fraternity whereof ſuch men are free, and each and every of them is free reſpectively into the livery of the ſaid company, guild or fraternity, whereof they reſpectively ſo as aforeſaid are freemen, which men, and every of them respectively so being elected, not having any reasonable cause or excuse to the contrary thereof, the office or place of a liveryman of that company, guild or fraternity respectively, in which every such man hath been elected to be of the livery thereof, for the whole time aforesaid, have been used and ought to take upon themselves, and to undergo and sustain that office and the burden of that office or place, which men so elected, and * sustaining that office, by reason of that office, or place greater burdens and expences and sums of money towards the support, and in and for the publick good, and better government of that company respectively, whereof every such man is of the livery thereof, than the other freemen of the said company respectively not being of the livery, for the whole time aforesaid, have paid and contributed, and have been used, and ought to pay and contribute; and we further certify, that within the said city there is had, and from the whole time aforesaid whereof the memory of man is not to the contrary, there was had a certain court of the lord the now king, and of his ancestors heretofore kings and queens of England of record, held weekly, on every Tuesday and every Thursday, before the mayor and aldermen of the said city for the time being, in the chamber of the Guildhall of of the said city, situate in the parish of St. Michael, Bassishaw, in the ward of Bassishaw, London, in which court the mayor and aldermen of the said city for the time being, for the whole time aforesaid, have managed, regulated and ordained, and have been used and accustomed to manage, regulate and ordain, all things the said several companies, guils and fraternities of the said city for the time being, touching, appertaining to, and in any manner concerning which have been brought before them, for the better rule and government thereof, to the support of the honour and dignity of the said city; and that the freemen being citizens and freemen of the city of London aforesaid, of every company, guild or fraternity of the city of London aforesaid, and each and every of them are, and for the whole time aforesaid have been, and have been accustomed to be, under the rule government, correction and punishment of the said mayor and aldermen of the said city for the time being, in the said court in the form aforesaid held, for all and singular the matters by any such freeman thereupon done, or omitted to be done, against or to the prejudice of the good rule and government of the said company, guild, or fraternity of the said city: And we further certify, that within the said city there is had, and also from the whole time aforesaid was had, a certain other custom within the

* P. 432.

said

ſaid city, from the whole time aforeſaid, hitherto uſed and approved, that if any complaint hath been made in writing, or by word of mouth, to the ſaid mayor and aldermen of the ſaid city for the time being, in the ſaid court ſo as aforeſaid, before them held according to the ſaid cuſtom, by the maſter and wardens of any company of the ſaid city within the ſaid city, or by the principal members of any company of the ſaid city within the ſaid city, in which there are not maſter or wardens, or any of them, ſhewing that any perſon being a citizen and freeman of the ſaid city, and a member of ſuch company, hath been elected by that company to the livery of the ſaid company whereof he is a member, and hath been requeſted to take upon himſelf the office or place of one of the livery of the ſaid company, and to undergo and ſuſtain the burden of that office or place, and that ſuch freeman and citizen of the ſaid city and member of ſuch company, without reaſonable cauſe or excuſe to the contrary thereof, hath refuſed to be of the livery of ſuch company, to take upon himſelf that office or place, and to undergo and ſuſtain the burden of that office or place, * and thereupon praying remedy, aid and juſtice * P. 433.
of the ſaid court, before the ſaid mayor and aldermen of the ſaid city for the time being, held as aforeſaid, according to the ſaid cuſtom, upon the premiſſes againſt ſuch perſon ſo refuſing, and thereupon ſuch perſon againſt whom ſuch complaint hath been made, being a citizen and freeman of the ſaid city, and a member of ſuch company, being before the mayor and aldermen of the ſaid city for the time being, in the ſaid court aſſembled, and before the ſaid mayor and aldermen of the ſaid city in the ſaid court hath acknowledged, or hath not denyed the premiſſes, but being admoniſhed by the ſaid court to conform himſelf in that behalf, and to take upon himſelf that office or place, and to undergo and ſuſtain the burden of that office or place, openly and wilfully, obſtinately and contemptuouſly without any cauſe or excuſe whatſoever to the contrary thereof, in the ſaid court ſhall have refuſed to be of the livery of that company whereof he ſo as aforeſaid is a member, and to take upon himſelf that office or place, then the ſaid mayor and aldermen of the ſaid city of London for the time being, in the ſaid court held as aforeſaid, have charged and committed ſuch perſon ſo refuſing to priſon under the cuſtody of the ſheriffs of London for the time being, there under cuſtody to remain and to be detained, until that the ſaid perſon ſo committed to priſon would conſent and declare that he would take upon himſelf the office and place aforeſaid, and would undergo and ſuſtain the burden of that office or place, or until ſuch perſon otherwiſe ſhould be delivered

livered and discharged out of prison, and out of the custody of the said sheriffs of the said city for the time being, by the due course of law: Which several customs above mentioned, and all the other customs and frank usages of the said city within the said city used, by the authority of the parliament of the lord Richard, late king of England, the second after the conquest, held at Westminster in the county of Middlesex, in the 7th year of his reign, to the mayor and commonalty and citizens of the said city were ratified and confirmed; and we further certify, that before the coming of the said writ of habeas corpus to us in this behalf directed, to wit, on the 18th day of June, in the 32d year of the reign of the said lord the now king, Jeremiah Taverner, in the writ to this schedule annexed named, who then and long before, and continually afterwards hitherto hath been, and as yet is a citizen and freeman of the said city, and a freeman and member of the said company of vintners, in the city of London aforesaid, by that company in the due manner, was elected into the livery of the said company, and thereof the said Jeremiah Taverner then had notice, and thereupon was requested to take upon himself the office or place of a liveryman of the said company, and to undergo and sustain the burden of that office or place according to the custom of the said city, from the whole time aforesaid hitherto used and approved in the same; but so to do he entirely refused, whereupon afterwards and before the coming of the said writ of habeas corpus to us in this behalf, to wit, on the 22d day of June, in the 32d year of the reign of the said lord the now king, a certain complaint was made by word of mouth, to Robert Clayton, knight, then and as yet mayor of the city of London aforesaid, and to the then aldermen of he said city, in the said court, by one John Billingsly, then master, and by Isaac Hodgkin, James Surrile, and Michael
* P. 434. Warring, then wardens of the * company of vintners in the city of London aforesaid, shewing that the said Jeremiah Taverner being a citizen and freeman of the said city, and being a member of the company of vintners aforesaid, in the city of London aforesaid, was elected by that company, into the livery of the said compananny, and as yet and long before, being a fit man as well to sustain that office as the burden of the said office, was requested to take upon himself the office or place of a liveryman of the said company, and to undergo and sustain the burden of that office or place, nevertheless the said Jeremiah Taverner, a citizen and freeman of the said city, and a member of the said company, without any reasonable cause or excuse to the contrary thereof, entirely has refused to be of the livery of the said company, and to take

take upon himſelf that office or place, and to undergo and ſuſtain the burden of that office or place, and thereupon the ſaid maſter and wardens by their complaint, prayed remedy, aid, relief and juſtice, of the ſaid court before the ſaid mayor and aldermen, held according to the cuſtom aforeſaid upon the premiſſes, againſt the ſaid Jeremiah Taverner, and thereupon the ſaid Jeremiah Taverner being before the ſaid mayor and aldermen of the ſaid city, aſſembled in the ſaid court, then and there held according to the cuſtom aforeſaid, and perſonally appearing before the ſaid mayor and aldermen of the ſaid city in the ſaid court, the premiſſes aforeſaid, to wit, that he being a citizen and freeman of the ſaid city, and being a member and freeman of the company aforeſaid laſt named, and alſo a fit man as well as to ſuſtain the ſaid office or place, as the burden of the ſaid office, was elected by the ſaid company into the livery of the ſaid company, and was requeſted to take upon himſelf the office or place, of one of the livery of the ſaid company, and to undergo and ſuſtain the burden of that office or place; and that he the ſaid Jeremiah Taverner being a citizen and freeman of the ſaid city, and a member of the ſaid company, and a fit man as aforeſaid had refuſed to take upon him that office or place, and to ſuſtain and undergo the burden of that office or place, before the mayor and aldermen of the ſaid city, in the open court aforeſaid, held before the mayor and aldermen aforeſaid, at the day and place laſt aforeſaid expreſsly acknowledged and confeſſed; whereupon the ſaid Jeremiah Taverner then and there in the ſaid court, by the ſaid mayor and aldermen of the ſaid city, oftentimes in the ſaid court there was admoniſhed to conform himſelf in that behalf, and to take upon himſelf that office or place, and to undergo and ſuſtain the burden of that office or place, nevertheleſs the ſaid Jeremiah Taverner not having, nor alledging any cauſe or excuſe whatſoever to the contrary thereof, after ſuch admonition to him in the form aforeſaid made, not having nor alledging any cauſe or excuſe, to be of the livery of the ſaid company laſt aforeſaid, or to take upon himſelf that office or place, and to undergo or ſuſtain the burden of that office or place in the ſaid court there, obſtinately, and wilfully and contemptuouſly, without any cauſe or excuſe whatſoever to the contrary thereof, expreſsly refuſed and denied; whereupon the ſaid mayor and aldermen of the city of London aforeſaid, then and there in the ſaid court, before the * coming of the ſaid writ of Habeas Corpus, him the ſaid Jeremiah Taverner ſo refuſing, according to the cuſtom aforeſaid did charge and commit to priſon, under the cuſtody of us the ſaid ſheriffs, there to remain and to be detained until the ſaid Jeremiah Taverner, would conſent and declare that he would take upon himſelf * P. 435.

himſelf that office or place, and that he would undergo and ſuſtain the burden of that office or place, or that the ſaid Jeremiah Taverner otherwiſe out of priſon, and out of the cuſtody of the ſheriffs of the ſaid city for the time being, by the due courſe of law ſhould be delivered and diſcharged; and we further certify, that the ſaid Jeremiah Taverner at any time hitherto hath not conſented, and declared that he was willing to take upon himſelf that office or place, or to undergo and ſuſtain the burden of that office or place, nor hath taken upon himſelf that office or place, and this is the cauſe of the caption and detention, of the ſaid Jeremiah Taverner in priſon, under the cuſtody of us the ſaid ſheriffs of the ſaid city, which, together with the body of the ſaid James Taverner, before the juſtices of the lord the king, of the bench, we have ready at the day and place in the writ to this ſchedule annexed mentioned, together with the ſaid writ, as by the ſaid writ we are commanded.

---

## Habeas Corpus *for* Cage.

Writ of Habeas Corpus to the keeper of Newgate, returnable before the lord chief juſtice of B. R.

JAMES the 2d &c. To the keeper of our goal of Newgate greeting: We command you, that the body of Thomas Cage in our priſon under your cuſtody committed and detained, as it is ſaid, together with the day and cauſe of his caption and detention, by whatſoever name the ſaid Thomas may be called in the ſame, you have before our beloved and faithful Edward Herbert knight, our chief juſtice, aſſigned to hold pleas before us, at his chamber, ſituate in Serjeant's-Inn, in Fleet-Street, London, immediately after the receipt of this writ, to ſubmit to all and ſingular the things, which our ſaid chief juſtice then and there ſhall ordain, concerning him in this behalf, and have there then this writ. Witneſs Edward Herbert knight, at Weſtminſter, the 12th day of February, in the 3d year of our reign.

By the court, RICHARD HOLLOWAY.

ASTRY.

* P. 436. * The execution of this writ appears in a certain ſchedule to this writ annexed.

The

## The Anſwer of William Richardſon Gent. Keeper of the Goal of Newgate, to the Chief Juſtice of the Lord the King, aſſigned to hold pleas before the King himſelf.

Return.—The like return for refuſing to be a livery-man of the merchant taylors company.

I WILLIAM RICHARDSON, keeper of the goal of the lord the king of Newgate, moſt humbly certify, that the city of London now is, and from the time whereof the memory of man is not to the contrary, hath been an antient city, and that the citizens and freemen of the ſaid city, from the whole time aforeſaid, whereof the memory of man is not to the contrary, until, to, and unto the term of the Holy Trinity, in the thirty-fifth year of the reign of our lord Charles II. the late king of England, have been incorporated as well by the name of the mayor, commonalty and citizens of the city of London, as by the name of the mayor and commonalty of the city of London; and that of the ſaid citizens from the whole time aforeſaid there have been, and as yet are ſeveral companies, guilds, and fraternities within the ſaid city, whereof the fraternity of merchant taylors, in the city of London, who from the whole time aforeſaid, being one ſeveral company, guild and fraternity within the ſaid city, have been incorporated by the name of the maſter and wardens of the merchant taylors the fraternity of St. John the Baptiſt, in the city of London, is and from the whole time aforeſaid was one; and that as well of and in the ſaid fraternity of merchant taylors, aforeſaid, as in all the other companies, guilds and fraternities within the ſaid city, there are and from the whole time aforeſaid have been certain men being citizens of the ſaid city, and freemen of the ſaid companies, guilds or fraternities reſpectively, called livery men, who from time to time from the whole time aforeſaid have been elected, and have been accuſtomed to be elected, by the company, guild or fraternity, whereof ſuch men are free, and each and every of them reſpectively is free, into the livery of the ſaid company, guild or fraternity whereof they reſpectively as aforeſaid were freemen, which men and each and every of them ſo reſpectively elected, (and not having any reaſonable cauſe or excuſe to the contrary thereof) the office or place of a livery man of the ſaid company, guild or fraternity reſpectively, in which every ſuch man hath been elected to be of the livery thereof, from the whole time aforeſaid, have been uſed, and ought to take upon themſelves that office, and the burden of that office or place, to ſuſtain; and greater burdens and expences and ſums of money towards the ſupport, and in and for the public good, and better government of the ſaid com-

London an antient city and a corporation by præſcription 'til Trinity term, twenty-fifth Charles II.

And time out of mind had ſeveral companies or guilds, whereof the merchant taylors is one.

In every one of which guilds there were certain men who were elected unto the office of livery men, and who upon their election, ought to undertake the office.

pany respectively, whereof every such man is of the livery thereof, than the other freemen of the said company respectively not being of the livery thereof, from the whole time aforesaid, have paid and contributed, and have been used, and ought to pay and contribute; and I further certify, that
* P. 437 within the said city there is had, and from the * whole time aforesaid whereof the memory of man is not to the contrary, was had, a certain court of the lord the now king, and of his ancestors, heretofore kings and queens of England, of record, held weekly on every Tuesday and every Thursday, before the mayor and aldermen of the said city for the time being, in the chamber of the Guildhall of the said city, situate in the parish of St. Michael Bassishaw, in the ward of Bassishaw London, in which court the mayor and aldermen of the said city for the time being, from the whole time aforesaid, have managed, regulated and ordained, and have been used and accustomed to manage, regulate and ordain, all things the said several companies, guilds, or fraternities of the said city for the time being, touching, appertaining to, or in any wise concerning, which hath been brought before them, for the better rule and government thereof, to the support of the honor and dignity of the said city; and that the freemen being citizens of the city of London aforesaid, of whatsoever company, guild, or fraternity of the said city, and each and every of them, from the whole time aforesaid have been, and have been accustomed to be, and as yet are under the rule, government, correction and punishment of the said mayor and aldermen of the said city for the time being, in the court aforesaid, in the form aforesaid held, for all and singular the matters by any such freeman of any company aforesaid, done or omitted to be done, against or to the prejudice of the good rule and government of the said company, guild or fraternity of the said city; and I further certify, that within the said city there is had, and from the whole time aforesaid was had, a certain other custom within the said city used and approved, that if any complaint hath been made in writing, or by word of mouth to the said mayor and aldermen of the said city for the time being, in the said court so as aforesaid held before them, according to the custom aforesaid, by the master and wardens of any fraternity of the said city, within the said city, or by the principal members of any fraternity of the said city within the said city, in which there are not master and wardens, or either of them, shewing that any person being a citizen of the said city, and a member of the said fraternity hath been elected by that fraternity into the livery of that fraternity whereof he is a member, and hath been requested to take upon himself the office or place of one of the livery of the said fraternity, and to sustain and undergo

undergo the burden of that office or place, and that ſuch citizen, freeman, and member of ſuch fraternity without any reaſonable cauſe or excuſe to the contrary thereof, hath refuſed to be of the livery of ſuch fraternity, to take upon himſelf that office or place, and to undergo and ſuſtain the burden of that office or place, and thereupon praying remedy, aid and juſtice of the ſaid court before the mayor and aldermen of the ſaid city for the time being, held as aforeſaid; according to the cuſtom aforeſaid, upon the premiſſes againſt ſuch perſons ſo refuſing, and thereupon ſuch perſon againſt whom ſuch complaint hath been made, being a citizen, freeman and member of ſuch fraternity, being before the mayor and aldermen of the ſaid city for the time aſſembled in the ſaid court, before the ſaid mayor and aldermen * in the ſaid court, ſhall have acknowledged or not denied the premiſſes, but being admoniſhed by the ſaid court to conform himſelf in that behalf, and to take upon himſelf that office or place, and to undergo and ſuſtain the burden of that office or place, openly and wilfully, obſtinately, and contemptuouſly without any cauſe or excuſe whatſoever to the contrary, ſhall have refuſed in the ſaid court to be of the livery of the ſaid company whereof he as aforeſaid is a member, or to undergo and ſuſtain the burden of that office or place, then the ſaid mayor and aldermen of the ſaid city of London aforeſaid for the time being, in the ſaid court as aforeſaid held according to the cuſtom for the whole time aforeſaid, uſed and approved, have charged and committed ſuch perſon ſo refuſing to priſon under the cuſtody of the ſheriffs of London for the time being, or of ſome other officers there, there to remain under cuſtody, and to be detained, until that the ſaid perſon who hath been ſo committed to priſon, would conſent and declare, that he would take upon himſelf the ſaid office or place, and would undergo and ſuſtain the burden of that office or place, or otherwiſe ſuch perſon ſhould be delivered and diſcharged by the due courſe of law, out of the priſon, and cuſtody of the ſaid ſheriffs or other officers of the ſaid city, which ſeveral cuſtoms aforementioned, and all the other cuſtoms and frank uſages of the ſaid city, within the ſaid city uſed, by the authority of the parliament of the lord Richard late king of England, the ſecond after conqueſt, held at Weſtminſter in the county of Middleſex, in the ſeventh year of his reign, to the then mayor and commonalty of the ſaid city were ratified and confirmed; and further, I moſt humbly certify, that in the term of St. Michael in the thirty-third year of the reign of our lord Charles II. &c. Robert Sawyer,

* P. 438.

Cuſtoms confirmed by parliament.

In the thirty-third year of Charles II. a quo warranto was brought againſt the mayor and citizens of London, judgment was thereupon given for the king, and their franchiſes and liberties were ſeized into the king's hands.



knight,

knight, attorney-general of the said late lord the king, who for the said late lord the king, did prosecute in that behalf, in his proper person, came into the court of the said late lord the king, before the said late lord the king himself, then at Westminster in the county of Middlesex, on the Monday next after fifteen days of St. Martin, in that same term, and for the said late lord the king, then exhibited in the court there, a certain information against the then mayor and commonalty and citizens of the city of London aforesaid, and in the said information gave the court there to understand and be informed, that the then mayor and commonalty and citizens of the city of London aforesaid, for the space of one month then last past and more had used, and until then did use and claim to have and use without any warrant or royal grant within the city of London aforesaid, and the liberties and precincts of the said city, divers liberties, privileges, and franchises in that information specified, without any commission or other authority from the said lord the late king in that behalf granted and obtained, all which liberties, privileges, and franchises, the said mayor and commonalty and citizens of the city of London aforesaid, for the whole time aforesaid, upon the said lord the late king had usurped, and until then did usurp; and thereupon afterwards, to wit, on the Monday next after the octave of St. Hilary, in the thirty-third year of the reign of the said lord the late king aforesaid, in the court of the said lord the late king before the king himself (the said court then being held at Westminster in the
* P. 439. county of * Middlesex) came the said mayor, and commonalty and citizens of the city of London, by Benedict Brown then their attorney, and having had oyer of the said information, the said mayor and commonalty and citizens of the city of London, prayed day to imparl thereto from the day of Easter in fifteen days then next ensuing, and it was granted to them, before the said late lord the king wheresoever, &c. And thereupon it was in such sort proceeded in the said court before the said late lord the king at Westminster aforesaid, that afterwards, to wit, in the said term of the holy Trinity, in the thirty-fifth year of the reign of the said late lord the king aforesaid, in the said court of the said late lord the king before the king himself then held at Westminster in the county of Middlesex, for this, because that it seemed to the said court then there, that the said mayor and commonalty and citizens of the city of London aforesaid, had forfeited to the said late lord the king their liberties, privileges and franchises aforesaid, it was considered by the said court there, that the liberties privileges and franchises of being in themselves one body corporate and politic, in deed in fact and in name, by the name of the mayor and commonalty and citizens of the city of London, and

and by the same name to plead, and to be impleaded, to answer and to be answered, by the said mayor and commonalty and citizens of the said city claimed, should be taken and seized into the hands of said late lord the king, whereof they are convicted as by the record and process thereof, in the court of the said lord the king, before the king himself now here, to wit, at Westminster aforesaid, more fully appears of record, which judgment as yet in its full force and effect remains not reversed or annulled, by virtue whereof the said lord the late king Charles, was seized of the liberties, and franchises aforesaid: And I further certify, that the most illustrious James the 2d, the now king of England, &c. afterwards, to wit, on the 17th day of January, in the 2d year of his reign, by his letters patent, bearing date on the day and year last mentioned, reciting his royal good pleasure to be, that the government and administration of the said city, and of the citizens of the said city, in all things should be continued, exercised, and used for the honour of the said city, and for the advantage of the citizens of the said city, and the other subjects of the said lord the now king, in the same manner in which at and before the time of the giving of the said judgment it was used; and that the good and laudable customs used and accustomed within the said city being in force before the giving of the said judgment, and at the time of the giving of the said judgment, as yet should be held, exercised, used and observed; by the said letters patent did assign, constitute and make his beloved John Peake, knight, then mayor, and William Turner, knight, John Moore, knight, &c. (and 23 others) then aldermen of the said city of London, to be aldermen of the said city, and to have, enjoy and execute all and the like authorities, powers and privileges, as the aldermen of the said city at or before the time of the giving the said judgment, of right had or could exercise, to have, enjoy, perform and execute, the same offices, authorities, powers and privileges, with all and singular the appendages and appurtenances, as well within their wards respectively, * as in any courts held or to be held before the mayor and aldermen of the said city, or elsewhere within the said city, and the liberties of the same, and in all other places, and to all intents and purposes, in as ample manner and form in all things, as they or any of them, or any other alderman or aldermen of the said city, before that time had had, enjoyed, performed and executed, or of right ought to have, enjoy, perform and execute: And the said lord James the 2d, by his said letters patent, further willed, constituted, established and declared, that the mayor, aldermen, recorder, sheriffs, chamberlain, and all the other officers

That James the 2d by letters patent granted to the citizens of London, that they should be governed in the same manner as before the said judgment, and enjoy all their customs, &c.

* P. 440

officers of the ſaid city, who then were, and afterwards ſhould be, and each and every of them, ſhould have, enjoy and exerciſe all courts as well of record as not of record, juriſdictions, powers and authorities reſpectively in their places as well within the city of London as without, which the mayor, aldermen, recorder, ſheriffs, chamberlain and the other officers of the ſaid city, or any of them, at the time of the giving of the ſaid judgment, or before or afterwards reſpectively had, or exerciſed, or lawfully could have and exerciſe, and alſo that the mayor and aldermen of the ſaid city for the time being, or any thirteen of them (of whom he willed that the mayor of the ſaid city or one of the two ſenior aldermen for the time being ſhould be one) could and might ordain, decree and provide for the good government of the ſaid city, and of the citizens of the ſaid city, and of his other ſubjects, or of the liberties of the ſame; and that they ſhould have the rule, government, and ordinance of all miſteries and companies within the ſaid city, and of all and ſingular the members of the ſame, and that they might and could appoint, and ordain, which of the ſaid companies ſhould have a livery, and alſo approve and allow, or refuſe at their pleaſure, any member of the ſaid ſeveral companies, elected, or to be elected into the ſaid livery before that they were or ſhould be admitted, and correct, chaſtize and puniſh the members of the ſaid companies for their diſobedience and contumacy, as they were then before uſed: And I further certify, that before the coming of the ſaid writ of habeas corpus to me in this behalf directed, to wit, on the 24th day of November, in the 2d year of the reign of the ſaid lord the now king, Thomas Cage, in the writ to this ſchedule annexed named, who then and long before, and continually afterwards hitherto hath been, and as yet is a citizen of the ſaid city, and a freeman and member of the fraternity of merchant taylors, in the city of London aforeſaid, by that fraternity was elected in the due manner, into the livery of the ſaid fraternity, and whereof the ſaid Thomas Cage had notice, and thereupon was requeſted to take upon himſelf the office or place of one of the livery of the ſaid fraternity, and to undergo and ſuſtain the burden of that office or place, according to the cuſtom of the ſaid city from the whole time aforeſaid, uſed and approved in the ſame, but ſo to do he entirely refuſed, whereupon afterwards and before the coming of the ſaid writ of habeas corpus to me in this behalf directed, to wit, on the 17th day * of February, in the 3d year of the reign of the ſaid lord the now king, a certain complaint was made, by word of mouth to the ſaid John Peake, then and as yet mayor, and to the then aldermen of the ſaid

That the defendant was a citizen of London, and a member of the company of merchant taylors, and was by the ſaid company elected a liveryman of the ſaid company but refuſed to accept the office. Complaint thereof made to the court of lord mayor and aldermen by the maſter and wardens of the company.

* P. 441

said city in the said court then held before the mayor and aldermen of the said city, by one William Dodson knight, then master, and by Hugh Nodin and John Page, then wardens of the fraternity of merchant taylors aforesaid, in the city of London aforesaid, shewing that the said Thomas Cage being a citizen of the said city, and a member of the fraternity of merchant taylors aforesaid, in the city of London aforesaid, was elected by that fraternity into the livery of that fraternity, and then and long before being a fit man, as well to undertake that office as the burden of that office, was requested to take upon himself the office or place of one of the livery of the said fraternity, and to undergo and sustain the burden of that office or place, neverthelefs that the said Thomas Cage, a citizen of the said city, and a member of the said fraternity, without any reasonable cause or excuse to the contrary thereof, had entirely refused to be of the livery of the said fraternity, and that office or place to take upon himself, and to undergo and sustain the burden of that office or place, and therefore the said master and wardens by that complaint prayed remedy, aid, and justice of the said court, before the said mayor and aldermen then held according to the said custom, upon the premisses against the said Thomas Cage: And thereupon the said Thomas Cage being before the said mayor and aldermen of the said city assembled, in the said court then and there according to the custom held before the said mayor and aldermen of the said city, and personally appearing before the said mayor and aldermen of the said city, in the said court, did not deny, but expressly acknowledged and confessed the premisses aforesaid, before the said mayor and aldermen of the said city, in the open court aforesaid, held before the said mayor and and aldermen, at the day and place last aforesaid, that he being a citizen of the said city, and a member and freeman of the said fraternity last mentioned, as well to the said office as to undergo the burden of that office, was elected by that fraternity into the livery of that fraternity, and was requested to take upon himself the office or place of one of the livery of the said fraternity, and to undego and sustain the burden of that office or place, and that the said mayor and aldermen aforesaid, approved of the said election of the said Thomas Cage made as aforesaid, neverthelefs that he the said Thomas Cage being a citizen of the said city, and a freeman and member of the said fraternity, and a fit man as aforesaid, had refused to take upon him that office or place, and to undergo and sustain the burden of that office or place, whereupon the said Thomas Cage then and there in the said court by the said mayor and aldermen of the said city in the said court there, oftentimes was admonished to conform himself in that behalf, and to take upon himself that office or place, and

The defendant appeared and confessed the election and refused to serve.

and to undergo and sustain the burden of that office or place nevertheless, the said Thomas Cage not having nor alledging any cause or excuse whatsoever to the contrary thereof, after such admonition to him in the form aforesaid made, to be of the livery of the said fraternity last aforesaid, or to
* P. 442. take upon himself that office or place, and * to undergo and sustain the burden of that office or place in the said court there, openly and wilfully, obstinately and contemptuously without any cause or excuse whatsoever to the contrary thereof denied and expressly refused; whereupon the said mayor and aldermen of the said city of London, then and there in the said court before the coming of the said writ of habeas corpus, him the said Thomas Cage so refusing, according to the custom aforesaid, in prison under my custody charged and committed, there to remain and to be detained until the said Thomas Cage consented and declared that he would take upon himself that office or place, and would undergo and sustain the burden of that office or place, or that the said Thomas Cage otherwise should be delivered and discharged out of prison by the due course of law; and I further certify, that the said Thomas Cage at any time hitherto, hath not consented, nor declared that he the said Thomas Cage was willing to take upon him that office or place, and to undergo and sustain the burden of that office or place, nor hath taken upon him that office or place. And this is the cause of the caption and detention of the said Thomas Cage in the said prison under my custody, which together with the body of the said Thomas Cage, before the said justice of the said lord the now king, assigned to hold pleas before the king himself, I have ready at the day and place in the writ to this schedule annexed named, together with the said writ, as I am by the said writ commanded.

---

## Excommunicato Capiendo.

## The King against Thwing.

### Easter, 18th Charles 2d.

Writ of habeas corpus.

THE lord the king hath sent to the warden of the Fleet, or to his deputy there, his writ close in these words: Charles the 2d, &c. to the warden of our prison of the Fleet, or to his deputy there, greeting: We command you, as before we have commanded you, that the body of Ferdinand Thwing, gent. in our prison under your custody detained

tained as it is said, together with the day and cause of his caption and detention, by whatsoever name the said Ferdinand may be called in the same, you have in our court before us at Westminster, immediately after the receipt of this writ, to submit to and receive those things which our court concerning him then and there shall ordain in this behalf, and this in no wise omit under the pain of 40l. and have there this writ; witness J. Kelyng, at Westminster, the 2d day of May, in the 18th year of our reign: And now, to wit, on the Thursday next after one month of Easter, in this same term, before the lord the king at * Westminster, comes the said F. T. brought before the lord the king at Westminster, by Bold Bonghey esquire, warden of the Fleet, by virtue of the said writ to him directed, with the cause, to wit, " *That the said F. T. in the said writ named, was committed to the prison aforesaid, on the Wednesday next after three weeks of the Holy Trinity, in the 16th year of the reign of the said lord the now king, by virtue of a writ of habeas corpus cum causâ, directed to the marshal of the marshalsea of the court of the lord the king, before the king himself at Westminster, and by the return thereof was committed to his custody by virtue of a certain writ of the lord the king of habeas corpus to the sheriff of Middlesex directed, and by the return of it was charged by virtue of a certain writ of the said lord the king, the tenor of which follows in these words, to wit. Charles the 2d &c.—To the sheriff of Middlesex greeting: The most reverend father in Christ, the archbishop of York, hath signified to us by his letters patent, that F. T. now or lately chaplain of Haddesly, in the county of York, gent. for his manifest contumacy in not appearing before Thomas Burwell, doctor of laws, official principal of the consistorial court of York, lawfully constituted, on a certain day, time and place now elapsed, personally to answer the allegations and articles of the libel on the behalf and by the party the lady Margaret Stapleton, otherwise Thwing his wife, against him given and exhibited, being lawfully cited, by the ordinary authority of the said archbishop is excommunicated, nor will by ecclesiastical censure be brought to justice, but because the holy church ought not to be without the royal power in their complaints, we command you, that you attach the said F. by the body, according to the custom of England, until that he satisfy the holy church as well of the contempt, as of the injury done by him to her, witness ourself at Westminster the 20th day of November, in the 14th year of our reign: And by virtue of another writ, the tenor of which follows in these words, Charles the 2d by the grace of God, &c.— To the sheriff of Middlesex greeting; The most reverend father in Christ, the archbishop of York, hath signified to us by his letters patent, that one F. T. late of H. in the county of Y. gent. for his manifest*

* P. 443.

Return. Commitment upon writs of excommuicato capiendo.

Tenor of the 1st writ.

And of the 2d writ.

*contumacy, in not paying nor satisfying to the lady M. S. otherwise T. his wife, the sum of 6l. 13s. 4d. of the lawful money of England, for her expences in a certain cause of alimony, by her the said Margaret against him the said F. in the consistorial court of the said archbishop of York, lawfully taxed, and also the sum of 40l. of the like money of England, for alimony to the said lady Margaret in the said cause adjudged, by the ordinary authority of the said archbishop is excommunicated, nor will be brought to justice by ecclesiastical censure, but because the holy church ought not to be without the royal power in their complaints, we command you, that you attach the said F. by his body, according to the custom of England, until he shall satisfy the holy church as well for the contempt, as for the injury done by him to her: Witness ourself at Westminster, the 6th day of May, in the 16th year of our reign*; Which T. F. is committed to the marshal, &c. and having had oyer of the return of the said writ of habeas corpus, and of the writs of excommunicato capiendo in the return aforesaid mentioned, saith that he doth not apprehend that the said lord the now king will or ought any further to impeach or trouble him the said F. by occasion of the said writs, because he saith that by a certain act of the parliament of the lady Elizabeth, the late queen of England, held at * Westminster, in the county of Middlesex, on the 12th day of January, in the 5th year of her reign, among other things, it is enacted, and provided by the authority of the said parliament, that from and after the first day of May next ensuing, every writ of excommunicato capiendo, which should be granted and should issue out of the high court of chancery against any person or persons within the kingdom of England, should be made in the time of term, and should be returnable before the lady the queen, her heirs and successors, in the court commonly called the king's bench, in the term next ensuing the test of the said writ; and that the said writ should be made to contain twenty days at the least between the test and return thereof; and after the said writ should be so made and sealed, that then the said writ forthwith should be brought into the said court of the king's bench, and there should be opened in the presence of the justices, and of record, should be delivered to the sheriff or other officer or officers to whom the execution thereof appertained, or to his or their deputy or deputies, as by the said statute, among other things, more fully appears; and the said F. T. further saith, that the several writs aforesaid, were not made returnable before the lord the king in the court of the lord the king, before the king himself, commonly called the king's bench, in the term next after the test of the same, and that after the said writs were made and sealed,

* P. 444

Defendant pleads that the writs were not made returnable into the king's bench, nor there recorded pursuant to the stat. of the 5th Elizabeth.

ſealed they were not brought into the ſaid court, of the lord the king called the King's Bench, and there in the preſence of the juſtices were not opened, nor thereupon were delivered of record to the ſheriff or other officer or officers, to whom the execution thereof appertained, or to his or their deputy or deputys, according to the form of the ſaid ſtatute, and this he is ready to verify, wherefore he prays judgment of the ſaid writs, and that he thereof may be diſmiſſed and diſcharged by the court, &c. Whereupon all and ſingular the premiſſes being ſeen, and by the court here underſtood for this, becauſe that the rolls of the ſaid court being examined, it doth not appear that the ſaid writs were brought into the court of the lord the king, called the King's Bench, nor were opened in the preſence of the juſtices, nor were delivered of record to the ſheriff or other officer or officers, to whom the execution thereof appertained, or to his or their deputy or deputys, according to the form of the ſaid ſtatute, it is conſidered that the ſaid F. T. be diſcharged of the ſaid writs, and that he go thereof without day.

*In this caſe the court would not diſcharge the defendant upon motion, but put him upon pleading the matter, it is reported* 1 *Siderfin* 285. 2 *Keble* 31. *Vide Croke. Cha.* 583. *John Parker*'s *caſe.*

---

## * The King *againſt* Cloberry. * P. 445.

## Michaelmas, 16th Charles.

*Plea to a writ of excommunicato capiendo, that the defendant was not excommunicated for any of the cauſes mentioned in the Stat. 5 Eliz.*

AND now &c.—Comes the ſaid J Cloberry, eſq; under the cuſtody of the marſhall of the lord king, before the king himſelf, by virtue of the writ of the lord the king, of habeas corpus ad ſubjiciendum, &c. in his proper perſon, who is committed to the ſaid marſhall, &c. and forthwith prays oyer of the writ of excommunicato capiendo to the marſhall directed, enrolled among the pleas before the lord the king, of the term of the Holy Trinity, in the fifteenth year of the reign of the lord the now king of England, and he hath it under this form, Charles, &c. which being read and heard, the ſaid J. C. ſaith, that he doth not apprehend the ſaid lord the now king, will or ought any further impeach or trouble him, by reaſon of the ſaid writ, becauſe proteſting that the ſaid writ is not ſufficient in law any longer, to keep or detain in priſon the ſaid J. C. by reaſon of the



ſaid

ſaid writ, for plea the ſaid J. ſaith, that in the ſtatute made in the parliament of the lady Elizabeth, late queen of England, held at Weſtminſter, in the county of Middleſex, the twelfth day of January, in the fifth year of her reign, by her the late queen, and the lords ſpiritual and temporal, and the commons in the ſaid parliament aſſembled, and by the authority of the ſame among other things it is enacted and eſtabliſhed, that from and after the firſt day of May then next following, every writ of excommunicato capiendo, which ſhould be granted and awarded out of the high court of Chancery, againſt any perſon or perſons within this kingdom of England, ſhould be made within the time of term, returnable before the lady the queen, her heirs and ſucceſſors, in the court commonly called the King's Bench, in the term next after the teſt of the ſaid writ, and that the ſaid writ ſhould be made to contain twenty days at leaſt between the teſt, and the return thereof, and that if the offender againſt whom any ſuch writ of excommunicato capiendo ſhould be awarded, ſhould not have ſufficient and lawful addition, according to the form of the ſtatute made in the firſt year of king Henry the 5d in caſes of certain ſuits whereupon proceſs of exigent are to be awarded, or if in the ſignificavit whereupon the writ of excommunicato capiendo iſſues out of the Chancery, it be not contained that the ſaid excommunication doth proceed upon ſome cauſe or contempt of ſome original matter of hereſy, or refuſing to have his or their child baptized, or to receive the holy communion as then commonly uſed in the ſaid church of England, or of error in matters of religion, or doctrine then received and allowed in the ſaid church of England, incontinency, uſury, ſimony, perjury in the eccleſiaſtical court or idolatry, that then the writ of excommunicato capiendo aforeſaid, and all and every pains and forfeitures limited againſt ſuch perſons excommunicated by the ſaid ſtatute, by colour of ſuch writ of excommunicato capiendo wanting ſufficient addition, or of ſuch writ of ſignificavit wanting in
* P. 446. all cauſes aforementioned, ſhould be entirely void in law *, and ſhould be allowed to the party aggrieved by way of plea, any thing in the ſaid ſtatute to the contrary thereof in any wiſe notwithſtanding, as by the ſaid ſtatute among other things more fully appears, and the ſaid J. further ſaith, that in the ſaid ſignificavit certified into the ſaid court of Chancery, and in the ſaid writ of excommunicato capiendo, it was not proceeded upon any cauſe or contempt or matter, of the matters aforſaid, and this, &c.

Quo

# QUO WARRANTO.

## The King *against* Lord Fitzwater.

## Michaelmas 26th Charles the 2d Roll. 1.

BE it remembered, &c. that whereas the river called Wallfleet, in the ſeveral vills and pariſhes of Southminſter, Burnham, C. A. L. N. S. F. T. P. E. H. A. and P. in the county of Eſſex, between the limits following, to wit, from a certain place called Rayland, unto a place called Clayclods, is and from the whole time whereof the memory of man is not to the contrary, hath been an arm of the ſea, in which the ſalt water of the ſea flows and ebbs, and the great veſſels of this kingdom of England can navigate between the limits aforeſaid, and in which every ſubject of the lord the king of this kingdom of England, there coming and willing to fiſh, with their nets of whatſoever kind, and with their drag-nets for oyſters and other fiſh of whatſoever kind, of common right ought freely to fiſh (except in certain weirs, and oyſter lanes) nevertheleſs Benjamin lord Fitzwater, for the ſpace of half of one year now laſt paſt, and more without any warrant or lawful grant hath uſed, and as yet uſes and claims to have and uſe in the ſaid river within the ſaid limits, the liberties, privileges, and franchiſes, following, to wit, to have in the ſaid water, in the arm of the ſea aforeſaid, and in the ſeveral vills and pariſhes aforeſaid, the ſole and ſeveral fiſhery for oyſters and for all other fiſh of whatſoever kind, ſo that no perſon may enter to fiſh or to take any thing in the ſaid river, within the limits aforeſaid, without the licence of the ſaid lord F. all and ſingular which liberties, privileges and franchiſes aforeſaid, the ſaid lord F. for the whole time aforeſaid, upon the ſaid lord the now king hath uſurped, and as yet uſurps, in contempt of the ſaid lord the king, and to the great damage and prejudice of his royal prerogative, and in contempt of the ſaid lord the now king his crown and dignity, whereupon the ſaid attorney-general * of the ſaid lord the king, for the ſaid lord the king prays the conſideration of the court in the premiſſes, and the due proceſs of law to be awarded againſt him the ſaid lord F. in this behalf, to make him to anſwer to the ſaid lord the king, by what warrant he claims to have the liberties, privileges, and franchiſes aforeſaid, &c. Whereupon the ſheriff is commanded, that he do not omit, &c. but that he cauſe him to come to anſwer, &c. and now to wit, on the Friday next, after three weeks of St. Michael in the ſame term, to which day the ſaid B. lord F. had leave to imparl to the ſaid bill, and

Quo warranto againſt defendant for claiming the liberty and franchiſes, of the ſole fiſhery for oyſters and other fiſh in an arm of the ſea

* P. 447.

Venire awarded.

Imparlance.

Plea—Defendant claims the fishery by præscription as appurtenant to his manor.

and then to anſwer, &c. before the lord king at Weſtminſter, comes as well the ſaid F. N. knight, who proſecutes as the ſaid lord F. by Philip Ward, his attorney, and having had oyer of the information aforeſaid, ſaith that he doth not apprehend that the ſaid lord the now king, will or ought any further impeach or trouble him by occaſion of the premiſſes, becauſe, proteſting that the ſaid information is not ſufficient in law, to which he hath no neceſſity, nor is he bound by the law of the land to anſwer, alſo proteſting that the river called Walfleet, in the ſaid information mentioned, between the limits in the ſaid information mentioned is not, nor from the time whereof the memory of man is not to the contrary, hath been an arm of the ſea, in which the ſalt water of the ſea ebbs and flows, and in which the great ſhips of this kingdom of England can navigate, nevertheleſs for plea as to the having and enjoying within the limits, and within the pariſhes and vills aforeſaid, in the information aforeſaid above mentioned, the liberties, privileges, and franchiſes, in the information aforeſaid ſpecified, to wit, the ſole and ſeveral fiſhery for oyſters, and for all other fiſh of whatſoever kind, ſo that no perſon may enter to fiſh, or to take any thing within the limits aforeſaid, in the river aforeſaid, without his licence in the manner and form as in the ſaid information is mentioned, ſaith, that long before the ſaid time in which the ſaid uſurpation of the ſaid liberties, privileges, and franchiſes above recited, is ſuppoſed to be committed by him the ſaid B. lord F. upon him the ſaid lord the king, the ſaid Benjamin lord F. was and as yet is ſeized in his demeſne, as of fee of and in the manor of Burnham, with the appurtenances in the county of E. aforeſaid, and that the ſaid B. lord F. and all thoſe whoſe eſtate the ſaid B. lord F. now hath, of and in the ſaid manor with the appurtenances, have had and from the time whereof the memory of man is not to the contrary, have been accuſtomed to have the liberties, privileges, and franchiſes in the ſaid information mentioned, to wit, the ſole and ſeveral fiſhery for oyſters, and all other fiſh of what kind ſoever, ſo that no perſon may enter to fiſh, or to take any thing in the ſaid rivers within the limits aforeſaid, without the licence of the ſaid B. lord F. as appendant and appurtenant to his manor of B. aforeſaid; and by that warrant the ſaid B. lord F. hath had and uſed, all and ſingular the liberties, privileges, and franchiſes aforeſaid, for the whole time aforeſaid, in the information aforeſaid ſpecified, as it was lawful for him, without this that the ſaid B. lord F. hath uſurped or as yet uſurps, in the manner and form as by the ſaid information above againſt him is ſuppoſed, all and ſingular which ſaid matters the ſaid B. lord F. is ready to verify as the court, &c. Wherefore he prays judgment, and that all and • ſingular the liberties,

• P. 448.

ties, privileges, and franchises above as aforesaid by him claimed, henceforth may be allowed and adjudged to him the said B. lord F. in the manner and form above specified, and that he of the premisses may be discharged by the court here, &c. And the said F. N. knight, attorney-general of the said lord the now king, who for the said lord the now king in this behalf prosecutes, having heard the plea aforesaid, of the said B. lord F. by him above pleaded as to the having and enjoying within the limits, and within the parishes and vills aforesaid, in the information aforesaid above specified, the liberties, privileges, and franchises, in the said information above specified, to wit, the sole and several fishery for oysters, and for all other fish of whatsoever kind, so that no person may enter to fish, or to take any thing within the limits aforesaid in the said river, without the licence of the said B. lord F. saith, that the said B. Lord F. for the said time in the information aforesaid specified, the said liberties, privileges, and franchises, upon the said lord the now king hath usurped, and as yet doth usurp, in the manner and form as by the said information above against him is supposed, without this that said B. lord F. and all those whose estate the said B. lord F. now hath in the said manor of B. with the appurtenances in the county of E. have had, and from the time whereof the memory of man is not to the contrary, have been accustomed to have the liberties, privileges, and franchises, in the said information mentioned, to wit, the sole and several fishery for oysters, and all other fish of whatsoever kind, so that no person may enter to fish, or to take any thing in the said river within the said limits, without the licence of the said B. lord F. as appendant and appurtenant to the manor of B. aforesaid, in the manner and form as the said B. lord F. above by pleading hath alledged, and this the said attorney-general of the said lord the now king who prosecutes, &c. for the said lord the king is ready to verify as the court, &c. wherefore he prays judgment, and that the said B. lord F. from the said liberties, privileges, and franchises aforesaid may be excluded, &c.

Replication. The attorney-general traverses the prescription.

And the said B. lord F. by P. W. his attorney aforesaid, as before saith, that he the said B. lord F. and all those whose estate the said B. lord F. now hath, in the manor of B. aforesaid, with the appurtenances in the county of E. aforesaid have had, and from the time whereof the memory of man is not to the contrary, have been accustomed to have the liberties, privileges, and franchises, in the information aforesaid mentioned, to wit, the sole and several fishery for oysters, and all other fish of whatsoever kind, so that no person may enter to fish, or to take any thing in the said river within the limits aforesaid, without the licence of the said B. lord F. as appendant

Rejoinder. Defendant takes issue upon the traverse.

appendant and appurtenant to the manor of B. aforeſaid, in the manner and form as the ſaid B. lord F. above by pleading hath alledged, and of this he puts himſelf upon the country; and the ſaid F. N. knight, attorney-general of the ſaid lord the now king, who for the ſaid lord the king in this behalf proſecutes doth the like, &c.

Iſſue.

*Reported 3 Keble 459, 465, 485, 519, and 2 Levinz 139. There was a verdict for the king, but the trial was ſet aſide upon affidavits, that the jury caſt lots.*
*This pleading may be found 2d Inſtructor Clericalis, 469.*

---

* P. 449.

## * The King *againſt* Bradley and others.

Quo warranto againſt ſeveral bakers, for ſelling and expoſing to ſale bread out of any market.

CHESTER. Be it remembered, that Robert Sawyer, knight, attorney-general of the lord the now king, who for the ſaid lord the king in this behalf proſecutes, in his proper perſon comes here into the court of the ſaid lord the king, before the king himſelf at Weſtminſter, on the Monday next after three weeks of St. Michael, in this ſame term, and for the ſaid lord the king, gives the court here to underſtand and to be informed, that George Bradley, of Farndon in the county of Cheſter, yeoman, Nathaniel Club of F. in the county of C. yeoman, and Thomas Birch of Kelſhall, in the ſaid county of C. yeoman, for the ſpace of one year now laſt paſt and more, have uſed and as yet uſe without any warrant or lawful authority, or grant, in a certain place called Gloverſtone, within the ſaid city of Cheſter, the liberties, privileges, and franchiſes following, to wit, to ſell and to expoſe to public ſale bread to whatſoever perſon or perſons are willing to buy bread in the ſaid place called Gloverſtone, and elſewhere within the city of C. aforeſaid, out of any ſhop and out of any market, as if in open market there, on the Wedneſday, and Saturday, weekly, and in every week throughout the year; and then and there out of any ſhop, and out of any market, for the whole time aforeſaid, on the ſaid days in every week, publicly have ſold bread as if in open market there; all which liberties, and privileges they the ſaid G. B. N. C. and T. B. for the whole time aforeſaid, upon the ſaid lord the now king have uſurped, and as yet uſurp in contempt of the ſaid lord the now king, and to the great damage and injury of his royal prerogative, whereupon the ſaid attorney-general of the ſaid lord the now king, for the ſaid lord the now king, prays the conſideration of the court here in the

the premisses, and the due process of law to be awarded against them the said G. B. N. G. and T. B. in this behalf, to make them to answer to the said lord the now king in this behalf, by what warrant they claim to have, use and enjoy the liberties, privileges and franchises aforesaid. Whereupon the chamberlain of the county palatine of Chester is commanded, that by the writ of the lord the king, under the seal of the county palatine aforesaid, duly to be made, and to the sheriff of the said county to be directed, that he command the said sheriff that he do not omit, &c. but that he cause them to come to answer, &c. And now, to wit, on the Monday next after the octave of St. Hilary in this same term, before the lord the king at Westminster, come the said G. B. N. C. and T. B. by Lionel Fanshaw their attorney, and having heard the said information severally say, that the said lord the now king, ought not any further to impeach or trouble them, the said G. N. and T. because of the premisses in the information aforesaid specified, because protesting that the said information is prosecuted against them the said G. N. and T. to vex and to impoverish them, and to exclude and terrify them from the use and exercise of the art of a public baker, and from the selling of bread by them * baked in their bake-houses, for plea the said G. N. and T. say that they are, and that each and every of them is a public baker, living in the country out of the city aforesaid, and in their bake-houses bake bread, and at the time in the information aforesaid mentioned, had sold that bread to the subjects of the lord Charles the 2d the now king of England, &c. willing to buy it, out of any shop at G. aforesaid, and in other places, as well without the said city as within, as it was lawful for them to do, and this they the said G. B. N. C. and T. B. are ready to verify as the court, &c. Wherefore they pray judgment, and that they of the premisses by the court here may be dismissed, &c.

Mandate to the chamberlain of Chester to issue a venire against the parties, directed to the sheriff.

* P. 450.

The defendants justify for, that they are common bakers and live in the country, and bake bread in their bake-houses and sell it out of any market to the king's subjects.

The attorney-general demurs.——And the defendants join in demurrer.

*Quo warranto only lies where men claim franchises not to question a mans trade or for selling his goods. Stat. quo warranto, 2d Inst. 495.*

Judgment given for the defendants.

 Mandamus,

# Mandamus, and returns thereto.

## Mandamus for Mannaton.

### Hilary 31 and 32 Charles II.

For admitting one into the office of mayor of Trevenna.

CHARLES the second by the grace of God, of England, Scotland, France and Ireland, king, defender of the faith, &c. To Charles Luxen, mayor of the borough of Trevenna Bofeny, in the county of Cornwall greeting; Whereas Ambrofe Mannaton, efq; into the place and office of mayor of the faid borough was duly elected according to the cuftom of the faid town, hitherto ufed, into which place or office of mayor of the faid borough the faid Ambrofe according to the cuftom of the faid town, ought to be admitted, neverthelefs you Charles Luxen, mayor of the faid borough, well knowing the premiffes, the faid Ambrofe Mannaton into the place and office of mayor of the faid borough have not as yet admitted, nor the oath to the faid Ambrofe Mannaton in that cafe always ufed to be adminiftered, have not adminiftered, but the faid Ambrofe to admit and fwear altogether have refufed, to the great damage and grievance of the faid Ambrofe, and to the manifeft injury of his eftate, as we have underftood by his complaint, we therefore willing that due and fpeedy juftice be done to the faid Ambrofe in this behalf, as is juft, command you firmly enjoining that immediately after the receipt of this writ, you admit without delay the faid Ambrofe into the place and office of mayor of the faid borough, into * which as aforefaid he was duly elected, with all liberties, privileges, pre-eminences and commodities to that place and office belonging and appertaining, and that you adminifter, or caufe to be adminiftered the oath to the faid Ambrofe according to cuftom in that cafe hitherto ufed, or fignify to us caufe to the contrary, leaft through your default complaint be again made unto us, and how you fhall execute this our command, certify to us on the octave of St. Hilary wherefoever we fhall then be in England, then returning to us this our writ; witnefs W. Scroggs, at Weftminfter, the twenty-eighth day of November in the thirty-firft year of our reign.

* P. 451.

By the court, ASTRY.

Return—That another person is duly elected and fworn.

The execution of this writ appears in a certain fchedule to this writ annexed, Charles Luxen. The borough of Trevenna Bofney, in the county of Cornwall, to wit, I Charles Luxen gent. to the moft ferene lord the king, in the court of the

the ſaid lord the king, before the king himſelf, moſt humbly certify, that before the coming of this writ to me the ſaid Charles Luxen directed, and alſo before the iſſuing of the ſaid writ, to wit, on the twenty-fifth day of October in the thirty-firſt year of the reign of our lord Charles II. by the grace of God of England, &c. king, &c. I the ſaid Charles Luxen from the place and office of the mayor of the borough of Trevenna Boſney, in the county of Cornwall aforeſaid, was amoved, and one William Amy of the ſaid borough gent. on the ſaid twenty-fifth day of October in the year aforeſaid, into the place and office of mayor of the borough of Trevenna Boſney, in the county aforeſaid was elected, admitted and ſworn, and thenceforth hitherto was and as yet is mayor of the ſaid borough, and by reaſon of his office from the time of his conſtitution and admiſſion aforeſaid into the ſaid office hitherto hath had, and now has in his cuſtody the common ſeal of the borough of Trevenna Boſney, by reaſon whereof I the ſaid Charles Luxen could not ſwear or reſtore the ſaid Ambroſe according to the command of the ſaid writ.

*The court was divided whether this return was inſufficient or not. Reported Raymond, 365.*

---

## * Mandamus for Duboys.

CHARLES the 2d &c. To the mayor and aldermen of the city of London greeting: Whereas John Duboys, eſq; freeman of the city of London, into the place and office of one of the ſheriffs of the ſaid city, and of the county of Middleſex, according to the liberties and privileges of the ſaid city in the due manner was elected, and oftentimes preſented himſelf to take the oath of ſheriff of the ſaid city, and of the county of Middleſex aforeſaid, into which place and office of one of the ſheriffs of the ſaid city of London, and of the county of Middleſex aforeſaid, the ſaid John Duboys according to the liberties and privileges of the ſaid city ought to be admitted and ſworn, nevertheleſs you the mayor and aldermen of the ſaid city, by whom of right ſuch oath of ſheriff of the city aforeſaid, and of the county of Middleſex aforeſaid, ought to be adminiſtered, well knowing the premiſſes, the ſaid John Duboys into the place and office of one of the ſheriffs of the ſaid city and of the ſaid county of Middleſex, have not as yet admitted, or the oath to the ſaid John Duboys in that caſe uſed to be adminiſtered have not adminiſtered, but the ſaid John Duboys to admit and ſwear altogether have refuſed, in contempt of us, and to the great damage and grievance

* P. 452.

To admit him to be ſworn ſheriff of London and Middleſex.

Pluries mandamus sub pena.

grievance of the said John, and to the manifest injury of his estate, as from his complaint we have understood, therefore we willing that due and speedy justice be done to the said John Duboys in this behalf as is just, we command you as we have oftentimes commanded you, firmly enjoining, that immediately after the receipt of this writ, you admit without delay the said John into the said place and office of one of the sheriffs of the said city, and of the said county of Middlesex, into which as aforesaid, he was duly elected, with all the liberties, privileges, pre-eminences, and commodities, to that place and office appertaining and belonging, and that you administer or cause to be administered the oath to the said John according to custom in that case hitherto used, or signify to us cause to the contrary, least through your default, complaint may be made agaiu to us, and how you shall execute this our command, make to appear to us at Westminster, on the Tuesday next after the octave of St. Hilary, under the pain of 80l. then returning to us this our writ; witness F. Pemberton at Westminster on the——day of November in the thirty-fourth year of our reign.

By the court, ASTRY.

Return—That he was not elected.

We the mayor and aldermen of the city of London, to the most illustrious lord the king within written, most humbly certify that J. D. within named was never elected into the place and office of one of the sheriffs of the said city, and of the county of Middlesex according to the liberties and privileges of the said city, therefore we cannot admit and swear the said J. D. into the place and office of one of the sheriffs of the said city, and of the said county of Middlesex.

The Answer of the Mayor and Aldermen of the City of London.

---

* P. 453.

## * Mandamus for Tourney.

To the juratts of Rye to administer to T. T. the oaths of the office of mayor, and to admit him to the office of mayor of Rye.

CHARLES the 2d &c. To Thomas Crouch, Thomas Burdett, Lewis Gillart, Benjamin Martin, Joseph Radford, and Michael Cadman gent. juratts of the antient town of Rye, in the county of Suffolk greeting: Whereas Thomas Tourney of the town aforesaid, gent. was duly elected and appointed, according to the custom of the said town, to the place and office of mayor of the said town, and although the said T. T. oftentimes hath presented himself to take his cor-

poral

poral oaths for his good behaviour in the ſaid office and place of mayor aforeſaid, nevertheleſs, you the ſaid jurats aforeſaid, to whom of right it belongs to adminiſter ſuch oaths to the mayor of the ſaid town, have denied, or at leaſt unduly have deferred to receive ſuch oath from the ſaid Thomas Tourney, to the great damage and grievance of the ſaid T. T. and to the manifeſt injury of his eſtate, as by his complaint we have underſtood, whereupon the ſaid Thomas Tourney hath beſought us to provide for him apt remedy in this behalf; we therefore willing that due and ſpeedy juſtice be done to the ſaid T. T. in this behalf, as is right; command you that the oaths which the mayor of the ſaid town hitherto hath been uſed to take, and which the ſaid T. T. ought to take before you, you adminiſter to the ſaid Thomas, and without delay you receive from the ſaid Thomas, and that you admit the ſaid Thomas Tourney, into the ſaid place and office of of mayor of the ſaid town, or ſignify cauſe to us to the contrary, leaſt through your default, complaint may be made again to us, and how you ſhall execute this our commanded, make to appear to us at Weſtminſter, on the Saturday next after the morrow of All Souls, then returning to us this our writ. Witneſs, F. Pemberton, at Weſtminſter, the 28th day of October, in the 33d year of our reign.

Return That it did not belong to the jurats to adminiſter the oaths.

To the moſt ſerene lord the now king, at the day and place within ſpecified, we moſt humbly certify, that it doth not appertain, nor ever did appertain to us the within named Thomas Crouch, Thomas Burdett, Lewis Gillart, Benjamin Martyn, Joſeph Radford, and Michael Cadman, to adminiſter any oaths to the mayor of the within writen town, nor have we, nor ever had we any power or authority to adminiſter or receive any ſuch oaths as by the ſaid writ is within ſuppoſed.

The anſwer of T. G. T. B. L. G. B. M. J. R. and M. C.

The ſecond mandamus which differs only in the direction.

CHARLES the 2d &c.—To the mayor, and jurats of the antient town of Rye, in the county of Suſſex, greeting: Whereas T. T. &c. "*word for word as in the preceding, returnable Tueſday after the morrow of the Purification, teſted the 3d. February, the 34th Charles 2d.*"

* P. 454. Return That they were ready to ſwear Tourney, but that the books containing the oath and the common ſeal of the town were in the cuſtody of T. C. who refuſed to deliver them, and ſo they could not further execute the ſaid writ.

* To the moſt ſerene lord the king, at the day and place within contained, we moſt humbly certify, that according to the command of the within written writ, we will ſum-

mon

mon before us the within written T. T. and are ready and willing to adminifter to the faid T. and to receive from the faid T. the oaths within mentioned, and to admit the faid T. T. to the place and office of mayor of the town of Rye aforefaid, as the faid writ in itfelf commands and requires; but the books in which the faid oaths are written and contained, and the common feal of the faid town, are in the cuftody of one Thomas Crouch, gent. and we have fent to him, for the books and feal aforefaid, that we might adminifter the faid oaths to the faid T. T. and might make return thereof under the faid feal, but the faid Thomas Crouch hath refufed to deliver to us the books and feal aforefaid, or to admit the faid T. T. to the faid office, whereby we cannot any further execute the faid writ; Thomas Burdett, Benjamin Martyn, Michael Cadman by his mark +.

A peremptory mandamus iffued thereupon, and was like the latter, fave only the words "*or fignify to us caufe to the contrary, left through your default, complaint may be made again to us*" were left out, it was returnable Thurfday next after the 15th days of Eafter, and tefted the 11th day of February.

---

## Mandamus for Veale.

To admit and fwear him into the office of mayor of Saltafh.

CHARLES the 2d &c.—To William Stephens, gent. mayor of the borough of Saltafh, in our county of Cornwall, greeting: Whereas Mathew Veale into the place and office of mayor of the faid borough was duly elected, into which place and office of mayor of the faid borough, the faid Mathew Veale according to the liberties and privileges of the faid borough, ought to be admitted and fworn, neverthelefs, you the faid William Stephens, mayor of the faid borough, on whom lies the burden and authority to adminifter the oath for the due execution of the faid office, well knowing the premiffes, have not as yet admitted the faid Mathew Veale to the office and place of mayor of the faid borough, nor according to the duty of your office, have adminiftered the oath to the faid Mathew Veale in this behalf, ufed to be adminiftered, but unduly have refufed to admit and fwear the faid Mathew Veale, to to great damage and grievance of the faid Mathew Veale, and to the manifeft fest injury of his estate, as we have understood from his complaint; we therefore willing that due and speedy justice be done the said Mathew in this behalf as is right, command you, firmly enjoining that immediately after the receipt of this writ, you admit without delay, the said Mathew, into the place and office of mayor of the said borough, into which as aforesaid, he was duly elected, with all liberties, privileges, preheminences and commodities to that office or place belonging and appertaining; and that you administer or cause to be administered to the said Mathew, the oath in this behalf hitherto used, or signify to us * the cause to the contrary, least through your default, complaint again be made unto us, and how you shall execute this our command, make to appear to us at Westminster on the Saturday next after one month of St. Michael, then returning to us this our writ; witness W. Scroggs, at Westminster, the 23d day of October, in the 32d year of our reign.

* P. 455.

By Rule of Court.

The execution of this writ appears in a certain schedule to this writ annexed, William Stephens.

Return that another was elected, admitted and sworn into the office.

The borough of Saltash in the county of Cornwall, to wit, I William Stephens, gent. to the most serene lord the king, in the court of the lord the king, before the king himself, most humbly certify, that before the coming of this writ to me William Stephens directed, and also before the issuing of the said writ, to wit, on the 29th day of September, in the 32d year of the reign of our lord Charles the 2d, by the grace of God, of England, &c. king, &c. I the said William Stephens, from the place and office of mayor of the borough of Saltash, in the county of Cornwall aforesaid, was amoved, and that one Andrew Willoughby, gent. being one of the aldermen and free burgesses of the said borough, on the said 29th day of September, in the year aforesaid, into the place and office of mayor of the borough of Saltash in the county aforesaid was elected, constituted admitted and sworn, and thenceforth, hitherto, was and as yet is mayor of the said borough, and by reason of his office from the time of his constitution and admission aforesaid, into the said office hitherto hath had, and now hath in his custody the common seal of the borough of Saltash aforesaid, by reason whereof, I the said William Stephens could not swear or admit him the said Mathew Veale according to the command of the said writ.

W. S

The

*The court held this to be but an argumentative and ill return, in not answering the election of Veale, and the mayor was taken upon an attachment, and fined for it, and paid the prosecutor his costs, and then a peremptory mandamus issued. Reported T. Jones, 177.*

---

* P. 456.

## * Mandamus for Prince.

Return—to a mandamus to admit him to the office of town-clerk of the city of Oxford; that he was not approved of by the king after his election.

WE the mayor and bailiffs of the city of Oxford, in the writ to this schedule annexed named, according to the command of the said writ, to the said lord the king, most humbly certify, that the city of Oxford aforesaid, from the time whereof the memory of man is not to the contrary, unto the first day of September, in the 34th year of the reign of the lord Henry the 8th, late king of England, was an antient town and borough, and the men and inhabitants within the said town and borough, from the whole time aforesaid, unto the said first day of September, were incorporated as well by the name of the Burgesses of Oxford, as by the name of the mayor, bailiffs, and burgesses of Oxford, otherwise Oxenford, and by the name of the mayor and bailiffs of the town of Oxford, and by the name of the mayor, bailiffs and burgesses of Oxford otherwise Oxenford, and by the name of the mayor and bailiffs of the town of Oxford, and by the said respective names for the whole time aforesaid, were commonly called and named; on which first day of September, in the 34th year aforesaid, the said late king Henry the eighth, by his letters patent, sealed under his great seal of England, bearing date at Westminster, on the said day and year, willed and ordained, among other things, that his whole town of Oxford aforesaid, in the county of Oxford, from thence afterwards should be a city, and willed and ordained that it should be called and named the city of Oxford, as by the said letters patent more fully appears: And further to the said lord the king, we most humbly certify, that in the said town and borough, from the whole time aforesaid, before the said time of the erection of the same into a city, and in the said city afterwards until the 29th day of July, in the 3d year of the reign of the lord James, late king of England, &c. there was a certain

Oxford a town and borough by prescription.

created a a city the 7th Sept. 34 H. 8.

antient

antient office of town-clerk of the ſaid borough or city aforeſaid, to the exerciſe of which office as often as it ſhould be vacant, one fit man by the freemen of the ſaid borough or city aforeſaid for the time being, within the borough or city aforeſaid, for this purpoſe aſſembled and collected, or by the greater part of the ſame hath been elected, and to which town-clerk ſo elected, after his election, the ſaid mayor and bailiffs of the borough or city aforeſaid for the time being, have adminiſtered, and have been accuſtomed to adminiſter from the whole time aforeſaid, the oaths for the due execution of that office. And further, we the ſaid mayor and bailiffs of the ſaid city moſt humbly certify, that the ſaid late king James, by his letters patent, ſealed with the great ſeal of England, bearing date at Weſtminſter aforeſaid, on the ſaid 29th day of July, in the 3d year of his reign aforeſaid, of his eſpecial grace, and of his certain knowledge and mere motion for himſelf, his heirs and ſucceſſors, among other things, willed, ordained, conſtituted, granted and declared that the ſaid city of Oxford, in the county of Oxford, ſhould be and ſhould remain from thence afterwards for ever, a free city in itſelf, and that the citizens of the ſaid city from thence afterwards for * ever, ſhould be one body politic and corporate in deed, fact, and in name, by the name of the mayor, bailiffs, and commonalty of the city of Oxford, in the county of Oxford; and by the ſaid letters patent, for himſelf, his heirs and ſucceſſors, erected, made, ordained, conſtituted, created, confirmed, ratified and declared them by that name, one body politick and corporate in deed, fact and in name fully and compleatly, and that by the ſaid name they ſhould have perpetual ſucceſſion, and that they by the name of the mayor, bailiffs, and commonalty of the city of Oxford, in the county of Oxford, ſhould be then and from thence for ever afterwards, perſons able, and in law capable, and a body corporate and politic, and in law capable to have, acquire, receive, enjoy and retain, lands, tenements, liberties, privileges, juriſdictions, franchiſes, and hereditaments of whatſoever kind, name, nature, quality, or ſort they ſhould or might be, to them and their ſucceſſors in fee, and in perpetuity, or for term of year or years, or otherwiſe in whatſoever manner; and alſo goods and chattles, and whatſoever other things of whatſoever kind, name, nature, quality or ſort they ſhould or might be; and alſo to give, grant, demiſe, alienate, aſſign, and diſpoſe of lands, tenements, and hereditaments, goods and chattles, and all and ſingular other deeds and things to be done and executed by the name aforeſaid; and that by

That there always has been in the ſaid city an antient office of town clerk.

Charter of James the 1ſt 29th July, in the 3d year of his reign.

* P, 457.

by the ſaid name of the mayor, bailiffs and commonalty of the city of Oxford in the county of Oxford, they might and could plead and be impleaded, anſwer and be anſwered, defend and be defended, in any courts, and places, and before any judges, and juſtices, and other perſons, and officers of the ſaid late king, his heirs and ſucceſſors, in all and ſingular actions and pleas, ſuits, complaints, cauſes, matters, and demands whatſoever of whatſoever kind, name, nature, quality, or ſort, they might or ſhould be in the ſame manner and form as any others, the liege ſubjects of the late king, of his kingdom of England, perſons able and in law capable, or any other body politic and corporate, within his realm of England, could or might have, acquire, receive, poſſeſs, enjoy, retain, give, grant, demiſe, alienate, aſſign, and diſpoſe, and plead and be implead, anſwer and be anſwered, defend and be defended, make, permit, or execute; and that the mayor, and bailiffs, and commonalty of the ſaid city, ſhould have for ever a common ſeal to be made uſe of, in their and their ſucceſſors cauſes and buſineſſes whatſoever; and that it ſhould and might be very lawful for the mayor, &c. and their ſucceſſors, to break, change, and make a-new that ſeal at their pleaſure from time to time, as it ſhould ſeem to them meet to be done; and further the ſaid late king willed, and by the letters patent aforeſaid, for himſelf, his heirs, and ſucceſſors, granted and ordained, that from thence afterwards for ever, there ſhould and might be within the ſaid city, one of the more honeſt and more diſcreet citizens of the ſaid city, to be elected in the form within in the letters patent aforeſaid mentioned, who ſhould be and ſhould be called mayor of the ſaid city, and that in like manner there ſhould and might be within the ſaid city, two honeſt and diſcreet citizens of the ſaid city, to be elected in the form within in the letters patent aforeſaid mentioned, who
* P. 458. ſhould be and ſhould be called * bailiffs of the ſaid city, and the ſaid late king alſo willed, and by the ſaid letters patent for himſelf, his heirs, and ſucceſſors, granted and ordained that thenceforth for ever, there ſhould and might be within the ſaid city from time to time, four honeſt and diſcreet men inhabiting and dwelling within the ſaid city, to be elected in the form within in the ſaid letters patent mentioned, who ſhould be and ſhould be called aldermen of the ſaid city, and alſo that from thenceforth for ever, there ſhould be within the ſaid city from time to time, eight others honeſt and diſcreet men inhabiting and dwelling within the ſaid city, to be elected in the form within in the ſaid letters patent mentioned, who ſhould be from time to time aſſiſtants of the ſaid city, and from time to time ſhould be aiding and

aſſiſting

assisting the mayor, bailiffs, and commonalty of the said city for the time being, in all causes and matters touching and concerning the said city; and further the said late king willed and by the said letters patent aforesaid, for himself, his heirs, and successors, granted and ordained, that from thenceforth afterwards there might be and for ever should be within the said city, twenty-four of the citizens of the said city, who should be and should be called the councellors or the common-council of the said city; and further the said late king willed, and by the said letters patent for himself, his heirs, and successors, granted to the said mayor, and bailiffs, and commonalty of the said city, and to their successors, that from time to time there should and might be within the said city, one honest and discreet man learned in the laws of England, who should be and should be called recorder of the said city, and should do and execute all and singular the things which belong, or ought to belong to the office of recorder, within the said city faithfully to be done; and further the said late king willed, and by his said letters patent granted to the mayor, bailiffs, and commonalty of the said city, and to their successors, that there should be in the said city one honest and discreet man, to be elected and nominated in the form within expressed, who should be and should be called the town-clerk of the said city, and that the town-clerk so as aforesaid elected and nominated, before that he should be admitted to execute that office, should take his corporal oath before the mayor, bailiffs, and commonalty of the said city for the time being, or the greater part of the same, of whom the said late king willed, that the mayor of the said city for the time being, should be one to execute the said office of town-clerk of the said city, rightly well and faithfully in all things touching the said office, and that after such oath so as aforesaid taken, he could exercise and should and might exercise the office of town-clerk of the said city, as by the said letters patent of the said late king James, among other things more fully appears;

James the 1st by the said patent granted, that there should be a town-clerk chosen by the mayor bailiffs, &c.

and further we the said mayor, and bailiffs of the said city, most humbly certify that the lord the now king Charles the 2d by his letters patent sealed under his great seal of England, bearing date at Westminster aforesaid, on the twentieth day of June, in the sixteenth year of his reign, of his especial grace and of his certain knowledge and mere motion willed, and by the said letters patent for himself, his heirs, and successors confirmed ratified and allowed to the then mayor, * bailiffs, and commonalty of the city of Oxford aforesaid, in the county of Oxford, &c. to their successors, all and all manner of messuages, mills, lands, tenements, tythes, meadows, pastures, feedings, commons, coroners, escheaters, courts of

King Charles the 2d by his letters patent dated 20th June, in the sixteenth year of his reign, confirms their franchises, &c.

* P. 459.

of record, cognizances of pleas, goods and chattles of felons and of felons of themselves, fugitives and outlaws, deodands, waifs, estrays, markets, feasts, fairs, tolls, customs, talliages, taxations, fines, redemptions, issues, amercements, forfeitures, perquisites of court, goal deliverys, and such tenements, and all such and the like liberties, and franchises, immunities, executions, privileges, acquittances, jurisdictions, wastes, commodities, profits, emoluments, and hereditaments whatsoever, as many as great such and which by the said letters patent of the said late king James, on the said twenty-ninth day of July, in the third year of his reign aforesaid, and by divers other letters patent, in the letters patent of the said lord the now king specified, were granted or were mentioned to be granted, or which the mayor, bailiffs, and commonalty of the city of Oxford, or their predecessors, by whatsoever name or names or by whatever incorporation, or under colour of whatever name or incorporation, before that time had held, used, or enjoyed, or occupied, or ought to have, hold, use or enjoy, or then had, held, used, enjoyed or occupied, to them and their successors, by reason or colour of any of the letters patent aforesaid, or of any of them, or of any other charters, grants, or letters patent, by any of the progenitors or ancestors of the said lord the now king, late kings or queens of England, howsoever before that time made, granted, confirmed, or mentioned to be made, granted, or confirmed, or by any other lawful manner, right, title, custom, use, or præscription whatsoever, before that time lawfully used, had, or accustomed, although the same or any of them were forfeited or lost, or although the same or any of them were misused, or not used, or abused, or discontinued, to have, hold, and enjoy to the said mayor, bailiffs, and commonalty of the city of Oxford aforesaid, and to their successors for ever, and yielding and paying thereout yearly to the said lord the now king, his heirs, and successors, as many such and the like fee farms, rents, services, sums of money and demands whatsoever, such as many and which ought to be rendered and payed to him before that time, for the same; wherefore the said lord the now king willed, and by the said letters patent for himself, his heirs, and successors, firmly enjoying commanded, that the said mayor, bailiffs, and commonalty of the said city, and their successors, should have, hold, use, and enjoy, and might and should have, hold, use, and enjoy for ever, all the liberties, authorities, jurisdictions, franchises, executions, immunities, acquittances, and hereditaments, aforesaid, according to the tenor and effect of his said letters patent, and of the said other letters patent above, in the said letters patent mentioned, without trouble or hindrance

drance of him the ſaid lord the king, his heirs and ſucceſſors, or of the ſheriffs, eſcheators, bailiffs, or miniſters of him his heirs and ſucceſſors whatſoever, willing that the * ſaid mayor, bailiffs, and commonalty of the ſaid city, or any of them, by reaſon of the premiſſes or any of them, by him his heirs or ſucceſſors, or by his or their juſtices, ſheriffs, bailiffs, or miniſters, ſhould not be troubled, moleſted or aggrieved, or in any manner diſturbed, provided always and the ſaid lord the now king willed, and by his ſaid letters patent for himſelf, his heirs, and ſucceſſors, ordained and firmly enjoining commanded, that the mayor, bailiffs, recorder, town--clerk, eſcheator, and all the officers and miniſters of the ſaid city, and their deputys, and alſo all juſtices to keep the peace of him, his heirs and ſucceſſors, within the ſaid city, by virtue or according to the tenor of the ſaid charter, or of any other letters patent or charters before that time made, then appointed, or afterwards to be nominated, elected or appointed, before that they were admitted to the execution or exerciſe of the office or offices, place, or places, to which they then were reſpectively appointed or conſtituted, or afterwards ſhould be reſpectively nominated, appointed, or conſtituted, or in any manner in that behalf ſhould intermeddle, or any of them ſhould intermeddle, ſhould take and each and every of them ſhould take upon the holy goſpel of God, as well the corporal oath, commonly called the oath of allegiance, as the corporal oath commonly called the oath of ſupremacy, before ſuch perſon or perſons as by the laws and ſtatutes of this kingdom of England, then were appointed and aſſigned, or afterwards ſhould be appointed and aſſigned to adminiſter, and receive ſuch oaths; and further the ſaid lord the now king willed, and declared his royal intention, that no recorder or town-clerk of the ſaid city, from thenceforth afterwards to be elected or conſtituted, ſhould intermeddle in ſuch office or offices, or either of them reſpectively before that they and every of them reſpectively were approved of, by the ſaid lord the now king, his heirs, and ſucceſſors, any thing in the ſaid charter, or any other thing cauſe or matter whatſoever, to the contrary thereof, in any wiſe notwithſtanding, as in the ſaid letters patent of the ſaid lord the now king, among other things is more fully contained. And further we the mayor, and bailiffs of the city of Oxford aforeſaid, moſt humbly certify, that Edward Prince gent. in the writ aforeſaid named, being a fit and honeſt man of the ſaid city, on the firſt day of Auguſt, in the thirty-third year of he reign of our lord the now king, according to the cuſtom of the ſaid city, from the whole time aforeſaid uſed, by the greater part of the freemen of the ſaid city, within the ſaid city for that purpoſe, being aſ-

ſembled

* P. 460

But orders that no recorder or town-clerk, ſhould intermeddle with their offices, until approved of by the king, his heirs and ſucceſſors, &c.

ſembled and collected, was duly elected into the place and office of town-clerk of the ſaid city, then vacant by the death of John Paynton gent. late town-clerk of the ſaid city; and the ſaid Edward Prince, on the day, &c. in the thirty-third year &c. aforeſaid, before R. B. then mayor, and A. B. and C. D. then bailiffs of the ſaid city, took the oath of allegiance and ſupremacy, in the ſaid letters patent of the ſaid lord the now king ſpecified, but by reaſon of the ſaid proviſion and will of the ſaid lord the king, in his ſaid letters patent ſpecified *, above mentioned, that no recorder or town-clerk of the ſaid city, from thenceforth to be elected or appointed, ſhould intermeddle or either of them reſpectively ſhould intermeddle in ſuch office or offices, before that they, and each of them reſpectively were approved by the ſaid lord the king, his heirs, and ſucceſſors, we the ſaid mayor, and bailiffs of the ſaid city, have not ſworn the ſaid Edward Prince, to exerciſe the place and office of town-clerk of the ſaid city, beeauſe the ſaid E. P. after his election aforeſaid, ſo as aforeſaid made into the place and office aforeſaid, hath not made appear to us the approbation of the lord the now king, that the ſaid E. P. ſhould be admitted into the ſaid office, as the ſaid lord the king by his charter aforeſaid hath commanded, and this is the cauſe wherefore we have not ſworn the ſaid E. P. into the place and office of town-clerk of the ſaid city, as by the ſaid writ we are commanded.

* P. 461.

But they could not admit or ſwear him, becauſe he did not produce the king's approbation of the ſaid election.

---

## MANDAMUS for TAVERNER.

### Hilary 31 and 32 Charles II.

To the maſter, wardens, and freemen, and alſo the aſſiſtants of the company of vintners, to admit him to be a liveryman of the ſaid company.

CHARLES the 2d by the grace of God of England, Scotland, France and Ireland, king defender of the faith, &c. To the maſter, wardens, and freemen, and to the commonalty of the myſtery of vintners of the city of London, and alſo to the maſter, wardens, and aſſiſtants of the ſaid company, and to every of them greeting: whereas Jeremiah Taverner who was, and as yet is a citizen and freeman of the city of London, and a freeman and member of the ſaid company of vinters of the city of London, by the ſaid company in

the

the due manner was elected into the livery of the ſaid company, and to the office and place of one of the livery-men of the ſaid company, to be taken upon himſelf, into which office and place, of one of the livery of the ſaid company, the ſaid Jeremiah according to the cuſtom of the ſaid city, ought to be admitted, nevertheleſs, you the maſter, wardens, and freemen, and commonalty, of the myſtery of vintners of the city of London, and alſo the maſter, wardens, and aſſiſtants of the ſaid company, well knowing the premiſſes, the ſaid Jeremiah into the ſaid place and office of one of the livery-men of the ſaid company have not as yet admitted, but the ſaid Jeremiah have refuſed to admit, to the great damage and grievance of the ſaid Jeremiah, and to the manifeſt injury of his eſtate, as from his complaint we have underſtood, we therefore willing that due and ſpeedy juſtic be done to the ſaid Jeremiah in this behalf as is right, command you and each and every of you, as heretofore we have commanded you firmly enjoying, that immediately after the receipt of this writ, you admit without delay, the ſaid Jeremiah to the ſaid office and place of one of the livery of the ſaid company, to which as aforeſaid he was duly elected, with all the liberties, privileges, pre-eminences, and commodities, to that office and place, appertaining and belonging, or thereupon ſignify to us cauſe to the contrary, leaſt through your default, complaint may be made again to us, and how you ſhall execute this our command, make to appear to us at Weſtminſter, on the Thurſday after the morrow of the purification of the bleſſed virgin Mary, then returning this our writ, * and this in no wiſe omit under the pain of 40l. to be levied of your goods and chattles, if you ſhall fail in the premiſſes and have there this writ; witneſs W. Scroggs, at Weſtminſter, the 1ſt day of February, in the thirty-ſecond year of our reign.

* P. 462.

ASTRY.

The anſwer of the maſter, wardens, and freemen, and commonalty, of the myſtery of vintners of the city of London, appears in a certain ſchedule to this writ annexed.

Return—That by a law made the 24th April 1656, every man when admitted into the livery, was bound to pay 31l. 13s. 4d. and that Taverner refuſed to pay that ſum on his election, wherefore they refuſed admit him.

We the maſter, wardens, and freemen, and commonalty, of the myſtery of vintners of the city of London, to the moſt ſerene lord the king, moſt humbly certify that the city of London is, and from the time whereof the memory of man is not to the contrary, hath been an antient city, and that the citizens and freemen of the ſaid city, from the whole time whereof the memory of man is not to the contrary, have been and as yet are incorporated as well by the

name

name of the mayor, and commonalty, of the city of London, as by the name of the mayor, and commonalty, and citizens of the city of London, and that of the ſaid citizens and freemen ſo incorporated, from the whole time aforeſaid, there have been ſeveral companies, guilds, and fraternities within the ſaid city, whereof the company of vintners in the city of London, now is, and from the whole time aforeſaid hath been one, and that as well of and in the ſaid company of vintners aforeſaid, as in all the other companies, guilds, and fraternities within the ſaid city, there are and from the whole time aforeſaid have been, certain men being citizens and freemen of the ſaid companies, guilds, or fraternities reſpectively called livery-men, who from time to time from the whole time aforeſaid, have been elected and have been accuſtomed to be elected by the company, guild, or fraternity, whereof ſuch men are free, and each and every of them is free reſpectively into the livery of the ſaid company, guild, or fraternity, whereſore they as aforeſaid reſpectively are freemen; and that the company of vintners aforeſaid, as well as the other companies aforeſaid, for the preſervation and maintenance as well of the honour, as of the ſtate and government of the ſaid city, in times of public meetings and attendance on the mayor and aldermen, and on other public occaſions, and for the preſervation of the honour, reputation, and government of the ſaid company, and for the relief of the poor members of the ſaid company, from time to time from the time whereof the memory of man is not to the contrary, divers great ſums of money and expences neceſſarily have been, and as yet are compelled to expend, lay out and ſuſtain; and we the ſaid maſter, wardens, freemen and commonalty, further certify, that the ſaid company of vintners anciently was incorporated, and called and known by divers names of incorporation, and that the moſt ſerene lord James late king of England, by his letters patent under his great ſeal of England, bearing date at Weſtminſter, the ſecond day of February, in the ninth year of his reign, of the eſpecial grace, certain knowledge, and mere motion of the ſaid late * king, for himſelf, his heirs, and ſucceſſors, gave and granted power and authority to his beloved and faithful liege ſubjects, the freemen of the myſtery of vintners, of the city of London, and of the ſuburbs of the ſame, and by the ſaid letters patent willed and ordained, and for himſelf, his heirs and ſucceſſors, did will and ordain, that they thenceforth ſhould be one body politic and corporate in themſelves, in deed, fact, and name, and one perpetual corporate community, of one maſter, three wardens, and the freemen and commonalty, of the vintners of the city of London,

That king James I. on the 2d February, in the 9th year of his reign, by letters patent, incorporated the vintners company, by the name of the maſter, wardens, and freemen,

* P. 463.

and commonalty, of the myſtery of vintners, of the city of London.

and

and them by the name of the maſter, wardens, and freemen, and commonalty of the miſtery of vintners of the city of London, for him, the ſaid late king his heirs and ſucceſſors, erected, ordained, made, conſtituted and eſtabliſhed, a body politic corporate for ever, realy and fully in all things, and for all things; and further, by the ſaid letters patent, granted and conſtituted that the maſter, wardens, and freeman, and commonalty, and their ſucceſſors, ſhould have perpetual ſucceſſion, and that they and their ſucceſſors for ever, ſhould be named, intitled and called by the name of the maſter, wardens, and freemen, and commonalty of the miſtery of vintners of the city of London, and by that name might plead and be impleaded, anſwer and be anſwered, defend and be defended, and might and could ſue, affirm and proſecute before any judges and juſtices, and other officers and miniſters of the ſaid late king, his heirs and ſucceſſors, and all other perſons whatſoever, in whatſoever courts and places, in all and ſingular matters, ſuits, complaints, actions, demands, and cauſes whatſoever; And that they ſhould have a common ſeal for their affairs and buſineſſes; And further, the ſaid late king of his moſt bountiful grace, willed, and by the letters patent aforeſaid, for himſelf, his heirs and ſucceſſors, granted to the ſaid maſter, wardens and freemen and commonalty, and their ſucceſſors, that the ſaid maſter, wardens and freemen and commonalty and their ſucceſſors, from time to time, for the ſupport, ſound government and better rule of the company and freemen and commonalty aforeſaid, and for the advantage, benefit and relief of the good and honeſt, and for the terror and correction of evil, deceitful and wicked, might make, ordain, and eſtabliſh orders, rules, proviſions, and ſtatutes, conſonant to the laws of this kingdom and to reaſon, as often as it would ſeem to them to be neceſſary: And we, the ſaid maſter, wardens, and freemen and commonalty further moſt humbly certify, that from the time whereof the memory of man is not to the contrary, the place and office of a liveryman was a place and degree of preheminence in the ſaid ſociety, and that for the whole time aforeſaid, as well before the making of the ſaid letters patent as afterwards, every brother of the ſaid company who hath been elected into the place and office of a liveryman, hath been accuſtomed, and ought to be a fit man, and of good eſtate and ſubſtance who well could, and at or before his admiſſion for the whole time aforeſaid hath been uſed and accuſtomed, and ought to pay for and towards the better and neceſſary ſupport and maintenance of the ſaid company, and the neceſſary burdens and expences thereof, a certain competent ſum of money; and that without the aſſiſtance and relief which the ſaid company had and received by ſuch payments, the ſaid company

Power by the letters patent to make bye laws.

and the good government and credit of the ſaid company could not be maintained; * And further, that for the ſpace of many years before the 24th day of April, which was in the year of our Lord one thouſand ſix hundred and fifty ſix, the ſum of money to be paid by every brother of the company who had been admitted into the ſaid office and place of the ſaid company towards the ſupport of their neceſſary burdens exceeded the ſum of thirty-one pounds, thirteen ſhillings, and four pence, and that upon the ſaid 24th day of April, in the year of our Lord 1656 aforeſaid, Henry Croone then maſter, and Thomas Langton, Edmund Waters, and John Clark, then wardens, and the then freemen and commonalty of the ſaid miſtery (upon public citation for that cauſe duly given by John Scotten, then bedell and officer of the ſaid company, for that intent lawfully appointed) aſſembled at their general court of the ſaid maſter, wardens, and freemen and commonality, held in their hall or council houſe, ſituate in the pariſh of St. Martin, in the Vintry, in the ward of Vintry, London, on the ſaid 24th day of April, in the year laſt aforeſaid, for the better preſervation, rule, order and government of the ſaid maſter, wardens, and freemen and commonalty of the ſaid miſtery, and of their ſucceſſors, and of the freemen of the ſaid company made and eſtabliſh their certain law and ordinance in writing, to endure to future times for ever; and by the ſaid law and ordinance then and there eſtabliſhed and ordained, that every perſon of the ſaid commonalty who thenceforth ſhould be elected into the ſaid livery, at or before his admiſſion into the ſaid livery, ſhould pay to the ſaid maſter, wardens, and freemen and commonalty of the ſaid miſtery for the time being, for their uſe, the ſum of thirty-one pounds, thirteen ſhillings and four pence, of the lawful money of England only; and we further moſt humbly certify to the ſaid lord the now king, that from the time of the ſaid ordinance aforeſaid made, the ſaid ſum of thirty-one pounds, thirteen ſhillings, and four pence, was and now is the ſum uſually paid by every perſon admitted into the place and office aforeſaid; and that before the coming of the ſaid writ of mandamus aforeſaid, and alſo before the coming of the ſaid firſt writ of mandamus to us in this behalf, directed, to wit, on the 8th day of June, in the year of our Lord 1680, the ſaid Jeremiah Taverner, in the writ to this ſchedule annexed named, who then and long before, and continually afterwards hitherto, was and as yet is a freeman of the ſaid city, and a member of the ſaid company, and a fit man to take upon him the office of a liveryman, by the ſaid company in the due manner was elected a liveryman of the ſaid company, and that the ſaid Jeremiah afterwards,

* P. 464.

Bye law made the 24th April 1656; and by it the ſum to be paid by a liveryman on his admiſſion was ſettled at 31l. 13s. 4d.

that Taverner was duly elected into the livery.

wards, to wit, on the day and year last aforesaid, by the then master and wardens of the said company was requested to take upon himself the office and place of a liveryman, and that the said master and wardens and freemen, and commonalty always were ready, and now are ready to admit the said Jeremiah to the office and place of a liveryman upon the payment of the said sum of thirty-one pounds, thirteen shillings, and four pence, and * which he ought to pay according to the ordinance aforesaid, and as the others of the said company when admitted into the said office and place have paid, nevertheless, the said Jeremiah Taverner the said sum of thirty-one pounds, thirteen shillings, and four pence, to the said master, wardens, and freemen and commonalty of the said mistery, altogether hath refused to pay, and as yet doth refuse, and thereupon we the said master, wardens, and freemen and commonalty of the said mistery, him the said Jeremiah Taverner to the office and place of a liveryman aforesaid, have refused to admit, until the said Jeremiah hath paid to us the said sum of thirty-one pounds, thirteen shillings, and four pence, according to the ordinance aforesaid; and this is the cause of refusing to admit the said Jeremiah to the place and office aforesaid.

* P. 465.

but hath refused to pay the sum of money due upon admission.

---

## Pluries Mandamus for Sherwin.

CHARLES the 2d, &c.—To the mayor and burgesses of our town of Nottingham, in the county of the said town greeting; Whereas John Sherwin, gent. into the place and office of one of the aldermen of the said town hath been duly elected according to the custom of the said town hitherto used, into which place and office of one of the aldermen of the said town, the said John Sherwin according to the custom of the said town, ought to be admitted and sworn, nevertheless you the mayor and burgesses of the said town, well knowing the premisses, the said John Sherwin into the place and office of one of the aldermen of the said town have not as yet admitted, nor have administered to the said John Sherwin the oath in such case, always used to be administered, but the said John Sherwin altogether have refused to admit and swear, to the great damage and grievance of said John, and to the manifest injury of his estate, as we have understood from his complaint; we therefore

To admit and swear him into office of an alderman of the town of Nottingham.



willing

willing that due and speedy justice be done to the John Sherwin in this behalf as is right, command you, and each and every of you, as we have often times commanded you, firmly enjoining, that immediately after the receipt of this writ, you admit without delay, the said John Sherwin into the place and office of one of the aldermen of the said town, into which as aforesaid, he hath been duly elected, with all the liberties, privileges, preheminences and commodities to that office and place belonging and appertaining, and that you administer, or cause to be administered, the oath to the said John Sherwin, according to custom in such case hitherto used, or signify to us cause to the contrary, least through your default complaint may be made again to us, and how you shall execute this our writ, make to appear to us at Westminster, on the Monday next after the octave of St. Hilary, then returning to us this our writ, and this in no wise omit under the pain of 80l. Witness F. Pemberton, knight, at Westminster, 22d day of November, in the 23d year of our reign.

By the Court. ASTRY.

* P. 466.

Return—By the mayor and Burgesses. That Sherwin the 24th Dec. 1661 was a burgess of the town and afterwards was removed and displaced from that office by commissioners for exercising the powers in the act for regulating corporations.

* We the mayor and burgesses of the town and county of the town of Nottingham within mentioned, to the most serene lord the king within written, most humbly certify, that John Sherwin in the within written writ named, upon the 24th day of December, in the year of our Lord 1661, was one of the burgesses of the town and county of the town aforesaid, and that the said John Sherwin afterwards, to wit, on the 24th day of March, in the 15th year of the reign of our lord Charles the 2d, within written, by Patrick viscount Chaworth, William Palmes, esquire, Cecil Cooper, esquire, Peniston Whalley, esquire, and Robert Pierrepoint esquire, five commissioners named and appointed by the lord the king within written, under his great seal of England, for the execution of the power and authority mentioned and expressed in a certain act of parliament, entitled an act for the better governing and regulating corporations, made and enacted at the parliament of the lord the king within written, begun at Westminster in the county of Middlesex, on the 8th day of May, in the 13th year of the reign of the king within written, and there continued until the 20th day of December then next following, and from that day adjourned unto the 7th day of January then next following, by virtue of the commission and act aforesaid, was amoved and displaced from his place and office aforesaid, of one of the burgesses of the town and county of the town of Nottingham aforesaid, for this because that it seemed to the said commissioners to be expedient for the public safety, that he

he the ſaid John Sherwin from his place and office aforeſaid, ſhould be amoved and diſplaced, and for this cauſe the ſaid commiſſioners by virtue of the commiſſion and act aforeſaid, him the ſaid John Sherwin, from the place and office aforeſaid did amove, and him the ſaid John Sherwin did declare to be amoved and diſplaced by their order and warrant, under their hands and ſeals; and to the ſaid moſt ſerene lord the king, we further moſt humbly ſignify that every alderman within the ſaid town, during the time of being an alderman, now and for the ſpace of twenty years now laſt paſt and more, by reaſon of his office hath been, and as yet is a juſtice of the lord the king, to preſerve the peace within the ſaid town, and alſo to hear and determine divers felonies, treſpaſſes, and other miſdeeds within the ſaid town, and that he the ſaid J. S. for many years now laſt paſt, hath been and as yet is, a ſtrenuous frequenter and maintainer of unlawful conventicles and aſſemblies, frequently convening and aſſembling within the ſaid town, under colour and pretence of the exerciſe of religion, in a different manner than according to the law and practice of the church of England, and againſt the ſtatutes, made and enacted againſt ſuch conventicles. and by reaſon of the premiſſes was incapable of being one of the aldermen and juſtices of the ſaid lord the king, to preſerve the peace within the ſaid town, and theſe are the cauſes wherefore we have refuſed to adminiſter the oath of one of the aldermen of the ſaid town, to the ſaid John Sherwin, or to admit him to the place of an alderman.

That every alderman of the town, is a juſtice of peace for the town by reaſon of his office, and that Sherwin is a frequenter and maintainer of conventicles, and therefore incapable to be an alderman and juſtice of the peace, and therefore they refuſed to mit and ſwear him.

---

## * Pluries Mandamus for Yolland.

* P. 467.

CHARLES the 2d by the grace of God, &c.—To the dean of the cathedral church of St. Peter, Exeter, or to his ſurrogate or deputy, greeting: Whereas John Yolland was duly elected into the place and office of one of the eight men of the pariſh of Aſhburton, in the county of Exeter, into which place and office of one of the eight men of the pariſh of Aſhburton aforeſaid, the ſaid John Yolland by you ought to be admitted and ſworn, neverthelefs you well knowing the premiſſes, have not as yet admitted the ſaid John Yolland, into the place and office of one of the eight men of the pariſh aforeſaid, nor have adminiſtered to the ſaid John Yolland, according to the duty of your office, the oath in

Mandamus directed to the dean of the cathedral church of St. Peter, Exeter, to admit and ſwear Yolland, into the place and office of one of the eight men of the pariſh of Aſhburton, in the county of Exeter.

this

this behalf used to be administered, but unjustly have refused to admit and swear the said J. Y. into that place and office, to the great damage and grievance of the said John, and to the manifest injury of his estate, as from his complaint we have understood, we therefore willing that due and speedy justice be done to the said J. Y. in this behalf as is just, command you as we have oftentimes commanded you, firmly enjoining that immediately after the receipt of this writ, you admit without delay the said John Yolland, into the place and office of one of the eight men of the parish of Ashburton aforesaid, into which as aforesaid he was duly elected, with all the liberties, privileges, pre-eminences, and commodities, to that office and place, belonging and appertaining, and that you cause to be administered to the said J. Y. the oath in this behalf hitherto used, or signify to us cause to the contrary, least through your default complaint may be made again to us, and how you shall execute this our command, make to appear to us from the day of Easter, in fifteen days wheresoever we shall then be in England, then returning to us this our writ, and this in no wise omit under the pain of 80l. Witness F. Pemberton, at Westminster, the thirteenth day of February, in the thirty-fourth year of our reign.

By the court, ASTRY.

Return— The execution of this writ appears in a certain schedule to this writ annexed; Richard Annesley Clerk, dean of the cathedral church of St. Peter, Exeter.

That by custom upon the death of any of the eight men, others used to be chosen into their places, upon the first Sunday after the sixth day of May, in every year after such death, and being elected should be tendered to the dean at his first visitation at Ashburton, after his election, that W F. one of the eight men died on the 1st May 1681, that Yolland was not elected on the 8th of May, which was the first Sunday after the 6th of the said May, and therefore he could not admit him.

To the most excellent lord the king, I most humbly certify that there is, and from the time whereof the memory of man is not to the contrary, there hath been, a certain antient and laudable custom, of choosing the said eight men in the parish of Ashburton, in the writ aforesaid specified, used and approved, to wit, that upon the death or deaths of one or more of the said eight men, some other person or persons from the whole time aforesaid, have been used and accustomed to be chosen, in the place or places of the person or persons so dying, upon the first * Sunday next, after the sixth day of the month of May, in every year after the death or deaths of such person or persons so dying, and not in and upon any other day or days, or any other time of the year next after such death or deaths, and that the person or persons so elected, should be tendered to the dean of the cathedral church of St. Peter, Exeter, or to his surrogate for the time being, at the next visitation of

* P. 468.

the

the dean and chapter, of the cathedral church aforesaid, held at Ashburton aforesaid, next ensuing, after such election or elections there to be admitted and sworn by the said dean, or by his surrogate, and that on the first of May 1681, one William Friend, then one of the said eight men of the parish aforesaid, at Ashburton aforesaid died, whereby the place aforesaid, of one of the eight men of the parish aforesaid became vacant; and that the said John Yolland, in the said writ named, was not elected into the place of the said William Friend, upon the 8th day of the month of May next following, after the said vacancy, after the said death of the said William Friend, the said eighth day of May, being the first Sunday next after the sixth day of the said month of May, in the year of our Lord aforesaid, according to the antient and laudable custom aforesaid, by reason whereof, I the said Richard Annesley, then and as yet dean of the cathdral church of St. Peter, Exeter, have refused to admit and swear the said John Yolland, into the said office as by the said writ I am commanded.

Richard Annesly, dean of the cathedral church of St. Peter, Exeter.

---

## A Mandamus for Yolland.

CHARLES the 2d &c.—To the dean of the cathedral church of St. Peter, Exeter, or to his surrogate or deputy, greeting: Whereas the parish of Ashburton, in the county of Devon, is an antient parish within which parish there is and is had, and also from the time whereof the memory of man is not to the contrary, there was and was had a certain body corporate, known by the name of the eight men, otherwise the eight men of Ashburton, having several liberties, privileges, pre-eminences, advantages, and commodities, thereto for the whole time aforesaid belonging and appertaining, and whenever the place and office of one of the said eight men, by death or otherwise hath been vacant, from time to time for the whole time aforesaid, one other fit and proper person, of the parishioners of the said parish, into the place so vacant, hath been elected and ought and hath been accustomed to be elected, to execute and exercise that office, and whereas the place and office of one of the said eight men being vacant, one John Yolland a fit and proper person

In another form directed to the said dean.

person, one of the parishioners of the said parish, according to the custom of the said parish was duly elected, into the place and office of one of the said eight men, of the parish of Ashburton aforesaid, into which place the said John Yolland, by you ought to be admitted and sworn, nevertheless you well knowing the premisses, the said John Yolland into the said place and office of one of the eight men aforesaid, * have not as yet admitted, and the oath in that behalf used to be administered to the said John Yolland, according to the duty of your office have not administered, but unjustly have refused to admit and swear the said John Yolland into that office and place, to the great damage and grievance of the said John, and to the manifest injury of his estate, as from his complaint we have understood, therefore we willing that due and speedy justice be done to the said John Yolland, in this behalf as is right, command you as we have oftentimes commanded you, firmly enjoining that immediately after the receipt of this writ, you admit without delay the said John Yolland, to the place and office aforesaid, into which as aforesaid he was duly elected, with all the liberties, privileges, and pre-eminences, and commodities, to that office and place belonging and appertaining, and that you cause to be administered to the said John Yolland, the oath in that behalf used, or signify to us cause to the contrary, least through your default complaint may be made again to us, and how you shall execute this our writ, make to appear to us from the day of Easter, in fifteen days wheresoever we shall then be in England, then returning to us this our writ, and this in no wise omit under the pain of 80l. Witness Edward Saunders knight, at Westminster, the twelfth day of February, in the thirty-fifth year of our reign.

* P. 469.

HENLY.

Return—That there is no such body corporate, as the eight men of Ashburton, as the writ supposes.

To the most excellent lord the king, I most humbly certify, that within the parish of Ashburton within mentioned, in the county of Devon within written, there is not nor is there had, nor ever was there, nor ever was there had any body corporate, known by the name of the eight men, otherwise the eight men of Ashburton, as by the said writ is within supposed.

The answer of Richard Annesley, dean of the cathedral church of St. Peter, Exeter.

*What passed in court upon the motion for this mandamus, is reported. 2 Shower 217.*

Mandamus

## Mandamus for Needham.

CHARLES the 2d &c.—To Andoenus Hughes, doctor of laws, archdeacon of the archdeaconry of Norwich, &c. Whereas the parochial church of St. Margaret, in Lynn Regis, in the county of Norfolk, is an antient church, and whereas the wardens of the ſaid church, from the time whereof the memory of man is not to the contrary, annually have been elected and choſen, and always hitherto ought and have been accuſtomed to be elected and choſen, by the major part of the pariſhioners of the ſaid pariſh, in the ſaid church aſſembled, on the Monday in Eaſter week, and whereas alſo the archdeacon of Norwich for the time being, or his official, ſurrogate, or deputy for the time being, from the whole time whereof the memory of man is not to the contrary, have been uſed and accuſtomed to admit and ſwear ſuch wardens ſo elected, well and faithfully to execute * the office of wardens of the church aforeſaid, during the time of their office of wardens of the church there, and whereas on the Monday in Eaſter week laſt paſt, one Jervais Needham, then and as yet one of the pariſhioners of the ſaid pariſh, by the major part of the pariſhoners of the ſaid pariſh, in the ſaid church then aſſembled, into the office of one of the wardens of the ſaid church for the year following, according to the cuſtom there uſed duly was elected, and the ſaid Jervais Needham, to the office of one of the wardens of the ſaid church ſo elected, to you at your next viſitation duly was preſented, nevertheleſs you diſregarding the premiſſes unduly and without any reaſonable cauſe, altogether have refuſed to admit and ſwear the ſaid Jervais, into the office of one of the wardens of the ſaid church, in contempt of us, and to the great damage and grievance of the ſaid Jervais Needham, and to the manifeſt ſubverſion of the cuſtom aforeſaid, as we have underſtood from his complaint in our court before us, thereſore we willing that due and ſpeedy juſtice be done to the ſaid Jervais, in this behalf as is right, command you that immediately after the receipt of this writ, you cauſe the ſaid Jervais to be admitted and ſworn into the office of one of the wardens of the church of St. Margaret, in Lynn Regis aforeſaid, to have and enjoy the ſaid office with all liberties, privileges, and commodities to that office belonging and appertaining, or ſignify to us cauſe to the contrary, whereſore you will not execute our command, leaſt thus your default complaint may be made to us again, and how you ſhall execute this our writ, make to appear to us from the day of St. Michael, in three weeks whereſoever we ſhall then be in England, and

To the archdeacon of Norwich, to admit and ſwear Needham, into the office of one of the church-wardens of the pariſh of St Margaret, in Lynn Regis.

* P. 470.

this in no wise omit at your peril. Witness M. Hale knight, at Westminster, the eighth day of July, in the twenty-sixth year of our reign.

Return—That by the canons all church-wardens should be chosen by the unanimous consent of the parishioners and their minister, or if they cannot agree; then the minister to choose one, and the parishioners another.

To the most serene and powerful prince in Christ, and our lord Charles the 2d by the grace of God of England, &c. king, &c.—answers Andoenus Hughes, doctor of laws, of the venerable man, master John Reynolds Clerk, archdeacon of the archdeaconry of Norwich, in and throughout the whole archdeaconry aforesaid, official, well, sufficiently, and lawfully appointed, greeting, in him by whom kings reign and princes bear rule, we have received with all humility and obedience your royal writ, annexed to these presents, on the seventh day of the present month of July, commanding us that we should cause Jervais Needham, in your said writ named, to be admitted and sworn into the office of one of the wardens of the church of St. Margaret, in Lynn Regis, in your county of Norfolk, or that we should signify to your royal majesty cause to the contrary, therefore to your royal highness by the tenor of these presents, we certify, that whereas it is provided by your royal ecclesiastical canons, that all wardens of churches should be elected by the united consent of the minister and parishioners, if that can be done, and if they should disagree in such election, then that it should be lawful for the minister to choose * one, and for the parishioners to choose another, nor that any one shall be held for the warden of a church, unless him whom such consent or devise shall elect, we because that a contrary custom of choosing wardens of the church of St. Margaret, in Lynn Regis aforesaid, did not appear to us in the first week after the feast of Easter last past, at the court of general inquisition, of the archdeacon of Norwich, held in the chapel of St. Nicholas, in Lynn Regis aforesaid, one Thomas Horwick, by master Mordant Webster Clerk, minister of the parochial church of St. Margaret aforesaid, and Thomas Tue elected by the parishioners of the said parish, presented to us to the office of wardens of the church aforesaid, for the year of our Lord 1674, now current, to the said office of wardens of the said church, then and there according to the said canon, in that behalf enacted have admitted, and caused to be sworn; and having examined the archives of the archdeacon of Norwich aforesaid, which are faithfully kept by his register, we cannot find more than two wardens of the said church, admitted and sworn for one and the same year; nor any custom of electing and admitting wardens of the said church of St. Margaret, in Lynn Regis, repugnant to the said canon, therefore because there are two wardens of the said church, to wit, Thomas Horwick, and Thomas Tue, long since as aforesaid, for

* P. 471.

That he had admitted two church-wardens, one chosen by the minister, and the other by the parishioners.

cannot find any custom repugnant to the said canon.

for this year 1674, admitted and ſworn, for that cauſe we have as yet deferred to admit, and cauſe to be ſworn the ſaid Jerveis Needham, into the office of warden of the ſaid church for the ſaid year, according to the tenor of your ſaid royal writ, until that the cauſe of this our delay being ſignified to you, we ſhall receive another command in that behalf from your royal majeſty, which may great and almighty God long preſerve in proſperity to the defence of his church, and to the happy government of your people, given under the ſeal which we uſe in this behalf, on the ſaid 7th day of the month of July, in the year of our Lord 1674, and in the 26th of your moſt happy reign of England, &c. &c. &c.

And therefore did not admit and ſwear Needham.

*The Canon mentioned in the return, is in the book called Conſtitutions and Canons Eccleſiaſtical. p. 61. Canon 89.*

THE king, &c.—To the keepers of our peace, and to our juſtices aſſigned to hear and determine divers felonies, treſpaſſes and other miſdeeds in the ſaid county of Bucks perperrated, and to every of them greeting: Whereas Thomas Harris, one of the inhabitants within the manor of Turviſton, within the three hundreds of Bucks, in the county of Bucks, to the office of conſtable of our manor of T. aforeſaid, within the three hundreds aforeſaid, in the county of B. in the court-leet, and view of Frank Pledge of the ſaid manor, at the feaſt of Eaſter, in the 20th year of our reign, there held according to the cuſtom there uſed, from the time whereof the memory of man is not to the contrary, hath been duly elected, and whereas one James Knight, into the office of conſtable of the ſaid manor, out of our ſaid court, and againſt the cuſtom aforeſaid, lately hath been elected, ſworn, and charged as by the relation and oath of perſons worthy of belief, in our court before us ſhewn we are informed, and whereas thereupon for the ſaid cauſe in our court before us, we have diſcharged the ſaid J. K. from the ſaid office, * and we have commanded the ſaid J. K. by our writ thereupon to him directed, firmly enjoining that he ſhould not intermeddle with the ſaid office, but that he ſhould be aiding and aſſiſting the ſaid T. H. duly to execute the ſaid office as was fit, or that he ſhould ſignify to us cauſe wherefore he would not or could not execute our command, and becauſe we are unwilling that our buſineſs touching the ſaid office ſhould any longer remain undone, or ſhould be retarded, we command you, and each of you (to whoſe hands this our writ ſhall come) firmly enjoining that you cauſe the ſaid T. H. to come before you, or ſome of you, immediately after the receipt of this writ, and that you adminiſter to the ſaid T. H. the oath

A mandamus to the juſtices of the peace to ſwear one Harris, conſtable for a manor being choſen at the leet in the room of one Knight who had been unduly choſen, and therefore turned out by the court of King's Bench.

* P. 472.

which the conſtables of our manor aforeſaid, hitherto have been accuſtomed to take, who have taken oath well and faithfully to execute that office until that another into the ſaid office ſhall be elected, or ſignify to us cauſe wherefore you will not or cannot execute this our command, and how you ſhall execute this our command make to appear to us on the morrow of the holy Trinity, whereſoever we ſhall then be in England, then returning to us this our writ: Witneſs Francis Bacon, at Weſtminſter, the 20th day of April, in the 22d year of our reign.

ASKE.

Mandamus to Knight to diſcharge him from that ſaid office, and to permit the ſaid Harris to execute it.

The king, &c.—To James Knight, conſtable of the manor of Turviſton, in the county of Bucks, greeting: Becauſe Thomas Harris, one of the inhabitants within the manor of T. in the county of B. in the court-leet, and view of Frank Pledge of the ſame manor, at the feaſt of Eaſter, in the 20th year of our reign, there held according to the cuſtom of the ſaid manor, from the time whereof the memory of man is not to the contrary, hath been duly elected into the office of conſtable of the ſaid manor, and becauſe you the ſaid James Knight, into the ſaid office of conſtable of the ſaid manor, out of our court, and againſt the ſaid cuſtom, have been lately elected and ſworn, as by the relation and oath of perſons worthy of belief, in our court before us we are informed, and we have diſcharged you thereupon for the cauſe aforeſaid, in our court before us from the ſaid office, therefore we command you firmly enjoining that you do not intermeddle with the ſaid office, but that you be aiding and aſſiſting the ſaid Thomas Harris, duly to execute the ſaid office, as is fit, or ſignify cauſe to us wherefore you will not or cannot execute this our command, and how you ſhall execute this our writ, make to appear to us on the morrow of the holy Trinity, whereſoever we ſhall then be in England, then returning to us this our writ: Witneſs Francis Bacon, at Weſtminſter, the 20th day of April, in the 22d year of our reign.

ASKE.

Mandamus,

## Mandamus for Patrick.

CHARLES the 2d &c.—To Richard Bryan, senior fellow of Queen's College, in the university of Cambridge, greeting: Whereas Simon Patrick, batchelor in divinity, in the due manner was elected president of the said college, and hath often times presented himself to be admitted into the place of president of the said college, * nevertheless, you Richard Bryan, being senior fellow of the said college, to whom it belongs to pronounce the president so elected, and to admit the person † so elected, and to make the elected president to be sworn, and personally to be presented before the community of the college in the chapel thereof, at the Lord's table, at the expence of the college, him the said Simon Patrick have refused, or at least have unduly deferred to admit into the office of president of the said college, according to the statutes of the said college, to the great damage and grievance of the said Simon, and to the manifest injury of his estate, as from his complaint we have understood, wherefore he hath besought us, that we would provide for him apt remedy in this behalf; we therefore willing that due and speedy justice be done to the said Simon Patrick in this behalf, as is just, command you, as we have oftentimes commanded you, that you pronounce the said Simon Patrick president of the said college, and that you admit him, and cause him personally to be presented before the community of the said college, in the chapel of the same, according to the statutes of the said college, or signify to us cause to the contrary wherefore you will not or cannot do these things, on the Friday next after 15 days of the holy Trinity, under the pain of 40l. and this in no wise omit at your peril: Witness Robert Foster, at Westminster, the 6th day of June, in the 14th year of our reign.

Mandamus to the senior fellow of Queen's college in Cambrige, to admit one Patrick to the office of president of the said college being duly elected.

* P. 473.

† *in the original it is inquiri, but see Sir Tho. Raymond 106, who states it to be Jurari.*

By the Court. FANSHAWE.

The execution of this writ appears in a certain schedule to this writ annexed.

The return.

The answer of the within named Richard Bryan, senior fellow of Queen's college, in the university of Cambridge within written.

RICHARD BRYAN.

I Richard

Henry 6th by letters patent in the 26th year of his reign granted licence to his queen Margaret to found and erect the said college as therein mentioned.

I Richard Bryan, batchelor of divinity, senior fellow of Queen's college, in the university of Cambridge, to the most serene lord Charles the 2d, the the now king of England, most humbly certify, that the lord Henry the 6th, late king of England, by his letters patent, sealed with his great seal of England, bearing date at Westminster, the 30th day of March, in the 26th year of his reign, granted and gave licence for himself, his heirs and successors, to Margaret then queen of England, the consort of the said late king, that she the said late queen might found, erect, make and establish to endure for ever, in a certain ground or place situate in the parish of St. Botolph, in Cambridge, lying between the dwelling-house of the brothers Carmelites, of the town of Cambridge on the north side, and the king's highway called small bridge-street, on the south side, and the wharf there at the west side, and the street called mill-street on the east side, lately in the possession of John Morys of Fromington, esquire, a certain perpetual college in and of the number of one president, and four follows, or more or less, as the case might be, to be increased or diminished, according to the estates and expences of the said college, to abide in the said university of Cambridge, to study and to pray; which president and fellows, and all and singular the presidents and fellows there being in their times successively the said late king willed should be elected, appointed, and instituted, ruled, directed and governed, corrected, punished and amoved, and deprived according to the statutes and ordinances thereupon, by the reverend father William, then bishop of Litchfield and Coventry, John Somerseth, chancellor of the said late king, Richard Cawdry, Peter Herford, Hugh Damlett, Thomas Boleyn, and William Millington, clerks, whilst they should live, or by the greater part of them, and after the decease of any one or more of them, by those * who should survive, or by the major part of those surviving, to be instituted, enacted, made and established; and that she might appoint, create and ordain master Andrew Dockett president of the said college, and John Lawe, Alexander Forklove, Thomas Haywood, and John Careway, clerks, fellows of the said college, to be governed, corrected, deprived and amoved according to the statutes and ordinances by the said bishop, John Somerseth, Richard Cawderay, Peter Herford, Hugh Damlett, Thomas Boleyn, and William Millington, as aforesaid, thereupon to be made and enacted; also the said late king willed and granted, that after the college aforesaid, by the late queen, in the form aforesaid should be founded, erected, made, and established, and the said president and fellows, by the said late queen in like manner should be appointed, made and ordained, they the

* P. 474.

the said president and fellows, and their successors, presidents and fellows of the said college, according to the ordinances and statutes as aforesaid, to be made and enacted, might elect, collect, and admit more fellows, to be governed, corrected, deprived and amoved, according to the said statutes and ordinances, which fellows and their successors so elected, collected, and admitted, to be governed, corrected, deprived, and amoved, according to the said statutes and ordinances, the said late king willed, and for himself, his heirs, and successors, granted for ever to the fellows of the said college, and should be had, held, and in all things reputed as fellows and members of the said college, and further the said late king willed and granted, that the college aforesaid so as aforesaid founded, erected, made and established, for ever should be called Queen's-college of St. Margaret, and St. Bernard, in the university of Cambridge; and that the president and fellows aforesaid for the time being, and their successors for ever, should be called for ever the president, and fellows of Queen's-college of St. Margaret, &c. by virtue of which letters patent, the said Margaret afterwards, to wit, on the fifteenth day of April, in the twenty-sixth year of the reign of the said late king aforesaid, by her letters patent sealed with her seal, bearing date the said day and year, in the said place or ground, which as aforesaid lately was in the possession of John Morys aforesaid, founded, erected, made and established, to endure for ever, a certain perpetual college, in and of the number of one president and four fellows, or more or less as the case might be, to be encreased or diminished, according to the estates and expences of the said college, to abide in the said university, to study and to pray in the form aforesaid, which president and fellows, and all and singular the president and fellows successively, in their times there being, she willed should be elected, appointed and instituted, ruled, governed and directed, corrected, punished, amoved and deprived, according to the laws and statutes thereupon by the said Bishop, * John Somerseth, Richard Cawdrey, Peter Herford, Hugh Damlett, Thomas Boleyn, and William Millington, whilst they should live, and by the greater part of them, and after the death of any one or more of them, by those who should survive, or by the major part of those so surviviving, to be instituted, enacted, made and established; and appointed, created and ordained, Andrew Dockett president, and the said John Lawe, Alexander Forklove, Thomas Haywood, and John Careway, clerks, fellows of the said college to be governed, corrected, deprived and amoved, according to the ordinances and statutes, by the said Bishop, John Somerset, Richard Cawderay, Peter Herford, Hugh Damlet,

That the queen by her letters patent, did found, &c. the same accordingly.

* P. 475.

let, Thomas Boleyn, and William Millington as aforesaid, to be made and enacted, also the said Margaret willed and granted, that the said president and fellows, and their successors, presidents, and fellows of the said college, according to the ordinances and statutes, as aforesaid to be made and enacted, might elect, collect, and admit, more fellows to be governed, corrected, deprived, and amoved, according to the said statutes and ordinances, which fellows and their successors so elected, collected, and admitted to be governed, corrected, deprived, and amoved, according to the said statutes and ordinances, she willed and for herself and her successors granted for ever, to be fellows of the said college, and to be had, held, and in all things reputed, as fellows and members of the said college, and further the said Margaret willed and granted, that the said college for ever should be called, Queen's-college of St Margaret, and St. Bernard, in the university of Cambridge, and that the president and fellows aforesaid, for the time there being, and their successors for ever, should be called for ever, the president and fellows of Queen's-college of St. Margaret, and St. Bernard, in the university of Cambridge; and moreover the said Margaret willed and granted, and gave licence by her said letters patent, for herself and her heirs, as much as in her lay, to the said Bishop, John Somerseth, Richard Cawdray, Peter Herford, Hugh Damlett, Thomas Boleyn, and William Millington, that they whilst they should live, or the greater part of them, and after the decease of any one or more of them, the major part of those surviving the statutes and ordinances aforesaid, might correct, amend, reform, or totally change and dispense with them, and publish new ordinances and statutes for the good government of the said college, according to which the presidents and fellows of the said college, being and from that time to be in the said college, should be ruled and governed, and should be amoved and deprived in the manner and form declared, and all and singular the premisses which did belong, or might belong to the said Margaret, under colour of the said letters patent of the said lord the king, and all other things consonant and convenient to the said creation, foundation and establishment, she the said Margaret for herself and her successors, as much as in her lay, by the tenor of the
* P. 476. said letters patent of the said * Margaret, made, ordained, and established, to endure for ever, according to the force, form, and effect, of the said letters patent, of the said lord the king. By virtue of which letters patent, the said Bishop, John Somerseth, Richard Cawdray, Peter Herford, Hugh Damlett, Thomas Boleyn, and William Millington, afterwards with the assent and consent, of the then president and fellows of the said college, made and founded, enacted and established, divers statutes

ſtatutes and ordinances, for the profitable eſtate and good government of the ſaid college; and for the regulation, government, order, and correction of the preſident and fellows of the ſaid college: And in the ſaid ſtatutes and ordinances to be adminiſtered for and in the ſaid college, made, enacted, and eſtabliſhed by the ſaid biſhop, John Somerſeth, Richard Cawderay, Peter Herford, Hugh Damlett, Thomas Boleyn, and William Millington, among other things it was enacted as follows: To wit, in the ſtatute concerning the name of the ſaid college, and the number to be maintained in the ſame, we [illegible] enact and ordain that the ſaid college ſhall be called Queen's College for ever, in which we will that there be one ſuperior, who ſhall be called Preſident, whom all the fellows, ſcholars, and other inhabitants, (by whatſoever name they may be called) in all lawful and honeſt things ſhall obey, and ſhall be bound to obey with effect. Moreover we will that in the ſaid college there be nineteen fellows, each of whom we will ſhall enter into holy orders within two years after that they have become maſters of arts, unleſs the proſident, and the major part of the fellows ſhall have given them longer time, under the pain of expulſion, ipſo facto. Alſo in the ſtatute for compoſing diſcords—nothing ſo much becomes Chriſtians as to live in mutual and laſting friendſhip, therefore we enact, that no fellow or elder of this college ſhall ſow diſcord between the preſident and fellows, nor between themſelves; and if any ſhall be found offending in this reſpect, for the firſt time, he ſhall be admoniſhed in a friendly manner, by the preſident or his deputy; if he ſhall offend a ſecond time, he ſhall be admoniſhed by the preſident or his deputy, and by the two ſenior fellows for the time being; if he ſhall offend the third time, he ſhall be for ever expelled from the college; ordaining, that as often as ſuch diſcords ſhall ariſe in this college, the preſident, if he be preſent, and all the fellows preſent, ſhall endeavour, with all their power, to appeaſe the ſaid diſcords, or in the abſence of the preſident, all the fellows preſent in the ſaid college, ſhall endeavour, with all their power, to appeaſe the ſaid diſcords, and that they ſhall labour to bring the diſagreeing members to brotherly love, who ſhall be bound to abide by the deciſion and judgment of the preſident and of the greater part of all the fellows, under the pain of perpetual expulſion from the college, ipſo facto. And if diſcord ſhould ariſe between the preſident and a fellow or fellows, the ſaid preſident ſhall be bound to aſſemble the fellows three different times, three being preſent, or two at the leaſt, that they may determine the controverſy among themſelves, which we chiefly wiſh; but if they cannot then remove it, then as well the preſident as the fellows aforeſaid, ſhall be bound to abide by

Statute that there ſhall be ſuperior called a preſident.

Statute for compoſing diſcords in the college.

the judgment of the chancellor, and of the greater part of the provosts of the colleges, under the pain of privation and expulsion from the college, *ipso facto*. And to the said lord the now king, I further most humbly certify that the lord James, late king of England, on the 9th day of March, in the second year of his reign, by his letters patent, sealed with his great seal of England, bearing date the said day and year of his especial grace, and of his certain knowledge and mere motion, ratified and confirmed all and singular endowments, gifts, grants, confirmations, and letters patent, whatsoever, before that time given, granted, and confirmed to the chancellor, masters, and scholars of the university of Cambridge, or to their or any of their predecessors, by any of his progenitors, predecessors, or ancestors, kings or queens of England, and those for himself, his heirs, and successors, as much as in him lay, accepted and approved: And by the said letters patent, for himself, his heirs and successors, to his beloved the then chancellor, masters, and scholars of the university of Cambridge aforesaid, and to their successors, granted, approved, ratified and confirmed: And further, the said late king James of his bountiful especial grace, and of his certain knowledge and mere motion, for himself, his heirs and successors, by his said letters patent, gave and granted to the said chancellor, masters, and scholars, and to their successors, that the chancellor of the said university, for the time being, if he should be present within the said town, or the suburbs of the same, or in his absence, the vice-chancellor of the said university, for the time being, (by the chancellor of the said university in that behalf deputed and appointed,) should be the ordinary visitor of all and singular the colleges, inns, or halls then being, or afterwards to be within the said university, (to which a special visitor otherwise was not or should not be appointed); and from time to time might, and should have, all and all manner of power and authority of visiting all and singular such colleges, inns, and halls, (to which as aforesaid a special visitor otherwise was not or should not be appointed) as often as it might seem necessary to him, and of doing and executing, by virtue of the said letters patent of the said late king James, in a summary manner, plainly and without noise, and without any form or figure of judgment, the truth of the fact alone being examined, all and singular the things which he should think necessary for the advantage of the said colleges, inns, or halls respectively, or for the reformation of their personal excesses. And further, to the said lord the king, I certify that there is no special visitor of the said college appointed. And to the said lord the king, I further certify, that one Edward Martin, doctor in divinity,

* P. 477

King James the 1st, in the 2nd year of his reign, by letters patent, granted, that the chancellor of the university if present, or the vice-chancellor in his absence should be visitor of all the colleges in the university of Cambridge, where there was not a special visitor appointed.

That this college has no special visitor.

ty, late and last president of this said college, on the 27th day of April, in the 14th year of the reign of the lord Charles the Second, the now king of England, at the town of Cambridge, in the county of Cambridge, died, and that at the time of the death of the said Edward Martin, and continually afterwards hitherto, Edward, earl of Manchester, was, and as yet is, chancellor of the said university, and out of the said town of Cambridge, and the suburbs of the same: And that Theophilus Dillingham, doctor in divinity, then, and continually afterwards hitherto, was, and as yet is, his deputy there, and vice-chancellor of the said university, elected, deputed and appointed, and present within the said * town of Cambridge; and that as well the town of Cambridge aforesaid, as the university aforesaid, are, and from the the time whereof the memory of man is not to the contrary were, within the diocess of the bishop of Ely; and that Mathew Wren, at the time of the death of the said Edward Martin, and continually afterwards hitherto, was, and as yet is, bishop of Ely aforesaid; but the said Simon Patrick hath not brought his appeal upon the premisses to the said chancellor, or to his deputy, being visitor of the said college, or to the said bishop, and for that cause I cannot pronounce or admit the said Simon Patrick president of the said college.

Death of the last president.

The earl of Manchester was and is chancellor of the university, but absent from Cambridge. Dr. Dillingham vice chancellor, and there present, that Cambridge and the university is within the diocess of Ely, whereof Wren was and is bishop, but Patrick hath not appealed to the chancellor vice chancellor, or to the said bishop.

RICHARD BRYAN.

*This case is largely reported in 1 Lev. 65. and Ray. 101. the court was divided, therefore no judgment was given herein.*

*. P. 478.

---

## Mandamus for Appleford.

CHARLES the 2nd, by the grace of God of England, &c. king, &c. to the warden and scholars of the college of St. Mary of Winchester, in Oxford, in the county of Oxford, commonly called New College, greeting, Whereas Daniel Appleford, master of arts, to the place of one of the fellows of the said college, according to the custom there hitherto used, hath been duly elected, admitted and constituted; in which place of one of the fellows of the said college, the said Daniel Appleford behaved and demeaned himself well, nevertheless you the warden and scholars of the said

Mandamus to the warden and scholars of Winchester college, commonly called New College, to restore Appleford to the fellowship of the said college.

ſaid college, well knowing the premiſſes, unjuſtly have removed the ſaid Daniel Appleford from the ſaid place of one of the fellows of the ſaid college, to the great damage and grievance of the ſaid Daniel, and to the manifeſt injury of his eſtate, as we have underſtood from his complaint: We therefore, willing that due and ſpeedy juſtice be done to the ſaid Daniel Appleford in this behalf as is juſt, command you, firmly enjoining, that, immediately after the receipt of this writ, you reſtore or cauſe to be reſtored without delay, the ſaid Daniel Appleford into his place of one of the fellows of the ſaid college, with all the liberties, privileges and commodities to that place belonging and appertaining, or ſignify to us cauſe to the contrary, leaſt through your default, complaint may be made to us again; and how you ſhall execute this our command, certify to us from the day of St. Michael in three weeks, whereſoever we ſhall then be in England, then returning to us this our writ. Witneſs, Mathew Hale, at Weſtminſter, the 12th day of July, in the 23d year of our reign.

By rule of court, FANSHAWE.

The execution of this writ appears in a certain ſchedule to this writ annexed.

MICHAEL WOODWARD, Warden.

* P. 479

Richard 2nd by letters patent licenſed William of Wickham, biſhop of Wincheſter, to found this college at Oxford.

* The anſwer of the warden and ſcholars, clerks of the college of St. Mary of Wincheſter, in Oxford, commonly called New College, to the writ to this ſchedule annexed; according to the command of the ſaid writ, to the ſaid lord the king, we moſt humbly certify, that the Lord Richard, the ſecond of his name after the conqueſt, late king of England, by his letters patent, ſealed with the great ſeal of England, bearing date at Weſtminſter the 30th day of June, in the third year of his reign, granted and gave licence, for himſelf, his heirs and ſucceſſors, to the reverend father in Chriſt William of Wickham, biſhop of Wincheſter, that he the ſaid William of Wickham, biſhop of Wincheſter, (then being ſeized in his demeſne, as of fee ſimple, in the right of his biſhoprick aforeſaid, of and in divers places in the town of Oxford aforeſaid, in the pariſh of St. Peter, in the eaſt of the ſaid town,) in the ſaid places might found anew a certain college, houſe, or hall; and that he might give a certain name to the ſame; and that there a certain warden, and the number of ſeventy ſcholars, ſtudying in the different arts in the univerſity of the town of Oxford aforeſaid, and their ordinances in this behalf to be made according to the will of the ſaid biſhop he might ordain and eſtabliſh; and the ſaid places by the name of ſuch college, houſe, or hall, to the

ſaid

ſaid warden and ſcholars might give and aſſign, to have and hold to the ſaid warden and ſcholars, and their ſucceſſors, for their abode and habitation, of the ſaid biſhops and their ſucceſſors in free, pure and perpetual frankalmoigne for ever: And the ſaid reverend father William of Wickham, biſhop of Winchester, afterwards, to wit, on the 30th day of November, in the third year of the reign of the ſaid king Richard, by his charter, ſealed with his ſeal, dated the ſaid 30th day of November, with the licence and authority of the apoſtolic ſee, (the gift being firſt aſſigned by the ſaid William, biſhop of Wincheſter, according to the form of the apoſtolic letters in this behalf granted) and alſo with the licence of the ſaid lord the king Richard, all others required by right, or otherwiſe howſoever, in that behalf concurring, really and effectually founded, conſtituted and eſtabliſhed a certain perpetual college of poor and indigent ſcholars clerks, by the name of the Warden and Scholars Clerks of St. Mary of Wincheſter: and alſo ordained, that the ſaid college ſhould conſiſt for ever of the number of ſeventy poor and indigent ſcholars clerks, living in the ſaid college, in the ſaid univerſity, by the grace of God to endure for ever; and by his ſaid charter appointed Nicholas of Wickham, archdeacon of Wincheſter, canon of the church of Saliſbury, and alſo rector of the parochial church of Wiltney, warden of the ſaid college, and admitted ſeventy poor and indigent ſcholars clerks, bound to ſtudy in the ſaid univerſity, and them aſſociated to the ſaid warden, really eſtabliſhed in the ſaid college, and them incorporated as a collegiate body; the names of which ſcholars clerks are more fully recited in the muniments of the ſaid college; and the ſaid college, by his * charter aforeſaid, named and called the College of St. Mary, commonly called St. Mary's College of Wincheſter, and willed that it ſhould be named and called by the ſaid name for ever. And the ſaid William, biſhop of Wincheſter, by his ſaid charter enacted, ordained, and willed that the ſaid warden and ſcholars clerks, and others to be choſen in their place in future times, into whoſe place we to whom the ſaid writ of the ſaid lord the king is directed, for the preſent time are choſen, as collegiate perſons, and in a collegiate manner, ſhould aſſociate together; and moreover willed and ordered that the ſaid ſcholars, and all and ſingular the future ſcholars, and the other officers and miniſters whatſoever of the ſaid college, ſhould be, and perpetually ſhould remain, under the care, order, and government of the ſaid warden, and of his ſucceſſors, wardens for the time being, according to his ſtatutes and ordinances in this behalf made or to be made. And further ordained and enacted, that the warden and ſcholars clerks of the ſaid college; and all and ſingular the ſucceſſors of the ſaid warden and ſcholars

The college founded by the biſhop.

* P. 480

ſcholars clerks, for the time being in their times ſucceſſively, ſhould obſerve and firmly keep all and ſingular the ſtatutes and ordinances of the ſaid college for ever: And that the ſaid warden and his ſucceſſors, upon their appointment, and the ſaid ſcholars clerks, and their ſucceſſors, upon their admiſſion, ſhould be held and ought to make their corporal oath upon the holy goſpels of God, well, fully, and faithfully in all things, to hold and inviolably obſerve all and ſingular the ſtatutes and ordinances aforeſaid: And by his ſaid charter gave, granted and confirmed to the ſaid warden and ſcholars clerks, and to their ſucceſſors, the ſaid places being in the pariſh aforeſaid, in the town aforeſaid, to have and to hold in common to the ſaid warden and ſcholars clerks, and to their ſucceſſors, for their abode and habitation in the ſaid college of the ſaid biſhop, and his ſucceſſors. biſhops of Wincheſter, in free, pure, and perpetual frankaimoigne; which charter, grant, or foundation laſt mentioned, of the ſaid biſhop of Wincheſter, the prior and convent of the cathedral church of Wincheſter, being the chapter of the ſaid biſhop, by their charter, bearing date the 7th day of December, in the third year of the reign of the ſaid king, ſealed with their common or publick ſeal, did allow and confirm. And we the ſaid warden and ſcholars clerks to the king's majeſty, further moſt humbly certify that the ſaid William of Wickham, biſhop of Wincheſter, founder of the ſaid college, further of and with the licence of the ſaid lord the king Richard, for the better rule, government and reformation of his ſaid college, and of the ſaid ſcholars clerks, and the members of the ſame whatſoever, who were or afterwards ſhould be admitted and elected into the ſaid college, certain ſtatutes or ordinances founded, eſtabliſhed and ordained, and by his ſaid ſtatutes or ordinances enacted and ordained, that all the ſaid ſcholars clerks, except his own kinſmen, for the firſt two years after their reſpective admiſſion into the ſaid college, ſhould be called ſcholars, and that always afterwards (the ſaid two years being finiſhed), they ſhould be * called fellows of the ſaid college, and into the number of the fellows ſhould be admitted; but by the ſaid ordinances willed, that his kinſmen immediately from their firſt admiſſion into the ſaid college, ſhould enjoy the names of fellows, and into the number of the ſaid fellows ſhould be admitted: And further ordained and eſtabliſhed, that all the ſaid ſcholars clerks of the ſaid college, after they had taken their ſeveral degrees in their reſpective faculties, ſhould cauſe themſelves to be advanced to holy orders, and to the prieſthood, under the pain of perpetual excluſion from the ſaid college. And the ſaid William of Wickham, biſhop of Wincheſter, the founder aforeſaid,

Confirmation by the prior and convent.

Statutes made by the founder.

* P. 481

ſaid, further enacted, ordained and willed, that if any of the ſcholars clerks, or ſcholars or fellows aforeſaid, ſhould commit any enormous crime or other fault, whereby great damage, prejudice, or ſcandal would be produced in the ſaid college, or infamy ſhould ariſe to the ſaid college, and ſhould appear manifeſtly convicted of the ſaid fault or crime, before the warden of the ſaid college, the vice-warden, five deans, three burſers, and five others of the ſeniors of the ſaid college, (one of whom he willed ſhould be a civilian and the other a canoniſt) ſitting together with the ſaid warden, either by his own proper confeſſion, or by evidence of the crime or fault, he willed that from thence he ſhould, by the force of the ſaid ordinance, without the remedy of any complaint, be perpetually excluded, and be ipſo facto expelled from the ſaid college. And further we moſt humbly certify, that the ſaid William of Wickham, biſhop of Wincheſter, the founder aforeſaid, further did ordain and enact, that the reverend fathers in Chriſt the lords biſhops of Wincheſter, his ſucceſſors, for ever ſhould be the true patrons and protectors of the ſaid college, and ſupervisors and preſervers of the ſtatutes of the ſaid college. And they are his viſitors of the ſaid college for ever; and he gave full power to the biſhops of Wincheſter, and to their ſucceſſors, upon all and ſingular the points and articles contained in the ordinances aforeſaid, and he gave power to the ſaid biſhops of Wincheſter, and to their ſucceſſors, of correcting and puniſhing the omiſſions, crimes and offences whatſoever of the ſcholars clerks, or of the ſcholars, or of the fellows of the ſaid college, and of doing and exerciſing all and ſingular other matters even to the deprivation or amotion of the ſcholars clerks, or of the ſaid fellows from the ſaid college. And further we moſt humbly certify, that the ſaid William of Wickham, biſhop of Wincheſter, the founder aforeſaid, by his ſtatutes aforeſaid, ordained that every ſcholar clerk of his ſaid college, upon his firſt admiſſion into the ſaid college, and alſo upon his admiſſion into the number of the fellows of the ſaid college, upon the holy goſpels of God ſhould take his corporal oath that he would inviolably maintain and obſerve all the ſaid ſtatutes and ordinances of the ſaid biſhop and founder, or otherwiſe without contradiction, would humbly ſubmit to the puniſhments inflicted for his non-obſervance of them; and that he ſhould further make oath, that if he ſhould happen to be expelled, excluded or amoved from the ſaid college, becauſe of his bad morals or other demerits, that he would never proſecute, moleſt or diſquiet, in any court ſecular or eccleſiaſtical, the ſaid college, warden, vice-warden, fellow or ſcholar of the ſaid college, by reaſon of the expulſion

If any of the ſcholars committed an enormous fault, and thereof ſhould be convicted before the warden vice-warden, &c. he ſhould be expelled from the college.

The biſhops of Wincheſter and their ſucceſſors viſitors of the ſaid college for ever.

from

from the ſaid college, but would expreſsly renounce in * writing, with the force of a contract, every action or ſuit, and the ſuing out of any letters, and the intreaties of princes, nobles and others whatſoever. And we further moſt humbly certify, that Daniel Appleford, in the writ to this ſchedule annexed, named in and upon his election and admiſſion into the place, and number of one of the ſcholars of the ſaid college, to wit, on the 30th day of Auguſt, in the 14th year of the reign of the ſaid lord the now king, and afterwards in and upon his admiſſion into the number of the ſaid fellows, and into the place of one of the fellows of the ſaid college, on the 30th day of Auguſt, in the 16th year of the reign of the ſaid lord the now king, upon the holy goſpel of God, and according to the command of the ſaid ſtatutes and ordinances of the ſaid biſhop of Wincheſter, the founder aforeſaid, took the ſaid oath, that he well and fully would obey and obſerve the ſaid ſtatutes and ordinances in all things; and that if he ſhould be amoved or expelled from the ſaid college, that he would never proſecute, moleſt, or diſquiet, in any courts ſecular or eccleſiaſtical, the ſaid college, warden, vice warden, fellow, or ſcholar, by reaſon of ſuch his expulſion, but would renounce and releaſe, in writing, all actions or ſuits to be made by him in that behalf. And we further moſt humbly certify, that the ſaid Daniel Appleford, being one of the ſcholars clerks and of the fellows of the ſaid college, on the 30th day of March laſt paſt, in the 23rd year of the reign of the ſaid lord the now king, being lawfully ſummoned, perſonally appeared before Michael Woodward, doctor in divinity, then warden of the ſaid college, ——— Hanbury, batchelor in divinity, then vice-warden of the ſaid college, and five deans of the ſaid college, to wit, Thomas Bewmont, Bennet Hobb, William Hemins, maſters of arts, Roger Stanley, and Joſeph Cox, batchelors of laws, and three burſars of the ſaid college, to wit, Edward Spencer, Chriſtopher Minſhall, maſters of arts, and John Longworth, batchelor of laws, and five of the ſeniors of the ſaid college, to wit, Edward Lawe, doctor of laws, ſenior canoniſt of the ſaid college, Benjamin Spurway, ſenior civilian of the ſaid college, and Richard Rowlandſon, Robert Seaſter, and Nathaniel Petham, maſters of arts, then being ſeniors of the ſaid college, ſitting together with the ſaid Michael Woodward, the warden aforeſaid; and the ſaid Daniel Appleford ſo ſummoned and appearing before the ſaid warden, vice-warden, five deans, three burſars aforeſaid, and the ſaid five ſenitors of the ſaid college, by evidence of the fact, manifeſtly appeared and is guilty of an enormous crime by him the ſaid Daniel Appleford perpetrated,

* P. 482

That Appleford took the oath to obſerve the college ſtatutes;

and afterwards was convicted of an enormous fault, and expelled.

trated, whereby great damage, prejudice, and ſcandal was produced to the ſaid college, and whereby infamy hath ariſen in the ſaid college; and of the ſaid crime, by their ſentence judicially pronounced, was convicted, whereby the ſaid Daniel Appleford from thenceforth from the ſaid college, and from the place of one of the ſcholars clerks, and of one of the fellows of the ſaid college, by force of the ſaid ordinance in that behalf as aforeſaid made, without the remedy of any ſuit, for ever was excluded, and ipſo facto was deprived; and alſo the reverend father in Chriſt, George then and now biſhop of Wincheſter aforeſaid, the ſucceſſor of William of Wickham, the true patron, ſuperviſor, protector and viſitor of the ſaid college, and the * final ordinary judge of all controverſies in the ſaid college (for this purpoſe ſpecially called upon, and upon the appeal and complaint made upon the premiſſes by the ſaid Daniel Appleford) by his viſitatorial authority, ſolemnly declared and adjudged, that the ſaid Daniel Appleford was guilty as aforeſaid, of the enormous crime, whereby great ſcandal did ariſe to the ſaid college, and decreed that the ſaid Daniel Appleford from the ſaid college ſhould be for ever amoved, excluded and expelled, and by his viſitatorial authority aforeſaid, decreed, allowed, and confirmed the expulſion and amotion of the ſaid Daniel Appleford from the ſaid college; and the name of the ſaid Daniel Appleford, by the ſaid Michael Woodward, warden of the ſaid college, (thoſe things concurring and being obſerved, which of right and by the ſtatutes and ordinances of the ſaid biſhop of Wincheſter the founder, are required) from the publick book of the ſaid college was eraſed and blotted out; and afterwards one Thomas Lee, kinſman of the ſaid William, biſhop of Wincheſter, the founder of the ſaid college, into the place of one of the fellows of the ſaid college, in the ſtead and place of the ſaid Daniel Appleford, in the due manner was elected and admitted, and now is one of the ſcholars clerks and fellows of the ſaid college, according to the command of the ſtatutes and ordinances aforeſaid, by the ſaid biſhop and founder in that behalf made: And the ſaid college now is full of and with the warden and ſeventy ſcholars clerks, into the ſaid college in the due manner admitted and elected; and therefore of the ſaid lord the king we moſt humbly pray judgment, whether the court of the ſaid lord the king, of and in the premiſes any further will intermeddle.

and confirmed by the viſitor upon an appeal.

* P. 483

His name raſed out of the college book.

Another choſen in his room.

And the college hath the full complement, and the return concludes to the juriſdiction.

*MICHAEL WOODWARD,*

Warden of the college of St. Mary of Wincheſter in Oxford.

*This caſe is reported 2 Levinz 14. and the return after ſeveral arguments was held good.*

## Mandamus for Ayloffe.

Mandamus to the warden of All Souls college Oxford, to admit Ayloffe to a fellowſhip of the ſaid college.

CHARLES the 2d. by the Grace of God, of England, Scotland, France, and Ireland, King, defender of the faith, &c. To the Warden of the College of All Souls of the faithful deceaſed in the Univerſity of Oxford, greeting: Whereas Joſeph Ayloffe, eſquire, to the place of one of the fellows of the college of All Souls of the faithful deceaſed in the Univerſity of Oxford, aforeſaid, according to the cuſtom and ordinance of the ſaid College hitherto uſed, was duly elected, into which place of one of the fellows of the ſaid College the ſaid Joſeph Ayloffe ought to be admitted, and according to his election, often times hath preſented himſelf, nevertheleſs you, the Warden of the ſaid College, not ignorant of the premiſſes, the ſaid Joſeph into the place of one of the fellows of the ſaid College, unjuſtly have refuſed to admit in contempt of us, to the great damage and grievance of the ſaid Joſeph, and to the manifeſt injury of his eſtate, as we have underſtood from his complaint, we therefore willing that due and ſpeedy juſtice be done to the ſaid Joſeph in this behalf, as is right, command you, as we have oftentimes commanded you, firmly enjoyning that immediately after the receipt of this writ, you admit or cauſe to be * admitted the ſaid Joſeph
* P. 484. Ayloffe into the ſaid place of one of the fellows of the ſaid College, with all the liberties, privileges, and commodities to the ſaid place belonging or appertaining, or ſignify to us cauſe to the contrary, leaſt through your default, complaint may be made to us again, and how you ſhall execute this our command, make to appear before us, from the day of Eaſter in fifteen days, whereſoever we ſhall then be in England, under the pain of eighty pounds, then returning to us this our writ, witneſs W. Scroggs, at Weſtminſter, the 12th day of February in the 33d year of our reign.

ASTRY.

The execution of this writ appears in a certain ſchedule to this writ annexed.

Return—Henry 6th by letters patent founded this college at the ſupplication and coſts of Chichely archbiſhop of Canterbury, and appointed a ſpecial viſitor to determin all offences, controverſies and complaints, and prays judgment if he ought to give any other anſwer

The anſwer of Thomas Jeames, Warden of the ſaid College.

To the moſt ſerene Lord the now King, I Thomas Jeames, profeſſor of divinity, warden of the college of all Souls, of the faithful deceaſed, in the univerſity of Oxford, moſt humbly certify, that before the erection aud founda-

tion

tion of the said college within written, the lord Henry the 6th, late king of England, by his letters patent, under his great seal of England, bearing date at his manor of Kennington, the 20th day of May, in the 16th year of his reign, reciting that the reverend father Henry Chichely, archbishop of Canterbury, primate of all England, and his godfather, by whose hands he had received the sign of holy baptism, wishing the increase of the clergy of his kingdom of England, which then it was known had greatly decreased, had supplicated him, that he the said late king at the proper costs, charges and expences of the said archbishop, a certain perpetual college of one warden, and certain scholars in Oxford, and in the university there, to study and to pray for the good estate of the said late king, and of his said godfather whilst they should live, and for the souls of the said late king, and his said godfather, and for the souls of the most renowned prince Henry, late king of England his father, and Thomas late duke of Clarence his uncle, and of the Dukes, Earls, Barons, Knights, Esquires, and the other nobles and subjects of his said late father, and of the said late king, who had ended their lives in war, and for the souls of all the faithful deceased, according to the ordinances of his said godfaher and of his successors would vouchsafe to found, make and erect, therefore the said late king Henry the 6th, animated by the supplications of his said godfather, for the honour of our Lord Jesus Christ, of the most glorious blessed Virgin Mary his mother, and of all the saints of God, erected, and by the tenor of his said letters patent founded, made and established, to endure for ever, a certain perpetual college, to be governed according to the tenor of the said letters patent, of one warden, and twenty scholars, abiding in the said town of Oxford, and in the university of the same, to study and to pray for his good estate, and for the good estate of his godfather whilst they should live, and for the souls of the said late king, and his said godfather, when they should depart this life, and for the souls of the said most renowned prince his father, and Thomas late duke of Clarence, and of the Dukes, Earls, Barons, Knights, Esquires, and subjects aforesaid, and for the souls of all the faithful deceased, upon a certain messuage called Berford Hall * then lately called Charletons inn, six shops, and one empty street annexed to the same in Oxford, upon a certain angle opposite to the east end of the parochial church of the blessed Virgin Mary, in the streets called Cat-street, and St. Mary-street, containing in length one hundred and seventy-two feet, and in breadth one hundred and sixty-two feet, which the said late king * P. 485.

 had

had by the appointment of his said godfather of the grant of Thomas Chichely archdeacon of Canterbury, Henry Penworth clerk, and Robert Danvers, feoffors thereof, to the use of his said godfather, to have and to hold to him and his heirs for ever, with the assent of his said godfather, for the building such college thereupon, whom and whose successors archbishops of Canterbury, for his pious designs, and his costs and expences about the erecting and founding of the said college, he made and intended to make as other founders of the said college, and created, made and ordained, Richard Andrew Clerk, warden of the said college, and Thomas Laventram, Thomas Lango, Thomas Winterborne, Robert Stoo, Thomas Lay, Richard Letoffe, William Hornedow, John Segour, John Porter, Walter Hest, Robert Carew, Simon Hoare, John Julian, Walter Hopton, Robert Stephens, Robert Sebrough, William Oneston, Thomas Elstor, Richard Ward, and Richard Penwortham, scholars of the said college, elected, and for this purpose chosen by his said godfather, to be governed, corrected, deprived and amoved according to ordinances and statutes of his said godfather, and of his successors archbishops of Canterbury; willing and granting by his said letters patent, that the said warden and his successors, wardens of the said college, according to the ordinances and statutes aforesaid might elect, collect and admit more scholars, even to the number of forty persons, to be governed, corrected, deprived and amoved according to the ordinances and statutes aforesaid, whom and whose successors so elected, collected and admitted, to be governed, corrected, deprived and amoved according to the said statutes and ordinances; † as scholars and members of the said college; and the said late king, for himself and his heirs, willed and granted by his letters patent aforesaid, that the said warden dying, or resigning, or being removed or deprived for any cause whatsoever, the scholars of the said college for the time being, according to the form and effect of the statutes and ordinances aforesaid, should and might elect another fit person into warden, and for warden of the said college, who should be admitted into the office of warden of the said College, by his said godfather, and his successors, archbishops of Canterbury, and not by the said late king, nor his heirs, to be governed, corrected, deprived and amoved according to the ordinances and statutes aforesaid, and in like manner such warden dying or resigning, or being deprived or amoved, in any manner whatsoever in future, the said scholars of the * said college should and might have, according to the ordinances and statutes aforesaid, the free election

† These words "*the said late king for himself, his heirs and successors for ever, willed and granted should be had, held and in all things reputed*," seem to be wanting here—see ante 474, line 26

* P. 485.

election of the new wardens, whom to be admitted, confirmed, governed, corrected, deprived and amoved, as aforesaid, and them in such manner into wardens elected, admitted and confirmed as aforesaid, the said late king willed and granted for himself, and his heirs for ever, as much as in him lay, should be perpetual wardens of the said college without licence sued or obtained from the said late king or his heirs, and no others, nor in any other manner; also willing that the scholars of the said college, or any of them dying or resigning, or being deprived or removed in future, that the said warden and his successors for ever, should have according to the ordinances and statutes aforesaid, the free election, admission and confirmation of the new scholars to be put in their stead, whom and no others so elected, confirmed and admitted, the said late king willed and granted for himself, and his heirs for ever, without licence sued and obtained from the said late king, or his heirs, should be scholars and members of the said college, to be governed, corrected, deprived and amoved according to the ordinances and statutes aforesaid, further willing that the warden and scholars aforesaid, for the time there being, and their successors for ever, should be called the Warden and College of All Souls of the faithful deceased of Oxford; and to the said Lord the now King, I further most humbly certify, that after the making of the said letters patent, to wit, within one year next after the date of the same, the said college, by the said late archbishop of Canterbury, upon the said ground in the letters patent aforesaid mentioned, was erected, founded, and by the said archbishop was endowed, and thereupon the said late archbishop by virtue of the letters patent aforesaid, afterwards to wit, on the first day of May, in the seventeenth year of the reign of the said late King Henry the 6th, founded, made, and published in writing, and established divers ordinances and statutes for the good and wholesome government, rule and correction of the warden and scholars of the said college, for the time being, and among others a certain ordinance or statute for the better rule, government and correction of the warden and scholars of the said college for the time being, in these words following, to wit, Likewise we enact, will and ordain, that the most reverend fathers in Christ, the archbishops of Canterbury, our successors, according to the will and ordinance of the most christian prince Henry the 6th, king of England, the illustrious and principal founder of the said college, as in his letters patent made upon the foundation of the said college is more fully contained, shall be co-founders with him for ever: and that they shall be the true patrons, and perpetual protectors

Laws made by the archbishop.

tectors of the ſaid college, and ſupervifors of the ſaid college, and of the perſons, poſſeſſions, rights ſpiritual and temporal, liberties and privileges of the ſaid college, and the ordinary preſervers of the obſervance of the ordinances and ſtatutes of the ſame, and viſitors of the ſaid college; wherefore we will, ordain and declare that it may be law-
* P. 487. ful for the lord archbiſhop of Canterbury * for the time being, as often as it ſhall ſeem neceſſary and expedient to him, freely to come to the ſaid college by himſelf, or by his commiſſaries, to wit, the prior or ſubprior of Chriſt's church of Canterbury, the official of the court of arches, or the dean of the ſaid court, whom and no others, we will and declare that he can depute his commiſſaries for this purpoſe, jointly and ſeverally as it ſeemeth good to him, and to ſummon the warden and all and ſingular the ſcholars and fellows of the ſaid college into one place within the ſaid college, to which moſt reverend father for the time being, and his commiſſaries only, by virtue of this our preſent ordinance and ſtatute, we grant full power of making the moſt exact inquiry upon all the points and articles contained in our ordinances and ſtatutes, by means of the warden and all and ſingular the fellows and ſcholars aforeſaid, even though it ſhould be neceſſary to do this under an oath to be taken before them, to declare the mere and full truth, if the force, orders and ſtatutes of the ſaid college have been duly executed and obſerved by them all, as far as concerned each of them, and alſo upon all and ſingular the matters concerning the ſtate, advantage and honour of the ſaid college, and which they knew or believed ſhould be reformed in the ſaid college, and in its members, beſides of making the moſt exact inquiry of ſecret matters, although they ſhould not be ſpecially examined upon theſe, of correcting and alſo of puniſhing according to the force, form and effect of the ſaid ordinances and ſtatutes, the exceſſes, negligences, crimes and offences of any of the members of the ſaid college howſoever committed, and of duly reforming attempts againſt the ſaid ordinances and ſtatutes, and of doing, exercifing, and alſo diſpatching the things which in the premiſſes and concerning them ſhall be neceſſary or conducive, even though they ſhould happen to proceed to the deprivation or removal of the warden, vice-warden, or any other whatſoever from his adminiſtration or office, or to the removal of any fellow or ſcholar of the ſaid college from the ſame, the ſtatutes and ordinances of the ſaid college requiring it. Which warden, vice-warden, fellows and ſcholars, and all the other officers of the ſaid college whatſoever, we will and

and command effectually to attend and obey the ſaid lord archbiſhop and his commiſſaries aforeſaid, as to all and ſingular the premiſſes aforeſaid, enacting moreover that no perſon in the viſitations or examinations to be made in our ſaid college ſhall ſay, depoſe or declare any thing againſt the warden, or any other fellow or ſcholar of the ſaid college, but what he ſhall believe to be true, or of which public report or fame hath prevailed againſt him; and we will that the ſame ſhould be obſerved by the warden, under the obligation of the oath to be taken by them all to the ſaid college, and we moſt ſtrictly charge the conſciences of the moſt reverend fathers our ſucceſſors whatſoever for the time being, and of his commiſſaries, that in doing and executing the premiſſes according to the doctrine of the Apoſtle, not ſeeking their own but what is Jeſus Chriſt's, they be content with moderate entertainment only, to wit, meat and drink, and having God alone before their eyes, laying aſide favour, hatred entreaty * fear, reward, pretences, occaſions and cauſes whatſoever, they duly attend, and faithfully execute in all things, the ſaid office of inquiſition, correction and due reformation, as they will in this caſe, give an account before God at his laſt judgment; moreover enacting, that the warden of the ſaid college upon exceſſes and delinquincies being diſcovered againſt him, and brought to the inquiſitions or viſitations to be held by the ſaid lord archbiſhop, and his commiſſaries as aforeſaid, in no manner ſhould require the preſence of the diſcoverers to be allowed to him, or the names of the diſcoverers to be explained to him, or the diſcoveries or names of ſuch perſons to be delivered to him, but upon ſuch diſcoveries that he immediately anſwer before the ſaid archbiſhop or his commiſſaries, and that he ſubmit to due correction for the ſame, according to the command and tenor of the ordinances and ſtatutes of the ſaid college, delays, appeals and complaints, and other remedies of law and fact being laid aſide, whereby his correction and puniſhment may be deferred or in any wiſe hindered, except the ſaid lord archbiſhop or his commiſſaries proceed againſt the ſaid warden to the deprivation of the benefice, or to the affecting of the perſon of the ſaid warden, in which caſes we allow all lawful defences to be ſaved to him notwithſtanding our ordinance aforeſaid: And to the ſaid lord the king, I now further certify, that by virtue of the letters patent of the ſaid late king Henry the 6th, the ſaid Henry Chichely, late archbiſhop of Canterbury, and all and ſingular his ſucceſſors archbiſhops of Canterbury, have been viſitors, and every of them for the time being hitherto hath

* P. 488.

hath been visitor of the said college, and of the warden and all the fellows and scholars there abiding, and for the time being, and have decreed, settled and determined all disputes, controversies and complaints of and concerning the election and appointment of the fellows and scholars in the said college, upon appeal being made to the said archbishop of Canterbury for the time being; and such elections, appointments and complaints in no other manner have been adjudged or determined; and to the said lord the now king I further most humbly certify, that at the time of issuing of the said writ to me directed, and to this schedule annexed, and long before the most reverend father in Christ, and the Lord, William by divine providence, was and as yet is lord archbishop of Canterbury, primate and metropolitan of all England, and visitor of the said college; and that the said Joseph Aylosse hitherto hath not appealed to the said archbishop to settle and determine the right of the election of said Joseph to the place of one of the fellows of the said college, as of right he ought, if it seemed to him expedient, all and singular which things, I the said warden most humbly submit to the judgment of the court of the said lord the king himself, and most humbly pray judgment of the said court, if I ought to be compelled to give any other or further answer to the said writ, &c.

That Aylosse hath not appealed to the visitor.

After several exceptions taken to this return, the court allowed it to be good.— *It is reported, T. Jones*, 174.

---

* P. 489.

## * Mandamus for Lee.

### Michaelmas the 2d. William and Mary.

Mandamus to the master warden or commissary of the prerogative court of Canterbury to restore Lee to the office of proctor of the said court.

WILLIAM and Mary by the Grace of God of England, Scotland, France, and Ireland, king and queen, &c.—To Richard Raines knight, doctor of laws, master, warden or commissary of the prerogative court of Canterbury lawfully appointed: Whereas Godfrey Lee into the place and office of one of the proctors general of the prerogative court of Canterbury of the arches London, duly was admitted and sworn, and in that place and office hath carried and demeaned himself well, nevertheless you Richard Raines, lightly regarding the premisses, the said Godfrey

frey Lee unduly, and without any reasonable cause, from that place and office have unjustly removed in contempt of us, and to the great damage and grievance of the said Godfrey, and to the manifest injury of his estate, as we have understood from his complaint, we therefore willing that due and speedy justice be done to the said Godfrey in this behalf as is right, command you, as we have often times commanded you, that immediately after the receipt of this writ, you restore or cause to be restored the said Godfrey Lee into the said office or place of one of the proctors general of the prerogative court of Canterbury aforesaid, with all the liberties, privileges, preheminences and commodities to that office and place belonging or appertaining, or signify to us cause to the contrary, least through your default, complaint may be made to us again, and how you shall execute this our command, make to appear to us at Westminster, on Monday after the morrow of All Souls, and this in no wise omit under the pain of 40l. then returning to us this our writ. Witness John Holt knight, at Westminster, the 27th day of October, in the second year of our reign. By the Court.

ASTRY.

The answer of the within named Richard Raines, knight, doctor of laws, master and commissary of the prerogative court of Canterbury, to this writ appears in a certain schedule to this writ annexed.

R. RAINES.

Return, That Lee was suspended for not paying a tax laid on him.

I Richard Raines, knight, doctor of laws, master and commissary of the prerogative court of Canturbury, by virtue of the writ to me directed, and to this schedule annexed, to the most serene lord the now king, and the lady the now queen, at the day and place in the said writ contained most humbly certify, that the prerogative court of Canterbury in the said writ mentioned, is an antient ecclesiastical court of the archbishop of Canterbury, and that the archbishop of Canterbury for the time being hath had, and hath been accustomed to have the government and regulation of the judges, advocates, proctors and other officers and ministers whatsoever of the said court; and further I most humbly certify, that the said prerogative court of Canterbury of the arches London, the high court of * admiralty of England, and also the consistorial court of the bishop of London, and the other ecclesiastical courts are held, and for a long time have been held in a certain Inn called Doctors Commons, situate in the parish of St. Benedict, near Paul's

* P. 490.

wharf, in the ward of Caſtle Baynard London, in which Inn the judges of the ſaid courts, and alſo very many doctors of law, advocates, proctors, and other officers attending the ſaid courts, conſtantly have reſided, and as yet do reſide for the exerciſe of their offices there reſpectively, and that the expences in and about the courts of juſtice, and the other public places within the ſaid Inn, and the other public neceſſary charges concerning the judges, advocates, proctors, and other officers aforeſaid are ſuſtained, and always hitherto have been accuſtomed to be ſuſtained at the coſts of the judges, advocates, proctors, and the other officers and and miniſters of the ſaid courts who have occupied, and have been accuſtomed to occupy the ſaid courts of juſtice, and other public places to tranſact their buſineſs, and for that reaſon, as often as it has been neceſſary the ſaid judges, advocates, proctors, officers and miniſters of the ſaid courts have aſſeſſed and levied, and have been accuſtomed to aſſeſs and levy upon themſelves certain rates or taxes to defray ſuch charges and expences, and that the ſaid Godfrey Lee being aſſeſſed as aforeſaid, ten ſhillings upon him to defray the public charges and expences aforeſaid, in and about the courts of juſtice, and the other public places aforeſaid, and the other public neceſſary charges concerning the judges, advocates, proctors, and other officers aforeſaid, ſo as aforeſaid taxed, had denied to pay the ſame, whereupon I Richard Raines, being judge and commiſſary of the ſaid prerogative court of Canterbury, and in the court of juſtice within the ſaid Inn, on the 30th day of July in the ſecond year of the reign of the within written lord and lady the now king and queen, for the ſaid cauſe, did deny audience to the ſaid Godfrey Lee, in a certain cauſe between George Gittins and Francis Moore, concerning the goods of Damaris Stane deceaſed, he requiring audience of me the judge then and there in that cauſe, until he ſhould ſubmit himſelf in the premiſſes, or the ſaid court ſhould otherwiſe ordain; and the Godfrey from the place or office of one of the proctors of the ſaid court, I have not otherwiſe nor in any other manner amoved: And I further certify, that the archbiſhops of Canterbury for the time being, and that ſee being vacant, the dean and chapter of the church of Canterbury, are the ſpiritual keepers of the archieopiſcopal ſee aforeſaid, and from the time whereof the memory of man is not to the contrary, have been viſitors of the ſaid prerogative court of Canterbury, and have heard and determined, and for the ſaid time have been accuſtomed to hear and determine all the appeals or plaints whatſoever, by the officers, proctors, or miniſters of the ſaid court brought to

That the archbiſhop of Canterbury & ſede vacante the dean & chapter of Canterbury are viſitors of the prerogative court.

to their visitations, and also have reformed, corrected, reversed and restored, and for the said time ought and have been accustomed to reform, correct, reverse, and restore all grievances whatsoever by the judge of the said court, against any of the officers, proctors, or ministers of the said court unduly committed or inflicted, and that the dean and chapter of the said cathedral church of Canterbury, who at the time of the refusal of the audience as aforesaid, to the said Godfrey, were, and as yet are, the spiritual keepers of the said archieopiscopal see of Canterbury, (the said see at that time and as yet being vacant) have had, and have full power and authority to hear, examine and determine the complaint of the said Godfrey in this behalf, and also to * restore the said Godfrey to the place and exercise of one of the proctors of the said court (if justice should require) and that the said Godfrey hath not brought his complaint in this behalf to the said visitors, nor hath submitted himself to the said court.

* P. 491. That Lee hath not appealed to the visitors.

*This case is reported* 3 *Mod.* 332. 3 *Lev.* 309. *Shower* 217, 251, 261. *It was adjudged that no mandamus lay for a proctor, and therefore the court would not grant a peremptory mandamus.*

---

## Mandamus for Lee.

### Michaelmas, the 2d William and Mary.

WILLIAM and Mary, &c. To Henry Newton, doctor of laws, of the reverend father in Christ, and the Lord, Henry by divine permission, lord bishop of London, vicar general in spirituals, and also of the consistorial court of the bishop of London, principal official lawfully constituted, whereas Godfrey Lee into the place and office of one of the proctors general of the consistorial court of the bishop of London aforesaid, duly was admitted and sworn, and in that office and place hath carried and behaved himself well, neverthelefs you Henry Newton, lightly regarding the premisses, the said Godfrey Lee unduly and without reasonable cause, from that office unjustly have amoved in contempt

Mandamus to the vicar general of the bishop of London and principal official of his consistory court to restore Lee to the office of one of the proctors of the said court.

tempt of us, and to the great damage and grievance of the said Godfrey, and to the manifest injury of his estate, as from his complaint we have understood, we therefore willing that due and speedy justice be done to the said Godfrey Lee in this behalf as is right, command you, as we have often commanded you, that immediately after the receipt of this writ, you restore, or cause to be restored, the said Godfrey Lee into the said place and office of one of the proctors general of the consistorial court of the bishop of London aforesaid, with all liberties, privileges, preheminences and commodities to that office and place belonging and appertaining, or signify to us cause to the contrary, least through your default, complaint may be made to us again, and how you shall have executed this our command, make to appear to us at Westminster, on the wednesday after the morrow of St. Martin, then returning to us this our writ, and in this in no wise omit under the pain of 80 pounds. Witness John Holt, knight, at Westminster, the 7th day of November, in the second year of our reign.

By the Court.

ASTRY.

The answer of the within named Henry Newton, doctor of laws, of the reverend father in Christ, and the Lord, Henry by divine permission, lord bishop of London, vicar general in spirituals, and also of the consistorial court of the bishop of London, official principal, to this writ appears in a certain schedule to this writ annexed.

HEN. NEWTON.

* P. 492. Return To the like effect as the former.

* I Henry Newton, doctor of laws of the reverend father in Christ, and the Lord, Henry by divine permission, lord bishop of London, vicar general in spirituals, and also of the consistorial court of the bishop of London, official principal, by virtue of the writ to me directed, and to this schedule annexed, to the most serene lord and lady the now king and queen, on the day and place in the said writ contained most humbly certify, that the consistorial court of the bishop of London in the said writ mentioned, is an antient ecclesiastical court, and the supreme consistory of the episcopal see of London; and I further do most humbly certify, that the said consistorial court of the bishop of London, and the court of Canterbury of the arches London, and also the prerogative court of Canterbury, and the high court of admiralty of England, and other ecclesiastical courts are held, and have been long held in a certain Inn called Doctors Commons, situate in the parish of S. Benedict,

St. Benedict, near Pauls wharf, in the ward of Castle Baynard London, in which Inn the judges of the said courts, and also very many doctors of law, advocates, proctors, and other officers attending the said courts constantly have resided, and as yet reside, for the exercise of their offices there respectively, and that the expences in and about the courts of justice, and the other public places within the said Inn, and the other public necessary charges concerning the judges, advocates, proctors and officers aforesaid, are sustained, and always hitherto have been accustomed to be sustained at the costs of the judges, advocates, proctors, and the other officers and ministers of the said courts, who have occupied, and have been accustomed to occupy the said courts of justice, and other public places, to transact their business, and for that reason, as often as there hath been need, the said judges, advocates, proctors, officers and ministers of the said courts have assessed and levied, and have been accustomed to assess and levy upon themselves certain rates or taxes, to defray such charges and expences, and that the said Godfrey Lee being assessed as aforesaid, to the sum of ten shillings upon him, to defray the publick charges and expences aforesaid, in and about the courts of justice aforesaid, and the other public places aforesaid, and the other public necessary charges concerning the judges, advocates, proctors and officers aforesaid, so as aforesaid taxed, had denied to pay the same; wherefore I Henry Newton, being judge of the said consistorial court of the bishop of London, and sitting in the court of justice in the said Inn, on the 5th day of July, in the second year of the reign of the within written lord and lady, the now king and queen, for the cause aforesaid, have denied audience to the said Godfrey Lee, in a certain cause between Mary Norris, otherwise Herbert, against Thomas Herbert, in a cause of nullity of marriage, by reason of the tender age of her the said Mary, (he requiring audience of me the judge then and there in the said cause) until he should submit himself in the premisses, or the said court should otherwise order therein, and the said Godfrey Lee, from the place or office of one of the proctors of the said court, I have not otherwise nor in any other manner amoved; and I further certify, that the bishop of London for the time being is, and from the time whereof the memory of man is not to the contrary, hath been supreme judge of the consistorial court of London aforesaid, and hath heard and determined, and for the whole time aforesaid hath been used to hear and determine all appeals or plaints whatsoever, by any of the * officers, proctors, or ministers of the said court * P. 493
to

to the biſhop of London aforeſaid brought, and alſo hath reformed, corrected, reverſed and reſtored, and for the ſaid time hath been uſed to reform, correct, reverſe and reſtore all grievances whatſoever, by the judge of the ſaid court, againſt any of the officers, proctors, or miniſters of the ſaid court unduly committed or inflicted, (if juſtice ſhould require) and that the ſaid Godfrey hath not brought any complaint in this behalf to the ſaid biſhop of London, nor hath ſubmitted himſelf to the ſaid court.

---

## Mandamus for Lee.

### Michaelmas the 2d William and Mary.

Another mandamus to the principal official of the court of arches to reſtore Lee to the office of proctor of the ſaid court.

WILLIAM and Mary, &c.—To George Oxendon, doctor of laws, of the court of Canterbury of the arches London, principal official lawfully conſtituted, whereas Godfrey Lee into the place and office of one of the proctors general of the court of arches aforeſaid, duly was admitted and ſworn, and in that place and office hath carried and behaved himſelf well, neverthelefs, you George Oxendon, lightly regarding the premiſſes, &c. *as in the former writ.*

The anſwer of the within named George Oxendon, doctor of laws of the court of Canterbury of the arches London, within written, principal official, to this writ appears in a certain ſchedule to this writ annexed.

GEORGE OXENDON.

Return to the like effect as the former with ſome variations.

I George Oxendon, doctor of laws of the court of Canterbury of the arches London, principal official lawfully conſtituted, by virtue of the writ to me directed, and to this ſchedule annexed, to the moſt ſerene lord and lady the now king and queen, at the day and place in the ſaid writ contained, moſt humbly certify, that the court of Canterbury of the arches London, in the ſaid writ mentioned, is an antient eccleſiaſtical court, and ſupreme conſiſtory of the archiepiſcopal ſee of Canterbury; that the archbiſhop of Canterbury for the time being, from the time whereof the

the memory of man is not to the contrary, hath had, and hath been accuſtomed to have the rule and government of the judges, advocates, proctors, and of the other officers and miniſters of the ſaid court whatſoever, and from time to time for the whole time aforeſaid, hath made, and hath been accuſtomed to make ſtatutes and ordinances for their better rule and government, as often as there hath been need, and that every perſon admitted a proctor of the ſaid court, at the time of his admiſſion into that place, hath taken, and always hath been accuſtomed to take oath before the judge of the ſaid court for the time being, to obſerve the ſtatutes and laudable cuſtoms of the ſaid court; which oath Godfrey Lee in the ſaid writ named, at the time of his admiſſion to be proctor of the ſaid court, before the judge of the ſaid court did take; and that among the ſtatutes of the ſaid court for the better rule and government of the ſaid proctors, officers, and miniſters of the ſaid court by Thomas Arundell * heretofore archbiſhop of Canterbury, made, there is one whereby it is enacted, that no proctor or proctors of the ſaid court, ſhould in any manner receive any cauſes or other buſineſs brought to the ſaid court, nor he nor they ſhould in any manner proſecute therein without the advice of ſome advocate, under pain of removal from his or their office or offices of proctor, or proctors, and that the ſaid court of Canterbury of the arches London, and alſo the prerogative court of Canterbury, and the high court of admiralty of England, and the conſiſtorial court of the biſhop of London, and other courts are held, and for a long time have been held in a certain Inn called Doctors Commons, ſituate in the pariſh of St. Benedict, near Pauls wharf, in the ward of Caſtle Baynard London, in which Inn the judges of the ſaid courts, and alſo very many doctors of laws, advocates, proctors, and other officers attending the ſaid court conſtantly have reſided, and as yet do reſide for the exerciſe of their offices there reſpectively, and that the expences in and about the courts of juſtice, and the other public places within the ſaid Inn, and the other public neceſſary charges concerning the judges, advocates, proctors and officers aforeſaid, are ſuſtained, and always hitherto have been accuſtomed to be ſuſtained, at the coſts of the judges, advocates, and the other officers and miniſters of the ſaid courts who have occupied, and have been accuſtomed to occupy the ſaid courts of juſtice, and the ſaid public places for tranſacting their buſineſs, and for that reaſon, as often as it hath been neceſſary, the ſaid judges, advocates, proctors, officers and miniſters of the ſaid courts have aſſeſſed, and have been accuſtomed to aſſeſs and levy

* P. 494.

levy upon themselves certain rates or taxes to defray such charges or expences; and that the said Godfrey Lee being assessed to 10 shillings upon him to defray the public charges and expences aforesaid, in and about the courts of justice, and the other public necessary charges concerning the judges, advocates, proctors and officers, so as aforesaid taxed, had refused to pay the same; and also the said Godfrey, as proctor of the said court of Canterbury of the arches London, did receive a certain cause between William Richards against William Beawe, brought into the said court of Canterbury of the arches London, and the same prosecuted in the said court without the advice of any advocate, against the form of the said statute; wherefore I George Oxendon, being judge of the said court of Canterbury of the arches London, and sitting in the judgment seat, within the said Inn, on the 2d day of July, in the 2d year of the reign of the lord and lady the now king and queen, denied audience to the said Godfrey Lee in the said cause, for the causes aforesaid, he the said Godfrey Lee then and there requiring audience of me the said judge in the said cause between the said William Richards against the said William Beawe, until he should submit himself in the premisses, or the said court should thereon otherwise order, and the said Godfrey from his place or office of one of the proctors of the said court, I have not otherwise, or in any other manner amoved: And I further certify, that the archbishop of Canterbury for the time being, and in the vacancy of the said see, the dean and chapter of the cathedral church of Canterbury, are the spiritual keepers of the archiepiscopal see aforesaid; and from the time whereof the memory of man is not to the contrary have been visitors of the said court of Canterbury of the arches London, and have heard and determined and for the time aforesaid have been accustomed to hear and determine all
* P. 495. appeals or plaints by any of the officers, * proctors, or ministers of the said court to the visitors brought, and also have reformed, corrected, reversed and restored, and for the said time have been accustomed to reform, correct, reverse and restore all grievances by the judge of the said court, against any of the officers, proctors, or ministers of the said court unduly committed or inflicted, and that the dean and chapter of the said cathedral church of Canterbury, who at the time of the denial of the audience as aforesaid, to the said Godfrey, were, and as yet are the spiritual keepers of the said archiepiscopal see of Canterbury, (that see at the said time, and as yet being vacant) have had, and have full power and authority to hear, examine, and determine the complaint

complaint of the ſaid Godfrey in this behalf, and to reſtore the ſaid Godfrey to the place and exerciſe of one of the proctors of the ſaid court (if juſtice may require it) and that the ſaid Godfrey hath not brought hitherto any complaint in this behalf to the ſaid viſitors, nor hath ſubmitted himſelf to the ſaid court.

GEO. OXENDON.

---

## Mandamus for Merrett.

To the preſident of the college of Phyſicians to reſtore Merrett to a fellowſhip of the ſaid college.

CHARLES the 2d. by the Grace of God of England, Scotland, France, and Ireland, King, defender of the faith, &c. To the preſident of the college or commonalty of the faculty of phyſick London, greeting: Whereas Chriſtopher Merrett, doctor of phyſick, to the place of one of the fellows of the college of phyſicians London, according to the cuſtom of the ſaid college hitherto uſed, duly was admitted and ſworn, with divers franchiſes, liberties, privileges and commodities, according to the cuſtom of the ſaid college appertaining, in which place of one of the fellows of the ſaid college he hath continually carried and behaved himſelf well; nevertheleſs you the preſident, lightly regarding the premiſſes, the ſaid Chriſtopher unduly and without reaſonable cauſe, from the ſaid place of one of the fellows of the ſaid college of phyſicians, and from the ſaid franchiſes, liberties, privileges and commodities to the fellows there belonging as aforeſaid, unduly have amoved in contempt of us, to the great damage and grievance of the ſaid Chriſtopher, and to the manifeſt injury of his eſtate, as from his complaint we have underſtood: We therefore willing that due and ſpeedy juſtice be done to the ſaid Chriſtopher in this behalf as is right, command you, firmly enjoyning that immediately after the receipt of this writ, you reſtore or cauſe to be reſtored the ſaid Chriſtopher Merrett into the ſaid place of one of the fellows of the ſaid college of phyſicians, with all the franchiſes, liberties, privileges and commodities aforeſaid to the ſaid place belonging or appertaining, or ſignify to us cauſe to the contrary thereupon, leaſt through your default, complaint may be made to us again, and how you ſhall execute this our command, make to appear to us at Weſtminſter, on the Wedneſday next after the morrow of All Souls next ensuing, then returning to us this our writ. Witness F. Pemberton, at Westminster, the 28th day of October, in the 33d year of our reign.

By Rule of Court.

ASTRY.

* P. 496. * The execution of this writ appears in a certain schedule to this writ annexed.

Return. The answer of J. M. knight, president of the college or commonalty within written.

Letters patent of Henry the 8th whereby the physicians of London were incorporated.

"*Vide 8th Report 212, and 3d Lord Raymond 289.*"

I J. M. knight, president of the college or commonalty of the faculty of physick London, to the lord the king, most humbly certify, that the lord Henry the 8th, late king of England, by his letters patent, sealed with his great seal of England, bearing date at Westminster the 23d day of September, in the 10th year of his reign, for the public good of his kingdom of England, and for the due exercise of the faculty of physick made, and incorporated John Chambre, Thomas Lineacre, Ferdinand De Victoria, Nicholas Halswell, John Francis, and Robert Yaxley, doctors of physick, and all the men of the said faculty of pyhsick of and in the city of London; and by his said letters patent granted, that they should be in thing and in name, one body and perpetual commonalty or perpetual college, and that the said commonalty or college, every year for ever, should elect and make some provident man of the said commonalty skilful in the faculty of medicine, president of the said college or commonalty, to supervise, review and govern for that year, the college or commonalty aforesaid, and all the men of the said faculty, and the businesses of the same, and that they should have perpetual succession, and a common seal to serve for the businesses of the said commonalty and president, for ever; and that they by the name of the president of the college or commonalty of the faculty of physick might plead, and be impleaded: And that the president and college or commonalty, and their successors, might make lawful and discreet assemblies of themselves, and statutes and ordinances for the good government, oversight and correction of the college or commonalty aforesaid, and of all the men exercising the said faculty in the said city, or within seven miles in the circuit of the said city, according to the exigence or necessity, as often as and when need should be, and that no person in the said city, or within seven miles in the circuit of the same, should exercise the said faculty unless that he should

ſhould be admitted to the ſame by the ſaid preſident and commonalty, or their ſucceſſors for the time being, by the letters of the ſaid preſident and college, ſealed with their common ſeal, under the pain of one hundred ſhillings for every month in which ſuch perſon not admitted as aforeſaid, ſhould exerciſe the ſaid faculty: And the ſaid late king, by his ſaid letters patent granted, that the preſident and college of the ſaid commonalty for the time being, and their ſucceſſors for ever, ſhould yearly, elect four perſons who ſhould have the overſeeing, ſearching, correction and government of all and ſingular the perſons uſing the ſaid faculty within the ſaid city and circuit aforeſaid, and the puniſhment of the ſame for their offences in not well executing, doing, and uſing the ſame, as by the ſaid letters patent more fully appears; and I further certify, that by a certain act made in the parliament of the ſaid late king Henry the 8th, begun and held at London, the 15th day of April, in the * 14th year of his reign, and from thence prorogued to Weſtminſter, in the county of Middleſex, to the laſt day of July, in the 15th year of the reign of the ſaid late king, and then and there held, it was enacted, That the ſaid corporation of the ſaid commonalty and fellowſhip of the faculty of phyſick aforeſaid, and all and ſingular the grants, articles, and other things contained and ſpecified in the ſaid letters patent, ſhould be approved, granted, ratified and confirmed, and clearly authorized and admitted, and ſhould be good, lawful and available to the ſaid body corporate, and to their ſucceſſors for ever, in as ample and large a manner as they could be underſtood, thought and conſtrued; and that by the ſaid act, it was further enacted and eſtabliſhed, that the ſaid ſix perſons in the ſaid letters patent, named as principals, and firſt named of the ſaid commonalty and fellowſhip, chooſing to themſelves two more of the ſaid commonalty afterwards for ever, ſhould be called and named Elects; and that the Elects annually ſhould chooſe one of themſelves to be preſident of the ſaid commonalty, and that as often as it ſhould happen that any of the places of the ſaid Elects ſhould be vacant by death or otherwiſe, that then the ſurvivors of the ſaid Elects, within 30 or 40 days next after the death of them or any of them, ſhould elect, nominate and admit one or more, as the caſe ſhould require, of the moſt learned and ſkilful of and in the ſaid faculty in London to ſupply the ſaid place and number of eight perſons, ſo that he or they who ſhould be ſo elected, ſhould be firſt ſtrictly examined by two of the ſurvivors, according to the form deviſed by the ſaid Elects, and approved by the ſaid ſurvivors, as by the ſaid act more fully appears; and I

Confirmed by act of parliament.

* P. 497.

 further

further certify, that by a certain other act made in the parliament of the said late lord king Henry the 8th, begun and held at Westminster aforesaid, on the 28th day of April, in the 32d year of his reign, it was among other things enacted by the authority of the said parliament, that the president of the said commonalty and fellowship for the time being, and the commonalty and fellows of the same, and every fellow thereof who then was, or afterwards should be, and their successors, and the successors of each and every of them at all time and times after the making of the said act, should be exonerated from watch and ward in the said city of London, as by the said act among other things more fully appears: And I further certify, that before the coming of the writ to this schedule annexed, to wit, on the 2d day of September, in the year of our Lord 1648, Christopher Merrett, doctor of physick, in the said writ named, by the then president and commonalty aforesaid, according to the tenor of the said letters patent, and of the said act first above mentioned, to exercise the said faculty in the due manner was licensed and admitted, which licence and admission remain in their full force and effect, and that the said Christopher from the free faculty and licence to exercise and practice the science and art of physick according to the form of the statute for this purpose enacted, or from his place of one of the said fellows of the said commonalty in no manner after his admission aforesaid ever was removed, as by the said writ is supposed, but the said Christopher as yet is one of the said fellows of the said commonalty; and I further certify, that the said * college or commonalty in no other manner was incorporated than as above is expressed, nor that any other fellows of the college or commonalty aforesaid, by the said letters patent, or the act of parliament aforesaid, or by any other grants of the said late king Henry the 8th, or of any of his ancestors or successors kings or queens of England, or by any other act of the parliament of this kingdom of England, were nominated or appointed except the fellows aforesaid: And I further certify, that after the making of the act of parliament last mentioned, and before the said 2d day of September in the year of our Lord 1648, by the then president of the college or commonalty aforesaid, of his own will, it was enacted, that there should be thirty persons of the college or commonalty aforesaid, who should be called fellows, of whom the president should be one, with intention that they should be aiding and assisting the president of the college or commonalty aforesaid for the time being, in the councils to be appointed by him; and I further certify, that on the 16th day

by another act exempted from watch and ward.

Merrett licenced by the president and commonalty to practice physick which licence is still in force.

* P. 498.

Council of 30 called fellows to assist the president.

day of May, in the year of our Lord 1651, the said Christopher by the then president of the college or commonalty aforesaid, was admitted to be one of the said thirty persons called fellows last mentioned, according to the ordinance aforesaid; and I further most humbly certify to the lord the now king, that upon the 28th day of September, in the 32d year of the reign of our lord the now king, I then being president of the said college, caused the said Christopher Merrett, and the other fellows, *made according to the ordinance aforesaid*, to be summoned to be present at the council to be held in and upon the 30th day of September, in the 32d year aforesaid, about the second hour after mid-day of the said day, in the Great Hall of the said college, situate in Warwick-lane, London, in the parish of Christ Church, in the ward of Farringdon within, to aid and assist me the then president of the said college or commonalty, in governing the college or commonalty aforesaid, and the other men exercising the said faculty of physick in the said city of London, or within seven miles in the circuit of the said city, according to the tenor of the letters patent and statute aforesaid; and although I the said president and the other fellows on the said 30th day of September, and at the hour aforesaid, and in the Hall aforesaid, in the council aforesaid, had collected and assembled ourselves, nevertheless the said Christopher Merrett on the said 30th day of September, in the Hall aforesaid did not appear, but without any just or reasonable cause, did absent himself from the said council then held as aforesaid, by reason of which I the said president and the other fellows then and there assembled, lost the aid and council of the said Christopher in governing the college or commonalty aforesaid, and the other men exercising the said faculty within the circuit aforesaid; and I further certify, that upon the 20th day of December, in the 32d year aforesaid, I then being president of the said college, caused the said Christopher Merrett and the other fellows made by virtue of the said ordinance, to be summoned to be present at the council to be held in and upon the 23d day of December, in the year aforesaid, about the 2d hour * after mid-day of the said day, in the Great Hall of the said college, situate in Warwick-lane London, aforesaid, in the parish and ward aforesaid, to aid and assist me the then president of the said college or commonalty, in governing the college or commonalty aforesaid, and the other men exercising the faculty of physick in the said city of London, or within seven miles in the circuit of the said city, according to the the tenor of the letters patent and statute aforesaid; and although

Several defaults of Merrett in not attending the council.

* P. 499.

although the ſaid preſident and the other fellows on the ſaid 23d day of December, and at the hour aforeſaid, in the Hall aforeſaid, in the council aforeſaid, had aſſembled and collected themſelves, nevertheleſs the ſaid Chriſtopher Merrett on the ſaid 23d day of December, in the Hall aforeſaid did not appear, but without any juſt or reaſonable cauſe, from the ſaid council then aſſembled did abſent himſelf, by reaſon of which, I the ſaid preſident and the other fellows then and there aſſembled, loſt the aid and council of the ſaid Chriſtopher in governing the college or commonalty aforeſaid, and the other men exerciſing the ſaid faculty within the ſaid city: And I further certify, that upon the 26th day of March, in the 33d year of the reign of the ſaid lord the now king, I then being preſident of the ſaid college, cauſed the ſaid Chriſtopher Merrett, and the other fellows made by virtue of the ordinance aforeſaid, to be ſummoned to be preſent at the council to be held in and upon the 28th day of March, in the 33d year aforeſaid, about the third hour after mid-day of the ſaid day, in the Great Hall of the ſaid college, ſituate in Warwick-lane London, aforeſaid, in the pariſh and ward aforeſaid, to aid and aſſiſt me the then preſident of the ſaid college or commonalty aforeſaid, in governing the college, and the other men exerciſing the ſaid faculty of phyſick in the ſaid city of London, or within ſeven miles in the circuit of the ſaid city, according to the tenor of the letters patent and ſtatute aforeſaid; and although the ſaid preſident and the other fellows, on the ſaid 28th day of March, and at the hour aforeſaid, in the hall aforeſaid, in the council aforeſaid had aſſembled and collected themſelves, nevertheleſs the ſaid Chriſtopher Merrett on the ſaid 28th day of March in the ſaid Hall did not appear, but without any juſt or reaſonable cauſe, himſelf from the council aforeſaid then aſſembled did abſent, by reaſon of which, I the ſaid preſident, and the other fellows then and there aſſembled, loſt the aid and counſel of the ſaid Chriſtopher in governing the college or commonalty aforeſaid, and the other men exerciſing the ſaid faculty within the circuit aforeſaid; and I further certify, that upon the 23d day June, in the 33d year aforeſaid. I then being preſident of the ſaid college; cauſed the ſaid Chriſtopher Merrett, and the other fellows made by virtue of the ordinance aforeſaid, to be ſummoned to be preſent at the council, to be held upon the 25th day of June, in the 33d year aforeſaid, about the third hour after mid-day of the ſaid day in the Great Hall of the ſaid college, ſituate in Warwick-lane London, aforeſaid, in the pariſh and ward aforeſaid, to aid and aſſiſt me the then preſident of the college

lege or * commonalty aforeſaid, in governing the college or commonalty aforeſaid, and the other men exerciſing the ſaid faculty of phyſick in the ſaid city of London, or within ſeven miles in the circuit of the ſaid city, according to the tenor of the letters patent and ſtatute aforeſaid; and although the ſaid preſident and the other fellows on the ſaid 25th day of June, and at the hour aforeſaid, in the Hall aforeſaid, in the council had aſſembled and collected themſelves, nevertheleſs the ſaid Chriſtophe Merrett, on the ſaid 25th day of June, in the Hall aforeſaid did not appear, but without any juſt or reaſonable cauſe, himſelf from the ſaid council then aſſembled did abſent, by reaſon of which I the ſaid preſident and the other fellows then and there aſſembled, loſt the aid and counſel of the ſaid Chriſtopher in governing the college or commonalty aforeſaid, and the other men exerciſing the ſaid faculty within the ſaid circuit; and I further certify to the ſaid lord the king, that at an aſſembly of me then preſident of the college or commonalty aforeſaid, and of the other fellows of the ſaid college held on the 30th day of September, in the 33d year of the reign of the ſaid lord the king, in the Great Hall aforeſaid, the ſaid Chriſtopher Merrett then preſent, was accuſed by me the then preſident of his abſence aforeſaid, from the ſaid council at the ſaid four ſeveral times; and his negligences by his abſence as aforeſaid, to the ſaid Chriſtopher Merrett then preſent in the ſaid aſſembly charged and objected were proved; and the ſaid Chriſtopher Merrett then preſent, was aſked by me the ſaid preſident in the ſaid aſſembly, if he the ſaid Chriſtopher could ſay any thing in juſtification or excuſe of his abſence aforeſaid, or of any of them, and the ſaid Chriſtopher Merrett could ſhow no cauſe or excuſe for his abſence aforeſaid, nor of any of them, from the council aforeſaid; therefore then and there by me the ſaid preſident and the other fellows at the aſſembly aforeſaid, from the place of one of the fellows, by virtue of the ordinance aforeſaid, he was amoved, and as yet is amoved, and I moſt humbly pray judgment of the court of the lord the king, if he to the ſaid place of one of the fellows aforeſaid, by virtue of the ordinance aforeſaid, ought to be reſtored, &c.

* P. 500.

and amoved from the place of one of the fellows of the council for his abſence.

*Upon motion for this mandamus the Lord Chief Juſtice Pemberton was ſtrongly of opinion that no mandamus lay as reported*, 2 Shower 178.—*But it ſeems it was nevertheleſs granted.*

* Mandamus

* P. 501.

## * Mandamus for Dunkins.

Dunkins executor in a will offers to prove the will in the prerogative court, the judge refuses to admit the probate or to grant administration, whereupon the executor appeals to the delegates, and this mandamus issues to them to admit the proving thereof before them, and to grant administration to the executor.

CHARLES the 2d by the grace of God, &c.—To our beloved in Christ Mathew Hale, knight, our chief justice, assigned to hold pleas before us, John Vaughan knight, our chief justice of the Bench, William Wild knight and baronet, one of our justices assigned to hold pleas before us, Timothy Littleton knight, one of the barons of our Exchequer, Timothy Baldwyn, Mondiford Brampton, and Edward Lowe knights, three masters of our court of Chancery, Richard Loyd, William Trumbull, Thomas Boucher, William Oldys, and Thomas Briggs, doctors of laws, respectively, our judges, delegates greeting: Whereas M. D. in his life time, to wit, on the 10th day of September, in the 25th year of our reign, at London, to wit, in the parish of St. Mary L'Bow, in the ward of Cheap, made his testament and last will in writing, and then and there did make and constitute one M. D. his son, sole executor of his last will and testament, and afterwards, to wit, on the 9th day of October, in the 25th year aforesaid, at London aforesaid, in the parish and ward aforesaid, the said M. D. the father died, having at the time of his death, bona notabilia to the value of one thousand pounds and more in divers dioceses of our kingdom of England; and whereas the said M. D. aforesaid, at the time of his death, at London aforesaid, in the parish and ward aforesaid, had divers great sums of money due to the said M. D. deceased, from divers subjects of our kingdom of England, and then and there was indebted to divers other our subjects in divers other great sums of money; and whereas afterwards, after the death of the said M. D. the father, to wit, on the 13th day of November, in the 25th year aforesaid, at London aforesaid, in the parish and ward aforesaid, the said M. D. the son, produced and exhibited the testament and last will aforesaid of the said M. D. the father, in the prerogative court of Canterbury, before Robert Wiseman, knight, doctor of laws, surrogate of the venerable man the lord Leoline Jenkyns, knight, doctor of laws, of the prerogative court of Canterbury master warden or commissary lawfully constituted, at that time judge of the said prerogative court, to prove the said testament according to the law and custom of England, in the due form of law, and then and there in the said court did offer to prove in the common form of law, the testament and last will aforesaid, by his oath, according to the use and custom of the said court,

and

and prayed administration of the goods and chattles of the said M. D. the father, by the said prerogative court, according to the command of the law to be decreed and committed to him; nevertheless the said judge of the said prerogative court (to whom the proving of the said testament, and the committing of the administration of the goods and chattles of the said M. D. the father, then and there of right belonged) no suit or controversy of or concerning the right and title of the said M. D. the son, to demand probate of the said testament in the said prerogative court, then or as yet depending, hath altogether refused to admit proof of the said testament, or to cause administration of the goods and chattles of the said M. D. the father to be decreed or committed to the said M. D. the son, according to the form of law, * and the said Leoline Jenkins, now judge of the said prerogative court, to whom of right it hath belonged to do these things, hath refused and denyed to do the same, which matter now by the appeal of the said M. D. the executor (because of the grievance done to him in the said prerogative court, in not admitting proof of the said testament) in this behalf had, before you the judges delegates in this behalf lawfully deputed, depends undetermined, and you the judges delegates, as yet have deferred to admit proof of the said testament, and to cause administration of the goods and chattles of the said M. D. the father, to the said M. D. the executor, according to the command of law, to be decreed and committed, by reason of which the said M. D. the executor is totally disabled and incapable to recover the debts of the said M. D. the deceased, or to pay the debts of the said deceased, in contempt of us, and to the great damage of the said M. the executor, and in obstruction of the faithful administration of the goods and chattles of the said M. D. deceased, as by the complaint of the said M. D. the executor we have understood, we herefore willing that due and speedy justice be done to the said M. D. the executor, command you, firmly enjoyning that immediately after the receipt of this writ, you cause and procure without delay, proof of the said testament by the said M. D. the executor, in the due and common form of law to be made, to be admitted, and administration of the goods and chattles of the said M. D. the decased, to the said M. D. the executor, according to the law and custom of our kingdom of England, to be decreed and committed, and that you do and execute without delay, all and singular the things to the speedy proving of the said testament, and to the commiting of the administration aforesaid, according to the command of law necessary, or signify to us

* P. 502.

cauſe wherefore you cannot do this, leaſt through your default complaint may be made to us again, and how you ſhall execute this our command, make to appear to us at Weſtminſter, on the day next after, &c.— then returning to us this our writ. Witneſs Mathew Hale, knight, at Weſtminſter, &c.

---

## Bromhall againſt Johnſon.

### Eaſter, 31ſt Charles IId.

Suggeſtion for mandamus.—The plaintiff's huſband made his will in writing and his wife executrix thereof which ſhe after his death proved in the prerogative court, but the judge refuſed to grant her a probate or adminiſtration under ſeal, but granted adminiſtration to the defendant cum teſtamento annexo, on pretence that the plaintiff had renounced the executrixſhip upon which plaintiff appealed to the delegates and ſuggeſts all this matter in the king's bench for a mandamus to the delegates to grant her the probate under ſeal.

ENGLAND, to wit,—Be it remembered, that on Thurſday next after fifteen days of Eaſter, in this ſame term, before the Lord the King at Weſtminſter, comes Elizabeth Bromhall, widow, relict and executrix of the teſtament and laſt will of Thomas Bromhall, eſquire, late her huſband, deceaſed, in her proper perſon, and gives the court of the Lord the King now here, to underſtand and to be informed, that whereas the ſaid Thomas Bromhall, in his life time, to wit, on the 15th day of June, in the year of our Lord one thouſand ſix hundred and ſeventy five, * at London, to wit, in the pariſh of St. Mary L'Bow, in the ward of Cheap, made his teſtament and laſt will in writing, and then and there thereupon did make and ordain the ſaid Elizabeth ſole executrix of his laſt will and teſtament aforeſaid, and afterwards, to wit, on the 17th day of June, in the 35th year of the reign of the lord the now king, at London aforeſaid, in the pariſh and ward aforeſaid, the ſaid Thomas Bromhall died, having at the time of his death, bona notabilia to the value of one thouſand pounds and more, in divers dioceſſes in this kingdom of England, and whereas alſo the ſaid Thomas Bromhall at the time of his death at London aforeſaid, in the pariſh and ward aforeſaid, had divers great ſums of money due and payable to

the

the ſaid Thomas Bromhall by divers ſubjects of the ſaid lord the now king of his kingdom of England, and then and there was indebted to divers other ſubjects of the ſaid lord the now king, in divers great ſums of money, amounting in the whole to one thouſand pounds and more; and whereas alſo the ſaid Elizabeth Bromhall afterwards, and after the death of the ſaid Thomas Bromhall, to wit, on the 24th day of June, in the 30th year aforeſaid, at London aforeſaid, in the pariſh and ward aforeſaid, produced and exhibited the ſaid teſtament and laſt will of the ſaid Thomas Bromhall in the prerogative court of Canterbury, before Richard Lloyd, knight, doctor of laws, ſurrogate of the venerable man the Lord Leoline Jenkins knight, doctor of laws, then maſter or commiſſary of the prerogative court of Canterbury lawfully conſtituted, (and then being judge of the ſaid prerogative court,) to prove in the due form of law, the ſaid teſtament according to the law and cuſtom of this kingdom of England, and to have and obtain letters teſtimonial of ſuch proof, and commiſſion of the adminiſtration thereon, under the ſeal of the ſaid prerogative court in that behalf atteſted, that thereupon according to the command of law, it ſhould appear that the ſaid Elizabeh Bromhall was the executrix of the laſt will and teſtament aforeſaid, and had the adminiſtration thereof as the law of this kingdom of England in itſelf commands and requires; and the ſaid Elizabeth then and there in the ſaid court proved the teſtament and laſt will aforeſaid, upon her oath, according to the uſe and cuſtom of the ſaid court, in the common form of law, and demanded adminiſtration in letters teſtimonial of ſuch proof, and adminiſtration in that behalf atteſted under the ſeal of the prerogative court aforeſaid, according to the command of law, that thereupon it might appear and be manifeſt that the ſaid Elizabeth was the executrix of the teſtament and laſt will aforeſaid, according to ſuch proof thereupon in the common form as aforeſaid made, and that ſhe had adminiſtration thereof like as the law of this kingdom of England in itſelf commands and requires; nevertheleſs the ſaid judge of the ſaid prerogative court (to whom the probate of the teſtament and laſt will aforeſaid, and the commiting of the adminiſtration thereupon, and the granting of ſuch letters teſtimonial of right belonged) no ſuit or controverſy of or concerning the validity of the ſaid teſtament, or of or concerning the right and title of the ſaid Elizabeth to be executrix, or to pray probate of the ſaid teſtament in the ſaid prerogative court then or as yet depending, entirely hath refuſed to certify under the ſeal of the ſaid court the letters * teſtimonial of * P. 504.

 ſuch

ſuch proof of the teſtament and laſt will aforeſaid, in the prerogative court aforeſaid, ſo as aforeſaid, upon her oath, in the common form proved, and admitted, and to grant or to cauſe to be granted the committing of the adminiſtration thereupon atteſted in that behalf, under the ſeal of the ſaid court, according to the command of law, or any probate of the teſtament and laſt will aforeſaid, in the prerogative court aforeſaid, in the common form as aforeſaid proved; and the ſaid Leoline Jenkins, now judge of the ſaid prerogative court (to whom of right it belonged to do theſe things) hath entirely refuſed and denyed to do, or to cauſe them to be done; which matter now by the appeal of the ſaid Elizabeth, becauſe of the grievance done to the ſaid Elizabeth in the ſaid court, in not granting or permitting the ſaid Elizabeth to have the letters teſtimonial aforeſaid, in this behalf had, before Robert Atkyns knight, one of the juſtices of the ſaid lord the now king of the bench. Thomas Jones knight, one of the juſtices of the ſaid lord the now king, aſſigned to hold pleas before the king himſelf, Vere Berty eſquire, one other juſtice of the ſaid lord the now king of the bench aforeſaid, William Dolbin knight, one other juſtice of the ſaid lord the now king, aſſigned to hold pleas before the king himſelf, Francis Brampton knight, one of the barons of the exchequer of the lord the now king, Charles Perrott, Henry Fauconbridge, Thomas Pinfold, Thomas Bridges, John Ediſbury, Robert Thompſon, Charles Hedges, Stephen Brice, and Robert Pepper, doctors of laws reſpectively, judges, delegates in this behalf lawfully deputed, depends undetermined, which judges, delegates as yet have deferred to make or to cauſe to be certified the ſaid letters teſtimonial of ſuch proof of the teſtament aforeſaid, in the common form as aforeſaid, made and admitted, and the committing of the adminiſtration thereon atteſted under the ſeal of the prerogative court aforeſaid, according to command of law in that behalf, to the ſaid Elizabeth to be granted, or any ſuch probate under the ſeal of the ſaid court, by reaſon of which the ſaid Elizabeth Bromhall is totally diſabled and incapable to recover or to pay the debts of the ſaid Thomas Bromhall, in contempt of the ſaid lord the now king, and to the great damage and grievance of the ſaid Elizabeth, and alſo in obſtruction of the execution of the ſaid teſtament, and of the adminiſtration of the goods and chattles of the ſaid Thomas Bromhall, and againſt the due form of the law of the land of this kingdom of England, and this the ſaid Elizabeth is ready to verify, whereupon the ſaid Elizabeth

Elizabeth most humbly imploring the aid and munificence of the court of the said lord now the king here prays relief; and the writ of the said lord the now king to the said judges delegates, or to some other competent judge in this behalf, commanding them and every of them that they may make and procure to be granted to the said Elizabeth without delay, and to be certified according to the law and custom of this kingdom of England, letters testimonial of the said proof of the testament and last will aforesaid in the Prerogate Court aforesaid, so as aforesaid upon her oath in the common form proved and admitted, and the committing of the administration thereon, attested under the seal of the said court, according to the command of law in that behalf, notwithstanding the confession of letters of administration with the testament annexed of the goods and chattles which belonged to the said Thomas * Bromhall at the time of his death to one Martha Johnson, or to any other person or persons whatsoever, under pretence of renunciation by the said Elizabeth; and also notwithstanding any inhibition from the judges delegates in or upon the cause or matter aforesaid in that behalf issued, and that they may do and execute without delay, all and singular the things necessary according to the command of law, to the compleat proof of the testament and last will aforesaid, and to the attesting and certifying the granting and committing of the administration in that behalf, or that they may signify to the said lord the now king cause wherefore they cannot or ought not do the same, at their peril; and it is granted to her, &c.

* P. 505.

Mandamus granted.

---

# Baker against Baker.

## Easter, 29th Charles IId.

Suggestion for a mandamus.

ENGLAND to wit —— Be it remembered that on the Wednesday next, after one month of Easter in the same term, before the Lord the King at Westminster, comes Jane

The widow of one who died intestate and had bona notabilia in divers diocesses, obtained decree in the Prerogative Court to have administration granted to her, and she gave security thereon according to the statute; nevertheless, the judge refused to grant her letters of administration under seal. All which is suggested in the King's Bench, to obtain a mandamus to the judge to grant her letters of administration.

Jane Baker, widow and relict of John Baker, late of the city of Exeter, gentleman, who died intestate, in her proper person, and gives the court of the said lord the now king here to understand and to be informed, that whereas the said John Baker, the younger, the husband of the said Jane, on the 15th day of January in the 28th year of the reign of the lord the now king at the city of Exeter aforesaid, within the diocess of Exeter died intestate, having while he lived and at the time of his death, the said Jane his wife, and divers goods and chattles, rights and credits, to the value of five hundred pounds and more in divers diocesses or jurisdictions within the province of Canterbury, whereby the commiting the administration of all and singular the goods and chattles, rights and credits, which belonged to the said John Baker, the younger, at the time of his death, of right belonged to Gilbert by Divine Providence then and as yet archbishop of Canterbury, primate and metropolitan of all England: and whereas the said John Baker at the time of his death aforesaid at the said city of Exeter aforesaid, had divers great sums of money from divers subjects of this kingdom of England due to the said John Baker, and then and there was indebted to divers other subjects of this kingdom of England, in divers other great sums of money; and by reason whereof she the said Jane being the widow of the said John Baker deceased, to whom the administration of all and singular the goods and chattles, rights and credits of of the said John, according to the form of the statute in such case lately made and provided, of right then belonged and appertained and as yet belongs and appertains; she the said Jane afterwards after the death of the said John Baker, to wit on the 29th day of March in the 29th year of the reign of the said lord the now king, came into the Prerogative Court of Canterbury before Richard Lloyd, knight, doctor of laws, surrogate of the venerable man the lord Leoline Jenkins, knight, doctor of laws of the said Prerogative Court of Canterbury, master, warden or commissary lawfully

* P. 506. appointed, then judge of the said * Prerogative Court, and then and there prayed that administration of all and singular the goods and chattles rights and credits of the said John, late while he lived the husband of the said Jane by the said Prerogative Court according to the laws of this kingdom of England, to her the said Jane should be committed and decreed, and thereupon afterwards to wit on the said 29th day of March in the 29th year of the reign of the said lord the now king aforesaid, the said judge of the said Prerogative Court decreed administration of all and singular the goods and chattles, rights and credits of the said John Baker to

the ſaid Jane, in the due manner and according to the law of this kingdom of England, and then and there took good ſecurity of the ſaid Jane for the true adminiſtration of the goods, chattles and debts which belonged to the ſaid John Baker at the time of his death, by the ſaid Jane to be made according to the form and effect of the ſtatute, in ſuch caſe made and provided. Neverthelefs the ſaid judge of the ſaid Prerogative Court, hitherto altogether hath deferred and as yet defers to make ſeal and delivers the letters of adminiſtration of the goods and chattles, rights and credits of the ſaid John Baker to the ſaid Jane, under the ſeal of the ſaid court, as the manner is, according to the command of law; by reaſon of which the ſaid Jane is totally diſabled and incapable to recover or pay the debts of the ſaid John Baker, deceaſed, in contempt of the ſaid lord the now king, and to the damage, prejudice and grievance of the ſaid Jane, and in obſtruction of the faithful adminiſtration of the goods and chattles of the ſaid John Baker. Whereupon the ſaid Jane moſt humbly imploring the aid and munificence of the court of the ſaid lord the now king here prays relief; and the writ of the ſaid lord the king of mandamus to the ſaid judge of the ſaid Prerogative Court or to ſome other competent judge in this behalf to be directed, commanding them and every of them that without delay they may make ſeal and deliver letters of adminiſtration of the goods and chattles, rights and credits of the ſaid John Baker, to the ſaid Jane, under the ſeal of the ſaid Prerogative Court, according to the law and cuſtom of this kingdom of England; and that they may cauſe and procure to be done all and ſingular the things in the like caſe uſed to be done, and neceſſary to be done, to the ſpeedy and perfect committing of the ſaid adminiſtration, according to the command of law, any appeal of or concerning the premiſſes heretofore had or made in any wiſe notwithſtanding: and it is granted to her, &c.

Mandamus granted.

---

## Mandamus for Eaſtwick.

Mandamus to the mayor, commonalty and citizens of London, to reſtore Eaſtwick to the office of common councilman.

CHARLES by the grace of God, &c. To the mayor and commonalty and citizens of the city of London greeting, Whereas Stephen Eaſtwick citizen of the ſaid city, according to the cuſtom in the ſaid city hitherto uſed, duly was elected and appointed one of the common council of the

the city of London, for the ward of Bridge within, London; in which office of one of the common council of the ſaid city for the ſaid ward, he conſtantly carried and demeaned himſelf well, nevertheleſs you the mayor and commonalty and citizens of the ſaid city lightly regarding the premiſſes, the ſaid Stephen unduly and without reaſonable
* P. 507 * cauſe from the ſaid office of one of the common council of the ſaid city and of the ſaid ward unduly have removed in contempt of us, and to the great damage and grievance of the ſaid Stephen, and to the manifeſt injury of his eſtate, as from his complaint we have underſtood, we therefore willing that due and ſpeedy juſtice be done to the ſaid Stephen in this behalf as is right, command you and every of you as we have often commanded you, that immediately after the receipt of this writ you reſtore or cauſe to be reſtored the ſaid Stephen, into the ſaid office of one of the common council of the ſaid city for the ſaid ward, with all liberties, privileges and commodities to the ſaid office belonging or appertaining, or ſignify to us cauſe wherefore you will not, or cannot do the ſame, leaſt through your default, complaint may be made to us again, and this in no wiſe omit under the pain of 40l. and how you ſhall execute this our command make to appear to us on the morrow of the Holy Trinity, whereſoever we ſhall then be in England, then returning to us this our writ. Witneſs Francis Bacon, at Weſtminſter, the 28th day of May, in the twenty-third year of our reign.

By the Court.

*ASKE.*

The execution of this writ appears in a certain ſchedule to the ſaid writ annexed.

Return.

The anſwer of the within named mayor and commonalty and citizens of the city of London.

That Eaſtwick being preſent in a court of common council and a queſtion in the ſaid court being moved concerning him, he was ordered to withdraw, which he refuſed to do, but made diſturbance in the court, for which reaſon they expelled him from the office of common councilman.

London to wit. — We John Gayer, knight, mayor of the city of London, and the commonalty and citizens of the ſaid city, to the lord the king at Weſtminſter; certify, that the city of London is an antient city, and that the freemen of the ſaid city from the time whereof the memory of man is not to the contrary, have been and as yet are incorporated

porated, as well by the name of the mayor and commonalty and citizens of the city of London, as by the name of the mayor and commonalty of the city of London; and that the said mayor and commonalty and citizens, so incorporated from the whole time aforesaid, have been, and as yet are, and consist of several companies, guilds, mysteries and fraternities, of freemen of the city of London aforesaid. And that the aldermen of the city of London aforesaid, from the whole time aforesaid, have been and as yet are parts and members, of the said mayor and commonalty and citizens of the said city; and that within the said city there is had, and from the whole time aforesaid was had, a certain court of the said lord the king, and of his progenitors and predecessors, kings and queens of England, of record, commonly called the court of the common council, held before the mayor or his deputy, the aldermen for the time being, and the commons of the said city, (for this purpose according to the custom of the said city elected,) within the said city assembled, upon reasonable summons thereto, according to the custom of the said city, which commons so elected, together with the mayor or his deputy and the aldermen have been, and have been accustomed to be of the * common * P. 508.
council of the said city, to consult of and upon the business, things and matters, concerning the said city, in such common council to be debated, and propounded, and to give and declare their assent and dissent to the same, as well for themselves as for the other freemen and inhabitants of the said city. And that every person so elected to be of the common council of the said city at the time of his election, makes and ought and hath been accustomed to make his corporal oath upon the holy gospel of God in these words following: To wit —— "*You shall swear that you shall be true to our sovereign lord the king, that now is, and to his heirs and successors, kings of England, and readily you shall come, when you be summoned to the common council of this city; but if you be reasonably excused; and good and true counsel you shall give in all things touching the common wealth of this city after your wit and cunning; and that for favour of any person you shall maintain no singular profit against the common profit of this city; and after you be come to the common council you shall not from thence depart till the common council be ended without reasonable cause, or else by the lord mayor's licence. And also any secret things that be spoken or said in the common council, which ought to be kept secret, in no wise you shall to disclose, as God you help.*" And we further certify, that from the whole time whereof the memory of man is not to the contrary every person being of the common council aforesaid, by the

judgment of the ſaid court of common council, may be ſuſpended or amoved, and hath been accuſtomed to be ſuſpended or amoved, and that all cauſes and matters whatſoever touching any ſuch perſon being of the common council aforeſaid, and the amotion and ſuſpenſion of ſuch perſon ought and have been accuſtomed to be examined by the ſaid common council in the ſaid court, and by the judgment of the ſaid court to be determined and adjudged. And we further certify, that from the whole time whereof the memory of man is not to the contrary, there hath been and as yet is a certain antient cuſtom; to wit, that if any matter, cauſe or thing in the court of common council aforeſaid, touching or concerning any perſon being member of the ſaid common council, duly elected and ſworn, according to the cuſtom aforeſaid, concerning his being of the ſaid common council, or any contempt by ſuch perſon in the ſaid court committed, ſhould happen to come into debate and diſpute, that then during the time of the debate and diſpute of the ſaid matter or cauſe (during ſuch ſitting) the ſaid court of common council then being aſſembled, by the command of the ſaid court, every ſuch perſon from the ſaid court of common council ought and hath been accuſtomed immediately to depart and withdraw himſelf, nor again to return or to enter the ſaid court for that time aſſembled before the end of the debate and diſpute aforeſaid, without the licence of the ſaid court; and alſo if any perſon ſo being member of the ſaid common council ſhould refuſe to obey and ſubmit to ſuch command, and from the court of common council aforeſaid according to the command aforeſaid, would not withdraw
* P. 509. himſelf or ſhould diſturb the ſaid court for the ſaid cauſe * in contempt of the ſaid court, that then for ſuch refuſal and contempt of the ſaid court it ſhall be lawful for the court of common council aforeſaid, and the ſaid court for the whole time aforeſaid hath been uſed and accuſtomed at their pleaſure for ſuch refuſal, diſturbance and contempt, to ſuſpend or amove every ſuch perſon from his office aforeſaid, until that the ſaid court ſhould otherwiſe ordain; which cuſtoms and all the other cuſtoms of the ſaid city by the authority of the parliament of the lord Richard late king of England, the 2d after the conqueſt, held at Weſtminſter in the 7th year of his reign, to the then mayor and commonalty and citizens of the ſaid city and to their ſucceſſors were ratified and confirmed. And we further certify that the office of a common councilman of the ſaid city is, and from the whole time aforeſaid hath been, only an office of the court, of advice and ſervice without any fee, reward, profit or benefit, thereto in any manner belonging or appertaining. And we

further

further certify that a certain league and covenant was ordained by the lords and commons in the parliament then and as yet assembled at Westminster, in the county of Middlesex, to be taken by every person within the cities of London and Westminster, and the suburbs and liberties of the same. and throughout all England, entitled "*A solemn league and covenant for reformation of religion, the honour and happiness of the king, and the peace and safety of the three kingdoms of England, Scotland, and Ireland,*" And we further certify that on the 20th day of December, in the 19th year of the reign of our said lord Charles the now king, &c. A certain ordinance of the lords and commons in parliament at Westminster. in the county of Middlesex assembled, was made and declared in these words following, to wit — "*The lords and commons taking into their consideration, that the well government and peace of the said city of London, and the liberties thereof doth chiefly depend upon, the faithfulness and integrity of the persons, that have and bear the publick offices, and places of trust therein. And that in these times of troubles more than ordinary care is to be taken in the choice and election of them, and that their true affection to the true protestant religion, and to the parliament, and the peace of the city and kingdom, should be openly testified and made known before they be admitted into any such place or office. And whereas by the antient customs and usages of the said city, those of the common council, and some other officers of the said city are to be chosen at or about the 21st day of this instant December. The lords and commons do ordain and declare, that no person shall be elected to any of the said offices, nor shall be capable thereof, nor shall have voice in any such election, whose person hath been imprisoned or his estate sequestered for malignancy against the parliament, or that before the election, or vote in such election respectively shall not have taken the late solemn league and covenant for reformation and defence of religion, the honour and happiness of the king, and the peace and safety of the three kingdoms of England, Scotland, and Ireland; and Sir John Woolaston, knight, lord * mayor of the city of London, and the aldermen in their several wards, and all other persons to whom the election of the said officers shall appertain, are hereby required to see this ordinance put in execution.*" And we further certify that in the common council of the said city held in the chamber of the Guildhall of the said city, on the 23d day of April, in the 23d year of the reign of our lord Charles the now king, &c.—It is enacted and established in these words following: "*This day was read here in court, an ordinance of the lords and commons in parliament assembled, dated the 16th day of this instant April, by which the common council is authorized to nominate and to present to both*" * P. 510.



*houses*

*houses of parliament, such thirty-one persons as they shall think fit to be a committee for the militia of the city of London, and liberties thereof, and all other places within the line of communication and weekly bills of mortality, &c.—Whereupon this court taking this business into serious consideration, as a matter of great concernment to this city, have thought fit to appoint Tuesday next, for nomination of the said persons, and to the end that the assistance and blessing of Almighty God may be supplicated upon so weighty a work, it is thought requisite, and so ordered by this common council that all the members of the same shall that day by eight of the clock in the morning, meet together at the parish of St. Laurence in the Old Jury; and that Mr. Burgis be intreated then to pray and to make a preparative sermon before them concerning this great business, and renewing of the covenant. And that after the sermon ended, the oath and covenant may be administered to the members of this common council, and then immediately afterwards to go into the chamber of the Guildhall, and there to proceed to the nomination aforesaid.*" And we further certify that the said Stephen Eastwick, in the said writ named on the 27th day of April, in the 23d year of the reign of our lord Charles the now king, &c. aforesaid, and for many years now past was, and as yet is a citizen and freeman of the said city, and inhabiting within the said city of London, to wit, in the parish, &c. in the ward of Bridge within, London. And that the said Stephen Eastwick on the said 27th day of April in the year last aforesaid, being one of the common council of the said city before that time, duly elected, appointed and sworn; in the court of the common council of the city of London aforesaid, held in the chamber of the Guildhall of the said city, within the said city, according to the custom of the said city, on the said 27th day of April, in the 23d year aforesaid, for the weighty and important business of the said city, a certain question arose in the said court of common council, whether the said Stephen Eastwick had received or had been willing to receive the said league and covenant of the lords and commons in the parliament assembled, and that during the examination of the said matter in the said court, the said Stephen Eastwick contemptuously disturbed the said court, whereby the said court could not examine and determine, and thereupon the said
* P. 511. Stephen being required by the said court, * that he should absent himself and withdraw and depart from the said court of common council until that it should be determined according to the custom of the said court, of the matter, disturbance and contempt aforesaid, (the said court of common council for that time assembled being sitting) which the said Stephen then and there entirely refused to do, calling out aloud

aloud and ſhouting againſt the ſaid command, to the great contempt and diſturbance of the ſaid court, and againſt the good rule and government of the ſaid city, wherefore the ſaid Stephen by the judgement of the ſaid court of common council from the place and office of one of the common council aforeſaid, was ſuſpended until the court of common council aforeſaid ſhould otherwiſe ordain; and ſo we the ſaid mayor and commonalty and citizens of the ſaid city cannot reſtore the ſaid Stephen Eaſtwick to the place or office of one of the common council of the ſaid city, or further execute the ſaid writ to us directed.

*Reſtitution was granted Trin. 23 Charles, and the caſe is reported at large in Styles, folio 32. 35. 42.*

---

## Mandamus for Smith.

The anſwer of the mayor and aldermen of the city of London within named, to this writ appears in a certain ſchedule to this writ annexed;

Return—to a mandamus to reſtore Sir James Smith to the office of one of the aldermen of the city of London. That he had not taken the oaths, according to the ſtatute of the 1ſt. Will. and Mary, whereby his office became void and he had not been again elected.

WE the mayor and aldermen of the city of London, to the moſt ſerene the lord the king, and the lady the queen, in the court of the ſaid king and queen, before the king and queen themſelves, moſt humbly certify that James Smith, knight, in the writ to this ſchedule annexed named, on the 13th day of February, in the year of our Lord, 1688, was one of the aldermen of the ſaid city, to that place and office according to the cuſtom of the ſaid city, before that time duly elected and appointed; and from the ſaid 13th day of February in the year of our Lord, 1688, aforeſaid, until the 1ſt day of Auguſt then next following, ſo did remain and continue one of the aldermen of the ſaid city, and that the ſaid James Smith at the time of the making of a certain act made in the parliament of the lord the now king, and the lady the now queen, held at Weſtminſter in the county of Middleſex, in the firſt year of their reign; to wit, on the 13th day of February in the 1ſt year of their reign, entitled "*An act for abrogating of the oaths of ſupremacy and allegiance, and appointing other oaths,*" and continually from thence until the ſaid firſt day of Auguſt, in the year of our Lord, 1689,

1689, the said place and office of one of the aldermen of the said city, did hold and occupy, and that the said James Smith at any time before the said first day of August, in the year of our Lord 1689 aforesaid, did not take the oaths by the said act appointed to be taken, but to take those oaths before the said first day of August, in the year of our
* P. 512. Lord 1689 aforesaid, * entirely omitted and neglected, whereby, by force of the said act, the said office and place of one of the aldermen of the said city became entirely vacant, and that the said James Smith at any time after his omission and neglect aforesaid, was not elected into the office of one of the aldermen of the said city, and for that cause, we the said mayor and aldermen cannot restore him the said James Smith into the said office or place.

The answer of the mayor and aldermen of the city of London.

*The arguments upon this return are in* 1 Shower 263, *and* 4*th* Mod. 53.—*The return was adjudged good, and the court would not grant any peremptory mandamus.*

---

## Mandamus for Edwards.

Return to a mandamus to restore Sir James Edwards to the office of alderman of London, That he had surrendered his office after the judgement in Quo warranto, and before the statute of the 2d of Will. and Mary reversing the said judgement.

The answer of the mayor and aldermen of the city of London within named, to this writ appears in a certain schedule to this writ annexed.

WE the mayor and aldermen of the city of London, to the most serene lord and lady, the now king and queen, the court of the said lord and lady the king and queen, before the said king and queen themselves at Westminster, most humbly certify, that by a certain act made and provided in the parliament of the said lord and lady the now king and queen, held at Westminster, in the county of Middlesex, on the 20th day of March, in the second year of their reign, intitled, "*An act for reversing the judgment in a Quo*

*Warranto*

*Warranto against the city of London, and forrestoring the city of London to its antient rights and privilges,"* reciting, that whereas a certain judgment had been given in the court of king's bench, in or about Trinity term, in the 35th year of the reign of the late king Charles the second, upon a certain information in the nature of a writ of Quo Warranto, exhibited in the said court against the mayor and commonalty citizens of the city of London, whereby the liberties, privileges, and franchises of the said mayor and commonalty and citizens, being a body politic and corporate, were seized into the hands of the king as forfeited, and in as much as the said judgment and the proceedings thereupon were, and had been illegal and arbitrary, and because that the restoration of the said mayor and commonalty and citizens, to their antient liberties of which they had been deprived, very much tended to the peace and good settlement of this kingdom, by the said act it was declared, and by the authority of the said parliament it was enacted, that the said judgment given in the said court of king's bench, in the said Trinity term, in the 35th year of the reign of the said late king Charles the 2d, or in any other term, and all and every other judgment given or recorded in the said court, for seizing into the hands of the said late king the liberties, privileges, or franchises of the mayor and commonalty and citizens * of the city of London, being in themselves a body politick and corporate, by the name of the mayor and commonalty and citizens of the city of London, and by that name to plead and to be impleaded, to answer and be answered, and in whatsoever manner or words such judgment had been, was, and might be entered, by the said act was reversed, annulled, and vacated to all intents and purposes whatsoever, and that vacates should be entered upon the rolls of the said judgments, for vacating and reversing the same accordingly; and further by the said act, it was declared and enacted by the authority aforesaid, that the mayor and commonalty and citizens of the city of London could, and might for ever from thence afterwards remain, continue and be, and prescribe to be a body corporate and politick in thing, fact and name, by the name of the mayor, commonalty and citizens of the city of London, and by that name, and all and every other name and names of incorporation whatsoever, by which they at any time before the said judgment had been incorporated, might sue, plead, and be impleaded, answer, and be answered without any seizure or forejudger of the said franchises, liberties or privileges, or being thereof ousted or excluded, for or upon any pretence of any forfeiture or misdemeanour

*P. 513.

meanour at any time before that time, or from thence afterwards to be done, committed or ſuffered; and that the ſaid mayor and commonalty and citizens of the ſaid city, could and might, as by law they ought, peaceably have and enjoy all and ſingular their rights, gifts, charters, grants, liberties, privileges, franchiſes, cuſtoms, uſages, conſtitutions, immunities, præſcriptions, markets, duties, tolls, lands, tenements, eſtates and hereditaments whatſoever, which they lawfully had, or had lawful right, title or intereſt of or in, at the time of the recording or giving of the ſaid judgment, or at the time or times of the ſaid pretended forſeitures. And by the ſaid act, it was further enacted by the authority aforeſaid, that all the officers and miniſters of the ſaid city who rightfully had held any office or place in the ſaid city or the liberties of the ſame, or in the borough of Southwark, at the time the judgment aforeſaid was given, ſhould have and enjoy the ſame in as ample a manner as they had held the ſame at the time of the giving of the ſaid judgment, (except ſuch as had voluntarily ſurrendered any ſuch office or place, or were removed for any juſt cauſe.) And that every perſon who after the giving of the ſaid judgment had been elected, admitted and ſettled in any office or employment within the ſaid city upon the death, ſurrender, or removal as aforeſaid, of the former officers ſhould be and by the ſaid act was confirmed in his ſaid office or employment, and ſhould have and enjoy the ſame in as ample and full a manner as if he had been admitted or ſettled in the ſame according to the antient cuſtoms of the ſaid city, as by the ſaid act more fully appears, and that the * within named James Edwards, at the time of the giving of the ſaid judgment, was one of the aldermen of the ſaid city of London, to which office and place he before that time, according to the cuſtom of the ſaid city, was duly elected and appointed; and that the ſaid James Edwards ſo as aforeſaid, being one of the aldermen of the ſaid city after the giving of the ſaid judgment, and before the making of the ſaid act, to wit, on the 18th day of October, in the year of our Lord 1688, freely and voluntarily ſurrendered the ſaid office of one of the aldermen of the ſaid city, and that afterwards and before the making of the ſaid act, to wit, upon the 19th day of October, in the year of our Lord 1688, one Thomas Lane, knight, citizen and freeman of the ſaid city into the ſaid office of one of the aldermen of the ſaid city in the place of the ſaid James Edwards, in the due manner, according to the cuſtom of the ſaid city, was elected and appointed, and the ſaid office always from thence hitherto hath exerciſed and as yet

* P. 514.

yet exercises, and at the time of the making of the said act was and as yet is one of the aldermen of the said city in the place of the said James Edwards, who the said office as aforesaid did surrender, and that the said James Edwards at any time after the surrender made was not elected into the said office or place of one of the aldermen of the said city, and for that cause, we the mayor and aldermen of the said city cannot restore the said James Edwards to the office or place of one of the aldermen of the said city.

The answer of the mayor and aldermen of the city of London.

---

## Mandamus for Pritchard.

WILLIAM and Mary, by the grace of God, of England, Scotland, France, and Ireland, king and queen, defenders of the faith, &c.—To the mayor and aldermen of our city of London greeting: Whereas upon the 26th day of May, in the year of our Lord 1690, a certain mayor of the city of London according to the provisions in a certain act made and provided in the present parliament begun and held at Westminster, in our county of Middlex, on the 20th day of March, in the 2d year of our reign, entitled an act for reversing the judgment in a quo warranto, against the city of London, and for restoring the city of London to its antient rights and privileges was not elected; and whereas also William Pritchard knight, at the time in which the judgment upon the information in the nature of a quo warranto, exhibited in the court of the lord the king, Charles the 2d, late king, &c. before the late king himself, and in the said act of parliament mentioned, was given, to wit, in the term of the holy Trinity, * in the 35th year of the reign of the said lord Charles the 2d, late king of England, &c. was mayor of the city of London aforesaid, according to the custom of the said city, duly elected and appointed; and whereas also the said William Pritchard in default, of the election of a mayor of the

Mandamus to the mayor and aldermen of London to swear Sir William Pritchard into the office of mayor of the said city, it recites that no mayor was elected on the 26th May 1690 according to the provision of the act of parliament reversing the judgment in the quo warranto, and that at the time of the judgment Sir William was mayor, and for default of the election he ought by virtue of the said act to continue in the said office of mayor till a new election.

* P. 515

ſaid city of London on the ſaid 26th day of May, in the year of our Lord 1690, being as aforeſaid, mayor of the ſaid city at the time of the giving of the ſaid judgment by virtue of the ſaid act of parliament, in the place and office of mayor of the ſaid city until that a new election of ſuch officer according to the antient uſe and cuſtom of the ſaid city ſhould be made, ought to be and continue; and although the ſaid William Pritchard on the 26th day of May, and from thence hitherto was ready and offered to take upon himſelf the ſaid office of mayor of the ſaid city, and to exerciſe and execute the ſaid office, and before you or ſome of you, offered to take his corporal oath of mayor of the ſaid city in that behalf to be taken and neceſſary to be taken; nevertheleſs, you to whom it belongs of right to adminiſter ſuch oath to the mayor of the ſaid city have denied, or at leaſt have unduly deferred to adminiſter the ſaid oath to the ſaid William, or to receive the ſame from the ſaid William, to the great damage and grievance of the ſaid William Pritchard, and to the manifeſt injury of his eſtate, as from his complaint we have underſtood, whereupon he hath beſought us, that we ſhould cauſe apt remedy to be provided for him in this behalf; we therefore willing that full and ſpeedy juſtice be done to the ſaid William Pritchard in this behalf as is right, command you and each and every of you, as we have before commanded you, that the ſaid oath by the mayor of the ſaid city in this behalf uſed to be taken, you adminiſter to the ſaid William Pritchard, mayor of the ſaid city of London aforeſaid, by virtue of the ſaid act of parliament as aforeſaid continued, and that you admit without delay the ſaid William ſo as aforeſaid, in the ſaid office continued, to the office and place of mayor of the city of London aforeſaid, or ſignify to us cauſe thereupon to the contrary, leaſt through your default, complaint may be made to us again, and how you ſhall execute this our command, make to appear to us at Weſtminſter, on the Tueſday next after three weeks of the holy Trinity next coming, then returning to us this our writ. Witneſs John Holt knight, at Weſtminſter, the 3d day of July, in the 2d year of our reign.

*Aſtry.*

WE

## Mandamus and Returns thereto.

WE the mayor and aldermen of the city of London to the most serene lord the king and the lady the queen, within written, most humbly certify that in and upon the within mentioned 26th day of May, in the year of our Lord, 1690, within specified, one Thomas Pilkington, knight, in the due manner and according to the provision in the statute within specified, was elected into the place and office of mayor of the city of London aforesaid, and into the said place and office afterwards, to wit, on the 2d day of June now last past, lawfully was sworn and admitted, and the said office and place from thence hitherto, hath exercised and as yet doth exercise as of right he ought, and for that cause we cannot administer the oath within written by the mayor of the said city in this behalf * used to be taken to the within named William Pritchard, knight, or admit the said William Pritchard into the office or place of mayor of the said city.

Return—That on the 26th of May Sir T. P. was chosen mayor, according to the said act and afterwards was sworn and still is in office.

* P. 516.

The answer of the mayor and aldermen of the city of London.

---

## Mandamus for Parker.

CHARLES &c.—To our chamberlain of our county Palatine of Chester, greeting. Whereas Samuel Parker, gentleman, unto the place and office of one of the attorneys of our Exchequer at Chester, duly was elected and appointed, in which place and office he continually carried and behaved himself well, nevertheless you our chamberlain, lightly regarding the premisses, the said Samuel Parker from the place and office of one of the attorneys of our Exchequer aforesaid, without any reasonable cause have removed, in contempt of us; and to the great damage and grievance of the said Samuel, and to the manifest injury of his estate, as from his complaint we have understood. We therefore willing that due and speedy justice be done to the said Samuel in this behalf as is right, command you, as before we have commanded you, that immediately after the receipt of this writ you restore or cause to be restored the said Samuel Parker, into the said place and office of one of the attornies of the the court of our Exchequer aforesaid, at Chester aforesaid, with all liberties, privileges, commodities and preheminences to that office or place belonging or appertaining, or signify to us cause to the contrary thereupon, least through your default

Mandamus to the chamberlain of Chester, to restore S. Parker to the office of one of the attorneys of the court of Exchequer, at Chester.

default complaint may be made to us, again, and how you shall execute this our command; make to appear to us on the octave of St. Hilary, wheresoever we shall then be in England, then returning to us this our writ, and this in no wise omit under the pain of 40l. Witness F. Raynsford, at Westminster, the 20th day of November in the 29th year of our reign.

By the Court.

*Astry.*

Return.

The answer of the most noble William earl of Derby, chamberlain of the County Palatine of Chester, appears in a certain schedule to this writ annexed.

By the chamberlain himself.

That he is suspended by the deputy baron, for disturbing him in the execution of his office, and speaking contemptuous words to him, and that he hath not submitted and asked pardon.

TO the most serene lord the king, I most humbly certify that the court of the Exchequer of the said lord the king, of the county palatine of Chester, is an antient court of record, and that the said court from the time whereof the memory of man is not to the contrary, in the absence of the said chamberlain of the county palatine of Chester, and of his vice chamberlain, and of the baron of the said lord the king of the said court, hath been held and hath been accustomed to be held before the deputy baron of the said lord the king of the said court; and that upon the 20th day of September in the 29th year of the reign of our said lord now the king, Samuel Parker in the said writ named, then being one of the attornies of the said court, came into the said court, then held in the castle of the said lord the king of Chester, before William Slater, gentleman, deputy of John Werden, baronet, then being * baron of the said court, in the said court judicially sitting, (the chamberlain of the said county palatine of Chester, his vice chamberlain, and the said baron then being absent) and him the said William Slater then and there in the exercise of his office, by his loud discourse with certain persons standing near him, did obstruct and disturb, against the duty of the office of him the said Samuel Parker, and the due respect from him to the said court due; whereupon the said William did command the said Samuel to be silent, and that he would desist further to disturb the said court; and the said Samuel Parker not desisting from his said discourse, the said William Slater further commanded the said Samuel to be silent; whereupon the said Samuel Parker in the full and open court aforesaid, and in the presence of very many of the suitors and officers of the said court, contemptuously answered the said William Slater in these words following, to wit—" *I care not a straw for*

* P. 517.

*for what you can do,"* and in further contempt of the ſaid William Slater and of the ſaid court of the ſaid lord the king, did continue his diſcourſe aforeſaid with a loud voice, and to ſhout out, and him the ſaid William Slater in the ſaid court, there judicially ſitting, then and there by his ſaid diſcourſe further did diſturb, and from exerciſing his ſaid office in the ſaid court then and there did hinder; whereupon the ſaid William then and there in the open court aforeſaid, him the ſaid Samuel from the exerciſe of his office of attorney aforeſaid in the ſaid court did ſuſpend, until that the ſaid Samuel ſhould ſubmit himſelf to the ſaid court, and ſhould acknowledge his inſolence aforeſaid, and ſhould beg pardon for the ſame from the ſaid court, which the ſaid Samuel at any time hitherto in any manner hath not done; and I further certify to the ſaid lord the king, that the ſaid Samuel from his place and office in the ſaid writ mentioned, otherwiſe or in any other manner is not removed, nor ever was by the chamberlain himſelf.

*Derby.*

---

## Mandamus for Thacker.

### Trinity the 30th Charles II.

CHARLES the 2d. &c. — To the mayor, ſheriffs, citizens and commonalty of the city of Norwich, greeting —Whereas Thomas Thacker into the place and office of one of the alderman of the ſaid city, according to the cuſtom of the ſaid city hitherto uſed, duly was elected, appointed and ſworn, in which place and office of one of the aldermen of the ſaid city, the ſaid Thomas Thacker continually hath carried and behaved himſelf well, neverthleſs you the mayor, ſheriffs, citizens and commonalty of the ſaid city not ignorant of the premiſſes, the ſaid T. T. from the ſaid place and office of one of the aldermen of the ſaid city, without any reaſonable cauſe unjuſtly have removed in contempt of us and to the great damage and grievance of the ſaid Thomas, and to the manifeſt injury of his eſtate, as from his complaint we have underſtood. We therefore willing that due and ſpeedy juſtice be done to the ſaid T. T. in this behalf,

Mandamus to the mayor, ſheriffs and citizens of Norwich, to reſtore Thacker to the office of one of the aldermen of the ſaid city.

* P. 518. behalf, as is right, * command you as before we have commanded you, firmly enjoining that immediately after the receceipt of this writ, you restore the said T. T. into the said place and office of one of the aldermen of the said city, with all and singular the liberties, privileges and commodities, to that place and office belonging and appertaining, or signify to us cause thereupon to the contrary, least through your default complaint may be made to us again, and how you shall execute this our command, make to appear to us from the day of the Holy Trinity in 15 days, wheresoever we shall then be in England, under the pain of 40l. then returning to us this our writ. Witness William Scroggs, at Westminster, the 1st day of June in the 30th year of our reign.

By the court,

*Astry.*

Return. The execution of this writ appears in a certain schedule to this writ annexed.

*John Richer*, mayor.

City of Norwich a corporation by prescription. Norwich to wit. — The answer of the mayor, sheriffs, citizens and commonalty of the city of Norwich, to the writ to this schedule annexed; according to the command of the said writ to the said lord the king, we most humbly certify that the city of Norwich is an antient city, and the citizens of the said city from the time whereof the memory of man is not to the contrary, have been incorporated by the name of the bailiffs, citizens and commonalty of the city of Norwich, and by the said name for the whole time aforesaid, until the 28th day of January, in the 5th year of the reign of the lord Henry the 4th, late king of England, have been called and named, and that on the said 28th day of January in the said 5th year of the reign of the said late king Henry the 4th, he the said late king by his letters patent sealed with his great seal of England, bearing date at Westminster, the said day and year; of his especial grace, granted for himself and his heirs to the citizens and commonalty of the said city of Norwich and to their successors for ever, that the said citizens and commonalty and their successors from thence for ever might have, appoint and elect in each year then successively for ever, one mayor of themselves, and that the citizens and commonalty and their successors for ever, (in the place of their four bailiffs of the said city, used from antient time, whom and whose names the said late king, then willed from thenceforth in the said city and elsewhere altogether, for the vulgar appellation should be abolished, and for er be ceased and omitted) might have,

Hen. the 4th in the 5th of his reign, incorporated them by the name of the mayor, sheriffs, citizens and commonalty.

have, and appoint and might elect in each year successively two sheriffs of themselves, and that they continually afterwards for ever should be named and called by the name of the mayor, sheriffs, citizens and commonalty of the city of Norwich, and by no other name whatsoever, as by the said letters patent more fully appears; and to the said lord the king, we further certify that the lord Edward late king of England, the fourth of that name after the conquest, on the 12th day of February in the first year of his reign, by his letters patent, sealed with his great seal of England, the date of which is at Westminster on the said day and year, among other things specified in the said patent granted for himself and his heirs, to the said mayor, * sheriffs, citizens and commonalty of the city of Norwich aforesaid, and to their successors for ever, that the said citizens and commonalty and their successors for ever in each year successively for ever, might elect, make and create four and twenty their fellow citizens of the said city into aldermen of the said city—which four and twenty fellow citizens, so elected and created should have and should bear for ever the name of aldermen of Norwich, who so elected and each and every of them should continue in their estate and degree during their life unless reasonable cause of removal should intervene, as by the letters patent last mentioned more fully appears; and to the said lord the now king, we further certify that the lord the now king on the 26th day of June in the 15th year of his reign, by his letters patent, sealed with his great seal of England the date of which is at Westminster on the said day and year, among other things specified in the said patent gave and granted for himself, his heirs, and successors, to the said mayor, sheriffs, citizens, and commonalty of the said city for ever, that the election of the said aldermen afterwards for ever might and should, be in the manner and form following, and not otherwise, to wit, whenever and as often as any one or more of the 24 aldermen of the said city should depart this life, or for any reasonable cause duly should be removed from that society, that then and so often the mayor of the said city for the time being or his deputy, within a convenient time after such decease or removal, should cause to be summoned all the citizens inhabiting within the great ward or wards for which such person or persons so lately deceased or removed was or were an alderman or aldermen of the said city, to meet at the Guildhall of the said city, to choose one or more into the place or places of him or them so dying or being removed, and that the said citizens or the major part of them so assembled, should choose and might and could choose one or more of the more worthy

Edward the 4th granted them licence to choose 24 alderman yearly.

* P. 519.

Charles the 2d by letters patent directed in what manner the aldermen should be chosen.

and

and more fit citizens or freemen of the said city to be alderman or aldermen, in the place or places of him or them so dying or being removed; and that all and every such person persons so elected from time to time, should take his and their corporal oath and oaths, upon the holy gospel of God, for the due execution of such office or place before the mayor and aldermen of the said city of Norwich for the time being or before such of them as should be present in the mayor's court to be held in the council chamber of the said city within a convenient time after such election and elections, so made or to be made; and from and after such oath and oaths so taken, he and they might and should be alderman and aldermen of the said city for and during his and their natural life and lives respectively, unless reasonable cause of removal should intervene, as by the said letters patent last mentioned in like manner appears; and to the said lord the king; we further certify, that by a statute made in the parliament of the said lord the now king, begun at Westminster the 8th day of May in the year of our Lord 1661, in the 13th year of his reign, and there continued until Friday the 20th day of December, and from that day adjourned to the 7th day of January then next following, reciting that, whereas questions were likely to arise concerning the validity of the elections of magistrates and * other officers and members, in corporations as well in respect of removing some as the placing others during the late troubles, contrary to the true intent and meaning of their charters and liberties, and to the end that the succession in such corporations might most probably be perpetuated in the hands of persons well affected to his royal majesty and to the established government, it being too well known that notwithstanding the endeavours of his majesty, and his unparalleled indulgence in pardoning all that was past nevertheless many evil spirits, then were working, therefore for the prevention of such mischief for the time to come and for the preservation of the publick peace, as well in church as in state, it was enacted by the said lord the king's most excellent majesty by and with the advice and consent of the lords spiritual, and temporal and of the commons in parliament assembled, and by the authority of the same, that before the 20th day of February next ensuing, commissions be issued forth under the great seal of England, to such persons as the said lord the king should appoint for the execution of the powers and authorities in the said statute afterwards expressed, and that all and singular the persons named commissioners in the said commissions respectively, should be by virtue of the said act commissioners respectively for and in the several cities, corporations and boroughs and cinque ports, and their members,

Statute 13th Charles 2d.

* P. 520

members, and the other port-towns within the kingdom of England, the dominion of Wales, or the town of Berwick upon the Tweed, for which they respectively should be nominated and appointed; and it was further enacted by the authority aforesaid, that no charters of any corporation, city, town, borough, cinque port and their members, and the other port towns in England or Wales, or the town of Berwick upon the Tweed, at any time afterwards should be avoided for or by reason of any act or thing done or omitted to be done before the 1st day of that present parliament; and it was further enacted by the authority aforesaid, that all persons who upon the 24th day of December in the year of our Lord 1661, should be mayors, aldermen, recorders, bailiffs, town clerks, common councilmen, and other persons then bearing any office or offices of magistracy, or places, or trusts or other employments relating to or concerning the government of the said respective cities, corporations, boroughs, cinque ports, and their members and other port towns at some time before the 25th day of March, in the year of our Lord 1663, when he or they should be required thereto by the respective commissioners or by any three or more of them, should take the oaths of allegiance and supremacy, and this oath following: to wit, "*I A. B. do declare and believe that it is not lawful upon any pretence whatsoever to take arms against the king; and that I abhor that traiterous position, of taking arms by his authority against his person, or against those that are commissioned by him, so help me God,*" and also at the same time should publickly subscribe before the commissioners or any three of them, this declaration following: "*I A. B. do declare, that I hold that there lies no obligation upon me or any other person from the oath * commonly called the solemn league and covenant, and that the same was in itself an unlawful oath, and imposed upon the subjects of this realm, against the known laws and liberties of the kingdom,*" * P. 521.
and that all such mayors and other persons aforesaid, by whom the said oaths are to be taken, and the declaration to be subscribed as aforesaid, who should refuse to take and subscribe the same within the time and in the manner aforesaid, from and immediately after such refusal should be by the authority of said act ipso facto removed and displaced, of and from their offices and places respectively, and that the said offices and places from and immediately after such refusal, be and are by the said act declared and adjudged void, to all intents and purposes, as if the said persons so refusing had been naturally dead; and it was further enacted by the authority aforesaid, that the said commissioners or any five or more of them should have full power by virtue of the said statute, by order and warrant under their hands and

ſeals to diſplace and remove any of the ſaid perſons from their reſpective offices, and places and truſts, aforeſaid, if the major part of them then preſent ſhould deem that to be expedient for the publick ſafety, although ſuch perſons ſhould take and ſubſcribe, and ſhould be willing to take and ſubſcribe the ſaid oaths and declaration; and it was alſo enacted that the ſaid reſpective commiſſioners or any five or more of them, as aforeſaid, ſhould have power to reſtore ſuch perſon or perſons as were illegally and unduly removed into the place or places from which he or they were removed, and alſo to put and place into the offices and places which by any of the means aforeſaid ſhould be vacant reſpectively, any other perſon or perſons then being or who had been members or inhabitants of the ſaid reſpective cities, corporations, boroughs and cinque ports, and their members and of other port towns, who before the ſaid reſpective commiſſioners or any three or more of them, ſhould take the ſaid oaths of obedience and ſupremacy and the ſaid other oath, and ſhould ſubſcribe the declaration thereupon above particularly mentioned; and that the ſaid perſons from and after the taking of the ſaid oaths, and ſubſcribing of the ſaid declaration ſhould hold, enjoy and ſhould be inveſted with the the ſaid offices and places as if they had been duly elected and choſen according to the charters and former uſages of the ſaid reſpective cities, corporations, and boroughs, and cinque ports, and their members, and the other port towns; and it was further enacted by the authority aforeſaid, that the ſaid commiſſioners or any three or more of them, reſpectively ſhould have power during the continuance of their reſpective commiſſions to adminiſter the ſaid oaths, and to tender the ſaid declaration to the ſaid perſons by the ſaid ſtatute required to take and ſubſcribe the ſame, and from and after the expiration of their ſaid reſpective commiſſions, that the ſaid three oaths and declaration ſhould be from time to time adminiſtered and tendered to ſuch perſon or perſons who by the true intent of the ſaid act or by any clauſe in the ſame contained, were to take the ſame, by ſuch perſon or perreſpectively, who by the charters or uſages of the ſaid reſpective cities, corporations, and boroughs and cinque ports,
* P. 522. and their * members and other port towns ought to adminiſter the oath for the due execution of the ſaid places and offices reſpectively, and in default of ſuch by two juſtices of the peace of the ſaid cities, corporations, boroughs and cinque ports, and their members, and other port towns for the time being, if ſuch ſhould be there, or otherwiſe by two juſtices of the peace for the time being of the reſpective counties, where the ſaid cities, corporations, or boroughs, or cinque ports or their members, or the other port towns ſhould

ſhould be; and it was in like manner ordained by the authority aforeſaid, that the ſaid commiſſioners, juſtices of the peace and other perſons by the ſaid act authoriſed to adminiſter the ſaid oaths, and to tender the ſaid declaration reſpectively ſhould cauſe memorandums or entries to be made of all the oaths taken before them, and of the ſubſcriptions made as aforeſaid, and ſhould deliver the ſame once in the year to the reſpective town clerks or regiſters, or clerks of the reſpective cities, corporations, and boroughs, and cinque ports and their members, and other port towns, who ſhould cauſe the ſame fairly to be entered in the books or regiſters belonging to the ſaid reſpective cities, corporations, or boroughs, or cinque ports or their members, or other port towns; and it was provided and enacted by the authority aforeſaid that from and after the expiration of the ſaid commiſſion, no perſon or perſons for ever afterwards ſhould be placed, elected or choſen into or to any offices or places aforeſaid, who ſhould not receive within one year next before the election or choice the ſacrament of the Lord's ſupper, according to the rites of the church of England, and that every ſuch perſon and perſons ſo placed, elected, or choſen in like manner ſhould take the ſaid three oaths, and ſhould ſubſcribe the ſaid declaration at the ſame time when the oath for the due execution of the ſaid places and offices reſpectively ſhould be adminiſtered, and in default thereof it was thereupon enacted and declared that every ſuch election and choice ſhould be void; provided always and it was enacted that every perſon who ſhould be placed in any corporation, by virtue of the ſaid act, upon his admiſſion ſhould take the ſeveral oath or oaths uſually taken by the members of ſuch corporation; alſo it was provided and thereupon enacted, that the powers granted to the commiſſioners by virtue of the ſaid act, ſhould continue and be in force until the 25th day of March in the year of our Lord 1663, and no longer, as by the ſaid act among other things more fully appears, and is manifeſt. And to the ſaid lord the king we further certify that Thomas Thacker in the ſaid writ named on the 7th day of December in the 16th year of the reign of the ſaid lord the now king, at the city of Norwich aforeſaid, according to the form of the letters patent aforeſaid, was elected, appointed and ſworn into the place and office of one of the aldermen of the city of Norwich in the place of William Tooke, alderman of the ſaid city then deceaſed, which T. T. then and there in the due manner took and ſwore the oath for the due execution of his office aforeſaid, and alſo the ſaid three oaths in the ſaid ſtatute reſpectively mentioned, and at the ſame time the ſaid declaration in the ſtatute aforeſaid *mentioned by the town clerk

On the 7th Dec. 16 Ch. 2. Thacker was choſen alderman, and took the oaths of office and the 3 oaths mentioned in the ſtatute and recited and pronounced the declaration mentioned in the ſtatute concerning the ſolemn league and covenant

* P. 523.

clerk of the ſaid city was read to the ſaid T. T. to be by him repeated, and he the ſaid Thomas then and there openly and willingly repeated and pronounced the ſaid declaration, which oaths and declaration then and there with the aſſent and approbation of the ſaid T. T. in the the regiſtry of the court of the ſaid city, by the ſaid town clerk were entered; but to the ſaid lord the king we further certify that the ſaid Thomas Thacker did not ſubſcribe the ſaid declaration at the ſaid time when he took the ſaid oaths and recited the ſaid declaration as in the ſaid ſtatute was appointed to be done; but afterwards, to wit, on the 9th day of March in the 30th year of the reign of the lord the now king, the ſaid declaration, by Bernard Church and John Mann, Eſquires, two juſtices of the ſaid lord the king in the due manner conſtituted to preſerve the peace in the ſaid city and in the county of the ſame at the Guildhall of the ſaid city, for the firſt time was tendered to the ſaid Thomas Thacker, to ſubſcribe, and at the ſaid time the ſaid Thomas Thacker ſubſcribed the ſaid declaration; and becauſe the ſaid Thomas Thacker did not ſubſcribe the ſaid declaration at the ſaid time when he was ſworn into the office of alderman aforeſaid, as by the ſaid ſtatute is required, therefore afterwards, to wit, on the laſt day of April in the 30th year of the reign of the ſaid lord the now king aforeſaid, at the Guildhall of the ſaid city and before the coming of the ſaid writ, Jehoſaphat Davy, a fit and proper perſon to be alderman of the ſaid city, and citizen of the ſaid city, into the place and office of the ſaid T. T. was elected according to the form of the letters patent aforeſaid and of the ſtatute aforeſaid, who ſo being duly elected then and there was ſworn into the place and office of one of the aldermen of the ſaid city, which Jehoſaphat Davy had received the ſacrament of the Lord's ſupper according to the rites of the church of England, within one year before his election aforeſaid, as in the ſaid ſtatute is ordained, and thereupon the ſaid Jehoſaphat Davy at the ſame time when he took the oath for the due execution of his office aforeſaid, alſo took and ſwore the ſeveral oaths in the ſaid ſtatute aforeſaid mentioned, and at the ſame time there ſubſcribed the ſaid declaration in the ſaid ſtatute contained, according to the form and effect of the ſaid ſtatute.

But did not then ſubſcribe the declaration as the ſtatute requires but it being firſt offered to him on the 9th of March, the 30th of Char. 2d. he ſubſcribed it then. And becauſe he did not ſubſcribe it when ſworn into office, they choſe another alderman who took the oaths and ſubſcribed the declaration at the ſame time.

*John Richer*, mayor.

Mandamus

## Mandamus for Haddock.

CHARLES the second, &c.—To the mayor, aldermen, bailiffs, and citizens of the city of Carlisle greeting: Whereas Timothy Haddock to the place and office of one of the aldermen of the city of Carlisle aforesaid, according to the custom of the said city, duly was elected and appointed, in which place and office of one of the aldermen of the said city, the said Timothy Haddock continually carried and behaved himself well, nevertheless you the mayor, aldermen, bailiffs, and citizens of the said city, lightly regarding the premisses, the said Timothy Haddock unduly, and without any reasonable cause, from the said place and office of one of the aldermen of the said city unjustly have removed, in contempt of us, and to the great damage and grievance of the said Timothy, and to the manifest injury of his estate, as from his complaint we have * understood; we therefore willing that due and speedy justice be done to the said Timothy Haddock, in this behalf, as is right, command you and every of you, as we have before commanded you, that immediately after the receipt of this writ, you restore or cause to be restored the said Timothy Haddock into the said office and place of one of the aldermen of the said city, with all liberties, privileges, and commodities to the said office and place belonging or appertaining, or signify to us cause to the contrary, least through your default, complaint may be made to us again, and how you shall execute this our command, make to appear to us on the Octave of St. Hillary, wheresoever we shall then be in England, then returning to us this our writ, and this in no wise omit, under the pain of 40l. Witness William Scroggs, at Westminster, the 28th day of November, in the 31st year of our reign.

Mandamus To the mayor, aldermen bailiffs and citizens of the city of Carlisle to restore Haddock to the office of one of the aldermen of that city.

* P. 524.

By the Court.

*Astry.*

The execution of this writ appears in a certain schedule of this writ annexed.

The answer of the mayor, aldermen, bailiffs, and citizens of the city of Carlisle within written to this writ.

*Tho. Jackson*, Mayor.

To

That the city of Carliſle is an antient city, and by preſcription the citizens thereof were incorporated by the name of the mayor and citizens until the 21 July 13 Charles the 1ſt, and in it till then there were 12 citizens called counſellors other wiſe aldermen out of whom annually a mayor was choſen, and every counſellor otherwiſe alderman was in for life, if he behaved himſelf well; the eleven remaining counſellors with 32 citizens of the guild of merchants were the common council of the city. Charles the 1ſt. by letters patent dated the 21 of July in the 13th year of his reign incorporated them by their preſent name.

To our moſt ſerene Lord Charles the ſecond, the now king of England, &c. on the day in the ſaid writ mentiontioned, we the mayor, aldermen, bailiffs, and citizens of the city of Carliſle, in the writ to this ſchedule annexed ſpecified, moſt humbly certify, that the city of Carliſle aforeſaid is, and from the time whereof the memory of man is not to the contrary, hath been an antient city, and that the citizens of the ſaid city for the time being from the time whereof the memory of man is not to the contrary until the 21ſt day of July in the 13th year of the reign of the Lord Charles the 1ſt late king of England, were incorporated, and were one body corporate and politick in thing in fact and in name, by the name of the mayor and citizens of the city of Carliſle, and from the whole time aforeſaid, until the ſaid 21ſt day of July, in the 13th year aforeſaid, within the ſaid city there were twelve of the more virtuous, and more proper citizens of the ſaid city for the time being who were named and called counſellors, otherwiſe aldermen of the ſaid city, and from which twelve counſellors otherwiſe aldermen, one annually and every year for the whole time aforeſaid, in the due manner, was elected, appointed and ſworn into the office of mayor of the ſaid city for one whole year next following ſuch election, and further until one other of the twelve counſellors otherwiſe aldermen aforeſaid, into the ſaid office of mayor was elected, appointed and ſworn; and that every one of the counſellors, otherwiſe aldermen aforeſaid, after that he into the office of one of the counſellors otherwiſe aldermen of the ſaid city reſpectively, had been elected and admitted, in the ſaid office continued during the term of his natural life, if he in the ſaid office ſo long behaved himſelf well: And we further certify, that from the whole time aforeſaid, until the ſaid 21ſt day of * July, in the 13th year aforeſaid, there were, and were accuſtomed to be thirty-two other virtuous and proper citizens of the ſaid city elected from the guild of merchants there, which thirty-two citizens together with the other eleven counſellors, otherwiſe aldermen of the ſaid city, (the mayor of the ſaid city not being one of them) from the whole time aforeſaid were, and were accuſtomed to be the common council of the mayor and citizens of the ſaid city; and we further certify, that the ſaid late king Charles the firſt, by his letters patent, ſealed with his great ſeal of England, bearing date at Cambury, the ſaid 21ſt day of July, in the 13th of his reign

* P. 525.

aforeſaid,

aforesaid, of his special grace, certain knowledge and mere motion for himself, his heirs, and successors, willed, ordained, constituted and granted by his letters patent aforesaid, that the said city of Carlisle, in the county of Cumberland, from thence for ever, should and might be a city in itself, and that the mayor and citizens of the said city by whatsoever name or names they or their predecessors, ever before that time were incorporated, and their successors from thence afterwards for ever, should and might be by force of the letters patent aforesaid, one body politick and corporate in thing, fact and name, by the name of the mayor, aldermen, bailiffs, and citizens of the city of Carlisle, and them by the name of the mayor, aldermen, bailiffs, and citizens of the city of Carlisle, the said late king for himself, his heirs and successors, erected, made, ordained, constituted, created and confirmed one body politick and corporate in thing, fact and name, really and fully, and by his letters patent aforesaid, declared that by that name they should have perpetual succession; and that they by the name of the mayor, aldermen, bailiffs, and citizens of the city of Carlisle, might and should be for ever, persons able and in law capable to have, acquire, receive and possess lands, tenements, liberties, franchises, privileges, jurisdictions, and other hereditaments whatsoever, of whatsoever kind, nature or species they might be, to them and their successors in fee, and perpetuity, and also goods and chattles, and other things whatsoever, of whatsoever kind or species they might be; and also to give, grant, demise and assign lands, tenements, and other hereditaments, goods and chattles, and all and singular their other deeds and things to be done and executed by the name aforesaid; and that by the said name of mayor, aldermen, bailiffs, and citizens of the city of Carlisle, they might and could plead and be impleaded, defend and be defended, in all courts and places whatsoever, and before whatsoever judges and justices, and other persons and officers of the lord the king, his heirs and successors, in all suits, complaints, pleas, causes, matters and demands whatsoever, real, personal and mixt, as well spiritual as temporal, of whatsoever kind, nature or species they might be, in the manner and form as the other liege subjects of the said lord the king, persons able and in law capable might and could plead and be impleaded, answer and be answered, defend and be defended, and might and could, have, acquire, receive, possess, give and grant; and that the said mayor, aldermen, bailiffs, and citizens of the said city and their successors, should have for ever a common seal to serve for transacting their causes and affairs

whatsoever,

whatsoever, and the causes and affairs of their successors;
* P. 526. and that it should and might be well lawful * for them and their successors from time to time to break, change and make anew the said seal at their pleasure, as it should seem to them to be meet and expedient: And further, the said late king willed, and by his letters patent aforesaid, for himself, his heirs and successors, granted to the said mayor, aldermen, bailiffs, and citizens of the said city and their successors, that from thence afterwards for ever, there should and might be within the said city one of the aldermen of the said city for the time being, who might be and should be named mayor of the said city, and that also there might and should be eleven honest men beside the mayor of the said city, who might be and should be called aldermen of the said city, and that in like manner there might and should be two other men of the said city to be elected in the form following in the letters patent aforesaid mentioned; who might be and should be called bailiffs of the said city; and that there might and should be within the said city two other discreet men to be elected in the form following in the letters patent aforesaid mentioned, who might be and should be called coroners of the said city; and that there might and should be within the said city twenty-four other men to be elected in the form following in the letters patent aforesaid mentioned; who might be and should be called the chief citizens of the said city, and might be from time to time of the common council of the said city, and assisting the mayor, aldermen, and bailiffs of the said city for the time being, in all causes, things, transactions and matters whatsoever, touching or any wise concerning the said city; and further the said late king willed, and by his letters patent aforesaid, for himself, his heirs and successors, granted to the said mayor, aldermen, bailiffs and citizens of the said city, and to their successors, that the said mayor, aldermen, bailiffs, and the twenty-four chief citizens of the said city for the time being, or the greater part of them, (of whom the said late king willed that the mayor of the said city for the time being should be one) upon publick summons by the mayor of the said city for the time being, thereupon to be had and made, should have full power, licence and authority, in the Guildhall of the said city from time to time to assemble, and there to found, constitute, ordain, make and establish from time to time reasonable laws, statutes, constitutions, decrees and ordinances in writing, which to them, or the greater part of them (of whom the said late king willed that

that the mayor of the said city for the time being should be one) should seem to be good, wholesome, useful, proper and necessary according to their sound discretion, for the good rule and goverment of the said city, and of all and singular the officers, ministers, artificers, inhabitants, and residents whatsoever within the said city for the time being, and for declaring in what mode and order the said mayor, aldermen, bailiffs, and chief citizens, and all and singular the officers, ministers, artificers, inhabitants and residents respectively within the said city should behave, demean and carry themselves in their offices, callings, misteries, arts and businesses within the said city, the liberties and precincts of the same, for the further publick good, common advantage and good government of the said city, and for supplying the same with food, and for all other matters and things whatsoever the said city touching or in any manner concerning; and that the mayor, aldermen, * bailiffs, and chief * P. 527.
citizens of the said city for the time being, or the greater part of them, (of whom the said late king willed that the mayor of the said city for the time being should be one) as often as they should found, make, ordain and establish such laws, institutions, rights, ordinances, and constitutions in the form aforesaid, might ordain, limit and provide such corporal pains, punishments and penalties, or impose and assess such fines and amercements, or both of them, upon all persons offending against such laws, institutions, rights, ordinances and constitutions, or any or either of them, as to the said mayor, aldermen, bailiffs, and chief citizens of the said city for the time being, or the greater part of them (of whom the said late king willed that the mayor of the said city should always be one) should seem necessary, convenient and requisite, for the observation of the said laws, ordinances and constitutions, and that they might and should levy and recover the said fines and amercements by their serjeant at mace, or other officer of the said city for the time being, by distress of the goods and chattles of the offenders in this behalf, or in any other lawful mode, and might keep and retain the same so levied and recovered to the use of the said mayor, aldermen, bailiffs and citizens of the said city and their successors, without hindrance of the said late king, his heirs and successors, or of any of the officers or ministers of the said late king, his heirs or successors whatsoever, and without making any account thereof, or in any other manner whatsoever, yielding or paying the same to the said king, his heirs or successors; all and singular which laws, institutions, ordinances, rights and constitutions so as aforesaid to be made, the said late

king willed, ſhould be obſerved under the pains in the ſame contained; and that from thence afterwards from time to time it ſhould and might be well lawful, and the ſaid late king by his letters patent aforeſaid, for himſelf, his heirs and ſucceſſors, gave and granted full and abſolute power and authority to the ſaid mayor, aldermen, bailiffs and citizens of the city of Carliſle aforeſaid, and to their ſucceſſors, that the ſaid mayor, aldermen, bailiffs and chief citizens, or the greater part of them, might and could change, annihilate, and abrogate the ſaid laws, ordinances and conſtitutions which they or their predeceſſors before had made, founded, ordained and conſtituted, which appeared to be inconvenient and inexpedient for them, and in the place of ſuch laws, ordinances and conſtitutions, might found, ordain and conſtitute ſuch other laws, ordinances and conſtitutions as to them, or to the greater part of them (of whom the ſaid late king willed that the mayor of the ſaid city for the time being ſhould be one) in like manner ſhould ſeem to be neceſſary and expedient, nevertheleſs ſo that the ſaid laws, ordinances, inſtitutions, conſtitutions, impriſonments, fines and amercements ſhould be reaſonable and not repugnant nor contrary to the laws, ſtatutes, cuſtoms, or rights of the kingdom of the ſaid late king of England; and for the better execution of the will and grant of the ſaid late king in that behalf, the ſaid late king aſſigned, named, created, conſtituted and made by his letters patent
* P. 528. aforeſaid, for himſelf his heirs and ſucceſſors, his * beloved Richard Barwiſe, eſquire, to be the firſt and modern mayor of the ſaid city, willing that the ſaid Richard Barwiſe ſhould continue in the ſaid office of mayor of the ſaid city until the monday next after the feaſt of St. Michael the Archangel, next enſuing the date of the letters patent aforeſaid, and from thence until one other of the eleven aldermen of the ſaid city for the time being to that office in the due manner ſhould be elected appointed and ſworn, according to the ordinances and proviſions following, in the letters patent aforeſaid expreſſed and declared, if the ſaid Richard Barwiſe ſhould ſo long live: the ſaid late king alſo aſſigned, nominated, erected, conſtituted and made by the letters patent aforeſaid, for himſelf his heirs and ſucceſſors, his beloved Richard Barwiſe then mayor of the ſaid city, Henry Bains, William Barwick the elder, Edward Aglionby, Thomas Blennerhaſſet, Thomas Gent, Mathew Cape, Peter Bains, George Dalton knight, Thomas Dacre knight, William Barwick the younger, and Ambroſe Nicholſon, to be the firſt and modern aldermen of the ſaid city, to continue in that office during their natural lives, unleſs in the mean time

time for their bad government or other reasonable cause by the mayor, aldermen, bailiffs and chief citizens of the said city for the time being, or by the greater part of them, (of whom the said late king willed that the mayor of the said city for the time being should be one) they or any of them should be removed; also the said late king assigned, nominated, created, constituted and made, by the letters patent aforesaid, for himself, his heirs and successors, his beloved Thomas Bushby and Thomas Kidd, to be the first and modern bailiffs of the said city, to continue in the said office until the Monday next after the feast of St. Michael the archangel next ensuing the date of the letters patent aforesaid, and from thence until others of the citizens of the said city in the due manner should be appointed and sworn to that office, according to the ordinances and provisions following in the said letters patent expressed and declared, if the said Thomas Bushby and Thomas Kidd should so long live, unless in the mean time for their bad conduct or for other reasonable cause they should be removed, as afterwards, he did limit and appoint; the said late king also assigned nominated, created, constituted and made by the letters patent aforesaid, for himself, his heirs and successors, his beloved William Atkinson and Leonard Milbyrne to be the first and modern coroners of the said city, to continue in that office until the Monday next after the feast of St. Michael the archangel next ensuing the date of the said letters patent, and from thence until others to the said office of coroners in the due manner should be elected, appointed and sworn; the said late king also assigned, nominated, created, constituted and made, by his letters patent aforesaid, for himself, his heirs, and successors, his beloved Edward Barwise, Henry Monck, Edward Dalton, Thomas Tallantyre, Thomas Willson, Robert Collyer, Simon Braithwaite, Robert Shepherd. Robert Jackson, Richard Dobson, Thomas Threweld, John Barker, Thomas Russel, Simon Jackson, James Knagg, Robert Watson, * Andrew Foster, Nicholas Hudson, Thomas Syde, Thomas Barnefather, Clement Barnefather, John Bell the elder, Thomas Dalton, and Hugh Gibson to be the first and modern chief citizens of the said city to continue in that office during their natural lives, unless in the mean time for their bad conduct, or for any other reasonable cause, by the mayor, aldermen, bailiffs, and chief citizens of the said city for the time being, or by the greater part of the same, they or any of them should be removed; and further the said late king willed, and by the letters patent aforesaid, for himself, his heirs and successors, granted to the said mayor, aldermen, bailiffs

* P. 529.

bailiffs and citizens of the ſaid city and to their ſucceſſors, that the mayor, aldermen, bailiffs and the twenty-four chief citizens of the ſaid city for the time being, or the greater part of them, from time to time for ever, ſhould and might have the ſole and full authority without the aſſiſtance or aid of the other citizens of the ſaid city or of any of them to chooſe and nominate, and that they might and could chooſe and nominate annually and every year on the Monday next after the feaſt of St. Michael the archangel for ever, collected and aſſembled in the Guildhall of the ſaid city, one of the ſaid aldermen for the time being to be mayor of the ſaid city, and if the number of electors in ſuch caſe ſhould be equal, then and ſo often the ſaid late king willed and ordained that the mayor for the time being in ſuch caſe ſhould have a double vote; and that he after that he ſhould be ſo elected and appointed before that he ſhould be admitted to execute that office, ſhould take his corporal oath before the laſt mayor his predeceſſor, if then alive, and if he ſhould be dead, then before the aldermen for the time being, or the greater part of the ſame in the preſence of as many aldermen, bailiffs and of the twenty-four chief citizens of the ſaid city for the time being, who then ſhould chooſe to be preſent; to execute the office of mayor of the ſaid city rightly well and faithful in all things touching the ſaid office; and that after ſuch oath ſo taken he might and ſhould execute the office of mayor of the ſaid city for one whole year then next following, and afterwards until one other of the aldermen aforeſaid for the time being, to that office in the due manner ſhould be elected, appointed and ſworn according to the ordinances and ſtatutes, in the letters patent aforeſaid expreſſed and declared; to which mayor of the ſaid city for the time being, and to the aldermen of the ſaid city for the time being, or to the major part of them, the mayor being dead, the ſaid late king gave and granted by his letters patent aforeſaid, full power and authority to give and adminiſter the reaſonable oath to the mayor of the ſaid city, ſo from time to time to to be nominated and elected well and faithfully to execute the office of mayor of the ſaid city, without any other warrant or commiſſion from the ſaid late king, his heirs or ſucceſſors in that behalf, to be procured or obtained; and further the ſaid late king willed, and by the letters patent aforeſaid, for himſelf, his heirs and ſucceſſors, granted to the ſaid mayor, aldermen, bailiffs, and citizens of the ſaid city and to their ſucceſſors, that the mayor, aldermen, bailiffs, and
* P. 530 twenty-four chief citizens of the * ſaid city for the time being, or the greater part of them from time to time for ever, might and ſhould have the power and authority to elect and

nominate,

nominate, and that they might and ſhould elect and nominate in the Guildhall of the ſaid city collected and aſſembled, on the ſaid Monday next after the feaſt of St. Michael the archangel in every year for ever, two of the citizens of the ſaid city to be bailiffs of the ſaid city, and that they ſo named and elected before that they ſhould be admitted to execute that office, ſhould take their and each of them ſhould take his corporal oath before the mayor and the reſt of the aldermen and the twenty-four chief citizens of the ſaid city, who ſhould chooſe to be preſent; to execute that office, rightly, well and faithfully in all things touching the ſaid office, and that after ſuch oath ſo taken they ſhould and might execute the ſaid office of bailiffs for one whole year from thence next following, and further until two other men in the due manner ſhould be elected, appointed and ſworn into that office, according to the ordinances in the letters patent aforeſaid, expreſſed and declared, and that the mayor of the ſaid city for the time being ſhould have full power and authority to give and adminiſter ſuch oath, to the ſaid bailiffs ſo elected and nominated, well and faithfully as aforeſaid to execute that office, without any other warrant from the ſaid late king, his heirs and ſucceſſors in that behalf to be procured; and further the ſaid late king willed, and by the letters patent aforeſaid for himſelf, his heirs, and ſucceſſors granted to the ſaid mayor, aldermen and bailiffs, and citizens of the ſaid city, and their ſucceſſors, that if the mayor of the ſaid city for the time being at any time then afterwards within one year after that he ſhould be elected, appointed and ſworn into the office of mayor of the ſaid city as aforeſaid ſhould happen to die, that then and ſo often it ſhould and might be lawful for the ſaid aldermen, bailiffs, and the ſaid twenty-four chief citizens of the ſaid city for the time being, or the major part of the ſame, in the Guildhall of the ſaid city for this purpoſe aſſembled, to nominate, elect and appoint one of the aldermen of the ſaid city for the time being to be mayor of the ſaid city, and that he ſo elected and appointed to the office of mayor of the ſaid city, ſhould have and exerciſe that office during the remainder of the ſame year, and afterwards until one other according to the ordinances aforeſaid in the ſaid letters patent declared, in the due manner ſhould be elected, appointed and ſworn, firſt taking his corporal oath before as many of the aldermen, bailiffs, and of the twenty-four chief citizens of the ſaid city for the time being, who ſhould then chooſe to be preſent, well and faithfully to execute the ſaid office, and ſo as often as the caſe ſhould ſo occur, and that it ſhould and might be well lawful the caſe ſo occurring, for any two

or

or more of the aldermen of the ſaid city in the preſence of ſuch of the aldermen, bailiffs, and of the ſaid twenty-four chief citizens of the ſaid city who then ſhould chooſe to be preſent to give and adminiſter ſuch oath to the mayor of the ſaid city ſo to be nominated and elected from time to time for the due execution of his office, without any other commiſſion or warrant from the ſaid late king, his heirs, or ſucceſſors in that behalf to be procured or obtained: and if an alderman or aldermen of the ſaid city for the time being, from thence afterwards ſhould * happen to die, that then and ſo often it ſhould and might be lawful for the mayor and ſurviving aldermen for the time being, or for the major part of the ſame, in the Guildhall of the ſaid city for this purpoſe aſſembled, to elect and appoint one or more of the more diſcreet and more honeſt citizens of the ſaid city into the place or places of ſuch alderman or aldermen ſo dying; and that he or they ſo appointed, the office of alderman or aldermen of the ſaid city, (having firſt taken his or their corporal oath or oaths, before the mayor of the ſaid city for the time being, well and faithfully to execute that office in all things touching the ſaid office) ſhould have and exerciſe during his or their natural life or lives, and ſo as often as the caſe ſhould ſo happen; to which mayor of the ſaid city for the time being, the caſe ſo happening the ſaid late king, gave and granted by his letters patent aforeſaid, full power and authority to adminiſter ſuch oath or oaths to the ſaid alderman or aldermen, ſo from time to time to be nominated and elected for the true execution of his or their office or offices, without any other warrant in that behalf to be procured; and further the ſaid late king willed, and by his letters patent aforeſaid, for himſelf, his heirs, and ſucceſſors, granted to the ſaid mayor, aldermen, bailiffs and citizens of the ſaid city and to their ſucceſſors, that the ſaid Richard Barwiſe, then mayor of the ſaid city, by the ſaid late king as aforeſaid nominated, ſhould make oath upon the holy goſpel of God, before the aldermen of the ſaid city before named, or the major part of them, well and faithfully to execute the office of mayor of the ſaid city; to which aldermen or to the greater part of them the ſaid late king by the letters patent aforeſaid, gave full power and authority to adminiſter ſuch oath, and that without any other warrant or commiſſion from the ſaid late king, his heirs, or ſucceſſors in that behalf to be procured; and further the ſaid late king willed, and by his letters patent aforeſaid, for himſelf, his heirs and ſucceſſors granted, to the ſaid mayor, aldermen, bailiffs and citizens of the ſaid city, that all others who from thence afterwards into the office of mayor of

* P. 531.

of the ſaid city, ſhould be appointed and elected as aforeſaid, ſhould take an oath before the laſt mayor, and the aldermen, or the greater part of them then willing to be preſent, well and faithfully to execute the ſaid office in all things and that without any other warrant, writ or commiſſion from the ſaid late king, his heirs or ſucceſſors in that behalf, to be procured or obtained; and further the ſaid late king willed, and by the letters patent aforeſaid for himſelf, his heirs, and ſucceſſors, granted to the ſaid mayor, aldermen, bailiffs and citizens of the ſaid city, and to their ſucceſſors, that whenſoever it might happen that the bailiffs of the ſaid city for the time being or either of them, at any time within one year after that, he or they ſhould be elected, appointed and ſworn to the office of bailiff and bailiffs of the ſaid city, ſhould die or ſhould be removed from that office, (which bailiffs or either of them the ſaid * late king willed, ſhould and might be removed by the mayor, aldermen, and twenty-four chief citizens of the ſaid city, or by the greater part of them, for reaſonable and juſt cauſes) that then and ſo often it ſhould and might be well lawful for the ſaid mayor, aldermen, bailiffs, and twenty-four chief citizens of the ſaid city for the time being, or the greater part of them, to nominate, elect and appoint one or two other of the citizens of the ſaid city for the time being, bailiff or bailiffs of the ſaid city; and that he or they ſo elected and appointed bailiff or bailiffs of the ſaid city ſhould have and exerciſe that office during the remainder of the ſaid year, firſt taking his or their corporal oath before the mayor and aldermen of the ſaid city for the time being, or the greater part of them willing to be preſent, to execute that office in all things well and faithfully, and ſo as often as the caſe ſhould ſo happen; to which mayor and aldermen or to the greater part of them for the time being, the ſaid late king by his letters patent aforeſaid gave full power to adminiſter ſuch oath, without any further warrant in that behalf to be procured or obtained; and if it ſhould happen that any one or more of the ſaid twenty-four chief citizens of the ſaid city for the time being ſhould die, or from that place be removed, which twenty-four citizens, or any one or more of them, the ſaid late king willed, ſhould and might be removed for juſt and reaſonable cauſe by the mayor and aldermen of the ſaid city or by the greater part of them for the time being, that then and ſo often it ſhould and might be well lawful for the mayor and aldermen of the ſaid city for the time being, or for the greater part of them, to aſſemble and collect themſelves in the Guildhall aforeſaid, and there to elect, nominate and appoint one or more other or others of the more honeſt and diſcreet citizens of the

* P. 532.

the ſaid city into the place or places of ſuch one or others of the twenty-four chief citizens aforeſaid, ſo dying or being removed, to ſupply the ſaid number of twenty-four chief citizens of the ſaid city, and that he or they ſo as aforeſaid elected and choſen to the place of chief citizen or citizens of the ſaid city, firſt taking his or their corporal oath before the mayor and aldermen of the ſaid city for the time being, or the greater part of them, well and faithfully to execute that place, ſhould have and exerciſe the ſaid place of chief citizen or citizens of the ſaid city during their natural lives, unleſs in the mean time by the mayor and aldermen of the ſaid city, or the greater part of them for juſt and reaſonable cauſes, he or they ſhould be removed according to the ordinance aforeſaid, in the letters patent aforeſaid declared; to which mayor and aldermen or the greater part of them for the time being, the ſaid late king by his letters patent aforeſaid gave full power to adminiſter ſuch oath to the ſaid chief citizen or citizens, ſo to be nominated and elected, without any other warrant from the ſaid late king, his heirs, or ſucceſſors in that behalf to be procured; alſo the ſaid late king willed, and by his letters patent aforeſaid for himſelf, his heirs, and ſucceſſors, granted to the ſaid mayor, aldermen, bailiffs and citizens of the ſaid city, and to their ſucceſſors, that they and their ſucceſſors from thence afterwards for ever, ſhould and might have within the ſaid city, one diſcreet man learned in the laws of England, who ſhould be and
* P. 533. ſhould be named * recorder of the ſaid city, and for the better execution of his will in that behalf, the ſaid late king aſſigned, nominated, conſtituted and made by his letters patent aforeſaid, for himſelf, his heirs, and ſucceſſors his beloved Thomas Carleton, knight, then recorder of the ſaid city, to be recorder of the ſaid city, to continue in that office during the pleaſure of the mayor, aldermen, bailiffs, and twenty-four chief citizens of the ſaid city for the time being, or the greater part of them; alſo the ſaid late king willed, and by his letters patent aforeſaid, for himſelf, his heirs, and ſucceſſors, granted that from time to time and at all times it ſhould and might be well lawful for the mayor, aldermen, bailiffs, and twenty-four chief citizens of the ſaid city for the time being, or for the greater part of them, for this purpoſe aſſembled and collected within the ſaid city, to chooſe and appoint from time to time one other diſcreet and proper perſon learned in the laws of England, to be recorder of the ſaid city, to continue in that office during the pleaſure of the mayor, aldermen, bailiffs, and twenty-four chief citizens of the ſaid city for the time being, or the greater

greater part of them; and that he ſhould take his corporal oath before the mayor of the ſaid city for the time being, well and faithfully to execute the office of recorder of the ſaid city in all things; and that the mayor and aldermen of the ſaid city for the time being, or the greater part of them, ſhould have full power by virtue of the letters patent aforeſaid to give and adminiſter as well to the ſaid Thomas Carleton then recorder of the ſaid city, as to ſuch other recorder to be choſen as aforeſaid, the reaſonable oath for the due, true and faithful execution of that office, without any other commiſſion or warrant whatſoever from thence afterwards to be procured and obtained, and ſo as often as the caſe ſhould ſo happen, as by the letters patent aforeſaid among other things appears; by virtue of which letters patent aforeſaid, the mayor and citizens of the ſaid city became a body corporate and politick, indeed, fact and in name, by the name of the mayor, aldermen, bailiffs, and citizens of the city of Carliſle, and ſo from thence hitherto have been and ſtill are incorporated; and we further certify that from the whole time aforeſaid, whereof the memory of man is not to the contrary, until the ſaid time of making the letters patent aforeſaid, every counſellor, otherwiſe alderman of the ſaid city, by the mayor and counſellors otherwiſe aldermen of the ſaid city, for the time being or the greater part of them, of whom the mayor for the time being hath been one, and after the making of the letters patent aforeſaid, every alderman of the ſaid city for the time being, by the mayor and aldermen of the ſaid city for the time being, or by the greater part of them, of whom the ſaid mayor hath been one, for juſt and reaſonable cauſe, hath been removable and hath been accuſtomed to be removed from his office of alderman of the ſaid city. And we further certify that the ſaid Timothy Haddock, after the ſaid time of the making of the letters patent aforeſaid, to wit, on the 2d day of October in the year of our Lord, 1673, then being a citizen of the ſaid city, at the * city aforeſaid in the Guildhall there, in the due manner was elected an alderman of the ſaid city, and then and there took his oath before the then mayor and the greater number of the aldermen of the ſaid city, well and faithfully to execute his office of alderman aforeſaid, to the effect following, to wit; that the advice, aid, and conſent of him the ſaid Timothy, ſhould be by him the ſaid Timothy given and ſpoken at all times afterwards to and with the greater part of the mayor and counſellors of the ſaid city, for the good government and increaſe of the publick weal, not regarding any private lucre or gain for himſelf, or any other perſon to the preju-

Every alderman as well before as after the letters patent, was removable for juſt and reaſonable cauſe by the mayor and the reſt of the aldermen for the time being.

* P. 534.

Haddock choſen an alderman after the letters patent.

And took the oath of office.

dice of the wealth, liberty, or liberties, goods, ordinances, constitutions and customs of the said city; and that the said Timothy would not disclose or discover to any person or persons at any time any words, talks, communications, or discourses, moved, spoken or heard by him, or by any of his fellow counsellors assembled together in any place to consult for the wealth or good government of the said city, and that he would yield and agree to all such causes and matters as the mayor and the greater part of his fellow counsellors should agree to; and also to the utmost of his power would suppress all such persons as should endeavour to make any factions, conspiracies or other disorder against the good government and constitution of the said city. all which points and articles he the said Timothy well and faithfully would keep according to the laws of this kingdom, and the constitutions, customs and liberties of the said city to the utmost of his power: under colour of which the said Timothy then became one of the aldermen of the said city. And we further certify that the said Timothy so being one of the aldermen of the said city, and one Thomas Jackson, esquire, being mayor of the said city, on the 6th day of October in the 31st year of the reign of the lord the now king, a common council was held in the Guildhall of the said city by the said Thomas Jackson, then being mayor of the said city as aforesaid, and the greater part of the aldermen, bailiffs, and chief citizens of the said city, for the election of a mayor for the year then next ensuing according to the form of the letters patent aforesaid, at which common council the said Timothy Haddock was present, and being about to depart from thence, the said Thomas Jackson so being mayor of the said city, spoke to him and requested the said Timothy not to depart from the said council before the election aforesaid was made, but that he should attend the said election then there to be made according to the duty of his office of alderman aforesaid, in that behalf; nevertheless the said Timothy from the said council instantly, contemptuously and without reasonable cause departed, and afterwards on the same day before the election aforesaid made, returned into the Guildhall aforesaid, bringing thither with him divers persons to the number of sixty of the inferior citizens of the said city, not having vote or suffrage in the said election, to disturb the said election; and the said Timothy and divers other persons of the said persons, at the instigation of the said Timothy, then and there * tumultuously, riotously, and in a threatning manner, required the said mayor, and the said aldermen, bailiffs, and chief citizens in the council aforesaid, for the cause aforesaid assembled, that

That at a common council held for the election of a mayor, Haddock misbehaved himself.

* P. 535.

that he and they, the other perſons ſo brought together with the mayor, aldermen, bailiffs, and chief citizens as aforeſaid aſſembled, ſhould chooſe the ſaid mayor ſo as aforeſaid to be choſen, againſt the form and effect of the letters patent aforeſaid, ſaying and with a great noiſe ſhouting and alledging that the letters patent aforeſaid concerning the election aforeſaid were void, to the great terror of the ſaid Thomas, then mayor, and of the aldermen, bailiffs, and chief citizens in the council aforeſaid, ſo as aforeſaid aſſembled: and the ſaid Timothy and all the other perſons ſo as aforeſaid by him brought with him, by and with the inſtigation and procurement of the ſaid Timothy, then and there in the preſence of the ſaid mayor, aldermen, bailiffs, and chief citizens for the cauſe aforeſaid as aforeſaid aſſembled, with ſuch and the like threats, ſtrifes, and riotous clamours, incommoded and diſturbed the ſaid mayor, aldermen, bailiffs, and chief citizens, ſo that they the ſaid mayor, aldermen, bailiffs, and chief citizens dare not and could not proceed, to the election of a mayor for a great ſpace of time, to wit, for the ſpace of two hours; wherefore afterwards to wit, on the 25th day of October, then next enſuing, in a council held in the Guildhall of the ſaid city, before the ſaid Thomas Jackſon, then mayor of the ſaid city, and the greater part of the aldermen of the ſaid city, it was ordained by the ſaid mayor and aldermen aforeſaid then there preſent, that the ſaid Timothy ſhould be ſummoned to be at the common council of the ſaid mayor and aldermen, to be held in the Guildhall aforeſaid on the 8th day of November then next enſuing, to anſwer for his miſdemeanour aforeſaid in that behalf, and to ſhow cauſe wherefore he for ſuch his miſdemeanour, from the office and place of alderman of the ſaid city ought not to be removed; at which council held on the 8th day of November, in the 31ſt year aforeſaid, in the Guildhall aforeſaid, before me the ſaid Thomas Jackſon and the greater part of the aldermen aforeſaid, the ſaid Timothy according to the ſummons aforeſaid appeared, and being aſked by the ſaid mayor if he could ſay any thing in his excuſe of and concerning the premiſſes, or could ſhow any cauſe wherefore he from the office of alderman of the ſaid city ought not to be removed, he the ſaid Timothy did not ſay any thing in excuſe of his miſdemeanour aforeſaid, nor ſhowed any cauſe wherefore he for his offence aforeſaid, from his place and office of one of the aldermen of the ſaid city ought not to be removed, therefore the ſaid Thomas Jackſon then mayor, and the ſaid greater part of the aldermen of the ſaid city, then there preſent, removed and diſcharged the ſaid Timothy Haddock, from his ſaid office of one

That he was ſummoned to appear at another common council to anſwer his miſdemeanour or ſhow cauſe why he ſhould not be turned out of his office for the ſame.

He appeared but ſhowed no cauſe and was therefore turned out of office.

one of the aldermen of the ſaid city, and declared him to be removed from that office, and for that cauſe, we the ſaid mayor, aldermen, bailiffs and chief citizens of the ſaid city have not reſtored, and cannot reſtore the ſaid Timothy Haddock to the place and office of one of the aldermen of the ſaid city.

---

* P. 536.

## * Mandamus for Sherman.

Return. to a mandamus to the archdeacon of of Exeter to reſtore Sherman to the office of regiſter of the archdeaconry. That the ſaid office is an antient office, to be exerciſed at Exeter in the dioceſs of the biſhop of Exeter by a proper perſon or perſons n perſon, or by ſufficient deputy or deputies.

TO wit—I Edward Lake, doctor in divinity, archdeacon of the archdeaconry of Exeter, in the county of the city of Exeter, and in the county of Devon, to the moſt ſerene and powerful prince in Chriſt Charles the ſecond, moſt humbly certify, that the ſaid place and office of regiſter of the archdeaconry of Exeter, in the county of the city of Exeter, and in the county of Devon aforeſaid, in the writ to this ſchedule annexed mentioned, now is, and alſo from the time whereof the memory of man is not to the contrary, hath been an antient office and place at Exeter aforeſaid, within the dioceſs of the biſhop of Exeter, to be held and exerciſed by a proper man, or by proper men, by himſelf or themſelves, or by his or their ſufficient deputy or deputies in that behalf, to be executed and enjoyed, and that to the ſaid office divers wages, fees, profits, rewards and emoluments for the acts and buſineſs in the court of the archdeaconry aforeſaid done, entered and regiſtered, from the time whereof the memory of man is not to the contrary, hitherto of right have appertained and belonged, and now do appertain and belong: And the regiſter of the archdeaconry aforeſaid for the time being, for the whole time aforeſaid, by reaſon of the execution of the office and place aforeſaid, hath been accuſtomed, and of right ought to have and receive divers wages, fees, profits, rewards and emoluments as belonging and appertaining to that office and place; and that from the whole time whereof the memory of man is not to the contrary, whenſoever that place and office hath happened to be vacant, the ſaid place and office of regiſter of the archdeaconry aforeſaid, with all wages, fees, profits, rewards and emoluments to the ſaid office belonging and appertaining, hath been granted and grantable, and hath been accuſtomed and of right ought

ought to be given and granted, by the archdeacon of the archdeaconry aforesaid for the time being, to some proper person or proper persons, willing and capable to take and exercise that office and place for the term of the life or lives of such person or persons: and that the archdeacon of the archdeaconry of Exeter aforesaid for the time being, and also from the time whereof the memory of man is not to the contrary bears the office, and for the whole time aforesaid hath born the office of ordinary within the archdeaconry aforesaid, for proving, registering and perfecting all and singular last wills, and testiments of all and singular the persons dying within the archdeaconry aforesaid, not having at the time of their death, goods, rights, or credits in divers or any diocesses or peculiar jurisdictions without the archdeaconry aforesaid, and for granting administration of the goods and chattles and credits of all and singular the persons within the archdeaconry aforesaid dying intestate, and not having at the time of their death goods, rights or credits in divers diocesses or peculiar jurisdictions; and that the archdeacon of the archdeaconry of Exeter aforesaid for the time being, is and also from the time whereof the memory of man is not to the contrary, hath been judge of the court of the archdeaconry aforesaid, held at Exeter aforesaid, within the archdeaconry aforesaid, from time to time for the whole time aforesaid, to hear and determine in the said court the causes, matters and suits belonging or appertaining to ecclesiastical jurisdiction and cognizance, and arising or springing within the said archdeaconry, as well at the * instance of the principal parties, as depending solely upon his office, and promotion, and also minister and officer to execute all things, which by the mandate of the bishop of Exeter, the archdeacons of the archdeaconry of Exeter aforesaid, within the diocess of the bishop of Exeter aforesaid, have been commanded and directed to execute within the said archdeaconry; and that the register of the archdeaconry aforesaid for the time being is, and from the time whereof the memory of man is not to the contrary, hath been an officer and minister of the archdeacon of the archdeaconry aforesaid, and by reason of his office hath been used and ought to enter and register in writing, and to reduce into writing all orders, memorandums, determinations and sentences to be made in that behalf, by the said archdeacon of and concerning the proving and registering of last wills and testaments, and the granting of administration as aforesaid, between the parties litigant in the said court of the archdeaconry aforesaid, or concerning other matters made, done, or published, pronounced or adjudged; and to make and reduce into writing the acts and

That the office of register is grantable by the archdeacon of Exeter who is ordinary within the archdeaconry,

for probate of wills,

granting administration,

and for hearing of causes of ecclesiastical cognisance.

* P. 537.

and an officer to execute the bishop's mandates.

That the register is the archdeacon's officer.

his duties.

and proceſs in that behalf; and that to the regiſter of the archdeaconry aforeſaid for the whole time aforeſaid, by reaſon of his office aforeſaid hath appertained, and was incumbent, and as yet appertains and is incumbent to examine as well the witneſſes produced upon any cauſe or cauſes, matter or matters, at any time depending undetermined in the court of the archdeaconry aforeſaid, as the principal parties, to wit, complainant and complained of, in the ſaid cauſes or matters or any of them, and this as well at the inſtance of the principal parties as of his own mere office and promotion; and to tranſmit the acts and proceedings of the court of the archdeaconry aforeſaid under the authentick form of law done and had in any cauſe buſineſs or matter in the ſaid court of the archdeaconry aforeſaid depending, to any other ſuperior eccleſiaſtical juriſdiction upon any application in that behalf made according to the command of the eccleſiaſtical law, and alſo to make out publick inſtruments and alſo to reduce into writing acts, ſentences and decrees of the judge of the ſaid court of the archdeaconry aforeſaid for the time being, according to the due form of law, and to enter and regiſter the ſame in writing, and to collect and receive for the lord the king ſeveral ſums of money due and payable to the ſaid lord the king for the acts and buſineſs in the ſaid court of the archdeaconry, entered done and regiſtered; and alſo to perfect, execute, diſpatch and perform all and ſingular the acts and buſineſs in any manner belonging and appertaining to the ſaid place and office of regiſter of the archdeaconry aforeſaid; and the office of regiſter aforeſaid touches and concerns, and for the whole time aforeſaid hath touched and concerned the adminiſtration and execution of juſtice as well in the ſeveral reſpects aforeſaid as in divers other reſpects; therefore the place and office of regiſter of the archdeaconry aforeſaid wants and requires a learned, ſkilful, diſcreet and honeſt officer; and to the ſaid lord the king, I further moſt humbly certify, that long before the coming of this writ to me in this behalf directed, to wit, on the 27th day of July, in the year of our Lord 1664, the place and office of regiſter of the archdeaconry of Exeter aforeſaid, by Robert Cary, doctor in divinity, then archdeacon of the ſaid * archdeaconry in the due manner was granted to the ſaid Edward Sherman and John Sherman, to be exerciſed by them, or by their ſufficient deputy or deputies, to wit, at the city of Exeter aforeſaid, by virtue of which they the ſaid Edward Sherman and John Sherman became entitled to the ſaid office and place of regiſter of the archdeaconry aforeſaid for the term of their lives, and that office there had, exerciſed and poſſeſſed

The office of regiſter concerns the adminiſtration of juſtice.

* P. 538. That the office of regiſter was granted to E. Sherman and J. Sherman by a former archdeacon.

possessed, and the execution of that office took upon themselves; and thy the said ES: and IS: so being register of the archdeaconry of Exeter aforesaid, they the said ES: and IS: on the 5th day of September in the year of our lord 1677 at the city of Exeter aforesaid, deputed assigned constituted, and appointed one Nicholas Eveleigh of the city of Exeter aforesaid gent. the deputy of them the said Edward and John, in the said office, to exercise and execute the said office of register of the archdeaconry of Exeter aforesaid, with all things whatsoever to the said office belonging or in any wise appertaining; and thereupon and against the form of the statute in such case made and provided, then and there they the said Edward Sherman and John Sherman corruptly and unduly took and received from the said Nicholas Eveleigh a writing obligatory, sealed with the seal of the said Nicholas, in which he the said Nicholas granted that he, his heirs and executors were holden and firmly bound to the said Edward Sherman and John Sherman in the penal sum of five hundred pounds, with a condition thereto annexed, that if he the said Nicholas at the request of them the said Edward Sherman and John Sherman, or either of them, should give to them the said Edward Sherman and John Sherman a true and just account of all and singular the monies, fees, and profits to that office appertaining which had come to the hands of the said Nicholas, and should pay over the same to the said Edward Sherman and John Sherman, then that the said writing obligatory should be void andof no effect, otherwise should remain in full force and vigour; by reason of which premisses he the said Nicholas Eveleigh, at the city of Exeter aforesaid, took upon himself the burden of the execution of that office and place, and the said office and place as the deputy of them the said Edward Sherman and John Sherman under colour of the premisses, there for the space of three years had, exercised and possessed, and during that time paid to the said Edward Shermen and John Sherman fifty pounds of the lawful money of England annually; And afterwards, to wit, on the third day of January, in the 23d year of the reign of the lord Charles the second, the now king of England, &c. by a certain other agreement made, it was concluded between them the said Edward Sherman and John Sherman and him the said Nicholas Eveleigh, against the form of the statute aforesaid in such case made and provided, to wit, at the city of Exeter aforesaid, that the said Nicholas should have and possess the said office as the deputy of them the said Edward Sherman and John Sherman, and should have the profits and issues thereof to his

that they made one N. Eveleigh their deputy and against the statute took from him a bond conditioned to account for and pay the fees and profits of the office to them.

" *the statute is the 5th and 6th of Ed. 6th, C. 16.*"

That Eveleigh executed the office for 3 years and paid the Shermans 50l. yearly.

afterwards another agreement between the Shermans and Eveliegh, that Eveleigh should have all the profits to his own use and should pay the Shermans * P. 539. 6l. 13s. 4d. monthly, which he did against the statute.

his own proper use, and that he the said Nicholas for his deputation of the said office so to be had, should pay to the said Edward Sharman and John Sherman by the month, for every month in which he the said Nicholas should have that office the sum of 6l. 13s. 4d. and * thereupon he the said Nicholas had and occupied the said office for twelve months, and in performance of the agreement last aforesaid, paid to the said Edward Sherman and John Sherman 6l. 13s. 4d. for every month, to wit, at the city of Exeter aforesaid, which 6l. 13s. 4d. for every month of the twelve months aforesaid, they the said Edward Sherman and John Sherman from the said Nicholas for his deputation to the said office there, had and received, against the form of the statute aforesaid; and afterwards, to wit, on the 13th day of February, in the 26th year of the reign of the lord Charles the 2d, the now king of England, &c. they the said Edward Sherman and John Sherman then pretending that they were seized of the office of register of the archdeaconry of Totnes, in the county of Devon and diocess of Exeter, a certain other agreement was made, to wit, at the city of Exeter aforesaid, between them the said Edward Sherman and John Sherman and the said Nicholas Eveielgh, or articles between them made and sealed, that one Philip Atherton gent. should receive annually for seven years, if the said Philip and the said Nicholas should so long live, out of the profits and emoluments of the said offices of register of the archdeaconries of Exeter and Totnes aforesaid, for the sole and proper use of the said Edward Sherman and John Sherman, the annual sum of one hundred and forty pounds by quarterly payments, and that the said Nicholas should have all the remaining profits of the said offices, for the execution thereof by him the said Nicholas to be executed; and that in pursuance of that agreement, he the said Nicholas had and possessed the said offices as the deputy of the said Edward Sherman and John Sherman for one half year, and seventy pounds were thereupon paid to the said Edward Sherman and John Sherman, to wit, at the city of Exeter aforesaid: And to the said lord the king I further most humbly certify, that afterwards, and after that he the said Nicholas Eveleigh left the exercise of the office and offices aforesaid, one Gilbert Eveleigh gent. by them and under them the said Edward Sherman and John Sherman, at the city of Exeter aforesaid, was made and constituted deputy of them the said Edward Sherman and John Sherman, to execute the office of register of the archdeaconry of Exeter aforesaid, and as their deputy on the 5th day of August, in the year of our Lord 1674, at the city of

Several corrupt agreements upon granting deputations of the said office of register of the archdeaconry of Exeter, and also of the archdeaconry of Totnes.

of Exeter aforefaid, took upon himfelf the execution of the office of regifter of the archdeaconry of Exeter aforefaid, and the faid place and office as the deputy of them the faid Edward Sherman and John Sherman there, for the fpace of one whole year in fact, had, exercifed, and poffeffed, and thereupon by agreement then and there between them the faid Edward Sherman and John Sherman, and the faid Gilbert Eveleigh made, it was corruptly and unlawfully concluded and agreed, that he the faid Gilbert, for and in confideration of the faid office, and of his deputation thereto, fhould pay to the faid Edward Sherman and John Sherman the fum of eighty pounds by the year, by quarterly payments; and thereupon he the faid Gilbert at the city of Exeter aforefaid, the faid eighty pounds to the faid Edward Sherman and John Sherman, according to the form and effect of the agreement aforefaid for that office and his * deputation thereto paid; and to the faid lord the king, I further moft humbly certify, that afterwards, and after that the faid Gilbert Eveleigh from the exercife of that office departed, they the faid Edward Sherman and John Sherman on the 17th day of Auguft, in the year of our Lord 1675, at the city of Exeter aforefaid, granted the execution of the faid office of regifter of the archdeaconry of Exeter aforefaid to the faid Philip Atherton, and to one John Atherton of the city of Exeter gentlemen, for a certain fum of money, to wit, eighty pounds, by them the faid Philip Atherton and John Atherton to them the faid Edward Sherman and John Sherman to be paid, and in confideration thereof by their deed of deputation fealed with the feal of the faid Edward and John, they deputed, affigned, conftituted and appointed the faid Philip Atherton and John Atherton the deputies of them the faid Edward Sherman and John Sherman in that office, to execute and exercife the faid office of regifter of the archdeaconry aforefaid, with all things whatfoever to that office belonging and any wife appertaining, under colour of which grant, appointment and deputation, they the faid Philip Atherton and John Atherton at the city of Exeter aforefaid, took upon themfelves the burden of the execution of the faid office, and the faid office and place in fact, had, exercifed and poffeffed for the fpace of one year and more, and they the faid Edward Sherman and John Sherman for the faid grant, appointment and deputation of the faid office to them the faid Philip Atherton and John Atherton, corruptly and againft the form of the ftatute in fuch cafe made and provided, at the city of Exeter aforefaid, demanded, had and received from them the faid Philip Atherton and John Atherton aforefaid, a fum of money,

* P. 540.

That the Shermans for the 12 last years have lived above 150 miles from Exeter, and the office being ill executed and the king's subjects prejudiced by the extortions of their deputies and complaints being made he hath removed the Shermans and their deputies from the said office.

to wit, eighty pounds of the lawful money of England; And to the said lord the king I further most humbly certify, that the said Edward Sherman and John Sherman for the space of divers years, to wit, twelve years last past at the least, live and reside at a distance beyond the space of one hundred and fifty miles from the city of Exeter, and committing and as aforesaid deputing the said office, and the exercise of that office to their deputies for sums of money to be thereout received, whereby and by the inattention and ignorance of their deputies, and by their exactions and extortions from the subjects and people of this kingdom of England coming to the said office, and transacting their acts and business in the said office of the register of the archdeaconry of Exeter aforesaid, the said office was ill executed to the damage, prejudice and oppression of the said subjects and people of the said kingdom, and upon very many complaints thereof being made, as well to the reverend father in Christ Anthony by divine permission, late lord bishop of Exeter, as to the reverend father in Christ Thomas by divine permission, now lord bishop of Exeter, as also to me the said archdeacon of the archdeaconry of Exeter aforesaid, of the misdemeanours, exactions, extortions and oppressions aforesaid, in the execution of the office aforesaid; I the said Edward Lake, doctor in divinity, who now am, and also continually for the space of two years and more, have been archdeacon of the archdeaconry of Exeter aforesaid, lawfully constituted and ordained, during the time in which as aforesaid, I have been archdeacon of the archdeaconry aforesaid, and before the coming of the said writ

* P. 541. of the * said lord the king to me in this behalf directed, the said Edward Sherman and John Sherman, and also the said Philip Atherton and John Atherton the deputies constituted in the manner and form aforesaid, for the causes and reasons aforesaid, as well from the office aforesaid as from the exercise thereof, on the 28th day of March, in the year of our Lord 1678, at the city of Exeter aforesaid, have removed; And by my certain writing sealed with my seal, bearing date the said day and year last mentioned, have given and granted to one Charles Heron gent. then and as yet a public notary, being a person proper and learned, skilful, honest and sufficient to exercise and execute the said office, the office of register of the archdeaconry of Exeter aforesaid, by the name of the office of register and clerk of the acts of the court of the archdeaconry of Exeter aforesaid, with all wages, fees, profits, emoluments and appurtenances whatsoever to the said office appertaining; and I have made and constituted the said Charles Heron register

Grant of the office to another for his life who is now register.

register and clerk of the acts of me, and of my successors archdeacons of the archdeaconry of Exeter aforesaid, to have, hold, exercise, and occupy the said office, with all wages, fees, profits, emoluments and appurtenances, to the said office belonging and appertaining to the said Charles Heron, by himself or by his sufficient deputy, immediately from and after that time, for and during the whole term of the natural life of the said Charles Heron, by virtue of which gift and grant, he the said Charles Heron, afterwards, to wit, on the 1st day of April in the year of our Lord, 1678, aforesaid, at the city of Exeter aforesaid, and in the absence of the said Edward Sherman and John Sherman from the said office, into the said office of register of the archdeaconry of Exeter aforesaid entered, and the burden of the execution of that office then and there took upon himself, and that office and the exercise thereof, continually from thence hitherto there hath had, exercised and possessed, and now is register of the archdeaconry of Exeter aforesaid, and the office of register of the archdeaconry of Exeter aforesaid, now is full with the said Charles Heron, and therefore, I the said archdeacon of the archdeaconry of Exeter aforesaid, cannot restore or cause to be restored the said Edward Sherman and John Sherman, or any further execute the said writ according to the command of the said writ.

---

## Mandamus for Lord Hawley.

### Easter, the 23d Charles the 2d.

Return to a mandamus to the mayor of the city of Bath, to restore lord Hawley to the office of recorder of that city. That queen Elizabeth by letters patent constituted

I EDWARD White, esquire, mayor of the city of Bath in the county of Somerset, to the most serene lord Charles the 2d, the now king of England, most humbly certify, that the lady Elizabeth, late queen of England, by her letters patent sealed with her great seal of England, bearing date at Westminster the 4th day of September, in the 32d year of the reign willed, ordained, constituted, granted and declared that the said city of Bath should be, and should remain afterwards for ever a city in * itself, and that the citizens and inhabitants of the said city afterwards for ever, should and might be one body corporate and politick, in thing, fact and name, by the name of the mayor, aldermen, and citizens of the city of Bath, and them by the name of the mayor, aldermen and citizens of the city of Bath, really and fully for herself, her heirs, and successors erected, made, ordained, constituted,

* P. 542.

Bath a city, and incorporated the inhabitants by the name of mayor, aldermen, and citizens.

conſtituted, declared and confirmed by her letters patent aforeſaid, one body corporate and politick, in thing, fact, and in name; and further the ſaid late queen of her further grace willed, and for herſelf, her heirs, and ſucceſſors, granted by the ſaid letters patent to the ſaid mayor, aldermen and citizens of the ſaid city of Bath and to their ſucceſſors, that there ſhould be within the ſaid city a mayor, aldermen, and a common council to be elected in the manner and form as in the ſaid letters patent aforeſaid is expreſſed, and that the ſaid mayor, aldermen, and citizens of the ſaid city and their ſucceſſors, ſhould have afterwards for ever in the ſaid city, one honeſt and diſcreet man learned in the laws of England, to be elected and nominated in the form expreſſed as follows, who ſhould be named and called recorder of the ſaid city; and that the mayor, aldermen, and common council of the ſaid city for the time being, or the greater part of the ſame might and could nominate, elect and appoint one good and diſcreet man from time to time to be recorder of the ſaid city, and that he who ſhould be nominated, elected and appointed recorder of the ſaid city as aforeſaid, might and ſhould, have, exerciſe and enjoy the office of recorder of the ſaid city, as long as he ſhould behave himſelf well in the ſame, and that the mayor, aldermen, and common council of the ſaid city for the time being, or the greater part of them, might and could remove ſuch recorder for the time being from his office for reaſonable cauſe, and might and could elect another into the place of ſuch recorder ſo removed in the manner and form above expreſſed, and for the better execution of the letters patent aforeſaid in that behalf, the ſaid queen aſſigned, nominated, conſtituted and made, and by the ſaid letters patent for herſelf, her heirs, and ſucceſſors, aſſigned, nominated, conſtituted and made, John Court, eſquire, to be the firſt modern recorder of the ſaid city, to continue in the ſaid office, and the ſaid office by himſelf to execute as long as he ſhould behave himſelf well in the ſame; and the ſaid late queen willed, and by the ſaid letters patent for herſelf, her heirs, and ſucceſſors, granted to the ſaid mayor, aldermen, and citizens of the ſaid city, that the ſaid queen and her ſucceſſors thenceforth afterwards for ever, ſhould and would have and hold, and might and could have and hold within the ſaid city a certain court of record on every Monday in every week throughout the year to be held before the mayor, recorder, and two aldermen who for the time ſhould be juſtices of the peace within the ſaid city, and the town clerk of the ſaid city, or before four, three, or two of them at the leaſt, of whom either the mayor or recorder of the ſaid city ſhould be one; and that

That they ſhould have one learned in the laws called a recorder, who ſhould hold his office quam diu ſe bene geſſerit.

That the mayor, aldermen and common council might remove the recorder for reaſonable cauſe.

that in the ſaid court they might hold by plaints in the ſaid court to be levied or proſecuted, all and all manner of pleas, actions, ſuits and demands, of all perſonal treſpaſſes with force and arms or otherwiſe, in contempt of the ſaid queen, her heirs, or ſucceſſors, committed or to be committed, and of all * other treſpaſſes upon the caſe, crimes and offences, done, ariſing, committed or perpetrated, or for ever afterwards to be done, committed, or perpetrated within the ſaid city, or within the late priory there, or their ſuburbs, liberties and precincts, or within any parcel thereof, and of all debts, accounts, covenants, detentions of goods or chattles, captions and detentions, of cattle and chattles, and all other contracts, whatſoever, from whatſoever cauſes or things perſonal, ariſing or occurring within the ſaid city and the precincts of the late priory there, or either of them, or their ſuburbs, liberties and precincts, or within any parcel thereof, although the ſaid treſpaſſes, debts, accounts, covenants, deceits, detentions or other contracts, ſhould amount to or exceed the ſum or value of forty ſhillings; and that ſuch pleas, plaints and actions, ſhould be there heard and determined, before the ſaid mayor, recorder and aldermen and town clerk of the ſaid city for the time being, or before four, three, or two of them in the abſence of the reſt by ſuch and the like proceſſes, methods, and means, according to the law and cuſtom of this kingdom of England, and as ſhould be conſonant to the law of the ſame, and in as ample manner and form as in any other court of the ſaid lady the queen, of record in any city, borough, or town corporate within this kingdom of England, was uſed and accuſtomed, or might or ought to be done, as by the ſaid letters patent among other things more fully appears; and I the ſaid mayor of the city of Bath aforeſaid, to the ſaid lord the king, further moſt humbly certify, that the ſaid Francis, lord Hawley, in the writ to this ſchedule annexed, named, on the firſt day of Auguſt in the 15th year of the reign of our lord Charles the 2d, the now king of England, at the city of Bath aforeſaid, in the due form of law, and according to the letters patent aforeſaid was elected to and into the office of recorder of the city of Bath, aforeſaid, upon the removal of one William Pryne, eſquire, before that time recorder of the ſaid city, by certain commiſſioners authorized according to to the form and effect of a certain ſtatute made at the parliament of our lord Charles the 2d, &c. begun and held at Weſtminſter, on the 8th day of May, in the year of our Lord, 1661, and in the 13th year of the reign of our lord Charles the 2d, and there continued until Friday the 20th day of December, then next following, entitled, "*an act for the well governing and regulating of corporations*," according to the form and effect of the ſaid ſtatute; and that the ſaid

* P. 543.

On the 1ſt of Auguſt 15th Char. the 2d. lord Hawley elected recorder of Bath, upon the removal of W. P. from that office.

And continued in his office till the 25th day of September in the 21st Charles 2d.

said Francis, lord Hawley, after his appointment to the said office, continued in that office according to his placing and appointment, until the 25th day of September in the 21st year of the reign of the said lord the now king; I further most humbly certify that the said Francis, lord Hawley at any time during the time in which he the said Francis, lord Hawley continued in the said office as aforesaid, was not, nor as yet is a barrister at law, nor in any wise learned in the laws of the land of this kingdom of England; and to the said lord the king, I further most humbly certify that the said Francis, lord Hawley, for the space of five years after the appointment of the said Francis, lord Hawley to the said office, and before the 20th day of * August in the 21st year of the reign of our said lord the now king without any reasonable cause whatsoever, absented and eloigned himself from the execution and exercise of that office aforesaid, and the execution and exercise of that office totally neglected, to the great impediment, and hindrance of justice in the said city to be administered, and of the good government of the said city; and to the said lord the now king, I further most humbly certify, that the said Francis, lord Hawley, upon the 20th day of August, in the 21st year aforesaid, was summoned by Robert Chapman, then mayor of the said city, by virtue of a certain order of the then said mayor, and the aldermen and common council of the said city in that behalf made, to appear before the mayor, alderman, and common council of the said city in the said city to be assembled upon the 30th day of the said month of August, to answer concerning his negligence and ignorance aforesaid, and to show cause if he had or knew any thing to say for himself, wherefore he the said Francis, lord Hawley for the ignorance, and so great negligence of him the said Francis, lord Hawley from his said office should not be removed, and that upon the said 30th day of August in the 21st year aforesaid, at the city of Bath aforesaid, the said Robert Chapman then mayor of the said city, and the aldermen and common council of the said city were publickly assembled, but the said Francis, lord Hawley, although as aforesaid, he was summoned, at that day did not appear before the said mayor, aldermen and common council of the said city there as aforesaid publickly assembled, nor any cause then and there did show wherefore he the said Francis, lord Hawley, from his office aforesaid, for the causes aforesaid, should not be removed, whereupon the said Francis, lord Hawley, then and there by the said mayor, and the major part of the aldermen and common council of the said city for the causes aforesaid, from the office of recorder of the said city was removed, and for

But was not any time a barrister at law.

* P. 544.

And absented himself five years from the execution of his office.

Summoned to show cause why he should not be removed for ignorance and negligence.

Did not appear or show any cause.

Removed from his office.

for that caufe the faid Francis, lord Hawley, I cannot re-ftore to his place of recorder of the faid city.

The anfwer of Edward White, efquire, mayor of the city of Bath, within written.

---

## Mandamus for Howfe.

CHARLES the 2d, by the grace of God, &c.—To the mayor, aldermen, and burgeffes of our borough of Reading, in our county of Berks, and to every of them greeting, whereas Samuel Howfe into the place of one of the aldermen of the faid borough, according to the cuftom of the faid borough hitherto ufed, duly was elected and appointed, in which place of one of the aldermen of the faid borough he hath continually carried and behaved himfelf well, neverthelefs you the mayor, aldermen and burgeffes of the faid borough, lightly regarding the premiffes, the faid Samuel unduly and without reafonable caufe, from the faid place of one of the aldermen of the faid borough, unjuftly have removed, in contempt of us, and to the great damage and grievance of the faid Samuel, and to the manifeft injury of his eftate as from his complaint we have underftood, we there * willing that due and fpeedy juftice be done to the faid Samuel in this behalf, as is right, command you and each of you, firmly enjoining, that immediately after the receipt of this writ, you reftore or caufe to be reftored the faid Samuel into the faid place of one of the aldermen of the faid borough, with all liberties, profits, and preheminences to that place belonging or appertaining, or fignify to us caufe to the contrary, leaft through your default complaint may be made to us again, and how you fhall execute this our command, make to appear to us from the day of St. Michael in three weeks, wherefoever we fhall then be in England, then returning to us their own writ, and this in no wife omit, under the pain of 8ol. Witnefs Mathew Hale, at Weftminfter, the 26th day of June, in the 24th year of our reign.

Mandamus to the mayor, aldermen and burgeffes of Reading, to reftore Howfe to the office of one of the aldermen of the faid borough.

* P. 545.

By the court,

*Fanfhawe.*

The execution of this writ appears in a certain fchedule to this writ annexed.

Return.

The

The anſwer of the mayor, aldermen, and burgeſſes of the borough of Reading within written.

Reading a borough by preſcription.

WE the mayor, aldermen and burgeſſes of the borough of Reading, to the writ to this ſchedule annexed, according to the command of the ſaid writ, to the ſaid lord the king, moſt humbly certify, that the borough of Reading is, and from the time whereof the memory of man is not to the contrary, hath been an antient borough; and that the lady Elizabeth, late queen of England, by her letters patent, ſealed with her great ſeal of England, bearing date at Weſtminſter the 23d day of September, in the ſecond year of her reign, for herſelf, her heirs and ſucceſſors ordained, that the men and burgeſſes of the ſaid borough thenceforth ſhould and might be for ever, one body corporate and politic in thing, fact, and in name, and by the ſaid letters patent, really and fully for herſelf, her heirs and ſucceſſors, conſtituted, created, and declared that they ſhould be one body corporate and politic in thing, fact, and in name, by the name of the mayor and burgeſſes of the borough of Reading, and that by the ſaid name they ſhould have perpetual ſucceſſion; and by the ſaid letters patent conſtituted and declared that there ſhould be for ever, within the ſaid borough one who ſhould be called mayor of the ſaid borough, and nine men who ſhould be named and called the chief burgeſſes of the ſaid borough, (of whom ſhe willed that the mayor ſhould be one.) And that afterwards, the lord Charles the firſt, late king of England, by his letters patent, ſealed with his great ſeal of England, bearing date at Weſtminſter the 17th day of December, in the 14th year of his reign, for himſelf, his heirs and ſucceſſors, ordained and declared that the ſaid borough thenceforth for ever, ſhould be a free borough, and that the men and free burgeſſes of the ſaid borough thenceforth for ever, ſhould and might be a body corporate and politic in thing, fact, and in name; and by his ſaid letters patent, really and fully for himſelf, his heirs and ſucceſſors, conſtituted, created and declared that they ſhould be a body corporate and politic in thing, fact, and in name, by the name of the mayor, aldermen and burgeſſes of the borough of Reading; and that by the ſaid name they ſhould have perpetual ſucceſſion; and further by his ſaid letters patent * for himſelf, his heirs and ſucceſſors, willed and declared, that from thenceforth for ever, there ſhould and might be within the ſaid borough one of the freemen of the ſaid borough who ſhould be called mayor, and

Queen Elizabeth by letters patent incorporated the burgeſſes of Reading by the name of the mayor and burgeſſes.

King Charles the firſt incorporated them by their preſent name,

* P. 546.

and thirteen who ſhould be called aldermen, (of whom he willed that the mayor ſhould be one) who ſhould be in the place and ſtead of thoſe who before were the chief burgeſſes of the ſaid borough, and twelve who ſhould be called aſſiſtants of the ſaid borough, who from time to time ſhould be aiding and giving of counſel to the mayor and aldermen of the ſaid borough in all cauſes, things and buſineſs touching or in any wiſe concerning the ſaid borough; And by the ſaid letters patent the ſaid late king aſſigned, conſtituted and made one Richard Burren firſt mayor of the ſaid borough, and Thomas Turner, Robert Mathews, Chriſtopher Turner, John Newman, Robert Bent, John Duck, George Thorne, Anthony Brackſtone, and the ſaid Richard Burren, John Jennings, Robert Dee, William Jacob, and Thomas Harriſon, firſt aldermen of the ſaid borough; and Peter Barneingham, Thomas Thackham, George Wooldridge, Richard Jeys, Edward Baker, William Turner the elder, William Brackſtone, Edward Hamlyn, Chriſtopher Blower, William Turner the younger, George Thorne and Thomas Duell firſt aſſiſtants of the ſaid borough: Alſo the ſaid late king willed, and by the ſaid letters patent for himſelf, his heirs and ſucceſſors, granted to the ſaid mayor, aldermen and burgeſſes of the ſaid borough. and to their ſucceſſors, that after the death or removal of any of the aldermen then being, or afterwards to be elected, that it ſhould be lawful for the mayor and the reſt of the aldermen of the ſaid borough for the time being, or the greater number of them, to chooſe and elect one of the aſſiſtants of the ſaid borough to be alderman of the ſaid borough, in the place and office of ſuch alderman ſo dying or being removed; and that ſuch aſſiſtant who ſhould be elected alderman of the ſaid borough, before that he ſhould be admitted to execute the office of alderman of the ſaid borough ſhould take his corporal oath before the mayor and the reſt of the aldermen of the ſaid borough for the time being, juſtly and faithfully to execute the ſaid office of alderman in all things touching the ſaid office; and further, by his ſaid letters patent, the ſaid late king willed, and for himſelf, his heirs and ſucceſſors, granted to the ſaid mayor, aldermen and burgeſſes, and to their ſucceſſors, that they for ever ſhould have and ought to have in the ſaid borough one diſcreet and fit man, learned in the law, who ſhould be called ſteward of the ſaid borough; and further, by the letters patent aforeſaid, the ſaid late king willed and ordained that it ſhould and might be lawful for the mayor and ſteward of the ſaid borough for the time being, to make, form and ordain apt forms of the oaths to be from time to time reſpectively taken by the officers and miniſters of

and ordained that they ſhould have one mayor and 13 aldermen inſtead of the former capital burgeſſes, and alſo 12 aſſiſtants.

and that the aldermen ſhould be elected out of the aſſiſtants who before admiſſion ſhould take oath. &c.

That they ſhould have one learned in the law who ſhould be called ſteward of the borough and that the mayor and ſteward ſhould ſettle the form of the oath to be taken by the officers &c. of the ſaid borough.

of the said borough afterwards to be chosen by virtue of the said letters patent; and further, the said late king by the said letters patent willed, and for himself, his heirs and successors, granted to the said mayor, aldermen and burgesses of the said borough, that it might and should be lawful for the said mayor and aldermen of the said borough for the time being, or for the greater part of them, to remove any alderman or assistant of the said * borough for the time being, from the said office, for his misbehaviour in the said office, or for any other reasonable and just cause; and the said late king by his letters patent aforesaid, further willed, and for himself, his heirs and successors, granted to the said mayor, aldermen and burgesses of the said borough, and to their successors, that from time to time for ever afterwards, it should and might be lawful for the mayor, aldermen and assistants of the said borough for the time being, or for the greater part of them, upon the summons of the mayor of the said borough for the time being, in the Guildhall of the said borough, or in any other convenient place within the said borough, to meet and collect together, and there to hold an assembly, and in the said assemblies so holden to confer, consult, and treat of statutes and laws in any manner touching the good rule, goverment, and estate of the said borough, and also to make, form, constitute, ordain and establish good, honest, wholesome, useful, necessary, and reasonable laws, ordinances and provisions, according to their sound discretion, for the good rule and government of the said borough, and of all and singular the officers, ministers, artificers, inhabitants, and residents within the said borough, the liberties and precincts of the same, and for the better care, disposition and demising of the lands and tenements, profits, and hereditaments, of which they the said mayor, aldermen and burgesses then were, or afterwards should be seized in their demesne, as of fee in their political capacity: And to the said lord the king we further certify, that on the 8th day of January, in the 14th year of the reign of the said late king Charles the first, the said Richard Burren being mayor, and one Edward Clark, Knight, being steward of the said borough, according to the power to them by the said letters patent delegated as aforesaid, made, formed and ordained this form of the oath following, to be taken by every alderman of the said borough then afterwards to be elected, before he should be admitted to exercise the office of alderman of the said borough, to wit, "*You shall swear that you shall truly exercise and perform the office of alderman of this borough of Reading, during the whole time in which you shall continue*

* P. 547.

The oath settled by the mayor and steward to be taken by every alderman.

to

*to be an alderman, and that you ſhall behave yourſelf towards the mayor of the ſaid borough for the time being, in a courteous and ſeemly manner, and you ſhall promote, aid, help, and aſſiſt all things and matters which will exalt and promote, or will tend to exalt and promote the publick good, the honour, eſtate and profit of the ſaid guild; and as much as in you lies, you ſhall prevent, or in convenient time reveal, and declare and make known to the ſaid mayor, or to his deputy, whatſoever, and whomſoever you ſhall know or conceive infringes, or may infringe, or is about to infringe the liberties, franchiſes, and lawful ordinances of the ſaid borough, and upon reaſonable ſummons you ſhall attend all councils and aſſemblies, to which you ſhall be ſummoned by the mayor or his deputy, and the counſel which you ſhall give at ſuch aſſemblies ſhall be good and ſound, according to your diligence and diſcretion; and the matters at ſuch aſſemblies diſcuſſed, the opinions, tranſactions and votes of the perſons diſcuſſing, and the ſecrets of the common-council of the borough and guild aforeſaid, you ſhall keep cloſe and ſecret, nor ſhall you publiſh, ſhow or declare them to any perſon unleſs to adviſe with an alderman or aſſiſtant of the ſaid borough, and all theſe things * and others belonging to the place of an alderman aforeſaid, you ſhall obſerve and truly keep in all points according to your power, ſo help you God."*——And to the ſaid lord the king we further certify, that the ſaid Samuel Howſe on the 17th day of July, in the 20th year of the reign of the ſaid lord the now king, duly was elected and appointed alderman of the ſaid borough, and on the ſame day before William Brackſtone the younger, gentleman, then being mayor of the ſaid borough, and alderman of the ſaid borough, took his corporal oath, to exerciſe the office of alderman of the ſaid borough well, in the words of the form of the oath above recited; And to the ſaid lord the king we further certify, that within the ſaid borough there is, and from the time whereof the memory of man is not to the contrary, there hath been an antient college or publick ſchool, founded and erected of royal foundation, to educate the ſons of the men inhabiting within the ſaid borough, and others in learning, by reaſon whereof the lady Elizabeth late queen of England, was the true patroneſs, and ought to have the appointing and conſtituting of the maſter, preceptor, or inſtructor of the college or publick ſchool aforeſaid; And the ſaid late queen by her letters patent aforeſaid, for herſelf, her heirs and ſucceſſors, granted to the mayor and chief burgeſſes of the ſaid borough, that they and their ſucceſſors for the time being, might and ſhould nominate, elect, and conſtitute one fit perſon to be maſter, preceptor or inſtructor of the college

* P. 54.

That there was time out of mind in the ſaid borough a publick ſchool of royal foundation.

That queen Elizabeth by her letters patent granted to the mayor and chief burgeſſes the election of the master of that school, and that they might remove him for reasonable cause.

lege or publick school aforesaid; and that it should and might be well lawful for the said mayor and chief burgesses and their successors for the time being, and for the greater part of them from time to time for any reasonable cause to remove and expel the said master, precepter, or instructor, and to constitute the same or any other in his stead, as it should seem expedient and necessary to them and to their successors; and further the late king Charles the 1st, by his said letters patent aforesaid, confirmed to the said mayor, aldermen, and burgesses the said power of nominating, electing, constituting and removing the master, preceptor or instructor of the college or publick school aforesaid, by reason of which the mayor and aldermen of the said borough for the time being have had, have, and ought to have the power of nominating, electing, constituting and removing the master, preceptor, or instructor of the college, or publick school aforesaid; and to the said lord the king, we further certify, that one Thomas Singleton, upon the first day of May in the 14th year of the reign of our lord the now king, and in the year of our Lord, 1662, lawfully was master preceptor or instructor of the said college or public school, and the said Thomas Singleton according to the form and effect of the statute made at the parliament begun and held at Westminster, in the county of Middlesex, upon the 8th day of May, in the 13th year of the reign of the said lord the now king, at some time before the feast of St. Bartholemew the apostle, in the said year of our Lord, 1662, before the bishop and ordinary of the diocess, refused to subscribe a certain declaration or acknowledgment by the said statute enacted and established to be taken and subscribed by every master, preceptor, or instructor of any public or private school, whereby he ought to have declared, "*that it was not lawful upon any pretence whatsoever to take up arms against the king, and that he* * *abhorred that traiterous position of taking arms by his authority against his person or against those commissioned by him; and that he would conform himself to the liturgy of the church of England as then established by law, and that he declared that he held that there lay no obligation upon him or any other person from the oath commonly called the solemn league and covenant to endeavour any alteration, or change of the government either in church or state, and that the same was in itself an unlawful oath, and imposed upon the subjects of this realm against the known laws and liberties of this realm*;" by reason of which refusal to make the said declaration, and to subscribe the declaration or acknowledgment aforesaid, the said Thomas Singleton, his place of master, preceptor, or instructor of the college or publick school aforesaid, by force of the

That king Charles the 1st confirmed the said grant.

That T. S. anno 1662, was schoolmaster, but did not subscribe the declaration appointed by the statute 13th Char. 2. whereby he was ipso facto deprived.

* P. 549.

statute

ſtatute aforeſaid, totally loſt, and of the ſame was ipſo facto deprived and removed, and was altogether rendered incapable to be maſter, preceptor or inſtructor of the ſaid college or publick ſchool, or of any other college or public ſchool until he ſhould ſubſcribe the declaration or acknowledgment aforeſaid, and ſhould conform himſelf to the order of the Engliſh church; and the ſaid Thomas Singleton never after the ſaid feaſt of St. Bartholomew, ſubſcribed the ſaid declaration or acknowledgment. And afterwards on the 14th day of October in the 14th year of the reign of the lord the now king, the mayor and aldermen of the ſaid borough elected, conſtituted and appointed one Thomas Thackham to be maſter, preceptor or inſtructor of the college or publick ſchool aforeſaid, nevertheleſs the ſaid Samuel Howſe well knowing all the premiſſes, and that the ſaid Thomas Singleton never conformed himſelf to the order of the church of England, nor ever ſubſcribed the ſaid declaration or acknowledgment, and lightly regarding the duty of his office, and his oath aforeſaid, on the 15th day of November in the 14th year of the reign of the lord the now king came to the houſe of the ſaid Thomas Thackham, then being maſter, preceptor, or inſtructor of the college or public ſchool aforeſaid, and in the name and under colour of a certain pretended order of the mayor and aldermen of the ſaid borough, endeavoured to perſuade the ſaid Thomas Thackham to receive and admit the ſaid Thomas Singleton, to be under-maſter or uſher of the college or publick ſchool aforeſaid, and his aſſiſtant in teaching his ſcholars of the college or publick ſchool aforeſaid, and then and there in the name of the ſaid mayor and aldermen, threatened the ſaid Thomas Thackham, that if he refuſed to receive and admit the ſaid T. S to be under-maſter or uſher of the college or publick ſchool aforeſaid, and his aſſiſtant as aforeſaid, that the ſaid mayor and aldermen, him the ſaid Thomas Thackham from the ſaid place of maſter, preceptor, or inſtructor of the college or publick ſchool aforeſaid, intended to remove and deprive, and with other threats terrified the ſaid Thomas Thackham, and ſo the ſaid Samuel Howſe by his perſuaſions and threats aforeſaid, procured the ſaid Thomas Thackham, (fearing the threats of the ſaid Samuel, and believing that the ſaid Samuel had an order and had received authority from the ſaid mayor and aldermen, him as aforeſaid to perſuade and threaten) to admit the ſaid Thomas Singleton to be under-maſter or uſher of the college or publick ſchool aforeſaid, * and his aſſiſtant in teaching his ſcholars; and the ſaid Thomas Thackham on the ſaid 15th day of November in the 14th year

The mayor, and aldermen choſe one T. Thackham ſchool-maſter.

That Howſe under pretence of an order from the mayor and aldermen, perſuaded and threatened Thackham, to admit Singleton to act as Uſher in the ſchool.

* P. 550.

year aforesaid, him the said Thomas Singleton against the form and effect of the statute aforesaid, by reason of the persuasions and threats of the said Samuel, received and admitted to be under-master or usher of the college or publick school aforesaid, and assistant in teaching his scholars: whereas in truth, the mayor and aldermen of the said borough never gave the said Samuel any order or authority to persuade and threaten as aforesaid, the said Thomas Thackham for the cause aforesaid, nor did they ever make any order to oblige the said Thomas Thackham to receive and admit the said Thomas Singleton to be under-master or usher of the college or publick school aforesaid, or assistant to the said Thomas Thackham in teaching his scholars; and to the said lord the now king, we further certify that the said Samuel Howse continuing his evil disposition, and lightly regarding the statutes of this kingdom, and also contriving to frustrate the effect of a certain statute made at a session of parliament held by prorogation at Westminster, in the county of Middlesex, upon the 14th day of February, in the 22d year of the reign of the lord the now king, entitled an act to prevent and suppress seditious conventicles, and knowing that one David Seymer of the said borough, taylor, was authorised by one William Armorer, knight, one of the justices of the lord the now king, to preserve the peace in the said borough, to enquire, and to give information to the said William, of all unlawful conventicles had and assembled within the said borough, against the form of the said statute, he the said Samuel Howse endeavoured to persuade and terrify the said David Seymer from making any inquiry and giving any information of the said conventicles, saying to the said David Seymour that if he would proceed in such inquiries, and in giving information, that he the said David would lose all his customers in his trade, and with many threats disturbed him the said David, in order to terrify him from making any inquiry and giving any information of the said seditious conventicles, by reason of which dissuasions and threatnings the said David entirely refrained and desisted from making any enquiries, and from giving any information, as aforesaid; and to the said lord the king, we further certify that Robert Tyrrell, being mayor of the said borough, on the 3d day of August in the 21st year of the reign of the lord the now king, by the serjeant at mace of the said borough, caused the said Samuel Howse to be summoned to go with the said mayor and the other aldermen of the said borough upon the 4th day of August next following to Streatly, to oversee divers messuages, lands, and tenements, of which the said mayor, aldermen, and burgesses of the said borough were seized in their demesne as of fee, and to ascertain

That the mayor and aldermen made no such order.

That Howse by his threatnings and persuasions prevailed upon one D. S. authorised to enquire after conventicles, to desist from making such enquiries.

That Howse being summoned to attend the mayor, &c. upon business, refused to attend, and uttered contemptuous words to the serjeant who summoned him.

ascertain the certain quantity of land and to treat and make agreements with the tenants of the said messuages concerning the repairs of the said messuages, and to aid and assist the said mayor and aldermen in all things, nevertheless the said Samuel Howse neglecting the duty of his office aforesaid, and of his oath aforesaid, without any just or reasonable cause, entirely refused to go to Streatly aforesaid with the said mayor and aldermen, according to the said summons, and to the said * serjeant at mace at the time in which he summoned the said Samuel as aforesaid, to go together with the said mayor and aldermen as aforesaid, maliciously and contemptuously said and published these words following, to wit, "*go tell Mr. Mayor I am none of the court, nor none of the council, and I will not go*;" and although the said mayor and the rest of the aldermen aforesaid, went together to Streatly aforesaid, upon the said fourth day of August upon the intention aforesaid, nevertheless the said Samuel did not go, but wilfully, entirely, and without any reasonable or just cause, absented himself, whereby the said mayor and aldermen then and there greatly wanted, and lost the council and aid of the said Samuel Howse; and to the said lord the king we further certify that on the 6th day of September in the 20th year of the reign of our lord the now king, William Brackstone, then mayor of the said borough, caused the said Samuel Howse and all the other aldermen and assistants of the said borough, lawfully to be summoned to appear and assemble upon the seventh day of the said month of September, at the ninth hour before midday of the said day in the Guildhall of the said borough, to consult with the said mayor of the estate and government of the said borough, and to establish and make good, wholesome, and honest laws and constitutions, for the advantage and benefit of the said borough, and although the said mayor and divers other aldermen and assistants, amounting only to the lesser part of the aldermen and assistants of the said borough upon the said seventh day of September, and at the said hour, in the Guildhall aforesaid, appeared and assembled, nevertheless the said Samuel Howse with divers other aldermen and assistants, who with the said Samuel Howse amounted to the greater part of the aldermen and assistants of the said borough, lightly regarding the duty of his office, wilfully and without any reasonable or just cause absented himself, and upon the said 7th day of September in the Guildhall aforesaid, did not appear; and so because of the absence of the said Samuel, as well as because of the said absence of the said other aldermen and assistants, at the day and place aforesaid, there was not a number of the aldermen and assistants of

* P. 551.

That being summoned to attend the mayor in the Guildhall, he wilfully absented himself

of the said borough assembled, amounting to the greater part of the aldermen and assistants of the said borough, by reason of which no consultation, nor any laws, constitutions or ordinances, for the advantage and benefit of the said borough could be had, made, or established; and to the said lord the king we further certify, that afterwards upon the twenty-seventh day of July, in the twenty-first year of the reign of the said lord the now king aforesaid, Robert Tyrrell being mayor of the said borough in like manner caused the said Samuel Howse and all the other aldermen of the said borough lawfully to be summoned to appear and assemble upon the 28th day of July aforesaid, and about the 9th hour before mid-day of the said day in the Guildhall aforesaid, to consult with the said mayor of the estate and government of the said borough, and to make and establish good, wholesome and honest laws and constitutions for the advantage and benefit of the said borough, and although the said mayor and the other aldermen and assistants of the said borough, upon the said 28th day of July, and at the hour aforesaid, in the place aforesaid, appeared and assembled, nevertheless the said Samuel Howse in like manner neglecting the duty

* P. 552. of his office aforesaid, wilfully * without any just or reasonable cause, on the said day absented himself, and at the place aforesaid did not appear, by reason of which absence of the said Samuel, the said mayor and the rest of the aldermen and assistants of the said borough, at the day and place aforesaid, greatly wanted and lost the counsel and assistance of the said Samuel in their consultations and deliberations for the good government and for the advantage and benefit of the said borough; and to the said lord the king.

*That he behaved himself contemptuously towards the mayor, by gesture and by words.*

We further certify that on the 6th day of July in the 22d year of the reign of the now king aforesaid, Michael Reading being mayor of the said borough, the said Samuel Howse, lightly regarding his oath aforesaid, and endeavouring and intending to bring the said mayor of the said borough and his authority into contempt, on the said day and year contemptuously as well by gesture as by words, behaved himself towards the said mayor, and then and there within the said borough in the like manner contemptuously, and without any just or reasonable cause, openly and publickly did say and publish these words following, to wit, "*you*" (meaning the said mayor) *are a pisspot mayor,*" And to the said lord the king we further certify that one Thomas Vachell, late of Coly in the said county, knight, was seized of one messuage in Reading aforesaid, and of all the lands and parcels

*That Howse endeavoured to raise differences and suits between the mayor, aldermen, and one T. Vachell, esquire, about the mayor and aldermen's right of placing poor people in an alms house in the said borough.*

cels of land, meadows and paſtures, commonly called and known by the name of Great Garſton, otherwiſe Gaſton, containing by eſtimation eighty acres, ſituate, lying and being in the pariſh of Shenefield, in the ſaid county of Berks, and of all that cloſe, paſture and land, commonly called and known by the name of Little Gaſton in the ſaid pariſh, in his demeſne as of fee, and the ſaid Thomas ſo being ſeized thereof at Reading aforeſaid, by his deed of feoffment indented, bearing date the 3d day of January in the 10th year of the reign of the lord Charles the 1ſt late king of England, did enfeoffe one Edward Barker, William Turner the elder, William Turner the younger, John Mills, James Winch, William Stretch, William White, Humfrey Evans, Chriſtopher Blower, Humphrey Mills, Andrew Wright, Edward Johnſon, William Wellder, and Ferdinand Clark of the whole ſaid meſſuage in Reading aforeſaid, and by the ſaid deed, the ſaid Thomas Vachell gave and granted to the ſaid Edward Barker, W. T. &c. one annuity or annual rent of forty pounds annually, iſſuing out of all the ſaid lands and parcels of land, meadows and paſtures, commonly called and known by the name of Great Garſton, otherwiſe Gaſton, in the pariſh of Shenefield aforeſaid, and out of all that cloſe, paſture and land, commonly called and known by the name of Little Gaſton, to have and to hold the ſaid meſſuage and the ſaid annuity or yearly rent to the ſaid Edward Barker, W. T. &c. their heirs and aſſigns for ever, nevertheleſs under the truſt and confidence, that they the ſaid Edward Barker, W. T. &c. after the feaſt of the nativity of St. John the baptiſt next following the date of the ſaid indenture, would permit the ſaid meſſuage to remain and be an alms-houſe, for the habitation and dwelling of ſix poor old men, having no wives, and that they would permit the ſaid Thomas Vachell during his life and after the deceaſe of the ſaid Thomas Vachell, the mayor and burgeſſes of * Reading aforeſaid, and their ſucceſſors, * P. 553. and Tanfield Vachell, nephew of the ſaid Thomas Vachell, and after the deceaſe of the ſaid Tanfield Vachell, ſuch perſon or perſons of the name, blood and kindred of the ſaid Thomas Vachell, who for the time being ſhould be proprietor or proprietors of the manor and land of Coly in the county aforeſaid, and for default of ſuch perſon or perſons who ſhould be proprietor or proprietors, then ſuch perſon or perſons who ſhould be proprietor or proprietors of the manor or farm of Coly aforeſaid, to have the placing, appointing and removing of the ſaid ſix poor and infirm old men in the ſaid houſe; and afterwards the ſaid Thomas Vachell died; and afterwards in like manner the ſaid Tanfield Vachell, died, and one Rebecca Vachell, widow, and relict of the ſaid Tanfield Vachell was ſeized of the ſaid manor or land of Coly, as of freehold, for the term of her natural life. And the ſaid Rebecca Vachell, ſo being ſeized upon the 23d day of July, in the 22d year of the reign of the ſaid lord the now king, the mayor, aldermen and burgeſſes of Reading aforeſaid, and the ſaid Rebecca Vachell placed one Mathew Jackſon, a poor and infirm old man having no wife, in the ſaid houſe, and appointed him one of the ſix poor and infirm old men to inhabit and dwell in the ſaid alms-houſe, according to the true intent of the ſaid Thomas Vachell above declared, nevertheleſs the ſaid Samuel Howſe, not ignorant of the premiſſes, of his own wicked diſpoſition, contriving and intending to promote and excite diſputes, controverſies and differences, between the ſaid mayor, aldermen and burgeſſes of Reading aforeſaid, and one Thomas Vachell, eſquire, being of the kindred of the ſaid Thomas Vachell, knight, on the 24th day of July in the 22d year aforeſaid, and at divers days and times after the ſaid 24th day of July, endeavoured to perſuade the ſaid Thomas Vachell, eſquire, that the ſaid mayor, aldermen and burgeſſes, and the ſaid Rebecca Vachell, widow, had no power, nor ought to have placed and appointed the ſaid Mathew Jackſon to be one of the ſix poor and infirm old men, to inhabit and dwell in the alms-houſe aforeſaid, without the conſent of the ſaid Thomas Vachell, eſquire, whereas in truth the ſaid Thomas Vachell, eſquire, by virtue of the indenture aforeſaid, had no power of conſenting to the placing and appointing of any poor and infirm old man in the alms-houſe aforeſaid, becauſe the ſaid Thomas Vachell, eſquire, was not proprietor, nor ſeized of the ſaid manor or land of Coly; and to the ſaid lord the king, we further certify, that

That Howſe revealed the ſecrets of the borough.

the ſaid Samuel, lightly regarding the duty of his office aforeſaid, and his oath aforeſaid, at divers days and times, after his appointment into the place of alderman of the ſaid borough did reveal and make known the ſecrets of the ſaid borough and the ſecrets and matters had and conſulted at the aſſemblies and common councils of the ſaid borough, to one John Harriſon, Thomas Blower, Samuel Jemmat, and to divers other perſons, none of them being aldermen or aſſiſtants of the ſaid borough.

* P. 554.

That Howſe behaved himſelf irreverently towards the mayor of the ſaid borough.

And to the ſaid lord the king, we further certify, that the ſaid Samuel Howſe, being infected * with his evil and malicious diſpoſition, deſpiſing the good government of the ſaid borough, and holding the authority of the mayor of the ſaid borough in contempt, and intending to draw it into contempt with the common people, behaved himſelf indecently and irreverently towards the ſaid Michael Reading at different days and times

times, during the time he continued to be mayor, and towards the persons of those who then before were mayors of the said borough, at the times in which they were mayors of the said borough, and them with many injuries, and reproaches disturbed, whereby the office of mayor was holden in great contempt among the common people, to the great damage and injury of the government of the said borough; And to the said lord the king we further certify, that the mayor, aldermen and burgesses of the said borough, to him the said Samuel Howse, (then being one of the chamberlains of the said borough) delivered two writings obligatory, to wit, one in which one John Jemmat, was bounden to the said mayor, aldermen, and burgesses in the sum of six pounds, thirteen shillings, and four pence, of the lawful money of England; and one other in which one John Burnham, was bounden to the said mayor, aldermen, and burgesses in the sum of three pounds, and ten shillings, of the like lawful money of England; which sums were in arrear and not paid to the said mayor, aldermen and burgesses of the said borough on the third day of April, in the 22d year of the reign of our lord the now king, separately to sue them the said John Jemmat and John Burnham at law, for recovering against them of the several debts aforesaid, nevertheless the said Samuel Howse from all prosecutions of them the said John Jemmat, and John Burnham, upon the said writings obligatory entirely desisted, and also unjustly intending to defraud them the said mayor, aldermen and burgesses of the said several debts, when one Richard Grover, clerk of the said borough, on the 3d day of July, in the 22d year aforesaid, and at divers days and times afterwards, at the command of the said mayor, aldermen and burgesses, had requested him the said Samuel Howse to deliver to him the said Richard Grover the said writings obligatory, for the use of the said mayor, aldermen, and burgesses, nevertheless the said Samuel then, and at all times afterwards, entirely refused to deliver to the said Richard the said writings obligatoy, and the said writings obligatory from the said mayor, aldermen, and burgesses detained, and as yet detains, and converts to his own proper use; And to the said lord the king, we further certify, that at a meeting of the mayor, and all the aldermen of the said borough, upon the 30th day of July, in the 22d year of the reign of the said lord the now king aforesaid, in the Guildhall aforesaid, the said Samuel Howse then present in the said assembly, was accused by the said mayor and aldermen of all the matters, offences and crimes above mentioned, and all the

That two bonds to the said corporation being put into his hands to put in suit, that he detained them to his own use.

That at a meeting of the mayor and all the aldermen Howse being present was accused of all the said misdemeanours and they all being proved, and he

 said

not offering any thing in excuse * P 555. or in extenuation, was turned out of his office by the said mayor and aldermen by virtue of the said letters patent.

said matters, offences and crimes, were charged objected and proved against him the said Samuel Howse then present in the said meeting, and the said * Samuel being asked by the said mayor and aldermen, if he could say any thing for himself in excuse or in extenuation of all the said matters to him charged or against him alledged; and the said Samuel could show no cause for his absence aforesaid, upon the days aforesaid above mentioned, nor could show any reason for his misbehaviour in all the said matters and things above recited; therefore then and there for the causes aforesaid, the said Samuel Howse by the said mayor and aldermen, according to the power aforesaid to them by the said letters patent, delegated, from the office of one of the aldermen of the said borough was entirely removed; And to the said lord the king we further certify, that by the statute made at the parliament begun and held at Westminster, in the county of Middlesex, upon the 8th day of May, in the 13th year of the reign of the said lord the now king, it was enacted, that no person afterwards should be placed or elected to any office or place of mayor, alderman, recorder, bailiff, or to any office of magistracy, or to any places, trusts, or employments relating to any corporation who within one year, before such election hath not received the sacrament of the Lords Supper, according to the rites of the church of England, and for default of such receiving of the said sacrament, such election and placing should be void; nevertheless the said Samuel House, at any time within one year now last past, before the issuing of the first writ of the said lord the king of mandamus, or at any time within the year before the issuing of the last writ of mandamus to restore the said Samuel to the place of alderman of the said bororough, hath not received the sacrament of the Lords Supper according to rites of the church of England, wherefore we pray judgment if the said Samuel be a person capable and fit to be restored to the place of alderman of the said borough.

That Howse did not receive the sacrament within one year before the issuing out the first or last writ of mandamus.

# * CERTIORARI. 

* P. 556.

## The King against the Mayor, Jurats and Commonalty of Winchelsea.

### Michaelmas, 24th Charles II.

CHARLES the second, by the grace of God of England, Scotland, France, and Ireland, king, defender of the faith, &c. to the mayor, justices, jurats and commonalty of the liberty of Winchelsea, in the county of Sussex, and to each of them greeting: We willing for certain causes, that all and singular the decrees and orders by you, or any of you made against the proprietors of lands for the relief of the corporation of Winchelsea aforesaid, be sent by you before us, command you and every of you, that you or one of you send all and singular the decrees and orders aforesaid, with all things touching them, as fully and entirely as by you or any of you they have been made, and before you or any of you now remaining, by whatsoever names the said proprietors of lands may be called in the same, before us, under your seals, or the seals of of you, from the day of St. Michael, in three weeks, wheresoever we shall then be in England, together with this writ, that we may further cause to be done thereupon, that which of right, and according to the law and custom of our kingdom of England, we shall see fit to be done. Witness Mathew Hale, at Westminster, the 26th day of June, in the 34th year of our reign.

Certiorari to remove all decrees and orders by the mayor, &c. made against land owners for the relief of the corporation of Winchelsea.

The answer of the mayor, jurats, and commonalty of the antient town of Winchelsea, within written.

Return.

WE the mayor, jurats, and commonalty of the antient town of Winchelsea to the said most serene lord the king, most humbly certify that in the counties of Kent and Sussex, there are and from the time whereof the memory of man is not to the contrary, there have been five antient towns, to wit, Hastings, Dover, Sandwich, New Romney and Hythe, which are commonly called the cinque ports, and that during the whole time aforesaid there have been and as yet are two antient towns called Rye and Winchelsea, being members of the said cinque ports, which antient town of Winchelsea

That Winchelsea is a member of the cinque ports, wherein the king's writ doth not run except, &c.

That the matters in the writ are civil matters, and do concern the the king's person, &c.

* P. 557.

Winchelsea is the one and the same town in the writ of certiorari thereto annexed mentioned, all which ports with their members for the whole time aforesaid are and have been ports and places for the ordering providing and preserving the ships of the kings and queens of this kingdom of England not for the time being specially * appointed, and whereas also for the whole time aforesaid the writs of the lord the king do not run nor ought to run into the said cinque ports, the said two antient towns with their members or into any of them for any cause or matter whatsoever arising within the said cinque ports, the said two antient towns with their members (matters concerning the person of the lord the king, felonies or appeals excepted,) And whereas the matters contained in the said writ of certiorari hereto annexed, have arisen within the said antient town of Winchelsea, and within the jurisdiction of the same, and are mere civil matters between party and party, and not concerning the person of the king, felonies or appeals whatsoever, and thereupon the said mayor, jurats, and commonalty of the said antient town of Winchelsea, pray judgment of the court here if they ought to make any other return to the writ of certiorari aforesaid, or to the matter in the same contained.

And pray judgment if they ought to make any other return.

---

## Return from Winchelsea to another Certiorari.

That in Kent and Sussex there are five antient ports, &c.

TO wit, we the mayor, jurats, and commonalty of the antient town of Winchelsea, in the writ to this schedule annexed mentioned, most humbly certify that in the counties of Kent and Sussex there are and from the time whereof the memory of man is not to the contrary there have been five antient towns to wit, Hastings, Sandwich, Dover, New Romney and Hythe, which towns from the whole time aforesaid have been the cinque ports of this kingdom of England, and that from the whole time aforesaid there have been and as yet are in the said county of Sussex two other antient towns called Rye and Winchelsea, which for the whole time aforesaid, have been and are members of the said cinque ports, and that the said town of Winchelsea for the whole time aforesaid hath been and as yet is incorporated by the name of the mayor, jurats, and commonalty of Winchelsea, all which ports with their members aforesaid, for the whole time aforesaid, are and have been ports and places

That there are two others called Rye and Winchelsea, members thereof, that Winchelsea is a corporation by prescription.

places for the ordering, providing, and preſerving of the ſhips of the kings and queens of this kingdom of England for the time being, ſpecially appointed, and that by reaſon of the ſituation of the ſaid cinque ports, and their members aforeſaid, nigh or upon the ſhores of the ſea, the inhabitants and reſidents within the ſaid cinque ports, and their ſaid members for the time being, as well for the ſafeguard of the ſaid cinque ports as of the ſaid kingdom of England, againſt the incurſions of the foreign enemies, of the lord the king and of his predeceſſors, from the ſea, there for the whole time aforeſaid have kept and ought and have been accuſtomed, and as yet are * accuſtomed to keep ſeveral beacons, and two watch-houſes, and great and conſtant watches and wards by night and day, as well by ſea as by land for preventing the incurſion of the enemies of the lord the king and of his predeceſſors, and for preventing other dangers by the ſea, and for the better maintenance of the ſaid beacons and watch-houſes, and watches and wards, by the ſaid town of Winchelſea, and the inhabitants of the ſaid town for the time being to be found, provided, and maintained, the mayor, jurats and commonalty of the ſaid town of Winchelſea for the time being, in their common hall there aſſembled, from the time whereof the memory of man is not to the contrary have made and aſſeſſed, and have been uſed and accuſtomed to make and aſſeſs, juſt and reaſonable, neceſſary and equal rates, and aſſeſſments upon every inhabitant or occupier of houſe or houſes, lands or tenements, lying or being within the ſaid town of Winchelſea or the liberties of the ſame, and to collect the ſaid rates and aſſeſſments for the uſes aforeſaid, all which cuſtoms were confirmed to the men of the ſaid cinque ports and their members aforeſaid by the ſtatute of magna charta; and we further certify that before the coming of the ſaid writ of the lord the king, to this ſchedule annexed, to wit, on the 21ſt. day of May, in the 32d. year of the reign of the ſaid lord the now king, a certain reaſonable, neceſſary, and

All which are ports and places for ordering and preſerving of the king's ſhips.

* P. 558.

That the inhabitants conſtantly keep beacons, watch houſes, watches, and wards, to prevent the incurſions of enemies, &c.

That for the maintenance of the ſaid beacons, &c. The corporation of Winchelſea in their common hall being aſſembled, have been uſed to lay an aſſeſſment upon every inhabitant or occupier of houſe or land there.

And to collect the ſame for the ſaid uſes.

That their cuſtoms were confirmed by Magna Charta.

That an equal assessment for the purposes aforesaid, was made by the corporation. Which assessment is annexed to the schedule. That there are no other decrees or orders.

and equal rate and assessment upon all the inhabitants and occupiers of the houses, lands and tenements within the town of Winchelsea aforesaid, and the liberties of the same, by us the said mayor, jurats and commonalty, in our common hall in Winchelsea aforesaid assembled, in the due manner, was made and assessed for the maintenance of the said beacons, watch-houses, watches and wards, which rate and assessment appears in a certain schedule hereto annexed, which rate and assessment to the said lord the now king, at the day and place in the said writ contained, we send as by the said writ we are commanded, and we further certify, that there are not other or more decrees or orders by us, or by any one or more of us, made against the proprietors of lands for the relief of the corporation of the town aforesaid, before us or any one or more of us remaining, which to the said lord the king we can send.

Answer by the mayor, jurats and commonalty, of the antient town of Winchelsea.

---

## The King against Hoopes.

Special subpœna after a pluries certiorari to the justices of the peace within the liberty of St. Peter, in the city of York, to remove all indictments before them against R. Hoopes and others.

* P. 559.

THE king &c.—To the keepers of our peace, and to our justices assigned to hear and determine divers felonies, trespasses and other misdeeds within the liberty of St. Peter, in the city of York, perpetrated, and to every of them greeting, whereas we lately being willing for certain causes that all and singular indictments of whatsoever trespasses and assaults, whereof Robert Hoopes of the city of York, Draper, and all others in the said * indictments named, are indicted before you (as it is said) before us and not elsewhere should be determined, have lately commanded you and every of you by our writ that you should send all and singular the said indictments, with all things touching the same by whatsoever names the said Robert and others may be called, in the same before us under your seals or the seal of one of you or that you should certify or that one of you should certify to us cause, wherefore you would not or could not execute our commands to you thereupon directed, and you have not taken care to certify to us, to the manifest contempt of us and of our commands aforesaid, because of which we are very much moved, therefore we command you and every of you firmly enjoyning that you send or that one of you send all and singular the indictments aforesaid, with all things touching

touching them by whatsoever names the said Robert and others may be called in the same, before us under your seals or the seal of one of you on the octave of St. Michael, wheresoever we shall then be in England according to the tenor of our commands aforesaid, to you and to every of you thereupon directed, that we may further cause to be done thereupon that which of right and according to the law and custom of our kingdom of England, we shall see fit to be done, and this in no wise omit under the pain of 40l. or be yourselves before us in your proper persons, or one of you to whom this our writ shall be delivered be before us in his proper person, to shew wherefore you have contemned to execute our commands so often to you and to every of you heretofore hereupon directed, and have there this writ. Witness J. Branpston, at Westminster, the 13th day of June, in the 14th year of our reign,

By the Court;

*F.* and *T.*

---

## The King, by his Majesty's Attorney General, against Read, baronet.

### Easter, 26th Charles the 2d.

HERTFORD to wit.——Be it remembered, that the writ of the lord the now king under the seal of his exchequer by the consideration of the barons here issued in these words, to wit—Charles the 2d &c. To our justices assigned to take assizes for the county of Hertford, to our justices assigned to deliver our gaol of the said county of the prisoners being therein, and also to our justices assigned to hear and determine divers felonies, trespasses and other misdeeds, in the said county perpetrated, greeting, we willing for certain causes that the barons of our exchequer at Westminster be certified by you of the tenor of a certain fine or amerciament lately imposed by you or one of you upon John Read, baronet, now or lately sheriff of the county aforesaid, command you that you have the tenor of the fine or amerciament aforesaid, together with all things touching the fine or amerciament aforesaid, as fully and entirely and in as ample manner and form as it now remains before you, by whatsoever name or addition of name the said *J. R.* may be

Certiorari from the court of Exchequer to the justices of assize, the justices of gaol delivery and the justices of oyer and terminer, to certify a fine imposed by them upon the sheriff of the county of Hertford for not doing his duty at the assizes.

be called in the same; before the barons of our exchequer at westminster, from the day of Easter in three weeks, that the
* P. 560. said * barons thereupon in our behalf may do that which of right and according to the law and custom of our kingdom of England they shall see fit to be done, and have there this writ, witness Edward Turner, knight, the 28th day of April, in the 26th year of our reign. By warrant of the attorney general of the lord the king, and by the barons.

*Fanshawe.*

Return to the writ a fine of 500l. imposed upon the sheriff, for not appearing at the assizes nor returning a precept to him directed.

At which day, Hugh Windham, knight, one of the justices of the lord the king of the bench, John Mounson, knight of the Bath, and Thomas Lee, esquire, the justices within written, return the said writ, thus indorsed, to wit—The execution of this writ appears in the tenor of the fine to this writ annexed, and the tenor of the said fine follows in these words, to wit——Hertford, to wit—A fine of five hundred pounds was imposed and assessed upon John Read, baronet, at the assizes and general delivery of the gaol of the lord the king, and also at the session of oyer and terminer of the said lord the king, held for the county of Hertford, before Hugh Windham, knight, one of the justices of the lord the king of the Bench, and Thomas Lee, for this time being associated to Thomas Twysden, knight and baronet, one of the justices of the lord the king, assigned to hold pleas before the king himself, and to the said Hugh Windham, justices of the said lord the king, assigned to take assizes in the said county, by the form of the statute, &c. the presence of the said Thomas Twysden not being expected, by virtue of the writ of the lord the king of si non omnes, &c. and before the said Hugh Windham and Thomas Lee, justices, assized to deliver the gaol of the said lord the king, of the county of Hertford aforesaid, of the prisoners being therein, and also before the said Hugh Windham, John Mounson, knight of the Bath, and Thomas Lee, esquire, justices of the said lord the king, by the letters patent of the said lord the king, to them and to others, and to any three or more of them, made under his great seal of England, assigned to enquire of all treasons, felonies, trespasses, contempts, offences, injuries, and other misdeeds whatsoever, and to hear and determine the said felonies, and the other premisses in the said county perpetrated; at the town of Hertford, in the county of Hertford aforesaid, on Friday the 27th day of March, in the 26th year of the reign of our lord Charles the 2d, by the grace of God of England, &c. king, &c.—for this because that he the said John Read, in the due manner being appointed sheriff for the said county, and having taken upon himself the office

fice of sheriff of the said county did not come before the said justices here at this day, to do these things which appertain to his office, nor hath returned now here before the said justices, as he ought, a certain precept to him on behalf of the said lord the now king, long before the return of the said precept duly directed and delivered to him, commanding, that he should not omit because of any liberty in his bailiwick, but that he should cause to come now here before the said justices all writs of assize, juries and certificates, before all justices whatsoever, as well by divers writs of the lord Charles late king of England, and by divers others writs under whatsoever name, stile, or test, as by divers writs of the said lord the now king, in the said county arraid to be taken, together with the pannels, attachments, reattachments, summons, resummons and all other * muniments in any manner touching the said assizes, juries, and certificates, under the provisoes in the said precept specified, and also that he should cause to come now here before the said justices, all prisoners in the said gaol being, together with their attachments, indictments, and all other muniments in any wise concerning the said prisoners, and of the neighbourhood of every town or placew here the felonies whereof the said prisoners are indicted, adjudged, appealed or arrested, were committed as well within liberties as without, twent-four good and lawful men by whom the truth of the matter may be the better known and enquired into, and who are in no wise of kin to the said prisoners, together with four selected men of those towns or places to do those things which on behalf of the said lord the now king, here now shall be commanded them; and also that he should make publick proclamation throughout his whole bailiwick, that all those who would prosecute the prisoners aforesaid, be here now to prosecute against them as is right, and that also he should give notice to all justices of the peace, mayors, coroners, escheators, stewards, and bailiffs of liberties and hundreds, in his county, and also to all and singular the chief constables of every liberty and hundred in his county, that they be here now in their proper persons, with their rolls, records, indictments, and their other remembrances, to do those things which appertain to their offices in that behalf to be done; and that he the said sheriff and his subsheriff, together with his bailiffs and his other attendants, be now here in their proper persons to do those things which appertain to their offices in that behalf to be done, and that he should have now here the names of the justices of the peace, mayors, coroners, escheators, stewards, bailiffs, chief constables, and of those whom he should cause to come, before whom and by whom he had given them no-

* P. 561.



tice

tice, and that he ſhould have now here the ſaid precept; but the duty of his office in the premiſſes he hath wilfully and entirely neglected and refuſed to execute, and although he was ſolemnly here called, nevertheleſs wilfully and entirely he hath abſented himſelf, to the manifeſt contempt and derogation of the authority of the ſaid lord the king, and of the ſaid juſtices of the ſaid lord the now king here at the town of Hertford aforeſaid, in the county aforeſaid, in the court of the ſaid lord the king, preſent and judicially ſitting, by virtue of the ſeveral commiſſions and letters patent of the ſaid lord the king abovementioned, and to the great hindrance of the adminiſtration of juſtice before the ſaid juſtices, and of the proceedings of the ſaid juſtices, to adminiſter juſtice between the ſaid lord the king and his ſubjects, and between the ſubjects of the ſaid lord the king now here in court, and to the great hindrance of juſtice.—As there is contained.

*Lee.*

Defendant appears.

And now in this term, in one month from the day of Eaſter, comes here into court the ſaid John Read, baronet, in the ſaid writ of certiorari named, by George Watts, his attorney, and prays oyer of the writ aforeſaid, and the return of the ſame, and alſo oyer of the tenor of the fine to the ſaid writ annexed, and they are read to him, which being read, heard and by him underſtood, he complains, that he is grievouſly vexed and diſquieted by colour of the premiſſes and this unjuſtly, becauſe

Proteſtation.

proteſting that the writ aforeſaid and the return of the ſame, and alſo the tenor of the fine aforeſaid, and the matters in the

* P. 562.

ſame contained are * not ſufficient in law to charge him the ſaid John Read, with the fine of five hundred pounds in the manner and form aforeſaid upon him impoſed and aſſeſſed, to which he hath no neceſſity nor is he bound by the law of the land to anſwer, nevertheleſs for plea ſaith; that by a certain act of parliament enacted in the parliament of the

Pleads the ſtatute of the thirty-third of Henry the eighth. c. 39. ſ. 30.

lord Henry the eighth late king of England, held at Weſtminſter in the county of Middleſex in the thirty third year of his reign, among other things it is provided and enacted by the authority of the ſaid parliament, that if any perſon or perſons, of whom any ſuch debt or duty as in the ſaid act ſpecified ſhould be demanded, ſhould alledge, plead or ſhew in any courts in the ſaid act mentioned good, perfect and ſufficient cauſe and matter in law, reaſon or good conſcience, in bar or diſcharge of the ſaid debt or duty, or wherefore ſuch perſon or perſons, ought not to be charged, or chargeable to, or with the ſame, and the ſaid cauſe or matter ſo alledged, pleaded, declared or ſhown, ſhould be ſufficiently proved in ſuch one of the ſaid courts as he or

they

they ſhould be impleaded, ſued, vexed, or troubled, that then the ſaid courts in the ſaid act mentioned and every of them ſhould have full power and authority, to accept, adjudge and allow the ſaid proof and wholly and clearly to acquit and diſcharge all and every perſon and perſons who ſhould be ſo impleaded, ſued, vexed or troubled for the ſame any thing in the ſaid act before mentioned to the contrary thereof notwithſtanding, as by the ſaid act among other things more fully appears: and the ſaid John Read for good ſufficient cauſe and matter in law, reaſon, and good conſcience in bar and diſcharge of the ſaid fine, in the tenor aforeſaid ſpecified, and of every part thereof upon him in the manner and form aforeſaid impoſed and aſſeſſed, and wherefore he the ſaid John with the ſaid fine or with any part thereof for the ſaid king, now ought not to be charged, nor is chargeable therewith, and now here in this court ſhews that although well and true it is that he the ſaid John Read, by virtue of certain letters patent of the ſaid lord the now king, made under his great ſeal of England bearing date at Weſtminſter in the county of Middleſex, on the 12th day of November in the 25th year of the reign of the ſaid lord the now king, in the due manner was appointed ſheriff of the county of Hertford aforeſaid as by the ſaid letters patent brought into court here more fully appeareth, and although the ſaid John by virtue of the letters patent aforeſaid had thereupon taken upon himſelf the office of ſheriff of the county aforeſaid, nevertheleſs the ſaid John to come before the ſaid juſtices at the day foreſaid to do thoſe things which appertained to the office of ſheriff of the county aforeſaid, or to return any precepts to him directed as ſheriff of the county of Hertford aforeſaid, was intirely diſabled and incapable in law, for this, to wit, becauſe long before the ſaid John Read, was appointed ſheriff of the county aforeſaid, to wit upon the 4th day of May, in the 25th year of the reign of our lord the now king, &c. at Biſhophatfield, in the county of Hertford, aforeſaid, in a certain eccleſiaſtical cauſe of appeal and complaint, there depending between the ſaid John Read, the party appellant and complainant, and one dame Charity Read, wife of the ſaid John, the party appellate and complained of, before John Mills, * David Budd, Edward Floyd and Edward Maſters, doctors of laws, reſpectively judges delegates of the lord the king in that behalf, by virtue of a commiſſion under the great ſeal of England, he the ſaid John Read, by the judges delegates aforeſaid, was excommunicated, and as yet remains and is excommunicated, after which excommunication and by force of the ſame, the ſaid John Read was totally excluded and incapable in law to receive the

Confeſſes he was choſen ſheriff, and took the office upon him.

* P. 563.

But was before his appointment excommunicated.

and therefore could not receive the facrament which is required by the teft act, enacted the 25th Charles 2.

Recital of the teft act, 25 Ch. 2. chapter 2.

the facrament of the lords fupper according to the rites of the church of England, and the faid John further faith, that by a certain other act of parliament made in the parliament began and held at Weftminfter in the county of Middlefex, on the 8th day of May in the 13th year of the reign of the faid lord the now king, and there continued by feveral prorogations to the 4th day of February in the 25th year of the reign of the faid lord the now king entitled "*an act for preventing dangers which may happen from popifh recufants*" it is enacted, by the faid lord the now king with the advice and confent of the lords fpiritual and temporal, and the commons in the faid parliament affembled among other things in the form following, to wit, "That all and every perfon or perfons as well peers as commoners who fhould bear any office or offices, civil or military or fhould receive any pay falary, fee or wages by reafon of any patent or grant from his majefty, or fhould have command or place of truft from or under his majefty or any of his majeftys predeceffors, or by his or their authority derived from him or them within the realm of England, the dominion of Wales, or the town of Berwick upon the tweed, or in his majefties navy, or in the feveral iflands of Jerfey and Guernfey, or fhould be of the houfhold, fervice or employment of his majefty or his royal highnefs the duke of York, who fhould inhabit, refide or be within the cities of London or Weftminfter, or within thirty miles diftant from the fame, on the firft day the term of Eafter which was in the year of our lord 1673, or at fome time during the faid term, all and every, the perfon and perfons aforefaid perfonally fhould appear before the end of the term aforefaid, or of the term of Trinity next enfuing in his majeftys high court of Chancery, or in his majeftys court of kings bench, and there in publick and open court between the hours of nine of the clock and twelve in the forenoon, fhould take the feveral oaths of fupremacy and allegiance, which oath of allegiance is contained in a ftatute made in the 3d year of king James by law eftablifhed, and during the time of the taking of the fame by the perfon and perfons aforefaid all pleas and proceedings in the refpective courts aforefaid fhould ceafe; and that all and every of the faid refpective perfons and officers not having taken the oaths aforefaid, in the faid refpective courts aforefaid, fhould on or before the 1ft day of Auguft 1673, at the quarter feffions for that county or place where he or they fhould be, inhabit or refide, on the 20th day of May,

* P. 564. * take the faid oaths in open court between the faid hours of nine and twelve of the clock in the forenoon, and the faid refpective officers aforefaid, alfo fhould receive the facrament

crament of the lords ſupper according to the uſage of the church of England at or before the 1ſt day of Auguſt 1673 in ſome pariſh church upon ſome lords day, commonly called Sunday, immediately after divine ſervice and ſermon; and it is further enacted by the authority aforeſaid that all and every perſon or perſons who ſhoud be admitted, entered, placed, or taken into any office or offices, civil or military, or ſhould receive any pay, ſalary, fee or wages, by reaſon of any patent or grant of his majeſty, or ſhould have command or place of truſt from or under his majeſty, his heirs, or ſucceſſors, or by his or their authority, derived from him or them within this realm of England, the dominion of Wales, or the town of Berwick upon the tweed, or in his majeſty's navy, or in the ſeveral iſlands of Jerſey and Guernſey, or who ſhould be admitted into any ſervice or employment in his majeſty's or Royal Highneſſes houſhold or family, after the firſt day of the term of Eaſter aforeſaid, and ſhould inhabit, be or reſide when he or they is or are ſo admitted or placed within the cities of London or Weſtminſter, or within thirty miles of the ſame, ſhould take the ſaid oaths in the ſaid reſpective court or courts in the term next after his or their, ſuch admiſſions, into the office or offices, employment or employments aforeſaid, between the hours aforeſaid and none other, and the proceedings to ceaſe as aforeſaid: and that all and every ſuch perſon or perſons to be admitted after the firſt day of the term of eaſter aforeſaid, not having taken the ſaid oaths in the courts aforeſaid, ſhould take the ſaid ſeveral and reſpective oaths as aforeſaid, at the quarter ſeſſions for that county or place where he or they ſhould reſide, next after his or their ſuch admittance or admittances into any of the reſpective offices or employments aforeſaid, and all and every ſuch perſon or perſons ſo to be admitted as aforeſaid, alſo ſhould receive the ſacrament of the lords ſupper according to the uſage of the church of England within three months after his or their admittance into or receiving the ſaid authority and employment in ſome publick church upon ſome lord's day, commonly called Sunday, immediately after divine ſervice and ſermon: and every of the ſaid perſons in in the reſpective court, where he ſhould take the ſaid oaths, ſhould firſt deliver a certificate, of ſuch his receiving the ſaid ſacrament as aforeſaid, under the hands of the reſpective miniſter, and church wardens, and ſhould then make proof of the truth of the ſame by two credible witneſſes at the leaſt, upon oath, all which ſhould be enquired of and put upon record in their reſpective courts; and it is further enacted by the the authority aforeſaid that all and every the the perſon and perſons who ſhould neglect or refuſe to take

the

the ſaid oaths and ſacrament in the ſaid courts and places and at the reſpective times aforeſaid, ſhould be ipſo facto
* P. 565. adjudged incapable and diſabled in law to all * intents and purpoſes whatſoever, to have, occupy or enjoy the ſaid office or offices, employment or employments, or any part of them or any matter or thing aforeſaid, or any profit or advantage appertaining to them or any of them, and every ſuch office and place, employment and employments, ſhould be void, and by the ſaid act are adjudged void; and by the ſaid act it is further enacted, that all and every ſuch perſon or perſons who ſhould neglect or refuſe to take the ſaid oaths or ſacrament as aforeſaid, within the times and in the places aforeſaid, and in the manner aforeſaid, and yet after ſuch neglect or refuſal, ſhould execute any of the ſaid offices or employments after the ſaid times expired in which he or they ought to have taken the ſame, and being thereupon lawfully convicted by or upon any information, preſentment or indictment, in any of the courts of the lord the king at Weſtminſter, or at the aſſizes, every ſuch perſon and perſons ſhould be diſabled thenceforth to ſue any action, bill, plaint or information in courſe of law or to proſecute any ſuit in any court of equity, or to be guardian of any child, or executor or adminiſtrator of any perſon, or capable of an legacy or deed of gift, or to bear any office within this realm of England, the dominon of Wales, or the town of Berwick upon the Tweed, and ſhould forfeit the ſum of five hundred pounds to be recovered by by him or them who would ſue for the ſame, to be proſecuted by any action of debt, ſuit, bill, plaint or information in any of his majeſty's courts at Weſtminſter, in which no eſſoign, protection or wager of law ſhould be allowed as by the ſaid act among other things in the ſame contained more fully appears. And the ſaid John Read, further ſaith, that he was admitted into the office of ſheriff of the county of Hertford aforeſaid, after the firſt day of the term of Eaſter, in the year of our Lord, 1673, in the act of parliament laſt mentioned ſpecified, to wit, on the ſaid twelfth day of November in the twenty-fifth year of the reign of the ſaid lord the now king aforeſaid, and afterwards, to wit, on the twelfth day of January in the twenty fifth year of the reign of the ſaid lord the now king aforeſaid, the quarter ſeſſions of peace were held for the ſaid county at the town of Hertford, being the next quarter ſeſſions held for the ſaid county after his admittance into the office of ſheriff of the county aforeſaid. And afterwards, to wit on the twenty-third day of January then next enſuing, the term of St. Hilary, being the term next after his admittance aforeſaid, into the office aforeſaid,

Defendant ſaith he was admitted into the office, after the 1ſt day of Eaſter term, 1673.

aforesaid, was held at Westminster aforesaid, and the respective courts in the act last mentioned, appointed to give and administer the oaths by the said act required, were at Westminster aforesaid, during the whole term of St. Hilary aforesaid. And the said John Read further saith, that he at the time in which he was appointed sheriff of the county of Hertford, aforesaid, and always afterwards hitherto, inhabited and resided at Bishophatfield, in the county of Hertford aforesaid, within thirty miles of the city of Westminster aforesaid, in the act aforesaid mentioned. And the said John Read further saith, that the office of sheriff of the county of Hertford is, and at the said time of the making of the act last aforesaid pleaded, and always afterwards was a civil office of great trust for the due execution of * justice within the said county, which to such office of sheriff of the county of Hertford belongs. And the said John Read further saith, that he at any time after he was appointed sheriff hitherto was not absolved from the excommunication aforesaid, and the sacrament of the Lord's supper, according to the command of the said act, did not receive nor could receive by occasion of the excommunication aforesaid, and by reason thereof the oaths aforesaid required in any of the courts of the said lord the king aforesaid, could not take in the manner and form as by the act aforesaid is required, whereby the office of sheriff of the county aforesaid, by the act aforesaid for not taking the oaths aforesaid according to the form of the act aforesaid, long before the coming of the justices aforesaid into the county aforesaid, to wit, on the twelfth day of February then next ensuing, being the last day of the term of St. Hilary aforesaid became void. And the said John thereupon became then incapable and disabled in law to all intents and purposes whatsoever to have, occupy or enjoy the said office of sheriff of the county of Hertford aforesaid, or to return before the justices aforesaid, any precepts to him on behalf of the said lord the now king, at any time directed or delivered, or any writs of assize, juries, or certificates before any justices by any writs whatsoever, or any pannels, attachments, reattachment, summonses, resummonses, or any other muniments the said assizes, juries and certificates any wise concerning, or to cause to come before the justices aforesaid, any prisoners being in the goal aforesaid, with any attachments, indictments, or any other muniments the said prisoners any wise concerning, or to cause to come of the neighbourhood of every town or place where any felonies whereof the said prisoners are indicted, judged, appealed or arrested were committed, as well within liberties as without twenty-four good and

That the office of sheriff is an office of trust.

* P. 566.

saith he was not absolved so could not receive the sacrament therefore could not take the oaths, whereby the office became void.

lawful men, by whom the truth of the matter might be the better known and enquired into, and who are in no wise of kin to the said prisoners, or four selected men of those towns and places, to do those things which on behalf of the said lord the king should be enjoyned them, and was incapable to make public proclamation that all those who would prosecute against the said prisoners, should be there, to prosecute against them, or to give notice to any justices of the peace, mayors, coroners, eschcaters, stewards, bailiffs of hundreds or liberties, within the county aforesaid, that they should be there, in their proper persons, with their rolls, records, indictments and other remembrances, to do those things which to their offices appertain in that behalf to be done, or to do those things which to the office of sheriff of the county aforesaid appertained in that behalf to be done, or to have the names of the justices of the peace, mayors, coroners, eschcaters, stewards, bailiffs, chief constables, or of any other persons whatsoever, or to have then there any precepts whatsoever, or to do any other thing appertaining to the office of sheriff of the county of Hertford aforesaid; But the said John Read, by the force of the act last aforesaid, on the coming of the justices aforesaid, into the county of Hertford aforesaid, was not sheriff of the said county, nor in the said office in any wise did intermeddle, nor ought to intermeddle. And the said John Read further saith, that the fine aforesaid in the tenor aforesaid to the said writ annexed, is such a debt as is specified in the said act of parliament first mentioned, to wit, a debt demanded for the said lord the king, and that the said court is one of the courts in the said act mentioned. And that the said cause and matter by him the said John Read, in bar
* P. 567. and discharge of the said fine of five hundred pounds * and every part thereof, in the tenor of the fine aforesaid demanded above pleaded is good, perfect, and sufficient cause and matter in law, reason and good conscience in bar and discharge of the said fine, and of every part thereof, and wherefore the said John ought not to be charged or to be chargeable to and with the same, or any part thereof, and that the said cause and matter by him above in this plea so alledged, pleaded, declared and shown in this court, by the affidavit of the said John Read to this plea annexed, and by the act of parliament in this plea last pleaded, is sufficiently proved: all and singular which things the said John Read is ready to verify as the court, &c. wherefore he prays judgment, and that the said proof, cause and matter in the premisses aforesaid, by the court here may be received, adjudged and allowed, and that he entirely and fully of the fine

fine aforesaid demanded in the tenor of the fine to the writ aforesaid annexed, and of every part thereof by the court here may be acquitted and discharged by virtue of the act aforesaid first pleaded, and that he the said John, as to the premisses by this court may be discharged. And the tenor of the affidavit in the plea aforesaid mentioned, follows in these words, to wit: In the term of Easter in the 26th year of the reign of Charles the second, &c. Be it remembered, that John Read of Brocket Hall in the county of Hertford, knight and baronet, came before the barons of the Exchequer, on the 26th day of May, in this term, in his proper person, and took his corporal oath in these words following, to wit, "That the writing hereunto annexed, is a true copy of the sentence or instrument of excommunication under the seal of the court of delegates, whereby this deponent is mentioned to be excommunicated. And this deponent further saith, that being thereby disabled he did not receive the sacrament of the Lord's supper, according to the act of parliament in his plea mentioned, neither did this deponent take the oaths prescribed by the said act in the court of Chancery or King's Bench, or either of them, or at the sessions, according to the command and direction of the said act, *John Read*; sworn the day and year first aforesaid before me *C. Spelman*." And the tenor of the writing aforesaid, in the affidavit aforesaid mentioned, follows in these words, "Charles the 2d. &c. To all and singular the rectors, vicars, curates, chaplains and clerks whomsoever, throughout our whole kingdom of England, wheresoever constituted, greeting: Whereas our beloved John Mills, David Budd, Edward Floyd and Edward Masters, doctors of laws respectively, in the business within written, and between the parties within named, our judges, delegates in a certain cause of appeal and complaint, which before them in judgment between Sir John Read, the party appellant and complainant on the one part, and Dame Charity his wife, the party appellate, and complained of on the other part, lately depended undetermined, rightly and duly proceeding the said Sir John Read, baronet, because of his manifest contumacy in not paying or causing to be paid truly and with effect to the said Dame Charity Read, or her proctor the sum of one hundred pounds of the lawful money of England, for her costs taxed in this cause, and the sum of one hundred pounds of the like lawful money of England, for alimony in this cause, at the rate of twenty pounds of the lawful money of England aforesaid, by the month, computing from the 16th day of May * 1668, to the 13th day of October 1668; and the sum of six hundred and fifty pounds

Affidavit of the truth of the plea.

Decree of excommunication.

* P. 568.

 of

of the like money for alimony, aforesaid, at the rate aforesaid, computing from the 13th day of October, 1668, to the 15th day of May, 1671, and the sum of four hundred pounds of lawful money aforesaid, for alimony aforesaid, at the rate aforesaid, computing from the 15th day of May, 1671, to the 15th day of November, 1672, amounting in the whole to the sum of 1265l. of the lawful money aforesaid, on a certain competent day appointed to him, and long since past, and being lawfully and peremptorily monished and cited, often publickly called and long and sufficiently waited for, and in no wise appearing, nor minding to pay the said respective sums amounting in the whole to the sum of 1265l. at the petition of the proctor of the said dame Charity Read, have pronounced him contumacious, and in pain of such his contumacy have decreed him to be excommunicated and have excommunicated him (justice so requiring). Therefore we empower and strictly enjoining, command you, jointly and severally, that you do in your parochial churches on the Lord's day, or on the festival day next and immediately ensuing the receipt of these presents, during divine service, while the greater part of the congregation are present to hear divine service, openly and publickly denounce and declare, or cause to be denounced and declared, the said Sir John Read to have been and to be excommunicated by our authority, under pain of the law, and contempt, and what you shall do in the premisses you shall duly certify to our delegates aforesaid, or to their condelegates, together with these presents, dated the 3d day of May in the 25th year of our reign. Thus indorsed, agreeable to the decree, John Clebury, royal register. " *The within named Sir John Read, was upon the fourth day of May, one thousand six hundred and seventy and three, being Sunday, in the time of divine service, openly denounced excommunicated, according to the tenor and effect of this excommunication, in the parish church of Bishop-hatfield, in the county of Hertford.*

*N. W. curate.*

Demurrer by the attorney general.

And Francis North, knight, attorney general of the said lord the now king, who for the said lord the now king in this behalf prosecutes, present here in court on the same day for the said lord the king saith, that the said lord the now king by any thing by the said John Read above, by pleading alledged from his execution for the said fine of five hundred pounds, ought not to be precluded, because he saith that the said plea of the said John Read, in the manner and form aforesaid, pleaded, and the matter in the same contained, are not sufficient in law to discharge or acquit the said John Read

Read from the ſaid fine of five hundred pounds, to which he hath no neceſſity, neither is he bound by the law of the land in any manner to anſwer, and this he is ready to verify, wherefore, becauſe of the inſufficiency of the ſaid plea, the ſaid attorney general prays judgment, and that the ſaid John Read with the ſaid fine of five hundred pounds may be * charged, and for the ſame may ſatisfy the ſaid lord the king, and that the ſaid lord the king may have his execution for the fine aforeſaid, &c. * P. 569.

And the ſaid John Read becauſe that he, ſufficient matter in law to diſcharge or acquit the ſaid John from the ſaid fine of five hundred pounds above, by pleading hath alledged, which he is ready to verify, which matter the ſaid attorney general of the ſaid lord the king, for the ſaid lord the king doth not deny, nor to the ſame in any wiſe doth anſwer, but altogether doth refuſe to admit that averment, as before prays judgment, and that he from the fine aforeſaid, and from every part thereof may be diſcharged. Therefore, &c. Joinder by defendant.

*This caſe was adjourned into the Exchequer chamber, for the opinion of all the judges: and judgment given for the king.*

---

# The Inhabitants of the County of Cornwall, at the ſuit of the Lord the King.

## Eaſter, 4th James 2d.

AND now, to wit, in one month from the day of Eaſter, come here into court, the ſaid inhabitants of the county of Cornwall aforeſaid, by J. S. their attorney, and pray oyer of the tenor of the fines aforeſaid upon them as aforeſaid impoſed, and aſſeſſed, and it is read to them, &c. which being read and heard, and by them underſtood, they complain that they under colour of the premiſſes are grieveouſly vexed and diſquieted and this unjuſtly, becauſe proteſting that the tenor of the fines aforeſaid in the charge aforeſaid mentioned, and the matter in the ſame contained are not ſufficient in law to charge them the ſaid inhabitants of the county of Cornwall aforeſaid

Plea in diſcharge of certain fines impoſed on the inhabitants of a county, for not keeping the county gaol in repair.

aforesaid with, the said several fines of fifty pounds and one hundred pounds in the manner and form aforesaid, upon them imposed and assessed, to which they have no necessity neither are they bound by the law of the land in any manner to answer. for plea nevertheless, they the said inhabitants say that by a certain act of parliament enacted in the parliament of the lord Henry the 8th late king of England, held at Westminster in the county of Middlesex in the 33d year of his reign, among other things it is provided and enacted by the authority of the said parliament, that if any person or persons of whom any such debt or duty as in the said act specified should be demanded, should alledge, plead or shew in any courts in the said act mentioned, good, perfect, and sufficient cause and matter in law reason, or good conscience, in bar or discharged of the said debt or duty; or wherefore such person or persons ought not to be charged or to be chargeable to or with the same, and the said cause or matter so alledged, pleaded, declared or shown should be sufficiently proved in such one of the said courts as he or they should be impleaded, sued, vexed, or troubled, that then the said courts in the said act mentioned, and every of them should have full power and authority to accept, adjudge, and allow the said proof, and wholly and * clearly to acquit and discharge all and every person and persons who should be so impleaded, sued, vexed or troubled, for the same, any thing in the said act aforesaid mentioned to the contrary thereof notwithstanding, as by the said act among other things more fully appears; and the said inhabitants for good and sufficient cause and matter in law reason and good conscience in bar and discharge of the several fines aforesaid, in the tenor and charge aforesaid specified, and of every part thereof upon them in the manner and form aforesaid imposed and assessed, and wherefore they the said inhabitants of the county of Cornwall; with the said several fines, or with any part thereof for the said lord the now king ought not to be charged nor are chargeable therewith further say, and now here in this court show that the castle of Lanceston otherwise Dunhead, in the said county of Cornwall, is and at the same time of the imposition of the several fines aforesaid, of fifty pounds, and one hundred pounds, and also from the time whence the memory of man is not to the contrary hath been an antient castle and that the office of constable of the castle aforesaid, is and for the whole time aforesaid hath been an antient office granted and grantable by our lord the King and his progenitors kings and queens of England when there is not a duke of Cornwall, and when there is a duke of Cornwall, then

Protestation. Act of the 33d Hen. 8th. c. 39. s. 30.

* P. 570.

That the office of constable of the castle at Lanceston, is grantable by the king when there is no duke of Cornwall and by the duke of Cornwall when there is one.

then by the duke of Cornwall, for the time being; to which office divers wages, fees and rewards from the whole time aforesaid have belonged and appertained, and as yet do belong and appertain; and the said inhabitants further say, that the said gaol of the said lord the now king of Lanceston in the county of Cornwall in the charge aforesaid mentioned, for the not repairing amending, and supporting of which gaol the said several fines of fifty pounds and one hundred pounds in the charge aforesaid mentioned were imposed, from the whole time aforesaid, hitherto hath been and is within the castle aforesaid, and parcel of the said castle of Lanceston otherwise Dunhead, and the antient, peculiar, sole and common gaol of the said county of Cornwall for the custody of malefactors, and of persons from the whole time aforesaid committed, or who ought to be committted within the county of Cornwall aforesaid, for any capital offences or crimes; and that the constable of the castle aforesaid, for the whole time aforesaid, by reason of his office aforesaid hath been and as yet is keeper of the said gaol of the said lord the king, within the said castle of Lanceston otherwise Dunhead, and by reason of his office aforesaid, divers wages, fees, and rewards of the prisoners in the gaol aforesaid from time to time kept and imprisoned, hath received and had, and hath been used and accustomed to receive and have: and that all and singular the constables of the Castle aforesaid, and every of them for the time being, by reason of his office aforesaid, from the whole time aforesaid, hitherto always have supported, repaired and amended, and have been used and accustomed and of right ought to support, repair and amend the said gaol for the safe and secure custody of the prisoners to the said gaol committed or to be committed; and that the sheriff of the county of Cornwall aforesaid for the time being, at any time hath not had the custody of the gaol aforesaid, nor of the prisoners in the same nor in the custody thereof in any wise hath intermeddled, nor ought or could intermeddle, but from the custody of the said gaol and of the prisoners being in the same hath been and is entirely excluded while such prisoners remain in the said * gaol: and that the whole profit and advantage arising from the said gaol and the custody of the same and from the prisoners being in the same, amounting annually to more than would repair, amend and support the said gaol, hath been received and had by the constable of the castle aforesaid, for the time being or his deputy or deputies and not by the sheriff of the county of Cornwall for the time being, or any of the officers or ministers of the said sheriff: and the said inhabitants further say that long before the imposition of the said several fines of fifty pounds and one hundred pounds, to wit, on the 3d day of April in the 19th year of the reign of the

That the gaol is within the said castle.

That the constable of the castle hath by reason of his office, divers fees, &c. from the prisoners.

That the constable hath been used to repair the said gaol.

That the sheriff of the county never had the custody of the gaol, &c.

* P. 571.

the lord Charles the 2d late king of England the said office then being vacant, and there being then no duke of Cornwall, the said lord Charles the 2d late king of England by his letters patent under his great seal of England made at Westminster in the county of Middlesex, gave and granted to one Hugh Pyper, knight, and Hugh Pyper, the younger, the said office of constable of the said castle of Lanceston otherwise Dunhead within the county of Cornwall aforesaid, to have and to hold the said office to the said Hugh Pyper, knight, and the said Hugh Pyper, the younger, and to him living the longer of them by themselves or their sufficient deputy or sufficient deputies, to and for the whole term of the natural lives of the said Hugh Pyper, knight, and Hugh Pyper, the younger, and for the natural life of him living the longer of them, as by the enrollment of the said letters patent in the court of the lord the now king of Chancery at Westminster, in the county of Middlesex, remaining of record more fully appeareth; by virtue of which letters patent they the said Hugh Pyper, knight, and Hugh Pyper the younger, were and as yet are seized of the office aforesaid, for the term of their lives, and for the life of him living the longer of them; and the office aforesaid and the custody of the gaol aforesaid, by themselves and their deputies, from the time of the making of the said letters patent, hitherto have exercised and had, and as yet do exercise and have, and all wages, fees, profits, and advantages to the said office belonging or appertaining continually from thence afterwards, hitherto have received and had, and as yet do receive and have, whereby the said Hugh Pyper, knight, and Hugh Pyper the younger, ought to repair, support and amend the said gaol, without this, that the inhabitants aforesaid, of the county of Cornwall aforesaid, the gaol of the lord the king at Lanceston aforesaid ought to repair support and amend in the manner and form as in the charge and constat aforesaid above is supposed: and the said inhabitants further say that the court of exchequer of the lord the king here is one of the courts in the act aforesaid above mentioned, and that the said fines of fifty pounds and one hundred pounds in the charge and constat aforesaid mentioned, are such debts as in the said act of parliament are mentioned, to wit, a debt demanded for the lord the king; and that the said cause and matter by the said inhabitants, of the county of Cornwall aforesaid, above in discharge of the several fines of fifty pounds and one hundred pounds and of every part thereof, above declared, alledged and shown, is good, perfect and sufficient cause and matter in law, reason and good conscience, in bar and discharge of the said debts of fifty pounds and one hundred pounds, and * every part thereof, and wherefore

That Char. the 2d granted the office of constable of the said castle to H. P. &c. for life.

Traverse that the inhabitants of the county ought to repair the gaol.

* P. 572.

wherefore the said inhabitants of the county of Cornwall aforesaid ought not to be charged nor to be chargeable to and with the said fifty pounds and one hundred pounds, or with any part thereof, all and singular which things the said inhabitants of the county of Cornwall aforesaid, are ready to verify and prove as the court, &c.—Wherefore they pray judgment, and that they entirely and fully of the fines aforesaid by the court here may be acquitted and discharged by virtue of the act aforesaid, and that they the said inhabitants of the county of Cornwall aforesaid as to the premisses by the court here may be dismissed.

*Hen. Pollexfen.*

---

# *CASES OF DEBT IN AID.

## The King against Hart, widow.

### Hilary, 1st, and 2d, James 2d. in the Exchequer.

Scire facias to the administratrix of the debtor of a conusor of a debt to the king, to show cause why the king should not have execution for the debt due his conusor.

Inquisition upon an extent, whereby the intestate of defendant was found to be indebted to one of the conusors.

BE it remembered, that the writ of the lord the now king, under the seal of this Exchequer, by the consideration the barons here issued in those words, to wit— James the 2d by the grace of God, &c. to the sheriff of Berks, greeting, whereas Heritage Harford, of London, merchant, Charles Gregory of London, merchant, and Henry Harford of London, pewterer, came before Edward Nevill, knight, one of the barons of our Exchequer, on the 30th day of October last past, in their proper persons; and jointly and severally acknowledged that they were indebted to us one hundred and eighty pounds, which they ought to have paid at a certain day past, and the same to us have not paid nor have caused to be paid as it is said: and whereas by a certain inquisition indented, taken at Guildhall, in the city of London, on the 23d day of September last past, before Thomas Kinsey, knight, and Benjamin Thorowgood, knight, sheriffs of the city aforesaid, by virtue of our writ of extent, under the seal of our exchequer to the said sheriffs directed, against the said Charles Gregory, it is found by the oath of Daniel Man and others good and lawful men of the bailiwick of the said sheriffs, that



* For the meaning of this term, see post, page 599.

that one John Hart, late of the Strand, in the county of Middlesex, vintner, deceased, at the time of his death was indebted to the said Charles Gregory, in the sum of one hundred and five pounds for divers goods and merchandizes by the said Charless Gregory, before the said time to the said John Hart, sold and delivered, which debt the said sheriffs by virtue of the writ aforesaid, on the said day of the taking of the writ aforesaid, into our hands, did, seize: and whereas by acerta in inquisition indented taken at

* P. 573. the Sugarloaf in Hatton Garden, in the county of Middlesex, on the 24th day of December last past, * before Benjamin

Inquisition of the death of the debtor of conusor. Thorowgood, knight, and Thomas Kinsey, knight, sheriff of the county aforesaid, by virtue of our writ of diem clausit extremum, under the seal of our exchequer to the said sheriff directed against the said John Hart, it is found by the oath of John Bradshaw and others, good and lawful men of the bailiwick aforesaid, that the said John Hart died the 27th day of December, in the 36th year of the reign of Charles the 2d late king, &c. and that at the time of his death he was possessed of several goods and chattles in a certain schedule to the said writ annexed mentioned, to the value of

And administration granted to defendant. 93l. 19s. 8d. and of several other goods and chattles to the value of 219l. 13s. 4d. and that after his death, to wit, on the 21st day of January, in the 36th year aforesaid, administration of all singular the goods and chattles, rights and credits, which were said John Hart's at the time of his death, to one Anne Hart, widow, in the due form of law was committed, by virtue of which administration all and singular the said goods and chattles came to the hands of the said Anne Hart, as by the several writs aforesaid, and the returns of the same and the several inquisitions aforesaid, into our Exchequer certified, and there in the custody of our remembrancer remaining more fully appears: and we being willing to be satisfied of the said one hundred and five pounds now due to us,

Scire facias. with all the speed with which we can, as is just, command you that you do not omit, because of any liberty, but that you enter the same and by good and lawful men of your bailiwick that you give notice to the said Ann Hart, widow, that she be before the barons of our Exchequer at Westminster on the 3d day of February, next ensuing, to show and propound if she hath and knoweth any thing to say for herself, wherefore we ought not to have execution against her of the goods and chattles of the said John Hart, for the said one hundred and five pounds, and have there then the names of those by whom you shall so give notice, and this writ, witness W, Montague, at Westminster, the 26th day of January, in the 1st year of our reign: by the writs and inquisitions aforesaid, and by the barons. *Ayloffe.*

And

And on the said third day of February, Edward Wiseman, the younger, esquire, sheriff of the county of Berks, aforesaid, returned this writ aforesaid, thus indorsed, to wit, to the barons within written I certify that by Richard Hart and John Oliver, good and lawful men of my bailiwick, I have given notice to the within named Anne Hart, widow, administratrix of the goods and chattles of the within named John Hart, that she be before the barons at the day and place within contained, to show, &c. as within I am commanded E. W. esquire, sheriff: as is more fully contained in the writ aforesaid, and the return of the same, which are in the file of the writs executed in Berks for the said lord the king of the term of St. Hilary, in the end of the first and beginning of the second year of his reign.

Return of the writ.

And now, to wit, on the said third day of February, in this term, comes here the said Anne Hart, widow, by Butler Buggin her attorney, and prays oyer of the writ of scire facias aforesaid, and the return of the same, and they are read to her which being read, heard and by her understood, she complains that the under colour of the premisses is grievously vexed and disquieted, and this unjustly, because protesting that the writ of scire facias aforesaid, and the return of the same and the matter in the same contained are not sufficient in law, to which * she hath no necessity neither is she bound by the law of the land to answer: for plea nevertheless the said Anne Hart saith, that the said John Hart in the writ of scire facias aforesaid named, in his life time, to wit, on the 17th day of July in the 36th year of the reign of the lord Charless the 2d late king of England, &c. at London, to wit, in the parish of the blessed Mary of the arches, in the ward of Cheap, by his certain writing obligatory sealed with his seal, bearing date the day and year aforesaid, for a true and just debt acknowledged that he was holden and firmly bounden to one Thomas Beachampe, in two hundred pounds of the lawful money of England, to be paid to the said Thomas when he should be thereto requested, and for this because that the said two hundred pounds to the said Thomas by the said John in his life time were not paid or satisfied, the said Thomas for the recovery of the said 200l. after the death of the said John, to wit, on the Wednesday next after fifteen days of Easter in the 1st year of the reign of the lord the now king, came into the court of the said lord the king before the king himself at Westminster, in the county of Middlesex, and produced in the said court then there his certain bill against the said Anne, by the name of Anne Hart, widow, administratrix of all and singular the goods and chattles, rights and credits which were the said John

Plea by the administratrix to the scire facias: that before the issuing of the writ of extent, two judgements for bond debts of the intestate to the amount of 300l. were recovered against her, and that there is now in full force a certain bond of her intestate for 1800l. That the said debts are unsatisfied, and that on the day of the issuing of the writ of extent, she had assets in her hands to the value of only 10l.

* P. 574.

which are bound with the payment of the said judgements, &c.

John Hart's at the time of his death, who died intestate as it is said, otherwise lately called John Hart of, &c. of a plea of debt of the said 200l. upon the writing obligatory aforesaid; upon which plea it was in such wise proceeded in the said court of the said lord the king, before the king himself, that afterwards and before the issuing of the writ of extent, in the writ of scire facias aforesaid mentioned, to wit, in the said term of Easter in the year aforesaid, he the said Thomas Beachampe by the judgment of the said court, in the said court recovered against the said Anne, as well the said debt of two hundred pounds, as thirty shillings for his damages, which he had by occasion of the detention of the said debt, as for his costs and charges by him about that suit in that behalf expended whereof she is convicted, of the goods and chattles of the said John Hart at the time of his death, in the hands of the said Anne, to be administered, if she had so much in her hands, and if she had not then the damages aforesaid, of the proper goods and chattles of the said Anne to be levied, as by the record and proceedings thereon in the said court of the said lord the king, before the king himself at Westminster, in the county of Middlesex aforesaid, remaining of record more fully appeareth; and the said Anne further saith that the said John in his life time, to wit, on the 17th day of July, in the 36th year of the reign of the lord Charles the 2d, late king of England, &c. at London, to wit, in the parish of the blessed Mary of the Arches, in the ward of Cheap, by his certain writing obligatory, sealed with his seal, bearing date the day and year last aforesaid, for a true and just debt acknowledged that he was holden and firmly bounden to one Philip Franklyn, gentleman, in one hundred pounds, to be paid to the said Philip when he should be thereto requested, and for this because that the said debt of one hundred pounds to the said Philip, by the said John in his life time, was not paid or satisfied, the said Philip for the recovery of the said one hundred pounds, after the death of the said John, afterwards, to wit, on the Wednesday next after fifteen days of Easter, in the first year of the reign of the lord the now king, came into the court of the said lord the king, before the king himself, at Westminster, in the county of Middlesex, aforesaid, and produced in the said court then there his certain bill

* P. 575. against the said Anne, by the name of Anne * Hart, widow, administratrix of all and singular the goods and chattles, rights and credits, which were the said John Hart's at the time of his death, who died intestate, as it is said, otherwise lately called J. H. of, &c. of a plea of debt of the said 100l. upon the writing aforesaid last mentioned, upon which plea

it

it was in such wise proceeded, in the said court, of the said lord the king, before the king himself, that afterwards and before the issuing of the writ of extent in the writ of scire facias aforesaid mentioned, to wit, in the said term of Easter, in the year aforesaid, he the said Philip by the judgment of the said court, in the said court recovered against the said Anne, as well the said debt of one hundred pounds as thirty shillings for his damages, which he had as well by occasion of the detention of the debt aforesaid, as for his costs and charges by him about that suit in that behalf expended, whereof she is convicted of the goods and chattles, which were of the said John, at the time of his death in the hands of the said Anne to be administered if she had so much in her hands, and if she had not so much, then the damages aforesaid of the proper goods and chattles of the said Anne to be levied, as by the record and proceedings thereupon in the said court of the said lord the king, before the king himself at Westminster aforesaid remaining, more fully appeareth: and the said Anne further saith, that the said John Hart in his life time, to wit, on the 20th day of August, in the 36th year of the reign of the Lord Charles the 2d. late king of England, &c. at L—, to wit, in the parish, &c. by the name of J. H. &c. by his writing obligatory, sealed with the seal of the said John in his life time, bearing date the said day and year, for a true and just debt, acknowledged that he was holden and firmly bounden to one Basil Firebrace, knight, in one thousand eight hundred pounds, to be paid to the said B— when he should be thereto requested; which several judgments in the form aforesaid, had and obtained, were for true and just debts, and as yet in their full force, vigour and effect, remain not reversed, paid or satisfied; and the said Anne further saith, that the writing obligatory aforesaid, as yet is in full force, and was made for a true and just debt as yet remaining not paid, discharged or satisfied: and that the said Anne hath fully administered all the goods and chattles which were the said John's at the time of his death in her hands to be administered; and that she at the time of the issuing of the said writ of extent, to wit, on the 8th day of November, in the 1st year of the reign of the said lord the now king James the 2d. nor ever afterwards had any goods or chattles, which were the said John's at the time of his death in the hands of the said Anne to be administered, except goods and chattles to the value of ten pounds, which are not sufficient to satisfy the several sums of money against her as aforesaid recovered, and due by the said writing obligatory, and which at the said time of the issuing of the said writ of extent, with the payment of the several debts in the

Averments. the judgments aforefaid, and in the writing obligatory aforefaid mentioned, are charged and bound, and this fhe is ready to verify, as the court, &c. with this that the faid Anne will verify that the faid John Hart in the judgments and writing obligatory aforefaid named, and the faid John Hart in the inquifitions aforefaid, and the writ of fcire facias aforefaid, in like manner named is one and the fame perfon, and not another, nor different, and that the faid Anne in the feveral judgments aforefaid named defendant, and the faid

* P. 576. Anne * in the faid writ of fcire facias aforefaid in like manner named, is one and the fame perfon and not another, nor different, wherefore fhe prays judgment if the lord the king ought to have or maintain his execution againft her, and that fhe the faid Anne as to the premiffes by the court here may be difmiffed, &c. &c.

The king demurs, and judgment given for the king.

---

## The King againft Butcher.

Scire facias. S. S. and W. became bound in feveral obligations to the king: upon an extent againft S. and S. B. H. was found to be indebted to them in feveral bonds: and upon another extent againft B. H. J. B. was found to be indebted to B. H. in 650l. by fimple contract, there-

BE it remembered, that the writ of the lord the now king under the feal of this exchequer, by the confideration of the barons here iffued in thefe words to wit, Charles the 2d &c. to the fheriff of Surry, greeting, whereas Hugh Surrey, Thomas Stevenfon, merchant, and Thomas Walton, wine cooper all of London, by their writing obligatory fealed with the feals, bearing date the 20th day of March in the 34th year of our reign, are holden to us jointly and feverally in two hundred and forty pounds of the lawful money of England, to be paid on a certain day paft: and whereas the faid Hugh Surrey, Thomas Stevenfon and Thomas Walton, by another writing obligatory fealed with their feals, bearing date the 15th day of April, in the 34th year of our reign aforefaid, are holden to us jointly and feverally in fixty pounds of the like lawful money of England, to be paid in like manner on a certain day now paft; and whereas the faid Hugh Surrey, Thomas Stevenfon and Thomas Walton, by another writing obligatory fealed with their feals, bearing date the 11th day of Auguft in the 34th year of our reign aforefaid are holden to us jointly, and feverally in one hundred and fixty pounds of the lawful money of England, to be paid in like manner on a certain day now paft; and whereas

whereas the faid Hugh Surrey, Thomas Stevenfon and Thomas Walton, by another writing obligatory fealed with their feals, bearing date the 29th day of November in the 34th year of our reign aforefaid, are holden to us jointly and feverally in fix hundred and forty pounds of the like lawful money of England to be paid in like manner on a certain day now paft, and the fame to us have not paid nor have caufed to be paid as it is faid: and whereas by a certain inquifition indented taken at the Guildhall of the city of London, fituate in the parifh of St. Lawrence in the old Jewry, in the ward of Cheap, of the faid city, on the 11th day of July laft paft, before Dudley North, knight, and Peter Rich efquire, late fheriffs of the city of London aforefaid, by virtue of our writ of extent under the feal of our exchequer, againft the faid Hugh Surrey and Thomas Stevenfon, to the faid late fheriffs directed, it is found by the oath of Daniel Man and others good and lawful * men of the bailiwick of the faid fheriffs, that one Benjamin Hinton of London, goldfmith, by his writing obligatory fealed with the feal of the faid Benjamin, bearing date the 19th day of March laft paft, became holden and bounden to the faid Hugh Surrey and Thomas Stevenfon, in eight hundred pounds of the lawful money of England, with a condition underwritten, for the true payment of four hundred and twelve pounds of the like good and lawful money of England, to the faid Hugh Surrey and Thomas Stevenfon, upon the 20th day of September next enfuing the date of the writing obligatory aforefaid; and that the faid Benjamin Hinton, by another writing obligatory fealed with the feal of the faid Benjamin, bearing date the faid 19th day March laft paft, became holden and bounden to the faid Hugh Surrey and Thomas Stevenfon in eight hundred pounds of the good and lawful money of England, with a condition underwritten, for the true payment to the faid Hugh Surrey and Thomas Stevenfon, of four hundred and eighteen pounds of the like lawful money of England upon the 20th day of December next enfuing the date of the writing obligatory aforefaid; and that the faid B. H. by another writing obligatory, fealed with the feal of the faid Benjamin, bearing date the faid 19th day of March laft paft, became holden and bounden to the faid H. S. and T. S. in eight hundred pounds of the good and lawful money of England with a condition underwritten for the true payment to the faid H. S. and T. S. of four hundred and twenty four pounds of the like good and lawful money of England, upon the 20th day of march in the year of our Lord 1683; which feveral writings obligatory aforefaid and the money thereon due, the faid fheriffs on the

fore fcire facias iffues to J. B. to fhow caufe why the king fhould not have execution for this debt.

* P. 577.

the faid day of the taking of the inquifition aforefaid by virtue of the writ aforefaid, into our hands have caufed to be feized and taken, as by the writ aforefaid, the return of the fame and the faid inquifition to the fame annexed into our exchequer certified, and there in the cuftody of our remembrancer remaining more fully appeareth; And whereas by another inquifition indented, taken at the Guildhall of the city of London fituate in the parifh of St. Lawrence in the Old Jewry, in the ward of Cheap, of the faid city, on the 21ft day of July laft paft, before the faid Dudley North, knight, and Peter Rich, efquire late fheriffs of London aforefaid, by virtue of our writ of extent under the feal of our exchequer againft the faid B. H. to the faid late fheriffs directed, it is found by the oath of William Church and others good and lawful men of the bailiwick of the faid fheriffs, that one John Butcher timber merchant, on the faid day of the taking of the inquifition aforefaid, was indebted to the faid Benjamin Hinton in fix hundred and fifty pounds of the good and lawful money of England, for fo much money by the faid Benjamin Hinton to the faid John Butcher before that time lent and advanced, and that the faid fum then remained due and not fatisfied, to wit, at the faid parifh of St. Laurence in the Old Jewry in the ward of Cheap, which fum of fix hundred and fifty pounds aforefaid, the late fheriffs aforefaid, on the day of the taking of the inquifition aforefaid, by virtue of the writ aforefaid, into our hands have caufed to be takne and feized as by the faid writ the return of the fame, and the faid inquifition to the faid writ annexed into our exchequer certified, and there in the cuftody of our remembrancer remaining more fully appeareth, and we being

* P. 578. willing to be fatisfied of the faid fix hundred and fifty * pounds to us now due, with all the fpeed with which we can, as is right, command you, that you do not omit becaufe of any liberty but that you enter the fame, and that by good and lawful men of your bailiwick; you give notice to the faid John Butcher, that he be before the barons of our exchequer at Weftminfter on the 31ft day of this prefent month of October, to fhow and propound if he hath or knoweth any thing to fay for himfelf wherefore we ought not to have execution againft him for the faid fix hundred and fifty pounds, and have there the names of thefe by whom you fhall fo give notice to him, and this writ, witnefs W. Montague, at Weftminfter, the 25th day October, in the 35th year of our reign: by the writs and inquifition aforefaid, and by the barons.

*Aviffe.*

At

At which day Anthony Rawlins, esquire, sheriff of the county of Surry aforesaid, returned here the writ aforesaid thus indorsed, to wit, by virtue of this writ to me directed by John Doe and Richard Roe, good and lawful men of my bailiwick, I have given notice to the within named John Butcher, that he be before the barons of the exchequer of the lord the king, at the day and place within contained as I am within commanded, Anthony Rawlins, esquire, sheriff. As is more fully contained in the said writ and return of the same, which are in the file of the writs executed in Surry for the said lord the now king, of this term on behalf of his remembrancer.

Return of the scire facias.

And now, to wit, on the said 31st of October in this term comes here the said John Butcher, in the said writ of scire facias and the return of the same named, by William Bathurst, his attorney, and prays oyer of the said writ of scire facias and of the said several writs of extendi facias, and of the returns of the same, and of the inquisitions aforesaid thereupon taken, and they are read to him, which being read and heard and by him understood, he complains that he under colour of the premisses is grievously vexed and disquieted, and this not justly, because he saith that the said lord the now king ought not to have execution against him, for the said six hundred and fifty pounds, because protesting that the said several writs of extendi facias, and the inquisitions aforesaid, taken, and the returns of the said writs, and also the said writ of scire facias, and the matter in the same contained are not sufficient in law, to which he hath no necessity, neither is he bound by the law of the land in any manner to answer, for plea nevertheless the said John Butcher saith, that the said Benjamin Hinton before the said time, in which he as aforesaid became holden and bounden to the said Hugh Surrey and Thomas Stevenson, to wit, on the last day of February in the 35th year of the reign of the said lord the now king aforesaid at London aforesaid, in the said Parish of St. Lawrence, in the Old Jewry, in the ward of Cheap, the said Benjamin Hinton then being indebted to one Richard Goffe in the sum of one thousand two hundred pounds and upwards, by a writing obligatory, and to divers others his creditors being natural born subjects of this kingdom of England, in divers other several sums of money, amounting to forty thousand * pounds and more became a bankrupt, the said Benjamin being a natural born subject of this kingdom of England, and as yet and for many years before that time seeking his living and his trade of living by way of buying and selling, to wit, at London aforesaid, in the parish and ward last aforesaid, and the said Benjamin Hinton so being indebted and a bankrupt, and the said John Butcher and other

Plea. That before Hinton became bound to Surrey and Stevenson he became a bankrupt and that the bonds were given by Hinton in consequence of a fraudulent agreement between Surrey, Stevenvenson and one Richard Goffe, a creditor of Hinton's, to obtain for Goffe a fraudulent preference in recovering his debt, and that defendants debt, was assigned over to the assignees by the commissioners of bankrupts.

* P. 579.

other persons being indebted to the said Benjamin Hinton, the said Richard Goffe, Hugh Surrey and Thomas Stevenson afterwards and before the said Benjamin Hinton as aforesaid became holden and bounden to the said Hugh Surrey and Thomas Stevenson, to wit, on the 18th day of March in the 35th year of the reign of the said lord the now king aforesaid, at London aforesaid, in the parish and ward last aforesaid, by fraud and covin among themselves, did conspire and devise, to gain to themselves the entire debts of one thousand two hundred pounds, due by the said Benjamin Hinton to the said Richard Goffe as aforesaid, and to deceive and to defraud the other creditors of the said B. H. of their true and just debts: and to fulfil their said conspiracies and purposes aforesaid, the said Richard Goffe, Hugh Surrey and Thomas Stevenson, on the day and year last aforesaid, at L. aforesaid, in the parish and ward aforesaid, among themselves fraudulently and deceitfully did agree that under colour of the sale of a certain parcel of casks of wines and of small value, by the said Hugh Surrey and Thomas Stevenson, to the said Richard Goffe, (who never dealt nor had dealing in wines for money amounting to the debt to him the said Richard Goffe, by by him the said Benjamin Hinton due as aforesaid,) the said writing obligatory in which the said Benjamin Hinton was bounden to the said Richard Goffe for the payment of the said debt, by the said Benjamin Hinton, to the said Richard Goffe as aforesaid due, should be delivered to the said Benjamin to be cancelled, And that thereupon, the said Benjamin should become bound to the said Hugh Surrey and Thomas Stevenson to pay to them the like sum of money; and that afterwards the said Hugh Surrey and Thomas Stevenson should procure out of the court here the said writ of the lord the king of extendi facias to the sheriffs of London, to be directed, against them the said Hugh and Thomas under pretence of the speedy obtaining the debt of the said lord the king, by the said Hugh and Thomas due by the writings obligatory aforesaid, in which they as aforesaid were holden debtors to the said lord the king, and by colour thereof to procure it to be found by the inquisition upon the said writ to be taken, that the said Benjamin Hinton by the said writings obligatory by him as aforesaid, to the said Hugh and Thomas to be made, was indebted to the said Hugh and Thomas, and thereupon to procure the money by the writings obligatory aforesaid, supposed to be due, by the sheriffs of London aforesaid, to be taken and seized into the hands of the said lord the king; and afterwards under colour of the loosing of the said debt unless speedy prosecution

should

should be commenced against the said Benjamin to procure out of the court here a certain other writ of the said king of extendi facias against the said Benjamin, and under pretence thereof to procure it to be found by a certain inquisition upon the said writ to be taken, that the said John Butcher and other persons indebted to the said Benjamin, were indebted to the said Benjamin and to procure those debts to be taken and seized by the sheriffs of London aforesaid, into the hands of the said lord the king: and thereupon in prosecution of the said corrupt agreement the said writing obligatory * in which the said Benjamin as aforesaid was holden to the said Richard afterwards, to wit, on the said 19th day of March in the 35th year of the said lord the now king at London aforesaid, in the parish and ward aforesaid, to the said Benjamin was delivered to be cancelled with intention that the said Benjamin should become bounden to the said Hugh Surrey and Thomas Stevenson, in satisfaction of so much money due to them by the said Richard Goffe for the wines aforesaid; and thereupon on the day and year last aforesaid, and at London aforesaid, in the parish and ward aforesaid, the said Benjamin became bound to the said Hugh and Thomas in the said three writings obligatory in the said first inquisition specified, and afterwards in further prosecution of the said corrupt agreement the said Hugh Surrey and Thomas Stevenson, at London aforesaid, in the parish and ward aforesaid, the said several writs of extendi facias and the inquisitions aforesaid thereupon taken, did procure unjustly in deceit of the other creditors of the said Benjamin Hinton: although the said Hughand Thomas at the time of the issuing of the said first writ of extendi facias and of the inquisition aforesaid thereupon, and from that time hitherto had and yet have sufficinet goods and Chattles within the city of London aforesaid, to wit, in the parish and ward aforesaid, whereof the said lord the king of his debt aforesaid, they could and yet can satisfy, and which by the sheriffs of London aforesaid, by virtue of the said first writ of extendi facias into the hands of the said lord the king, could have been seized and taken; and the said John Butcher further saith, that as well the said debt of six hundred and fifty pounds by him the said John to the said Benjamin as aforesaid due, as the other debts goods and chattles of the said Benjamin, afterwards to wit on the 24th day of October, in the 35th year of the reign of the said lord the now king aforesaid, at London aforesaid, in the parish and ward aforesaid, by certain commissions by virtue of a certain commission of the lord the king in that behalf, lately issued out of the court of Chancery of the said lord the king at Westminster, according to the form of the statute made and provided

* P. 580.

 against

against bankrupts, made at the humble petition of divers creditors of the said Benjamin, by the Lord Keeper of the great seal of England, by their certain indenture were granted and assigned to one Jonas Sish and John Hill, for and towards the satisfaction of the creditors of the said Benjamin, for the debts due by the said Benjamin, and this he is ready to verify, wherefore he prays judgment if the said lord the now king, against him ought to have execution of the said six hundred and fifty pounds into his hands by pretence of the inquisition aforesaid, seized as aforesaid, by fraud and covin, &c. &c.

*Robert Gilmore.*

Demurrer. And Robert Sawyer, knight, attorney general of the said lord the now king, who for the said lord the now king prosecutes, present here in court on the same day in his proper person, protesting, not acknowledging any thing in the plea of the said John Butcher by him above pleaded to be true, for the said lord the king saith that the said plea of the said John Butcher by him in the manner and form aforesaid pleaded, is not sufficient in law to preclude the said lord the now
* P. 581. king * from having his execution against the said John Butcher, for the said six hundred and fifty pounds in the said writ of scire facias mentioned, and for causes of demurrer in law, the said attorney general shows to the court here, the causes following, to wit, that the said plea of the said John Butcher is double; uncertain; and wants form, and upon which no certain issue can be joined, and this the said attorney general for the said lord the now king is ready to verify, wherefore for the insufficiency of the said plea and the matter in the same contained the said attorney general of the said lord the now kng, for the said lord the king, prays judgment, and that the said lord the now king may have his execution against the said John Butcher for the said six hundred and fifty pounds in the said writ of scire facias specified, &c.

Joinder. And the said John Butcher, because that he, sufficient matter in law to preclude the said lord the king from having his execution against the said John Butcher for the said 650l. in the said writ of scire facias mentioned, above by pleading hath alledged which he is ready to verify, and which matter the said attorney general for the said lord the king, doth not deny, nor to the same in any wise doth answer but altogether doth refuse to admit the said averment as before prays judgment: therefore, &c.

The

# The King against Woodhouse.

## Hilary, 34th and 35th Charles 2d.

LONDON, to wit—Be it remembered that the writ of lord the now king, under the seal of this Exchequer, by the consideration of the barons here issued in these words, to wit, Charles the 2d, &c. to the sheriffs of London, greeting, whereas Anthony viscount Faulkland, in the kingdom of Scotland, treasurer of our royal fleet and of our navy, and receiver general of all our monies assigned or to be assigned and payable for the support, maintenance and repairing of our royal fleet and of our navy, for the buying provisions appertaining to and necessary for the said fleet and navy, or for the wages and salaries of the officers, ministers, and all others whatsoever belonging to the fleet aforesaid, or navy aforesaid, or for any other thing or matter whatsoever, our royal fleet or our navy in any wise touching and concerning, to us now is indebted in divers sums of money amounting in the whole to the sum of three thousand pounds and upwards, by reason of his office aforesaid, as by record of our Exchequer at Westminster more fully appeareth, and whereas by a certain inquisition indented, taken at the Guildhall of the city of London, situate in the parish of St. Laurence, in the Old Jewry, in the Ward of Cheap of the said city, on the 23d day of December, last past, before you Dudley North, esquire, and Peter Rich, esquire, now sheriffs of the city of London, by virtue of our writ of extent under the seal of our Exchequer, against Anthony viscount Faulkland, to you lately directed by the oath of J. P. and others good and lawful men of the city aforesaid, it is found * that one John Bolithoe and John Wilson late of London, goldsmiths, on the said day of the taking of the inquisition aforesaid, were indebted to the said Anthony viscount Faulkland, in divers sums of money amounting in the whole to four hundred and thirteen pounds of the good and lawful money of England, for so much sums of money of the said Anthony, viscount Faulkland for the use of the said Anthony, by the said John Bolithoe and John Wilson, before that time had and received, which several sums of money amounting in the whole as aforesaid, to four hundred and thirteen pounds, remaining unpaid and not satisfied, by the said J. B. and J. W. you the said sheriffs on the said day of the taking of the inquisition aforesaid, have caused to be taken and seized into our hands, and whereas

Scire facias to the debtor of a debtor of the king's treasurer of the fleet, &c. to show cause why the king should not have execution for the said debt.

* P. 582.

whereas by a certain other inquisition indented, taken at the Guildhall of the city of London, situate in the parish of St. Lawrence in the Old Jewry, in the ward of Cheap of the said city, on the 3d day of the present month of January, before you Dudley North, esquire, and Peter Rich, esquire, now sheriffs of the city of London, aforesaid, by virtue of our writ of extent under the seal of our Exchequer, against the said J. B. and J. W. to you lately directed, by the oath of D. M. and others good and lawful men of the city aforesaid, it is found among other things that one Jonathan Woodhouse, of London, merchant, on the said day of the taking of the inquisition last mentioned was indebted to the said J. B. and J. W. in the sum of one thousand six hundred pounds of the lawful money of England, for the like sum of money, by the said J. B. and J. W. to the said Jonathan Woodhouse, before that time lent and advanced, which debt and also the money thereupon due you the said sheriffs on the said day of the taking of the inquisition aforesaid, by virtue of the said writ of extent, have caused to be taken and seized into our hands as by the several writs aforesaid, and the returns of the same and the said several inquisitions to them annexed into our Exchequer certified, and there in the custody of our remembrancer remaining more fully appeareth: and we being willing to be satisfied of the said one thousand six hundred pounds to us now due, with all the speed with which we can as is just, command you that you do not omit because of any liberty but that you enter the same, and by good and lawful men of your bailiwick, that you give notice to the said Jonathan Woodhouse, that he be before the barons of our Exchequer at Westminster, on the first day of February next ensuing, to show and propound if he hath or knoweth any thing to say for himself, wherefore we ought not to have execution against him for the said one thousand six hundred pounds, and have there then the names of those by whom you shall give notice to him and this writ, witness W. Montague at Westminster, the 23d day of January in the 34th year of our reign. By the writs and inquisitions and by the barons.

*Ayloffe.*

Scire facias returned. At which day Dudley, North, esquire, and Peter Rich, esquire, sheriffs of the city of London aforesaid, return here the writ aforesaid thus indorsed to wit, by virtue of this writ to us directed by Charles Hargrave, and John Doe, good and lawful men of our bailiwick, we have given notice to the within named Jonathan Woodhouse, that he be before
* P. 583. the barons of the * exchequer, of the lord the king at the day

day and place within contained, to show, &c. as within we are commanded, the answer of Dudley North, esquire, and Peter Rich, esquire,——as is there contained.

And now, to wit, on the said 1st day of February comes here the said Jonathan Woodhouse, in the writ of scire facias aforesaid, and the return of the same mentioned by B. B. his attorney, and prays oyer of the writ of scire facias aforesaid, and the return of the same, and they are read to him, which being read, heard, and by him understood, he complains that he under colour of the premisses is grievously vexed and disquieted and this unjustly, because protesting that the said writ of scire facias aforesaid, and the matter in the same contained, are not sufficient in law to which he hath no necessity, neither is he bound by the law of the land to answer for plea, nevertheless, the said J. W. saith, that the said lord the now king ought not to have execution against him, for the said one thousand six hundred pounds because as to one thousand three hundred fifty and three pounds and nine shillings, of the said one thousand six hundred pounds in the writ of scire facias aforesaid mentioned, and by the inquisition aforesaid, in the writ of scire facias aforesaid last mentioned supposed to be due to the said J. B. and J. W. by the said Jonathan Woodhouse, the said Jonathan saith, that he the said Jonathan on the day of the taking of the said inquisition, or at any time afterwards was not indebted to the said J. B. and J. W. in the said 1353l. 9s. nor in one penny thereof, as by the said inquisition is above supposed and this he is ready to verify, wherefore he prays judgment if the said lord the now king ought to have execution against him, for the said one thousand three hundred fifty and three pounds and nine shillings, &c. And as to two hundred and forty six pounds and eleven shillings, the residue of the said one thousand six hundred pounds in the said writ of scire facias aforesaid mentioned, supposed to be due to the said J. B. and J. W. the said Jonathan saith that the said writ of scire facias and the matter in the same contained, are not sufficient in law for the said lord the king to have or maintain execution for the said 246l. 11s. against him the said Jonathan and that he to the said writ in the manner and form aforesaid obtained, hath no necessity neither is he bound by the law of the land in any manner to answer, and this he is ready to verify, wherefore for want of a sufficient writ of scire facias in this behalf the said Jonathan prays judgment of the said writ of scire facias aforesaid, that the said writ may be quashed &c.

Plea That as to part of the sum found by the inquisition he was not indebted, prout. &c.

And as to the residue demurs.

Demurrer.

And Robert Sawyer knight, attorney general of the said lord the now king, who for the said lord the king prosecutes, present here in court on the same day in his proper person, protesting

proteſting, not acknowledging any thing in the plea of the ſaid Jonathan Woodhouſe, by him in the manner and form aforeſaid, above pleaded to be true, nevertheleſs for replication the ſaid attorney general of the ſaid lord the now king, for the ſaid lord the king ſaith, that the plea of the ſaid Jonathan Woodhouſe in the manner and form aforeſaid above pleaded, and the matter in the ſame contained are not ſufficient in law to preclude the
* P. 584. ſaid lord the king from having execution * againſt the ſaid Jonathan, for the ſaid one thouſand ſix hundred pounds in the ſaid writ of ſcire facias ſpecified or of any part thereof; wherefore for the inſufficiency of the ſaid plea and of the matter in the ſame contained, the ſaid attorney general of the ſaid lord the now king, for the ſaid lord the king prays
Cauſes of demurrer. judgment, and that the ſaid lord the now king may have his execution againſt the ſaid Jonathan for the ſaid one one thouſand ſix hundred pounds in the ſaid writ of ſcire facias ſpecified, and for cauſe of demurrer in law upon the ſaid plea the ſaid attorney general of the ſaid lord the now king, for the ſaid lord the king, ſets down and to the court here ſhows the cauſes following, to wit, that the ſaid plea is double and incertain and wants form and that upon the ſaid plea no certain iſſue can be joined; and that part of the ſaid plea admits the ſaid writ of ſcire facias and is in bar of the execution of the ſaid lord the king, thereupon to be had for part of the ſaid ſum of one thouſand
Joinder in demurrer. ſix hundred pounds, and another part of the ſaid plea is in abatement of the ſaid writ of ſcire facias.

And the ſaid Jonathan ſaith, that the ſaid plea of the ſaid Jonathan in the manner and form aforeſaid pleaded, is ſufficient in law to preclude the ſaid lord the king from having his execution againſt him for the ſaid one thouſand ſix hundred pounds in the ſaid writ of ſcire facias ſpecified, which he is ready to verify, which matter the ſaid attorney general of the ſaid lord the king, for the ſaid lord the king doth not deny nor to the ſame in any manner doth anſwer, but, altogether doth refuſe to admit the ſaid averment, therefore as before prays judgment, and that the ſaid lord the king from having his execution aforeſaid, for the ſaid one thouſand ſix hundred pounds againſt him may be precluded, and that he the ſaid Jonathan as to the premiſſes by this court may be diſmiſſed; therefore &c.

The

## The King against Thorpe and others.

TO wit.——Be it remembered, that the writ of the lord the now king under the seal of this Exchequer by the consideration of the barons here issued in these words, to wit; Charles the 2d by the Grace of God of England, Scotland, France and Ireland, king defender of the faith, &c. to the sheriffs of London and Middlesex greeting, whereas Philip Thorpe of James Deeping, in the county of Lincoln, gentleman, William Collins of Peterborough in the county of Northampton, gentleman, John Blythe of Stamford in the county of Lincoln, gentleman, Henry Thriste of Bottlebridge in the county of Huntingdon, gentleman, John Seale of the parish of St. Bartholomew, London, upholsterer, Adam Buddle of the parish of St. Dunstan in the east, London, gentleman, Godfrey Norris of the Parish of St. Sepulchre, London, gentleman, and John Bressey of the parish of St. Andrew Holborn, London, gentleman, by their writing obligatory sealed with their seals bearing date the 28th day of March in the year of our Lord 1657, are holden to Oliver lately called lord protector of the commonwealth of England, Scotland and Ireland, and of the dominions belonging to the same in four thousand one hundred and fifty pounds of the * lawful money of England to be paid on a certain day past, and the same to the said Oliver, or to Richard late pretended ord protector of the commonwealth of England, Scotland, and Ireland, and of the dominions and teritories belonging to the same, or to the late pretended keepers of the liberties of England, by the authority of parliament, or to us have not yet paid, nor caused to be paid, as it is said, and we willing to be satisfied of the said four thousand one hundred and fifty pounds to us now due with all the speed with which we can, as is right, command you that you do not omit because of any liberty but that you enter the same, and by good and lawful men of your bailiwick that you give notice to said John Seale, A. Buddle. G. Norris and J. Bressey, that they be before the barons of our Exchequer, at Westminster, on the 16th day of November next ensuing, to show and propound if they have or know any thing to say for themselves, wherefore we ought not to have execution against them for the said four thousand one hundred and fifty pounds, and have there then the names of those by whom you shall give notice to them and this writ, witness, Mathew Hale, at Westminster, the 3d day of July, in the 13th year of our reign. By the writing obligatory aforesaid and by the barons.

Scire facias against several obligees upon bond given to Oliver, lat-ly called lord protector.

* P. 585.

*Fanshawe.*

 The

The sheriffs of London return as to two, scire facias.

Nichil as to the other two.

Nichil as to two of the defendants returned by the same persons as sheriff of Middlesex.

The obligors appear and pray oyer of the writ of scire facias, and of the return.

And oyer of the bond.

At which day Samuel Starling and Francis Meynell, sheriffs of London, aforesaid, returned the said writ thus indorsed, to wit, "by virtue of this writ to us directed by J. S. and J.C. good and lawful men of our bailiwick, we have given notice to the within named J. Seale and J. Bressey, that they be before the barons within written on the day and place within contained to show and propound as the said writ in itself commands and requires: the within named Adam and Godfrey, have nothing, nor hath either of them any thing in our bailiwick where or whereby, we could give notice to them or either of them, nor are they found nor is either of them found in the same, Samuel Starling and Francis Meynell, sheriffs of the city of London; the within named John and Adam have nothing nor hath either of them any thing in my bailiwick, whereby I could give notice to the them or either of them, nor are they found nor is either of them found in the same, Samuel Starling and Francis Meynell sheriff of Middlesex. As in the said writ and return of the same is more fully contained, which are in the file, of the writs executed in London and Middlesex for the said lord the now king of this term, on the behalf of his remembrancer. And now, to wit, on the 16th day of November in this term come here the said Philip Thorpe, &c. in the said writ named, by Charles Keepe, their attorney, and pray oyer of the said writ of scire facias and the return of the same and it is read to them, also they pray oyer of the said writing obligatory whereof in the said writ mention is made, and in like manner it is read to them in these words, to wit, "be it known unto all men by these presents that we Philip Thorpe, of &c. do stand and hold ourselves firmly bound and indebted unto his highness Oliver, lord protector of the commonwealth of England, Scotland and Ireland, and the dominions and territories thereunto belonging in the sum of 4150l. of good and lawful money of England, to be paid to the said lord protector and his successors, to which payment well and truly to be made and done, we bind ourselves and every of us, jointly and severally, in the whole and for the whole, and every one of our executors and administrators, and every of them, firmly by these presents, * sealed with our seals dated the 28th day of March, in the year of our Lord, 1657. The condition of the above obligation is such that if the above-bound Philip Thorpe, John Collins, William Blyth and Henry Thrift or any of them, their or any of their executors administrators or assigns, every or any of them, shall and do according to certain articles of agreement indented, of the date abovesaid, made between John Ireton and Thomas Alleyn, aldermen of the city of London,

* P. 536.

Richard

Richard Bury, William Puckle, and Nathaniel Manton, esquires, commissioners and governors of the excise and new imposts, for and on the behalf of his highness the lord protector of the commonwealth of E. S. and I. and the dominions thereunto belonging, and his successors of the one part, and the said Philip Thorpe, William Collins, John Blyth and Henry Thrift of the other part, well and truly satisfy, content and pay, or cause to be well and truly satisfied, contented and paid unto the said commissioners and governors of the excise and new impost, their survivors, successors or assigns, at the grand office of excise and new impost, situate and kept within the city of London aforesaid, the full sum of 2075l. of good and lawful money of England, being in full payment of the sum or farm-rent of 8300l. in the said articles of agreement mentioned, upon the 25th day of March which shall be in the year of our Lord, 1658, being one of the proportions and times in the said articles of agreement mentioned, for payment of the said 8300l. without fraud, covin or delay, that then this obligation to be void and of none effect, or else to remain in full force, power, strength and virtue." Which being read and heard, and by them fully understood, they complain that they under colour of the premisses are grievously vexed and disquieted, and this unjustly, because protesting that the writ of scire facias aforesaid, and the return of the same, and the matter in the same contained, are not sufficient in law, to which they have no necessity, neither are they bound by the law of the land to answer for plea, nevertheless they the said Philip Thorpe, &c. say, that by a certain act, made in the parliament held at Westminster, in the county of Middlesex, on the 25th day of April, in the 12th year of the reign of the lord Charles the 2d, the now king of England, &c. it was enacted by the said lord the now king, with the advice and consent of the said lords and commons in the said parliament assembled, among other things in the form following, to wit. That all and every the subjects of these his majesty's realms of England and Ireland, the dominion of Wales, the isles of Jersey, Guernsey and the town of Berwick upon the Tweed, and other his majesty's dominions, the heirs, executors and administrators of them, and every of them, and all and singular bodies in any manner of wise corporated, cities, boroughs, shires, ridings, hundreds, laths, rapes, wapentakes, towns, villages, hamlets and tythings, and every of them, and the successor and successors of every of them should be and were by the authority of the said parliament, acquited, pardoned, released, indemnified and discharged against the king's royal majesty, his heirs and successors, and every of them, of and from all manner of treasons,

They then plead the act of indemnity and oblivion, the 12th Charles 2d. c. ii.

treasons, misprisons of treasons, felonies, trespasses, offences, contempts, entries, injuries, * deceits, misdemeanours, forfeitures, penalties and sums of money, intrusions, mesne profits, wardships, marriages, reliefs, liveries, ousterlemains, mesne rates, respites of homage, fines and seizures for alienation, without licence, arrearages of rents (other than arrearages of rents due from the late farmers, or pretended farmers of the excise or customs respectively, and other than such arrearages of rents or mesne profits as were or should be otherwise disposed by any act or by any acts of the parliament aforesaid,) and of and from all arrearages of tenths and first fruits, fines, post fines, issues and amerciaments, and all recognizances, obligations, or other securities, given for the payment of them or any of them, concealment of customs and excise, arrearages of purveyance, and compositions for the same and of and from all pains of death, pains corporal and pecuniary, and of and from all others things, causes, quarrels, suits, judgments and executions in the said act afterwards not excepted, nor foreprized, which by his majesty in any wise or by any means could be pardoned, before and unto the 24th day of June, in the year of our Lord, 1660, to every or any of the said subjects of the said lord the king, bodies corporate, cities, boroughs, shires, ridings, hundreds, laths, rapes, wapentakes, towns, villages and tythings, or to any of them, as by the said act among other things in the same contained more fully appears. And the said Philip Thorpe, W. C. &c. further say, that by a certain other act made in this present parliament, begun and held at Westminster, aforesaid, in the said county of Middlesex, on the 8th day of May, in the year of our Lord, 1661, and in the 13th year of the reign of the said lord Charles the 2d, the now king, &c. and there continued until Tuesday the 30th day of July, in the year of our Lord, 1661, and from that time adjourned until the 20th day of November, then next ensuing, it is enacted by the said lord the now king, by and with the advice and consent of the lords and commons in the said parliament assembled and by the authority of the same, among other things; that all and singular the acts made or mentioned to be made by the said lord the king, by and with the advice or consent of the lords and commons, upon and after the 25th day of April in the said act particularly mentioned and expressed, to wit, among others one act entitled, "an act of free and general pardon, indemnity and oblivion;" and all singular the clauses, sentences and articles in them and every of them contained were and by the said last mentioned act of parliament are ratified and confirmed and enacted and declared to have the force and effect

* P. 587.

The act for confirming publick acts: the 13th Char. 2d. c. 7.

effect of an act of parliament, according to the tenor and purpose of the same, and so were adjudged, deemed and taken to all intents and purposes whatsoever, as if the same had been made, declared and enacted by the authority of that present parliament, as by the said last mentioned act of parliament more fully appeareth; and the said Philip Thorpe, W. C. &c. further say, that they the said P. T. &c. are not the persons, nor is any of them a person in any manner excepted or foreprized by the said first mentioned act of parliament, and that neither the said writing obligatory in the said writ of scire facias mentioned, is an obligation * excepted or foreprized in the said act, nor is the said sum of 4150l. in the said writing obligatory, and in the said writ of scire facias expressed, a sum or debt excepted or foreprized in the said act, and that they the said Philip Thorpe, W. C. &c. are and at the time of the beginning of the said first mentioned parliament, and of the enacting of the said first mentioned act of parliament were subjects, and every of them was a subject of his majesty, of his kingdom of England, born under the obedience of the said lord the now king, to wit, at Westminster aforesaid, in the county of Middlesex aforesaid, all and singular which things they the said Philip Thorpe, W. C. &c. are ready to verify as the court, &c. wherefore they pray judgment, and that they of the said 4150l. in the said writing obligatory specified, may be entirely discharged, and that every of them may be discharged, and that the said writing obligatory may be cancelled, and made void, and may be delivered to them, and thereupon that they the said P. &c. as to the said premisses by the court here may be dismissed, and that every of them may be dismissed. And because the court will advise of the plea aforesaid, before further, &c. day is given here to the said Philip Thorpe, &c. in the same state in which now until the octave of St. Hilary, on which day the said Philip Thorpe, &c. come here as before, and for the cause aforesaid, have day further until from the day of Easter in fifteen days, on which day the said Philip Thorpe, &c. and for the cause aforesaid, have day further until the morrow of the Holy Trinity, on which day the said Philip Thorpe, &c. come here as before, and for the cause aforesaid, have day further until from the day of St. Michael in three weeks, on which day the said Philip Thorpe, &c. come here as before, and for the cause aforesaid have day further, until the octave of St. Hilary, on which day the said Philip Thorpe, &c. come here as before and for the cause aforesaid, have day further until from the day of Easter in fifteen days: on which day they the said Philip Thorpe, &c. come here as before, and

That the obligors nor the bond, nor the money therein mentioned are excepted in the said act of oblivion.

* P. 588.

And that the obligation may be cancelled.

Continuances.

Geoffry

Geoffry Palmer, knight and baronet, attorney general of the faid lord the now king, who for the fame lord the king profecutes prefent here in court on the faid day in his proper perfon, for plea or replication for the faid lord the king, faith, that the faid lord the now king from having his execution againft the faid Philip, &c. for the faid 4150l. or for any part thereof, becaufe of any thing in the plea of the faid Philip, &c. mentioned, ought not to be precluded, becaufe he faith that well and true it is that by the faid act made in the parliament held at Weftminfter aforefaid, in the faid county of Middlefex, on the 25th day of April in the 12th year of the reign of the faid lord Charles the 2d the now king, it was enacted by the faid lord the now king, with the advice and confent of the lords and commons in the faid parliament affembled, as the faid Philip, &c. above have alledged, but the faid attorney general of the faid lord the now king, for the faid lord the now king, further faith, that by the faid act among other things, the arrearages of rent due from the late farmers or pretended farmers, of excife, are excepted out of the faid free and general pardon, as by the faid act among other things in the fame contained more fully appeareth: And that by the faid articles of agreement in the faid condition of the faid writing obligatory above mentioned, made at Weftminfter aforefaid, in the faid county of Middlefex, on the 28th day of March in the year of our Lord, 1657, between the faid John * Ireton, Thomas Alleyn R. B. W. P. and N. M. then commiffioners and governors of the excife and new impofts aforefaid, by the names of John Ireton, T. A. &c. commiffioners and governors of the excife and new impofts, for and on behalf of his highnefs the lord protector of the commonwealth of E. S. and J. and of the dominions thereunto belonging, and his fucceffors of the one part; and the faid Philip Thorpe, &c. by the names of Philip Thorpe, of James Deeping, in the county of Lincoln, gentleman, W. C. of &c. of the other part, one part of which articles of agreement fealed with the feals of the faid P. T. &c. bearing date the faid day and year, the faid attorney general of the faid lord the king, brings here into court, it was covenanted concluded and agreed by and between the parties aforefaid to the articles of agreement, aforefaid and the faid commiffioners and governors of the excife and new impofts, according to and in purfuance of the order, confent and approbation of the commiffioners of appeal fignified by their order, made the 23d day of the then prefent month of March, in purfuance of the order and declaration of his highnefs the then lord protector and of his council, entitled the order and declaration of his highnefs the lord protector with the advice and confent of

Replication by the attorney general, that well and true it is that by the faid act it was enacted as the defendants have alledged.

But that the arrears of rent due by the late farmers of excife are excepted.

* P. 589.

The articles of agreement whereby the excife of beer, ale, &c. in the county of Lincoln, &c. was let to farm to four of the obligors.

of his council, touching the continuance of the duty of the excise and new imposts, bearing date the 28th day of February, 1654, (and the said then commissioners of excise were enabled by any act ordinance, order or declaration as well of his highness and council as of the parliament to convey set over and invest the power and authorities to them granted, or let to farm the excise of all or any of the commodities chargeable with the same to any sub-commissioner, farmers, or other persons whatsoever) and not otherwise, had, covenanted, promised and agreed to and with the said William Collins, Philip Thorpe, Henry Thrift, and John Blythe, their executors and administrators by the said articles of agreement, that the said W. C. P. T. H. T. and J. B. their executors and administrators for and in consideration of the sum of eight thousand three hundred pounds of the lawful money of England, to be paid as afterwards expressed in the said articles of agreement, should have and hold in farm, and should take, receive, recover and enjoy to their proper use for ever, all and all manner of rates, charges and duties of excise, which had accrued due or payable for and upon all beer, ale, hops and soap, which had been made, grown, consumed and spent within the city in the county of the city of Lincoln, together with the bailiwick and close of Lincoln, and the county of Lincoln, together with the city of Ely, and the town of Wisbeech, and the whole isle of Ely in the county of Cambridge, and in all the towns corporate, vills, hamlets, parishes, parts and places whatsoever, as well within liberties as without, within the limits, parts, and places aforesaid, to have, levy, receive, recover, collect, and perceive all, every, or any of them from and after the the 25th day of the then present month of March, exclusive, until the 25th day of March inclusive, which would be in the year of our Lord, 1658, as before was directed and appointed in and by any of the said acts, ordinances orders and declarations as well of his highness and council as of the parliament, * which had been in force and being on the 2d day of September, 1654, or afterwards had been or at any time afterwards might be directed, appointed and established by his highness and his council, or by the parliament, for the better collection and receipt of the several rates, charges and duties of excise; as fully and largely as the said commissioners, sub commissioners or their deputies by any act, ordinance law or declaration had been enabled to do or cause to be done, by themselves, the sub-commissioners or their deputies; in consideration whereof the said W. Collins, P. T. H. T. and J. B. for themselves, their executors and administrators had covenanted, promised and granted to and with the said commissioners

* P. 590.

missioners and governors of excise and new imposts, their survivors and successors, by the said articles of agreement in the manner following: To wit, that they the said W. C. P. T. H. T. and J. B. their executors, administrators, or assigns well and faithfully would satisfy, or well and faithfully would cause and to be satisfied and paid to the said commissioners or governors of excise and of the new imposts, their survivors, successors, or assigns, at or in the office of excise, situate and being in London, for the use of his highness the lord protector of the commonwealth of E. S. and J. and of the dominions belonging to the same, and his successors, the said sum or farm rent of eight thousand three hundred pounds of lawful money, on the days and places of payment afterwards mentioned; to wit, at or upon the 24th day of June next ensuing the date of the said articles of agreement, the sum of 2075l. part of the sum or farm rent of 8300l. before mentioned, at or upon the 29th day of September then next ensuing the sum of 2075l. another part thereof; at or upon the 25th day of December then next ensuing, the sum of 2075l. another part thereof; and at or upon the 25th day of March in the year of our Lord, 1658, the sum of 2075l. the remainder of and in full payment and satisfaction of the said sum or farm rent of 8300l. by the said articles of agreement covenanted, to be satisfied and paid as aforesaid, without fraud or delay as by the said articles of agreement among other things more fully appears and is manifest. By colour of which demise afterwards, to wit, on the 29th day of the said month of March, in the year of our Lord 1657, at James Deeping, aforesaid, in the said county of Lincoln they the said P. T. W. C. H. T and J. B. into the premisses aforesaid, so to them in the form aforesaid demised, entered and were thereof possessed; and the said attorney general of the said lord the now king, for the said lord the king further saith, that at the said time of the enacting of the act aforesaid, and on the day of the issuing of the said writ of scire facias, the sum of ten pounds of the lawful money of England, was due and as yet is due from the said W. C. P. T. H. T. and J. B. late farmers of the excise aforesaid, for arrearages of rent, to wit, at Westminster in the county of Middlesex; and that the said writing obligatory was delivered on the said 28th day of March, in the year of our Lord, 1657, at Westminster aforesaid, in the county of Middlesex aforesaid, by the said P. T. W. C. H. T. and J. B. for the security of the payment of the said sum of 2075l. in full payment of the said sum or farm of rent of 8300l. in the said articles of agreement mentioned: And by the said John Seale, A. B. N. G. and J. B. as the sureties of the said

That there was on the day of the enacting the said act, and on the day of the issuing the writ of scire facias 10l. of the said rent in arrear.

That by the said act are excepted all recognizances, &c. given or entered into after the 25th day of March, 1642, by any receiver, accomptant, in the Exchequer, &c.

said P. T. W. C. J. B. and H. T. for the security of the payment of the said 2075l. in * full payment of the said sum or farm rent aforesaid of 8300l. in the said articles of agreement mentioned: and the said attorney general of the said lord the now king, for the said lord the king further saith, that by the said act there are excepted out of the pardon in the said act mentioned, all recognizances, obligations and other securities given or entered into after the 25th day of March, in the year of our Lord, 1640, by any receiver, reeve, bailiff, collector or other accomptant in the court of the publick Exchequer, and their sureties and accounts respectively as by the said act among other things in the same contained more fully appeareth.——And the said attorney general of the said lord the now king, for the said lord the king further saith, and will verify that the said P. T. W. C. J. B. and H. T. are and at the same time of the making and enacting of the act aforesaid were accomptants, and each and every of them was an accomptant in the said court of Exchequer, to wit, at Westminster aforesaid, in the said county of Middlesex, and that the said John Seale, Adam Buddle, Godfrey Norris and John Bressey, are, and at the said time of the making and enacting of the said act were sureties for the said P. T. W. C. J. B. and H. T. to wit, at Westminster aforesaid, in the said county of Middlesex: And the said attorney general of the said lord the now king, for the said lord the king further saith, that after the said octave of St. Hilary, last past, from which day the process aforesaid was last continued to the said fifteen days of Easter, to wit, on the 18th day of February now last past by a certain act made in the parliament of the said lord the now king, begun and held at Westminster aforesaid, in the county of Middlesex aforesaid, on the 8th day of May, in the 13th year, &c. and there continued until the 19th day of May, in the 14th year, &c. and from that time prorogued until the 18th day of February, then next ensuing, at the 2d session of the said parliament, held by prorogation at Westminster aforesaid, in the said county of Middlesex, on the 18th day of February now last past, it is declared and enacted by the most excellent majesty of the said lord the now king, by and with the advice and consent of the lords spiritual and temporal, and the commons in the said parliament assembled, and by the authority of the same, that when any commissioner, sub-commissioner, treasurer, and all the other officers who before that time were employed in the receipt of the excise; farmer or collector of excise, then were or stood charged with or accountable for any duties of excise by him or them received, farmed or detained, or

* P. 591.

That P. T. &c. were accomptants at the time of passing the said act.

That J. S. &c. were their sureties.

That by an act of parliament made after the last continuance the sureties of all commissioners, &c employed in the excise and not pardoned by the act of oblivion, should be liable according to the nature of their securities.

13th and 14th of Charles 2d c. 16.

in any manner due by the persons above named or by any of
them, and not pardoned by the late act entitled, "*an act of
free and general pardon, indemnity and oblivion*," that then and
in such case all and singular the sureties of such person and
persons charged or chargeable as aforesaid, should be deemed
and taken to beliable and responsible according to the nature
of their respective securities, any doubt or question made, touching the construction of the said late act of free and general
pardon to the contrary thereof notwithstanding, as in the said
act is more fully contained: and the said attorney general of
the said lord the now king, for the said lord the king further
* P. 592. saith, that the said Philip Thorpe, William Collins, * J. B.
and H. T. before the enacting of the said act of parliament
last mentioned, to wit, on the said 28th day of March, in
the year of our Lord 1657, at Westminster aforesaid, in
the county of Middlesex, aforesaid, were farmers of excise,
to wit, of all and all manner of rates, charges and duties
of excise, which accrued due or payable for and upon all
beer, ale hops, and soap, which had been made, grown,
consumed and spent within the city and county of Lincoln,
together with the bailiwick and close of Lincoln, and the
whole county of Lincoln, together with the city of Ely and
the town of Wisbeech, and the whole isle of Ely, in the
county of Cambridge, and in all the towns corporate, vills,
Hamlets, parishes parts and places, whatsoever, as well
within liberties as without, within the limits, parts and places
aforesaid, and that the said writing obligatory was sealed
and delivered on the said 28th day of March, 1657, at Westminster, aforesaid, in the county of Middlesex aforesaid, by
the said P. T. W. C. J. B. and H. T. for the security of the
payment of such sum as the said P. T. W. C. J. B. and
H. T. should stand charged, for any duties of the excise
aforesaid, by them within the cities, counties and places aforesaid, farmed, and by the said J. S. A. B. G. N. and J. B.
as the sureties of the said P. T. W. C. J. B. and H. T.
for security of the payment of such sum as the said
P. T. W. C. J. B. and H. T. should stand charged for any
duties of excise aforesaid, by them within the cities, counties and places aforesaid farmed, and that the said J. S.
A. B. G. N. and J. B. on the said 29th day of March, in
the year of our Lord 1657, and at the said time of the enacting
of the act aforesaid last mentioned, at Westminster, aforesaid, in the county of Middlesex aforesaid, were sureties
for the said P. T. W. C. J. B. and H. T. for the security of
such sum as the said P. T. W. C. J. B. and H. T. should
stand charged, for any duties of the excise aforesaid, by
them within the cities, counties and places aforesaid farmed,
and that at the said time of the enacting of the act aforesaid
last

laft mentioned, at Weftminfter, aforefaid, in the county of Middlefex aforefaid, the faid P. T. W. C. J. B. and H. T. ftood charged with the fum of twenty fhillings, of the lawful money of England, for the faid duties of excife by them within the cities, counties and places aforefaid farmed, to wit, at Weftminfter, aforefaid, in the county of Middlefex aforefaid, and that the faid fum of twenty fhillings fo charged upon the faid P. T. W. C. J. B. and H. T. for the faid duties of Excife by them within the cities, counties and places aforefaid farmed, was not pardoned by the faid late act, entitled "*an act of free and general pardon, indemnity and oblivion*" all and fingular which things the faid attorney general of the faid lord the now king for the faid lord the king, is ready to verify as the court, &c. wherefore he prays judgment, and that the faid lord the now king may have execution againft the faid P. T. W. C. J. B. H. T. J. S. A. B. G. N. and J. B. for the faid 4150l. in the faid writ of fcire facias and writing obligatory mentioned.

* And the faid P. T. W. C. J. B. H. T. J. S. A. B. G. N. and J. B. rejoining, fay that the faid lord the now king, ought not to have his execution againft them the faid P. T. W. C. J. B. H. T. J. S. A. B. G. N. and J. B. or any of them, for the faid four thoufand one hundred and fifty pounds in the faid writ of fcire facias fpecified, or for any part thereof, becaufe they fay that the faid replication of the faid attorney general of the faid lord the now king, in the form aforefaid replied, and the matter in the fame contained are not fufficient in law, to which they have no neceffity neither are they bound by the law of the land to anfwer, for this, to wit, that although well and true it is, that by the faid laft mentioned act of parliament in the faid replication mentioned, it is declared and enacted by the moft excellent majefty of the faid lord the now king, by and with the advice and confent of the lords fpiritual and temporal and the commons in the faid parliament affembled, and by the authority of the fame, that when any commiffioner, fub-commiffioner, treafurer, and all other officers who then before were employed in the receipt of the excife; farmer or collector of excife, then were and ftood charged with or accountable for any duties of excife by him or them farmed, received or detained or due in any manner by the perfons above named or any of them, and not pardoned by the late act entitled "*an act of free and general pardon, indemnity and oblivion*" that then and in fuch cafe all and every the fureties of fuch perfon and perfons charged or chargeable as aforefaid fhould be deemed and taken to be liable and refponfible according to the nature of their refpective fecurities, any doubt or queftion made, touching the conftruction of the faid

* P. 593. Demurrer to the replication and fhews for caufe, that although well and true it is that it was enacted by the act of parliament laft mentioned as in the replication, yet that the bond was pardoned by the act of oblivion.

ſaid late act of free and general pardon to the contrary notwithſtanding; as by the replication aforeſaid is ſuppoſed; nevertheleſs the ſaid obligation of 4150l. by them the ſaid P. T. W. C. J. B. H. T. J. S. A. B. G. N. and J. B. for the ſaid duties of exciſe by them the ſaid P. T. W. C. J. B. and H. T. within the counties and cities aforeſaid farmed, was and is pardoned by the ſaid late act of free and general pardon, indemnity and oblivion, in the manner and form as the ſaid P. T. W. C. J. B. H. T. J. S. A. B. G. N. and J. B. above by pleading have alledged, wherefore for the inſufficiency of the replication aforeſaid, and the matter in the ſame contained, they the ſaid P. T. &c. pray judgment upon the premiſſes, and that they of the ſaid 4150l. in the ſaid writ of ſcire facias ſpecified, againſt the ſaid lord the now king, his heirs and ſucceſſors, may be diſcharged, and that each and every of them may be diſcharged, and that the ſaid obligation may be cancelled, and made void and held for nought.

Joinder in demurrer.

And the ſaid Geoffrey Palmer, knight and baronet, attorney general of the ſaid lord the now king, who for the ſaid lord the king proſecutes, preſent here in court, on the ſame day in his proper perſon for the ſaid lord the king ſaith, that he above by replying hath alledged ſufficient matter in law to have execution for the ſaid lord the king againſt the ſaid P. T. &c. for the ſaid 4150l. which he for
* P. 594. the ſaid lord the king is ready to * verify, which matter the ſaid P. T. &c. do not deny, nor the ſame in any wiſe anſwer, but altogether refuſe to admit the ſaid averment, therefore as before he prays judgment and that the ſaid lord the now king may have execution againſt the ſaid Philip Thorpe, Willam Collins, John Blythe, Henry Thrifte, John Seale, Adam Buddle, Godfrey Norris and John Breſſey for the ſaid four thouſand one hundred and fifty pounds. Therefore &c.

The

# The King against Lady Newton.

## In the 15th Year, Charles 2d.

GLOUCESTER, to wit, be it remembered that the writ of the lord the now king, under the seal of this Exchequer, by the consideration of the barons here, issued in these words, to wit: Charles the 2d, by the grace of God of England, Scotland, France and Ireland, king defender of the faith, &c. to the sheriff of Gloucester greeting, whereas George Benyon, late esquire, now knight, receiver general of our late father, Charles the first, late king of England, &c. of the revenues of his crown, in the counties of Northampton and Rutland, to our said late father was indebted in divers sums of money, by reason of his office aforesaid, as by record of our Exchequer at Westminster more fully appeared; and whereas John Newton, of Bascourt, in the county of Gloucester, esquire, and Denham Hunlocke, citizen and merchant taylor of London, by their writing obligatory, sealed with their seals, bearing date the 22d day of July, in the year of our Lord, 1638, and in the 14th year of the reign of our said late father, &c. jointly and severally became bound to the said George Benyon, in four hundred pounds of the lawful money of England, to be paid on a certain day past, which writing obligatory, together with the said sum of four hundred pounds in the same contained, the said G. B. by his good and sufficient conveyance in law, bearing date the 12th day of July in the 16th year of the reign of our said late father, &c. in and towards the payment and satisfaction of so much of his debts to our said late father did give, grant and assign: and whereas by virtue of our writ of scire facias under the seal of our Exchequer against the executor of the testament and last will of the said John Newton, deceased, and the administrators of the goods and chattles which were the said John Newton's at the time of his death, and also against the heir and tenants of the lands and tenements of the said John Newton, which were his at the time of the assignment of the writing obligatory aforesaid; to the sheriff of the county of G. aforesaid directed, Humfrey Hooke, knight, late sheriff of the county aforesaid, hath certified to us that by W. P. and T. S. good and lawful men of his bailiwick, he had given notice to Edward Briglade, esquire, tenant of the manors of Bitton and Hannam, in the county of Gloucester, with their rights, members

Writ of capias in manus. To enquire into the yearly value of the manors of Bitton and Hannam, and to seize the same into the king's hands, until that he is satisfied for a certain debt by bond, entered into to the king's receiver general, and by him assigned over to the king.

members and appurtenances, which premiffes were the within named John Newton's at the time of the affignment of the writing obligatory within mentioned, and of which the faid John Newton was feized in his demefne as of fee; as more
* P. 595. fully * may appear by the writ aforefaid, and the indorfement of the fame which are in the file of writs executed for us in Gloucefter of the term of St. Michael, in the 14th year of our reign, on behalf of our remembrancer. And becaufe the faid manors of Bitton and Hannam with their rights, members and appurtenances are not taken and feized into our hands, and we being willing to be fatisfied of the faid four hundred pounds to us now due, with all the fpeed with which we can, as is juft; command you that you do not omit becaufe of any liberty, but that you enter the fame, and as well by the oath of good and lawful men of your bailiwick, or otherwife by the oath and evidence of any good and lawful men of your faid bailiwick, by whom the truth of the matter may be the better known, as by all other ways, method, and means by which you may or can know better: that you diligently enquire of the clear yearly value of the faid manors of B[illegible]d H. with their rights, members and appurtenances, and that you caufe the fame to be taken and feized into our hands fo that we may have them until we are fully fatisfied of the debts aforefaid, according to the form of the ftatute for recovering fuch our debts thereon lately enacted and provided, and further we alfo empower you by thefe prefents, to call before you and diligently to examine of and touching the premiffes all perfons whatfoever, proper to be examined concerning the premiffes, leaft this our prefent command may remain to be executed further, and how you fhall execute this our command, certify diftinctly and plainly to the barons of our Exchequer at Weftminfter, on the octave of the Holy Trinity next enfuing, and have there then this writ; witnefs Mathew Hale, knight, at Weftminfter, the firft day of June, in the 15th year of our reign; by the writ of fcire facias aforefaid, and the return aforefaid, and by the faid act of parliament enacted in the 33d year of the reign of the late king Henry the 8th and by the barons.

*Fanfhawe.*

Return. At which day Thomas Eftcourt, efquire, fheriff of the county aforefaid, returns the writ aforefaid, thus indorfed, to wit: the execution of this writ appears in a certain in-
Inquifition. quifition to this writ annexed: and the tenor of the faid inquifition follows in thefe words, to wit, Gloucefter to wit, an inquifition indented taken at Cirencefter in the county aforefaid, on the 15th day of June, in the 15th year of the reign

reign of our Lord, Charles the 2d by the grace of God of England, Scotland, France and Ireland, king defender of the faith, &c. before me Thomas Estcourt, esquire, sheriff of the county aforesaid by virtue of the writ of the lord the king to me directed and to this inquisition annexed, by the oath of Richard Trotman, Thomas Stephens, Henry Freeman, (and nine others) good and lawful men of the county aforesaid, who upon their oath aforesaid say, that the manors of Bitton and Hannam in the county aforesaid, with all their rights, members and appurtenances are of the clear yearly value in all their issues above reprisals, of one hundred pounds, which manors with appurtenances, I the said sheriff on the day of taking of this inquisition into the hands of the lord the king have caused to be taken and seized as the said writ in itself commands and requires, in testimony whereof as well I the said sheriff as jurors aforesaid, to this inquisition severally have set our seals on the day and year and place first aforesaid, Thomas Estcourt, esquire, sheriff. As more fully is contained in the said writ and the return of the same, and in the inquisition aforesaid thereto annexed, which are in the file of writs executed * in Gloucester for the king, of the term holy Trinity in the 15th year of the reign of the lord the now king on behalf of his remembrancer. And now, to wit, from the day of St. Michæl in three weeks in this term comes here Dame Grace Newton, widow and relict of the said John Newton, lately deceased, tenant of the lands of the said manor of Bitton and Hannam with the appurtenance in the county aforesaid, by W. H. her attorney, and prays oyer of the said writ of capias in manus and the return of the same, and the inquisition aforesaid thereto annexed and they are read to her which being read, heard and by her fully understood, she complain that she under colour of the premisses is griveously vexed and disquieted, and that the said manors are taken and seized into the hands of the said lord the now king, and this unjustly, because protesting that the said writ, the return of the same, and the inquisition aforesaid, to the same annexed are not sufficient in law, to which she hath no necessity neither is she bound by the law of the land to answer, for plea nevertheless the said dame Grace Newton, saith that by a certain act made in the parliament begun and held at Westminster, in the county of Middlesex on the 25th day of April, in the 12th year of the reign of the lord Charles the 2d the now king, &c. entitled "*an act of free and general pardon, indemnity and oblivion*" it is enacted by the said lord the now king, with the advice and consent of the lords and commons in the parliament aforesaid, assembled, among other things in the form following, to wit, that all and every the subjects

* P. 596.

Plea by Grace Newton, of the act of oblivion, the 13th Char. 2.

Protestation.

subjects of those his majesty's realms of England and Ireland the dominion of Wales the isles of Jersey and Guernsey, and the town of Berwick upon the Tweed, and the other dominions of his majesty, the heirs, excutors and administrators of the said subjects, and of every of them, and all and singular bodies in any manner of wise corporated, cities, boroughs, counties, ridings, hundreds, lathes, rapes, wapentakes, towns, vills, hamlets, and tythings, and every of them, and the successor and successors, of every of them, should be and were by the authority of the said parliament acquitted, pardoned, released, indemnified and discharged against the said lord the king his heirs and successors, and every of them, of and from all manner of treasons, misprisons of treasons, felonies, offences, contempts, trespasses, entries, injuries, deceits, misdemeanours, forfeitures, penalties and sums of money, intrusions, mesne profits, wardships, marriages, reliefs, liveries, ousterlemains, mesne rates, respits of homage, fines and seizures for alienation without license, arrearages of rent, (other than the arrearages of rent due from the late farmers or pretended farmers of excise or customs respectively and other than such arrearages of rent or mesne profits as were or might be otherwise disposed of by any act or acts of the parliament aforesaid) and of and from all arrearages of tenths and first fruits, fines, post fines, issues and amerciaments and of all recognizances, obligations or other securities, given for the payment of them or any of them, concealments of customs and excise, arrearages of purveyance and composition for the same, and of and from all pains of death, pains corporal and pecuniary, and generally of and from all other things, causes, quarrels, suits, judgments and executions in the said act afterwards not excepted, which by his majesty in any wise or by any means could be pardoned before and until the 24th day of June, in the year of our Lord, 1660, to every or any of them the said lord the king's subjects, bodies corporate,
* P. 597. cities, boroughs, counties, ridings, * hundreds, lathes, rapes, wapentakes, towns, vills, hamlets and tythings or any of them; and it further pleased the king's majesty, that it should be enacted, and it was and is enacted, that the said free pardon indemnity and oblivion by the general words, clauses and sentences before recited should be decreed, adjudged, expounded, allowed and taken in all courts of the said lord the king and elsewhere most beneficially and availably for all and singular his subjects aforesaid, bodies corporate and others before recited, and every of them in the said act not excepted nor foreprized, without any ambiguity, question, or other delay whatsoever to be made, pleaded, objected or alledged

alledged by the ſaid lord the king, his heirs or ſucceſſors, or by his or their attorney general or attorney generals, or by any other perſon or perſons for the ſaid lord the king, or any of his heirs or ſucceſſors, as in the ſaid act of free and general pardon and the exceptions and proviſions of the ſame among other things is more fully contained; and the ſaid Dame Grace Newton, further ſaith, that ſhe at the time of the enacting of the act aforeſaid, and long before, was and as yet is a ſubject of the ſaid lord the now king of this his kingdom of England born under the obedience of the ſaid lord the now king, to wit, at B. in the county of Glouceſter; and the ſaid Dame Grace Newton, further ſaith, that neither the ſaid John Newton, baronet, lately deceaſed, nor the ſaid Denham Hunlocke, nor either of them, nor ſhe the ſaid Dame Grace Newton, now here pleading, nor any of them, is or are a perſon or the perſons in the ſaid act or by the ſaid act in any manner excepted or foreprized, and that neither the ſaid writing obligatory in the ſaid writ of capias in manus mentioned, nor the ſaid ſum of four hundred pounds in the ſaid writing obligatory mentioned, nor the ſum of two hundred pounds in the condition of the ſaid writing obligatory mentioned, nor any part thereof is excepted or foreprized, in or by the act aforeſaid in any manner: all and ſingular which things the ſaid dame Grace Newton is ready to verify as the court, &c. wherefore ſhe prays judgment, and that the hands of the ſaid lord the now king from the poſſeſſion of the ſaid manors of Bitton and Hannam with the appurtenances in the ſaid county of Glouceſter may be removed, and that ſhe the ſaid dame Grace Newton to her poſſeſſion thereof, together with the iſſues and profits thereof, whereof the ſaid lord the now king is not as yet anſwered may be reſtored, and that as well the ſaid T. Eſtcourt, eſquire, now ſheriff of the county aforeſaid, as all others, from that time, now, and who afterwards ſhall be ſheriffs of the ſaid county, of the iſſues and profits of the premiſſes and of every part thereof, in their accounts againſt the ſaid lord the now king, his heirs and ſucceſſors, may be diſcharged, and that each and every of them may be diſcharged and that ſhe the ſaid dame Grace Newton as to the premiſſes by the court may be diſmiſſed.

*That the defendant at the time of the making of the act was, and is the king's ſubject.*

*That neither J. Newton nor his co-obligor, nor ſhe are excepted in the act of oblivion.*

*Nor is the money or bond excepted in the ſaid act.*

*Prays an amoveas manus.*

*Replication.*

*Proteſtations.*

And Geoffrey Palmer, knight and baronet, attorney general of the ſaid lord the now king, who for the ſaid lord the now king proſecutes, preſent here in court on the ſame day in his proper perſon proteſting, not acknowledging any thing in the ſaid plea, of the ſaid dame Grace Newton, by her in the manner and form aforeſaid, pleaded to be true, proteſting alſo that the ſaid plea of the ſaid dame Grace Newton, by her in the manner and form aforeſaid, pleaded, and the mat-

ter in the same contained are not sufficient in law to remove
* P. 598. the hands of the said lord the * now king, from the possession of the said manors of Bitton and Hannam, with the appurtenances in the inquisition specified, to which he hath no necessity, neither is he bound by the law of the land to answer: for replication, nevertheless, the said attorney general of the said lord the now king, for the said lord the king, saith, that

That by the said act all issues, &c. received for the use of his majesty, &c. and not accounted for, are excepted.

in the said act of parliament in the plea of the said dame Grace Newton, mentioned, all issues, fines, and amerciaments, rents and other publick duties, being levied, received or collected by any sheriff, sub-sheriff, bailiff, minister or officer, to or for the use of the late king, or the said keepers of the liberties of England, or any other person stiling himself protector, or for his present majesty, and not accounted for and discharged, are excepted; and further by the said act of parliament it was and is further provided, that the act aforesaid should not extend to pardon any obligation taken in the name of his late majesty, before the month of May in the year of our lord, 1642, for security of the proper debt of any servant or receiver of the revenues aforesaid of his late ma-

That by the said act it was provided that it should not extend to any bond taken in the name of his majesty for the security of the proper debt of any servant or receiver general, &c.

jesty, which was not paid to any lawful or pretended authority, or by the order of such authority; and the said attorney general of the said lord the now king, further saith, that long before the time of the making of the writing obligatory aforesaid, to wit, on the 20th day of June, in the 7th year of the reign of the said Charles, late king of England, &c. the said late king by his letters patent, sealed with the great seal of England, bearing date at Westminster, in the county of Middlesex, the same day and year, brought here into court, did give and grant to the said George Benyon, now knight, by the name of George Benyon, esquire, the office of receiver general of the issues and revenues of all and singular the honours, castles, lordships, manors, tenements, rents, services and other possessions, and the other hereditaments whatsoever, of the said lord the late king, his heirs and succes-

That before the making of the said writing obligatory, Charles the 1st, by patent, created Benyon his receiver general of his revenues in Northampton and Rutland for his life.

sors, in the counties of Northampton and Rutland, and in all cities, towns and places whatsoever, as well within liberties as without, within the precincts, limits and circuit of the said counties and each of them, lately being in the care and government of the late court of augmentation of the revenues of the crown of England, and then being or afterwards in any manner happening to be assigned and appointed to the inspection and government of the court of Exchequer of the said lord the now king, and of the officers and ministers of the said Exchequer, to have, hold, enjoy, exercise and occupy the said office of receiver general of the issues and revenues of all and singular the honours, castles, lordships, manors, tenements, rents, services, possessions and

hereditaments,

hereditaments, of the ſaid late king, in the ſaid counties of Northampton and Rutland, to the ſaid George Benyon as well by himſelf as by his ſufficient deputy, or deputies, for and during the whole term of the natural life of the ſaid George Benyon: by virtue of which letters patent, the ſaid George Benyon at the time of the making of the letters patent aforeſaid, was receiver of the revenues of the ſaid late king, and as yet is receiver of the revenues of the ſaid lord the now king, according to the form of the letters patent aforeſaid. And the ſaid attorney general of the ſaid lord the now king, further ſaith, that the ſaid George Benyon being indebted to the ſaid late king in divers ſums of money, by reaſon of his office aforeſaid, as by the record of the Exchequer of the ſaid lord the late king, at Weſtminſter, more fully appeareth, and the ſaid John Newton and Denham * Hunlocke, by their writing obligatory aforeſaid, being indebted to the ſaid G. B. in the ſaid ſum of four hundred pounds, the ſaid G. B. at Weſtminſter, aforeſaid, in the county of Middleſex aforeſaid, before the month of May, 1642, the ſaid writing obligatory together with the ſaid ſum of four hundred pounds in the ſame contained, by his good and ſufficient conveyance in law, bearing date the 12th day of June in the 16th year of the reign of the ſaid late king, &c. to the ſaid late king and in this Exchequer enrolled of record did give, grant and aſſign for ſecurity of the ſaid proper debt of the ſaid George Benyon, (then being as aforeſaid receiver general of the iſſues and revenues of the ſaid late king in the counties aforeſaid, in the manner and form aforeſaid) due to the ſaid George Benyon, by the ſaid John Newton and Denham Hunlocke ſo as aforeſaid: upon which writing obligatory ſo in the form aforeſaid aſſigned, the ſaid George Benyon proſecuted the ſaid writ of capias in manus for the ſaid four hundred pounds in the ſaid writing obligatory mentioned, and to the ſaid late king in the form aforeſaid aſſigned, which proceſs ſo in the manner and form had and proſecuted, was at the inſtance of the ſaid George Benyon, *and in aid* of the ſaid George Benyon, receiver general of the iſſues and revenues aforeſaid; with this that neither the ſaid four hundred pounds by the writing obligatory aforeſaid, ſo as aforeſaid due, and in the form aforeſaid given, granted, and aſſigned, nor the ſaid 200l. in the condition of the writing obligatory aforeſaid mentioned were paid, nor was any part of them paid to any lawful or pretended authority or by the order of ſuch authority; all and ſingular which things the ſaid attorney general of the ſaid lord the now king, for the ſaid lord the now king, is ready to verify, as the court, &c. Wherefore he prays judgment, and that the ſaid manners of E. and H. with the appurtenances in the hands of the

That Benyon being indebted to the king by reaſon of his office, as appears, &c.

* P. 599.

And Newton and Hunlocke being indebted to Benyon by their bond aforeſaid, in the ſum aforeſaid, he Benyon to ſecure the ſaid debt aſſigned it over to the king, and that the ſaid Benyon proſecuted the ſaid writ of capias in manus, and that the ſaid proceſs was in aid of the ſaid Benyon.

Averment of the nonpayment of the money.

the said lord the now king, may remain, and that the said lord the king of the issues and profits of the manors of B. and H. may be answered, until &c.

Rejoinder.

That Benyon did not assign the bond to the king. &c.

Protestations.

And the said Dame Grace Newton, protesting, saith, that the said George Benyon, did not give, grant or assign the said writing obligatory together with the sum of four hundred pounds in the same contained in the said writ of capias in manus, and in the said replication of the said attorney general mentioned, to the said late lord the king for the security of the said proper debt of the said George Benyon: protesting also that the said George Benyon did not prosecute the said writ of capias in manus, for the said 400l. in the said writing obligatory mentioned: protesting also that the process so in the form aforesaid had, was not had and prosecuted at the instance of the said George Benyon, and in aid of the said George Benyon: for plea, the said dame Grace Newton saith, that the said plea by the said attorney general so in the form aforesaid, by replying, pleaded, is not sufficient in law and to which the said Grace Newton is not bound to answer, for this because that the said replication so in the form aforesaid pleaded, is a departure from the said writ of capias in manus and from the matter in the said writ contained, as also for want of sufficient matter in the said replication contained, and this the said dame Grace Newton is ready to verify, wherefore for want of a sufficient replication the said dame Grace Newton, prays judgment as before, and that the hands of the said lord the now king from the possession of the said manors of B. and H. with the appurtenances in the said county of Gloucester, may be removed, and that she the said dame Grace Newton, to his possession thereof, together with the issues and profits thereof, of which the said lord the now king is not as yet * answered may be restored, and that as well the said T. E. esquire, now sheriff of the said county as all other sheriffs from that time, and who afterwards shall be sheriffs of the said county, of the issues and profits of the premisses and of every part of them in their accounts against the said lord the now king, his heirs and successors, may be discharged, and that the said general pardon may be allowed to her the said dame Grace Newton, in the premisses, and that she the said dame Grace Newton, as to the premisses by the court here may be dismissed.

Demurrer, and cause that the replication is a departure from the writ of capias in manus.

* P. 600.

Joinder.

And the said attorney general, of the said lord the now king, because that he in the replication aforesaid, above hath alledged sufficient matter in law to hold the said manors of B. and H. with the appurtenances in the said county of Gloucester, in the hands of the said lord the king, until, &c. which he is ready to verify as the court, &c. which

matter

matter the said Dame Grace Newton doth not deny, nor to the same in any manner doth answer, but altogether doth refuse to admit that averment as before prays judgment, and that the said several manners of B. and H. with the appurtenances may remain in the hands of the said lord the now king, and that the said lord the king of the issues and profits of the said manors of B. and H. with the appurtenances may be answered until, &c. Therefore, &c.

---

## The King against Greenhill and others.

### 13th Charles the 2d.

To wit London and Middlesex } BE it remembered that the writ of the lord the now king, under the seal of this exchequer, by the consideration of the barons here issued in these words, to wit, Charles the 2d &c. to the sheriffs of London and Middlesex, greeting whereas by a certain inquisition indented taken at the Savoy, in the county of Middlesex, the 12th day of February, in the 13th year of our reign, before the most noble Thomas, earl of Berks, Lewis Kirke, knight, Francis Burghill and Thomas Newland, esquires, by virtue of our commission under the seal of our Exchequer, to them and others directed, by the oath of John Clendon and others, good and lawful men of the county aforesaid, it is found that William Greenhill of Islington, in the county of Middlesex, Richard Hutchinson of Stepney in the county of Middlesex, aforesaid, and John Pocock of the Parish of St. Martin in the county of Middlesex, aforesaid, gentleman, between the first day of November in the year of our Lord, 1652, and the — day of — in the — year, &c. being treasurers for the relief and support of the sick soldiers wounded in the service of the then pretended parliament belonging to the infirmary in the parish of St. Andrew, Holborn, in the county of Middlesex aforesaid, and to the hospital of the Savoy, in the said county of Middlesex, did collect, levy and receive the sum of three hundred and forty thousand, four hundred and twenty-two pounds from the several treasurers of excise, of customs, of prize goods and of the monthly taxes, and that there remains in the hands of the said W. G. R. H. and J. P. thereof the sum of two thousand,

Scire facias, to the treasurers for the relief of the sick soldiers wounded in the service of the late pretended parliament, to show cause why the king should not have execution for part of the money which remains in their hands, for which they have not satisfied the king, nor accounted for to him.

thousand, two hundred and seventy-four pounds, ten shillings and five pence, halfpenny * which they the said W. G. R. H. and J. P. have not as yet paid, satisfied, nor for the same have accounted nor are they discharged, but the same remains to be paid to us as by the commission and inquisition aforesaid into our Exchequer returned and there in the custody of our remembrancer remaining more fully appears, and we willing to be satisfied, of the said 2274l. 10s. 5dh. to us in the form aforesaid due, with all the speed with which we can, as is just, command you that you do not omit because of any liberty but that you enter the same, and by good and lawful men of your bailiwick that you give notice to the said W. G. R. H. and J. P. that they be before the barons of our Exchequer at Westminster, the first day of July next coming, to show and propound if they have or know any thing to say for themselves wherefore, we ought not to have execution against them for the said 2274l. 10s. 5dh. to to us so due, and in their hands remaining, and further to do and receive in the premisses what our court then there may order; and have there then the names of those by whom you shall give notice to them and this writ. Witness, Mathew Hale, at Westminster, the 21st day of June, in the 13th year of our reign. By the commission and inquisition aforesaid returned and by the barons.

* P. 601.

*Fanshawe.*

Return.

Sheriffs of Middlesex returns scire facias to two.

And nichil to the third defendant.

The two defendants summoned appear and plead the act of oblivion, the 12th Char, 2d.

And on the said first day of July William Bolton and William Peake, sheriffs of Middlesex aforesaid, return here the writ aforesaid, thus indorsed, to wit, by virtue of this writ by J. M. and J. D. good and lawful men of my bailiwick I have given notice to the within named Richard and John that they be before the barons within written on the day and place within contained, to show according to the command of the said writ, and I further certify that the said within named W. hath not any thing in my bailiwick, whereby I can give him notice, nor is he found in the same; the answer of W. B. and W. P. sheriffs: as is contained in the said writ and in the return of the same which are in the file of writs executed for the said lord the now king, in the 13th year of his reign, in Middlesex, on the behalf of his remembrancer, and now to wit, on the said first day of July in the same term, come here the said R. H. and J. P. in the said writ of scire facias and in the return of the same named; by T. H. their attorney and pray oyer of the said writ of scire facias and the return of the same and they are read to them, which being read, heard and by them understood, they complain that they under colour of the premisses

fes are grieveoufly vexed and difquieted and this not juftly, becaufe protefting that the writ aforefaid, and the return of the fame, and the matter in the fame contained are not fufficient in law, to which they have no neceffity neither are they bound by the law of the land to anfwer, for plea neverthelefs the faid R. and J. fay that the faid lord the now king ought not to have further execution againft them for the faid 2274l. 10s. 5dh. in the faid writ mentioned, becaufe they fay that by a certain act made in the parliament begun and held at Weftminfter, in the county of Middlefex, the 25th day of April, in the 12th year of the reign of Charles the 2d the now king, &c. entitled "*an act of free and general pardon, indemnity and oblivion*" it is enacted by the faid lord the king, with the advice and confent of the lords and commons in the faid parliament affembled, * among other things in the form following, to wit, "That all and every the fubjects of thefe his majefty's realms of England and Ireland, the dominion of Wales, the ifles of Jerfey and Guernfey, the town of Berwick upon the Tweed, and other his majefty's dominions, the heirs, executors and adminiftrators of the faid fubjects, and of every of them, and all and fingular bodies in any manner of wife corporated, cities, boroughs, counties, ridings, hundreds, lathes, rapes, wapentakes, towns, villages, hamlets and tythings, and every of them, and the fucceffor and fucceffors of every of them fhould be and were by the authority of the faid parliament acquitted, pardoned, releafed, indemnified and difcharged, againft the king's majefty, his heirs and fucceffors and every of them, of and from all manner of treafons, mifprifons of treafon, felonies, offences, contempts, trefpaffes, entries, injuries, deceits, mifdemeanours, forfeitures, penalties and fums of money, intrufions, mefne profits, wardfhips, marriages, reliefs, liveries, oufterlemains, mefne rates, refpits of Homage, fines and feizures for alienation without licence, arrearages of rent, (other than the arrearages of rent due from the late farmers or pretended farmers of the excife or cuftoms refpectively, and other than fuch arrearages of rent or mefne profits as were or fhould be otherwife difpofed of by any act or any acts of the parliament aforefaid) and of and from all arrearages of tenths and firft fruits, fines, poft fines, iffues, and amerciaments, and all recognizances, obligations or other fecurities, given for the payment of them or any of them, concealments of cuftoms and excife, arrearages of purveyance and compofition for the fame, and of and from all pains of death, pains corporal and pecuniary, and generally of and from all other things, caufes, quarrels, fuits, judgments and executions in the faid act afterwards not excepted nor forceprized

Proteftation.

* P. 602.

prized which by his majesty in any wise or by any means could be pardoned, before and unto the 24th day of June in the year of our Lord, 1660, to every or any of the said lord the kings subjects, bodies corporate, cities, boroughs, counties, ridings, hundreds, lathes, rapes, wapentakes, towns, villages and tythings, or to any of them as by the said act among other things in the same contained more fully appeareth; and the said R. H. and J. P. further say, that by a certain other act made in the parliament begun and held at Westminster aforesaid, in the said county of Middlesex, on the 8th day of May in the 13th year of the reign of the lord Charles the now king of England, &c. entitled "*an act for confirming publick acts*" it is enacted by the most excellent majesty of the said lord the now king, by and with the advice and consent of the lords and commons in the said parliament assembled, and by the authority of the same, that all and singular the acts made or mentioned to be made by his said majesty by and with the advice or consent of the lords and commons upon or after the said twenty-fifth day of April in the 12th year of the reign of the said lord the now king, in the said act last mentioned and expressed, to wit, among others, one act entitled "*an act of free and general pardon indemnity and oblivion*" and all and singular the the clauses sentences and articles in the same and every of them contained, should, be and were by the said act last mentioned, ratified and confirmed, and enacted and declared to have the force and * strength of an act of parliament, according to the tenor and purport of the same, and so should be adjudged, deemed and taken to all intents and purposes whatsoever, as if the same had been made, declared and enacted by the authority of the said parliament last mentioned, as by the said act last mentioned among other things in the same contained more fully appears: and the said R. H. and J. P. further say, that neither he the said R. H. nor he the said J. P. nor the said W. G. is or are, nor at the time of the making of the act aforesaid first mentioned, was or were attainted or convicted of any offence or offences in the said act first mentioned excepted, and that the said accompt in the said writ named, is not the accompt of any person or of any persons appointed by any authorities or by any pretended authorities whatsoever, to be treasurer, receiver, farmer or collector, who have received or collected, any subsidies, customs, subsidies of tunnage or poundage, prize goods, assessments, sequestrations, new imposts, or excise, any rents or revenues of any lands or hereditaments of or belonging to the late lord the king, queen or prince, or to the lord the now king, or belonging to the late archbishopricks, bishopricks,

They also plead the act for confirming publick acts the 13th Charles 2d.

* P. 603.

That neither the nor any of them are or is, were or was attainted of any offence, &c. excepted in the said first mentioned act.

That the accompt in the said writ mentioned, is not the accompt of any Treasurer, &c.

ſhopricks, deans, or deans and chapters, canons, prebends, and the other officers belonging to any cathedral or collegiate church, or popiſh recuſants convict, or to any perſons ſequeſtered for their recuſancy, or other ſequeſtered eſtates, received or collected by them or paid to them after the 30th day of January, 1642, or of any monies or other duties grown due or contracted, upon the ſale or diſpoſition of them or any of them; and that the ſaid ſum of 2274l. 10s. 5dh. is not nor is any part thereof, the iſſues fines or amerciaments, rents, or other publick duties levied received or collected by any ſheriff or ſub-ſheriff, bailiff, miniſter or other officer to or for the uſe of the ſaid late king, the parliament or the keepers of the liberties of England or of any other perſon ſtiling himſelf protector, or for his majeſty that now is, and not accounted for and diſcharged; and that the ſaid ſum of 2274l. 10s. 5dh. is not, nor is any part thereof, iſſues returned upon any proceſs concerning any high ways or bridges, after the 30th day of January, 1741: and that neither the ſaid R. H. nor the ſaid J. P. nor the ſaid W. G. are, nor ever were the perſons, nor any of them is or was a perſon who have or hath had a hand in pleading, contriving or deſigning the great and henious rebellion mentioned in a certain act made in the parliament begun at Weſtminſter aforeſaid, the 3d day of November in the 16th year of the reign of the ſaid late king Charles, entitled "*an act for the ſpeedy and effectual reducing of the rebels in his majeſty's kingdom of Ireland to their due obedience to his majeſty and the crown of England*" nor in aiding aſſiſting or abetting the ſame; and that the ſaid ſum of 2274l. 10s. 5dh. is not nor is any part * thereof, any ſum or ſums of money received for the ſervice or ſupply the now king, after the year of 1648; and that the ſaid ſums of 2274l. 10s. 5dh. is not, nor is any part thereof anyſum or ſums of money received for that illegal tax of decimation, or upon the account of any militia, ſettled or acted in ſince the year, 1648; and that neither the ſaid R. H. nor the ſaid J. P. nor the ſaid W. G. are nor were perſons nor any of them is nor was a perſon who being his majeſtys menial ſervant or ſervants, or who having or pretending to have received particular inſtructions or directions from his majeſty, the lord the now king, during the time of ſuch, his or their relation to his majeſty, or while he or they were acting or pretending to act for the intereſts of his majeſty in purſuance of the ſaid inſtructions or directions, wilfully, maliciouſly and traiterouſly held intelligence with any foreign prince or princes, ſtate or ſtates, or with any perſon or perſons uſurping the ſupreme authority in this

And in like manner they anſwer all the exceptions of the ſaid act of oblivion, as follows.

* P. 604.

this kingdom, or in any other his majesty's dominions, or with their or either of their ministers or agents, and without his majesty's licence, and to the intent to betray his majesty's person or councils, or who have received any sum or sums of money or any pension for any such treachery; and that the said sum of 2274l. 10s. 3dh. is not nor is any part thereof a debt or debts, a sum or sums of money due to or for the excise of any goods or merchandizes, of which any entries were made in the custom house which accrued due after the 25th day of March, in the year of our Lord, 1658; or a debt, sum of money due by farmers or pretended farmers of excise, after the 25th day of March, in the year of our Lord 1657, and that neither the said R. H. nor the said J. P. nor the said W. G. are nor were, nor any of them is, nor was, these two persons or either of them who being disguised by frocks and vizors appeared upon the scaffold erected before Whitehall, the 30th day of January, in the year of our Lord, 1648.—And that neither the said R. H. nor the said J. P. nor the said W. G. are, nor ever were, nor any of them is, nor ever was any of the persons who were appointed trustees in a late pretended act or ordinance made in the year of our Lord, 1649, for or concerning tythes appropriate, oblations, obventions, pensions, portions of tythes appropriate, offerings, fee farms, rents issuing out of the tythes, in the said pretended act or ordinance mentioned, first fruits and other things, and enacted or mentioned to be enacted, to be vested, established, adjudged or deemed in the actual seizen or possession of such person and persons in the said pretended act or ordinance mentioned, and their heirs; nor the said R. H. nor the said J. P. nor the said W. G. are or ever were, nor any of them is, nor ever was any
* P. 605. agent or receiver under the order of the * said trustees, or any of the occupiers or tenants of any of the said premisses, who have taken the premisses or the profits thereof into their own hands without agreement to pay rent therefore, and have made no accompt or satisfaction to the trustees aforesaid, or to any other or others by their orders; nor any of the persons who have held the said premisses or any part thereof, or have taken the profits of the same or any part thereof under any agreement to pay rent or money for the same, and have not paid the rent or money aforesaid; and that the said sum of 2274l. 10s. 3dh. is not, nor is any part thereof any sum or sums of money of any of the rents or profits of the tythes appropriate, oblations, obventions, pensions, portions of tythes appropriate, offerings, fee farm rents issuing out of the tythes in the said pretended act or ordinance mentioned, first fruits or other things aforesaid, whatsoever, which ever came to the hands of the said trustees or of any of

them,

them, or any fum or fums of money received for the premif fes aforefaid, or for the profits of the premiffes aforefaid, or of any part thereof, nor the arrearages of rent or money remaining unpaid upon any fuch agreement aforementioned; and that neither the faid R. H. nor the faid J. P. nor the faid W. G. are nor ever were, nor any of them is, nor ever was any of thofe perfons, nor the heir or heirs, nor the executor or executors, nor the adminiftrator or adminiftrators, nor the affignee or affignees, of any of the perfons who have not paid their proportions which they ought to contribute to the payment of one hundred and fifty thoufand pounds, which by the order of the 16th day of May, 1641, the then houfe of commons accepted as a compofition from the farmers of the feveral cuftoms voted to be illegally taken; and that the faid fum of 2274l. 10s. 5dh. is not, nor is any part thereof any fum or fums of money due and in arrear for the excife of beer, ale, or of any other native or inland commodities after the 24th day of June, in the year of our Lord, 1659: and the faid R. H. and J. P further fay that the faid fum of 2274l. 10s. 5dh. is not, nor is any part thereof in the faid act firft mentioned, excepted, or foreprized; and that he the faid R. H. is and at the time of the beginning of the parliament aforefaid firft mentioned, and of the enacting of the act aforefaid firft mentioned, was a fubject of his majefty of this kingdom of England, born under the obedience of the faid king, to wit; at &c. and that the faid J. P. is, and at the time of the beginning of the parliament aforefaid firft mentioned, and of the act aforefaid mentioned, was a fubject of his majefty of this kingdom of England, born under the obedience of the faid lord the king, to wit; at, &c. and that the faid W. G. is and at the time of the beginning of the parliament aforefaid firft mentioned, and of the enacting of the act aforefaid firft mentioned, was a fubject of his majefty of this kingdom of England, born under the obedience of the faid lord the king to wit, at, &c. and that neither faid R. H. nor the * faid J. P. nor the faid W. G. are, nor were, nor is, nor was any of them the perfon or perfons in the faid act firft mentioned, by name or by any other manner excepted or foreprized; all and fingular which things the faid R. H. and J. P. are ready to verify as the court, &c. wherefore they pray judgment if the faid lord the now king will or ought to have execution againft them for the faid 2274l. 10s. 5dh. or for any part thereof, and that the faid general pardon be allowed to them, and that they the faid R. H. and J. P. of the faid 2274l. 10s. 5dh. and of every part thereof againft the faid lord the now king, his heirs and fucceffors, may be difcharged, and each

That at the time of the making of the act of oblivion, they were and as yet are, the king's fubjects.

* P. 606.

And pray judgment if the king ought to have execution, and that the general pardon [illegible] be allowed.

each of them may be difcharged, and that they, and each of them as to the premiffes, by the court here may be difmiffed.

Replication. And Geoffrey Palmer, knight and baronet, attorney general of the faid lord the now king, who for the faid lord the king in this behalf profecutes, by protefting, not acknowledging any thing by the faid R. H. and J. P. above alledged to be true, by protefting alfo that the faid fum of 2274l. 10s. 5dh. in the faid writ of fcire facias fpecified by the faid W. G. R. H. and J. P. the treafurers aforefaid, received within the time aforefaid, in the faid writ of fcire facias mentioned, by the faid act of free and general pardon indemnity and oblivion, is not remitted, releafed or pardoned, for plea, for the faid lord the now king faith, that by a certain other act made in the faid parliament, begun and held at Weftminfter, in the county of Middlefex, aforefaid, on the 8th day May, in the 13th year of the reign of the faid lord the now king, entitled "*an act for declaring, vefting and fettling of all fuch monies goods and other things in his majefty which were received, levied or collected in thefe late times, and are remaining in the hands or poffeffion of any treafurers, receivers, collectors or others, not pardoned by the act of oblivion*" reciting, that whereas divers doubts had been made whether the monies, goods, chattles and other things excepted to be accounted for in the act of free and general pardon, indemnity and oblivion, made and enacted in the parliament begun at Weftmifter, on the 25th day of April, in the 12th year of his majefties reign, belonged to and of right were in his majefty, for that the fame were not levied, received, collected, or taken, by his majefties authority or for his majefties ufe, for remedy and clearing, whereof, the lords and commons affembled in the parliament aforefaid, had humbly befought his majefty that it fhould be enacted, and it was declared enacted and ordained by the king's moft excellent majefty, by and with the advice and confent of the lords and commons in the faid parliament affembled, and by the authority of the fame, that every fum and fums of money, goods, plate, jewels, horfes, arms, ammunition, and all other things whatfoever, levied, received or taken after the 30th day of January, 1642, by any of the late pretended authorities, or by pretence or colour of any power or authority derived or pretended to be derived from them or any of them, for any publick ufe, which were * not pardoned by the act aforefaid, which were not otherwife vefted and fettled in the kings majefty, and all obligations and other fecurities, entered into for the fame or any part thereof, fhould be and were by the authority of

Protestation. The attorney general replies, the 13th Char. 2. c. 3. (made for explaining doubts upon the act of oblivion, the 12th of Charles 2) by which act the defendants are made liable to account for the money.

* P. 607.

of the faid act vefted and fettled in the kings majefty, his heirs and fucceffors; and that his facred majefty, his heirs and fucceffors might from time to time and at all times afterwards have, demand, fue for and recover the fame from all and every the perfon and perfons, their heirs executors, adminiftrators and affigns, who fhould be accountable for the fame, or in whofe hands or poffeffion foever the fame were or fhould be, as if the fame had been levied, received, collected or taken in his majefties name or to his majefties ufe, any law or ftatute, ufe or cuftom to the contrary in any wife notwithftanding; and that it was further enacted by the authority aforefaid that all and every the perfon and and perfons who had received any the aforefaid fum or fums of money of any treafurer or receiver for any publick ufe by way of impreft to be accounted for, which are not pardoned and difcharged by the faid act, fhould be liable to account and to be called to account, in fuch manner and form as if they had received the fame out of his majefties exchequer or any other publick treafury, as by the faid act of parliament laft mentioned, among other things more fully appears; with this that the faid attorney general of the faid lord the now king, for the faid lord the king, will verify that the faid R. and J. were perfons who within the time in the faid writ fpecified, at Weftminfter, in the county of Middlefex, received the faid fum of 340422l. in the faid writ of fcire facias fpecified from the faid feveral treafurers of excife cuftoms, prize goods and monthly taxes in the faid writ mentioned, for the faid public ufe in the faid writ fpecified, by way of impreft; and that the faid fum of 340422l. and every part thereof was to be accounted for; and that on the faid day of the iffuing of the writ aforefaid, the faid fum of 2274l. 10s. 5dh. remained and as yet remains in the hands of the faid Richard and John to be accounted for to the faid lord the now king; and that the faid fum of 2274l. 10s. 5dh. in the hands of the faid Richard and John fo remaining to be accounted for, is and was part of the faid fum of 340422l. in the faid writ fpecified, received from the faid feveral treafurers of the excife, cuftoms, prize goods and monthly taxes in the faid writ fpecified, for the faid publick ufe in the faid writ mentioned, by way of impreft to be accounted for and whereof they the faid R. and J. to the faid lord the now king have not as yet accounted, nor hath either of them accounted; all and fingular which things the faid attorney general of the faid lord the now king, for the faid lord the king, is ready to verify, as the court, &c. wherefore he prays judgment and that the faid R. and J. of the faid 2274l. 10s. 5dh. * and of every part thereof againft the faid

Averments.

* P. 608.

said lord the now king, his heirs and successors, may be charged and each of them may be charged.

Demurrer. And the said R. H. and J. P. say that the said plea of the said attorney general of the said lord the now king, above by replying pleaded and the matter in the same contained are not sufficient in law, to which they have no necessity, neither are they bound by the law, of the land to answer, wherefore for the insufficiency of the said plea, and the matter in the same contained, they the said R. and J. as before pray judgment, if the said lord the now king, will or ought to have execution against them for the said two thousand two hundred seventy-four pounds, ten shillings, and five pence halfpenny, or for any part thereof; and that the said general pardon may be allowed, and that they the said R. and J. of the said 2274l. 10s. 5dh. and of every part thereof against the said lord the now king, his heirs and successors may be discharged, and each of them may be discharged.

Joinder. And the said attorney general of the said lord the now king, because that he by his replication aforesaid above by replying, hath alledged sufficient matter in law, which he is ready to verify as the court, &c. which matter the said R. H. and J. P. do not deny, nor to the same in any manner answer, but altogether refuse to admit that averment, for the said lord the king prays judgment, and that the said R. and J. of the said 2274l. 10s. 5dh. and of every part thereof against the said lord the now king, his heirs and successors, may be charged, and each of them may be charged. Therefore, &c.

---

## The King against Broadnax and others.

### Michaelmas, 14th Charles 2d.

Scire facias upon a bond entered into to the king, by three obligors. SURRY, to wit—Be it remembered that the writ of the lord the now king, under the seal of this Exchequer by the consideration of the barons here issued in these words, to wit: Charles the 2d, &c. to the sheriff of Surry, greeting, whereas Henry Broadnax, of the parish of St. Olave, Southwark, in the county of Surry, gentleman, Josias Nicholson of of the parifh of St. Mary, Overeys, Southwark, in the county of Surry aforefaid, brewer, and John Goodwyn of St. Olave, Southwark, in the county of Surry, aforefaid, diftiller, by their writing obligatory, fealed with their feals, bearing date the 6th day of March in the 13th year of our reign, are holden to us in two thoufand pounds of the lawful money of England, to be paid upon a certain day paft, and the fame to us have not as yet paid nor have caufed to be paid, as it is faid, and we being willing to be fatisfied of the faid two thoufand pounds to us now due with all the fpeed with which we can, as is juft, command you that you do not omit becaufe of any liberty but that you enter it, and by good and lawful men of your bailiwick, that you give notice to the faid Henry B. J. N. and J. G. that they * be before the barons of our Exchequer, at Weftminfter, on the 6th day of May next coming, to fhow and propound if they have or know any thing to fay for themfelves, wherefore we ought not to have execution againft them of the faid two thoufand pounds, and have there then the names of thofe by whom you fhall give them notice, and this writ. Witnefs, Mathew Hale, knight, at Weftminfter, the 12th day of February, in the 14th year of our reign; by the writing obligatory aforefaid, &c. and by the barons. * P. 609.

*Fanfhawe.*

At which day Roger Duncombe, efquire, fheriff of the county aforefaid, returns the writ aforefaid, thus indorfed, the within named Henry, Jofias, and John, have not any thing in my bailiwick, whereby I can give them notice, nor are they found in the fame. Be it remembered alfo that another writ of the lord the now king, under the feal of this Exchequer, by the confideration of the barons here, iffued in thefe words, Charles the 2d, &c. to the fheriff of Surry, greeting, whereas Henry Broadnax of the parifh of St. Olave, Southwark, in the county of Surry, gentleman, Jofias Nicholfon, of the parifh of St. Mary Overeys, Southwark, in the county of Surry, aforefaid, brewer, and John Goodwyn, of St. Olave, Southwark, in the county of Surry, aforefaid, diftiller, by their writing obligatory, fealed with their feals, bearing date the 6th day of March, in the 13th year of our reign, are holden to us in two thoufand pounds, of the lawful money of England, to be paid upon a certain day now paft, and the fame to us have not as yet paid, nor have caufed to be paid, as it is faid, and we being willing to be fatisfied of the faid two thoufand pounds to us now due, with all the fpeed with which we can, as is juft, command you that you do not omit, becaufe of any liberty within your

Return nichil.

A fecond fcire facias upon the fame bond.

your bailiwick, but that you enter it, and by good and lawful men of your bailiwick, that you give notice to the faid Henry Broadnax, Jofias Nicholfon and John Goodwyn, that they be before the barons of our Exchequer, on the morrow of All Souls, next coming, to fhow and propound if they have or know any thing to fay for themfelves, wherefore we ought not to have execution againft them for the faid two thoufand pounds, and have there then the names of thofe by whom you fhall fo give them notice, and this writ. Witnefs, Mathew Hale, knight, at Weftminfter, the 18th day of June, in the 14th year of our reign; by the writing obligatory aforefaid, and by the barons.

*Fanfhawe.*

Return fcire facias to two and nichil as to the third defendant.

On which day the faid Roger Duncombe, fheriff of the county aforefaid, returns here the writ aforefaid, thus indorfed, to wit; by virtue of this writ, to me directed by Thomas Salmon and Thomas Browne, good and lawful men of my bailiwick, I have given notice to the within named Henry and Jofias, that they be before the barons within written, on the day and place within contained, to fhow as the faid writ in itfelf commands and requires; and the within named John Goodwyn, hath not any thing in my bailiwick whereby I can give him notice, nor is he found in the fame. As is more fully contained in the faid feveral writs and the returns of the fame, which are in the file of writs executed for the faid lord the king of the 14th year of the faid lord the now king, on behalf of his remembrancer.

* P. 610. The three defendants appear and pray oyer of the writs of fcire facias and of the bond, and the condition thereof.

* And now, to wit; on the faid morrow of all Souls, in this term come here the faid Henry Broadnax, Jofias Nicholfon and John Goodwyn, in the faid writs and in the returns of the fame named, by C. K. their attorney, and pray oyer of the faid feveral writs of fcire facias, and of the faid feveral returns of the fame, and they are read to them, alfo they pray oyer of the faid writing obligatory whereof in the faid writs mention is made, and of the condition of the fame, and they are in like manner read to them in thefe words, to wit; "know all men &c." (reciting the obligation) "the condition of the within obligation is fuch, that whereas fir George Benyon, knight, Francis Finch, Nathaniel Manton and Edward Wingate, efquires, commiffioners and governors of his majefties revenue of the excife or new impoft, have by commiffion under their hands and feals, bearing date the day of the date within written, deputed, conftituted, authorized and appointed the within-bounden Henry Broadnax, together with Roger Clarke and John Windebanke,

Oyer of the condition of the bond.

Windebanke, gent. to be subordinate commissioners, under them, to erect, settle and continue an office of excise or new impost, in and for the towns of Kingston, Guilford and Croydon, in the county of Surry, and in all towns corporate, towns, villages, hamlets, parishes, parts and places whatsoever, as well within liberties, as without, lying and being within the same, except the borough of Southwark and weekly bills of mortality. If therefore the said Henry Broadnax for his part shall, and do from time to time and at all times hereafter, well and truly observe, perform, fulfil and keep all and every the clauses, articles and conditions of the said commission, and shall and do truly execute the same according to the present laws of excise, or such as shall hereafter be appointed and established, and well and truly from time to time observe such instructions as are, or shall be given by his majesties commissioners and governors of the excise or new imposts aforesaid, by order of the lord high Treasurer of England; and shall and do also upon the twenty-fourth day June next ensuing the date within written, and so from that day afterwards at and upon every of the usual quarter days of the year, during the whole term that the said commission shall be in force, make due and true accompt, satisfaction, content and payment, or cause the same to be well and truly made and done unto the said commissioners of excise or new impost, or to the major part of them, their survivors, successors or assigns, of all such sum and sums of money, and other goods and things, as either at or before the said 24th day of June, or at or before every of the usual quarter days of the year aforesaid, which he the said Henry Broadnax, or any other person or persons, for him, or by his means, assent, consent, privity or procurement, shall have received, collected and gathered by virtue and force, and under colour and pretence of the said commission, the same to be made and done at or in the head office of excise, situate and kept within the said city of London, that then this obligation to be void and of none effect, or else to remain in full force and virtue;" which being read, heard and by them fully understood, they complain that they under * colour of the premisses, are griveously vexed and disquieted, and this unjustly, because protesting that the said several writs of scire facias and the returns of them, and the matter in the same contained, are not sufficiant in law, to which they have no necessity, neither are they bound by the law of the land to answer, for plea, nevertheless, they the said Henry Broadnax, Josias Nicholson and John Goodwyn, say that from the 6th day of March, in the 13th year of the reign of the lord Charles the now king, &c. until the 9th day of August from

* P. 611.

Protestation

Plea. Performance of the condition of the bond from the

date of the bond, viz. the 6th of March, 13th of Charles 2d, until the 9th of Auguſt following.

from that time next enſuing, he the ſaid Henry Broadnax, at the head office of exciſe, ſituate and kept within the city of London aforeſaid, to wit; in the pariſh of St. Bartholomew, near the Royal Exchange, in the ward of Broad-ſtreet, for his part from time to time and at all times, in all things well and truly hath obſerved, performed, fulfilled and kept all and every the clauſes, articles and conditions, of the ſaid commiſſion, and well and truly hath executed the ſame, according to the laws of exciſe then appointed and eſtabliſhed, and well and truly from time to time hath obſerved ſuch inſtructions as were given by his majeſty's commiſſioners and governors of the exciſe or new impoſt aforeſaid, by the order of the lord high treaſurer of England; and at the pariſh and ward aforeſaid, he the ſaid Henry Broadnax, upon the 24th day of June, next after the date of the ſaid writing obligatory, and ſo from thence to and unto the ſaid 9th day of Auguſt from that time next enſuing, hath made due and true accompt, ſatisfaction, content and payment to the ſaid George Benyon, knight, Francis Finch, Nathaniel Manton and Edward Wingate, eſquires, then commiſſioners and governors of the exciſe or new impoſt aforeſaid, of all ſuch ſum and ſums of money and of other goods and things as either at or before the ſaid 24th day of June, or at or before the ſaid 9th day of Auguſt aforeſaid, he the ſaid Henry Broadnax, or any other perſon or perſons for him or by his means, aſſent, conſent, privity or procurement, had received, collected and gather by force and virtue and under colour and pretence, of the ſaid commiſſion, according to the tenor, form and true intent of the ſaid condition of the writing obligatory aforeſaid; and the ſaid H. B. J. N. and J. G. further ſay, that afterwards, to wit; on the ſaid 9th day of Auguſt in the 13th year aforeſaid, the ſaid George Benyon, knight, Francis Finch, Nathaniel Manton and Edward Wingate, eſquires, commiſſioners and governors of the exciſe and new impoſt as aforeſaid, by their certain writing under their ſeveral hands and ſeals, bearing date the ſaid day and year laſt mentioned, at the pariſh and ward aforeſaid, revoked the ſaid commiſſion as to the ſaid Henry Broadnax, and by their ſaid writing at the pariſh and ward aforeſaid, did diſmiſs him the ſaid Henry Broadnax from any further acting as a ſubordinate commiſſioner for the exciſe, within the county of Surry, aforeſaid, whereby the ſaid commiſſion ſo as aforeſaid in the ſaid condition of the ſaid writing obligatory * mentioned, to be granted to the ſaid Henry Broadnax, as to him the ſaid Henry became void and of no force and effect, all and ſingular which things they the ſaid Henry Broadnax, Joſias Nicholſon and John Goodwyn, are ready to verify,

And that on the 9th day of Auguſt aforeſaid, the commiſſioners by their writing under their ſeals, revoked the defendant Broadnax's commiſſion and diſmiſſed him from acting under the ſame

* P. 612.

rify, as the court, &c. wherefore they pray judgment, and that they of the said two thousand pounds in the said writing obligatory, and in the said several writs of scire facias mentioned and expressed, and of every part thereof, may be discharged, and that the said writing obligatory may be cancelled, and made void, and may be delivered to the said H. J. and J. and also that they the said H. J. and J. as to the premisses by the court here may be dismissed, and every of them may be dismissed.

And Geoffrey Palmer, knight and baronet, attorney general of the lord the now king, who for the said lord the king prosecutes present here in court on the same day in his proper person, by protesting, not acknowledging any thing in the plea of the said Henry Broadnax, Josias Nicholson and John Goodwyn, by them above pleaded to be true, in the manner and form as the said H. J. and J. above by pleading have alledged, nevertheless, for plea or replication, the said attorney general of the said lord the now king, for the said lord the king, saith, that the said lord the king ought not to be precluded from having his execution against them the said H. J. and J. and every of them, for the said two thousand pounds or for any part thereof, because of any thing in the plea aforesaid mentioned, because he saith that between the 8th day of March in the 13th year aforesaid, and the 23d day of June in the 13th year aforesaid, the said Henry Broadnax, received, collected and gathered by force, and virtue and under colour and pretence of the said commission, the sum of twenty shillings of the lawful money of England, to wit; at the said parish of St. Bartholemew, nigh the Royal Exchange, in the ward of Broad-street, London, and that the said H. B. did not make true payment to the said George Benyon, knight, Francis Finch, Nathaniel Manton and Edward Wingate, esquires, then commissioners and governors of the excise and new impost aforesaid, nor to any of them, of the said sum of twenty shillings of the lawful money of England, so by him received, collected and gathered, by force and virtue, and under colour and pretence of the said commission upon the said 24th day of June next, after the date of the writing obligatory aforesaid, according to the tenor, form and effect of the said condition of the said writing obligatory in the manner and form as the said Henry, Josias and John above, by pleading have alledged, all and singular which things the said attorney general of the said lord the now king, for the said lord the king, is ready to verify as the court, &c. wherefore, he prays judgment, and that the said lord the now king may have execution against the said Henry, Josias and John and every of them, of the said two thousand

Replication that Broadnax between the 8th of March, the 13th of Cha. 2. and the 23d of June following received twenty shillings, by virtue of his commission, which he did not pay to the commissioners and governors of excise upon the 24th of June following, according to the form of the condition of the obligation.

thousand pounds in the said writ of scire facias, and writing obligatory mentioned.

Demurrer. And the said Henry Broadnax, Josias Nicholson and John Goodwyn, rejoining say, that the replication aforesaid of the said attorney general of the said * lord the now king above, by replying pleaded, and the matter in the same contained are not sufficient in law to have the execution of the said lord the king against them the said Henry, Josias and John, to which they have no necessity, neither are they bound by the law of the land to answer, wherefore for the insufficiency of the said replication and the matter in the same contained, they the said Henry, Josias and John as before pray judgment, and that they of the said two thousand pounds in the said writing obligatory mentioned, against the said lord the now king, his heirs and successors may be discharged, and that the writing obligatory aforesaid may be cancelled and made void, and to the said Henry, Josias and John may be delivered.

* P. 613.

Joinder. And the said attorney general of the said lord the now king, because that he hath alledged sufficient matter in law to have the execution of the said lord the king against the said Henry Broadnax, Josias Nicholson and John Goodwyn, which for the said lord the now king he is ready to verify, which matter the said Henry, Josias and John do not deny, nor to the same in any wise answer, but altogether refuse to admit that averment, as before prays judgment and that the said lord the now king may have execution against the said Henry, Josias and John, for the said two thousand pounds in the said writ of scire facias and writing obligatory mentioned. Therefore, &c.

Scire facias upon recognizance of 20l. entered into to the king in the court of King's Bench.

The king, &c. to the sheriff of Gloucester, greeting, we command you that you do not omit because of any liberty in your county, but that by good and lawful men of your said bailiwick, you give notice severally to A. B. of C. in your county, gent. and to G. H. of the same, merchant, that they be before us on the morrow of All Souls wheresoever we shall then be in England, severally to show to us if they have or know any thing to say for themselves, to wit; to the said A. B. wherefore twenty pounds of his lands and chattles, and of the lands and chattles of each of them ought not to be made and levied to our use and behoof according to their several recognizances in our court before us acknowledged, and further to do and receive what our court aforesaid shall consider in this behalf and have there then the names of those by whom you shall so give them notice, and this writ. Witness, J. Brampston, at Westminster, &c.

By the court, *F. K.*

The

## The King against Morris and others,

BE it remembered, that on the Wednesday next after three weeks of the Holy Trinity, in this same term, the court here is given to understand and to be informed that John Morris of G. in the county of Salop, yeoman, on the 22d day of April, in the 17th year of the reign of the reign of the lord Charles the now king of England, &c. with force and arms, at the parish of Cloubry, in the county aforesaid, in and upon one Thomas Browne of the parish of C. aforesaid, in the county aforesaid, yeoman, in the peace of God and of the said lord the king then and there being made an assault and affray and * him the said Thomas then and there beat, wounded and ill-treated, so that his life was despaired of, and other wrongs to the said T. B. then and there did, to the great damage of the said T. &c. and further, that the said J. M. on the 12th day of June, in the 17th year aforesaid, at C. in the parish of C. in the county aforesaid, with force and arms, &c. in and upon one J. B. in the peace of God and of the said lord the king, then and there being, made an assault and affray, and him the said J. B. in like manner beat, wounded and ill-treated, and other wrongs to the said J. B. then and there did, to the great damage of the said J. B. against the peace of the said lord the now king, his crown and dignity, and against the force, form and effect of the undertaking and mainprize in the court of the said lord the king before the king himself, acknowledged, &c.

Suggestion of the breach of a recognizance.

* P. 614

Salop, to wit: The lord the king hath sent to the sheriff of the county aforesaid his writ close in these words, Charles, &c. to the sheriff of Salop, greeting, whereas J. M. of C. in the county of Salop, yeoman, on the Saturday next after 15 days of St. Martin, in the 16th year of our reign, in our court before us at Westminster, was delivered on bail to Silvanus Price, of L. in the county aforesaid, gent. and to Hugh Owen of the parish aforesaid in the county aforesaid, gent. until the morrow of the Holy Trinity then next ensuing, wheresoever we should then be in England, which S. P. and H. O. then and there undertook for the said John Morris, and he the said John Morris then and there undertook for himself, that he the said John Morris should personally appear before us at the said term, and that he in the mean time would demean himself well towards us and all our people, according to the form of the statute in such case made and provided: to wit: each of the pledges aforesaid, for the said John

Scire facias thereupon against the principal and his sureties, reciting the breach of his recognizance, &c.

John under the pain of 20l. and he the said John under the pain of 40l. which sums of 20l. the said Silvanus and Hugh as aforesaid, severally for themselves and the said John the said sum of 40l. acknowledged to owe us, and to be made and levied of their lands and chattles, and of the lands and chattles of every of them to our use and behoof, if it should happen that the said John in any wise should fail in the premisses, and in the lawful manner should be convicted thereof, as in our court before us fully appeareth of record; and now in our court before us on our behalf we have understood that the said J. M. after the taking of the recognizance aforesaid, and before the said morrow of the Holy Trinity, to wit, on the 22d day of April, in the 17th year of our reign, with force and arms, &c. at the parish of C. in the county aforesaid, in and upon one T. B. of the parish of C. aforesaid in your county, yeoman, in the peace of God and in our peace, then and there being made an assault an affray. and him the said T. then and there beat, wounded and ill-treated, so that his life was despaired of and other wrongs to the said T. B. then and there did, to the great damage of the said T. against our peace, and against the force, form and effect of the mainprize, undertaking and recognizance aforesaid; and further, that the said J. M. afterwards and before the said morrow of the Holy Trinity, to wit; on the 12th day of June, in the 17th year of our reign aforesaid, at C. in the parish of C. in your county, with force and arms, &c. in and upon one J. B. in the peace of God and our peace, then and there being made an assault and affray, and him the said J. B. then and there in like manner beat, wound-
* P. 615. ed and ill-treated and other wrongs to the said * J. B. then and there did, to the great damage of the said J. B. against the force, form and effect, of the mainprize and undertaking aforesaid, and against our peace, our crown and dignity, and we being willing to provide for our indemnity in this behalf as we are bounden, command you that you do not omit because of any liberty within your bailiwick, but by good and lawful men of your said bailiwick that you give notice severally as well to the said J. M. as to the said S. P. and H. O. that they be before us on the morrow of All Souls, wheresoever we shall then be in England, severally to show to us, if they have or know any thing to say for themselves, to wit; to the said J. M. wherefore 40l. of his lands and chattles, and of the lands and chattles of every of them, ought not to be made and levied for the causes aforesaid to our use and behoof, according to their several recognizances aforesaid in our court before us acknowledged, and further to do and receive what our court aforesaid shall consider in this behalf

behalf and have there the names of those by whom you shall so give them notice and this writ: Witness, T. Brampston, at Westminster, the 14th day of July, in the 17th year of our reign. At which morrow of All Souls, before the lord the king at Westminster, Thomas Nicholls, esquire, sheriff of the county aforesaid, returns that the said John Morris, Silvanus Price, and Hugh Owen, have not any thing in his bailiwick, whereby he could give them notice; Whereupon the said John Morris on the fourth day of pleading, being solemnly called, comes by Richard Marston his attorney, and having had oyer of the writ aforesaid and of the record by which the said writ will be warranted, the said John as well for his own indemnity as for the indemnity of his pledges in this behalf saith, that neither the said sum of 40l. of the goods and chattles of the said S. P. and H. O. for the said John for the occasion aforesaid, nor &c. &c. ought to be made and levied, because he saith that the said T. B. at the said time on which the assault, beating, wounding and ill-treating is supposed to be committed, at the parish of C. in the county of S. aforesaid, with force and arms in and upon the said J. M. made an assault and him the said John would have beaten, wounded and ill-treated, unless the said J. M. himself then and there immediately in this behalf had defended, wherefore the said J. M. then and there did defend himself against the said T. B. so that if any damage then and there happened to the said T. it was of his own proper assault and in the defence of the said J. and the said J. M. further saith that the said J. B. at the said time in which the assault, beating, wounding and ill-treating is supposed to be committed at C. in the parish of C. aforesaid, with force and arms in and upon the said J M. in like manner made an assault and him the said John would have beaten, wounded and ill-treated, unless the said J. M. himself then and there immediately had defended, wherefore the said J. M. then and there did defend himself against the said J. B. so that if any damage then and there happened to the said J. B. it was of his own proper assault and in the defence of the said J. M. and this the said J. M. is ready to verify, as the court, &c. wherefore he doth not apprehend that the said lord the now king, him the said J. M. or his pledges aforesaid, because of the premisses, will or ought to impeach, nor that the said several sums or any of them ought to be made and levied of his lands and chattles, or of the lands and chattles of his pledges aforesaid, to the use and behoof of the said lord the king, wherefore he prays judgment, and that he and his pledges aforesaid of the premisses by the court here may be dismissed, &c. And Thomas Fanshawe, esquire, coroner and

Return nichil.

Morris the principal appears and having had oyer of the scire facias and the record, &c. for his own and his bails indemnity, pleads son assault demesne to each of the assaults.

* P. 616. and attorney of the lord the king in the * court of the lord the king, before the king himself, who for the said lord the king in this behalf prosecutes for the said lord the king, saith, that the said sum of forty pounds of the lands and chattles of the said S.P. and H. O. for the said I. M. for the occasion aforesaid, ought to be made and levied, because he saith that the said J. M. of his own proper injury, without any such cause as by the said J. M. above by pleading is alledged, on the said 22d day of April, in the 17th year aforesaid, with force and arms, &c. at the parish of C. in the county aforesaid, in and upon the said T. B. in the peace of God and of the said lord the king, then and there being made an assault an affray and him the said T. B. then and there beat, wounded and ill-treated, so that his life was despaired of and other wrongs to the said T. B. then and there did to the great damage of the said T. against the peace of the said lord the king, and against the force, form and effect of the mainprize, undertaking and recognizance aforesaid, in the manner and form as by the said writ of the lord the king of scire facias above, against him is supposed, and further the said attorney of the said lord the king for the said lord the king saith, that the said J. M. on the said 12th day of June, in the 17th year aforesaid, of his own proper injury without any such cause as by the said J. above by pleading is alledged at C. in the parish of C. in the county aforesaid, with force and arms, &c. in and upon the said J. B. in the peace of God and of the said lord the king, then and there being made an assault an affray and him the said J. B. then and there in like manner beat, wounded and ill-treated and other wrongs to the said J. B. then and there did, to the great damage of the said J. B. against the force, form and effect of the mainprize and undertaking aforesaid, and against the peace of the said lord the now king, his crown and dignity, in the manner and form as by the said writ of the lord the king of scire facias above against him is supposed, and this the said coroner and attorney of the said lord the king for the said lord the king, prays may be enquired of by the country; and the said J. M. doth the like. Therefore let a jury come thereupon before the lord the king on the octave of St. Hilary, wheresoever, &c. and who neither, &c. to recognize, &c. because as well, &c. the same day is given as well to the said T. F. who prosecutes, &c. as to the said J. M. &c. at which octave of St. Hilary, before the lord the king, at Westminster, come as well the said T. F. esquire, who prosecutes, &c. as the said J. M. by his attorney aforesaid, and the sheriff returns the names of 12 jurors of whom none, &c. therefore the sheriff aforesaid is

Replication of de injuria sua propria, to each justification.

Petit quod inquiratur.

Venire facias awarded.

is commanded that he do not omit, &c. but that he diſtrain them by all their lands, &c. and that of the iſſues, &c. ſo that he have their bodies before the lord the king at Weſtminſter, from the day of Eaſter in 15 days, whereſoever, &c. or before the beloved and faithful Edward Hendon, knight, one of the barons of the Exchequer of the lord the king, the juſtice of the ſaid the king aſſigned to take aſſizes in the county of S. if firſt on Monday the 21ſt day of March, at Bridgnorth, in the county aforeſaid, by the form of the ſtatute, &c. he ſhall come for the default of jurors, &c. therefore that the ſheriff have their bodies, &c. to recognize in the form aforeſaid, the ſame day is given as well to the ſaid T. F. who proſecutes, &c. as to the ſaid John Morris, &c.

---

# TRAVERSES AND SPECIAL PLEAS TO INQUISITIONS AND OFFICES FOUND. * P. 617.

## The King againſt the Earl of Warwick.

HERETOFORE, to wit, on the 30th day of June in the 21ſt year of the reign of our lord Charles the 2d. by the grace of God of England, &c. it was found by a certain inquiſition taken for our moſt ſerene lord the king, at C. in the county of E. aforeſaid, before Joſhua Oyer, one of the coroners of the ſaid lord the king, for the county aforeſaid, on view of the body of William Finch, gent. of C. aforeſaid, in the county aforeſaid, then and there lying dead, by the oath of twelve jurors, good and lawful men of the county aforeſaid, who then and there being ſworn and charged to enquire for the ſaid lord the king, when, where, how, and by what means the ſaid William Finch came to his death, upon their oath aforeſaid, ſaid that he the ſaid William Finch, on Thurſday the 10th day of June, in the 21ſt year aforeſaid, about the eighth hour in the night of the ſaid day, not having the fear of God before his eyes, but being moved and ſeduced by the inſtigation of the devil, of his malice aforethought at C. aforeſaid, in the county of Eſſex aforeſaid, then and there being alone, into a certain ditch

Recital of an inquiſition before the coroner ſupervíſum corporis, whereby it was found that one Finch was felo de ſe by drowning himſelf in a ditch.

of water there, of the depth of ten feet, himself then and there wilfully and feloniously did cast and drown, and so the jurors aforesaid, upon their oath aforesaid said, that the said William Finch in the manner and form aforesaid, then and there wilfully and feloniously as a felon of himself, himself did murder, against the peace of the said lord the now king, his crown and dignity, and so the said William Finch came to his death and not otherwise, and further the jurors aforesaid, upon their oath aforesaid said, that the said William Finch at the time of the felony aforesaid, had goods and chattles in the inventory to the said inquisition annexed, which remain in the custody of the most noble Charles earl of Warwick, who claims the goods and chattles aforesaid, the tenor of which schedule follows in these words and figures, to wit, an inventory of the goods and chattles of William Finch, in the inquisition annexed named who drowned himself, viz. in the hall, two tables, &c.

That Finch at the time of the felony, &c. had divers goods which are in the custody of the earl of Warwick who claims them.

And also it was found by another inquisition indented, taken for the most serene lord the king, at —— in the county of Essex, aforesaid, on the 8th day of December, in the year, &c. before J. G. gent. one of the coroners of the said lord the king, of the county aforesaid, upon view of the body of one Andrew Baker of T. in the county of Essex aforesaid, husbandman, then and there lying dead, by the oath of twelve jurors, good and lawful men of the county aforesaid, who then and there being sworn and charged to enquire for the said lord the king, when, where, how and by what means the said Andrew Baker came to his death, said upon their oath that the * said A. B. on Tuesday the 7th day of December, in the year, &c. about the seventh hour after mid-day of the said day, riding in a certain waggon of one J. G. of T. aforesaid, yeoman, in a certain lane nigh to a certain place called P. which is within the manor of A. in the parish, &c. in the county aforesaid, the said waggon accidentally overturned and fell upon the head of the said A. B. and so crushed his head, and that of that crushing he the said A. B. then and there instantly died, and so the jurors aforesaid upon their oath aforesaid said, that the said A. B. in the manner and form aforesaid by misfortune came to his death, and not otherwise, and further the jurors aforesaid upon their oath aforesaid said, that then and there the waggon aforesaid and one horse of a bay colour moved to the death of the said A. B. and that the waggon aforesaid is of the value of 40 shillings, and the horse aforesaid with the harness is of the value of 20 shillings, and they remain in the custody of the most noble Charles earl of Warwick, who claims the deodand aforesaid.

* P. 618.

Recital of another inquisition whereby it was found that A. B. came to his death by misfortune, and that a cart and one horse moved to his death, and that the said earl claims the deodand.

Which

Which inquisitions J. G. gent. one of the coroners of the lord the king, of the county of Essex aforesaid, by his proper hands, on the Saturday next after three weeks of St. Michael in the 21st year aforesaid, in the court of the lord the king, before the king himself, delivered of record to be determined, &c. whereupon the sheriff of the county aforesaid is commanded that he do not omit, &c. but that because the said Charles earl of Warwick, to come to answer, &c.

The inquisitions delivered by the coroner into B R. Venire to answer awarded against the earl of Warwick.

And now, to wit: on the Monday next after the octave of St. Hilary, in this same term before the lord the king, at Westminster, comes the said Charles earl of Warwick, by P. W. his attorney, and having had oyer of the several inquisitions aforesaid, saith, that he doth not apprehend that the said lord the now king, will or ought impeach or trouble him Charles earl of Warwick for the premisses in the several inquisitions aforesaid above specified, because he saith, that the several villages of C. and others, &c. are and from the time whereof the memory of man is not to the contrary, have been parcel of the hundred or half hundred of Harlowe, in the the county of Essex aforesaid, and that long before the taking of the several inquisitions the lord Edward the 6th late king of England was seized of and in the hundreds of Onger and Harlowe with the appurtenances in the said county of Essex, in his demesne as of fee in right of his crown of England, and so being thereof seized, the said lord Edward the 6th, on the first day of May, in the year, &c. by his letters patent, sealed under his great seal of England, the date of which is the same day and year, gave and granted to Richard Rich, lord Rich, his heirs and assigns, among other things the said hundreds of H. and O. with the wardstaff of the said hundreds and the services of the said wardstaff, with all and singular their rights, jurisdictions, liberties, privileges, franchises, exemptions and all their appurtenances in the said county of Essex, and also the courts leet or view of frankpledge, chattles waived, estrays, and deodands, and the goods and chattles of felons of themselves, felons, fugitives, and all other felons whatsoever, and also wardships, marriages, knights fees, escheats and reliefs and fines and amerciaments of all and every the tenant's and resiants, and the return of writs, and all and every other rights, jurisdictions, liberties, privileges and franchises, profits, commodities, * benefits, possessions and hereditaments whatsoever, with the appurtenances in the hundreds of O. and H. and elsewhere wheresoever in the said county of Essex, to the said hundred of O. and H. in any wise belonging or appertaining; as by the said letters patent among other things more

Plea. That the places where the deaths happened are time out of mind part of the hundred of Harlowe, in the county of Essex.

That Edw. the 6th being seized of the hundreds of O. and H. granted them by letters patent to Richard lord Rich in fee with all deodands and goods and chattles of felons of themselves, &c.

* P. 619.



fully

And shows that they came to him by by descent.

fully appears; by virtue of which letters patent of the said lord Edward the 6th late king of England, the said Richard lord Rich into the hundreds aforesaid, with the appurtenances entered and was thereof seized in his demesne as of fee, and of and in the liberties, privileges and franchises aforesaid as of fee and right, and he the said Richard Lord Rich so being seized thereof, he afterwards and before the time in which, &c. to wit, on the first day of September, in the 10th year of the reign of the lady Elizabeth, late queen of England, &c. at L. in the county aforesaid, died seized of such estate; after whose death the hundreds aforesaid with their appurtenances and liberties, privileges and franchises aforesaid descended, as of right they ought to descend to Robert lord Rich, as son and heir of the said lord Rich, whereby the said Robert lord Rich into the hundreds aforesaid with the appurtenances entered and was thereof seized in his demesne as of fee, and of the liberties, privileges and franchises aforesaid as of fee and right, and he the said Robert lord Rich so being thereof seized afterwards and before the time in which, &c. to wit, on the —— day of —— in the year, &c. at L. aforesaid, in the county aforesaid, died so seized of such estate, after whose death the hundreds aforesaid with their appurtenances and liberties, privileges and franchises aforesaid, descended as of right they ought to descend, to Robert then lord Rich, afterwards earl of Warwick, as the son and heir of the said Robert lord Rich, whereby the said Robert lord Rich, earl of Warwick into the hundreds aforesaid with the appurtenances entered and was thereof seized in his demesne as of fee, and of the liberties, privileges and franchises aforesaid as of fee and right, and he the said Robert lord Rich earl of Warwick, so being thereof seized, &c. died, &c. after whose death, &c. descended to Robert earl of Warwick, as the son and heir of the said Robert, &c. after whose death, &c. descended, &c. to Robert late earl of Warwick, &c. after whose death the hundreds aforesaid with the appurtenances and the liberties, priveleges and franchises, aforesaid descended as of the right they ought to descend, to Charles now earl of Warwick, whereby the said Charles now earl of Warwick into the Hundreds aforesaid, with the appurtenances entered, and was thereof seized in his demesne as of fee, and of the liberties, privileges and franchises aforesaid as of fee and right, and he the said Charles earl of Warwick so being thereof seized, the said William Finch in one of the inquisitions aforesaid named, at C. in the county of Essex aforesaid, within the hundred of H. aforesaid, himself feloniously did kill and murder, in the manner and form in the said inquisition mentioned. And the said A. B. in the said

That the deaths of the persons mentioned in the inquisitions happened within the hundred of H.

ſaid other inquiſition mentioned, at S. and A. aforeſaid, within the hundred of H. aforeſaid, was killed in the manner and form in the ſaid inquiſition mentioned, and that the goods and chattles aforeſaid in the ſaid inquiſitions mentioned, were within the hundred of H. aforeſaid, in the county aforeſaid; and that the ſaid Charles earl of Warwick, the goods and chattles aforeſaid in the ſaid inquiſitions ſpecified at the ſeveral villages of C. S and A. aforeſaid, within the hundred of H. aforeſaid, as his proper goods and chattles, did ſeize as it was * well lawful for him, wherefore he prays judgment and that he as well of the ſeveral inquiſitions aforeſaid, as of the duty in the ſaid ſeveral inquiſitions above ſpecified, and in the hands of the ſaid Charles earl of Warwick being, by the court here may be diſmiſſed and diſcharged; And Thomas Fanſhawe, knight, coroner and attorney in the court of the ſaid lord the king, before the king himſelf, who for the ſaid lord the king in this behalf proſecutes, having ſeen and inſpected the plea of the ſaid Charles earl of Warwick, and the ſame being diligently examined by him, for this, to wit; becauſe that it well appears to him by evidence and the record to the ſaid coroner and attorney ſhown that the plea aforeſaid of the ſaid Charles earl of Warwick above pleaded is true, he doth not deny it but confeſſeth the ſaid plea to be true in all things; and the letters patent aforeſaid are produced here in court, ſealed under the great ſeal of England, &c.

* P. 620.

The king's coroner confeſſeth the plea.

---

## The King againſt Butler.

TO wit: and the ſaid J. Butler comes by J. H. his attorney, and having had oyer of the inquiſition aforeſaid ſaith, that he doth not apprehend that the ſaid lord the king will impeach him for occaſion of the premiſſes, becauſe he ſaith, that before the death of the ſaid J. J. the ſaid lady Elizabeth, late queen of England, by her letters patent made under her great ſeal of England, bearing date at Greenwich, the 25th day of July, in the 39th year of her reign, which the ſaid J. B. produces here in court, granted to one William Paget, then eſquire, afterwards William lord Paget, all deodands within the manor of Longden, aforeſaid, to have and to hold to the ſaid W. P. and his heirs, by virtue of which grant the ſaid W. P. was ſeized of the franchiſe aforeſaid, to have and take to his own proper uſe, all deodands within

Supra 270.

Plea to an inquiſition. That the defendant delivered a deodand found by the inquiſition to be in his hands to the royal patentee.

within the manor aforeſaid as of fee and right, and ſo being thereof ſeized, the ſaid W. P. afterwards, to wit: on the 1ſt day of May in the 3d year of the reign of the lord Charles the 1ſt, late king of England, &c. at L. aforeſaid, died ſo ſeized thereof, after whoſe death the franchiſes aforeſaid deſcended to the ſaid W. lord Paget, in the inquiſition aforeſaid named, as the ſon and heir of the ſaid W. P. deceaſed, whereby the ſaid W. lord P. the ſon was and as yet is ſeized of all the ſaid franchiſes of having and taking to his own proper uſe all deodands within the manor aforeſaid, whereupon the ſaid J. B. after the taking of the inquiſition aforeſaid, to wit: on the 1ſt day of May, in the 3d year aforeſaid at the manor aforeſaid, the oak aforeſaid to the ſaid W. lord P. the ſon did deliver, and the ſaid W. lord P. the ſaid oak from the ſaid J. B. then and there had and received, and this he is ready to verify, wherefore he prays judgement, and that he of the premiſſes by the court here may he diſmiſſed, &c.

---

* P. 621

## * The King againſt Jewell.

KENT, to wit: heretofore, to wit, on the 15th day of March, in the 21ſt year of the reign of our lord Charles the 2d, the now king of England, &c. it is found by a certain inquiſition indented, taken for the moſt ſerene lord the king at Weſterham, in the county of Kent aforeſaid, before Robert Heath, gentleman, one of the coroners of the ſaid lord the king, of the county aforeſaid, on view of the body of Richard Green, then and there lying dead, by the oath of 12 jurors, good and lawful men of the county aforeſaid, who then and there being ſworn and charged to enquire for the ſaid lord the king, when, where, how and by what means the ſaid R. G. came to his death, ſay upon their oath, that the ſaid R. G. on the 11th day of March, at W. aforeſaid, about the third hour after mid-day, of the ſaid day, going with a wain drawn by two horſes and ſix plow oxen, then and there fell upon the ground, and then and there the ſaid wain paſſed over the right leg of the ſaid R. G. of the bruiſing and cruſhing of which he the ſaid R. G. from the ſaid 11th day of March in the 21ſt year aforeſaid until the 14th day of March, in the 21ſt year aforeſaid, did languiſh, and languiſhing did live, on which 14th

Inquiſition, whereby it was found that a wain drawn by two horſes and 6 oxen, run over one Green and killed him.

day

day of March in the 21st year aforesaid, he the said R. G. at W. aforesaid in the county aforesaid, of the mortal bruising and crushing aforesaid died, and so the jurors aforesaid upon their oath aforesaid say, that the said R. G. in the manner and form aforesaid came to his death, and the jurors aforesaid upon their oath aforesaid further say, that the two horses and six plow oxen aforesaid, of the value of 4l. and the wain aforesaid of the value of 40 shillings moved to the death of the said R. G. and remain in the custody of Thomas Jewell of Oxteed, in the county of Surry, husbandman, in witness whereof as well the said coroner as the jurors aforesaid to this inquisition have set their hands and seals the day and year and place first mentioned; which inquisition, Robert Heath, gentleman, one of the coroners of the lord the king of the county aforesaid, by his proper hands hath delivered here in the court of the said lord the king before the king himself of record to be determined, &c. whereupon the sheriff is commanded that he do not omit, &c. but that he cause come to answer, &c.

That the wain, &c. moved to his death, and that they remain in the custody of defendent Jewell.

Venire awarded.

And now, to wit, on the Wednesday next after three weeks of Easter, in the same term before the lord the king, at Westminster, comes the said Thomas Jewell, by J. G. his attorney, and having had oyer of the inquisition aforesaid, saith, that he doth not apprehend that the said lord the now king will or ought any further impeach or trouble him the said T. J. for the premisses in the inquisition above specified, because he saith that Westerham, aforesaid, in the inquisition aforesaid above mentioned is, and from the time whereof the memory of man is not to the contrary, hath been an antient village, within the manor of Westham, otherwise Westerham in the said county of Kent, and that long before the taking of the inquisition aforesaid, the lord Edward the first, heretofore king of England, was seized of and in the said manor of W. otherwise W. with its rights, members and * appurtenances, in the said county of Kent, in his demesne *as of fee* in right of his crown, and so being thereof seized, the said Edward the 1st heretofore king of England with a regard to charity and the health of the soul of Elinor of fair memory, heretofore queen of England his consort, by his charter duly made under the great seal of England, for the consideration in the same contained, gave, granted and confirmed for himself and his heirs, to God and to the church of St. Peter, Westminster, and to Walter, then abbot and prior, and to the convent of the same place, among other things the manor aforesaid by the name of the manor of Westerham, with the appurtenances in the county of Kent, aforesaid, to have and to hold to the said church, abbot, prior

Plea. That Westerham the place where the death happened is within the manor of Westerham.

* P. 622.

*The king cannot be said to be seized in his demesne as of fee, but "in his demesne." Vid 2 Bla. Com. 105.*

That Ed. the 1st being seized of the said manor

granted it to the abbot and prior and convent of St Peter's Westminster.

prior and convent and their successors, with all its appurtenances, together with the return of writs and all the liberties and free customs which they then had in any other of their lands or other things whatsoever, by the charters of his progenitors then late kings of England, and of him the said king, as by the said charter here in court produced more fully appeareth: by virtue of which charter the then abbot and convent of the place aforesaid, were seized of the manor aforesaid with the appurtenances to them and their successors, in their demesne as of fee in the right of their church aforesaid. And so being thereof seized the lord Richard the 2d, late king of England, by his charter duly made under the great seal of England, bearing date the 18th day of December, in the 17th year of his reign, reciting, that whereas among the other liberties and franchises, to the beloved in Christ of the late lord the king, the abbot and convent of the church of St. Peter's, Westminster, by the charters of St. Edward and others his progenitors, formerly king's of England granted, and by the said late king to the said abbot and convent confirmed, it was granted that they should have all liberties for ever, and that if any of their men or tenants who were not earls or barons, ought to lose his life or member for his crime, or should fly and would not abide judgement, or should commit any crime for which he ought to lose his chattles, wheresoever justice ought to be done, whether in his court or in other courts, the chattles should belong to the said abbot and convent, and that it should be lawful for them without the hinderance of his sheriffs, or bailiffs or others, to put themselves into seizin of the said chattles in the said cases and others, whensoever his bailiffs if those chattles should belong to him the said late king, should and ought to seize them into his hands; and if any tenant of the said abbot and convent and of their house should forfeit his fee, which he then held of the said abbot and convent and their house, that it should be lawful for them to put themselves into seizin of the said fee, and that fee with the appurtenances to possess notwithstanding that the said late king and his progenitors had been accustomed to possess the fees of fugitives and offenders for one year and one day; and if any of their men or tenants, (earls and barons excepted) should be amerced before the said late lord the king, his justices, sheriffs, constables, foresters, bailiffs or any other his ministers of whatsoever condition they might be, for whatsoever cause, crime or forfeiture, the said abbot and convent should have all amerciaments and fines for licence to agree without any hindrance or obstruction from them, and if perchance in any case the said * amerciaments

The abbot and convent seized.

That Richard the 2d by his charter reciting that it was granted to the said abbot, &c. by the charters of St. Edward, &c. that they should have all liberties, &c.

* P. 623.

ments by his bailiffs, or the bailiffs of his heirs, should be collected into the Exchequer of the said lord the king or of his heirs they should be restored by the vice-treasurer for the time being to the said Abbot, Convent and their successors, without dimunition, which liberties and franchises were granted and confirmed to the said Abbot and Convent, by the said progenitors of the said lord the king in pure and perpetual frankalmoigne with all liberties and free customs which the royal power could bountifully bestow upon any religious house, as in the charters and confirmation of the said lord the king aforesaid, is more fully contained, and that the said late lord the king, Richard the 2d was given to understand that the said Abbot and Convent, of their said liberties and franchises in the Exchequer, of the said late lord the king, and in the court of the marshal, and elsewhere, then lately were impeached, for this because it seemed to the officers of the said places as they then said, that divers words contained in the said charters, were not general enough and also were not sufficiently special, to have an allowance of the liberties and franchises aforesaid; the said late king, at the intreaty of the said Abbot and convent, and in consideration of the great devotion and especial affection which his said progenitors had to the same place and of their good and pious intention in granting the franchises and liberties aforesaid, and willing for the greater quiet and security of the said Abbot and convent, and their successors to take away, blot out, and entirely to remove such ambiguity, for the honour of God and St. Peter and also of St. Edward, of his especial grace and with the consent of his council declared, granted and confirmed, for himself and his heirs, to the said Abbot and Convent and their successors, the said liberties and franchises in the manner and form following, to wit; that the said Abbot and Convent and their successors, and their house for ever should have and hold all the goods and chattles of their men and tenants, as well freeman as villains, and of all the resiants within and upon their lands, demesnes and fees, felons of themselves and other felons whatsoever, fugitives or offenders, so that if any man or tenant or resiant as aforesaid, for any felony or for any occasion whatsoever, ought to lose his life or member, or should fly and would not abide judgment, or should be outlawed, or should commit any crime or forfeiture or any other thing for which he ought to loose his goods and chattles, wheresoever justice should be done thereupon, whether it should be before the said late lord the king, or his heirs, the justices of the said lord the king or of his heirs of the one bench or

And that the said Abbot &c. had been impeached because the words in the charters were neither sufficiently general nor special.

the said king Richard by the said charter confirmed the said liberties franchises &c. and granted them to the said Abbot &c. by special words and among the rest deodands expresly.

the other in the Chancery or Exchequer, of the ſaid lord the king and of his heirs, or before the ſteward, marſhall and and comptroller of the houſehold of the ſaid lord the king, and of his heirs or before the juſtices in Eyre of the ſaid lord the king, and of his heirs, aſſigned to take common pleas and pleas of the crown and pleas of the foreſt, or before the juſtices of the ſaid lord the king and of his heirs, aſſigned to hear and determine felonies, treſpaſſes and all other things whatſoever at the ſuit of the ſaid lord the king and of his heirs and to take aſſizes, juries and certificates and all other inquiſitions whatſoever, and to deliver gaols, or before the keepers of the peace and the juſtices of the ſaid lord the king and of his heirs aſſigned to preſerve the ſtatutes and ordinances concerning artificers, labourers, ſervants and victuallers and alſo of
* P. 624. * weights and meaſures, or before whatſoever other juſtices officers and miniſter of the ſaid lord the king, and of his heirs, as well in the preſence of the ſaid lord the king and of his heirs, as in the abſence of the ſaid lord the king, and of his heirs, and in all other courts and places, the ſaid goods and chattles ſhould belong to the ſaid abbot and convent and their ſucceſſors, and that it ſhould be well lawful for them and their ſervants and miniſters without the hindrance of the ſaid lord the king or his heirs, or of all the officers, juſtices and miniſters aforeſaid or of the ſheriffs, coroners, eſchetators, mayors, bailiffs, or other officers whatſoever of the ſaid lord the king and of his heirs, to put themſelves into ſeizin of the ſaid goods, chattles, in all caſes whatſoever, whenſoever the officers, bailiffs or miniſters of the ſaid lord the king, or of his heirs ſhould and ought to ſeize the ſaid goods and chattles into his hands or into the hands of his heirs, if they ſhould belong to the ſaid lord the king or his heirs, and to retain the ſaid goods and chattles to the uſe and benefit of the ſaid abbot and convent, and that the ſaid abbot and convent, and their ſucceſſors and their houſe for ever, ſhould have all fines for treſpaſſes, oppreſſions, extortions, deceits, conſpiracies, concealments, regrating and foreſtalling, maintenances and other offences and miſpriſons whatſoever, and all fines for licence to agree, and alſo all amerciaments, redemptions, forfeited iſſues and all forfeitures as well of attainder as of all other things, year day and waſte, deodands and treaſure trove, and all things which to the ſaid lord the king or his heirs, might or ought to belong as well for the ſaid year, day and waſte as for all murders and felonies whatſoever, of all their men and tenants and reſiants aforeſaid, in whatſoever courts of the ſaid lord the king and his heirs as well to wit; before the ſaid lord the king and his heirs, and the chief juſtices of the

the said lord the king and of his heirs, and in the Chancery of the said lord the king, and of his heirs and before the treasurer and barons of the Exchequer, of the said lord the king and of his heirs and before the justices of the said lord the king, and of his heirs of the common bench, and before the steward, marshal and comptroller of the household, of the said lord the king and of his heirs, and before the justices in Eyre of the said lord the king, and of his heirs assigned to take common pleas and pleas of the crown and pleas of the forest and also before the justices of the said lord the king, and his heirs assigned to hear and determine felonies, trespasses, extortions, oppressions and other grievances and misdeeds at the suit of the said lord the king, and of his heirs and to take assize, jurys and certificates, and all other inquisitions whatsoever, and to deliver gaols, and also before the justices of the peace and the justices of the said lord the king and his heirs assigned to preserve the statutes and ordinances concerning artificers, labourers, servants, victuallers, hostlers and of weights and measures, as before whatsoever other justices, officers and ministers of the said lord the king, and his heirs as well in the presence of the said lord the king and his heirs, as in the absence of the said lord the king and his heirs, wheresoever if it should happen that the said men, and tenants, and resiants, should be fined or amerced, or should forfeit their issues, or that the year day, and waste, forfeitures, deodands, murders and felonies should be adjudged, which fines and amerciaments, redemptions, year day and waste, * forfeitures, deodands, treasure trove, murders and felonies to the said lord the king and his heirs would belong, if they had not been granted to the said Abbot and Convent and their successors; and that they and their successors, and their house should have and preceive all and singular the premisses in the form aforesaid, and that it should be well lawful for the said Abbot and Convent, their successors, by themselves, their bailiffs and ministers, to levy, collect, perceive and have all the said fines, amerciaments and redemptions, forfeited issues, forfeitures, deodands, treasure trove and all things which might belong to the said lord the king, or his heirs, for the said year day and waste, murders and felonies without any challenge, impeachment or hinderance of the said lord the king, or his heirs, and of all the officers, justices and ministers aforesaid, and of all the other justices, escheators, sheriffs, coroners, bailiffs or ministers whatsoever of the said lord the king, or his heirs, as by the said charter in court here, in like manner produced more fully appeareth, by virtue of which the said Abbot and Convent of the monastery of St. Peter's, Westminster, aforesaid, were

Deodands.

* P. 265.

By virtue of which the said abbot and convent were seized of the said liberties &c.

were seized of the liberties, privileges, royalties, and franchises aforesaid, above in the form aforesaid, given, granted and confirmed to them and their successors, as of fee and right, in right of their monastery aforesaid, and all the liberties, privileges, royalties and franchises aforesaid, had and enjoyed, according to the form and effect of the grant aforesaid; And the said T. J. further saith, that the abbot and convent of the place aforesaid, of the monastery aforesaid, and among other things of the manor of W. otherwise W. aforesaid, with its rights, members and appurtenances, and of the liberties, privileges and franchises aforesaid, to them and their successors being seized, afterwards, to wit; on the 16th day of January, in the 31st year of the reign of the lord Henry the 8th, late king of England, one William, then abbot of the monastery of St. Peter, Westminster, aforesaid, and the convent of the said place, by their writing sealed with the common seal of the said abbot and convent, bearing date the said day and year and in the court of Chancery of the said late king, in the due manner enrolled of record, with their unanimous assent and consent, and of their free will, gave, granted and confirmed, to the said lord the late king Henry the 8th, their entire monastery aforesaid, and the church, cloister, scite, circuit, compass and precincts of the same, and also all and singular their lordships, manors, messuages, lands, tenements, liberties, privileges, possessions and hereditaments, whatsoever, as well spiritual and temporal, (among others) in the said counties of Middlesex and Kent, and elsewhere wheresoever with all their rights, members and appurtenances, to have, hold and enjoy the entire monastery aforesaid, and all the lordships, lands, tenements, and hereditaments, and the other premisses aforesaid, with the appurtenances aforesaid, to the said late king Henry the 8th, his heirs, and successors for ever, by virtue of which and by force of the statute made and enacted in this behalf in the parliament of the said late king Henry the 8th, held at Westminster, aforesaid, the said late king Henry the 8th, was seized of the monastery, lordships, manors, lands, tenements and the other premisses aforesaid, with the appurtenances in his demesne as of fee in right of his crown of England, and so being thereof seized the said late king Henry the 8th by his letters patent made under the great seal of England, bearing date at Terling, the 16th day of * August, in the 32d year of his reign, for the consideration in the same mentioned, gave and granted among other things to John Gresham, knight, the said manor of Westram otherwise Westerham and Etonbrigg, with all their rights, members and appurtenances in the said county of Kent, by the name of all those his manors of W. otherwise

that the said abbot and convent afterwards by their deed granted their monastery, manors liberties &c. to king Henry the 8th.

* P. 626.

otherwise

otherwise W. and E. otherwise E. otherwise E. with all their rights, members and appurtenances in his county of Kent, then lately belonging and appertaining to the monastery of St. Peter Westminster in his county of Middlesex then lately dissolved, and being parcel of the possessions of the said late monastery, and of all those his lands, tenements, meadows, pastures and hereditaments, called Charmir, and his two water mills with their appurtenances in Westram, in his said county of Kent, to the late monastery lately belonging appertaining and being parcel of the possessions of the late monastery and also of all those his messuages, lands, tenements, mills, tofts, cottages, meadows, feedings, pastures, woods, underwoods, waters, fishings, commons, furze, brush-wood, marshes, wastes, moors, rents, reversions, services, rents reserved upon any demises and grants, knights fees, escheats, reliefs, and all other his rights, benefits and hereditaments whatsoever with the appurtenances situate lying and being in the towns, fields, parishes and hamlets of Westram otherwise W. and Etonbrigg, otherwise Edullenburgh, otherwise E. in his county of Kent and elsewhere wheresoever, to the said manors or either of them, in any manner belonging and appertaining, or as members or parcel of the said manors or either of them, being had, known, used and reputed; also he gave and for the consideration aforesaid by the said letters patent granted to the said John Gresham, within the manors aforesaid and the other premisses, and every parcel thereof, as many, such, and the like fairs, issues and profits of fairs, and courts leet or view of frankpledge, and free warrens and all things to the view of frankpledge and free warrens or either of them belonging or appertaining, and also the assize and essay of bread, wine and beer, chattles waived, estrays and other rights, profits, commodities and advantages whatsoever, as many, such, and the like, and as fully and entirely and in as ample manner and form as the last abbot and the late convent, of the said monastery or any of their predecessors in the right of the said late monastery or before the said monastery came to the hands of the said late late king, ever had, held or enjoyed, or any of them ever had, held or enjoyed, or ought to have, hold, or enjoy in the said manors, lands, tenements, and the other premisses, or in part thereof, by reason or pretence of any prescription, use or customs before that time had or used, or by reason or pretence of any grant or confirmation or letters patent by the said late king, or by any of his progenitors, to the said late last abbot and convent, of the said late monastery or to any of their predecessors in any wise made or granted, or in any wise, in any other manner, and as fully and entirely and

That king Henry the 8th granted the said manor and another to Sir John Gresham, with all rights, members and appurtenances, as fully as the abbot and convent ever enjoyed the same.

and in as ample manner and form as the ſaid laſt abbot and late convent of the ſaid late monaſtery or any of their predeceſſors, in the right of that * monaſtery, at any time before the diſſolution of the ſaid late monaſtery had, held or enjoyed, or ought to have, hold, and enjoy the ſaid manors, lands, tenements, courts leet or view of frankpledge, chattles waived, eſtrays, free warrens and all and ſingular the premiſſes above expreſſed and ſpecified, with the appurtenances or any parcel thereof, and as fully and entirely and in as ample manner and form as all and ſingular the premiſſes had come or ought to have came to the hands of the ſaid late lord the king, by reaſon or pretence of the diſſolution of the ſaid late monaſtery, or by reaſon or pretence of any charter, gift, grant and confirmation by the ſaid late abbot and convent, of the ſaid late monaſtery, under the ſeal of their convent to the ſaid lord the king made, or otherwiſe in any other manner, and as fully and entirely as in the hands of the ſaid late king they then were or ought to be; to have, hold and enjoy the ſaid manors, lands, tenements, courts leet or view of frankpledge, free warrens, rents, reverſions, ſervices and all and ſingular the other premiſſes above expreſſed and ſpecified, with all their appurtenances, to the ſaid John Greſham, his heirs and aſſigns, for ever, to be held of the ſaid late king his heirs and ſucceſſors, in capite by the ſervice of the twentieth part of one knights fee, and yielding and paying thereout yearly to the ſaid late king, his heirs and ſucceſſors, nine pounds, ſix ſhillings and nine pence ſterling, at the court of the augmentations of the revenue of the crown of England, to be paid on the feaſt of St. Michael the archangel, in every year, for all rents, ſervices and demands whatſoever, thereout to the ſaid late king his heirs and ſucceſſors in any manner to be yielded, paid, or to be made, as by the ſaid letters patent among other things in the ſame contained more fully appeareth: by virtue whereof the ſaid John Greſham, was ſeized of the ſaid manor of Weſtram, otherwiſe W. with its rights, members and appurtenances, in his demeſne as of fee and of the liberties, privileges and franchiſes aforeſaid, to him in the form aforeſaid granted, and by the abbot and convent aforeſaid, ſo as aforeſaid enjoyed, as of fee and right; and the ſaid liberties, privileges and franchiſes had and enjoyed according to the form and effect of the letters patent aforeſaid; the eſtate, title, intereſt, inheritance, claim and demand of which John Greſham, by good and ſufficient conveyances and aſſurances in the law, came to Marmaduke Greſham, baronet, and the ſaid Marmaduke Greſhham, baronet, on the ſaid 11th day of March, in the 21ſt

* P. 627.

By virtue whereof Sir John Greſham was ſeized in fee.

That the eſtate, &c. of Sir John Greſham by conveyance came to Sir Marmaduke Greſham.

21st year of the said lord the now king aforesaid, and long before and from that time hitherto was and as yet is seized of the said manor of W. otherwise W. with its rights, members and appurtenances in his demesne as of fee, and of the liberties, privileges and franchises aforesaid, as of fee and right, and so being thereof seized, the goods and chattles aforesaid, to wit; the said two horses, six plow oxen and the wain in the inquisition aforesaid, above mentioned by the death of the said Richard Green, in the form and for the cause aforesaid in the said inquisition above specified, so as aforesaid happening at W. aforesaid, within the manner aforesaid, became and were * forfeited, and that thereupon the said Marmaduke Gresham, before the taking of the inquisition aforesaid, to wit; on the said 15th day of March, in the 21st year aforesaid, at W. aforesaid, within the manor aforesaid, the goods and chattles aforesaid for the cause aforesaid so as aforesaid forfeited, and to the said Marmaduke of right belonging, seized, and the goods and chattles so seized to the said Thomas for the use of the said Marmaduke safely to be kept, did deliver, and that the said goods and chattles, at the said time of the taking of the inquisition aforesaid, in the hands of the said Thomas Jewell in the form and for the cause aforesaid, were and remained as by the inquisition aforesaid is found, nevertheless for the use and benefit of the said Marmaduke Gresham, and this the said Thomas Jewell is ready to verify, wherefore he prays judgment, and that he because of the goods and chattles aforesaid, in the inquisition aforesaid above specified in his hands in the form and for the cause aforesaid, so as aforesaid remaining, by the court here may be dismissed and discharged, &c.

Who thereby became seized of &c.

* P. 628.

And so being seized, the said wain, horses and oxen, became forfeited.

That Sir Marmaduke seized them and delivered them to defendant to keep.

Wherefore, &c.

And Geoffrey Palmer, knight and baronet, attorney general of the said lord the now king, who for the said lord the king, in this behalf prosecuteth, having seen the plea of the said Thomas Jewell, and the several charters and letters patent in the same plea mentioned, being seen and by him fully understood and diligently examined, for this, because that if sufficiently appears to him that the liberties, franchises and royalties aforesaid were granted and confirmed, and according to the grants thereof aforesaid from time to time within the manor aforesaid were had and enjoyed in the manner and form as the said Thomas Jewell, above, by pleading hath alledged, the said attorney general of the said lord the now king, doth not deny it, but the plea aforesaid by the said Thomas, in the form aforesaid pleaded, confesses and in all things acknowledges to be true, and saith, that he will not any further prosecute for the said lord the king in the premisses, against the said Thomas Jewell.

Confession and non vult ulterius prosequi.

*Geoffrey Palmer.*

The

## The King against the Borough of Great Torrington.

Recital of three inquisitions found before the coroner 1st found Dennis, felo de se, and that his goods, &c. are in the hands of Blackmore to the use, &c. 2d that Blake died per infortunium, and that the deodand is in the hands of the mayor, &c. 3d, That Randle died per * P. 629. infortunium, and that the deodand is in the hands of Mortimer to the use of the borough.

Venire to answer awarded.

Plea That James the 1st by letters patent granted the said forfeitures to the mayor, aldermen, and burgesses of the said borough.

DEVONSHIRE, to wit,—Heretofore, to wit, on the 10th day of January, in the 21st year of the reign of our lord Charles the 2d, by a certain inquisition taken at Great Torrington, *and so throughout the whole inquisition and schedule thereto annexed*, this inquisition was taken upon the body of Abraham Dennis, who was a felon of himself, and returns that the goods are in the hands of Thomas Blackmore, to the use of the borough and town of Torrington: The borough of Great Torrington, in the county of Devon, to wit,—likewise heretofore, to wit, on the first day of February in the —— year &c. by a certain other inquisition taken at Great Torrington, &c. "*and so throughout the whole inquisition*," this inquisition was taken upon the body of Christopher Blake, who died by misadventure, and returns that the deodand was in the hands of the mayor, &c. of the borough and town of Great Torrington; The borough and town of Great Torrington, to wit, likewise heretofore to wit, on the 17th day of March, &c. by a certain other inquisition taken at Great Torrington, &c. *and so throughout the whole inquisition*; this inquisition was taken upon the body of Theophilus Randle * who died by misadventure, and returns that the goods are in the hands of William Mortimer, to the use of the borough and town aforesaid; which several inquisions, the several coroners aforesaid afterwards, for certain causes, by their proper hands, severally delivered here in the court of the said lord the king, before the king himself of record to be determined, &c. whereupon the sheriff of the county aforesaid was commanded that he do not omit, &c. but that he cause them to come to answer, &c. And now, to wit, on the wednesday next after the morrow of the Holy Trinity, in this same term, before the lord the king at Westminster, come the mayor, aldermen, and burgesses of the borough and town of T. in the said county of D. by W. M. their attorney, and having had oyer of the several inquisitions aforesaid, severally say that they do not apprehend that the said lord the now king will or ought any further impeach or trouble them the said mayor, aldermen, and burgesses, or the said T. B. and W. M. for occasion of the premisses, because they say that the borough and town of Torrington aforesaid, is an antient and populous borough and town, and the said mayor,

mayor, aldermen and burgesses of the said borough and town have had, used and enjoyed, and have use and enjoy divers liberties, franchises, privileges, preheminences and other hereditaments by divers charters, and letters patent of divers of the kings and queens of this kingdom of England; and that long before the said times in which, &c. to wit; on the 22d day of December, in the 15th year of the reign of the lord James, late king of England, F. and J. and in the 51st year, &c. of Scotland, the said lord James, late king, by his letters patent, sealed with his great seal of England, and in court here produced, the date of which is at Westminster the said day and year last mentioned, for himself, his heirs and successors, gave and granted among other things in the said letters patent mentioned, to the said mayor, aldermen, and burgesses of the borough and town aforesaid, and to their successors, all and all manner of goods and chattles forfeited, waifs and estrays, and the goods and chattles of all felons, and fugitives whatsoever, and also of felons of themselves, of all and singular the burgesses, resiants, and inhabitants, within the borough and town aforesaid, and the whole and entire residue of the parish of T. being without the limits and jurisdiction of the borough and town aforesaid, by the letters patent aforesaid, to the said borough and town annexed and united, and within the liberties and precincts of the same, from time to time happening and arising; and that it should be well lawful for the said mayor, aldermen and burgesses of the borough and town and parish aforesaid, and for their successors, according to the law and custom of this kingdom of England, to put themselves into seizin and possession of the said goods and chattles, emoluments, advantages, and the other premisses by the said letters patent granted, and to collect, levy, receive, and retain all and singular the premisses to the use and behoof of the said mayor, aldermen, and burgesses, and their successors, of the borough and town aforesaid, without the hindrance of the said late king, his heirs and successors, or of any of his officers or ministers, or of the officers or ministers of his heirs or successors, by virtue of which letters patent the said mayor, aldermen, and burgesses of the borough and town aforesaid, of the liberties, privileges, and franchises aforesaid, in the said plea above recited, were, and as yet are seized as of fee and right, and so being thereof seized, the said mayor, aldermen and burgesses, the goods and chattles aforesaid, which were the cause of the * death of the said Christopher Blake, in the inquisition aforesaid, above specified, taken upon view of the body of the said

Whereby they are seized in fee of the said liberties, &c.

* P. 630.

And being so seized they took the goods of Blake within the borough and Blackmore and Mortimer respectively seized the deodands by their command and to their use.

C. B. took and seized within the borough and town aforesaid, to their own proper use as it was and is well lawful for them to do, and the said T. Blackmore, the goods and chattles which were the said Abraham Dennis's, a felon of himself, mentioned in the said inventory to the inquisition aforesaid taken upon the view of the body of the said A. B. annexed, took and seized within the borough and town aforesaid, by the command and to the use of the said mayor, aldermen and burgesses; and the said William Mortimer, the goods and chattles aforesaid which were the cause of the death of the said T. R. in the inquisition aforesaid, above specified, taken upon view of the body of the said T. R. took and seized within the said borough and town, by the command and to the use of the said mayor, aldermen and burgesses of the said borough and town, with this that the borough and town of Great Torrington, in the several inquisitions mentioned, and the borough and Town of T. in the letters patent aforesaid, and in the said plea mentioned, is one and the same borough and town, and not another nor different, and the said A, Dennis, C. Blake and T. Randle, at the said times of their several deaths aforesaid, were burgesses, residents and inhabitants within the borough and town aforesaid, all and singular which things in the said plea above contained, the said mayor, aldermen and burgesses, and the said T. B. and W. M. are ready to verify, as the court &c. wherefore they pray judgment, and that all and singular the liberties, privileges and franchises, aforesaid, to the said mayor, aldermen and burgesses, and their successors for ever afterwards may be allowed and adjudged and that the said mayor, aldermen and burgesses, and the said T. B. and W. M. of the premisses by the court here may be dismissed, &c.

Averments.

The

## The King against the Hundred of Chippenham.

The Liberty of the Hundred of Chippenham, to wit; } HERETOFORE, to wit, on the 26th day of March in the 24th year of the reign, &c. by a certain inquisition taken at the parish of Box, within the liberty of the hundred aforesaid, &c. "*and so throughout the whole inquisition,*" this inquisition was taken upon view of the body of dame Martha Hungate, widow, who died by misadventure, and returns that the goods are in the hands of William Lord, bailiff to the duke of York, &c. which inquisition, &c. whereupon the sheriff was commanded, &c. And now, to wit; on the Wednesday next after fifteen days of Easter, in this same term, before the lord the king, at Westminster, comes the said William Lord, by W. M. his attorney, and having had oyer of the inquisition aforesaid, saith, that he doth not apprehend that the said lord the now king will or ought any further impeach or trouble him the said W. L. because of the premisses in the inquisition aforesaid mentioned, because he saith that John Danvers, knight, now deceased, in his life time was seized of and in the hundred of C. aforesaid, in the county of W. aforesaid, with all rents, jurisdictions and profits whatsoever, to the said hundred in any wise belonging or appertaining in his demesne as of fee, and so being thereof seized, the said John Danvers among other things had, took, and enjoyed the goods and * chattles of felons of themselves and deodands, as it was well lawful for him to have, take and enjoy, and that the said John Danvers, so of the hundred aforesaid, with the appurtenances being seized, afterwards and before the taking of the inquisition aforesaid above specified, the hundred aforesaid with the appurtenances among other things came to the said lord Charles the 2d, now king of England, &c. by the forfeiture of the said J. D. by virtue of a certain act made and provided in the parliament begun and held at Westminster, in the county of Middlesex, on the 8th day of May in the 13th year of the reign of the said lord Charles the 2d, &c. entitled "*an act declaring pains penalties and forfeitures, imposed by the statute upon some notorious offenders, excepted, out of the act of free and general pardon, indemnity and oblivion.*" And in the hands of the said lord the king, were by virtue of the said act, and that the said lord the king was thereof seized in his demesne as of fee, in right of his crown of England, and so being thereof seized, the said lord the king, afterwards and before

Recital of inquisition wherein lady Hungate was found to have died per infortunium, and that four horses and a chariot moverunt ad mortum, which remain in the hands of William Lord, bailiff to the duke of York. Who appears and pleads that Sir J Danvers was seized of the hundred of C—, and inter alia had deodands, &c.

* P. 631.

That the said hundred came to Ch. 2d, by the stat. of the 12th of his reign.

That the ſaid king afterwards granted the ſaid hundred, &c to the duke of York in fee, and all deodands, &c.

before the taking of the inquiſition aforeſaid, to wit; on the 20th day of September, in the 14th year of his reign, by his letters patent bearing date the ſame day and year, ſealed with his great ſeal of England, of his royal and free gift, for and towards the better ſupport of the eſtate of his moſt dear brother James, duke of York, and his heirs, and for divers other good cauſes and conſiderations, the ſaid lord the king ſpecially moving of his eſpecial grace, certain knowledge and mere motion, among other things gave and granted, and for himſelf, his heirs and ſucceſſors gave and granted to his moſt dear brother James, duke of York, his heirs and aſſigns, the whole ſaid hundred of C. in the county of Wilts, aforeſaid, with all rents, juriſdictions and profits whatſoever to the ſaid hundred in any wiſe belonging or appertaining, and all and ſingular meſſuages, houſes, edifices, ſtructures, barns, ſtables, dove cotes, orchards, gardens, crofts, curtillages, lands, tenements, meadows, paſtures, commons, demeſne lands, woods, underwoods, coppices, waſtes, furze, bruſh-wood, moors, marſhes, waters, watercourſes, pools, parks, fiſh-ponds, fiſhing, ſuits to mills, mulctures, mines, quarries, rents, reverſions, remainders, rents-charge, rents-ſeck, rents of aſſize, and rents and ſervices as well of free as of cuſtomary tenants, farms, fee farms, annuities, knights fees, wards-ſhips, marriages, eſcheats, reliefs, heriots, deodands, fines, amerciaments, courts leet, and view, of frank-pledge and courts baron, with the appurtenances, waifs and the chattles of felons and fugitives, and felons of themſelves, of thoſe put in the exigent, outlaws and convicts, neifs and villains, with their ſeveral eſtovers, fairs, markets, tolls, cuſtoms, rights, juriſdictions, franchiſes, liberties, privileges profits, commodities, advantages, emoluments, and hereditaments whatſoever, of whatſoever kind, nature or ſpecies, or by whatſoever names or additions of name they were known, called or named within the ſaid hundred of C. as by the ſaid letters patent among other things more fully appeareth; by virtue of which letters patent the ſaid duke of York entered into the hundred aforeſaid, with the appurtenances and was and yet is thereof ſeized in his demeſne as of fee, and right, and of the liberties, privileges and franchiſes aforeſaid, as of fee and right and the ſaid duke of York ſo being thereof ſeized, that ſaid dame Martha Hungate in the * inquiſition aforeſaid above mentioned, came to her death by miſadventure, in the manner and form as by the inquiſition aforeſaid is ſpecified, and the ſaid four horſes and chariot in the ſaid inquiſition mentioned, which moved to the death of the ſaid dame Martha

Deodands.

* P. 632.

That lady Hungate came to her death as aforeſaid, that the horſes and tha Hungate, were within the hundred of C. aforeſaid, and that the ſaid W. L. in the inquiſition aforeſaid in like manner mentioned, at the time of the death of the ſaid M. H. and long before and as yet is the ſervant and bailiff of the ſaid duke of York, within the hundred aforeſaid, to take and ſeize goods and chattles forfeited to the ſaid duke of York, within the hundred aforeſaid, to the uſe and behoof of the ſaid duke, wherefore the ſaid W. L. ſaith, that he as the ſervant and bailiff of the ſaid duke of York as aforeſaid, within the hundred aforeſaid, the horſes and chariot in the inquiſition aforeſaid mentioned, which were the cauſe of the death of the ſaid dame M. H. as aforeſaid, to the uſe and behoof of the ſaid duke of York, took and ſeized, and not otherwiſe, and the ſaid horſes and chariot to the ſaid James duke of York delivered, wherefore the ſaid W. L. prays judgment and that he as well of the inquiſition aforeſaid as of the duty aforeſaid, in the inquſition aforeſaid ſpecified, by the court here may be diſmiſſed and diſcharged, &c.

chariot which moved to her death were within the hundred and that defendant as the duke of York's bailiff, ſeized them to his uſe, and delivered them to him.

Wherefore, &c.

---

# The King and Trethewy againſt Northcote and Crooke.

## Hilary, 33d and 34th Charles 2d.

DEVON—It is found among the memorandums of this Exchequer of the 33d and 34th years of the reign of Charles the 2d, &c. to wit; among the rolls of the term of St. Hilary, in the 33d and 34th years aforeſaid, on behalf of this remembrancer, in theſe words, to wit; be it remembered that Richard Anwill, gent. clerk of the outlawries preſent here in court, on the 12th day of February, in this term, in his proper perſon delivered here the tranſcript of a certain writ of outlawry pronounced againſt Halſwell Northcote, gent. for further execution to be done thereupon for the ſaid lord the king, the tenor of which tranſcript follows in theſe words, to wit; Charles the 2d, &c. to the ſheriff of Devon, greeting, we command you that you do not omit becauſe of any liberty of your county, but that you diligently enquire by the oath of good and lawful men of your county, what goods and chattles, lands and

Pleading to on outlawry tranſcribed into the Exchequer.

Writ of capias utlagatum.

and tenements, Halswell Northcote, of Great Torrington in your county, gent. hath, or had in your bailiwick on the 28th day of October, in the 31st year of our reign, or at any time afterwards on which day he was outlawed in your county, at the suit of Anthony, Trethewy, of a plea of debt, whereof he is convicted, as the sheriff of our county of Devon, to our justices at Westminster on a certain day now past, hath returned, and them by their oath cause to be extended and appraised, according to the true values of the same, and those which you shall find by that inquisition take into our hands and cause to be safely kept, so that you answer to us of the true values and issues of the same, and these being so extended and appraised, what you shall do therein certify to our justices at Westminster, on the octave of St. Martin, distinctly and plainly, under your seal and the seals of those by whose oath you shall make that extent and appraisments, and because that the said Halswell
* P. 633. * Northcote, so outlawed secrets himself and runs up and down in your county, in contempt of us and to the prejudice of our crown, as we have understood, we command you that you take the said Halswell wheresoever he may be found in your bailiwick, as well within liberties as without, and him safely keep so that you may have his body before our justices at Westminster, in the said term to do and receive what our court concerning him shall con- consider in this behalf, and have there this writ. Witness, Francis North, at Westminster, the 30th day of June in the 32d year of our reign.

*Cotton.*
*Levinz.*

Return. Non est inventus. The within named Halswell Northcote, is not found in my bailiwick, the residue of the execution of this writ appears in a certain inquisition to this writ annexed, Edward Seymour, baronet, sheriff of the county of Devon, to

Inquisition. wit; an inquisition, indented taken at Great Torrington in the county aforesaid, on the 20th day of September, in the 32d year of the reign of our Lord Charles the 2d. &c. before me, Edward Seymour, baronet, sheriff of the county aforesaid, by virtue of the writ of the said lord the king to me directed, and to this inquisition annexed, by the oath of Richard Tucker, &c. good and lawful men of the county aforesaid who say upon their oath that Halswell Northcote, in the said writ named, on the day of the

Which finds defendant seized in the right of his wife of, &c. taking of this inquisition was seized in his demesne as of freehold, in the right of Mary, his wife, of and in one capital messuages called Great Weeke, situate, lying and being,

ing, within the parish of Great Torrington, aforesaid, in the county aforesaid, of the clear yearly value in all its issues above reprisals, of forty pounds, which capital messuage, I the said sheriff into the hands of the said lord the king have seized and taken; also the jurors aforesaid, say upon their oath aforesaid that the said Halswell on the 28th day of October, in the 31st year of the reign of the said lord the king, or ever afterwards, on which day the said Halswell was outlawed in the county of Devon aforesaid, had no other lands or tenements, goods or chattles within the said county of Devon, which in any manner could come to the knowledge of the said jurors in witness whereof, as well I the said sheriff as the jurors aforesaid, have caused our seals to be put to this inquisition, on the day, year and place aforesaid, Edward Seymour, baronet; as is there contained; And now, to wit; on the octave of the purification of the blessed virgin Mary, in this term comes here one Unton Crooke, gent. tenant of the said one capital messuage, called Great Weeke, situate, lying and being, within the parish of Great Torrington, in the inquisition aforesaid mentioned, by Anselem Beaumont, his attorney, and prays oyer of the transcript of the writ and inquisition aforesaid, and it is read to him, which being read, heard, and by him understood, he complains that he under colour of the premisses is grievously vexed and disquieted, and that the said capital messuage are taken and seized into the hands of the said lord the king, and this not justly, because protesting that the transcript aforesaid and the matter in the same contained, are not sufficient in law to which he hath no necessity, neither is he bound by the law of the land to answer, for plea, nevertheless the said Unton Crooke, saith, that long before the said 28th day of October, in the * 31st year, &c. aforesaid, on which day the said Halswell Northcote, gent. is supposed to have been outlawed at the suit of the said Anthony Trethewy, of a plea of debt whereof he is convicted, to wit; on the 20th day of March in the year of our Lord 1648, and in the 24th year of the reign of our late lord Charles the first, one William Hockin was seized of the said capital messuage in his demesne as of fee, and so being thereof seized by his indenture made at the parish of Great Torrington, aforesaid, between the said William Hockin, by the name, &c. of the one part, and one Thomas Chase, by the name, &c. of the other part, one part of which sealed with the seal of the said William Hockin, the date of which is the said day and year, the said Unton Crooke produces here in court, for the consideration in the said indenture mentioned, the said William, at

The tenant appears.

Protestation.

* P. 634.

And pleads a lease made to T. C. before the outlawry.

at Great Torrington, in the said county of Devon, demised, granted, bargained, sold, aliened, assigned and set over to the said Thomas Chase, the said capital messuage by the name, &c. to have and to hold to the said Thomas Chase, his executors, administrators and assigns, from the 23d day of June, then next ensuing unto the end and for and during the term of one hundred years, from that time next ensuing, fully to be compleated and ended, yielding thereout yearly to the said William Hockin, his heirs and assigns, during the term aforesaid, one pepper corn if the same should be lawfully demanded, by virtue of which the said Thomas Chase into the said capital messuage entered, and was thereof possessed for the term aforesaid and so being thereof possessed, the said Thomas Chase, by his indenture made at Great Torrington, aforesaid, bearing date the 25th day of March, in the year of our Lord, 1653, between the said Thomas Chase by the name, &c. and the said William Hockin, by the name, &c. of the one part, and the said Unton Crooke, by the name of Unton Crooke, of the inner temple, London, gent. of the other part, one part of which sealed with the seals of the said Thomas and William, the said Unton produces here in court, for the consideration in the said indenture mentioned, they the said Thomas Chase and William Hockin, granted, bargained, sold, aliend, assigned and set over to the said Unton Crooke, now here pleading, his executors, administrators and assigns, the said capital messuage to have and to hold to the said Unton Crooke, his executors, administrators and assigns, for and during the residue of the said term of one hundred years, as yet to come and unexpired; by virtue of which the said Unton Crooke, into the said capital messuage entered and was and as yet is thereof possessed, during the residue of the term of one hundred years, as yet to come and unexpired, all and singular which things the said Unton Crooke is ready to verify, as the court, &c. wherefore he prays judgment, and that the hands of the said lord the king, from the possession of the said capital messuage during the residue of the said term of one hundred years, as yet to come and unexpired, may be removed, and that he the said U. C. to his possession thereof together with the issues and profits thereof, whereof the said lord the king is not as yet answered may be restored, and also that as well the said Edward Seymour, baronet, late sheriff aforesaid, as also all others from that time now, and who afterwards shall be sheriffs of the said county of Devon, of the issues and profits of the said capital * messuage during the term aforesaid, may be discharged, and also that the said Unton Crooke,

That T. C. bargained and sold to this defendant.

Who entered and was and yet is possessed.

And prays an amoveas manus.

* P. 635.

Crooke, as to the premisses by the court here may be dismissed, &c.

And Robert Sawyer, knight, attorney general of the said lord the now king, who for the said lord the king in this behalf prosecutes, saith, that the said plea of the said Unton Crooke, above pleaded, and the matter in the same contained are not sufficient in law to remove the hands of the said lord the king, from the possession of the premisses in the said inquisition mentioned, and that he to the said plea in the manner and form above pleaded hath no necessity, neither is he bound by the law of the land to answer, and this he is ready to verify, as the court, &c. wherefore for want of a sufficient plea of the said Unton Crooke, in this behalf, the said attorney general of the said lord the king prays judgment, and that the said premisses in the hands of the said lord the king may remain, and that the said lord the king may be answered for the issues thereof, and for causes of demurrer in law upon the said plea, the said attorney general for the said lord the king according to the form of the statute in such case made and provided, sets down and to the court here shows the causes following, to wit: that the said plea doth not answer to the title and estate of the said Halswell Northcote, in the inquisition aforesaid mentioned, and found, and is double and incertain and wants form, and also this that the said Unton, in the said plea doth not confess and avoid nor traverse or deny the estate and interest of the said Halswell Northcote, in and by the inquisition aforesaid mentioned and found. And the said Unton Crooke because that he above by pleading hath alledged, sufficient matter in law to remove the hands of the said lord the king, from the possession of the premisses in the inquisition aforesaid mentioned, which he is ready to verify which matter the said attorney general of the said lord the king doth not deny, nor to the same in any wise answer, but altogether refuseth to admit that averment, as before prays judgment, &c.

Demurrer.

Causes of demurrer.

Joinder.

## Pearſe and others, at the ſuit of the King,

Plea, by certain tenants to an inquiſition finding certain premiſſes to be the property of one Sampſon Larke, and to be forfeited for treaſon by him committed.

AND now, to wit; on the 12th day of February, in this term, comes here one Adam Pearſe, of the city of Exeter, merchant, William Bennet, of Gabrels, in the county of Dorſet, eſquire, John Bennet, of Lime Regis, in the county of Dorſet, gent. and William Forſe, of Ayleſbury, in the county of Devon, yeoman; tenants of the ſaid two meſſuages and tenaments called Wingate, otherwiſe W. with the appurtenances, and of the ſaid three acres of wood, and of the thirty-two acres of paſture with the appurtenances, ſituate, lying and being in the pariſh of Coombe, Rawleigh, in the county of Devon, parcel of the premiſſes in the inquiſition aforeſaid mentioned, by F. B. their attorney, and pray oyer of the commiſſion aforeſaid, and of the ſchedule thereto annexed, as to the ſaid Sampſon Larke, and the return of the ſaid commiſſion, and the inquiſition thereupon taken, and they are read to them, &c. which being read, heard, and by them underſtood, they complain that they under colour of the premiſſes are grievouſly vexed and diſquieted, and that the ſaid two meſſuages and tenements with the appurtenances, and the other premiſſes * in this plea before mentioned, parcel of &c. into the hands of the ſaid lord the now king, are taken and ſeized and this not juſtly, &c. becauſe proteſting that the commiſſion aforeſaid and the ſchedule to the ſame annexed, and the inquiſition aforeſaid, and alſo the matters in the ſame contained are not ſufficient in law, to which they have no neceſſity, neither are they bound by the law of the land in any manner to anſwer, for plea nevertheleſs the ſaid Adam, William, John and William ſay, that long before the ſaid 11th day of July aforeſaid, in the firſt year of the reign of James the 2d, the now king, &c. on which day the high treaſon aforeſaid by him the ſaid Sampſon Larke, againſt the ſaid lord the now king was committed and perpetrated, to wit; on the 8th day of April, in the 54th year of the reign of the lord Charles the 2d late king of England, &c. one Thomas Drew, eſquire, was ſeized of and in the ſaid two meſſuages and tenements with the appurtenances and the other premiſſes in this plea before mentioned, parcel of, &c. in his demeſne as of fee, and ſo being thereof ſeized, the ſaid Thomas Drew, afterwards and before the ſaid time in which, &c. to wit; on the ſaid 18th day of April, in the 34th year, &c. aforeſaid, at Coombe Rawleigh, aforeſaid, demiſed granted

Oyer.

* P. 636.

Proteſtation.

That T. D. was ſeized in fee.

granted and to farm let to the said John Bennet the said two messuages and tenements, and the other premisses in this plea before mentioned, parcel of, &c. to have and to hold to the said John Bennet and his assigns, from the said 18th day of April, in the 34th year, &c. aforesaid, until the full end and term of 99 years from that time next ensuing and fully to be compleated and ended, if one Elizabeth Raddon wife of one William Raddon, Davy Raddon, John Raddon and Johanna Larke, wife of the said Sampson Larke, or any of them should so long live, which Davy Raddon, John Raddon and Johanna Larke as yet are living and in full life, to wit; at Coombe Rawleigh, aforesaid, by virtue of which demise the said John Bennet into the said two messuages and tenements and the other premisses in this plea before mentioned, parcel of, &c. entered and was thereof possessed for the term aforesaid, and so being thereof possessed the said John Bennet, afterwards and before the said time in which, &c. to wit; on the first day of May, in the 34th year, &c. aforesaid, at Coombe Rawleigh aforesaid, granted and assigned to the said Sampson Larke in the inquisition aforesaid mentioned, the entire estate and term of years which he then had of and in the said two messuages and the other premisses in this plea before mentioned, parcel of, &c. by virtue of which grant the said Sampson Larke, into the said two messuages and tenements and the other premisses in this plea before mentioned, parcel of, &c. entered and was thereof possessed, and so being thereof possessed, the said Sampson afterwards and before the time in which, &c. to wit; on the 10th day of May, in the 34th year, &c. aforesaid, at Coombe Rawleigh, aforesaid, granted and assigned to the said Adam Pearse, William Bennet, John Bennet, and William Forse, their executors and assigns, his whole estate and term of years which he the said Sampson then * had of and in the said two messuages and tenements and other premisses in this plea before mentioned, parcel of, &c. by virtue of which they the said Adam, William, John and William, into the said two messuages and the other premisses in this plea before mentioned, parcel of, &c. entered and were and as yet are thereof possessed for and during the residue of the said term of 99 years as yet to come, and unexpired, if the said Elizabeth Raddon, Davy Raddon, John Raddon and Johanna Larke or any of them shall so long live; the reversion thereof to the said Thomas Drewe and his heirs, immediately belonging, and appertaining; without this, that the said Sampson Larke at the time of the high treason aforesaid by him committed, or at any time afterwards was seized of the said two messuages

Who being so seized demised by indenture to one of the defendants for 99 years if E.R. D. R. J. R. and J. L. or any of them should so long live.

That D. R. J. R. and J. L. are yet alive.

That the lessee entered and granted away his estate in the premisses to S. Larke.

That Larke entered.

And before the time in which, &c. granted to the present defendants.

* P. 637.

Who entered and were possessed.

And traverse the seizin of Larke at the time of the high treason committed, or at any time afterwards prout the inquisition.

meſſuages and tenements and the other premiſſes in this plea before mentioned, parcel of, &c. or of any parcel thereof in the manner and form as by the inquiſition aforeſaid is above found, all and ſingular which things they the ſaid Adam Pearſe, William Bennet, John Bennet, and William Forſe, are ready to verify as the court, &c. wherefore they pray judgment, and that the hands of the ſaid lord the now king from the poſſeſſion of the ſaid two meſſuages and tenements and other premiſſes in this plea before mentioned, parcel of, &c. may be removed, &c. and that they the ſaid Adam Pearſe, William Bennet, John Bennet and William Forſe, to their poſſeſſion thereof, together with the iſſues and profits thereof, whereof the ſaid lord the king is not as yet anſwered may be reſtored, and that all who have been, now are and afterwards ſhall be ſheriffs of the ſaid county of Devon, of the iſſues and profits of the ſaid two meſſuages and the other premiſſes in this plea before mentioned, parcel of, &c. during the term aforeſaid, may be diſcharged, and alſo that they the ſaid Adam, William, John and William, as to the premiſſes in this behalf may be diſmiſſed, &c.

And pray an amoveas manus.

---

# The King againſt Lewys.

## Eaſter, 20th Charles 2d.

Writ of extent iſſued out of the Exchequer upon a bond entered into to the king by Lewys.

MONMOUTH, to wit;—Be it remembered that the writ of the lord the now king under the ſeal of this exchequer, by the conſideration of the barons here iſſued in theſe words, to wit;—Charles the 2d, by the grace of God, of England, &c.--King, to the ſheriff of Monmouth, greeting, whereas Edward Lewys, of Abergavenney, in the county of Monmouth, gent. by his writing obligatory, ſealed with his ſeal, bearing date the 13th day of March, in the 19th year of our reign, and in the year of our lord, 1666, is holden to us in one thouſand pounds of the good and lawful money of England, to be paid upon a certain day now paſt, and the ſame to us hath not paid nor cauſed to be paid, as it is ſaid, and we being willing to be ſatisfied of the ſaid one thouſand pounds to us now due with all the ſpeed

ſpeed with which we can, as is juſt, command you that you do not omit becauſe of any liberty but that you enter it, and as well by the oath of good and lawful men of your bailiwick or otherwiſe by the oath of teſtimony of any good and lawful men of your ſaid bailiwick, by whom the truth of the matter may be the better known, * as by all other ways, methods and means, by which you can or may know better, that you diligently enquire what lands and tenements, and of what yearly value, the ſaid Edward Lewys, had in your ſaid bailiwick on the ſaid 13th day of March, in the 19th year of our reign aforeſaid, on which day he firſt became a debtor to us or at any time afterwards hitherto, and what goods and chattels, and of what value, and what debts, credits, and ſpecialties, and in whoſe hands they now are, and by the oath of good and lawful men, that you diligently cauſe them to be appraized and extended, and taken and ſeized into our hands, that we may have them until we are fully ſatisfied of our debt aforeſaid, according to the form of the ſtatute for recovering ſuch our debts, thereupon lately made and provided; and we further command and empower you, by theſe preſents, to ſummon before you all perſons whatſoever, fit to be examined touching the premiſſes, and diligently to examine them of and touching the premiſſes, leaſt this our command may remain to be executed further, and how you ſhall execute this our command, certify to the barons of our exchequer, at Weſtminſter, in one month from the day of Eaſter, next coming openly and plainly provided that you ſhall not ſell nor cauſe to be ſold, the goods and chattels which you ſhall take into our hands by reaſon of this writ, until you ſhall have other command from us. Witneſs Matthew Hale, knight, the 21ſt day of March, in the 20th year of our reign. By the ſaid act made in the parliament held in the 33d, year of the reign of king Henry the 8th, and by the warrant of Rainsford, baron; and by the barons; Fanſhawe. At which day William Herbert, eſquire, ſheriff of the county aforeſaid, returns here the writ aforeſaid thus indorſed, to wit; the execution of this writ appears in a certain inquiſition to this writ annexed: and the tenor of the inquiſition aforeſaid follows in theſe words, to wit; Monmouth, to wit; An inquiſition indented taken at Abergavenney, in the county of Monmouth, aforeſaid, on the 15th day of April, in the 20th year of the reign of our lord Charles the 2d, the now king of England, &c. before me William Herbert, eſquire, ſheriff of the county aforeſaid, by virtue of the writ of the lord the king to me directed and to this inquiſition annexed, by the oath of William Gibbs, gent. &c. good

* P. 638.

Inquiſition finds that Lewys was ſeized of divers tenements in fee at the time he became the kings debtor, good and lawful men of the county aforesaid, who say upon their oath, that Edward Lewys, on the writ aforesaid named, on the 5th day of August, in the 19th year of the reign of our lord Charles the 2d, the now king, &c. on which day he became a debtor to the said lord the king, was seized in his demesne as of fee, of and in one messuage, one stable, and one garden with the appurtenances, situate, lying and being in the town of Abergavenney aforesaid, in the county aforesaid, in a certain street there called Rythergh-street, now in the tenure or occupation of one Thomas Lewys, of the clear yearly value in all issues above reprisals of eight pounds, and of and in, &c. (reciting all the lands in the inquisition) And the jurors aforesaid further say upon their oath aforesaid, that the said Edward Lewys, on the day of the taking of this inquisition, was possessed of and in divers parcels of goods, grocery, and saltery as of his proper goods to the value of two hundred and thirty pounds, which goods and wares afterwards came to the hands and possession and now remain in the hands and possession of one John Stevens, and the jurors aforesaid further say upon their oath aforesaid, that the said Edward, on the day of the acknowledgement of the debt aforesaid, or at any time afterwards, had no goods or chattles, debts, credits or specialties, nor other or more lands or tenements in the county aforesaid, to their * knowledge, which could be extended and appraized, or taken and seized into the hands of the said lord the king; which lands and tenements goods and wares, I the said sheriff on the day of the taking of this inquisition, have taken into the hands of the said lord the king, by the extent aforesaid, in testimony whereof as well I the said sheriff as the jurors aforesaid, to this inquisition have severally put our seals, the day, year and place aforesaid, &c. William Herbert esquire, sheriff— as is more fully contained in the said writ and in the return of the same, and in the said inquisition, thereupon taken in the county of Monmouth, into this Exchequer certified, and there of this term remaining in the custody of this remembrancer.

And that at the time of taking the inquisition he was possessed of divers goods which afterwards came to the hands of J. S. who still retains them.

* P. 639.

Plea by Crump, Bristow, Pindar and Hanbury, that before the issuing of the extent, Lewys became a bankrupt,

And now, to wit; in one month of Easter, in this term, come one Richard Crump, Richard Bristow, Michael Pindar, and Capel Hanbury, proprietors and possessers of the said several parcels of goods, and wares, grocery, and saltery in the said inquisition specified, by Charles Keepe, their attorney and pray oyer of the said writ of extent and of the return of the same and of the said inquisition, thereupon taken, and they are read to them which being read, heard and by them understood, they complain that they under co-

lour

lour of the premisses are grievously vexed and disquieted, and that the said goods and wares, out of their hands, and possession by the said William Herbert, the sheriff aforesaid, under colour of the premisses, are taken and detained, and this not justly, because protesting that the said writ of extent and the return of the same, and the said inquisition thereupon taken, and the matter in the same contained are not sufficient in law to which they have no necessity neither are they bound by the law of the land to answer, for plea nevertheless they the said Richard Crump, Richard Bristow, Michael Pindar, and Capel Hanbury, say that the said Edward Lewys, for the space of divers years next before the issuing of the said writ of extent, at the town of Abergavenny aforesaid, in the said county of Monmouth, endeavoured to obtain his living by buying and selling of divers goods and merchandizes, and that by reason thereof the said Edward Lewys, within said space of the said years, at Abergavenny aforesaid, became indebted and as yet is indebted, to wit; to the said Richard Crump, in four hundred pounds and to the said Richard Bristow, Michael Pindar, and Capel Hanbury, and to divers other persons his creditors in divers other sums of money, and that the said Edward Lewys, so being indebted afterwards, and before the issuing of the writ of the said lord the now king of extent, to wit; on the 5th day of March in the 20th year of the reign of the lord the now king, at A: aforesaid, became a bankrupt to all purposes, within the intention of the statutes made and provided against bankrupts; And the said Richard Crump, Richard Bristow, Michael Pindar, and Capel Hanbury, further say, that long before the said day of the taking of the said inquisition, to wit; on the said 5th day of March in the 20th year of the reign of the lord Charles the 2d, &c. a commission of the said lord the king under his great seal of England, bearing date, at Westminster, in the county of Middlesex, the same day and year, grounded upon the several statutes made concerning bankrupts, issued against the said Edward Lewys, in the said writ of extent and the return of the * same, and in the said inquisition thereupon taken, named, directed to one Richard Adams, esquire, Hugh Philips, and George Johnson, gentlemen, Henry Bedingfield, esquire, and Mathew Pedley, gent. by the said commission giving full power and authority to the said commissioners or to four or three of them, (of whom the said Richard Adams, or Henry Bedingfield to be one) to execute the same as by the said commission, more fully appeareth; by virtue of which commission, the said Richard Adams, Hugh Philips, and George Johnson, three of the commissioners

that a commission of bankruptcy was sued out against him, and that the commissioners assigned the said goods, &c. mentioned in the said inquisition to them for the benefit of the creditors of Lewys.

* P. 640.

commiſſioners aforeſaid afterwards, to wit; on the 6th day of the ſaid month of March, in the 20th year aforeſaid, having begun to put the ſaid commiſſion in execution, upon the due examination of witneſſes, and other good proofs upon oath taken before them, found that the ſaid Edward Lewys, had ſought and endeavoured to acquire his living by buying and ſelling of divers and ſeveral goods, wares, and commodities, as grocery, ſaltery, and haberdaſhery, as a grocer or country chapman, for the ſpace of eighteen years laſt paſt, or thereabout, before the date and iſſuing of the ſaid commiſſion, at his late manſion houſe and ſhop, ſituate and being in the town of Abergavenny, in the ſaid county of Monmouth, and dominion of Wales, and that by reaſon of the dealing and trading of the ſaid Edward Lewys, as aforeſaid, he the ſame Edward became indebted to the ſaid Richard Crump, Richard Briſtow, Michael Pindar, and Capel Hanbury, now here pleading and to divers and ſeveral other perſons his creditors, in divers and ſeveral ſums of money amounting to the ſum of three thouſand pounds and upwards of the lawful money of England, and ſo being indebted as aforeſaid, he the ſaid Edward Lewys, at the town of Abergavenny aforeſaid, in the ſaid county of Monmouth, before the date and iſſuing of the ſaid commiſſion, became a bankrupt to all intents and purpoſes, within the compaſs and true intent of the ſeveral ſtatutes in the ſaid commiſſion mentioned, or of ſome one of them; and the ſaid Richard Crump, R. B. M. P. and C. H. further ſay that the ſaid Richard Adams, Hugh Philips, and George Johnſon, the commiſſioners, aforeſaid in further execution of the ſaid commiſſion, afterwards, to wit; on the 12th day of the ſaid month of March, in the 20th year aforeſaid, at the town of Abergavenny, aforeſaid, in the ſaid county of Monmouth, by their warrant of ſeizure, under their hands and ſeals, bearing date the ſame day and year, laſt mentioned, cauſed divers and ſeveral goods and wares of the ſaid Edward Lewys, and of and belonging to his eſtate to be ſeized, which then were remaining in his houſe and ſhop aforeſaid, and the ſame to be received, valued, and appraized by honeſt men of knowledge and induſtry, in that behalf, who upon their corporal oaths, taken before the ſaid commiſſioners valued, rated, and appraized the ſame to be worth to be ſold the ſum of two hundred and ſeventy pounds, and nineteen ſhillings; of the lawful money of England, which goods and wares, * and other things of the ſaid Edward Lewys, which came to and remain in the hands and poſſeſſion of the ſaid John Stevens, grocer, are firſt, three caſks and one bag of ginger, groſs, three hundred, one

* P. 641.

one quarter and fifteen pounds, tare, two quarters and sixteen pounds; neat, two hundred two quarters and twenty seven pounds, at twenty eight shillings by the hundred 3l. 16s. 9d. likewise, &c. [*reciting the goods and wares*] total 270l. 19s. All which goods and wares then were remaining in the hands, custody, and possession of John Stevens of Abergavenny aforesaid, grocer; and the said Richard Crump, R. B. M. P. and C. H. further say that the said Richard Adams, Hugh Philips, and George Johnson, the commissioners aforesaid, in further prosecution of the said commission and by force and virtue of the same, and of the statutes in the same mentioned, for and in consideration of the covenants, in the indenture of bargain aud assignment, between the said Richard Adams, Hugh Philips, and George Johnson, and the said Richard Crump, R. B. M. P. and C. H. mentioned to be made on the part of the said R. R. M. and C. their executors and administrators, to be performed, they the said commissioners by their said indenture of bargain and assignment, bearing date at Abergavenny aforesaid in the said county of Monmouth, the 21st day of March, in the year of our lord 1667, and in the 20th year of the reign of our lord Charles the 2d, the now king, &c. made between the said Richard Adams, by the name &c. Hugh Philips, by the name &c. George Johnson, by the name &c. of the one part, and them the said Richard Crump, by the name &c. Richard Bristow, by the name &c. Mathew Pindar, by the name &c. and Capel Hanbury, by the name &c. of the other part, [one part of which sealed with the seal of the said, R. A. H. P. and G. J. they the said R. C. R. B. M. P. and C. H. bring here into court,] bargained, sold, assigned, and demised, to them the said Richard Crump, &c. their executors, administrators and assigns, to and for the use benefit and advantage of all the creditors of the said Edward Lewys, who then had sought and afterwards in due time should come in and seek relief by virtue of the said commission, and should contribute towards the charges of the same, according to the limitation of the statutes in the same mentioned, all and singular the said goods, wares, and other things mentioned and expressed, in the schedule, or inventory indented aforesaid, to have, hold, ask, demand, sue for, recover and receive all and singular the said goods, wares, and other things mentioned, contained and expressed in the said schedule, or inventory indented to them the said R. C. R. B. M. P. and C. H. their executors, administrators, and assigns, to and for the use intention and purpose before declared and to and for no other use intention or

purpoſe whatſoever, by virtue of which indenture of bargain and aſſignment, they the ſaid R. C. R. B. M. P. and
Averments. C. H. became poſſeſſed of and in the ſaid ſeveral, goods wares and other things aforeſaid, under the truſt aforeſaid, with this that the ſaid goods wares and other things in the ſaid ſchedule, and inventory, and in the ſaid indenture of
* P. 642. ſale and aſſignment mentioned * and expreſſed, and the ſaid divers parcels of goods wares and grocery, and ſaltery in the ſaid inquiſition ſpecified, are one and the ſame and not another nor different, and that the ſaid Edward Lewys in the ſaid writ, of extent and the return of the ſame, and in the ſaid inquiſition thereupon taken, named, and the ſaid Edward Lewys in the ſaid commiſſion and in the ſaid indenture of bargain and aſſignment, in like manner named is one and the ſame perſon, and not another nor different,
Traverſe. without this that the ſaid Edward Lewys on the ſaid day of the taking of the inquiſition aforeſaid, was poſſeſſed of and in the ſaid divers parcels of goods and wares, grocery and ſaltery, as of his proper goods in the manner and form as by the ſaid inquiſition is above found, all and ſingular which things they the ſaid, R. C. R. B. M. P. and C. H.
And pray an amoveas manus. are ready to verify as the court, &c. wherefore they pray judgment and that the hands of the ſaid lord the now king, from the poſſeſſion of the ſaid divers parcels of goods and wares, grocery and ſaltery, in the ſaid inquiſition mentioned, may be removed, and that they the ſaid R. C. R. B. M. P. and C. H. may be reſtored to their poſſeſſion thereof, and alſo that as well the ſaid William Herbert, eſquire, the ſaid ſheriff, as all others from that time now and who afterwards ſhall be ſheriffs of the ſaid county of Monmouth, and each of them of the ſaid goods and wares, in their accounts in the great roll of this exchequer, may be diſcharged, and thereupon that they the ſaid R. C. R. B. M. P. and C. H. and each of them, as to the premiſſes by the court here may be diſmiſſed.

*The attorney general demurs, and the defendants join in demurrer: judgment was given for the king. Vide Parkers Reports, 126.*

The

## The King againſt Band and Wife.

PLEAS before the lord the now king, in his chancery at Weſtminſter, in the county of Middleſex, in the term of St. Michael, in the 2d, year of the reign of our lord James the 2d, by the grace of God, of England, Scotland, France, and Ireland, king, defender of the faith, &c.

It is found by a certain inquiſition indented taken at the guildhall, of the city of London, on the 21ſt day of July, in the 2d, year of the reign of our lord James the 2d, by the grace of God, of E. S. F. and I. King, defender of the faith, &c. before Robert Brent, Richard Graham, Philip Burton, Thomas Hall, and Aron Pengry, eſquires, commiſſioners of the ſaid lord the now king, by virtue of the the commiſſion of the ſaid lord the king, ſealed under his great ſeal of England bearing date at Weſtminſter, the 13th day of July aforeſaid, to them and to others in the ſaid commiſſion named, directed, and to the ſaid inquiſition annexed to enquire on behalf of the ſaid lord the king, of certain articles things and circumſtances in the ſaid commiſſion ſpecified, by the oath of Daniel Mann, Richard Dowley, William Haywood, John Timms, Thomas Timms, Thomas Yates, Charles Pepys, John Barraby, Richard Beauchampe, George Hill, William Church, Thomas Cowles, Thomas Penſett, Matthew Fuller, John Pope, * Adam Crumpton, Edward Benſon, William Bird, Richard Lord, William Pender, and Hezekiah Brome, good and lawful men of the city aforeſaid, that the ſaid Edward Peckham in the commiſſion aforeſaid named on the firſt day of June, in the firſt year of the reign of the ſaid lord the now king, at London aforeſaid dyed, and that on the day on which he dyed he was ſeized in his demeſne as of fee, of and in one meſſuage or tenement, with the appurtenances commonly called or known by the name of the graſhopper brew-houſe, ſituate and being in a certain lane, called Long-lane, in the pariſh of St. Sepulchre, London, then or late in the tenure or occupation of —— Fellowes his aſſigns or undertenants, of the clear yearly value in all the iſſues above repriſals of fifty five pounds, and alſo of and in one other meſſuage or tenement, with the appurtenances ſituate and being in Long-lane aforeſaid, in the pariſh aforeſaid, then or late in the tenure or occupation of —— Moryſon, or his undertenants, of the clear yearly value in all iſſues above repriſals of eleven pounds, and alſo of and in one

Inquiſition upon a commiſſion out of the Chancery, whereby it is found that E. Peckham at the time of his death was ſeized of ſeveral meſſuages, &c. that he died without heir, and that the ſame after his death, * P. 643. ought to revert to the king as his eſcheat.

 other

other meſſuage or tenement with the appurtenances in Long-lane aforeſaid in the pariſh aforeſaid, nigh adjacent to the meſſuage laſt mentioned then or late in the tenure or occupation of —— Stretton, his aſſigns or undertenants, of the clear yearly value in all iſſues above repriſals of four pounds, and alſo of and in nine other meſſuages or tenements, with the appurtenances ſituate and being in Long-lane aforeſaid, in the pariſh aforeſaid, then or late in the tenure or occupation of —— Emerye, his aſſigns or undertenants, of the clear yearly value in all iſſues above repriſals of thirty five pounds, and alſo of and in a certain paſſage with the appurtenances, leading from Long-lane a foreſaid, into a certain court called the carpenters yard, within the city aforeſaid, in the pariſh aforeſaid, then or late in the tenure or occupation of —— Ruſſel, his aſſigns, or undertenants, of the clear yearly value in all iſſues above repriſals of thirty five pounds, and alſo of and in one other meſſuage or tenement with the appurtenances ſituate and being in a certain court within the pariſh aforeſaid, called graſhopper court, then or late in the tenure or occupation of —— Goodman, widow, her aſſigns or undertenants, of the clear yearly value in all iſſues above repriſals of four pounds, and alſo of and in three ſeveral meſſuages or tenements, with the appurtenances ſituate lying and being in Long-lane aforeſaid, in the pariſh aforeſaid, nigh adjacent to the ſaid court called graſhopper court, then or late in the tenure or occupation of ————, of the clear yearly value in all iſſues above repriſals of twenty ſhillings, and alſo of and in two other meſſuages or tenements with the appurtenances, ſituate lying and being in Long-lane aforeſaid, in the pariſh aforeſaid, then or late in the ſeveral tenure or occupation of —— Painter and —— Symons, of the clear yearly value in all iſſues above repriſals of twenty pounds, and that the ſaid Edward Peckham, of all and ſingular the premiſſes aforeſaid, ſo as aforeſaid being ſeized, of ſuch his eſtate therein dyed ſeized without any heir, and that the premiſſes aforeſaid with their appurtenances, after the death of the ſaid Edward Peckham, ought to revert to the ſaid lord the king as his eſcheat, becauſe the ſaid Edward Peckham dyed thereof ſeized without heir, and therefore the commiſſioners aforeſaid, the premiſſes aforeſaid, have taken and have cauſed to be ſeized into the hands of the ſaid lord the now king, as by the * commiſſion aforeſaid, they were commanded as by the inquiſition aforeſaid, together with the commiſſion aforeſaid, to the ſaid inquiſition annexed into the chancery here returned, and in the files of the ſaid court, here remaining of record more fully appeareth;

* P. 644.

Band and Ann his wife, appear in Chancery,

eth. And now here at this day to wit Thurſday the 11th day of November, in the 2d, year of the reign of the ſaid lord the now king aforeſaid, before the ſaid lord the king, in his ſaid chancery, here to wit; at Weſtminſter aforeſaid come Ferdinand Band and Ann his wife, by Littleton Powell, eſquire, their atrorney, and pray oyer of the commiſſion aforeſaid, and of the return of the ſame, and alſo of the inquiſition aforeſaid, and they are read to them, &c. which being read and heard they complain, that they under colour of the premiſſes are grievouſly vexed and diſquieted, and this not juſtly becauſe proteſting that the commiſſion aforeſaid, and the inquiſition aforeſaid, thereupon taken are not ſufficient in law, to which they have no neceſſity neither are they bound by the law of the land, to anſwer for plea neverthleſs they the ſaid Ferdinand and Ann, ſay that ſhe the ſaid Ann is and at the ſaid time of the death of the ſaid Edward Peckham, and at the ſaid time of the taking of the inquiſition aforeſaid, was the couſin and next heir of the ſaid Edward, and that the ſaid meſſuages or tenements aforeſaid, with the appurtenances after the death of the ſaid Edward, did deſcend and ought to deſcend to the ſaid Ann as the couſin and heir of the ſaid Edward, to wit the daughter of Ann Allen, the ſiſter of Elizabeth Peckham, the mother of Robert Peckham, the father of the ſaid Edward Peckham without this that the ſaid Edward Peckham, died without heir as by the inquiſition aforeſaid was found, all and ſingular which things they the ſaid Ferdinand and Ann, are ready to verify, as the court of the ſaid lord the now king here ſhall conſider, wherefore they pray judgment, and that the hands of the ſaid lord the king may be therefrom removed, and that they to their poſſeſſion thereof together with the iſſues and profits thereof, in the mean time may be reſtored by writ, &c.

*and plead that Ann is next heir to Edward Peckham, and that the premiſſes deſcended to her as heir.*

*Proteſtation.*

*And traverſe that Peckham died without heir.*

And Robert Sawyer, knight, attorney general, of the ſaid lord the now king, who for the ſaid lord the now king in this behalf proſecutes, ſaith that the ſaid plea by the ſaid Ferdinand and Ann, now in the form aforeſaid pleaded, and the matter in the ſame contained, are not ſufficient in law to remove the hands of the ſaid lord the king, from his poſſeſſion, of the tenements aforeſaid, and that he to the ſaid plea, in the manner and form aforeſaid pleaded, hath no neceſſity neither is he bound by the law of the land, in any manner to anſwer, and this he is ready to verify, wherefore for want of a ſufficient plea, in this behalf the the ſaid attorney general, of the ſaid lord the now king, who for the ſaid lord the king in this behalf proſecutes prays judgment, and that the tenements aforeſaid in the inquiſition

*Demurrer.*

inquisition aforesaid specified, with the appurtenances in the hands and possession of the said lord the king, may remain.

Joinder. And the said Ferdinand and Ann, say that they above by pleading have alledged sufficient matter in law, to have the premisses aforesaid, out of the hands of the said lord the now king, which they are ready to verify, which matter the said attorney general of the said lord the now king, who for the said lord the now king, in this behalf prosecutes, doth not deny, nor to the same in any wise answer, but al-
* P. 645. together doth refuse to * admit that averment, wherefore they the said Ferdinand and Ann, as before pray judgment, and that the hands of the said lord the now king, may be removed therefrom, and that they to their possession thereof together with all issues and profits thereof, in the mean time by writ may be restored, &c. But because the said court of the said lord the now king, here will advise themselves of and concerning, the premisses aforesaid, before that they proceed to give judgment thereon, therefore day is given to the parties aforesaid, before the said lord the now king, in his said Chancery, until the octave of St. Hilary, next &c. wheresoever, &c. to hear their judgment thereupon, because the said court of the said lord the now king, here thereupon not as yet, &c. At which octave of St. Hilary, before the said lord the now king, in his said Chancery, here to wit; at Westminster aforesaid, come as well the said Robert Sawyer, knight, attorney general of the said lord the now king, who, &c. in his proper person, as the said Ferdinand and Ann, by their attorney aforesaid, but because the said court of the said lord the now king, here will further advise themselves of and upon the premisses aforesaid, before that they proceed to give judgment hereupon, therefore day is further given to the parties aforesaid, before the said lord the now king, in his Chancery until fifteen days of Easter next, &c. wheresoever, &c. to hear their judgment thereupon, because the said court of the said lord the now king, here thereupon not as yet, &c. At which fifteen days of Easter, before the said lord the now king, in his said Chancery, here to wit; at Westminster aforesaid, come as well the said Robert Sawyer, knight, attorney general of the said lord the now king, who, &c. in his proper person as the said Ferdinand and Ann, by their attorney aforesaid, but because the said court of the said lord the now king, here will advise themselves further of and upon the premisses aforesaid, before that they proceed to judgment thereupon, therefore day is further given to the parties aforesaid, before the said lord the now king, in his Chancery aforesaid, until the morrow of the Holy Trinity next,

Continuances by curia vult advisare.

next, &c. wheresoever, &c. to hear their judgment thereupon, because the said court of the said lord the now king, here thereupon not as yet, &c. At which morrow of the Holy Trinity, before the said lord the now king in his Chancery, here to wit; at Westminster aforesaid, come as well the said Robert Sawyer, Knight, attorney general of the said lord the now king, who, &c. in his proper person, as the said Ferdinand and Ann, by their attorney aforesaid, but because the said court of the said lord the now king, here will advise themselves further of and upon the premisses aforesaid, before that they proceed to give judgment thereupon, therefore day is further given to the parties aforesaid, before the said lord the now king, in his Chancery aforesaid until three weeks of St. Michael next, &c. wheresoever, &c. to hear their judgment thereupon, because the said court of the said lord the now king, here thereupon not as yet, &c.

---

## * The King against Phillips.

* P. 646.

### Hilary 19th James 1st.

SURRY to wit. Be it remembered, that the writ patent of the lord the king James, under his great seal of England, issued in these words to wit, James by the grace of God of England, Scotland, France, and Ireland, king, defender of the faith, &c. to our beloved and faithful Thomas Lowe, knight, Thomas Grymes, knight, Edward Farrand, Hamlet Clarke, Clement Mosse, and Thomas Latham, gentlemen, greeting, know ye that we very much confiding in your fidelity, industry and prudent circumspection, in doing our affairs, have assigned you diligently to enquire, and to you or to two or more of you give and commit full power and authority, by these presents, to enquire as well by the oath of good and lawful men, of our

A commission out of the Chancery, to enquire whether Agnes Philips late wife of W. Philips was cousin and heir of one Cuthbert Beeston, deceased or not and whether she is dead or not, and if dead, when and where she died, whether she died without heir, and of what tenements, &c. she died seized, and what title she had to any tenements &c. and in whose tenure, and of what annual value, and who received or receives the profits of them, and of whom held, and if the same ought not to come to the king by the death of the said A. P.

county

county of Surry, as by the examination and depoſition of all witneſſes whatſoever, worthy of belief, and by all other ways, methods, and means, by which you or two or more of you, may or can know better, whether Agnes Philips, late the wife of William Philips, was the couſin and heir of Cuthbert Beeſton, deceaſed, or not, and alſo whether the ſaid Agnes be dead or not, and if ſhe be dead, then when and where ſhe died, and whether the ſaid Agnes died without heir, and of what manors, meſſuages, lands, tenements, and hereditaments, the ſaid Agnes was ſeized at the time of her death, and what right or title the ſaid Agnes had to any manors, meſſuages, lands, tenements, and hereditaments, at the time of her death, and in whoſe tenure or occupation the ſaid manors, meſſuages, lands, tenements, and hereditaments, now are and what are their annual values, and who hath had or perceived the iſſues and profits of the premiſſes aforeſaid, or of any parcel thereof from the ſaid time of the death of the ſaid Agnes hitherto, and from whom the ſaid manors, meſſuages, lands, and tenements, were holden at the time of the death of the ſaid Agnes, and alſo to enquire whether the manors, meſſuages, lands, tenements, and hereditaments, rights, or titles aforeſaid, by reaſon of the death of the ſaid Agnes without heir, in the form aforeſaid, or for other cauſes or reaſons whatſoever, came or ought to come to us or not, and alſo to enquire of all other articles and circumſtances, concerning the truth and certainty of the premiſſes aforeſaid, and therefore we command you that at ſuch day and place or days and places, as you or two or more of you, for this purpoſe ſhall appoint, that you or two or more of you, diligently enquire concerning the premiſſes, and that you or two or more of you, do and execute all thoſe things, with effect in the form aforeſaid, ſo that as well the inquiſition thereon, before you or two or more of you, diſtinctly, and openly taken and made, as the entire reſidue of your acts or the acts of two or more of you, may be had before the barons of our Exchequer at Weſtminſter, as ſoon as you or two or more of you can, and at leaſt in * 15 days of St. Hilary next coming, to be delivered to our court, then there, under your ſeals, or the ſeals of two or more of you, and the ſeals of thoſe by whom that inquiſition ſhall be made, together with this our commiſſion, for we command the ſheriff of the ſaid county of Surry, that at ſuch day and place or days and places as you or two or more of you, ſhall appoint, and which on our behalf you ſhall make known to him, that he cauſe to come before you or two or more of you, ſo many and ſuch good and lawful men of his

Commiſſion returnable into the Exchequer.

* P. 647.

his bailiwick, by whom the truth of the matter may be better known and enquired into, also we give to you and to two or more of you, full power and authority by these presents, to summon and cause to appear before you or two or more of you, all persons whatsoever fit to be examined, touching the premisses, and diligently to examine them of and touching the premisses, upon their corporal oaths, to be taken upon the Holy Gospel of God, least this our present command may remain further to be executed, moreover we give in charge, firmly by the tenor of these our presents, to all and singular our mayors, sheriffs, bailiffs, constables, and all our officers, ministers, and subjects, that they observe, obey, and attend, you and every of you in the execution of the premisses, as is right at their peril, in witness whereof we have caused these our letters to be made patent; witness, ourself at Westminster, the 9th day of January, in the 19th year of our reign of England, France, and Ireland, and of Scotland the 55th. Edmunds. At which day the commissioners aforesaid, return the commission aforesaid, thus indorsed, to wit; the execution of this commission appears in a certain inquisition, to this commission annexed; the answer of Edward Farrand, Clement Mosse, and Thomas Latham, commissioners, within named. Surry to wit; an inquisition indented taken at Southwark, in the county of Surry, aforesaid, on the 21st day of January, in the 19th year of the reign of our lord James by the grace of God, of England, Scotland, France, and Ireland, king, defender of the faith, &c. to wit; of England, France, and Ireland, and of Scotland, the 55th, before Edward Farrand, esquire, Clement Mosse and Thomas Latham, gentlemen, commissioners of the said lord the king, by virtue of the commission of the said lord the king, sealed with his great seal of England, issuing out of his court of Chancery, to the said Edward Farrand, Clement Mosse, and Thomas Latham, and to Thomas Lowe, knight, Thomas Grymes, knight, and Hamlet Clarke, gent. in the said commission named, directed, and to this inquisition annexed, to enquire whether Agnes Phillips, in the said commission named, late the wife of William Philips, gent. was the cousin and heir of Cuthbert Beeston, deceased, or not, and whether the said Agnes, be dead, or not, and if she be dead, then when and where she died, and whether the said Agnes died without heir, and of what manors, messuages, lands, tenements, and hereditaments, the said Agnes was seized, and what right or title the said Agnes had to any manors, messuages, lands, tenements, or hereditaments, at

Return of the commission.

Inquisition

Recital of the points in the commission to be enquired into.

the time of her death, and in whose tenure or occupation the ſaid manors, meſſuages, lands, tenements, and hereditaments, then were, and what was their annual value, and who had or perceived the iſſues and profits of the premiſſes aforeſaid, or of any part thereof, from the ſaid time of the death of the ſaid Agnes, until the making of the commiſſion aforeſaid, and of whom the ſaid manors, meſſuages, lands, and tenements, were holden at the time of the death of the ſaid Agnes, and alſo to enquire whether

* P. 648. the manors, * meſſuages, lands, tenements and hereditaments, rights or titles aforeſaid, by reaſon of the death of the ſaid Agnes, without heir in the form aforeſaid, or for any other cauſes or reaſons whatſoever, came or ought to come to the ſaid lord the now king, or not, and alſo to enquire of all other articles and circumſtances concerning the truth and certainty of the premiſſes aforeſaid; by the oath of Thomas Oveman, John Heyman, Michael Nicholſon, John Jones, Thomas Miller, Thomas James, Thomas Royden, Edward Farthing, Joſeph Cooper, Henry Auſtell, Gregory Clarke, Thomas Bagnell, Gilbert Walpoole, William Wells, Humphry Cholmely, and Thomas Edge, good and lawful men of the county aforeſaid, who being ſworn and charged of and upon the premiſſes ſay upon their oath aforeſaid, that the ſaid Agnes Phillips, in the commiſſion aforeſaid named, and late the wife of William Phillips, gent. in the ſaid commiſſion, in like manner named, was the couſin and next heir of the ſaid Cuthbert Beeſton deceaſed, in the commiſſion aforeſaid named, to wit; the daughter and heir of William Beeſton, the brother of Adam Beeſton, the father of the ſaid Cuthbert, and that the ſaid Agnes died on the 29th day of April, in the 14th year of the reign of our lord James, the now king of England, &c. at the pariſh of St. Olave, in Southwark, aforeſaid in the ſaid county of Surry, without heir, and the jurors aforeſaid further ſay upon their oath aforeſaid, that the ſaid Cuthbert Beeſton, in his life time was ſeized in his demeſne as of fee of and in one meſſuage with its appurtenances, called the wallnut-tree, ſituate, lying, and being in the pariſh of St. Olave, in Southwark, in the county of Surry, aforeſaid, now or late in the ſeveral tenure or occupation of John Buckworth, John Clarke, John Battie, Edward Ducket, John Allen, Ralph Male, Robert Marſhrother, William Lynne and Jacob Barlow, or their aſſigns, or the aſſigns of ſome one or more of them, and of and in fifteen other meſſuages with their appurtenances, ſituate, lying and being in Wallnut-tree-lane, otherwiſe, Charter-lane, in the ſaid pariſh of St. Olave, in Southwark, aforeſaid,

Jury find that Agnes Phillips was the couſin and heir of Cuthbert Beeſton: the couſinage found, the place where and time when ſhe died.

That Cuthbert in his life-time was ſeized of divers meſſuages, &c.

aforesaid, in the said county of Surry, now or late in the several tenure or occupation of Richard Held, Christopher Woodburne, Margaret Hill widow, George Thompson, Henry Johnson, John Backer, —— Shale widow, Henry Brayford, Robert Abdey, William Barley, —— Grey, Ralph Holmes, and Anthony Witherings, or their assigns, or the assigns of some one or more of them: and the jurors aforesaid upon their oath aforesaid, further say, that the said Cuthbert Beeston, so being seized of the messuages aforesaid and the other premisses on the 5th day of July in the 22d. year of the reign of the lady Elizabeth, late queen of England, at the said parish of St. Olave, Southwark, aforesaid, in the said county of Surry, made and composed his last will and testament, in writing, and by the said last will and testament, willed and bequeathed two parts of all and singular the messuages and tenements aforesaid in these words following, to wit;—" *Therefore for a full and perfect declaration to be had and made touching the order and disposition of two parts of the said capital messuage or tenement, called the wallnut-tree, and of two parts of the said other messuages and tenements with their appurtenances in Charter-lane, aforesaid, last before mentioned and expressed, I will give,* * *demise and bequeath the said two parts of the said capital messuage or tenement called the wallnut-tree, and the said other messuages or tenements with their appurtenances in Charter-lane, aforesaid, unto the said George Ward, my wife's son, to have and hold the said two parts of the said capital messuage or tenement, called the wallnut-tree, and also two parts of all the other said messuages or tenements with their appurtenances in Charter-lane, aforesaid, last before expressed, to the said George Ward, immediately from and after the decease of the said Alice my wife, and to his heirs and assigns for ever, to these intents, and under these conditions, hereafter mentioned, that is to say, that the said George Ward, his heirs, executors or assigns, shall with the rents issues and profits thereof coming and growing every year, yearly from and after the decease of the said Alice my wife, for and during the space of ten years then next ensuing, if the Gospel of our Saviour Jesus Christ shall be by all the said time and space truly and sincerely preached within this realm of England, as it now is, make or cause to be made within the aforesaid parish church of St. Olave four sermons, that is to say every quarter, one of the same sermons; and give and pay to the preacher of every such sermon five shillings; and that if at any time during the said term and space of ten years as God defend, the Gospel shall cease, and not be truly and sincerely preached*

That he on the 5th of July in the 22d year of Elizabeth made his last will and testament, and thereby bequeathed two parts of the said messuages to George Ward his wife's son

* P. 649.

after the death of the testator's wife in fee simple.

To the intents and upon the conditions that the said G. W. for ten years after the decease of testator's wife, should make and cause to made four quarterly sermons to be preached in the parish church of St. Olave, and should pay 5s. to every preacher and if at any time during the said term the Gospel should cease then to pay the said 20 shillings to the poor of St. Olaves quarterly: and also during the said term to distribute to the prisoners in 3 several prisons 30 shillings quarterly in bread, and every year during the said 10 years to give to eight poor maidens 10 shillings apiece towards their marriages.

*preached within this realm of England, as it now is, then during that time only, the aforesaid twenty shillings so given and appointed to the preacher of the same sermons as is aforesaid, shall be given and distributed yearly to and amongst the poorest people of the said parish of St. Olave's, where most need shall appear, quarterly, by equal portions; and also shall every quarter, quarterly, for and during all the said space and term of ten years; that is to say, at the feast of the birth of our Lord God, the Annunciation of our Lady; the Nativity of St. John the Baptist, and St. Michael the Archangel, or within 21 days next before or after every of the said feasts give and distribute to and amongst the poor prisoners being within the prison of the King's Bench, the Marshalsea and the White Lyon, in Southwark, aforesaid, thirty shillings in bread, that is to say, to every of the same prisons ten shillings apiece; and shall every year, yearly, during the said term and space of ten years give and distribute to eight poor maidens, for and towards their marriages, such as shall be known to be of honest and good name and fame, four pounds, that is to say, to every of the said poor maidens ten shillings apiece,"* As by the last willand testament aforesaid, to the jurors aforesaid shown in evidence more fully appeareth; and the jurors aforesaid, further say upon their oath aforesaid, that afterwards the said Cuthbert Beeston, so being seized of all and singular the premisses, as aforesaid, at the parish of St. Olave, in Southwark, aforesaid, on the 6th day of February, in the year of our Lord 1581, died seized of his estate aforesaid, and the said Alice in the testament aforesaid named, survived him; after the death of which Cuthbert, the said Alice into the said two parts of the messuages * and tenements aforesaid entered, and was thereof seized in her demesne as of freehold for the term of her life, remainder thereof belonging to the said George Ward, in the testament aforesaid in like manner named and his heirs, by virtue of the said last will and testament of the said Cuthbert Beeston; and the third part of all and singular the messuages aforesaid, descended to the said Agnes as the cousin and heir of the said Cuthbert Beeston, to wit; the daughter and heir of the said William Beeston, the cousin and next heir to the said Cuthbert Beeston, and that the said Agnes into the said third part of the messuages tenements and other premisses aforesaid entered, and was thereof seized in her demesne as of fee; and that afterwards the said George Ward, in the life time of the said Alice, on the 9th day of December, in the year of our Lord 1593, of

That Cuthbert died seized and his wife Alice survived him, who entered into the 2 parts and was seized for her life.

* P. 650.

Remainder to George Ward in fee.

That one third descended to Agnes Phillips as cousin to Cuthbert Beeston who entered and was seized in fee.

of the remainder aforesaid, so as aforesaid seized, at the said parish of St. Olave, in Southwark aforesaid died, after whose death the remainder of the messuages, tenements and the other premisses aforesaid, descended to one Cuthbert Ward, as the son and heir of the said George Ward; and the jurors aforesaid further say upon their oath aforesaid, that afterwards, to wit; on the 22d, day of November, in the 45th year of the reign of the said late queen Elizabeth, a certain inquisition indented was taken within the borough of Southwark, aforesaid, before Thomas Woodgate, gent. and then escheator of the county aforesaid, by virtue or colour of a writ of the said late queen to the said escheator after the death of the said George Ward, directed, the tenor of which writ follows in these words, to wit;— Elizabeth by the grace of God of England, France and Ireland, queen, defender of the faith, &c. to our escheator in the county of Surry, greeting, we command you that by the oath of good and lawful men of your bailiwick by whom the truth of the matter may be the better known, you diligently enquire what lands and tenements George Ward, deceased, held of us in capite as well in demesne as in service in your bailiwick, on the day on which he died, and what of others, and by what services, and what is the value of those lands and tenements by the year in all issues, and on what day the said George died, and who is his next heir, and of what age and who hath occupied the said lands and tenements from the time of the death of the said George, and hath perceived the issues and profits thereof by what title, quality and by what means, and without delay, send to us into our Chancery the inquisition thereon openly and distinctly made, under your seal and the seals of those by whom it shall be made, and this writ witness ourself at Westminster, the 18th day of November, in the 45th year of our reign; the execution of this writ appears in a certain inquisition to this writ annexed, Thomas Woodgate, gent. escheator, by which inquisition among other things it was found that the said George Ward, on the 9th day of December, in the year of our Lord 1593, at Southwarke aforesaid, died, and that the said two parts of the said messuage called Walnut-tree, and of the said fifteen messuages in Walnut-tree-lane, otherwise Charter-lane, aforesaid, then and at the time of the death of the said George Ward, were held of the said lady the queen, by military service and in capite, and that the said Cuth-

That George Ward died in the life-time of Alice, and his remainder descended to Cuthbert Ward his son.

They find an inquisition taken at Southwark the 22d Nov. the 45 of Eliz. after the death of George Ward, before the escheator of Surry, upon a writ of diem clausit extremum to enquire what lands G. Ward held in capite the day he died and who is his next heir, and of what age, &c.

By which inquisition it was found that G. W. died the 9th Dec. 1593. That at that time the said two parts were held of the queen in capite, by military service, that Cuthbert Ward was his heir and within age; and that he was within age at the death of Alice.

bert

bert Ward, was the son and heir of the said George Ward, and was within the age of twenty-one years, at the time of

* P. 651.

the death of his * father, to wit; of the age of five years and ten months, and that at the time of the death of the said Alice, he was of the age of fourteen years and eight

But the jurors first named find that Edward the 6th granted to the mayor and commonalty and citizens of London, that the mayor of London for the time being shall be the king's escheator in the borough of Southwark, &c.

months and seven days; but the said jurors first above named upon their oath aforesaid say, that Edward the 6th late king of England, by his letters patent, sealed with his great seal of England, bearing date at Westminster, the 23d, day of April, in the 4th year of his reign, gave and granted to the mayor and commonalty and citizens of the city of London, and to their successors, that the mayor of the said city for the time being should be escheator of the said lord the late king Edward, and of his heirs in the borough of Southwark, aforesaid, and in the precincts thereof, and in the said parish of St. Olave, in Southwarke, aforesaid, and that the said mayor should have full power and authority to make precepts and commissions to all the sheriffs of the county of Surry, for the time being, and to do, execute and perform there all and singular the things which belong or appertain to the office of escheator in any county of his kingdom of England, and that no other escheator of the said lord the late king Edward or of his heirs should enter nor presume to enter there to do any thing to the office of escheator belonging, nor should intermeddle in any wise in any thing there to the office of escheator appertaining; and the jurors aforesaid first above

And that at the time of the taking the said inquisition Robert Lee was mayor of London.

named, further say, upon their oath aforesaid, that upon the said, 22d day of November, in the 45th year of the reign of the said late queen Elizabeth, aforesaid, and also at the said time of the taking of the inquisition aforesaid, before the said Thomas Woodgate, and long before and afterwards, one Robert Lee, was mayor of the city of London, in the due manner elected, appointed, admitted and sworn; and that the said Alice so being seized as aforesaid, with remainder thereof over as aforesaid, on the 4th day

They then find the death of Alice.

of October, in the year of our Lord, 1602, at the parish of St. Stephen Coleman-street, London, died, so being thereof seized, and that the said several sums of money, in the testament of the said Cuthbert Beeston, mentioned, were not paid after the death of the said Alice, and in the

And that Cuthbert Ward did not fulfil the conditions of Cuthbert Beestons will.

life time of the said Cuthbert Ward, according to the form and effect of the last will and testament, aforesaid, and the jurors first above named further say upon their oath aforesaid, that afterwards the said Agnes entered into the said two parts of the messuages and other premises, aforesaid, by virtue of the condition aforesaid, and was thereof seized

as

as the law requires, and by reason thereof had right, title, estate and interest of and in all and singular the messuages tenements and the other premisses as here is above found, as the law requires, and afterwards the said Agnes, so as aforesaid, being seized of all and singular the messuages, tenements and premisses aforesaid, on the 29th day of April, in the 14th year of the reign of the said lord the now king James of England, at the parish of St. Olave, in Southwark, aforesaid; died, so thereof seized as the law requires, without heir, and that the said two parts are of the value of 6l. by the year in all issues above reprisals, and that the premisses aforesaid at the time of the death of the said Cuthbert Beeston, the testator, were held of the said lady Elizabeth, late queen of England, by military service in capite, and also at the said time of the death of the said Agnes were held of the said lord the now king by military service in capite, but who hath had and perceived the issues and profits of the premisses aforesaid, from the time of the death of the said Agnes, to the day of the taking of this inquisition, the jurors aforesaid are * ignorant; in witness whereof, as well the commissioners aforesaid, as the jury aforesaid, to this inquisition, have put their seals the day, year and place first aforesaid mentioned. As is contained in the commission aforesaid and the inquisition thereto annexed, which remain in the custody of the king's remembrancer.

That Agnes Phillips entered for the condition broken.

And died seized the 24th April. in the 14th James the 1st without heir.

They find the value of the two parts and and the tenure.

But know not who hath received the profits, &c.

* P. 652.

---

# The King against Stone.

## Trinity Term 24th Charles 2d, Roll. 131.

ENGLAND, to wit,—Be it remembered, that Orlando Bridgman, knight, and baronet, lord keeper of the great seal of England, on the 7th day of June, in this same term before the lord the king, at Westminster, by his proper hands, delivered here in court, a certain record had, before the said lord the king in his Chancery in these words to wit. Pleas before the lord the now king in his Chancery,

An issue joined in Chancery upon a traverse of an inquisition [whereby Margaret Stone is found to be a lunatick] is delivered by the lord keeper of the great seal into B. R. to be tried.

at

at Westminster in the county of Middlesex, in the term of Easter, in the 24th year of the reign of our lord Charles the 2d, by the grace of God of England, Scotland, France, and Ireland, king, defender of the faith, &c. to wit;—

The inquisition recited.

Worcester, to wit;—It is found by a certain inquisition taken at the Chequer in Droitwich, in the county aforesaid, on the 4th day of May, in the 21st year of the reign of our lord Charles the 2d, by the grace of God of England, Scotland, France, and Ireland, king, defender of the faith, before G. Dannett, esquire, T. H. gent. and T. W. gent. commissioners of the said lord the now king, by virtue of the commission of the said lord the king, bearing date at Westminster, the 10th day of February, in the 21st year aforesaid, to them and to others in the said commission named, directed, and to the said inquisition annexed, to enquire of the lunacy of Margaret Stone, widow, in the said commission named, and of other things and circumstances in the said commission mentioned, by the oath of J. D. gent. (and 11 others) good and lawful men of the

Margaret Stone found a lunatick.

county aforesaid, that the said Margaret Stone, at the time of the taking of the inquisition aforesaid, was lunatick, and enjoyed lucid intervals, so that she is not capable of the government of herself, her messuages, lands, tenements, goods and chattles, and so hath continued for the space of twelve years then past and upwards, and that she became lunatick by the visitation of God, and not otherwise to the knowledge of the jurors aforesaid, and that the said Margaret Stone at the time of the taking of the inquisition,

Seized of divers tenements.

was seized for term of her life, of the grant of one Walter Stone, deceased, the father of John Stone, deceased, late the husband of the said Margaret, of and in the moiety of a certain messuage, and of the moiety of one yard land with the appurtenances in Astley, in the said county of Worcester, and of and in the moiety of one part of a certain wood with the appurtenances in Astley aforesaid, called Penny-park, into 33 parts to be divided, and of and in the moiety of one other part of a certain other wood, with the appurtenances in Astley, aforesaid, called Astley-wood, into 33 parts to be divided, all and singular which premisses with the appurtenances were of the clear yearly value of in all issues above reprisals of 10l. and it is further found by the

And possessed of chattles.

inquisition aforesaid, that the said Margaret Stone, had no other or more lands or tenements, nor was possessed of any goods or chattles to the knowledge of the jurors aforesaid, except a certain writing obligatory, dated the 10th day of

* P. 653. * April, in the year of our Lord, 1655, whereby one Richard Portman, deceased, acknowledged that he was indebted

indebted to the said Margaret in 200l. conditioned for the payment of 103l. upon the 12th day of October, next after the date of the said writing, and a certain other writing obligatory, dated the 3d day of February, in the year of our Lord, 1658, whereby Henry Longmore and Francis Longmore, acknowledged that they were indebted to the said Margaret Stone, in 100l. conditioned for the payment of 50l. with interest, upon the 3d day of February, in the year of our Lord, 1659, and divers other goods and chattles, to the value of five pounds, or thereabouts, and not more, as by the said inquisition together with the said commission to the said inquisition annexed, in the Chancery here returned, and in the files of the said court here of Record remaining, more fully appeareth. And now at this day, to wit; the 24th day of April, in the 24th year of the reign of our lord Charles the 2d, by the grace of God of England, Scotland, France, and Ireland, king, defender of the faith, &c. before the said lord the now king, in his Chancery aforesaid, here, to wit; at Westminster, comes the said Margaret in her proper person, and complains that she under colour of the premisses is grievously vexed and disquieted, and this not justly, because protesting that the inquisition aforesaid and the matter in the same contained are not sufficient in law, to which she hath no necessity neither is she bound by the law of the land, to answer in any manner, for plea nevertheless, the said Margaret saith, that she the said Margaret, at the said time of the taking of the inquisition aforesaid, and also always before and continually afterwards, hitherto was and yet is of sound mind, good understanding and sane memory, and sufficiently capable for the government of herself and her estate aforesaid, without this that she the said Margaret, at the said time of the taking of the inquisition aforesaid, or at any time before or afterwards, was, or now is lunatick, so that she is not capable of the government of herself and her estate aforesaid, and this the said Margaret is ready to verify as the court here shall consider, wherefore she prays judgment and that the inquisition aforesaid may be quashed, made void, and entirely held for nought, and that she to all things which she hath lost by occasion or colour of the inquisition aforesaid, may be restored, and that she by occasion or colour of the inquisition aforesaid may not be any further disturbed, but of the premisses by the court here may be entirely discharged: &c. And H. Finch, knight and baronet, attorney general of the said lord the now king, who for the said lord the king in this behalf prosecutes, present here in court in his proper person for the said lord

M. Stone appears in Chancery and pleads that she is compos mentis.

Protestation.

Traverse of the lunacy.

And prays that the inquisition may be quashed.

Replication of the attorney general and issue.

the king, saith, that by any thing by the said M. S. above by pleading alledged, the hands of the said lord the now king, from the several moieties of the messuage, lands, meadows and woods, aforesaid, and from the divers writings obligatory aforesaid, ought not to be removed and that the said M. S. to the possession of the said moieties, together with the issues and profits thereof in the mean time ought not to be restored, because by protesting not acknowledging any thing by the said M. S. pleaded to be true, for plea the said attorney general of the said lord the now king who, &c. for the said lord the king, saith, that she the said M. at the said time of the taking of the inquisition aforesaid and continually afterwards hitherto, was not, nor as yet is of sound mind, good understanding and sane memory, nor sufficiently capable of the government of herself and her estate aforesaid as she the said M. above by pleading hath alledged, and this the said attorney * general of the said lord the now king, who, &c. for the said lord the king prays may be enquired of by the country, and the said M. S. doth the like, &c. therefore day is given as well to the said M. S. as to the said attorney general of the said lord the now king, who, &c. before the said lord the king, until the morrow of the Holy Trinity, wheresoever he shall then be in England, to do and receive what is just in the premisses, and the sheriff of Worcester is commanded, that he cause to come before the said lord the now king, on the same day, twelve good and lawful men of the neighbourhood of Droitwich in his bailiwick, every of whom hath four pounds of land, tenements or rent, by the year at the least, by whom the truth of the matter in the premisses may be the better known, and who are in no wise of kin to the said M. S. to recognize upon their oath more fully the truth of and concerning the premisses. At which day before the lord, at Westminster, come as well the said M. S. by F. S. her attorney, as the said attorney general of the said lord the now king, who, &c. in his proper person, and the sheriff of the county aforesaid returns the said writ of venire facias in all things served and executed, together with the pannel of the names of the jurors to the said writ annexed, of whom none, &c. therefore the sheriff is commanded that he distrain the jurors aforesaid, by all their lands, &c. and that of the issues, &c. so that he may have their bodies before the lord the king from the day of St. Michael, in three weeks, wheresoever, &c. or before the justices of the said lord the king, assigned, to take assizes in the county of Worcester, aforesaid, if they shall first come on Thursday the first day of August, at W. in the

p P. 654.

Issue joined.

Venire awarded.

Parties appear in B. R.

Writ returned.

Destringas awarded.

the county aforesaid, by the form of the statute, &c. for the default of jurors, &c. the same day is given to the said M. S. as to the said attorney general of the said lord the now king, who, &c. and be it known that the writ of the said lord the king, thereupon, upon record, on the 26th day of June, in this same term was delivered to the under sheriff of the county aforesaid, in the form of law to be executed at his peril; At which three weeks of St. Michael, before the said lord the king, at Westminster, come as well the said H. F. knight and baronet, attorney general of the said lord the now king, as the said M. S. by her attorney aforesaid, and the justices before whom, &c. have sent here their record before them had, under the form of following to wit; Afterwards at the day and place within contained, before E. T. knight, chief baron of the Exchequer, of the lord the king, and J. A. knight, one of the justices of the said lord the king of the bench, justices of the said lord the king, assigned to take assizes, in the county of W. by the form of the statute, &c. come as well the within named H. F. knight and baronet, attorney general of the said lord the now king, who for the said lord the now king, in this behalf prosecutes, as the within written M. S. by her attorney within named, and the jurors of the jury whereof within mention is made, being called in like manner come, who being elected tried and sworn to speak the truth of the within contained, say upon their oath aforesaid, that the said M. within written, at the time of the taking of the inquisition aforesaid, and continually afterwards, hitherto was, and is of sound mind, good understanding, and sane memory and sufficiently capable for the government of herself and her estate within written, as the said M. within by pleading hath alledged.

Le sciendum.

Postea.

Verdict that at the time of taking the inquisition she was and now is of sound mind &c.

---

## • The King against Dancey.

P. 655.

CHARLES, by the grace of God, of England, Scotland, France and Ireland, king, defender of the faith, &c. to our beloved and faithful Edward Deering, knight and baronet, Peter Hayman; knight, Thomas Welford, knight, and James Oxendon, knight, and also to our beloved Lancelot Lovelace, esquire, one of the masters of our Chancery, Thomas Hales, esquire, Francis Rogers, doctor

A commission of king Charles 1st out of the Chancery to enquire of the forfeiture of offices granted by letters patent.

doctor in divinity, and Edward Bayes, esquire, greeting; whereas we by our letters patent, sealed under our great seal of England, bearing date at Westminster, the 3d day of January, in the second year of our reign, reciting in the same that whereas our most dear late father king James, of blessed memory, by his letters patent, bearing date at Westminster, the 24th day of February, in the first year of his reign, of England, France and Ireland, and in the 37th of Scotland, had given and granted to one Emanuel Alley of the town of Dover, in the county of Kent, gent. the office of water bailiff of the town of Dover aforesaid, in the said county of Kent, to have, enjoy, exercise and occupy the office aforesaid, to the said Emanuel Alley, by himself or by his sufficient deputy or deputies, from the date of his said letters patent, to the term and for the term of the natural life of the said Emanuel Alley, and that whereas our said most dear father, by his said letters patent, had given and granted to Jeremiah Alley, the son of the said Emanuel, the said office of water bailiff of the said town of Dover, in the said county of Kent, to have, enjoy, exercise and occupy, the office aforesaid to the said Jeremiah Alley, by himself or by his sufficient deputy or deputies, from the time in which the said office of water bailiff of the town of Dover aforesaid, by the death, surrender or forfeiture, of the said Emanuel Alley, or by any other manner whatsoever, or by any cause or occasion whatsoever should become vacant, or should happen to be in his hands or disposal, to the term and for the term of the natural life of the said Jeremiah Alley: and that whereas in and by a certain indenture, made the 22d day of July, in the 10th year of the reign of the said lord, our most dear father of England, France and Ireland, and the 45th of Scotland, between our said most dear father of the one part, and the said Emanuel Alley, and Jeremiah Alley, of the other part, our said father among other things, had given and granted to the said Emanuel Alley, the said office of water bailiff, of the said town of Dover in the county of Kent, to have, enjoy, exercise and occupy, the office aforesaid, to the said Emanuel Alley, his executors, administrators and assigns, by himself or themselves, or by his or their or any of their sufficient deputy or deputies, from the time in which the said office of water bailiff, of the town of Dover aforesaid, after the death, surrender, or forfeiture of both of them the said Emanuel Alley and Jeremiah Alley, or in any manner whatsoever or by any cause or occasion whatsoever, should become vacant or should happen to be in the hands and disposal of our said father, for the term

The commission recites that the said king Charles had by his letters patent reciting that James 1st by his patent had granted to E. Alley the office of water bailiff of Dover for his life, and the same office to J. Alley his son for his life after death, &c. of E. Alley.

And that by indenture between the said king James and E. Alley and J. Alley the said king had granted to E. Alley his executors, &c. the said office for 60 years next after determination of the said former estate.

term and during the whole term of ſixty years, from that time next enſuing, and fully to be compleated, yielding thereout * yearly to our ſaid father his heirs and ſucceſſors, from the time in which the ſaid Emanuel Alley, his executors adminiſtrators, or aſſigns, ſhould have or enjoy the office aforeſaid, by virtue of the indenture aforeſaid, twenty ſhillings of the lawful money of England, to be paid by equal portions at the feaſts of St. Michael the archangel, the Nativity of our Lord, the Annunciation of the Bleſſed Virgin Mary, and the Nativity of St. John the Baptiſt; as by the letters patent aforeſaid, and indenture aforeſaid more fully appeareth: and that whereas the ſaid Emanuel Alley, and Jeremiah Alley, by their indenture dated the 18th day of March, in the 19th year of the reign of our ſaid moſt dear father of England, &c. the ſaid office of water bailiff of the town of Dover aforeſaid, and alſo the ſaid letters patent and indenture aforeſaid, and all the right title claim intereſt and demand of them the ſaid Emanuel Alley, and Jeremiah Alley, and of each of them of and in the premiſſes to one Richard Dancey, had granted and aſſigned, as by the indenture of the ſaid Emanuel Alley, and Jeremiah Alley, more fully appeared: and that the ſaid letters patent and indenture, firſt recited, then being in the hands and poſſeſſion of the ſaid Richard Dancey, the ſaid Richard Dancey had ſurrendered and reſtored them to us in our Chancery, to be cancelled, nevertheleſs for the intention that we our other letters patent to one Maximilian Dancey, the brother of the ſaid Richard Dancey, for the term of his life, and after the death, ſurrender, or forfeiture of the ſaid Maximilian Dancey, to the ſaid Richard Dancy, for the term of his life, in the form following, would vouchſafe to make and grant, which ſurrender and reſtitution with the intention aforeſaid made, we accepting by our ſaid letters patent, and cauſing the ſaid letters patent to be cancelled, and the ſame remaining cancelled, we of our eſpecial grace, and certain knowledge and mere motion by our ſaid letters patent, gave and granted to the ſaid Maximilian Dancey, the office of water bailiff of our town of Dover, in the county of Kent in our hands and diſpoſal by the cancelling of the letters patent aforeſaid, or by whatſoever other means then being, and him the ſaid Maximilian Dancey, our water bailiff of the ſaid town made ordained and created by our letters patent aforeſaid, to have, enjoy, exerciſe and occupy the office aforeſaid, to the ſaid Maximilian Dancey, by himſelf or by his ſufficient deputy or deputies from the date of our ſaid letters patent to and for the term of the natural life of the ſaid Maximilian

P. 656.

And that the ſaid Alleys had by indenture granted their intereſt in the ſaid office and the ſaid letters patent and indenture to one Richard Dancey.

And that the ſaid Dancey had ſurrendered the ſame to ſaid king Charles to be cancelled to the intent to have the ſaid office regranted to M. D. for life; and after his death to the ſaid R. D. for life.

That the ſaid king had accordingly granted the ſaid office to M. D. for life.

imilian Dancey, together with all and ſingular houſes, edifices, ſtructures, profits, commodities and advantages whatſoever, to the ſaid office in any wiſe belonging or appertaining, in as ample manner and form as Richard Linch, Thomas Andrews, Emanuel Alley, or afore-time John Finch, Nicholas Stretley, Thomas Cheney, Thomas Portway, Edward Mody or Thomas Vaughan, or any or either of them or any other or others poſſeſſing the ſaid office before that time had or received, or ought to have had or received to and for the exerciſe or occupation of the office aforeſaid, and that without yielding, paying or making any account or any other thing whatſoever thereout to us our heirs and ſucceſſors, provided always that the ſaid Maximilian Dancey, or his ſufficient deputy in that behalf, ſhould continually reſide upon the ſaid office from time to

Provided he or his deputy ſhould continually reſide upon his office.

P. 657. * time during the life of the ſaid Maximilian Dancey; and further of our bountiful eſpecial grace, and of our certain knowledge and mere motion for the conſideration aforeſaid, by our ſaid letters patent, for us our heirs and ſucceſſors, we gave and granted to the ſaid Richard Dancey, the office of water bailiff of the town of Dover, in the county of Kent, aforeſaid, and him the ſaid Richard Dancey our water bailiff of the ſaid town made, ordained and created by our ſaid letters patent to have, enjoy, exerciſe and occupy the ſaid office to the ſaid Richard Dancey, by himſelf or by his ſufficient deputy or deputies, from the time in which the ſaid office of water bailiff of the town of Dover aforeſaid, by the death, ſurrender or forfeiture of the ſaid Maximilian Dancey or by any other means whatſoever or by any cauſe or occaſion whatſoever ſhould become vacant, or ſhould happen to be in our hands and diſpoſal to the term and for the term of the natural life of the ſaid Richard Dancey, together with all and ſingular houſes, edifices, ſtructures, profits, commodities and advantages whatſoever, to the ſaid office in any wiſe belonging or appertaining, in as ample manner and form as Richard Linch, Thomas Andrews, Emanuel Alley, or afore-time, John Finch, Nicholas Stretley, Thomas Cheney, Thomas Portway, Edward Mody or Thomas Vaughan, or any or either of them or any other or others poſſeſſing the ſaid office before that time had or received, or ought to have had or received, to and for the exerciſe and occupation of the ſaid office, and that without yielding paying or making any account or any other thing thereout to us, our heirs and ſucceſſors, provided always that the ſaid Richard Dancey, or his ſufficient deputy in that behalf after that the ſaid Richard Dancey ſhould enjoy the ſaid office by virtue of our ſaid letters

And by the ſaid patent granted the ſame office to R. Dancey for his life after the death, &c. of Maximilian Dancey with the like proviſo.

letters patent, should continually reside upon the said office from time to time during the natural life of the said Richard Dancey; also further reciting by our said letters patent that whereas our said most dear father, by his letters patent bearing date at Westminster, the 19th day of May, in the 14th year of his reign, of England, France and Ireland, and in the 50th of Scotland, as well in pursuance of his contract in a certain indenture made the 22d day of July, in the 10th year of his reign, of England, France and Ireland, and in the 46th of Scotland, between our said father of the one part, and the said Emanuel Alley of the town and port of Dover, in the county of Kent, gent. of the other part, as for divers good causes and considerations our said father specially moving, had willed, ordained and appointed, that from that time afterwards for ever a certain house or prison by the said Emanuel at his proper costs and charges then lately built and constructed, in the parish of St. Mary, in the ward of Mary Ann, in the town of Dover, aforesaid, should be a prison for the detaining and imprisoning malefactors and delinquents and all other persons whatsoever, for felony, debt, or other cause whatsoever, within the jurisdiction of the town and port of Dover, aforesaid, to be taken or arrested, and that all persons so within the jurisdiction of the said town and port, * after that time to be taken or arrested should be sent and committed to the said prison and to no other prison, there to remain until they should be delivered thereout in the lawful manner according to the law of the kingdom of England, and that there should be one or more persons or persons by our said father, his heirs and successors, from time to time to be nominated and appointed, who should be and should be called keeper or keepers of the prison of the town of Dover; also further reciting in our said letters patent, that whereas our said father, by his said letters patent, had given and granted to the said Emanuel Alley, the said office of keeper of the prison of the town and port of Dover, aforesaid, to have, hold, enjoy and exercise the said office to the said Emanuel and his assigns, by himself and themselves or by his or their sufficient deputy or deputies, for and during the natural life of the said Emanuel Alley: and also had given and granted by the said letters patent to the said Jeremiah Alley, the son of the said Emanuel Alley, the said office of keeper of the prison of the town and port of Dover, aforesaid, to have, hold, exercise, and enjoy the said office to the said Jeremiah Alley, and his assigns, by himself and themselves, or by his or their sufficient deputy or deputies, immediately after the death, surrender or forfeiture of the said Emanuel Alley, for and during the natural life of the said Jeremiah

And further reciting that whereas king James by other letters patent in pursuance of a contract between him and E. Alley, had ordained that a house lately built by E. Alley, in Dover, should be a prison for malefactors and debtors, &c. and that the keeper thereof should be appointed by the king. &c.

* P. 658.

And that by the said letters patent king James had granted the office of keeper of the said prison to E. Alley for his life, and to J. Alley for his life after the death, &c. of E. Alley.

And to E. Alley and his executors, &c. after the deaths of E. and J. Alley for the term of 60 years.

Jeremiah Alley, and further by his said letters had given and granted to the said Emanuel Alley, his executors, administrators and assigns, the said office of keeper of the said prison of the town and port of Dover, aforesaid, to have, hold, exercise and enjoy the said office to the said Emanuel Alley, his executors, administrators, and assigns, by himself, his heirs, executors, administrators and assigns, or by his or their sufficient deputy or deputies, immediately after the death, surrender or forfeiture of both of them the said Emanuel Alley and Jeremiah Alley; to the term and for the term of sixty years from that time next ensuing, fully to be compleated, as by the said letters patent of our said father more fully was manifested and appeared; also further reciting, that whereas the said Emanuel Alley and Jeremiah Alley, by their certain indenture, dated the 18th day of March, in the 19th year of the reign of our said most dear father of England, &c. the said office of keeper of the prison aforesaid, and also the said letters patent and the whole right, title, interest, claim and demand of the said Emanuel Alley, and Jeremiah Alley, and of each of them had granted and assigned to the said Richard Dancey, as by the indenture aforesaid more fully was manifested and appeared, and that the said letters patent in the hands and possession of the said Richard Dancey, being, he the said Richard Dancey, had surrendered and restored them to us in our Chancery to be cancelled, nevertheless for the intention that we our other letters patent to the said Maximilian Dancey for the term of his life, and after the decease, surrender or forfeiture of the said Maximilian Dancey, to the said Richard Dancey for the term of the life of the said Richard Dancey, of the said office of keeper of the prison of the town of Dover, aforesaid, in the form following, would vouchsafe to make and grant which surrender and restitution with the intention aforesaid made, we accepting by our said letters patent, and causing the said letters patent to be cancelled, and the same remaining * cancelled, we of our especial grace and of our certain knowledge and mere motion, and by our royal prerogative, willed, ordained and constituted by our said letters patent, for us, our heirs and successors, that afterwards for ever the said tenement or prison so as aforesaid, by the said Emanuel Alley, within the said town of Dover, built and constructed should be a prison for the detaining and imprisoning malefactors and delinquents, and all other persons whatsoever, for felony, debt or any other cause whatsoever, within the jurisdiction of the town and port of Dover, aforesaid, to be taken or arrested; and that all persons so within the jurisdiction of the town and port of Dover, afterwards to be taken

And also reciting that the said Alleys had by indenture granted the said office of keeper, and the said letters patent to R. Dancey, and that the said Dancey had surrendered the said patent to the said King Charles, for the intention, &c.

* P. 659.

That the said King Charles by the said letters patent ordained that the said prison should be a prison for the town of Dover, for imprisoning ma-

or

or arrested, should be sent and committed to the said prison and to no other prison, there to remain until that thereout they should be delivered in the lawful manner, according to the law of our kingdom of England, any statute, act, ordinance, or provision, or any other thing, cause or matter whatsoever to contrary thereof notwithstanding; and that the said prison from that time afterwards for ever should be called the prison of the town and port of Dover, and that from that time afterwards for ever, there should be one office which should be called and named the office of keeper of the prison of the town and port of Dover, aforesaid, and that in like manner there should be one or more person or persons, by us, our heirs and successors, from time to time to be nominated and appointed, who should be and should be called keeper or keepers of the prison of the town and port of Dover, and for the better execution of our will in that behalf, and of our bountiful especial grace, and of our certain knowledge and mere motion for the considerations aforesaid, (whether the office aforesaid of keeper of the prison of the town and port of Dover, by reason of the surrender aforesaid, or by whatsoever other means was vacant or should happen to be vacant) we by our said letters patent for us, our heirs and successors, gave and granted to the said Maximilian Dancey, the said office of keeper of the prison of the town and port of Dover, and him the said Maximilian Dancey, keeper of the prison of the town and port of Dover, aforesaid, for us, our heirs and successors, made, ordained and appointed by our said letters patent, to have, hold, exercise and enjoy the said office, to the said Maximilian Dancey, and his assigns, by himself and themselves, or by his or their sufficient deputy or deputies, for and during the natural life of the said Maximilian Dancey, and of our bountiful especial grace, and of our certain knowledge and mere motion willed and granted that the said Maximilian Dancey and his assigns, or his or their sufficient deputy or deputies for the exercise and occupation of that office, should have, take, perceive and enjoy to his or their proper use and behoof, all and singular such and the like fees, rewards, perquisites, profits, allowances, and sums of money as by the keeper of our gaol or prison of our city of Canterbury, or by the keeper of our gaol or prison of our borough of Maidstone, in the county of Kent, for the prisoners to them or to either of them committed were usually had, taken or received, and that without yielding, paying, or making any account thereof, or any other thing whatsoever to us, our heirs, or successors, and moreover of our especial grace and of our certain

lefactors, &c. and by the said patent granted the office of keeper to M. Dancey, for his life, and to R. Dancey for his life after the death, &c. of M. Dancey.

 knowledge

* P. 660. knowledge * and mere motion for the considerations aforesaid, by our said letters patent, for us, our heirs and successors we gave and granted to the said Richard Dancey, the said office of keeper of the prison of the town and port of Dover, aforesaid, and him the said Richard Dancey, keeper of the prison of the town and port of Dover, aforesaid, for us, our heirs and successors, made, ordained and appointed, by our said letters patent, to have, hold, exercise and enjoy the said office to the said Richard Dancey, and his assigns, by himself and themselves, or by his or their sufficient deputy or deputies, immediately after the death, surrender or forfeiture of the said Maximilian Dancey, for and during the life of the said Richard Dancey, and of our bountiful especial grace, and of our certain knowledge and mere motion for us, our heirs and successors, we willed and granted that the said Richard Dancey and his assigns, or his or their sufficient deputy or deputies for the exercise and occupation of the said office, should have, perceive and enjoy to his or their proper use and behoof, all and singular such and the like fees, rewards, perquisites, profits, allowances and sums of money as by the keeper of our gaol or prison of our city of Canterbury, or by the keeper of our gaol or prison of our borough of Maidstone, in the county of Kent, for the prisoners to them or to either of them committed were usually had, taken, or received, and that without yielding, paying, or making any account thereof or any other thing whatsoever, to us, our heirs, or successors; as by the said letters patent among other things more fully appeareth and is manifest; which office of water bailiff of the town of Dover, aforesaid, and the said office of keeper of the prison of the town and port of Dover, aforesaid, he the said Maximilian Dancey after the making of our letters patent aforesaid, to the said Maximilian, of the said several offices so as aforesaid made, by himself or by his sufficient deputy or deputies, rightly and duly hath not exercised, for this, because the said Maximilian Dancey from the time of the making of our said letters patent to him, of the several offices so as aforesaid made, neither by himself nor by his sufficient deputy or deputies, the said offices or either of them in the due manner did serve or attend, and for this, because the said Maximilian Dancey, or his sufficient deputy in that behalf, upon the said office of water bailiff aforesaid, from the time of the making of our said letters patent, continually and from time to time did not reside according to the tenor and effect of our said letters patent to him thereon as aforesaid made, and for this, because the said Maximilian Dancey, divers persons to the said prison of the town and port of Dover, aforesaid, under his custody committed

*Prout the said letters patent.*

*Then the commission suggests that M. Dancey, hath not rightly and duly executed the said offices of water bailiff and keeper of the prison of Dover, either by himself or deputy, &c.*

*1st He did not serve or attend the said offices or either of them.*

mitted, and in the ſame priſon under his cuſtody detained, wilfully and negligently did permit to eſcape and go at large out of the ſaid priſon, by reaſon of which the ſaid Maximilian Dancey, the ſeveral offices aforeſaid, and his whole eſtate, right, title and intereſt of and in the ſaid offices and each of them, hath entirely forfeited to us, as we are certainly informed: which office of water bailiff of the town of Dover, aforeſaid, and alſo the ſaid office of keeper of the priſon of the town and port of Dover, aforeſaid, he the ſaid Richard Dancey, after the forfeiture of the ſaid ſeveral offices by the ſaid M. D. to us as * aforeſaid forfeited, by himſelf or by his ſufficient deputy or deputies, rightly and duly hath not exerciſed, for this, becauſe the ſaid R. D. from the ſaid time of the ſaid forfeiture of the ſaid office of water bailiff, and of the ſaid office of keeper of priſon of the town and port aforeſaid, neither by himſelf nor by his ſufficient deputy or deputies, the ſaid offices or either of them in the due manner did ſerve or attend, and for this, becauſe the ſaid R. D. or his ſufficient deputy, upon the ſaid office of water bailiff from the ſaid time of the forfeitture of the ſaid office to us by the ſaid M. D. in the form aforeſaid forfeited, continually from time to time did not reſide according to the form and effect of our ſaid letters patent to him thereof as aforeſaid made, and for this, becauſe the ſaid R. D. divers perſons to the ſaid priſon of the town and port of Dover, aforeſaid, under his cuſtody committed, and in the ſame priſon under his cuſtody detained, wilfully and negligently did permit to eſcape and go at large out of the of the ſaid priſon, by reaſon of which the ſaid R. D. the ſeveral offices aforeſaid, and his whole eſtate, right, title and intereſt, of and in the ſaid offices and each of them to us in like manner hath entirely forfeited, as we in like manner are certainly informed: we therefore bebeing willing to provide as well for our ſecurity as for our peoples ſecurity in this behalf, as we are bounden and very much relying in your fidelity and prudent circumſpection, have aſſigned you, and by the tenor of theſe preſents give you, and to ſeven, ſix, five, four, three or two of you, full power and authority to enquire as well by the oath of good and lawful men of our cinque ports, as well within liberties as without, by whom the truth of the matter may be the better known, as by all other ways, methods and means by which you may or can know better, whether the ſaid M. D. from the ſaid time of the making of our ſaid letters patent of the offices aforeſaid, to him as aforeſaid made, by himſelf, or by his ſufficient deputy or deputies, the ſaid offices or either of them rightly and duly hath exerciſed, ſerved or attended or not, and alſo whether the ſaid M. D. or his ſufficient

2d, He did not reſide upon the office of water bailiff according to the proviſo, &c.

3d, He ſuffered ſeveral perſons to eſcape out of priſon.

* P. 661.

By reaſon of which he hath forfeited his ſaid offices.

And that R. Dancey after the ſaid forfeiture hath not rightly and duly exerciſed the ſaid offices: and the ſame matters aſſigned as cauſes of forfeiture.

Therefore the commiſſioners or any two of them empowered to enquire.

1ſt, Whether M. D. hath rightly and duly exerciſed the ſaid office.

2d, Whether he did reside upon the office of water bailiff.

sufficient deputy in that behalf upon the said office of water bailiff, from the said time of the making of our said letters patent, of that office to the said M. D. as aforesaid made, continually from time to time, according to the tenor and effect of our said letters patent did reside or not: and whether the said Richard Dancey from the said time of the forfeiture of the said office of water bailiff, and of the said office of keeper of the prison of the town and port aforesaid, by himself or by his sufficient deputy or deputies, the said offices or either of them rightly and duly hath exercised, served or attended, or not: and whether the said R. D. from the said time of the forfeiture of the said office of water

3d and 4th the same as to R. D.

bailiff to us, by the said M. D. as aforesaid forfeited, by himself or by his sufficient deputy in that behalf, upon the said office of water bailiff, continually from time to time according to the tenor and effect of our said letters patent

5th, Whether M. D. and R. D. or either of them suffered any person to escape out of prison.

did reside or not: and whether the said M. D. and R. D. or either of them or the deputy or deputies of either of them, at any time after the making of our said letters patent, any person or persons to the said prison of the town and port of Dover, aforesaid, under the custody of the said M. or R. committed and under the custody of the said M. and R. or either of them detained wilfully * or negligently did permit

* P. 662.

to escape and go at large out of the said prison or not: and whether they the said M. D. and R. D. or either of them or any person or persons by them or either of them deputed at any time, in or concerning the exercise and execution of

6th, Whether they or either of them or their deputies, &c. have in any manner failed in their duty.

the said offices or either of them, in any wise hath or have failed in his or their duty; and of all other forfeitures of the offices aforesaid or either of them, by the said M. D. and R. D. or either of them committed or perpetrated, and more fully the truth of all other things, matters, articles and circumstances, the premisses or any of them in any wise touching or concerning: therefore we command you that at certain days and places which for this purpose you shall appoint, or any seven, six, five, four, three or two of you

7th, Of all other forfeitures, &c.

shall appoint, you or seven, six, five, four, three or two of you diligently make inquisition in the premisses, and the same so made distinctly and plainly to us in our Chancery, under your seals, or of any seven, six, five, four, three or two of you, and the seals of those by whom it shall be made

Command to the constable of Dover, and the warden of the cinque ports.

without delay send, or seven, six, five, four, three or two of you send, and these our letters patent: for We command by the tenor of these presents, the constable of our castle of Dover, and the warden of our cinque ports, that at certain days and places which you shall appoint, or any seven, six, five, four, three or two of you shall appoint, and

and shall make known to him on our behalf or any seven, six, five, four, three or two of you shall make known to him that he cause to come before you, or seven, six, five, four, three or two of you, so many and such good and lawful men of the cinque ports aforesaid, as well within liberties as without, by whom the truth of the matter in the premisses may be the better known and enquired into, in witness whereof we have caused these our letters to be made patent. Witness ourself at Westminster, the 26th day of August, in the second year of our reign. Test.

*Cesar.*

An inquisition indented taken at the Guildhall of the town and port of Dover, within the liberties of the cinque ports in the county of Kent, on the 23d day of September, in the 5th year of the reign of our lord Charles by the grace of God of England, Scotland, France and Ireland, king defender of the faith, &c. before Edward Deering, knight and baronet, Peter Hayman, knight, Lancelot Lovelace; esquire, one of the masters of the Chancery of the lord the now king, and Francis Rogers doctor in divinity, four commissioners of the said lord the now king, by virtue of the commission of the said lord the king, under his great seal of England to them and to others in the commission to this inquisition annexed, named, to enquire of the forfeiture of the offices of water bailiff of the town of Dover, in the county of Kent, and of keeper of the prison of the town and port of Dover, aforesaid, and of all other things, matters, articles and circumstances, in the said commission mentioned and specified, by the oath of Richard Lutham, George Blackboy, Thomas Browne, Daniel Billiard, John White, William Epps, John Bell, Francis Gamon, Richard Sprye, Simon Dugdale, Robert Stone, Edward * Baylon, John Nathersole, Francis Barrington, Richard Heiling, Henry Turner, Robert Smith and Humphrey Mantle, good and lawful men of the cinque ports, aforesaid, who being sworn and charged, say upon their oath aforesaid, that the said Maximilian Dancey, in the commission aforesaid named, by himself or by any his sufficient deputy in that behalf, after the making of the said letters patent, bearing date the 3d day of January, in the 2d year of the reign of the said lord the now king in the said commission specified, to wit; on the 27th day of October, in the 3d year of the reign of the said lord the now king, and continually afterwards until the 21st day of November, from that time next ensuing, upon the office of water bailiff of the town of Dover, aforesaid, in the county of Kent, aforesaid, in the commission aforesaid named did not reside according to the form and effect of the proviso

Inquisition.

* P. 663.

The jury find that M. D. the 27th of Oct. 3d year of the king, and from thence to the 21st of November following, did not reside upon his office of water bailiff.

And that from the 26th of Oct. to the 21ſt of Nov. in the 3d of the king, he did not attend his ſaid office whereby many affairs remained unperformed.

proviſo in the ſaid letters patent mentioned: and that the ſaid M. D. and his deputies from the office aforeſaid, for the whole time aforeſaid, abſented themſelves and each and every of them abſented himſelf: and that the ſaid M. D. by himſelf or by his ſufficient deputy or deputies the ſaid office for the whole time aforeſaid, to wit; from the 26th day of the ſaid month of October, in the 3d year of the reign of the ſaid lord the king aforeſaid unto the ſaid 21ſt day of November, from that time next enſuing, did not ſerve nor attend, whereby divers affairs as well the ſaid lord the now king, as divers liege ſubjects of the ſaid lord the now king very much concerning, and by him the ſaid M. or by his ſufficient deputy or deputies within and during the time aforeſaid ſpecially to be performed, entirely remained unperformed: and the jurors aforeſaid, further ſay, upon their oath aforeſaid, that the ſaid M. D. by himſelf or by any his ſufficient deputy in that behalf, after the making of the letters patent aforeſaid, bearing date the 3d day of the month of January in the 2d year of the reign of the ſaid lord the now king, in the ſaid commiſſion ſpecified, to wit; on the 25th day of November, in the 3d year of the reign of the ſaid lord the now king aforeſaid, and continually afterwards until the 20th day of February from that time next enſuing upon the ſaid office of water bailiff of the town of Dover, aforeſaid, in the county of Kent, aforeſaid, in the commiſſion aforeſaid mentioned, did not reſide according to the form and effect of the proviſo in the ſaid letters patent mentioned: and that the ſaid M. D. and his deputies from the office aforeſaid for the whole time aforeſaid abſented themſelves and each and every of them abſented himſelf, and that the ſaid M. D. by himſelf or by his ſufficient deputy or deputies, that office for the whole time aforeſaid, to wit; from the 24th day of the ſaid month of November in the 3d year of the reign of the ſaid lord the now king aforeſaid until the ſaid 20th day of February, from that time next enſuing, did not ſerve nor attend, whereby divers other affairs as well the ſaid lord the now king as divers liege ſubjects of the ſaid lord the now king very much concerning, and by the ſaid M. or by his ſufficient deputy or deputies within and during the time aforeſaid ſpecially to be performed entirely remained unperformed: and the jurors aforeſaid, further ſay upon their oath aforeſaid, that the ſaid M. D. in the commiſſion aforeſaid named, by himſelf or by any his ſufficient deputy in that behalf after the making of the ſaid letters patent, bearing date the ſaid 3d day of January in the 2d year of the reign of the ſaid lord the now king * aforeſaid, in the ſaid commiſſion ſpecified, to wit; on the 24th day of February, in the 3d year of the reign

Did not reſide upon his ſaid office upon the 25th of Nov. the 3d of the king, nor from that unto the 20th of February following.

Did not attend his ſaid office from the 24th of Nov. in the 3d year of the king, until the 20th of February following, whereby, &c.

* P. 664.

reign of the said lord the now king and continually afterwards until the 24th day of June from that time next ensuing upon the said office of water bailiff of the town of Dover, aforesaid in the county of Kent aforesaid, in the commission aforesaid mentioned, did not reside, according to the form and effect of the proviso in the letters patent, aforesaid mentioned: and that the said M. D. and his deputies from the said office for the whole time aforesaid absented themselves and each and every of them absented himself: and that the said M. D. by himself or by his sufficient deputy or deputies that office for the whole time aforesaid, to wit; from the 23d day of February in the 3d year of the reign of the said lord the now king, aforesaid, until the 24th day of July, from that time next following, did not serve nor attend whereby divers other affairs as well the said lord the now king as divers liege subjects of the said lord the now king, very much concerning, and by the said M. D. or by his sufficient deputy or deputies within and during the time aforesaid, specially to be performed, remained unperformed: and the jurors aforesaid upon their oath aforesaid, further say, that after the making of the said letters patent, bearing date the 3d day of January, in the 2d year of the reign of the said lord the now king aforesaid, to wit; on the 3d day of August in the second year of the reign of the said lord the now king, one John Wright, late of the city of London, gent. by virtue of a certain commission de restringendo passagio, in the town and port of Dover, aforesaid, by George, late duke of Buckingham, then warden of the cinque ports, and of the antient towns and members of the same, lawfully granted to the mayor of the town and port, aforesaid, for the time being or his deputy, to the rectors of the several parishes of the blessed virgin Mary, and St James the apostle, in the town and port aforesaid, for the time being, to Francis Wilford and William Ham, esquires, to George Bing, William Leonard, Henry Steed, and Nicholas Elve, jurats of the town and port aforesaid, to Thomas Linhill, clerk of the castle of Dover, to Francis Raworth, town clerk of the town and port aforesaid, and to William Jones, passage clerk, or to any three or more of them, by John Pringle, then mayor of the town and port aforesaid, John Reading, clerk, then rector of the said parochial church of the blessed virgin Mary, aforesaid, and the said George Bing and Henry Steed, jurats of the town and port, aforesaid, four of the said commissioners was lawfully committed to the said prison of the said lord the king, of the town and port aforesaid, under the custody of the said M. D. then keeper of the prison aforesaid, safely and securely in the said prison to be kept, until from thence he should be

Did not reside upon his said office upon the 24th of February, the 3d of the king, nor from that to the 24th of June following.

Did not attend his said office from the 23d of Feb. in the 3d year of the king, to the 24th of June following, whereby, &c.

The jury find that one John Wright on the 3d of August in the 2d year of the king was committed by certain commissioners to the prison of Dover in keeping of the said M. D. for refusing to take the oath of allegiance, and that on the 14th of March in the 3d year of the king, M. D. suffered him to escape.

be lawfully delivered, because that the said John Wright did refuse to take the oath of allegiance to the said the king, to him by the said commissioners then and there lawfully tendered, and that the said John Pringle, John Reading, George Bing, and Henry Steed, the four commissioners aforesaid, at the time of the committal of the said John Wright, had sufficient power and authority to commit the said John Wright, to the prison aforesaid under the custody of the said M. D. for the cause before mentioned, and the said John Wright to the custody of the said M. D. so thereto being lawfully committed, and in the prison * aforesaid, under the custody of the said M. D. the keeper of the said prison, then and there being, he the said M. D. him the said John Wright out of the prison aforesaid, and out of the custody of the said M. D. afterwards, to wit; on the 14th day of March in the 3d year of the reign of the said lord the now king, at the said town of Dover, in the conuty of Kent, aforesaid, wilfully did permit to escape and go at large wheresoever he would, without any lawful warrant by him the said M. D. thereupon had; and the jurors aforesaid upon this oath aforesaid, further say, that after the making of the said letters patent, bearing date the 3d day of January in the 2d year of the reign of the said lord the now king, aforesaid, to wit; on the third day of August, in the 2d year of the reign of the said lord the now king, aforesaid, one George Thompson, late of London, Gentleman by virtue of a certain commission de restringendo passagio, in the town and port of Dover, aforesaid, by the said George, late duke of Buckingham, then warden of the cinque ports, aforesaid, and of the antient towns and members of the same; lawfully granted to the mayor of the said town and port aforesaid, for the time being, or to his deputy, to the rectors of the several parishes aforesaid, of the blessed virgin Mary, and St. James the apostle, in the town and port aforesaid, for the time being, to Francis Wilford, and —— Harrington, esquires, to G. B. W. L. H. S. T. F. and N. Eaton, jurats of the town and port aforesaid, to T. L. clerk of the castle of Dover, to Francis Raworth, town clerk of the town and port aforesaid, and to William Jones, passage clerk, or to any three or more of them, by John Pringle, then mayor of the town and port aforesaid, John Reading, clerk, rector of the said parochial church of the blessed virgin Mary, and the said George Bing and Henry Steed, jurats of the town and port aforesaid, four of the said commissioners was lawfully committed to the said prison of the said lord the king, of the town and port aforesaid, under the custody of the said M. D. then keeper of the prison aforesaid, safely and securely in the said prison to be kept, until he should be thereout

* P. 665.

That in like manner he suffered one George Thompson to escape.

thereout delivered, because that the said George Thompson, did refuse to take the oath of allegiance to the said lord the king, then to him by the said commissioners then and there lawfully tendered; and that the said John Pringle, John Reading, George Bing, and Henry Steed, the four commissioners aforesaid, at the time of the committal of the said George Thompson, had sufficient power and authority to commit the said G. T. to the prison aforesaid, under the custody of the said M. D. for the cause aforesaid, and the said G. T. to the custody of the said M. D. so thereto being lawfully committed, and in the said prison under the custody of the said M. D. keeper of the said prison, then and there being, the said M. D. him the said G. T. out of the prison aforesaid and out of the custody of the said M. D. afterwards, to wit; on the 14th of day of March, in the 3d year of the reign of the said lord the now king, at the said town of Dover, in the county of Kent, aforesaid, wilfully did permit to escape and go at large, wheresoever he would, without any lawful warrant by him the said M. D. thereupon before had. And the jurors aforesaid further say, upon their oath, aforesaid, that after the making of the letters patent aforesaid, bearing date the 3d day of January, in the 2d year aforesaid, to wit; upon the 14th day of March, in the 2d year of the reign of the said * lord the now king, aforesaid, at the general session of the peace and gaol delivery, in the town and port of Dover, aforesaid, in the Guildhall of the said town, before John Pringle, then mayor of the town and port aforesaid, John Waad and Edward Kempe, jurats, of the town and port aforesaid, justices of the said lord the now king, in the due manner assigned, to preserve the peace within the town and port aforesaid, and the members and precincts of the said town and port, and also to hear and determine divers felonies, trespasses, and other misdeeds there perpetrated, there lawfully held on the said 14th day of March, in the 2d year of the reign of the said lord the now king, aforesaid, one John Westward, by the name of John Westward, late of the town and port of Dover, aforesaid, in the county of Kent, gent. was indicted for this, that he on the 10th day of February, in the 2d year of the reign of our lord the king, aforesaid, with force and arms, to wit; with swords and knives, between the ninth and tenth hours of the night of the same day, in the king's high-way, leading from Dover, aforesaid, to a certain place called Fardinglowe, in the parish of Huffam, in the county aforesaid, within the liberties of the town and port of Dover, in the county aforesaid, and within the jurisdiction of the said court, upon one Valentine Harvey, in the parish of Huffam, in the county of Kent, yeoman, and Frances his wife, then and there in the peace of

* P. 666.

The jury find further that at the sessions of peace and gaol delivery for Dover, held the 14th March, in the 2d year of the king, one John Westward was indicted, tried, convicted and attainted of an highway robbery, and thereupon was committed to the said prison, and that the said M. D. on the 24th of March permitted him to escape.

of God, and of the said lord the king, being made an assault and them beat, wounded and ill-treated, and one silver spoon of the value of 12 shillings, and one horse of the value of 10l. of the lawful money of England, and one saddle, one bridle, one pillion, and one saddle-cloth of the value of 20 shillings, of the lawful money of England, of the goods and chattles of the said Valentine, and three shillings in monies, numbered, then and there found from the person of the said Valentine, feloniously took and carried away, against the peace of the said lord the king, his crown and dignity, as by the said indictment more fully appeareth, to which indictment the said John Westward, then and there pleaded that he was not guilty of the robbery and felony aforesaid, to him above supposed, and thereupon issue in the due manner was joined between the said lord the now king, and the said John Westward, whether the said John Westward was guilty of the said robbery and felony in the said indictment mentioned or not; and afterwards at the said general session of the peace and gaol delivery, held in the form aforesaid, on the said 14th day of March, in the 2d year of the reign of the said lord the now king aforesaid, at the town and port of Dover, in the county of Kent, aforesaid, before the said justices, the said John Westward was lawfully arrested, and by certain jurors then an there duly elected, sworn and charged to give their verdict of and upon the issue aforesaid, was found guilty of the robbery and felony aforesaid, whereupon the justices aforesaid then and there gave their judgment thereupon, that the said John Westward should be hanged, until, &c. and thereupon the said J. W. for the said cause, then and there by the justices aforesaid, to the custody of the said M. D. then being keeper of the prison aforesaid, of the town and port of Dover, aforesaid, was lawfully committed there to remain until, &c. and the said John Westward. so thereupon to the custody of the said M. D. being committed and in the prison aforesaid, under the custody of the said M. D. keeper
* P. 667. of the * said prison then and there being, he the said M. D. him the said J. W. out of the said prison and out of the custody of the said M. D. afterwards, to wit; on the 24th day of March, in the 2d year of the reign of the said lord the now king, did permit to escape and go at large, wheresoever he would, without any lawful warrant by him the said M. D. thereupon before had. And the jurors aforesaid now sworn further say, upon their oath aforesaid, that after the making of the letters patent aforesaid, bearing date the 3d day of January, in the 2d year of the reign of the said lord the now king, aforesaid, at the general session of the peace and gaol delivery, in the town and port of Dover, aforesaid, in the

the Guildhall of the ſaid town, before John Pringle, then mayor of the town and port aforeſaid, John Waad and Edward Kempe, jurats of the town and port aforeſaid, juſtices of the ſaid lord the now king, in the due manner aſſigned, to preſerve the peace within the town and port aforeſaid, and within the members and precincts of the ſaid town and port, and alſo to hear and determine divers felonies, treſpaſſes, and other miſdeeds there perpetrated, there lawfully held on the 30th day of Auguſt, in the 3d year of the reign of the ſaid lord the now king, one John Burke, by the name of John Burke, late of Conrock, in the kingdom of Ireland, and then of the town and port of Dover, aforeſaid, in the county of Kent, yeoman, was indicted for this, that he on 16th day of Auguſt, in the 3d year of the reign of the ſaid lord the now king, aforeſaid, at the town and port of Dover aforeſaid, within the juriſdiction of the ſaid court, with force and arms upon one Thomas Hogben, late of the town and port aforeſaid, mariner, in the peace of God and of the ſaid lord the king, then and there being of his malice aforethought, made an an aſſault, and with a certain dagger of the value of two ſhillings, which he in his right hand then and there had and held, him the ſaid Thomas Hogben then and there in the left part of his breaſt, feloniouſly did ſtrike, and gave to him one mortal wound of the depth of four inches, and of the breadth of one inch, of which mortal wound the ſaid Thomas Hogben inſtantly died, and ſo the ſaid J. B. him the ſaid T. H. at the town and port aforeſaid, within the juriſdiction of the ſaid court, of his malice aforethought, feloniouſly and wilfully did kill and murder, againſt the peace of the ſaid lord the king, his crown and dignity, as by the ſaid indictment more fully appeareth: to which indictment the ſaid J. B. pleaded that he was not guilty of the murder and felony aforeſaid to him above charged, and thereupon iſſue in the due manner was joined, between the ſaid lord the king and the ſaid John Burke, whether the ſaid J. B. was guilty of the felony and murder aforeſaid, in the ſaid indictment laſt mentioned or not, and afterwards at the ſaid general ſeſſion of the peace and gaol delivery in the form aforeſaid, on the ſaid 30th day of Auguſt, in the 3d year aforeſaid, at the town and port of Dover aforeſaid, in the ſaid county of Kent, before the juſtices aforeſaid lawfully held, the ſaid J. B. was lawfully arreſted, and by certain jurors then and there duly elected, ſworn, and charged to give their verdict of and upon the iſſue aforeſaid, was found guilty of the murder and felony aforeſaid, whereupon the juſtices aforeſaid, then and there gave their judgment thereon, that the ſaid John Burke ſhould be hanged until, &c. and thereupon the

The jury alſo find that he permitted one John Burke attainted of murder, to eſcape from his cuſtody out of ſaid priſon on the 16th Sept. the 3d of the king.



ſaid

ſaid J. B. for that cauſe then and there by the juſtices aforeſaid to the cuſtody of the ſaid M. D. then being keeper of the priſon within the town and port of Dover aforeſaid, was * P. 668. * lawfully committed, there to remain until, &c. and the ſaid John Burke to the cuſtody of the ſaid M. D. ſo thereupon being committed and in the priſon aforeſaid, under the cuſtody of the ſaid M. D. the keeper of the priſon aforeſaid, then and there being, he the ſaid M. D. him the ſaid J. B. out of the priſon aforeſaid and out of the cuſtody of the ſaid M. D. afterwards, to wit; on the 16th day of September, in the 3d year of the reign of the ſaid lord the now king aforeſaid, wilfully did permit to eſcape and go at large whereſoever he would, without any lawful warrant by him the ſaid M. D. thereupon before had. And the jurors aforeſaid now ſworn further ſay upon their oath aforeſaid, that the ſaid M. D. by himſelf or by any his ſufficient deputy in that behalf after the making of the letters patent aforeſaid, bearing date the 3d day of January, in the 2d year of the reign of our lord the now king, aforeſaid, to wit; on the 27th day of October, in the 3d year of the reign of the ſaid lord the king aforeſaid, and continually afterwards unto the ſaid 21ſt day of November, from that time next euſuing, upon the ſaid office of keeper of the priſon of the town and port of Dover, in the county of Kent, aforeſaid, in the commiſſion aforeſaid in like manner mentioned did not reſide, and that the ſaid M. D. and his deputies from that office for the whole time aforeſaid, abſented themſelves, and each and every of them abſented himſelf: and the ſaid M. D. by himſelf or by his ſufficient deputy or deputies that office for the whole time aforeſaid, to wit; from the 26th day of the month of October, in the 3d year of the reign of the ſaid lord the king aforeſaid, until the ſaid 21ſt day of November, from that time next enſuing did not ſerve nor attend, whereby divers affairs as well the ſaid lord the king as divers liege ſubjects of the ſaid lord the king very much concerning, and by the ſaid M. or by his ſufficient deputy or deputies, within and during the time aforeſaid ſpecially to be performed, remained entirely unperformed. And the jurors aforeſaid now here, ſworn further, ſay upon their oath aforeſaid, that the ſaid M. D. by himſelf or by any his ſufficient deputy in this behalf, after the making of the ſaid letters patent, bearing date the 3d day of January, in the 2d year of the reign of our ſaid lord the now king aforeſaid, to wit; upon the 25th day of November, in the 3d year of the reign of the ſaid lord the king aforeſaid, and continually afterwards until the 20th day of February from that time next enſuing, upon the ſaid office of keeper of the priſon of the town and port aforeſaid

That M. D. by himſelf or his deputies did not reſide upon his office of keeper of the priſon of Dover, upon the 27th of Oct. in the 3d year of the king, nor from that continually unto the 21ſt of Nov. following.

And that from the 26th of Oct. ſame year to the 21ſt of Nov. following he did not attend ſaid office, whereby, &c.

Did not reſide upon the 25th Nov. in the 3d year of the king nor from that unto the 20th of February following, whereby, &c.

said did not reside, and that the said M. D. and his deputies from the office aforesaid for the whole time aforesaid, absented themselves and each and every of them absented himself: and that the said M. D. by himself or by any his sufficient deputy or deputies that office for the whole time aforesaid, to wit; from the 24th day of the said month of November, in the 3d year of the said lord the king aforesaid, until the said 20th day of February, from that time next ensuing did not serve nor attend, whereby divers affairs as well the said lord the king as divers liege subjects of the said lord the king, very much concerning, and by the said M. D. or by his sufficent deputy or deputies within and during the said time specially to be performed, remained entirely unperformed. And the jurors aforesaid now sworn further say upon their oath aforesaid, that the said M. D. by himself, or by any his sufficient deputy in that behalf, after the making of the said letters patent, bearing date the 3d day of January, in the 2d year of the reign of the said lord the now king, aforesaid, to wit; on the 23d day of February, in the 3d year of the reign of the said * lord the now king aforesaid, and continually afterwards, until the 23d day of June from that time next ensuing, upon the said office of keeper of the said prison of the town and port of Dover aforesaid, did not reside, and that the said M. D. and his deputies from the said office for the whole time aforesaid, absented themselves, and each and every of them absented himself: and that the said M. D. by himself or by any his sufficient deputy or deputies, the said office for the whole time aforesaid, to wit; from the 22d day of February in the 3d year of the reign of the said lord the king aforesaid unto the 23d day of June, from that time next ensuing, did not serve nor attend, whereby divers affairs as well the said lord the king as divers liege subjects of the said lord the king very much concerning, and by the said M. or by his sufficient deputy or deputies, within and during the said time specially to be performed remained entirely unperformed. And the jurors aforesaid now sworn, further say upon their oath aforesaid, that the said Richard Dancey in the commission aforesaid named, on the —— day of June in the 4th year of the reign of our said lord the now king, at the town and port of Dover aforesaid, took upon himself the execution as well of the said office of water bailiff of the town aforesaid, as the said office of keeper of the prison of the town and port aforesaid, and was of the offices aforesaid the seized as the law requires: and they further say upon their oath aforesaid, that the said R. D. by himself or by any his sufficient deputy in that behalf, after the making of the said letters patent, bearing date the 3d day of January, in the 2d year

Did not attend said office from the 24th Nov. 3d of the king, unto the 20th of Feb. following, whereby, &c.

Did not reside upon said office upon the 23d of February nor from that to the 23d of June following.

* P. 669.

Did not attend said office from the 22d of Feb. in the 3d year of the king, unto the 23d of June following whereby, &c.

The jury then find that R. Dancey in June, in the 4th year of the king, took upon himself the said offices and was seized prout lex postulat.

That R. D. upon the 15th day of June, in the 4th year of the king, and from that to the 25th day of the said month did not reside upon his office of water bailiff.

year aforesaid, to wit; on the 15th day of June, in the 4th year of the reign of the said lord the king, and continually afterwards until the 25th day of the said month of June, in the 4th year aforesaid, upon the office of water bailiff of the town of Dover aforesaid, in the county of Kent, aforesaid, in the commission aforesaid mentioned, did not reside according to the form and effect of the proviso in the said letters patent mentioned, and that the said R. D. and his deputies from the office aforesaid, for the whole time absented themselves, and each and every of them absented himself: and that the said R. D. by himself or by any his sufficient deputy or deputies, the said office for the whole time aforesaid, to wit; from the 14th day of the said month of June in the 4th year aforesaid unto the said 25th day of the said month of June in the 4th year aforesaid, did not serve nor attend, whereby divers affairs as well the said lord the king as divers liege subjects of the said lord the king, very much concerning, and by him or by his sufficient deputy or deputies, within and during the time aforesaid, specially to be performed, remained entirely unperformed. And the jurors aforesaid now sworn, further say upon their oath aforesaid, that the said R. D. by himself or by any his sufficient deputy in that behalf, after the making of the letters patent aforesaid, bearing date on the 3d day of January in the 2d year of the reign of the said lord the king aforesaid, to wit; on the 2d day of July in the 4th year of the reign of the said lord the king aforesaid, and continually afterwards until the 5th day of August in the 4th year of the reign of the said lord the king aforesaid, upon the office of water bailiff of the town of Dover aforesaid, in the county of Kent aforesaid, in the commission aforesaid mentioned, did not reside according to the form and effect of the proviso in the said letters patent mentioned, and that the said R. D. and his deputies from the office aforesaid, for the whole time aforesaid, absented himself and each and every of them absented himself: and that the said R. D. by himself or by any his sufficient deputy or deputies, that office for the whole time aforesaid, to wit; from the first day of the month of July, in the 4th year of the reign of the said lord the now * king aforesaid, unto the 5th day of August in the 4th year aforesaid, did not serve nor attend, whereby divers other affairs as well the said lord the king as divers liege subjects of the said lord the king, very much concerning, and by the said R. D. or by his sufficient deputy or deputies, within and during the time aforesaid, specially to be performed, remained entirely unperformed. And the jurors aforesaid now sworn, further say upon their oath aforesaid, that after the making of the said letters patent bearing date the 3d day of January,

That from the 14th of June in the 4th year of the king, to the 25th of the same month, he did not attend his said office, whereby, &c.

That he did not reside on his office on the 2d day of July, nor from that time till the 5th of August following.

* P. 670.

That he did not attend his said office from the 1st of July in the 4th year of the king, to the 5th of August following, whereby, &c.

January, in the 2d year of the reign of the ſaid lord the now king aforeſaid, to wit; upon the 22d day of December, in the 4th year of the reign of the ſaid lord the now king aforeſaid, one Richard Griffin, late of the pariſh of St. John the Baptiſt, in the iſland of Thanet, in the county of Kent, beer-brewer, was taken and arreſted at the ſaid pariſh of St. John the Baptiſt in the iſland aforeſaid, for felony and burglary, and then and there was brought before Stephen Monyns, eſquire, then mayor of the town and port of Dover, aforeſaid, John Waad and Nicholas Eaton, jurats of the ſaid town and port, in the county of Kent, and juſtices of the ſaid lord the king aſſigned to preſerve the peace in the town and port aforeſaid, and in the members and precincts of the ſame, whereof the ſaid pariſh of St. John the Baptiſt is and then was parcel, and alſo to hear and determine divers felonies, treſpaſſes and other miſdeeds in the ſaid town and port aforeſaid perpetrated; and after his examination taken by the ſaid mayor and jurats, afterwards, to wit; on the 23d day of the ſaid month of December, in the 4th year of the reign of the ſaid lord the now king, aforeſaid, by the ſaid mayor and juſtices of the town and port aforeſaid, at the ſaid town and port was committed to the ſaid R. D. keeper of the ſaid priſon of the ſaid lord the now king of the town and port aforeſaid, and of the priſoners in the ſaid priſon then being, for the felony and burglary aforeſaid, by him the ſaid Richard Griffin, ſuppoſed to have been perpetrated, in the priſon aforeſaid to remain until that according to the law and cuſtom of this kingdom of England, he ſhould be delivered, and the ſaid Richard Griffin in the cuſtody of the ſaid R. D. keeper of the ſaid priſon then and there being, he the ſaid R. D. him the ſaid R. G. out of the priſon aforeſaid and out of the cuſtody of the ſaid R. D. afterwards, to wit; on the —— day of —— in the 5th year of the reign of the ſaid lord the now king, at the ſaid town of Dover in the county of Kent aforeſaid, did permit to eſcape and to go at large whereſoever he would without any lawful warrant by him the ſaid R. D. thereupon before had. And the jurors aforeſaid, now here ſworn, further ſay upon their oath aforeſaid, that after the making of the letters patent aforeſaid, bearing date the 3d day of January in the 2d year aforeſaid, at the general ſeſſion of the peace and gaol delivery in the town and port of Dover aforeſaid, in the Guildhall of the ſaid town aforeſaid, before Stephen Monyns, eſquire, then mayor of the town and port aforeſaid, John Waad and Nicholas Eaton, then jurats of the ſaid town and port and juſtices of the ſaid lord the now king in the due manner aſſigned, to preſerve the peace within the town and port aforeſaid,

That he permitted one Richard Griffin, who was committed to his cuſtody and to the ſaid priſon for burglary, upon examination before juſtices of the peace to eſcape.

aforesaid, and also to hear and determine divers felonies, trespasses and other misdeeds there perpetrated, there held on the 7th day of August in the 5th year of the reign of the said lord the now king, one George Astey was committed to the said prison of the said lord the king in the town and port aforesaid, under the custody of the said R. D. then keeper of the said prison, safely and * securely in the said prison to be kept until from thence he should be lawfully delivered, because that the said George Astey did refuse to take the oath of allegiance to the said lord the now king, to him by the said justices then and there lawfully tendered, and the said George Astey to the custody of the said R. D. so thereupon being lawfully committed, and in the prison aforesaid, under the custody of the said R. D. keeper of the said prison then and there being, he the said R. D. him the said G. A. out of the prison aforesaid and out of the custody of the said R. D. to wit; on the 25th day of August in the 5th year of the reign of the said lord the king at the said town of Dover, in the county of Kent, aforesaid, wilfully did permit to escape and go at large wheresoever he would, without any lawful warrant by the said R. D. thereupon before had. And the jurors aforesaid now sworn, further say upon their oath aforesaid, that the said R. D. by himself or by any his sufficient deputy in this behalf, after the making of the said letters patent, bearing date the 3d day of January in the 2d year of the reign of the said lord the now king, aforesaid, to wit; on the 15th day of June, in the 4th year of the reign of the said lord the now king, and continually afterwards until the 25th day of the said month of June in the 4th year of the reign of the said lord the now king aforesaid, upon the said office of keeper of the prison of the town and port aforesaid did not reside, and that the said R. D. and his deputies from the office aforesaid for the whole time aforesaid, absented themselves and each and every of them absented himself: and that the said R. D. by himself or by any his sufficient deputy or deputies, that office for the whole time aforesaid, to wit, from the 14th day of the month of June aforesaid, in the 4th year aforesaid, unto the 25th day of the said month of June in the 4th year aforesaid, did not serve nor attend, whereby divers affairs as well the said lord the now king as divers liege subjects of the said lord the now king very much concerning, and by the said R. D. or by his sufficient deputy or deputies, within and during the time aforesaid specially to be performed remained entirely unperformed. And the jurors aforesaid, now sworn, further say upon their oath aforesaid, that the said R. D. by himself or by any his sufficient deputy in this

That he permitted one George Astey committed to the said prison for refusing to take the oath of allegiance to escape.

* P. 671.

That R. D. on the 15th of June and from that to the 25th of the same month in the 4th year of the king, did not reside upon his office of keeper of the prison of Dover.

That from the 14th of June to the 25th of same month in the 4th year of the king, he did not attend the said office, whereby, &c.

this behalf, after the making of the letters patent aforeſaid, bearing date the 3d day of January, in the 2d year, &c. aforeſaid, to wit; on the 2d day of July in the 4th year, &c. aforeſaid, and continually afterwards unto the 20th day of December in the 4th year, &c. aforeſaid, upon his ſaid office of keeper of the priſon of the town and port aforeſaid, did not reſide, and that the ſaid R. D. and his deputies from that office for the whole time aforeſaid, abſented themſelves, and each and every of them abſented himſelf: and that the ſaid R. D. by himſelf or by any his ſufficient deputy or deputies that office for the whole time aforeſaid, to wit; from the firſt day of the ſaid month of July in the 4th year aforeſaid, unto the ſaid 20th day of the month of December, in the 4th year aforeſaid, did not ſerve nor attend, whereby divers affairs as well the ſaid lord the king as divers liege ſubjects of the ſaid lord the king very much concerning and by the ſaid R. D. or by his ſufficient deputy or deputies within and during the time aforeſaid ſpecially to be performed, remained totally unperformed. And the jurors aforeſaid, now here * ſworn, further ſay upon their oath aforeſaid, that the ſaid M. D. and R. D. as yet are alive and in full life, to wit; at the ſaid town and port of Dover in the county of Kent, aforeſaid. In witneſs whereof as well the ſaid commiſſioners as the jurors aforeſaid, to this inquiſition have put their ſeals the day, year and place firſt aforeſaid, &c.

That on the 2d of July, and from that time to the 20th of Dec. in the 4th year of the king he did not reſide upon his ſaid office of keeper of the priſon.

And that from the 1ſt day of July unto the 20th day of Dec. in the 4th year of the king, he did not attend ſaid office, whereby, &c.

* P. 672.

# INFORMATIONS IN THE EXCHEQUER UPON SEIZURES OF SHIPS, GOODS, &c. AS FORFEITED, AND PROCEEDINGS THEREON.

## The King and Martyn against Verdjuice.

### Trinity, 20th Charles 2d.

Information in the Exchequer, upon seizure of a ship, &c. for having goods imported in her contrary to the form of the statute of the 12th Cha. 2d, c. 18. s. 4.

*Vide Hardress*, 511.

MIDDLESEX, to wit; be it remembered that William Martyn, of London, gent. who as well for the said lord the king as himself prosecutes, comes before the barons of this Exchequer, on the 10th day of May in the 20th year of the reign of our lord Charles the 2d the now king, &c. in his proper person, and as well for the said lord the king as for himself gives the court here to understand and to be informed that he between the first day of June last past and the day of the exhibition of this information, at Ratcliffe, in the county of Middlesex, within the port of London, seized, and to the use of the said lord the king, and of the said William arrested as being forfeited, a certain ship or vessel called the James, with all her guns, tackle, ammunition, furniture and apparel, for this, to wit; that between the said first day of June last past, and the time of the seizure of the said ship or vessel twenty hogsheads of French wine, twenty hogsheads of vinegar, and twenty hogsheads of spirits, called brandy wine, were imported in the said ship or vessel from foreign parts and parts beyond the seas into this kingdom of England, to wit; unto Ratcliffe aforesaid, in the county aforesaid, within the port aforesaid, which ship or vessel at the said time of the importation of the said goods truly and without fraud, did not belong to the people of England, Ireland, and Wales, or the town of Berwick upon the Tweed, or of any of them, as the true owners and proprietors thereof and of which the master and three-fourths of the mariners at least were not English, and that the said ship or vessel was not of the built of that place or country, whereof the said goods were of the growth, production or manufacture, nor of such port where such goods can be only or more usually are first shipped for transportation, and whereof

whereof the maſter and * three-fourths of the mariners at leaſt were of the ſaid country or place, againſt the form of the ſtatute in ſuch caſe made and provided, whereupon the ſaid William Martyn, as well for the ſaid lord the king as for himſelf, prays the conſideration of the court in the premiſſes, and that the ſaid ſhip or veſſel with all her guns, tackle, ammunition, furniture and apparel, for the cauſes aforeſaid, may remain forfeited, and that he the ſaid William Martyn may have the moiety thereof according to the form of the ſtatute aforeſaid. Whereupon proclamation being made for the ſaid lord the king, (as the cuſtom is) if any one here could inform the court wherefore the veſſel or ſhip aforeſaid, with all her guns, tackle, ammunition, furniture and apparel, to the ſaid lord the king, (for the cauſes aforeſaid) ought not to remain as being forfeited, that he ſhould come forth and ſhould be heard; and no one appeared to do this; it is ordered that Nehemiah Rogers and Thomas Rivers, gent. be commanded by the writ of the lord the now king, under the ſeal of this Exchequer, to cauſe the ſaid ſhip or veſſel to be juſtly and faithfully appraiſed by the oath of good and lawful men of the county of Middleſex, aforeſaid, and indentures thereof, &c. ſo that they may have one part of the ſaid indentures here, &c. and to the court here to be delivered: and the ſaid Nehemiah and Thomas in the form aforeſaid are commanded ſo, &c. on the 23d day of the month of May. At which day the appraiſers aforeſaid return here the writ aforeſaid, together with a certain indenture to the ſaid writ annexed, which are in the file of writs executed for the ſaid lord the king and others of this term on behalf of this remembrancer, the tenor of which indenture follows in theſe words, to wit; "*This indenture made the 21ſt day of May, in the year of our Lord God, 1668, and in the 20th year of the reign of our ſovereign lord Charles the 2d, by the grace of God of England, Scotland, France and Ireland, king, defender of the faith, &c. witneſſeth that we Nehemiah Rogers and Thomas Rivers, his majeſty's appraiſers according to a writ unto us directed, and hereunto annexed, have viewed and appraiſed the ſhip James, with all her guns, ammunition, furniture and apparel, at the ſum of 330l. in witneſs whereof we have hereunto ſet our hands the day and year above written.*" Whereupon proclamation being made a ſecond time for the ſaid lord the king, (as the cuſtom is) if any one here could inform the court wherefore the ſhip or veſſel aforeſaid with all her guns, tackle, ammunition, furniture and apparel, for the cauſes aforeſaid) ſhould not remain to the ſaid lord the king as being forfeited, and if any one would give more for the ſaid ſhip or

* P. 673.

Proclamation.

Writ of appraiſment awarded.

Return of the writ of appraiſment and indenture.

2d proclamation.

 veſſel,

vessel, with all, &c. than as aforesaid appraised, that he should come forth and should be heard. Whereupon here comes one Peter Verdjuice, by Anselem Beaumont, his attorney, and claims the property of the ship or vessel aforesaid, with all her guns, tackle, ammunition, furniture and apparel, in the information aforesaid specified, to belong to him: and prays oyer of the information aforesaid, and it is read to him, which being read, heard, and by him understood, he complains that he under colour of the premisses is grieveously vexed and disquieted, and this not justly, because protesting that the information aforesaid, and the matter in the same contained are not sufficient in law, to which he hath no necessity neither is he bound by the law of the land to answer; for plea, neverthelesss the said Peter Verdjuice saith, that the goods aforesaid, in the information aforesaid specified were not * imported in the ship or vessel aforesaid, contrary to the form of the statute aforesaid, in the manner and form as by the said information is above supposed, and of this he puts himself upon the country. And Geoffry Palmer, knight and baronet, attorney general of the said lord the now king, who for the said lord the now king, prosecutes present here in court on the same day in his proper person for the said lord the king, in like manner prays that it may be enquired of by the country. Therefore let an inquisition be thereupon had, and the sheriff of the county of Middlesex is commanded that he do not omit, &c. and that he cause to come here on the 5th day of the month of June, twelve free and lawful men of his bailiwick of the neighbourhood of Ratcliffe, each of whom, &c. by whom, &c. and who are not, &c. to recognize upon the premisses, and the same day is given here to the said Peter Verdjuice: at which day the said Peter comes here as before and the sheriff, to wit; Dionysius Gauden, knight, and Thomas Davies, knight, return here the writ aforesaid, together with the pannel of the names of jurors to the said writ annexed, which are in the file of writs executed for the said lord the king of the said 20th year of the reign of the said lord the now king on behalf of this remembrancer, in Middlesex, and the jurors come not; therefore the sheriff is commanded that he distrain those jurors, by their lands, &c. so that, &c. on the ninth day of the month of June; or in the mean time before the beloved and faithful of the lord the king, Mathew Hale, knight, chief baron of this Exchequer, at Westminster, in the place where the court of this Exchequer is commonly kept, on Monday the 8th day of the said month of June, about the first hour after mid-day of the

said

Defendant appears and claims property.

* P. 674. Plea That the goods were not imported contrary to the form of the statute.

Attorney general joins issue.

Venire facias awarded.

Destringas awarded with nisi prius.

ſaid day, if he ſhall firſt come there then. And it is ſaid to the ſaid Peter Verdjuice, that he keep his day before the ſaid chief baron at the ſaid days and place, and that he be here on the ſaid 9th day of the month of June, to hear his judgment, if &c. At which day the ſaid Peter Verdjuice comes here as before, and the ſaid chief baron before whom &c. hath ſent here his record before him had thus indorſed, to wit.

Afterwards at the day and place wthin contained, before Mathew Hale, knight, chief baron of the Exchequer of the lord the king within written, Robert Langley, gent. being aſſociated to him according to the form of the ſtatute, &c. come as well the within named William Martyn, gent. in his proper perſon, as the within named Peter Verjuice, by his attorney within named, whereupon publick proclamation being ſolemnly made, (as the cuſtom is) if there was any one who could inform the chief baron, the ſerjeant at law of the ſaid lord the king, the attorney-general of the ſaid lord the king, or the jurors of the jury whereof mention is within made of the matters within contained, that he ſhould come forth and ſhould be heard, and thereupon Robert Sawyer, eſquire, who proſecutes for the ſaid lord the king in this behalf, offered himſelf to do this: and the jurors of the jury aforeſaid being called in like manner come, who being elected, tried and ſworn to ſpeak the truth of the matters within contained, ſay upon their oath: That the ſhip or veſſel in the information within contained mentioned, was a foreign and Dutch built ſhip, and bonâ fide, bought by ——— Greenway, and his co-partners, Engliſhmen, and certified, and tranſmitted into the Exchequer of the ſaid lord the now king, before the firſt day of October 1662, according to the form of the ſtatute in ſuch caſe made and provided: and the jurors * aforeſaid, further ſay upon their oath aforeſaid, that the ſaid lord the now king, by and with the advice of his privy council, by his declaration bearing date at his court of Whitehall, in the county of Middleſex, on the 22d day of February, in the year of our Lord 1664, in the due and uſual form publiſhed, did declare that as well the ſhips and fleets of the ſaid lord the king, as all other ſhips and veſſels which then ſhould be commiſſioned by letters of marque from the moſt dear brother of the ſaid lord the king, the duke of York lord high admiral of England, might and could lawfully fight with, ſubdue, ſeize and take all ſhips, veſſels and goods belonging to the ſtates of the united Provinces, or of any of their ſubjects or inhabitants within any of their territories, and the ſame being taken, ſhould be condemned as good and lawful prizes, the

Poſtea.

Proclamation.

The jury find a ſpecial verdict

That the ſhip was Dutch built and bona fide bought before the 1ſt October 1662 by Greenway and co.

* P. 675.

They find the king's proclamation whereby it is declared that his majesty's ships and other vessels commissioned by the lord high admiral might fight with and take Dutch vessels, &c.

the tenor of which declaration follows in these words, to wit, "*Whereas upon complaint of the several injuries, affronts, and spoils done by the East and West India Companies, and other the subjects of the united provinces, unto and upon the ships, goods, and persons of our subjects, to their grievous damages, and amounting to vast sums, instead of reparation and satisfaction, which hath been by us frequently demanded, we found that orders had been given to De Ryter not only to abandon the consortship against the pirates of the Mediterranean seas, (to which the States General had invited us) but also to use all acts of depredation and hostility against our subjects in Africa: We thereupon gave orders for the detaining of the ships belonging to the States of the United Provinces, their subjects and inhabitants, yet notwithstanding we did not give any commission for letters of marque, nor were there any proceedings against the ships detained until we had a clear and undeniable evidence, that De Ryter had put the said orders in execution, by seizing several of our subjects ships and goods. But now, since finding by these fresh injuries and actings of theirs, and the intelligence we had of their great preparations for war, and their granting of letters of marque against our people, that both our forbearance, and the other remedies we have used to bring them to a compliance with us have proved ineffectual, and that they are resolved what they have done by wrong to maintain by arms and war against us, we have thought fit by and with the advice of our privy council, to declare and do hereby declare to all the world, that the said States are the aggressors, and that they ought in justice to be so looked upon by all men. So that as well our fleets and ships, as also all other ships and vessels that shall be commissioned by letters of marque from our dear brother the Duke of York, lord high admiral of England, shall and may lawfully fight with, subdue seize and take all ships, vessels and goods belonging to the said States of the united provinces, or any of their subjects or inhabitants within their territories: And we do hereby command as well all our own subjects, as advertise all other persons of what nation soever, not to transport or carry any soldiers, arms, powder, ammunition or any other contraband goods to any of the territories, lands, plantations or countries of the said States of the united * provinces, declaring that whatsoever ship or vessel shall be met withal transporting or carrying any soldiers, arms, powder, ammunition, or other contraband goods, to any the territories, lands, plantations or countries of the States of the united provinces, the same being taken, shall be condemned as good and lawful prize. And we do further declare that whatsoever ship or vessel of what nation soever, shall be met withal having any goods, merchandizes, or any number of persons belonging to the*

* P. 676.

*the ſaid States of the united provinces, or any of their ſubjects or inhabitants, the whole being taken, ſhall be adjudged as good and lawful prize, as likewiſe all goods and merchandizes of what nation ſoever, whether of our own or of foreigners, that ſhall be laden aboard any ſhip or veſſel, that ſhall belong to the States of the united provinces, or any of their ſubject, or any inhabiting within them, and ſhall be taken, the whole ſhall be condemned as good and lawful prize, except the ſaid ſhip or veſſel hath ours, or our dear brothers letters of ſafe conduct granted to them. And to the end due intimation and publication of this our declaration may be made, and publick notice thereof be taken, it is our will and pleaſure that this our preſent declaration ſhall be publiſhed in due and uſual form."* And the jurors aforeſaid upon their oath aforeſaid, further ſay that in proſecution of the declaration aforeſaid, afterwards open war was between the ſaid lord the king and the States of the united provinces, and that during the ſaid war, the ſaid ſhip in the information aforeſaid ſpecified, was taken, condemned and confiſcated by the ſubjects of the united provinces aforeſaid, according to the laws there uſed; and that the ſaid ſubjects of the States of the united provinces became proprietors of the ſame; and the jurors aforeſaid upon their oath aforeſaid, further ſay that the ſaid ſubjects of the States of the united provinces aforeſaid, afterwards ſold the ſaid ſhip truly and bona fide, to one Arnold Beake, merchant, a native of this kingdom of England, and the ſaid Arnold Beake is and from the time in which, &c. was proprietor of the ſaid ſhip by virtue of the ſaid ſale; and the jurors aforeſaid, upon their oath aforeſaid, further ſay that the ſaid lord the now king, by his proclamation under his great ſeal of England, bearing date at his court of Whitehall aforeſaid, the 24th day of Auguſt, in the 19th year of his reign, did declare that all ſhips, and all moveable goods whatſoever which then ſhould appear to be taken from the ſubjects of the States general of the united provinces, after the 26th day of the month of Auguſt, in the Britiſh and northern ſeas, and after the 24th day of September then next enſuing, from the mouth of the channel to Cape St. Vincent, without any form of proceſs, immediately and without damage, ſhould be reſtored to the proprietors, according to the treaty concluded at Breda, between the ſaid lord the king and the States General of the united provinces aforeſaid, and the ratifications thereof exchanged, and the publication thereof made upon the 14th day of the ſaid month of Auguſt; and the jurors aforeſaid, upon their oath aforeſaid, further ſay that after the ſale of the ſaid ſhip or veſſel aforeſaid to the ſaid

That open war was between the king and the united States in which war the ſaid ſhip was taken and confiſcated by the ſubjects of the united States, and was by them ſold to one Arnold Beake a native of this kingdom, who is and from the time in which, &c. was proprietor of ſaid ſhip, the jury then find another proclamation whereby all ſhips &c. taken from the Dutch after certain times, &c. mentioned ſhould be forthwith reſtored purſuant to [illegible]

Arnold

* P. 677.

That the veſſel in queſtion was navigated from France into England with the goods, &c. mentioned in the information by the maſter and three fourths of the mariners who were Engliſh, that no new oath or certificate was taken by Arnold Beake, that Peter Verdjuice claimed in right of Arnold Beake. But whether upon the whole matter the ſhip be forfeited or not the jury doubt, &c.

Arnold Beake, the ſaid ſhip or veſſel was navigated from the kingdom of * France into this kingdom of England, to wit, to Ratcliffe, in the ſaid county of Middleſex, within the port of London, with the goods and merchandizes in the ſaid information mentioned, by the maſter of the ſaid ſhip or veſſel, and three fourth parts of the mariners who were Engliſh, and that the navigation aforeſaid, is one and the ſame navigation with the importation in the information aforeſaid ſpecified, and not another or different, and and the jurors aforeſaid upon their oath aforeſaid, further ſay that no new oath by the ſaid Arnold Beake, or new certificate by the officers of the cuſtoms of the port of London aforeſaid, were made after the ſaid ſale to the ſaid Arnold Beake; and the jurors aforeſaid upon their oath aforeſaid, further ſay that the ſaid Peter Verjuice, claimed the property of the ſaid ſhip or veſſel, with all her guns, tackle, ammunition, furniture, and apparrel in the right of the ſaid Arnold Beake the proprietor thereof, but whether upon the whole matter aforeſaid, by the jurors aforeſaid, in the form aforeſaid found the ſhip or veſſel aforeſaid with all her guns, tackle, ammunition, furniture and apparel is forfeited in the manner and form as by the ſaid information is within ſuppoſed, the jurors aforeſaid are entirely ignorant, and pray the advice of the court of the lord the king here in the premiſſes; and if upon the whole matter by the jurors aforeſaid in the form aforeſaid, found it ſhall ſeem to the court here, that the ſaid goods in the ſaid information ſpecified, were imported in the ſaid ſhip or veſſel from foreign parts and parts beyond the ſeas into this kingdom of England, againſt the form of the ſtatute in ſuch caſe made and provided, then the jurors aforeſaid ſay upon their oath aforeſaid, that the ſaid ſhip or veſſel with all her guns, tackle, ammunition, furniture and apparel at the ſaid time of the importation of the ſaid goods was forfeited as by, &c. &c.

*In this caſe judgment was given for the defendant.—See Hardreſs* 511.

The

# The King and Martyn against the Ship called the Griffin.

## Trinity, 21ft Charles II.

Information in the Exchequer upon a forfeiture of the ship under the 12th Ch. 2. c. 18. f. 3 4.

BE it remembered that William Martyn of London, gent. who as well for the faid lord the king as for himfelf profecutes, comes before the barons of this Exchequer on the 15th day of June in this term, in his proper perfon, and as well for the faid lord the king as for himfelf, gives the court here to underftand, and to be informed, that he between the firft day of July laft paft, and the day of the exhibition of this information, at Ratcliffe, in the county of Middlefex feized, and to the ufe as well of the faid lord the king as of him the faid William Martyn, arrefted as being forfeited, a certain fhip or veffel called the Griffin, of Amfterdam, with the furniture of the fame, for this, to wit, that a parcel of drugs called camphire and agarick, and a parcel of fpices, being goods and merchandizes which are of foreign growth, production or manufacture, to wit, of Africa, Afia or America, or which are defcribed or laid down in the ufual maps or cards of the faid places, or fome one of them, and which are to be imported into England, * Ireland, Wales, the iflands of Jerfey and Guernfey, or the town of Berwick upon the Tweed, in fhips or veffels which in truth and without fraud belong to the people of England or Ireland, or the dominion of Wales, or the town of Berwick upon the Tweed, or of the lands, iflands, plantations, and territories belonging to the faid lord the king in Africa, Afia, or America, as the proprietors and right owners of the fame, and whereof the mafter and three fourths of the mariners at leaft are Englifh: between the times aforefaid, in the faid fhip were imported from the port of Amfterdam, in the country of Holland, in foreign parts and parts beyond the feas, not being the place or country of the growth, production or manufacture of the faid goods or commodities, or of any part thereof, nor the faid port of Amfterdam being that port where the faid goods and commodities can only be, or are, or ufually were firft fhipped for tranfportation: contrary to the form of the ftatute in fuch cafe made and provided, wherefore the faid William Martyn as well for the faid lord the king as for himfelf, prays the confideration of the court here in the

* P. 678.

premiſſes, and that the ſaid ſhip and the furniture thereof for the cauſes aforeſaid, may remain forfeited, and that he the ſaid William Martyn may have the moiety of the value thereof, according to the form of the ſtatute aforeſaid.

Delivered the day and year firſt aforeſaid before me
*Edward Atkins.*

---

## The King and Salmon againſt Waller.

### Michaelmas, the 19th Charles II.

Information where the goods are not ſeized but a ſubpena is awarded againſt defendant upon a ſuggeſtion that the goods came to his hands.

NORFOLK, to wit. Be it remembered, that Peter Salmon, gent. who as well for the lord the king as for himſelf proſecutes, comes before the barons of this Exchequer on the 20th day of November, in this term, in his proper perſon, and as well for the ſaid lord the king as for himſelf, gives the court here to underſtand and to be informed, that certain merchants whoſe names to the ſaid Peter Salmon are yet unknown, between the firſt day of December laſt paſt, and the day of the exhibition of this information, imported or cauſed to be imported from the Netherlands into this kingdom of England, to wit, to the town of Yarmouth, in the county of Norfolk, within the port of Yarmouth, in certain ſhips or veſſels to the ſaid Peter Salmon in like manner being unknown, five thouſand pounds weight of ſpices, every pound weight thereof of the value of ten ſhillings; of their own proper goods and merchandizes, againſt the form of the ſtatute in ſuch caſe made and provided, by reaſon of which the ſaid goods became and are forfeited, and ſo being forfeited, the ſaid goods afterwards, to wit, between the time aforeſaid, at the town of Yarmouth aforeſaid, in the county of Norfolk aforeſaid, to the hands and poſſeſſion of Benjamin Waller, merchant, came and each and every parcel thereof came, * wherefore the ſaid Peter Salmon, as well for the ſaid lord the king as for himſelf prays the conſideration of the court here in the premiſſes, and that the goods aforeſaid for the cauſes aforeſaid, may remain forfeited, and that he the ſaid P. S. may have a moiety thereof

*The information laid this way by virtue of the 13th and 14th Charles the 2d, c. 11. ſ. 17.*

* P. 769.

of according to the form of the ſtatute aforeſaid, and alſo that the ſaid Benjamin Waller may come here to anſwer of the forfeited goods aforeſaid, ſo come to his hands, or of 2500l. of the lawful money of England for the value thereof. Whereupon it is ordered that it be given in charge to the ſaid Benjamin Waller, by the writ of the lord the now king of his Exchequer to be here, &c. to anſwer upon the premiſſes, and this under the pain of 100l. which, &c. if not, &c. and the ſaid Benjamin Waller is commanded in the form aforeſaid, ſo, &c. on the octave of St. Hilary. Subpeona awarded.

At which day the ſaid Benjamin Waller comes here, by Charles Keepe, his attorney, and prays oyer of the information aforeſaid, and it is read to him, which being read, heard, and by him underſtood, he complains that he under colour of the premiſſes is grievouſly vexed and diſquieted, and this not juſtly, becauſe proteſting that the information aforeſaid and the matter in the ſame contained are not ſufficient in law, to which he hath no neceſſity, neither is he bound by the law of the land to anſwer, for plea nevertheleſs the ſaid Benjamin Waller ſaith, that the goods aforeſaid in the information aforeſaid ſpecified, did not come, nor did any parcel thereof come to his hands and poſſeſſion in the manner and form as by the information aforeſaid above againſt him is ſuppoſed, and of this he puts himſelf upon the country. And G. P. knight and baronet, attorney general of the ſaid lord the now king, who for the ſaid lord the king proſecutes preſent here in court, on the ſame day in his proper perſon for the ſaid lord the king, prays in like manner, that it may be enquired of by the country; therefore let an inquiſition be thereupon: and the ſheriff of the county of Norfolk is commanded that he do not omit, &c. and that he cauſe to come here on the 8th day of the month of February, twelve free and lawful men of his bailiwick, of the of the neighbourhood of the town of Yarmouth, aforeſaid, in the county aforeſaid, each of whom, &c. by whom, &c. and who neither, &c. to recognize upon the premiſſes. And the ſame day is given here to the ſaid B. W. At which day B. W. comes here as before, and the ſheriff, to wit; Edward Barkham, baronet, returns here the writ aforeſaid, together with the pannel of the names of jurors to the ſame writ annexed, which are in the file of writs executed for the ſaid lord the king, in the end of the 19th and beginning of the 20th year of his reign, on behalf of this remembrancer in Norfolk; and the ſaid jury come not; therefore the ſheriff is commanded that he diſtrain the ſaid jurors by all their lands, &c. ſo that, &c. from the day of Eaſter in

Defendant appears. Oyer. Proteſtation. Plea. That the goods did not come to his hands. Iſſue. Venire awarded. Diſtringas awarded.

 15 days

15 days or in the mean time before the beloved and faithful of the lord the king, his justices assigned to take assizes in the county of Norfolk, aforesaid, (who by letters patent of the said lord the now king under the seal of this Exchequer, are assigned to take the said inquisition) at Thetford, on Saturday the 29th day of the month of February, if then they shall first come there; and it is said to the said B. W. that he keep his day before the justices of assize aforesaid, at the said day and place; and that he be here at the said fifteen days of Easter, to hear his judgement if, &c. At which day the said B. W. comes here as before, and the said justices of assize, before whom, &c. have sent here their record before them had thus indorsed, to wit; afterwards at the day and place * within contained, before William Moreton, knight, one of the justices of the said lord the king, assigned to hold pleas before the king himself, and John Harvey, esquire, to the said William Moreton and Wadham Windham, knight, one other justice of the said lord the king assigned to hold pleas before the king himself, justices of the said lord the king assigned to take assizes in the county of Norfolk, aforesaid, by the form of the statute, &c. for this time being associated, the presence of the said Wadham Wyndham not being expected, by virtue of the writ of the said lord the king of si non omnes, &c. come as well the within named Peter Salmon, gent. who as well for the said lord the king as for himself, prosecutes in his proper person, as the within named B. W. by his atattorney within named. And thereupon here in court publick proclamation being made for the said lord the king (as the custom is) that if there be any one here who could inform the said justices, or the serjeant at law of the said lord the king, or the attorney general of the said lord the king, or the jury within written of the matters within contained, or could challenge the said jury that he should come forth and should be heard, and thereupon George Cure, esquire, for the said lord the king, offered himself to do this; and the jurors of the jury whereof mention is within made, being called in like manner come, who being elected, tried, and sworn to speak the truth of the matters within contained, as to all the goods and merchandizes in the information within written specified, except 625 pound weight of spices called nutmegs, to the hands and possession of the said Benjamin, by the information aforesaid, supposed to have come, say upon their oath that the said goods and merchandizes did not come to the hands and possession of the said Benjamin Waller, as the said Benjamin Waller for himself within, by pleading hath alledged; and as to the said

Postea.

* P. 680.

Verdict that the goods, &c. except 625 pound weight of nutmegs, came not to the hands of defendant.

ſaid 625 pounds weight of ſpices in the information aforeſaid ſpecified, the jurors aforeſaid upon their oath aforeſaid ſay, that the ſaid Benjamin Waller at the ſaid time in the information aforeſaid within ſpecified, was a ſubject of the ſaid lord the now king, and born within the allegiance of the the kingdom of England, and the ſaid 625 pounds weight of ſpices called nutmegs, at the ſaid time in the information aforeſaid within ſpecified, were imported from the Netherlands, in parts beyond the ſeas, in a certain ſhip called the Tobias of Newport, and were imported at the port of Yarmouth, within this kingdom of England, and that all the cuſtoms and duties due for the ſame in the due manner were paid: and the jurors aforeſaid upon their oath aforeſaid further ſay, that before the ſaid time in the information within written ſpecified, to wit; by a certain act made in the parliament of the lord the now king, begun and held at Weſtminſter, in the county of Middleſex, on the 25th day of April in the 12th year of the reign of the ſaid lord the now king, and there continued until the 29th day of December then next enſuing, entitled, "*an act for the encouraging and encreaſing of ſhipping and navigation,*" among other things it was enacted by the authority of the ſaid parliament; that no goods or commodities which were of foreign growth, production or manufacture, and which were to be imported into England, Ireland, Wales, the iſlands of Jerſey and Guernſey, or the town of Berwick upon the Tweed, in Engliſh built ſhipping, or other ſhipping belonging to ſome of the ſaid places, and navigated by Engliſh mariners as aforeſaid, ſhould be ſhipped or brought from any other place or places, country or countries, but only from thoſe of the * ſaid growth, production or manufacture, or from thoſe ports where the ſaid goods and commodities, could only or were, or uſually had been firſt ſhipped for tranſportation, and from no other places or countries under the penalty of the forfeiture of all the ſaid goods which were imported from any other place or country contrary to the true intent and meaning of the ſaid act, as alſo of the ſhip in which they were imported, with all her guns, furniture, ammunition, tackle and apparel, one moiety to the ſaid lord the now king, his heirs, and ſucceſſors, and the others moiety to him or them who would ſeize, inform or ſue for the ſame in any court of the ſaid lord the king of record, by bill, plaint, information, or other action in which no eſſoin, protection or wager of law ſhould be allowed; as by the ſaid act to the jurors aforeſaid here ſhown in evidence more fully appeareth. And the jurors aforeſaid further ſay upon their oath aforeſaid, that

And as to the ſaid 625 pound of nutmegs they find that they were imported from the Netherlands, and that the duties were paid.

They then find part of the navigation act, viz. the 12. Charles 2d, c. 18. ſ. 4.

* P. 681.

The jury find part of the ſtatute of the 13th Ch. 2. c. 11. ſ. 23.

that afterwards and before the ſaid time in the ſaid information within ſpecified by a certain act made in the parliament of the ſaid lord the now king, begun and held at Weſtminſter aforeſaid, in the county of Middleſex aforeſaid, on the 8th day of May in the 13th year of the reign of the ſaid lord the now king, and from that time prorogued until the 28th day of February then next enſuing, intitled, "*an act for preventing frauds and regulating abuſes in his majeſty's cuſtoms*," among other things it was enacted by the authority of the ſaid parliament, that no ſort of wines other than rheniſh wines, no ſort of ſpicery, grocery, tobacco, potaſhes, pitch, tar deal boards, fir, timber, or olive oil, ſhould be imported into England, Wales, or Berwick, from the Netherlands or Germany, upon any pretence whatſoever, in any ſort of ſhip or veſſel whatſoever, upon penalty of the loſs of all the ſaid goods, and alſo of the ſhip and furniture," as by the ſaid act laſt mentioned and to the jurors here ſhown in evidence more fully appeareth; and the jurors aforeſaid upon their oath aforeſaid further ſay, that after the making of the ſeveral acts of parliament aforeſaid, and before the time in the information aforeſaid within ſpecified, to wit; at the court of the lord the king, at Whitehall, in the county of Middleſex, held on the 6th day of March in the 16th year of the reign of the ſaid lord the now king, before the ſaid lord the now king and his privy council, by a certain order then and there made, the ſaid lord the king by and with the advice of his privy council, did declare and ordain that the act of the parliament begun at Weſtminſter the 25th day of April in the 12th year of his reign, and confirmed by the parliament begun at Weſtminſter, the 8th day of May, in the 13th year of his reign, intitled, "*an act for encouraging and encreaſing navigation*," and all proceedings upon the ſame or therein directed, ſhould be totally ſuſpended in all matters and things concerning or relating to any ſhips or veſſels, their maſters or mariners, guns, * furniture, tackle, ammunition and apparel, or any goods or commodities imported or exported to or from Norway or the Baltick ſea, and further, that the ſaid act and all proceedings upon the ſame or therein directed, ſhould be totally ſuſpended in all matters and things in the ſame contained, concerning or relating to any ſhips or veſſels, their maſters or mariners, guns, furniture, tackle, ammunition and apparel, or to any goods or commodities imported or exported to or from any parts of Germany, Flanders or France, the merchants and owners of which ſhould be ſubjects of the ſaid lord the now king, born within his allegiance, and further, the ſaid lord the now king, by his ſaid order, further did ordain, declare and grant that not

The jury then find an order of council ſuſpending the operation of two acts of parliament

* P. 682.

not only his natural born ſubjects, but alſo all merchants of any nation in amity with the ſaid lord the now king, might import from any parts whatſoever, hemp, pitch, tar, maſts, ſalt petre, and copper, and upon any importation thereof, ſhould be liable to pay only ſuch duties as by the act of tonnage and poundage are impoſed upon the natural born ſubjects of the ſaid lord the king, and no other, any thing in the ſaid act to the contrary notwithſtanding; and further the ſaid lord the now king by his ſaid order did ordain that notwithſtanding the act aforeſaid for the encouraging and encreaſing ſhipping and navigation, and another act made in the ſaid parliament begun at Weſtminſter in the county of Middleſex, on the 8th day of May in the 13th year of his reign, entitled "*an act for the encouragement of trade*," or either of them, or any clauſe or clauſes in them or either of them to the contrary it ſhould and might be lawful for any Engliſh merchants, and by the ſaid order they were authorized freely and without interruption to uſe and employ any foreign ſhips or veſſels whatſoever, navigated by ſailors or mariners of any nation in amity with the ſaid lord the now king, for the importation or exportation of goods or commodities to or from any port in England, Ireland or Wales, to or from any of the ſaid lord the now king's plantations, provided that no goods or commodities whatſoever ſhould be imported by them into any of the ſaid lord the now king's plantations, but which without fraud ſhould be laden and ſhipped in England, Ireland or Wales, and from thence directly carried, and from no other place to the plantations of the ſaid lord the now king, and provided always that ſuch goods and commodities which by them ſhould be laden or taken on board at the ſaid plantations of the ſaid lord the now king, or at any of them ſhould be brought directly from thence to any of the ports of the ſaid lord the now king, in England, Ireland or * Wales, and all governors and officers of the cuſtoms by the order aforeſaid were charged and required ſtrictly to obſerve all regulations, directions, and orders for the taking of writings obligatory or other ſecurities, and for the examination of all forfeitures and penalties by the ſaid acts or either of them required; the clauſes in both of them always being excepted, touching Engliſh ſhips and Engliſh mariners, in the ſame order before diſpenſed with; and finally the ſaid lord the now king did ordain that the order aforeſaid ſhould continue and be in force during his good pleaſure, and when the ſaid lord the now king ſhould think proper to determine the diſpenſation by the order aforeſaid, granted by his royal proclamation, he would give ſix months notice thereof, for the

*There is no act of this title in the 13th or 14th of Charles 2d, therefore it is ſuppoſed that the 13th of Charles 2d, already found by the jury is intended. See ante 681.*

* P. 683.

the intention that no merchants or other perſons in the order aforeſaid concerned might be ſurpriſed: as by the order aforeſaid to the jurors here ſhown in evidence more fully appeareth, and the jurors aforeſaid upon their oath aforeſaid further ſay, that the ſaid 625 pounds weight of ſpices called nutmegs, parcel of the ſpices aforeſaid in the information aforeſaid within written ſpecified, after the making of the order aforeſaid, the ſaid order being in its full force and effect, and within the time in the information ſpecified, were ſhipped, imported, and came to the hands of the ſaid Benjamin Waller. And that the true value of the ſaid 625 pounds weight of ſpices aforeſaid called nutmegs, at the ſaid time in the information within written ſpecified, was after the rate and price of four ſhillings by the pound for every pound weight thereof; but whether upon the whole matter by the jurors aforeſaid in the form aforeſaid, found the ſaid 625 pounds weight of ſpices called nutmegs, in the information aforeſaid within ſpecified, came to the hands and poſſeſſion of the ſaid Benjamin Waller, in the manner and form as by the information aforeſaid is within ſuppoſed or not, the jurors aforeſaid are entirely ignorant, and pray the advice of the court thereupon, and if upon the whole matter aforeſaid, by the jurors aforeſaid, in the form aforeſaid found, it ſhall ſeem to the court here that the ſaid 625 pound weight of ſpices called nutmegs, came to the hands and poſſeſſion of the ſaid Benjamin Waller, the now defendant, in the manner and form as by the information aforeſaid is within ſuppoſed, then the jurors aforeſaid ſay upon their oath aforeſaid, that the ſaid 625 pound weight of ſpices aforeſaid called nutmegs, came to the hands and poſſeſſion of the ſaid Benjamin Waller in the manner and form as by the information aforeſaid is within ſuppoſed, and if upon the whole matter aforeſaid by the jurors aforeſaid, in the form aforeſaid found, it ſhall ſeem to the court here that the ſaid 625 pound weight of ſpices called nutmegs did not come to the hands and poſſeſſion of the ſaid Benjamin Waller, in the manner and form as by the information aforeſaid is within ſuppoſed, then the jurors aforeſaid ſay upon their oath aforeſaid, that the ſaid 625 pound weight of ſpices called nutmegs, did not come to the hands and poſſeſſion of the ſaid Benjamin Waller in the manner and form as by the ſaid information is within ſuppoſed. Therefore, &c.

Jury doubt, &c.

Writ

# * Writ de Rege inconfulto.

* P. 684.

## Squibb *v.* Loveing.

CHARLES the 2d, &c. To our barons of our Exchequer and every of them greeting, whereas Charles the firft late king of England, our moft dear father, for himfelf, his heirs and fucceffors, by his letters patent made under his great feal of England, bearing date at Weftminfter the 29th day of January in the 15th year of his reign, had given and granted to one Arthur Squibb the younger, gent. the office of the four tellers of the receipt of the Exchequer of the faid lord the late king, his heirs, and fucceffors, to wit; that office of one of the four tellers of the faid Exchequer of the faid late lord the king, his heirs and fucceffors, which firft and next after the date of of the faid letters patent, fhould become vacant, and to the gift, grant and difpofition of the faid late king, his heirs or fucceffors, fhould or would belong, if that grant of the faid lord the late king had not been made: and the faid Arthur Squibb, the younger, an officer of the faid late king, his heirs and fucceffors, in the faid office of one of the four tellers of the receipt of the faid Exchequer of the faid late king, his heirs and fucceffors, which firft and next as aforefaid fhould become vacant, and to the gift, grant or difpofition of the faid late king, his heirs or fucceffors, fhould or would belong, if that grant of the faid lord the king had not been made, ordained, conftituted and created, for himfelf, his heirs and fucceffors, by the faid letters patent: and all fees, wages, rewards, allowances, poffeffions, houfes, habitations and profits whatfoever, to the office of officer aforefaid, which firft and next as aforefaid fhould become vacant, and to the gift, grant and difpofition of the faid late king, his heirs or fucceffors fhould or would belong, if that grant of the faid late king had not made, due, accuftomed, ufed or occupied, and to be due, ufed or occupied, to the faid Arthur Squibb in the manner and form aforefaid, in like manner gave and granted by the faid letters patent: to have and to hold the faid office of one of the four tellers of the receipt of the Exchequer, of the faid lord the late king, his heirs and fucceffors, which firft and next as aforefaid fhould become vacant, and to the gift, grant or difpofition of the faid late king,

Writ de rege in confulto, out of the Chancery, directed to the barons of the Exchequer, reciting that whereas king Charles the 1ft by letters patent had granted to A. Squibb, the firft office of one of the four tellers of the Exchequer, as fhould become vacant, and all fees, houfes, habitations, &c. thereunto belonging for life.



king,

king, his heirs or ſucceſſors, ſhould or would be belong, if that grant of the ſaid lord the king had not been made, to the ſaid Arthur Squibb the younger, and his aſſigns, as well by himſelf as by his ſufficient deputy or deputies, during the natural life of the ſaid Arthur Squibb the younger, immediately and as ſoon as the ſaid office of one of the four tellers of the ſaid Exchequer of the ſaid lord the late king, his heirs and ſucceſſors, ſhould become vacant, and to the gift, grant or diſpoſition of the ſaid late king, his heirs or ſucceſſors, ſhould or would belong, if that grant of the ſaid late king had not been made: together with all fees, wages, rewards, allowances, poſſeſſions, houſes, * habitations and profits to that office belonging or appertaining, uſed or occupied, provided always that if the ſaid Arthur Squibb the younger, by virtue of the ſaid letters patent of the ſaid late king, in any manner ſhould enter upon and execute and uſe or exerciſe the ſaid office of one of the four tellers of the Exchequer of the ſaid late king, his heirs and ſucceſſors, in the form aforeſaid granted, or in any wiſe by virtue of the ſaid letters patent of the ſaid late king, ſhould intermeddle in the execution or exerciſe of the ſaid office before the ſaid Arthur Squibb the younger, and ſo many and ſuch his ſufficient mainpernors, as many and ſuch as the treaſurer or chancellor of the ſaid Exchequer by his writing ſigned with his hand, ſhould limit and approve, in the ſaid Exchequer of the ſaid late king, ſhould acknowledge and make lawful recognizances and obligations in the ſum or ſums by the ſaid treaſurer or chancellor, or either of them in writing, in like manner ſigned, to be preſcribed, for making his account concerning the office aforeſaid, as by the laws and ſtatutes he ſhould be thereupon bound to make, then that the ſaid grant of the ſaid late king ſhould entirely ceaſe and be void, any thing in the ſaid letters patent of the ſaid late king to the contrary thereof notwithſtanding, as by the ſaid letters patent among other things more fully appeareth: by virtue of which letters patent, the ſaid Arthur Squibb the younger, was ſeized of the intereſt in the office aforeſaid, to him as aforeſaid granted as of freehold; and the ſaid Arthur Squibb ſo being thereof ſeized, afterwards, to wit, on the 28th day of May, in the year of our Lord 1750, and in the ſecond year of our reign, Arthur Squibb the elder, gent. then and long before one of the four tellers of the receipt of the Exchequer aforeſaid died, by reaſon of which the ſaid office of one of the four tellers of the receipt of the Exchequer aforeſaid, to the ſaid Arthur Squib granted as aforeſaid became vacant, and thereupon the ſaid Arthur Squibb

* P. 685.

Provided that if he ſhould exerciſe the ſaid office therefore giving ſecurity, &c. to make his account, that the ſaid grant ſhould be void.

by virtue of which he was ſeized as of freehold.

A. S. one of the 4 tellers dies.

Squibb the younger, claimed to have and poſſeſs the ſaid office, together with the fees, wages, rewards, allowances, houſes, habitations and profits to the ſaid office appertaining: And whereas alſo it is found by a certain inquiſition indented, taken at the queſt-houſe, in the pariſh of St. Andrew, in Holborn, in the county of Middleſex, on Monday the 14th day of September, in the 15th year of our reign, before Hugh Cartwright, knight, Anthony Jackſon, knight, William Gery, eſq; Richard Newman, eſq; and William Bowles, eſq; our commiſſioners, by virtue of our certain commiſſion out of our court of Chancery, at Weſtminſter, aforeſaid, iſſuing to them and to one Robert Long, baronet, Charles Herbert, knight, our Surveyor General, Richard Franklyn, baronet, Edmund Sawyer, knight, William Roberts, baronet, Joſeph Aſh, baronet, Thomas Ingram, knight, Thomas Robinſon, eſquire, chief prothonatory of our court of the bench, Richard Aldworth, Charles Whiteacre, John Phillips, and William Gouldſborough, eſquires, or to two or more of them directed; by the oath of twelve, &c. that from the ſaid time of the death of the ſaid Arthur Squibb the elder, unto the day of the taking of the ſaid inquiſition, the ſaid Arthur Squibb the younger, by himſelf, or by his ſufficient deputy or deputies, did not exerciſe, ſerve or attend the ſaid office, but the execution of the ſaid office for the whole time aforeſaid, totally neglected, and then did neglect: and that the ſaid Arthur Squibb the younger, or his ſufficient deputy in that behalf, upon the ſaid * office of one of the tellers of the receipt of our Exchequer, from the ſaid time of the death of the ſaid Arthur Squibb the elder, late one of the tellers of the receipt of the Exchequer aforeſaid, from time to time according to the tenor and effect of the ſaid letters patent of the ſaid lord the late king, to the ſaid Arthur Squibb the younger, late thereupon made, was not reſident, but the ſaid Arthur Squibb the younger, from the ſaid time of the death of the ſaid Arthur Squibb the elder, unto the day of the taking of the ſaid inquiſition, from the ſaid office abſented himſelf, and the execution of the ſame by himſelf or by his ſufficient deputy for the whole time aforeſaid, did not regard but entirely neglected; and further, it is found by the inquiſition aforeſaid, that the ſaid Arthur Squibb the younger, from the ſaid time of the death of the ſaid Arthur Squibb the elder, unto the ſaid day of the taking of inquiſition aforeſaid, did not take the oath of renunciation of all foreign juriſdictions, according to the tenor and effect of certain acts thereupon made and enacted in the parliaments of the lady Elizabeth, late queen of England, held in

reciting alſo an inquiſition taken before certain commiſſioners by virtue of a commiſſion out of chancery by which it was found that A. S. after the death of A. S. the elder did not attend but neglected the ſaid office and that he was not a reſident upon the ſaid office.

* P. 686.

that he did not take the the oath of ſupremacy

nor the oath of allegance.

in the firſt and fifth years of her reign, or the oath of allegiance, according to the tenor and effect of certain acts made and enacted in the parliament of the lord James, late king of England, held in the 3d and 7th years of his reign, but the ſaid oaths, or either of them to take until that time, entirely neglected and refuſed, and then did neglect and refuſe; and further, it is found by the inquiſition aforeſaid, that the ſaid Arthur Squibb the younger, after the death of the ſaid Arthur Squibb the elder, to wit, on the 10th day of May, in the 4th year of our reign, at Weſtminſter, in the pariſh of St. Margaret, in the county aforeſaid, by the hands of Edmund Squibb, the brother of the ſaid Arthur Squibb the younger, received fees and wages, to wit, 113l. 3s. 4d. to the ſaid office appertaining, before that he had taken his corporal oath well and truly to execute the office aforeſaid, and that the ſaid Arthur Squibb the younger, was admitted to exerciſe the ſaid office before that he the ſaid Arthur Squibb the younger, with his ſufficient mainpernors by the treaſurer or chancellor of our Exchequer, by his writing, ſigned with his hand, limitted and approved, in our Exchequer, had acknowledged and made lawful recognizances or obligations in any ſum or ſums by the ſaid treaſurer or chancellor, or either of them, in writing, in like manner ſigned, preſcribed for making his accounts concerning the office aforeſaid, as by the laws and ſtatutes he was bound to make: as by the inquiſition aforeſaid, into our ſaid court of chancery at Weſtminſter aforeſaid returned, and in the files of the ſaid court of chancery remaining of record more fully appeareth: Whereupon afterwards, to wit, on Wedneſday the 27th day of April, in the 16th year of our reign, came into our court of chancery at Weſtminſter aforeſaid, one Edmund Squibb, gent. by his then attorney, being the aſſignee of the ſaid Arthur Squibb the younger, of the office aforeſaid, and complained that he by reaſon and colour of the inquiſition aforeſaid, from his admiſſion to the ſaid office, and from the exerciſe and occupation of the ſame, was hindred and precluded. and this not juſtly, becauſe he then ſaid that * well and true it is that Arthur Squibb the elder, on the ſaid 28th day of May, in the year of our Lord 1650 aforeſaid, and in the 2d. year of our reign died, as by the inquiſition aforeſaid is found; and the ſaid Edmund Squibb then ſaid that the ſaid Arthur Squibb the younger, after the death of the ſaid Arthur Squibb the elder, by virtue of the letters patent aforeſaid, to the ſaid Arthur Squibb the younger as aforeſaid made, was ſeized of the office aforeſaid, to him as aforeſaid, granted as of freehold,

that before he was ſworn into office by the hands of his brother he received fees belonging to the ſaid office, and that he was admitted to exerciſe the ſaid office before he had given ſecurity to account.

prout the inquiſition.

That afterwards Edmund Squibb the aſſignee of Arthur Squibb came into the chancery and

* P. 687.

pleaded that the ſaid A. Squibb after the death of A. Squibb the elder aſſigned the office to him.

freehold, and he the ſaid Arthur Squibb the younger, ſo being thereof ſeized, he the ſaid Arthur Squibb the younger, afterwards, to wit, on the 21ſt of February, in the year of our Lord 1653, at Weſtminſter, aforeſaid, by his certain writing ſealed, bearing date the ſame day and year, and afterwards, to wit, on the 18th day of May, in the year of our Lord 1660, in the court of our Exchequer at Weſtminſter aforeſaid, in the due manner enrolled of record, aſſigned and ſet over to the ſaid Edmund Squibb the ſaid office, and all other things to the ſaid Arthur by the ſaid letters patent granted as aforeſaid, and the entire eſtate, intereſt, right, title, claim and demand whatſoever, which he the ſaid Arthur had or could have by force and virtue of the ſaid letters patent, or otherwiſe, together with the ſaid letters patent, to have, hold, and enjoy and exerciſe the ſaid office to the ſaid Edmund Squibb and his aſſigns, by himſelf or his ſufficient deputy or deputies, during the life of the ſaid Arthur Squibb the younger, together with all the premiſſes aforeſaid, in as ample and beneficial manner, and to all intents and purpoſes whatſoever as he the ſaid Arthur Squibb could or might; by virtue of which the ſaid Edmund Squibb as the aſſignee of the ſaid Arthur Squibb the younger ought to hold, enjoy exerciſe and occupy the ſaid office during the natural life of the ſaid Arthur Squibb the younger, which Arthur Squibb the younger, then was living and in full life, to wit, at Weſtminſter aforeſaid, in the county of Middleſex aforeſaid, and prayed that our hands might be removed from the office aforeſaid: and it was in ſuch wiſe proceeded in our ſaid court of chancery at Weſtminſter aforeſaid, and by the ſaid court of chancery it was adjudged, that the office aforeſaid was forfeited, and that the ſaid office together with all and ſingular the fees, wages, rewards, profits, commodities, advantages, houſes and poſſeſſions to the ſaid office belonging and appertaining into our hands ſhould be taken and ſeized, as forfeited, as by the ſaid record thereof in our ſaid court of chancery at Weſtminſter aforeſaid, in the county of Middleſex aforeſaid remaining more fully appeareth; and we are given to underſtand that one Henry Dennis our debtor before you hath complained by bill againſt one John Loving, of a plea of treſpaſs and ejectment of a farm, for this, to wit, that whereas the ſaid Edmund Squibb on the 10th day of January, in the 14th year of our reign, at Weſtminſter, in the county of Middleſex, had demiſed to the ſaid Henry one meſſuage and one garden, with the appurtenances, ſituate in Weſtminſter aforeſaid, in the county of Middleſex aforeſaid, to have and to hold the tenements aforeſaid, with the appurtenances, to the ſaid Henry and his

to hold for the life of the ſaid A. Squibb the younger who is ſtill living.

That an ejectment upon the demiſe of Edmund Squibb was commenced in the Exchequer for a houſe and garden belonging to the ſaid office and there now depends.

his assigns, from the 20th day of November, in the 14th year aforesaid, until the end and term of seven years from that time next ensuing, fully to be compleated and ended, by virtue of which demise the said Henry into the tenements aforesaid with the appurtenances entered, and was thereof possessed until the said John Loving afterwards, to wit, on the said 10th day of January, in the 14th year aforesaid, with force and arms into the tenements aforesaid with the appurtenances, which the * said Edmund to the said Henry in the form aforesaid demised for the term aforesaid, which then had not elapsed, entered, and him the said Henry from his farm aforesaid ejected, expelled, and removed: which messuage and garden in the bill aforesaid mentioned are, and from the time whereof the memory of man is not to the contrary, were belonging and appertaining to the said office of one of the four tellers of the Exhequer aforesaid, to the said Arthur Squibb the younger, so as aforesaid granted: which matter in the bill aforesaid before you remaining, as yet depends undetermined, and because we are willing for our indemnity in this behalf, to apply convenient remedy hereupon, understanding that if you proceed to examine and determine the matter in the bill aforesaid before you remaining, great damage can easily be done to us, and willing as much as we can to provide against such damage, we command you and every of you, that you, or any of you in no wise proceed to examine and determine the matter aforesaid in the bill aforesaid contained, before as aforesaid remaining, without our advice; witness ourself at Westminster, the 7th day of June, in the 19th year of our reign.

* P. 688.

that great damage may thereby be done to the king,

therefore the barons are hereby commanded not to proceed therein without the king's advice.

FINIS.

# THE KING, AGAINST THOMAS AMERY, AND JOHN MONK.

The Editor was favoured with the printed Copy of these Pleadings by Mr. SNOW, the Attorney for the Relator; the Case is reported 2d Durnford and East. 515, and 4th Durnford and East. 112. The Court of King's Bench gave Judgements for the Defendants, but they were reversed by the House of Lords.

# IN THE KING's BENCH.

The KING againſt THOMAS AMERY—one of the *twenty-four aldermen* of the city of Cheſter.

The like againſt JOHN MONK—one of the *forty common-council-men* of the ſaid city.

Upon ſeveral informations in the nature of a Quo Warranto *for exerciſing the ſeveral offices abovementioned*, on the proſecution of James Templar, Eſquire, his Majeſty's coroner.

RALPH EDDOWES, merchant, a freeman and citizen of Cheſter, is the relator.

CITY OF CHESTER, AND COUNTY OF THE SAME CITY.

Trinity Term, 25th Geo. III.

Information againſt *Amery*, as an alderman.

BE it remembered, that James Templar, eſquire, coroner and attorney of our preſent ſovereign lord the king, in the court of our ſaid lord the king, before the king himſelf, who for our ſaid lord the king, in this behalf proſecutes in his proper perſon, comes here into the court of our ſaid lord the king, before the king himſelf at Weſtminſter, on Friday next after the morrow of the Holy Trinity, and for our ſaid lord the king, at the relation of Ralph Eddowes, of the city of Cheſter, merchant, according to the form of the ſtatute in ſuch caſe made and provided, gives the court here to underſtand and be informed, that *the city of Cheſter is an antient city*, and that the *mayor and citizens* of the ſaid city now are and for the ſpace of ten years now laſt paſt have been and long before were, *a body corporate* and politic, in deed, fact and name, *by the name of the mayor and citizens of the city of Cheſter* (that is to ſay) at the city of Cheſter, in the county of the ſame

Cheſter an antient city.

Body corporate by the name of *the mayor and citizens of the city of Cheſter.*

fame city. And the faid coroner and attorney of our faid prefent fovereign lord the king, for our faid prefent fovereign lord the king, gives the court here further to underftand and be informed, that for and during the whole time aforefaid, there have been divers, to wit, *twenty-four aldermen within and for the faid city of Chefter* (that is to fay) at the city of Chefter aforefaid, in the county of the fame city; and that the *office of an alderman* of the faid city of Chefter is, and for and during the whole time aforefaid hath been, a public office, and a *place of great truft and pre-eminence within the faid city of Chefter, touching the rule and government of the faid city, and the adminiftration of public juftice within the fame city*, that is to fay, at the city of Chefter aforefaid, in the county of the fame city; and that *Thomas Amery*, of the faid city of Chefter, in the county of the fame city of Chefter, linen-draper, upon the *firft day of December, in the year of our Lord* 1784, at the city of Chefter aforefaid, in the county of the fame city, *did ufe and exercife*, and from thence continually afterwards, to the time of exhibiting this information at the city of Chefter aforefaid in the county of the fame city, hath there ufed and exercifed, and yet doth there ufe and exercife, *without any legal warrant*, royal grant, or right whatfoever, *the office of an alderman of the faid city of Chefter*; and for and during all the time laft above mentioned, hath there claimed, and yet doth there claim, without any legal warrant, royal grant, or right whatfoever, to be one of the aldermen of the faid city of Chefter, and to have, ufe, and enjoy, without any legal warrant, royal grant, or right whatfoever, all the liberties, privileges, and franchifes, to the office of an alderman of the faid city of Chefter belonging and appertaining; which faid office, liberties, privileges,

*Twenty-four aldermen.*

Office of alderman an office of truft touching the rule and government of the city.

*Amery* on 1ft Dec. 1784.

exercifed the office of alderman without legal warrant *&c.*

vileges, and franchises, he the said Thomas Amery, for and during all the time last aforesaid, upon our said present sovereign lord the now king, hath usurped, and still doth usurp (that is to say) at the city of Chester aforesaid, in the county of the same city; in contempt of our said present sovereign lord the king, and to the great damage and prejudice of his royal prerogative, and also against his crown and dignity: Whereupon the said coroner and attorney of our said present sovereign lord the king, for our said present sovereign lord the king, prayeth the consideration of the court here in the premises, and that due process of law may be awarded against him the said Thomas Amery, in this behalf, to make him answer to our said present sovereign lord the king, to shew by what warrant he claimeth to have, use, and enjoy, the office, liberties, privileges, and franchises aforesaid, in manner aforesaid, *&c.*

*GEO. WOOD.*

*The information against Monk, as a common-council-man, is exactly the same—mutatis mutandis.*

---

## Plea of defendant Amery, as an alderman.

### Of Trinity Term, 25th year of King George the 3d.

AND now, that is to say, on Friday next after the morrow of the Holy Trinity aforesaid, before our said lord the king at Westminster, cometh the said Thomas Amery, by Gabriel Lepipre, his attorney comes, and having heard the said information, complains, that he is by colour thereof grievously vexed and disquieted, and this unjustly, because protesting that the information, aforesaid, and and the matters therein contained, are not sufficient in

Plea of defendant *Amery, as an alderman.*

in law; to which ſaid information, he the ſaid Thomas Amery is not bound by the law of the land to anſwer; yet for plea in this behalf; the ſaid Thomas Amery ſaith, that true it is that the city of Cheſter is an antient city, and that the mayor and citizens of the ſaid city, now are, and for the ſpace of ten years now laſt paſt have been, and long be-

Mayor and citizens a corporation.

fore were, a body corporate and politic, in deed, fact, and name, by the name of *the mayor and citizens of the city of Cheſter*, And the ſaid Thomas Amery further ſaith, that our ſovereign lord *Charles the Second*, late king of England, *by his letters patent* under *the great ſeal of England*, bearing date at Weſtminſter, the fourth day of February, in *the*

4th February, 37th Cha. II. (A.D. 1684) Letters patent creating.

*thirty-ſeventh year of his reign*, (and now brought here into court) by reaſon of the great affection which he had and bore to his ſaid city of Cheſter, and the citizens of the ſaid city, and in conſideration of the good behaviour and great coſts and expences of the citizens of the ſame city, and alſo the generous ſervices to him and his dearly beloved father of bleſſed memory, by them, againſt his the ſaid late king's adverſaries and rebels, diverſly employed, *and being deſirous of the improvement of his ſaid city of Cheſter, and of the citizens thereof, and eſpecially to provide for their benefit and quiet*, out of his ſpecial favor, and of his certain knowledge and mere motion, the ſaid late king Charles the ſecond willed, and by the ſaid laſt mentioned letters patent, for himſelf, his heirs and ſucceſſors, did declare, ordain, conſtitute, and *grant*, that the *ſaid city, and all the ground within the ditch* of the ſame city, with *its ſuburbs and hamlets in the precinct* and circuit of the ſame, *and all the ground in the precinct and circuit of the ſame city of Cheſter*, and of its aforeſaid ſub-

city of Cheſter (except the caſtle and Glover-ſtone)

urbs and hamlets (his caſtle of Cheſter, within the the walls of the ſame city ſituated, and his liberty within

within the boundaries commonly called Le Gloverftone, altogether excepted) *fhould be* from the county of Chefter thenceforth exempt, feparate, and in all things, and by all things, wholly exempt and feparate, as well by land as by water; and that the faid city and fuburbs, and hamlets thereof, and all the ground within the precinct and circuit of the fame (except as before excepted) fhould be from thenceforward *a county by itfelf*, in itfelf diftinct from the county of Chefter, and be thenceforth named and called the county of the city of Chefter for ever; and that *the citizens and inhabitants* of the city aforefaid *(Roger Whitley, efquire*, Thomas Whitley, fon of the faid Roger, John Mainwaring, efquire, William Williams, then late recorder of the city aforefaid, George Booth, efquire, William Street, George Mainwaring, and Michael Johnfon, alone, *excepted) fhould be* by themfelves one community and *body corporate* and politic, in deed, name, and in fact, and be for ever thereafter named and called *by the name of "the mayor and citizens of the city of Chefter*; and that by *the fame name* of the mayor and citizens of the city of Chefter, *they* were, and *fhould be* in all times then to come, perfons able and in law *capable to have, demand, receive, and poffefs manors, lands*, tenements, liberties, privileges, jurifdictions, franchifes, and hereditaments, of whatfoever fort or kind they were, to themfelves and their fucceffors, in fee and in perpetuity, or in any other manner, *and alfo goods*, credits, and chattels, and whatfoever other things, of what kind, nature, or fort foever they were; *and alfo to give, grant, demife, and affign manors, lands*, tenements and hereditaments, *goods*, debts, credits, and chattels, *and to do and execute all other acts and things*, by the aforefaid name of the mayor and citizens of the city of Chefter, and that they and their fucceffors

a county by itfelf — Citizens and inhabitants of Chefter (except Roger Whitley and feven others) made a body corporate, by the name of the *mayor and citizens* of the city of Chefter.

Powers and capacities under that defcription.

fucceffors might, by the fame name, *plead and be impleaded*, anfwer and be anfwered, defend and be defended, in any courts and places, and before any judges and juftices, and other perfons and officers of the faid laft mentioned king, his heirs and fucceffors, and might in all and all forts of actions, fuits, plaints, pleas, caufes, matters and demands whatfoever, and of what kind, nature, or fort foever, in the fame manner and form as others the faid laft-mentioned king's liege fubjects of that his realm of England, be perfons able and in law capable to plead and be impleaded, anfwer and be anfwered, defend and be defended; and that the mayor and citizens of the city aforefaid, for the time being, *fhould have for ever a common feal* kept, to be made ufe of in their caufes, and any other their bufineffes; and that it fhould and might be very lawful for the fame mayor and citizens aforefaid and their fucceffors from time to time, *at their pleafure to break and change that feal*, and to make it anew, as it fhould feem meet to them to do or to be done: And further, the faid laft-mentioned king willed, and by the faid laft-mentioned letters patent, for himfelf, his heirs and fucceffors, did grant and ordain, that there fhould be thenceforth for ever within the faid city *one principal magiftrate* or officer, who fhould be and fhould be *called mayor* of the city of Chefter; and alfo an honeft and difcreet perfon, learned in the laws of England, who fhould have been a barrifter by the fpace of three years at leaft, who fhould be and fhould be called *recorder* of the city of Chefter; and that there might and fhould be within the fame city, *twenty-four* honeft and difcreet perfons, who were and fhould be called *aldermen* of the fame city, of *whom the mayor* of the city aforefaid, and *the recorder* of the city aforefaid, for the time being, fhould

A common feal.

To be changed at pleafure, and to have a new one.

A mayor.

A recorder.

Twenty-four aldermen, including the mayor and recorder.

ſhould be *two:* and that there ſhould be within the city aforeſaid, *forty* other honeſt and diſcreet perſons, who were and ſhould be called the *common-council* of the city aforeſaid; and alſo *two* honeſt and diſcreet perſons, who were and ſhould be called *ſheriffs* of the city of Cheſter, and county of the ſame city, and *one* fit perſon who ſhould be and ſhould be called the *common clerk* of the city aforeſaid; and alſo *two* honeſt and diſcreet perſons, who were and ſhould be called *coroners* of the city of Cheſter, and county of the ſame city; and alſo an *eſcheator*, clerk of the market, two ſurveyors of the walls of the city aforeſaid, called *murengers*, two *treaſurers* of the city aforeſaid, two officers called *leave-lookers*, a *ſword-bearer* of the city aforeſaid, a *mace-bearer* of the city aforeſaid, one officer called the *yeoman of the pentice*, and a *cryer of the courts* of the city aforeſaid: And the ſaid late king Charles the ſecond did, by the ſame letters patent, appoint, nominate, conſtitute, and make his dearly beloved and faithful kinſmen, William George Richard earl of Derby, and Thomas Groſvenor, Peter Pindar, baronet, Richard Dutton, knight, Edward Lutwych, knight (the ſaid king's ſerjeant at law) Peter Shakerly, eſquire, Hugh Groſvenor, eſquire, Robert Werden, eſquire, Robert Murray, Thomas Wilcock, Thomas Simpſon, William Ince, William Wilme, John Sparke, William Wilſon, Edward Oulton, Hugh Starkie, Ralph Burroughs, Francis Skellerne, William Starkie, William Allen, Henry Bennet, William Bennett, and Valentine Short, in the ſaid letters patent mentioned, to be then and thereafter the firſt and new aldermen of the city aforeſaid. And the ſaid Thomas Amery further ſaith, that the ſaid late king Charles the ſecond, by the ſaid laſt-mentioned letters patent, for himſelf, his heirs and ſucceſſors, alſo willed, conſtituted

Forty common council. Two ſheriffs. A common-clerk. Two coroners. An eſcheator, and clerk of the market. Two murengers, two treaſurers, two leave-lookers, a ſword-bearer, a mace-bearer, a yeoman of the pentice and crier of the courts. The twenty-four aldermen firſt appointed.

Mode of electing mayor, on Friday after the feaſt of St Dennis yearly.

ſtituted, ordained, and declared, that *upon Friday next after the feaſt of Saint Dennis, every year, the mayor, aldermen, and common-council of the city aforeſaid; or the greater part of them, might, without any contradiction, aſſemble and meet together in the common-hall of the city aforeſaid; and that they, ſo aſſembled, or the greater part of them, might by ſcrutiny, nominate and elect one of the aldermen of the city aforeſaid, who ſhould by no means have ſerved the office of ſheriff for three years before the ſaid Friday next after the feaſt of Saint Dennis immediately preceding, to be mayor of the city aforeſaid*, to continue in that office until another perſon ſhould be nominated, elected, and made, in due form, in and to the office of mayor of the city aforeſaid; and alſo two *of the common council* of the city aforeſaid, who *ſhould by no means have ſerved the office of ſheriff for three years. before the ſaid Friday* next after the feaſt of Saint Dennis immediately preceding, to be the *ſheriffs* of the city aforeſaid, and county of the ſame city, and to *continue in that office until two other perſons ſhould in due form be nominated*, choſen, and made, to and in that office; and alſo out *of the moſt diſcreet and honeſt citizens* of the city aforeſaid, *two perſons to be coroners* of the city aforeſaid, and of the county of the ſame city, and to continue in that office until two other perſons were choſen and made, in due form, in and to that office, which ſame coroners, ſo choſen, and made, ſhould have, uſe, and exerciſe, and might have, uſe, and exerciſe, the power and authority as the ſaid laſt-mentioned king's corners of the county palatine of Cheſter, or in any other county in the ſaid laſt-mentioned king's realm of England had uſed and exerciſed: And further, that the *mayor, aldermen and common-council* of the city aforeſaid, or the greater part of them, ſo as aforeſaid aſſembled, might *chooſe*

Alſo two ſheriffs, on ſame day.

Two coroners.

*two*

*two of the aldermen* of the city aforefaid, *to be* furveyors of the walls of the city aforefaid, called *murengers*, to continue in that office till two other perfons were in due form chofen and made, to and in that office, and *that they, fo elected, fhould yearly collect* and receive a certain *fubfidy* or cuftom in the city aforefaid, commonly *called murage, as it had been antiently levied in the city aforefaid, for the fupport and building of the walls aforefaid*; and alfo *two others out of the moft difcreet and honeft citizens* of the city aforefaid, to be *treafurers* of the city aforefaid; and alfo *two* others out of the *moft difcreet and honeft citizens* of the city aforefaid, to be officers called *leave-lookers* of the city aforefaid, to continue in that office till two other perfons were in due form elected and made to and in that office: And further, the faid laft-mentioned king willed, and by the faid laft-mentioned letters patent, for himfelf, his heirs and fucceffors' did grant, conftitute, and ordain, *that if it fhould happen that the mayor of the aforefaid city during his mayoralty, died or fhould be removed from that office, at any time before the Friday next after the feaft of Saint Dennis in any year, that then and fo often, the aldermen and common-council of the city aforefaid, or the greater part of them, immediately after the death or removal of fuch mayor, might, without any hindrance or contradiction affemble and meet together in the common-hall aforefaid; and that they, fo affembled, or the greater part of them, might nominate and choofe, by fcrutiny, one of the aldermen of the city aforefaid, who fhould in no wife have ferved the office of fheriff for three years immediately preceding the day of fuch election, to be mayor of the city aforefaid, in the place and ftead of fuch mayor fo dead or removed, to continue in that office until Friday next after the feaft of Saint Dennis, next enfuing his election aforefaid,*

Two murengers.

Two treafurers.

Two leave-lookers.

Mode of electing mayor, in cafe of death or removal during his year of office.

*aforesaid, and until another person to and in that office should be chosen and made in due form, and according to the ordinances, forms, and provisions therein before mentioned*; and further, that as often as it should happen that one or more of the aldermen of the city aforesaid, *should die, or be removed from the office or offices, place or places, of aldermen*, that then and there, and so often, the mayor, *or* the residue of the *aldermen and common-council* of the city aforesaid, or the greater part of them, *immediately* after the death or removal of such alderman or aldermen, might, without any hindrance or contradiction, *assemble* and meet together in *the common-hall* aforesaid; and that they, so assembled, or the greater part of them, might, *by scrutiny elect and make one or more* (as the case should require) *of the common-council* of the city aforesaid, to *be an alderman or aldermen*, in the place or places of him or them so dead or removed: And further the said last-mentioned king willed, and by the said last-mentioned letters patent, for himself, his heirs and successors, did ordain, and firmly enjoin and command, that the aforesaid mayor, recorder, aldermen, common-council, sheriffs, coroners, common-clerk, the officers called murengers, treasurers, the officers called leave-lookers, sword-bearer, mace-bearer, and crier of the courts of the city aforesaid, by the said last mentioned letters patent nominated and appointed; and also all and singular persons who, after the completion of the said letters patent, and by virtue of the same, should be nominated, chosen, or appointed, to or in any office or place, offices or places, of the officers aforesaid, or to or in any other office within the city aforesaid, or should be the deputy of any of the officers in the same letters patent before-mentioned; and also all and every persons who should be nominated and appointed, by the said last-mentioned letters patent,

Mode of electing aldermen, on death of or removal.

*Out of the common-council.*

Officers to take oaths, viz.

patent, justices to keep the peace within the said city, and all and every other persons who by virtue of the same letters patent, should afterwards be justices to keep the peace in the said city; *before they were admitted to the execution or exercise of the office* or offices, place or places, to which they were or should be so respectively nominated, appointed, or constituted, or any otherwise, in that respect, should intermeddle, or any of them respectively, *take*, as well the corporal oath commonly called *the oath of allegiance*, as the corporal oath called *the oath of supremacy*, and also their *oaths for the due execution of their offices*, before such persons as afterwards were appointed by the same letters patent to give and adminster the same, or any two or more of them; and for the better execution of the said last-mentioned king's will, as to the giving and administering the several oaths aforesaid, the same king did give and grant, for himself, his heirs and successors, by the same letters patent, full power and authority to the honourable Thomas Needham, esquire, and to his the same king's dearly beloved and faithful Richard Myddleton, baronet, John Werden, baronet, Philip Egerton, knight, Jeoffrey Shakerley, knight, Thomas Wainwright, doctor of laws, Kenrick Eyton, esquire, John Grosvenor, esquire, William Venables, esquire, Peter Dutton, esquire, John Massey, esquire, and Ralph Graham, esquire, or to any two or more of them, to give, perform, and administer, the several oaths before appointed and directed to be given, to all and singular the persons beforementioned in the same letters patent, and appointed in the same letters patent to be mayor, recorder, aldermen, common council, sheriffs, coroners, common clerk, officers called murengers, treasurers, officers called leave lookers, sword-bearer, mace-

Of allegiance and supremacy, and also oaths of office.

Commissioners appointed to administer oaths to the persons before appointed.

 mace-

mace-bearer, and crier of the courts of the city aforesaid; and also, by the said last-mentioned letters patent, for himself his heirs and successors, the said last-mentioned *king did give* and grant full power and authority to the respective persons in the same letters patent before-mentioned, and appointed to be *mayor and recorder* of the city aforesaid for the time being, *and* to the respective persons by the same letters patent before mentioned to be *justices* to keep the peace in the said city, *and also* all other persons who afterwards should be *mayor, deputy mayor, recorder, deputy recorder*, of the city aforesaid, *or justices assigned* to keep the peace in the said city, *or to any two or more of them*, from time to time, to *give, perform, and administer, the several oaths before-mentioned, to such persons* respectively who afterwards should be named, chosen, or *appointed to any* office or *offices*, place or places, of officer or officers, in *the same letters patent mentioned* or constituted, *or to any other officer within the city* aforesaid, or county of the same city; and also *to all other persons* who *afterwards should be justices* to keep the peace in the said city, or *should be admitted freemen* of the city aforesaid; and *also to* give, perform, and *administer the* oath aforesaid, called the oath of *supremacy*, to *any persons within the city* aforesaid, or county of the same city, who, by the laws or statutes of the said last-mentioned king's kingdom of England, ought to take that oath, as by the said last mentioned letters patent (among other things) more fully appears: *Which said last-mentioned letters patent, were duly accepted and agreed to, by the said citizens and inhabitants.* And the said Thomas Amery further saith, that the said earl of Derby, Thomas Grosvenor, Peter Pindar, baronet, Richard Dutton, knight, Edward Lutwych, knight, Peter Shakerly, Hugh Grosvenor, Robert

Mayor, recorder, and justices, in future, to administer them.

Acceptance of charter.

Robert Werden, Robert Murray, Thomas Wilcock, Thomas Simpson, William Ince, William Wilme, John Sparke, William Wilson, Edward Oulton, Hugh Starkie, Ralph Buroughs, Francis Skellerne, William Starkie, William Allen, Henry Bennett, William Bennett, and Valentine Short, in the said last-mentioned, letters patent mentioned, after *the granting and acceptance of the said last-mentioned letters patent* (to wit) *on the fifth day of February, in the said thirty-seventh year of the reign of* the said late king *Charles the second, became and were aldermen of the said city respectively*, according to the form and effect of the said last-mentioned letters patent (that is to say) at the city of Chester aforesaid; and *from that time hitherto there ought to have been, and still are, twenty-four aldermen of the said city*; as is in and by the said information alledged (to wit) at the city of Chester aforesaid. And the said Thomas Amery further saith, that on the first day of March, in the twenty-second year of the reign of our lord the now king, he the said Thomas *Amery was a citizen and one of the common-council* of the said city of Chester, then inhabiting in the same city (that is to say) at the city of Chester aforesaid, and county of the said city; and the said Thomas *Amery*, so being a *citizen and one of the common-council* of the said city, *and inhabiting there*, as aforesaid, afterwards, to wit, on the said first day of March, in the twenty-second year aforesaid, at the city of Chester aforesaid, and county of the same city, *by the major part of the then mayor, aldermen and common-council of the said city, then and there in the common-hall of the said city in due manner assembled and met together, was lawfully, and in due manner, elected and made one of the aldermen of the said city*, after the death, and in the room and place, of one Thomas Astle, lately one of the aldermen

That the first twenty-four aldermen, named in the charter, became so.

And that ever since there have been, and still are, 24 aldermen.

That Amery was elected an alderman on 1st March, 22d Geo. 3.

aldermen of the faid city, and then deceafed; and the faid Thomas *Amery*, *fo being elected* and made an alderman of the faid city, as aforefaid, afterwards, to wit, on the *firft day of April*, in the twenty-fecond year aforefaid, at the city of Chefter aforefaid, *did*, in due manner, take *an oath for the due execution of his duty* of fuch alderman of the faid city, and did then and there alfo take the corporal oath commonly called the oath of *allegiance*, and the corporal oath commonly called the oath of *fupremacy*, *before* Pattifon Ellames, efquire, (then *mayor* of the faid city) *and* Jofeph Snow (then *one of the aldermen, and a juftice* of the peace of the fame city) *who had then and there a lawful and competent authority to adminifter the fame* in that behalf: And thereupon he the faid Thomas Amery was then and there *duly admitted* into the faid place and office of one of the aldermen of the faid city; by reafon of which faid premifes, he the faid Thomas Amery *then and there became, and was, and ftill is, one of the aldermen of* the faid city (to wit) at the city of Chefter aforefaid, and county of the fame city; by virtue whereof, he the faid Thomas Amery for all the faid time in the faid information in that behalf mentioned, hath ufed and exercifed, and ftill doth ufe and exercife, the faid office of alderman of the faid city of Chefter, and hath there claimed, and yet doth there claim, to be one of the aldermen of the faid city of Chefter, and to have, ufe, and enjoy, all the liberties, privileges, and franchifes, to the faid office of an alderman of the faid city of Chefter belonging and appertaining, as it was and is lawful for him to do, *without this, that the faid Thomas Amery hath ufurped* the faid office, liberties, privileges, and franchifes, upon our faid prefent fovereign lord the king, in manner and form as by the faid information is above fuppofed.

And that he took the neceffary oaths the firft of April following.

pofed. All and fingular which faid matters and things, he the faid Thomas Amery is ready to verify as the court fhall confider: Whereupon he prays judgment, and that the aforefaid office, liberties, privileges, and franchifes, in form aforefaid, claimed by him the faid Thomas Amery, may, for the future, be allowed to him; and that he may be difmiffed and difcharged by the court here of and from the premifes aforefaid, &c.

F. BOWER.

N. B. *Monk's plea, as a common-councilman, is exactly the fame—mutatis—mutandis.*

Replication to Plea of Defendant Amery (as an Alderman.)

AND the faid James Templar, efquire, coroner and attorney of our faid fovereign lord the now king, in the court of our faid lord the now king, before the king himfelf, who for our faid lord the now king, in this behalf profecutes, being now prefent here in court, and having heard the faid plea of the faid Thomas, in manner and form aforefaid above pleaded in bar, faith, that by reafon of any thing by the faid Thomas in that fame plea alledged, the faid lord the now king ought not to be barred from profecuting his aforefaid information against the faid Thomas Amery; becaufe *protefting* that the faid plea by the faid Thomas in manner and form aforefaid above pleaded, and the matters therein contained, are not fufficient in law to bar the faid lord the now king from having his aforefaid information againft the faid Thomas, the faid coroner and attorney of our faid lord the now king, for

Proteftations.

Plea bad.

for the said lord the now king, saith, that our sovereign lord *Charles the second*, late king of England, by his letters patent under the great seal of England, bearing date the fourth day of February, in *the thirty-seventh* year of his reign, *did not grant, in manner and form as the said Thomas hath above in that behalf by his said plea alledged:* And this the said coroner and attorney of our said lord the now king, for our said lord the now king, prays may be inquired of by the country, &c. *And* the said coroner and attorney of our said lord the now king, for our said lord the now king, also saith, that the aforesaid *letters patent*, by the said Thomas above in his said plea mentioned, *were not duly accepted and agreed to by the said citizens and inhabitants of the said city of Chester*, as the said Thomas hath above in pleading alledged: and this the said coroner and attorney of our said lord the now king, for our said lord the now king, prays may be inquired of by the country, &c. *And* the said coroner and attorney of our said lord the now king, for our said lord the now king, also saith, that the said *Thomas* at the time in the said plea in that behalf mentioned, was not *by the major part of the then mayor, aldermen, and common council* of the said city of Chester, then and there in the common-hall of the said city, in due manner assembled, and met together, lawfully, and in due manner *elected and made one of the aldermen* of the said city, in manner and form as by the said Thomas is above in pleading alledged: and this the said coroner and attorney of our said lord the now king, for our said lord the now king, prays may be inquired of by the country, &c. *And* the said coroner and attorney of our said lord the now king, for our said lord the now king further saith, That the said *Thomas was not duly admitted into the office and place of one of*

Non concessit to the charter of Charles 2d.

That said charter was not accepted

Non fuit electus—an alderman.

Non fuit admissus.

*of the aldermen* of the city of Chester, in manner and form as the said Thomas hath by his said plea above alledged: And this the said coroner and attorney of our said lord the now king, for our said lord the now king, prays may be inquired of by the country, *&c.*

1st Replication.

*And* the said coroner and attorney of our said sovereign lord the now king for our said sovereign lord the now king, for further replication in this behalf, saith, that the said late king Charles the second, in and by the said letters patent, in the said plea of the said Thomas above-mentioned, further willed, and by the same letters patent did provide and reserve *full power* and authority to himself, his heirs and successors, from time to time, and at all times thereafter, at the free will and pleasure of the said late *king* Charles the second, his heirs or successors, the mayor, recorder, common clerk, or any one or more of the aldermen, common-council-men, sheriffs, coroners, and justices of the peace, of the said city, for the time being, *by any order of the said late king, his heirs or successors, in privy-council made, and under the seal of the said privy-council, to them respectively signified, to amove or declare them or any of them, to be amoved accordingly. And* that as often as the said late king, his heirs or successors, by any such order made in privy-council, should declare any such mayor, recorder, common-clerk, and any one or more of the aldermen, common-council-men, sheriffs, coroners, or justices of the peace, of the said city, for the time being, to be amoved from his or their respective offices; that then, and *from thenceforth*, the mayor, recorder, common clerk, aldermen, and common-council-men, sheriffs, coroners, and justices of the peace, for the time being; and all or any of them so amoved or declared to be amoved from their re-

Power of amotion reserved to the crown in charter of 37th Charles 2d.

ſpective offices, ſhould in deed and in fact, and *without any further proceſs, actually*, and to all intents and purpoſes whatſoever, be *amoved* from their reſpective offices, and ſo from time to time, as often as the caſe ſhould ſo happen, any thing in the ſaid letters patent contained to the contrary notwithſtanding. *And* that in every ſuch caſe, *other fit perſon* or perſons, *within a convenient time* after any ſuch amotion or amotions, ſhould be *choſen*, *ſworn* and *appointed* in ſuch manner as by the ſaid letters patent was before directed, into the place and office or places and offices reſpectively, of any ſuch perſon or perſons ſo amoved, as in and by the ſaid letters patent (amongſt other things) it doth and may more fully appear. *And* the ſaid coroner and attorney of our ſaid lord the now king for our ſaid lord the now king, further ſays, That *after the making of the ſaid letters patent* of the ſaid late king Charles the ſecond, in the ſaid plea of the ſaid Thomas above-mentioned, to wit: on the 12th *day of Auguſt*, which was in the year of our Lord 1688, under and by virtue of the ſaid laſt mentioned letters patent, Hugh Starkey, eſquire, was one of the aldermen of the ſame city, and a juſtice of the peace of and within the ſaid city of Cheſter, and county of the ſame city; and that Richard Leving, eſquire, was then and there recorder of the ſaid city, and alſo one of the aldermen of the ſaid city, and a juſtice of the peace of and within the ſaid city of Cheſter, and county of the ſame city; and that the right hon. William earl of Derby, col. Robert Werden, Sir Thomas Groſvenor, Sir Peter Pindar, Sir Richard Dutton, Peter Shakerley, Thomas Simpſon, William Ince, Thomas Wilcock, and Robert Murrey, ſeverally were *adlermen*, and each of them was an alderman of the ſaid city, and alſo ſeverally *juſtices of the peace* within the ſaid city

12th Auguſt 1688, corporate officers then in being.

city of Chefter, and county of the fame city; and that William Wilme, Hugh Grofvenor, John Spark, William Wilfon, Randal Oulton, Francis Skellerne, William Allen, William Starkey, Henry Bennett, William Bennett, Valentine Short, and Peter Bennett, feverally were alfo aldermen, and each of them was an alderman of the faid city of Chefter; and that Edward Starkey and Jonathan Whitby, then fheriffs, James Hutchinfon and Randal Vaufe, then leave-lookers, John Johnfon, John White, Randal Holme, Elizeus Lloyd, Bradford Thropp, John Gouldborun, Richard Taylor the elder, Richard Taylor the younger, John Minfhall, Jofeph Dyafon, John Crichley, Caldecot Alderfey, Edward Partington, Randal Oulton, John Burroughs, Pulefton Partington, Samuel Heath, Richard Oulton, Thomas Maddockes, Thomas Warringham, Henry Crofby, William Francis, Theodorus Aldcroft, Richard Brett, Thomas Holland, Mathew Anderton, Thomas Johnfon, John Warrington, Nathaniel Bullen, Charles Pindar, Hugh Bartley, Griffith Trygan, John Hale, Robert Moulfon, Ralph Poole, and Edward Croughton, feverally were *common-council men* of the faid city of Chefter, to wit; on the fame day and year laft abovementioned, at the city of Chefter aforefaid, in the county of the fame city; and that *no other perfons or perfon whatfoever then were or was aldermen or common-council-men*, or an alderman or common-council-man of the faid city of Chefter. *And* the faid coroner and attorney of our fovereign lord the now king for our faid lord the now king, further fays, that the faid laft-mentioned perfons fo being aldermen and common-council-men of the faid city, and there being no other perfon or perfons whatfoever aldermen or common-council-men, or an alderman or common-council-man of the faid city

And that there were no others.

 of

of Chester, his said late majesty king *James the second* afterwards, to wit: on the 12*th day of August*, which was in the year of our Lord 1688, *by his order in privy-council made in execution of the power reserved to the said late king Charles the second*, his heirs or successors, in and by the said letters patent, made in the thirty-seventh year of the reign of the said late king Charles the second, in the said plea of the said Thomas above-mentioned, was pleased to order, and *did thereby order*, that the said Hugh Starkey, esquire, and Richard Leving, esquire, recorder, aldermen and justices of the peace, the said right hon. William earl of Derby, col. Robert Werden, Sir Thomas Grosvenor, Sir Peter Pindar, Sir Richard Dutton, Peter Shakerley, Thomas Simpson, William Ince, Thomas Wilcock, and Robert Murrey, aldermen and justices of the peace; the said William Wilme, Hugh Grosvenor, John Sparke, William Wilson, Randal Oulton, Francis Skellerne, William Allen, William Starkey, Henry Bennett, William Bennett, Valentine Short, and Peter Bennett, aldermen; the said Edward Starkey, and Jonathan Whitby, sheriffs; James Hutchinson, and Randal Vause, leave-lookers; John Johnson, John White, Randal Holme, Elizeus Lloyd, Bradford Thropp, John Gouldbourne, Richard Taylor senior, Richard Taylor junior, John Minshall, Joseph Dyason, John Crichley, Caldecott Aldersey, Edward Partington, Randal Oulton, John Burroughs, Puleston Partington, Samuel Heath, Richard Oulton, Thomas Maddockes, Thomas Waringham, Henry Crosby, William Francis, Theodorus Aldcroft, Richard Brett, Thomas Holland, Matthew Anderton, Thomas Johnson, John Warrington, Nathaniel Bullen, Charles Pindar, Hugh Bartley, Griffith Trygan, John Hale, Robert Moulson,

12th August 1688, king James's order of amoval, of all the officers.

Moulfon, Ralph Poole, and Edward Croughton, common-council-men, *fhould be, and they were, thereby removed* and difplaced from their aforefaid offices and employments in the faid city of Chefter, to wit, at the city of Chefter aforefaid, in the county of the fame city. *And* the faid coroner and attorney of our faid lord the now king for the faid lord the now king, alfo fays, that afterwards, to wit, on the faid twelfth day of Auguft, in the faid year of our Lord 1688, *the faid order in council, under the feal of the faid privy-council, was fignified* to the faid Hugh Starkey, Richard Leving, the right hon. William earl of Derby, colonel Robert Werden, Sir Thomas Grofvenor, Sir Peter Pindar, Sir Richard Dutton, Peter Shakerley, Thomas Simpfon, William Ince, Thomas Wilcock, Robert Murrey, William Wilme, Hugh Grofvenor, John Sparke, William Wilfon, Randal Oulton, Francis Skellerne, William Allen, William Starkey, Henry Bennett, William Bennett, Valentine Short, Peter Bennett, Edward Starkey, Jonathan Whitby, James Hutchinfon, Randal Vaufe, John Johnfon, John White, Randal Holme, Elizeus Lloyd, Bradford Thropp, John Gouldbourne, Richard Taylor fenior, Richard Taylor junior, John Minfhall, Jofeph Dyafon, John Crichley, Caldecott Alderfey, Edward Partington, Randal Oulton, John Burroughs, Pulefton Parting, Samuel Heath, Richard Oulton, Thomas Maddockes, Thomas Waringham, Henry Crofby, William Francis, Theoderus Aldcroft, Richard Brett, Thomas Holland, Matthew Anderton, Thomas Johnfon, John Warrington, Nathaniel Bullen, Charles Pindar, Hugh Bartley, Griffith Trygan, John Hale, Robert Moulfon, Ralph Poole, and Edward Croughton, refpectively and thereby, *they and each of them feverally and refpectively became and were amoved from their refpective offices*

Which was fignified to them.

*offices and places of aldermen and common-council-men* before-mentioned: *Wherefore the faid power in the faid laft-mentioned letters patent, as to the election of aldermen* of the faid city of Chefter, *ceafed, and determined,* to wit, at the city of Chefter aforefaid, in the county of the fame city; all which matters and things, the faid coroner and attorney of our faid lord the now king for the faid lord the now king, is ready to verify, and prays, that the faid Thomas Amery may be convicted of the premifes above charged upon him by the faid information, by the faid coroner and attorney of our faid lord the now king, exhibited againft him; and that the faid Thomas Amery may be forejudged, and excluded from the aforefaid office of an alderman of the faid city of Chefter, and from the liberties, privileges, and franchifes, belonging and appertaining to the faid office.

Wherefore the power of electing aldermen, ceafed.

2d. Replication.

*And* the faid coroner and the attorney of our faid lord the now king, for our faid lord the now king, for further replication in this behalf, faith, That the fovereign lord Henry the feventh, late king of England, *by his letters patent, under the feal of his county palatine of Chefter,* bearing date at Chefter, upon the *6th day of April, in the twenty-firft year of his reign,* out of the great affection which he bore and had to his city of Chefter, and the citizens and commonalty of the fame city; and in confideration of the good behaviour and the great cofts and expences of the citizens of the fame city, and alfo of the grateful fervices to the faid late king by them againft the adverfaries and rebels of the faid late king, many times beftowed, willing the bettering of the fame city; and alfo efpecially to provide for the advantage and quiet of the fame citizens, their heirs and fucceffors, out of his fpecial grace, and on his certain knowledge and mere motion, *gave and granted,* and, by

6th April, 21 Henry 7th, Original charter of incorporation.

by the said letters patent, confirmed for himself and his heirs, to the aforesaid citizens and commonalty, and their heirs and successors, for ever, *that the said city*, and all the ground within the ditch of the same city, with its suburbs and hamlets in the precincts and circuit of the same, and the whole ground in the precincts and circuit of the same city of Chester, and its aforesaid suburbs and hamlets (his castle of Chester, situated within the walls of the same city, altogether excepted) *should be from the county of Chester from that time exempted*, separated, and in all things, and by all things, wholly exempted and separated, as well by land as by water: And that the said city and suburbs and hamlets of the same, and all the lands within the precincts and circuit of the same, (except before excepted) should be *for the future, a county by itself*, and in itself distinct and separate from his county of Chester, and for the future should be named and called the county of the city of Chester, for ever: And the said late king Henry the seventh, by his said letters patent, also willed, and gave, and granted, for himself and his heirs, to the *said citizens and commonalty*, their heirs and successors, *that they and their successors, for ever, in every year successively, might elect, make, and choose twenty-four fellow citizens of the same city, to be aldermen, and also forty other citizens, of the same city, for the common-council of the same city, which said twenty-four fellow citizens so to be elected and chosen, should have and bear the name of aldermen of the city of Chester, for ever*, of which said twenty-four aldermen, also one, by the unanimous consent and assent of the mayor, aldermen, sheriffs, and also of the other citizens of the common-council aforesaid, to *the office of recorder* of the city aforesaid, should be elected and appointed: And the said late king Henry the seventh, also willed and granted. for himself and his heirs, that the said

Mode of electing 24 aldermen, and 40 common council.

One of these aldermen, to be recorder.

*citizens*

*citizens and commonalty*, and their heirs and succeffors, fhould and might *have, appoint, and elect out of them-*

The mayor, *felves in every year* fucceffively, for ever, *a mayor*, and that every mayor of the fame city, for the time being, fhould himfelf, *fo foon* as he fhall be *elected* and appointed mayor of the faid city, be his *efcheator and clerk of the market* there. *And* that the faid may-

to be efcheator and clerk of the market.

or and commonalty, and their heirs and fucceffors, for ever, fhould be one community by themfelves, and fhould be for ever named, and called *by the name* of the *mayor and citizens of the city of Chefter*, and

Name of incorporation.

by the fame name fhould be perfons able and capable in law, and by the fame name might *plead and be impleaded*, anfwer and be anfwered unto, before the faid late king, his heirs and fucceffors, earls of Chefter, and before every of the faid king's juftices, in whatfoever of his faid courts. *And* that the aforefaid *mayor and citizens, might have, appoint, and elect* out of themfelves every year fucceffively, *two citizens to be fheriffs* of the fame county of the city of Chefter, which mayor and fheriffs fhould be in the form underwritten elected and appointed, (that is to fay) All *the fellow citizens* of the faid city, and the fuburbs, and hamlets aforefaid, dwelling within the

Form of electing mayor,

fame city, fuburbs, and hamlets of the fame city, who would interfere in the election of mayor, *might every year upon Friday next after the feaft of Saint Dennis, at the common-hall of the city* aforefaid, freely and without any contradiction, *affemble together*, who being fo there, or the major part of them, might *nominate two citizens inhabiting* in the faid city, of of the moft able, difcreet, and honourable perfons *out of* the number of *the twenty-four aldermen* in the fame city, fuburbs, and hamlets aforefaid, in form following, likewife to be elected, *either of whom had or had not before been* mayor, or fheriff of the faid city, and *who had by no means enjoyed the office of fheriff*,

*riff within three years* immediately preceding the faid Friday next after the feaft of Saint Dennis, out *of which two fo named, the major part of the faid aldermen and fheriffs* then prefent there, by fcrutiny fhould nominate, elect, and appoint a *mayor*; and if in fuch election or nomination of that one perfon to be mayor, the voices fhould be in number *equal*, difagreeing from each other, then, the faid late king willed, that *the voice of the mayor* of the faid city for the time being fhould be had and held for *two voices*. But in the election of the fheriffs of the faid city, the faid late king willed, that the form following fhould be obferved, to wit, that *the mayor, fhereffs, aldermen, and other citizens* of the fame city and county, inhabiting in the fame, who fhould be willing to interfere in the election of the fheriffs, fhould, on *Friday next after the feaft of Saint Dennis, annually*, without any contradiction whatfoever, affemble and meet together; and the *mayor, fheriffs, and aldermen, for the time being*, or the major part of them, then being perfonally there, fhould *freely elect* and appoint *one able and fufficient perfon to be one fheriff of the faid city*; and then the *faid other fellow citizens* being there then likewife prefent, or the major part of them, fhould on the fame day freely elect and *appoint another* able *and fufficient perfon* to be the other fheriff of the faid city, which two fo elected fheriffs of the fame county and city, fhould be, and remain from the faid Friday next after the feaft of Saint Dennis, for *one whole year*: And that the faid *mayor, and efcheator, and clerk of the market, and fheriffs*, of the city aforefaid, for the time being, fhould yearly, *immediately after* their appointment, *take their oaths before him who preceded the fame mayor* fo elected in his office the year preceding, and *before the commonalty* of the faid city, in manner and form, as theretofore they had been accuftomed: And this

and the fheriffs, one by the mayor, fheriffs, and aldermen, the other by the commonalty,

Oaths to be taken by mayor and fheriffs.

this without the ſaid late king's writ of dedimus poteſtatem, to be ſued out of the chancery or exchequer of the ſaid late king, his heirs or ſucceſſors, or waiting for other mandates of the ſaid late king, his heirs or ſucceſſors. *And* the ſaid late king Henry the ſeventh, by the ſaid laſt-mentioned letters patent, further granted to the ſaid *mayor* of the ſaid city, and his ſucceſſors, that they might yearly *elect out of the moſt diſcreet and honeſt citizens* of the ſaid city, *two citizens to be the coroners* of the ſaid late king, his heirs and ſucceſſors, within the ſaid city, and the limits and liberties of the ſame city, who before the mayor and aldermen of the ſaid city, ſhould yearly *take their corporal* oaths, that they for one whole year, the office of coroner within the ſaid city, and the limits and boundaries aforeſaid, would well and truly execute and ſerve: And that the ſaid coroner, ſo elected and ſworn, ſhould *have power and authority in like manner as the coroner* of the ſaid late king, in the county palatine *of Cheſter, or in any other county of his kingdom of England*, had uſed or exerciſed. *And* the ſaid late king Henry the ſeventh, by the ſaid letters patent, further gave, and granted to the aforeſaid *mayor and citizens*, and their ſucceſſors, that they ſhould elect yearly out of the citizens of the ſaid city, *two citizens to be ſurveyors of the walls* of the ſaid city, to be called murengers, as antiently they had been accuſtomed to do there; and that they ſhould yearly ſurvey the walls of the ſaid city, and repair them; and that they, ſo elected, ſhould annually collect and *receive a certain ſubſidy* or cuſtom in the ſaid city, commonly called *murage*, as it had antiently been levied in the ſaid city, for the upholding and building of the walls of the ſaid city. *And* the ſaid late king Henry the ſeventh, did moreover grant, for himſelf, his heirs and ſucceſſors, and by the ſaid letters patent, confirm, that if perchance any

Mode of electing coroners,

their oath of office;

and murengers.

Power of making bye laws, by mayor, ſheriffs, and aldermen.

any customs or ordinances in the same city of Chester thitherto obtained and used, should be difficult or defective in any part of them, so that on account of any thing newly happening within the same city, *wherein fit remedy did not clearly exist before*, such ordinances might stand in need of correction, that then, and in such case, the *mayor and sheriffs* of the said city, for the time being, *and the aldermen*, or the major part of them, for the time being, should have full *power and authority to apply and ordain a new remedy*, agreeable to good faith and consonant to reason, for the common good of the citizens of his said city of Chester, and other his faithful people resorting to the said city, with the common assent of the aforementioned, and by *the advice of the mayor, sheriffs, and forty other fellow-citizens of the said city, for the common council of the said city in form aforesaid to be annually elected, or the greater part of them*, and to require due execution of such their ordinances, so often and at such time as need should require, or to them should seem expedient; provided those ordinances were beneficial to him and his people, and consonant to good faith and reason, as by the said letters patent of the said late king Henry the seventh (amongst other things) it more fully appears: *Which said last-mentioned letters*-patent, the said *citizens and commonalty* of the said city of Chester, afterwards (to wit) on the same day and year last above mentioned, at the city of Chester aforesaid, in the county of the same city, *did agree to and did duly accept*. *And* the said coroner and attorney of our said lord the now king, for our said lord the now king, further saith, that our sovereign lady *Elizabeth*, late queen of England, by *her letters*-patent, under the great seal of England, bearing date at Westminster, the *fourteenth day of June, in the sixteenth year of her reign*, reciting as therein is recited, *did*

Charter of 21st Hen. 7th accepted.

14th June, 16th Elizabeth, (A.D. 1574) Confirmation (by inspeximus) of charter of 21st Henry 7th.

*did by infpeximus of the faid letters-patent of the faid late king Henry the feventh*, holding as ratified the fame letters-patent, as alfo all and fingular the things contained and fpecified in them, for herfelf, her heirs and fucceffors, allow and approve them, and did *then ratify and confirm them to the mayor, aldermen, and fheriffs of the faid city, and alfo the citizens and commonalty of the faid city*, their heirs and fucceffors: And *moreover the faid late queen Elizabeth did*, by her faid letters-patent, for herfelf, her heirs and fucceffors, *confirm* to the aforefaid mayor, citizens, and commonalty of the city aforefaid, their heirs and fucceffors, for ever, that *fo oft as* it fhould fall out that the *mayor or fheriffs* of the faid city, or any of them *fhould die within the year* of their offices, the *aldermen, citizens and commonalty* of the city aforefaid, who would be prefent at the new election, fhould *affemble and meet together* in the common-hall of the faid city, on the *Friday next after the death* of the deceafed mayor or fheriffs, and *then and there*, after the death of every mayor or fheriff fo departing, they might choofe and *appoint fome one of the moft* difcreet and fit perfons in the number *of the twenty-four aldermen*, in fuch manner and form as in *the yearly election of the mayor* of the faid city, they *were accuftomed to do*; which mayor, fo chofen and made, fhould before all the aldermen prefent, *take the fame oaths* which the mayors before were wont to take; and if the *mayor fo chofen* and appointed, was *not prefent* at the election, then on the *Friday next after his return home he fhould take the oaths* before the aforefaid aldermen, or at the leaft four of them, in the common hall of the faid city: And that after *the death of every fheriff*, dying as aforefaid, *they fhould elect and name one of the forty who were the common-council of the faid city for fheriff*, in fuch manner and

Additional power to elect a mayor or fheriffs in cafe of death.

and form as in the yearly election of sheriffs in the said city they were accustomed to do; which *sheriff so chosen, should take the oaths before the then mayor*; and the sheriff *or sheriffs* so chosen, should *continue in his or* their offices from the day and time of the election aforesaid, until the *Friday next after the feast of Saint Dennis, when they were wont to choose new officers* of the said city: As by the said letters patent of the said late queen Elizabeth (amongst other things) more fully appears: Which *said last mentioned letters patent*, the said, *mayor, citizens, and commonalty* of the said city of Chester, did *afterwards agree to, and did duly accept* (to wit) on the same day and year last aforesaid, at the city of Chester aforesaid, in the county of the same city. *And* the said coroner and attorney of our said sovereign lord ths now king, for our said lord the now king, further says, *that the said several letters patent of the said late king Henry the seventh, and the said letters patent of the said late queen Elizabeth, confirming the same, were, and each of them was, and did remain and continue, in full force, strength, and effect, before and until and at the time of the judgment herein after next mentioned being given against the said mayor and citizens* (that is to say) at the city of Chester aforesaid, in the county of the same city. *And* the said coroner and attorney of our said sovereign lord the now king for our said lord the now king, further says, that after the granting of the said letters patent of the said late king Henry the seventh, and the said late queen Elizabeth, herein before mentioned (to wit) on *Friday next after the morrow of the Holy Trinity, in the thirty-fifth year of the reign* of the said sovereign lord Charles the second, late king of England, *&c.* Sir *Robert Sawyer*, knight, then attorney-general of the said late sovereign lord king Charles the second, who

Charter of confirmation accepted.

Charters in force at the time of the judgment in quo warranto.

Trinity Term, 35th Cha. 2d. (A.D. 1683) Information in quo warranto by Sir Robert Sawyer (attorney-general) v. the mayor and citizens.

who for the said late sovereign lord the king prosecuted in that behalf, came in his proper person in the court of the said late sovereign lord the king, before the said late king himself, at Westminster, in the county of Middlesex, and for the said late sovereign lord king Charles the second, brought into the said court of the said late king Charles the second, before the said late king himself then and there, a certain *information against the said mayor and citizens*, by the name of the mayor and citizens of the city of Chester, by which said information the said attorney-general of the said late king gave the said court there to understand and be informed, *that the said mayor and citizens* of the said city of Chester, by the space of one month then last past, and longer, had *used and did then* use, and claimed to have and use *without any warrant* or royal grant, within the said city, and the liberties and precincts of the same city, *divers liberties, privileges*, and franchises, in the said information mentioned, that is to say, to be in themselves one body-corporate and politic, in law, fact and name, by the name of the mayor and citizens of the city of Chester, and by the same name to plead and be impleaded, answer and be answered unto; and also to have sheriffs of the said city, and county of the same city, and to nominate and choose from amongst themselves two persons to be sheriffs of the said city, and of the county of the same city, and to execute and return all writs, bills, and precepts, of our said lord the said late king, touching the administration and execution of justice within the same city, and county of the same city, and to do and execute all and singular other things within the said city, and the county of the said city, which to the office of sheriff appertained, without any commission, or other letters patent, from the said lord the late king in that behalf obtained

For claiming to be a body-corporate, &c.

tained, or to be obtained; and also that the mayor and recorder of the said city, and the aldermen who had been mayors of the said city, were jointly and severally justices of the said lord the said late king, to keep the peace within the same city, and to hold sessions of the peace and pleas of the crown within the same city, and to enquire, hear, and determine, all manner of felonies, riots, routs, and unlawful assemblies, within the same city, of their own proper authority, without any commission or other authority, from the said late lord the king in that behalf granted or obtained: All and singular which liberties, privileges, and franchises, the *said mayor and citizens* of the said city, for all the time aforesaid, against the said lord the late king *had usurped*, and did then usurp, in contempt of the said lord the late king, and to the great injury and prejudice of his royal prerogative: And thereupon the said attorney general of the said lord the late king, for the said lord the late king, prayed the advice of the court there in the premises, and that due process of law might issue in that behalf against the said mayor and citizens, to answer to the said lord the late king, to shew by what warrant they claimed to have and exercise the liberties, privileges, and franchises aforesaid, &c. *And* the said coroner and attorney of our said lord the now king, for our said lord the now king, further saith, that *such proceedings were thereupon had* in the same court, that afterwards, to wit, in the *term of Saint Hilary, in the thirty-fifth and thirty-sixth* years of the said reign of the said late king Charles the second, for *the default of the said mayor and citizens in not appearing* in the said court of the said lord the late king, before the king himself, to answer to the said lord the late king, touching and concerning the premises; *it was* then and there, by the same court of the said lord the late king,

Hilary Term, 35th and 36th Charles 2d. (A. D. 1683. 4)

Judgment by default in not

appearing and seizure quo us que pro ut patet &c.

king, before the king himself, *considered, that the liberties, privileges, and franchises, in the said last-mentioned information above specified, should be seized into the hands of the said lord the late king, until the said court there further ordered*, as by the record and proceedings thereof, remaining in the court of our said lord the now king, before the king himself, at Westminster aforesaid, appears. *And* the said coroner and attorney of our said lord the now king, for the said lord the now king, further saith, that after the said judgment, and after the making of the said letters patent, in the said plea of the said Thomas mentioned (to wit) on the 19th day of October, which was in the year of our lord 1688, his late majesty king James the second, by *a certain order in council bearing date the nineteenth day of October*, which was in the said year of our lord 1688, being graciously resolved, that *the city of Chester, and the mayor, and citizens thereof, should be restored* to their antient charters, rights, and franchises, *notwithstanding the judgment and proceedings against them in an information in the nature of a quo warranto* in the court of the king's-bench, in the reign of the late king Charles the second, of blessed memory; his said majesty king James the second was, by the said order last mentioned, made in council, graciously pleased to order according to the power to him reserved in the late charters, patents, and grants; *and it was thereby ordered* accordingly, that *all mayors, sheriffs*, recorders, aldermen, clerks of the pentice, town clerks, common-council-men, and all other officers and members of the said city of Chester, constituted, named, appointed, or *elected by virtue of any charter, patent, or grant, since the year* 1679, from the late king, or his then majesty, and all, and every person and persons, having or claiming any office or place by the same, be

19th October, 1688, king James 2d's order in council for restoring mayor and citizens of Chester.

be *removed*, difplaced, and difcharged, and they and every of them were thereby removed, difplaced and difcharged accordingly; *And it was further ordered* by his faid late majefty king James the fecond, by the faid order in council, that *Mr. Attorney, or Mr. Solicitor-General, fhould prepare a bill*, inftrument, or inftruments for his majefty's royal fignature, *for the granting, confirming, and reftoring of the faid city of Chefter, and the mayor, and citizens thereof, to their ancient charters*, rights, franchifes, offices, and places had or ufed by them before the faid judgment given, and proceedings againft them, and to pardon, difcharge, vacate, annul, and reverfe the faid judgment, and proceedings.—*And* the faid coroner and attorney of our faid lord the now king, for the faid lord the now king, further faith, that afterwards (to wit) on the *twenty-fixth day of October*, which was in the faid year of our *Lord* 1688, the faid late fovereign lord *king James the fecond*, late king of England, *&c. by his letters patent* under the great feal of England, bearing date at Weftminfter, the faid twenty-fixth day of October, which was in the faid year of our Lord 1688, in the fourth year of his reign, in confideration of the good fervice which the faid mayor and citizens of the faid city of Chefter, had done to him, and alfo for the good government of the faid city, did pardon, remife and releafe; and by thofe prefents *aid for himfelf, his heirs and fucceffors, amongft other things, pardon, remife and releafe to the mayor and citizens of the faid city of Chefter, the judgment given againft the faid mayor and citizens* of the faid city of Chefter, or againft the aforefaid citizens, by the name of the mayor and citizens of the faid city of Chefter, or by any other name or names, in the term of St. Hilary, in the *thirty-fifth and thirty-fixth years of the* reign of his moft dearly beloved

26th October, 1688, Charter of reftoration, purfuant to the laft-mentioned order in council.

 brother

Judgment in quo warranto is pardoned.

brother *Charles the fecond, late* king of England, upon an information of quo warranto, in the nature of a quo warranto, thentofore exhibited by Sir Robert Sawyer, knight, attorney general of his faid brother, in the court of his faid brother (then late king) before the king himfelf, at Weftminfter, in the county of Middlefex, againft the mayor and citizens of the city of Chefter; and alfo, all feizures and procefs thereupon had, *and all and fingular forfeitures, pains* and penalties, forfeited, had, or incurred by the faid citizens, or by the mayor and citizens of the faid city of Chefter, by reafon of the faid judgment; and *alfo all and fingular claims* and demands of him the faid late king James the fecond, his heirs and fucceffors, to any liberties, privileges, or franchifes lawfully had or enjoyed by the faid citizens, or by the mayor and citizens, of the faid city of Chefter, before the time of the rendering of the faid judgment. — *And the faid late king James the fecond*, did alfo, by his faid letters patent, for himfelf, his heirs and fucceffors, wholly remife, *releafe, and quit claim, to the faid mayor and citizens of the city of Chefter aforefaid, the information aforefaid, and all, and all manner of procefs, judgment, and feizure, thereupon* had and rendered. *And* moreover, the faid late king James the fecond, of his fpecial grace, and of his certain knowledge, and mere motion, *reftored and granted*, and by his faid letters patent, for him, his heirs and fucceffors, did reftore and grant to the *faid mayor and citizens* of the faid city of Chefter, *all and fingular liberties, franchifes*, lands, tenements, rents, jurifdictions, hereditaments, goods, chattels, intereft, reverfions, profits, offices, rights, emoluments, cuftoms, exemptions, privileges, eafements, benefits and advantages whatfoever, which the faid citizens, or the mayor and citizens of the faid city of Chefter, enjoyed,

Former liberties reftored to the mayor and citizens, by their ancient name of incorporation.

joyed, or of right ought or could enjoy, or which to them were by any means whatfoever belonging, at *or before the time of the rendering of the aforefaid judgment, by the name*, or in the right *of the mayor and citizens of the city of Chefter*, or by the name, or in the right of the *citizens of the faid city, or by any other name of incorporation, by which* the faid citizens were called: in as ample manner and form to all intents and purpofes, as though the information aforefaid, had never been exhibited, and the judgment aforefaid, or any procefs upon the information aforefaid, had not been given, or had; and that the faid mayor and citizens of the faid city of Chefter, might be and fhould be *one body corporate, and politic in* deed, fact, and name, by the name of the mayor and citizens of the city of Chefter, and by all and fingular, fuch other name and names as they lawfully had, and claimed to have, at the time of the rendering of the faid judgment, and *in fuch and as ample manner* and form, *as they were* incorporated or claimed to be incorporated, at the time of the rendering of the faid judgment, or before. *And* the faid late king James the fecond, by his faid letters patent, alfo willed and commanded, that all and fingular, *the officers*, mayor, recorder, aldermen, fheriffs, and citizens, being of the common-council of the faid city, and all officers and minifters whomfoever, and each of them, who were in fuch offices or places, at *the time of rendering of the faid judgment*, that they and each of them, fhould take upon themfelves and *execute the fame* offices and places refpectively, as they held and executed the fame, and each of them before the rendering the judgment aforefaid. *And* moreover, the faid late king James the fecond, by the faid letters patent for him, his heirs and fucceffors, did conftitute and reftore *to William Street*, efquire, (who

William Street, Efq; (the old mayor) and aldermen, are reftored.

(who was *mayor* of the ſaid city of Cheſter, at the time of the rendering the ſaid judgment, in the ſaid term of Saint Hilary, in *thirty-fifth and thirty-ſixth years* of the reign of the ſaid late king Charles the ſecond) the *office of mayor* of the ſaid city; and did alſo *conſtitute and reſtore* to Sir William Williams, knight and baronet, the ſolicitor-general of his ſaid late majeſty king James the ſecond, (who was *recorder and alderman* of the ſaid city at the time of rendering of the ſaid judgment) the *office* and place, and offices and places, of *recorder and aldermen* of the ſaid city; and did conſtitute and *reſtore to William earl of Derby*, Thomas earl Rivers. Thomas Groſvenor, baronet, Peter Pindar, baronet, Roger Whitley, eſquire, the ſaid William Street, Thomas Wilcock, Richard Wright, Thomas Sympſon, Henry Lloyd, William Ince, John Anderſon, George Mainwaring, Peter Edwards, Nathaniel Williamſon, William Wilſon, Edward Oulton, and Hugh Starkey, gentlemen, (who were aldermen of of the ſame city at the ſame times of rendering of the ſaid judgment) the ſame ſeveral and reſpective *offices of aldermen*; and did conſtitute and reſtore to * *Robert Murren* (who was ſheriff of the ſaid city at the ſame time of rendering of the ſaid judgment) the *office of ſheriff* of the ſaid city—To have and exerciſe the ſame ſeveral and reſpective offices and places, in ſuch and as ample manner and form as they had the ſame offices and places reſpectively before the rendering the ſaid judgment. *And did thereby authoriſe*, command, and require them, and each of them, to take upon themſelves, *exerciſe and perform the ſaid ſeveral offices* and places of mayor,

And alſo Robert Murren, the ſurviving ſheriff.

* John Wilme, co-ſheriff with Robert Murren at the time of the judgment in quo warranto, was dead before this charter of reſtoration paſſed.

mayor, recorder, aldermen and sheriffs respectively, in such and as ample manner and form as they had and exercised the same, at or before the time of rendering the said judgment; and also that they should cause the citizens of the said city to be assembled in the common-hall of the said city, to make elections, and to do all other things requisite and accustomed, and to be done in the usual manner. And moreover the said late king James the second, by his said letters patent, also willed and granted, that the mayor, recorder, aldermen, sheriffs and citizens of the said city, for the time being, the common-council, citizens in common-hall assembled, and also all other officers of the said city, should do and perform all such other like things, and should respectively have and exercise the same powers, authority and jurisdiction as the mayor, recorder, aldermen and common-council-men, or other officers respectively were accustomed, or could do, exercise or perform respectively, at or before the time of rendering the said judgment, and in as ample manner and form as though no such judgment had ever been rendered, as by the said letters patent of the said late king James the second, amongst other things, more fully appears; *which said letters patent the said mayor and citizens* of the said city of Chester afterwards, to wit, on the said *twenty-sixth day of October*, in the said year of our Lord 1688, and in the said fourth year of the reign of his said late Majesty king James the second, *did accept and agree unto*, to wit, at the city of Chester aforesaid, in the county of the same city. *And* the said coroner and attorney of our said lord the now king, for our said lord the now king, in fact says, that the said *information in the said letters patent* last aforesaid mentioned and referred to, was and is *the said information*, in the nature of a quo warranto, exhibited

Acceptance of said charter of restoration.

exhibited by the said Sir Robert Sawyer, knight, as aforesaid, to wit, at the city of Chester aforesaid, in the county of the said city. *And* the said coroner and attorney of our said lord the now king, for our said lord the now king, also in fact says, that the *judgment* in and by the said *letters patent* of the said late king James the second, mentioned to be given against the said mayor and citizens of the said city of Chester, in the term of St. Hilary, in the 35th and 36th years of the reign of the late sovereign lord king Charles the second was and is *the said judgment* given and pronounced by the court of the said late king Charles the second, before the king himself, against the said mayor and citizens, *upon the said information*, exhibited by the said Sir Robert Sawyer, knight, attorney-general of the said late king Charles the second, against the said mayor and citizens as aforesaid, to wit, at the city of Chester aforesaid, in the county of the same city. Wherefore the said coroner and attorney of our said sovereign lord the now king for our said lord the now king says, *That the said letters patent of the said late king Charles the second, by the said Thomas above in his said plea mentioned, from and after the granting and acceptance* of *the said letters patent of the said late king James the second herein-before mentioned, did cease, determine and become void, and of no further effect, to wit*, at the city of Chester aforesaid, in the county of the same city; all which matters and things the said coroner and attorney of our said sovereign lord the now king, for our said sovereign lord the now king, is ready to verify, and prays that the said Thomas Amery may be convicted of the premises above charged upon him in and by the said information, by the said coroner and attorney of our said lord the now king, exhibited against him; and that the said Thomas may be forejudged, and excluded from the aforesaid office of an

Judgment quousque is that before mentioned.

Wherefore the charter of 37th Charles 2d, after the granting and acceptance of the charter of restoration, was of no further effect.

an alderman of the city of Chefter, and from the liberties, privileges, and franchifes, belonging and appertaining to the faid office.

GEORGE WOOD.
JAMES TOPPING.

N. B. *The replication to Monk's plea, as a common-council-man, is exactly the fame—mutatis mutandis.*

---

## Rejoinder of Defendant Amery, as Alderman.

### Of Eafter Term, 26th George III.

AND the faid Thomas Amery, as to the faid feveral matters, which the faid coroner and attorney hath above prayed, may be enquired of by the country, doth fo likewife. *And* as to the faid plea of the faid coroner and attorney, by him firft above in reply, pleaded to the faid plea of the faid Thomas Amery, by him above pleaded in bar, the faid Thomas Amery faith, that our faid lord the king ought not by reafon of any thing therein alledged, further to profecute his faid information againft him the faid Thomas Amery, becaufe he faith, that the faid order in council, under the privy feal of the faid privy council, in that plea above in reply pleaded mentioned, was not fignified to the faid Hugh Starkey, Richard Leving, the right hon. William earl of Derby, col. Robert Werden, Sir Thomas Grofvenor, Sir Peter Pindar, Sir Richard Dutton, Peter Shakerley, Thomas Simpfon, William Ince, Thomas Wilcock, Robert Murren, William Wilme, Hugh Grofvenor, John Sparke, William Willon, Randal

Similiter.

To 1ft replication.

Order in council under privy feal, not fignified to the felect body.

Randal Oulton, Francis Skellerne, William Allen, William Starkey, Henry Bennett, William Bennett, Valentine Short, Peter Bennett, Edward Starkey, Jonathan Whitby, James Hutchinson, Randal Vause, John Johnson, John White, Randal Holme, Elizeus Lloyd, Bradford Thropp, John Gouldbourne, Richard Taylor senior, Richard Taylor junior, John Minshall, Joseph Dyason, John Crichley, Caldecott Aldersey, Edward Partington, Randal Oulton, John Burroughs, Puleston Partington, Samuel Heath, Richard Oulton, Thomas Maddocks, Thomas Waringham, Henry Crosby, William Francis, Theodorus Aldcroft, Richard Brett, Thomas Holland, Matthew Anderton, Thomas Johnson, John Warrington, Nathaniel Bullen, Charles Pindar, Hugh Bartley, Griffith Trygan, John Hale, Robert Moulson, Ralph Poole, and Edward Croughton, in manner and form as the said coroner and attorney hath by that plea above in reply pleaded, alledged, and of this he puts himself upon the country, &c. *And* the said coroner and attorney of our said lord the king, for our said lord the king, doth so likewise. *And* the said Thomas Amery, as to the said plea of the said coroner and attorney, by him, 2*dly*. above in reply pleaded, saith, that our lord the king ought not, by reason of any thing therein alledged, further to prosecute the said information against him the said Thomas Amery, because he saith that such further proceedings were had upon the said information in that replication mentioned in the said court of the said lord the late king Charles the 2d before the king himself; that afterwards (to wit) in the term of the Holy Trinity, in the 36th year of the reign of the said lord the late king, it was considered by the said court of the said lord the late king before the king himself, that the said liberties, privileges,

As stated in the replication, &c.

*Similiter.*

To 2d replication.

Pleads a final judgment in Trinity term, 36th Charles 2d.

vileges, and franchifes, in the faid laft-mentioned information fpecified, fhould be feized into the hands of the faid lord the king, and the faid mayor and citizens be excluded and amoved therefrom; *the record of which faid laft-mentioned judgment is loft or deftroyed, and is not now remaining in the faid court of our lord the now king, before the king himfelf.* *And* the faid Thomas further faith, that the faid laft-mentioned judgment, always, from the time of giving thereof, until now, was, and ftill is, in full force, ftrength, and effect; not reverfed, annulled, vacated, or made void; by reafon whereof the faid community and body corporate of the mayor and citizens of the city of Chefter, in that replication mentioned, became and was totally diffolved and deftroyed, long before, and until, and at the time of, the fuppofed granting and acceptance of the faid fuppofed letters patent of the faid late king James the 2d, in that replication mentioned (to wit) at the city of Chefter aforefaid. *And* this the faid Thomas Amery is ready to verify. Wherefore he prays judgment, and that the aforefaid office, liberties, privileges, and franchifes, in form aforefaid, claimed by him the faid Thomas Amery, may, for the future, be allowed to him, and that he may be difmiffed and difcharged, by the court here, of and from the premifes aforefaid.

FOSTER BOWER.

N. B. *The rejoinder of defendant Monk, as a common-council-man, is exactly the fame — mutatis mutandis.*

## Surrejoinder to Rejoinder of Defendant Amery.

AND the faid coroner and attorney of our faid lord the king, for our faid lord the king, as to the faid rejoinder of the faid Thomas Amery, by him made to the faid plea of the faid coroner and attorney, by him fecondly above in reply pleaded to the faid plea, of the faid Thomas Amery, fays, that by reafon of any thing by the faid Thomas Amery, in that fame plea alledged, the faid lord the king ought not to be barred from profecuting his aforefaid information againft the faid Thomas Amery, becaufe protefting that the faid rejoinder of the faid Thomas Amery, and the matters therein contained, are not fufficient in law to bar the faid lord the king from having his aforefaid information againft the faid Thomas Amery, the faid coroner and attorney of our faid lord the king, for our faid lord the king, for furrejoinder in this behalf fays, That there was not any fuch record of fuch judgment, as by the faid Thomas Amery is above in pleading alledged. And this the faid coroner and attorney of our faid lord the king, for our faid lord the king, prays may be inquired of by the country, &c. And the faid Thomas Amery doth fo likewife, &c.

Iffue on final judgment of Trinity Term, 36th Charles 2d.

*Similiter.*

GEO. WOOD.

N. B. *The furrejoinder to the rejoinder of defendant Monk, as a common-council-man, is exactly the fame—mutatis mutandis.*

# INDEX

TO

PART the SECOND,

Being from PAGE 351 (inclusive) to the End.

---

## AFFIDAVIT.



## ASSAULT.



## BAKERS.



## CAPIAS IN MANUS.



## CAPIAS UTLAGATUM.



## CERTIORARI.



N 2 Special

## COMMISSION.



## CONDITION.



## CONFESSION.



## CONTINUANCES.



## DECREE.



## DEMURRER.



To

EX-

# I N D E X.

## EXTENT.



## HABEAS CORPUS.



INFOR-

# I N D E X.

## INFORMATION.



## INQUISITION.



## LE SCIENDUM.



## LUNACY.



## MANDAMUS.

# I N D E X.



To

# INDEX.

# INDEX.



## POSTEA.



PRE-

## PRESCRIPTION.



## QUO WARRANTO.



## REJOYNDER.



## REPLICATION.



## RETURN.





To

To

SCIRE FACIAS.



SEIZURE.



SUGGESTION.

## TRAVERSE.



## UTLAGATUM.



## VENIRE.



## VERDICT.



## WRIT.

www.ingramcontent.com/pod-product-compliance
Lightning Source LLC
Chambersburg PA
CBHW031816270326
41932CB00008B/441

* 9 7 8 3 3 3 7 2 6 8 0 2 2 *